The Inner Brain Conceptualization
and the System Mind

The Inner Brain Conceptualization and the System Mind

VOLUME II THE SYSTEM MIND

———

D. D. Wells

ISBN-13: 9781537107820
ISBN-10: 1537107828

Table of Contents

The System Mind and Economic and Political Systems

———

23.1 The System

We have spent a whole book talking about the millions of extraordinary and mystifying things the mind/brain can do. Looking at one single ability, memory, it is incredible how much we can remember. Sometimes, at an odd moment, a memory experience will simply pop into our heads from 20 years ago that we have never before thought about until now. There seem to be billions of little memory representations that can be activated in real time. Little things people say, little pictures of things we lived through, etc. We remember scenes from hundreds of movies we have seen. How does all that fit into one relatively small skull? On the other hand, as we saw in Ch. 11, the brain, although very complex, is made of a relatively small number of different kinds of pieces: nodes and wires connecting them. The nodes are little packages of chemicals called neurons. You might want to go back and reread Ch. 11 so as to better follow this chapter. Of course, as was pointed out there, the neuron is greatly underrated in terms of complexity. There are billions of different macromolecules in a neuron. But from a larger point of view, they look pretty much alike: a neuron is a neuron is a neuron.

The wires connecting these neurons are even simpler: very fine nerves. And the means of communication between neurons are simpler yet. They communicate simply by sending little electrical impulses back and forth. And that's it for the brain. And yet out of all this comes a *mind* which has as one of its major qualities, consciousness. Of course, it is true that the brain has over a hundred billion neurons and a hundred *trillion* connections. That's a lot of complexity. But the *parts* are relatively simple — neurons and connecting wires.

As we saw in Vol. I, it is the very complex system of neurons communicating via electrical impulses zipping between neurons that creates a mind that supervenes on the physical brain. So we could ask a very simple question. If we had a system with nodes like the brain's neurons and a means of communication between nodes, why wouldn't a system like this have a mind? Well, in this volume, we will explore evidence that any node-communication complex system resembling the brain creates a mind of sorts. In this chapter, we will look into the possibility that communication and information flows between nodes of our economic system creates a kind of mind, a *system mind* analogous to the mind created by the human brain. This theory would be a natural consequence of the *functionalist* theory of mind discussed in Sect. 13.5. Recall, functionalism states that any system of components that are causally related as in the brain, will also have a mind just as the human mind supervenes on the physical brain. Well, it seems to me that the components of an economic system are causally related by communicating information transfers pretty much the same way that neurons in the brain are causally related by flows of information in the form of electrical impulses going back and forth between billions of neurons. The functionalist, if he really means what he says, should approve of a system mind of the economic system.

Now there are some differences. Unlike the brain which has neurons as nodes, nodes of an economic system are any entities that take part in the game of economics and sends flows of information to other nodes. This would include individual consumers because they buy goods and services. It would include any business that produces or sells a good or service, whether a tiny little retail outlet, to a gigantic corporation like General Motors or Motorola. It includes all farms and cattle ranches. It includes all means of transportation to distribute goods and services to local populations, like trucking companies, railroads and airline freight companies. It includes all outlets selling goods and services to the public like small stores, fast food outlets, large department stores like Macy's and large retail stores like Target. The economic system also includes banks, investment houses, and brokerage firms that facilitate the movement of money. Some of these nodes, like a large corporation, can be considered independent systems themselves with their own subnodes and subcommunication channels. But we will be considering each of the entities in the above categories as nodes of the entire economy.

Of course, nodes of the economic system have a much higher degree of complexity than a neuron. As we have stressed in Ch. 11, a neuron is a lot more complex than most people realize. In my opinion, it's most underrated entity in the entire universe. But a single node in the economic system like a human person is made of billions of neurons and other body cells and is considerably more complex than a single neuron of the brain. And what about nodes like large corporations made up of a whole army of humans interacting in complex ways? This is why the system mind of the economy is clearly much more complex than the mind of the brain and why it is just as hard to predict the economy as it is an individual person.

Another important difference lies in the flows of information. For one thing, the kinds of communication of information between nodes in the economy are much more complex than the communication between nodes of the brain. In the brain, all information flows are simply trains of impulses going between neurons. In the economy, the information flows are buying and selling in markets, labor effort flowing to companies, paychecks, investments, government taxing and spending, advertising that communicates a message between sellers and consumers, money and goods, and most importantly information from newspapers, TV and radio.

Take a simple purchase. When you buy something in a store, you are communicating to the store as well as the maker of the item. They are communicating a good or service to you and you are communicating your preferences. This communication has information.

By tendering over money to the store and maker of an item, you are communicating the message that you approve of their product and its price. If you don't buy a product, you are communicating to the maker and seller that you don't need the product or the price is too high.

There are millions of other means of communicating between nodes of the economy. Individual consumers gossip to each other about products in the market. However, as a node in a *system* mind, the individual does things simply as an information processor without necessarily being aware of being part of a system mind. Advertisers communicate to consumers to show them new products. Most of the venues for communication between nodes are called markets. Markets have replaced churches as places of worship in recent years. But they provide a medium for information to be exchanged between nodes of the system. All of these are very complex flows of information and involve much higher information content than is contained in the simple impulse flows in the brain.

Of course, there are many subsystems of nodes with communication between them *within* the economy. These subsystems can be viewed somewhat like Jerry Fodor's modules. For example, there are subgroups such as political parties, associations, labor unions, etc. There is special communication among the individual elements *within* these associations. Do any of these systems have something like a mind the way the brain system of neurons and interconnecting nerves creates the human mind? Perhaps so, but this volume will be mostly concerned with evidence and illustrations of a system mind of the entire economy.

A good question is, are politicians nodes of the system mind? Well, the view taken here is that information flowing between citizens and politicians are pretty tenuous. We vote for politicians once in a while and we sometimes talk to our representatives. However, these flows are very minimal. Our view is that the political system of a country should not be part of the system mind but should be a kind of overseer making sure the economic system runs smoothly and effectively for the benefit of all of society. However, as we shall explain, sometimes the flows between many nodes of the economy and political nodes in Washington become so intertwined that these nodes do become part of the system mind.

Also, what we will be describing as a system mind should not be confused with Karl Jung's concept of *universal consciousness*. This latter concept as I understand it, is where a large group or population of people have a similar view towards a phenomenon in the world, but they do it spontaneously without communication between them. This is an entirely different concept. It comes as a result of similarities in peoples' perceptual apparatuses that cause reactions towards a phenomenon that are similar.

23.2 NATURE OF THE SYSTEM MIND

We should realize that the system mind is very similar to the human mind. All the qualities of the human mind can be found in the system mind. Just as the human mind has values, interests, goals, needs and wants, so also does the system mind. However, mindedness does not necessarily entail consciousness. Animals below mammals have minds of sorts, but they probably cannot project enough meaning to causal objects to reach the threshold of consciousness. Similarly, there is probably no consciousness in the system mind. Why is this so? This might point to our explanation of consciousness described in Ch.13, which is that consciousness might be the result of high information density in the brain underlying the mind. This can only be achieved in a human brain composed of trillions of large macromolecules. But the system mind lacks this degree of information density which might explain why the system mind is not conscious.

What this implies is that the system mind may be like the mind of a reptile. This has some very interesting ramifications that we will get to. Without consciousness, the system mind does not have concepts like the concept of self or of time; cannot entertain propositional attitudes, so it doesn't have beliefs or intentions as the human mind has. Also, without a sense of self, the system mind has a weak concept of morality. It doesn't know right from wrong and is very bad at maintaining justice in the system. Its main priority is to perpetuate itself. However, it does have interests, drives, needs and wants just like a reptile. It has a need for sustenance, to control its environment, to tell the difference between what is conducive to its continued existence and what is detrimental.

However, the interests and needs of *sub*minds of the system mind can be different from those of the overall system mind. This means that the system mind is somewhat schizophrenic. It has different personalities corresponding to its various subminds. This leads to the question of what determines the interests, values and goals of the system mind as a whole. In the first volume we discussed this question regarding the human mind. Basically the way the human mind reacts to states of affairs in its environment is determined by how it conceptualizes these states of affairs. This in turn depends of where in the brain representations of the state of affairs is located. But the physical causal underpinnings of the system mind are the whole economic/political system. So it may be just a category mistake to talk about the location of concepts and representations in the system mind. However, there may still be an analogy in this regard. The way the system mind reacts to states of affairs in its world may not depend on the location in the underlying system brain, which is the whole physical economic/political system. But it does depend on the more important nodes in the system. Let's explain this.

All the nodes of the brain, its neurons, are pretty much alike — little sacks containing billions of macromolecules. But the nodes of the economy vary greatly in size and importance. Some of them are only individual persons and households. But some are large financial firms, corporate conglomerates, and very wealthy individuals. For this reason, the values, interests and goals of the larger nodes will be more influential in determining the values, interests and goals of the entire system mind than smaller nodes. This can happen in a number of ways. Corporations have the resources to buy advertising to influence the choices of key nodes of the system. Wealthy individuals and corporations can buy up and control media outlets that promote theories that favor the larger nodes. And finally larger nodes can greatly affect the actual rules of the economic game, by influencing the political process. In the most important study of this century so far, the authors showed that in terms of public policy, "ordinary citizens have little or no independent influence on policy at all". [1] In order to show how the system mind works in an economy, we should first categorize economic and political systems.

23.3 Society's Two Major Systems — First, the Economic

The two main systems in any society are the economic and political systems. The political system consists of government entities. For example, in the US, our political system is composed of a Senate and a House of Representatives, an executive and a judiciary. European countries have parliaments. Let's talk about the economic system first. Many of you either don't like economics or are afraid that it's too complicated. However, the basic model of the entire economy is really quite simple. Remember, it is in the interests of rich and powerful elements of the economy to give you the impression that economic events occur because of cosmic forces that nobody understands nor can do anything about. I am writing this after the great financial meltdown of 2008. The almost universal claim we get from every communication venue, regardless of political views, is that nobody saw this coming, and nobody understands why it happened — we just have to fix it. Well, we're not going to fix it without some idea of how it works.

The *Economic System* of a society is composed of all the structures, institutions, businesses and even individuals that are organized towards the production and distribution of goods and services that satisfy the wants and needs of society's individual members. Thus the economic system consists of the *means of production* of goods and services, the means of distributing those goods and services and individual citizens who purchase them. The political system is concerned with communicating the state of society, preserving the rights and freedoms we enjoy, and designing rules governing how production of goods and services are to be made and distributed. There are a few new concepts to explain.

The first concept is the idea of *surplus*. Any population of peoples will produce some amount of goods and services. But if the amount of goods and services produced is just enough to keep everyone barely alive, there is no *surplus*. Whatever goods and services are produced *over and above* the bare subsistence needs of the people in the population is called an economic *surplus*. We don't hear much about this idea in modern times because modern economies are so efficient at producing things that there is plenty of surplus. However, there are still a few countries and tribes in the world where they have very little surplus. They are mostly agricultural or hunting societies and this is where we can find malnutrition and starvation at various times. What creates surplus is *productivity*, which is a simple concept. Productivity is the amount of goods and services a worker can produce in an hour. As productivity goes up, the economy can produce more goods and services in an hour of labor time and so its surplus will increase.

Now there are really two kinds of goods and services people want and need. Those that exist to grant and support *rights* of citizens, and those that support our *discretionary* wants and needs. The latter are goods and services we buy in a marketplace and are called *commodities*. For example, cars, houses, and hair-driers are commodities. (Some economists reserve the word 'commodity' to agricultural products, minerals, and other natural resources that are mined.) However, the *rights* we have like freedom of speech and freedom of religion are not commodities. We don't buy and sell *rights* in a marketplace, at least not in theory. In practice, of course, things are different. In the US, a rich person can *buy* the right to a fairer trial than a poor person; but in theory, the Constitution stipulates that the right to a fair trial is not a commodity that can be bought and sold.

23.4 THE POLITICAL SYSTEM AND THE FOUR PILLARS

Before we get into the basic roles of government, we'll mention the major principles of liberty that our country was founded on. In my opinion, these are the pillars that support our form of government and were implemented by the founding fathers as a direct result of the abuses that they saw in the British monarchy. The four liberty pillars are to be found in the Declaration of Independence, which was, in effect, one big blast at the British king for his "Injuries and Usurpations". You wouldn't believe the anger expressed in the Declaration at the British king. Here's a sample: "He is, at this Time, transporting large armies of foreign Mercenaries to compleat the Works of Death, Desolation, and Tyranny, already begun with circumstances of Cruelty and Perfidy, scarcely paralleled in the most barbarous Ages...." What would they have thought about Bush's invasion of Iraq? It is very clear from the Declaration the issues the founders intended to redress in writing the Constitution. Of course, when various Supreme Courts want to decide an issue that the Constitution is unclear about, the last place they look is the Declaration for the simple reason that it very clearly delineates what the founders intended. We can refer to the four pillars as the 4 P's, two positive and two negative.

PRIVACY. One of the most important abuses the founding fathers addressed was that the British king could send his men into people's houses to search for evidence of anti-king beliefs or actions. Not only that, but the king could force Americans to quarter "...large Bodies of Foreign Troops...". They could say and do anything they wanted in a citizen's house. The only freedom of speech that existed in Europe was that the king's men could invade your house and exercise their "freedom of speech". To prevent these abuses and "usurpations", the Constitution contains the IV Amendment against illegal searches and seizures. It appears that the founding fathers deemed that there is *some* part of our lives that should remain private beyond the reach of other institutions, especially government.

PROPERTY. Property rights have been articulated for hundreds of years under the British system of common law and was specified in the 14th amendment which says, "...nor shall any state deprive any person of life, liberty, or property, without due process of law...". Most international economists deem that a necessary ingredient for economic development is the protection of private property rights. This shows the intentions of the founders to guarantee property rights against the abuses of a king or any kind of government who might want to take a citizen's property. The next two are negatively expressed principles.

PECULATION TAXES. The important ostensible reason for the American Revolution was the practice of the British king taxing Americans. The American claim was that you cannot tax citizens unless they are *represented* in government. It is called taxation without representation and is a foundational axiom in the establishment of our country. When you tax citizens who are not represented, you are effectively stealing their moneys, which is peculation.

PRIVATE WARS. Another important abuse the Founding fathers addressed was the making of wars. In Europe, the king could make his own private war at his discretion and waste the lives of tens of thousands of people. Charles I of England is a perfect example. The founding fathers specifically gave the powers to make and declare wars to *congress*. The palpable proof of their motivation was indicated in the Declaration of Independence where it complained that the king "...has kept among us, In Times of Peace, standing armies, without the consent of our Legislatures". This precluded the president from making his own private war as the British king had been doing for centuries. War is important stuff. Human beings die in wars, many of whom are innocent of anything international. Children die in wars who have no knowledge of nor any responsibility for the issues and conflicts between nations. War is really a big deal. And the founding fathers made it clear that something as important as war should be the responsibility of the direct representatives of the people, the *legislature*, which is Congress. This would insure that more than one person was responsible for a war, that there would be careful deliberations and that the people responsible would be the people's direct representatives. Even though the Constitution gives too many powers to the president, in my opinion, it clearly stops short of giving him the power to make wars. Under current Supreme Courts, we all know what has happened to that principle: down the toilet along with most else important in the Constitution.

These are the 4 important bedrock pillars of liberty that create the foundation for the establishment of the United States of America. They are enumerated in the words and intent of the founding fathers as expressed in the Constitution. It is the purview of the Supreme Court to maintain and enforce these bedrock principles. But when we look at the performance of various Supreme Courts, especially in modern times, it is perfectly obvious that we have very little left of the Constitution.

The groundwork for the total annihilation of the Constitution was laid down by the worst American who ever lived: Oliver Wendell Holmes. This guy was the mother of all scumbags. Holmes was a very influential Supreme Court justice around the turn of the last century. Recall in Sect. 3.3, we talked about the *message* of a piece of communication. The message is the intended *meaning* of the communication regardless of the exact words used. The *message* Holmes intended to all future Supreme Court justices was, when you have a difficult case, simply flush the Constitution down the toilet and rule as you dam well please. Of course, Holmes didn't put it in these terms. He used all kinds of fancy language. But this is *message* he communicated. This is exactly the practice that various Supreme Courts have carried out ever since. Holmes set the standard with a ruling on a Sedition law against freedom of speech during WWI, by reaching up his butt to pull out the idea from his reason box to the effect that the Constitution really didn't mean what it said about freedom of speech in time of war. Not only does the Constitution not make any such exception, but in modern times, war can be defined as anything the government undertakes.

Now the way this is done is through "*interpretation*". Supreme Court justices no longer *read* the Constitution — they *interpret* it, which gives them a chance to do exactly as Holmes suggested. When the court wants to decide a case in one way, they call themselves "originalists"; when they want to rule in another way, they call themselves "contextualists"; and when they want to rule in still another way, they call themselves "revisionists". All the reason box crap they spew forth to justify their ideological droppings is just that. Now admittedly there are hard cases, usually involving concepts in modern life that simply did not exist at the time of the Constitution. The abortion issue might be a case in point. But in many cases the Constitution is very clear about what is intended. But with reason box rationalizations, there is almost nothing left of the Constitution that hasn't been "interpreted" away. This is especially the case with the four pillars.

Regarding privacy, we see monitors and secret cameras popping up everywhere. Of course, I would say that the owners of property like homes, stores, restaurants, etc. have to right to cameras directed towards their property because this is part of the process of *securing* their property. But public streets and parks are places where people are conducting their *private* lives. And yet, cameras are popping up everywhere that spy on people's private lives. Now we're getting drones, no less. The Supreme Court has continually "interpreted" away constitutional guarantees for privacy to the point where we have very little inherent right to privacy at all. And this will get much worse.

As far as private wars, the president has achieved pretty much the power of medieval kings in their power to make war. Every war, military adventure and military offensive since WWII has been initiated by the president, the latest being the Iraq war. Wars really are big deals involving killing of thousands. They should be deliberated upon by more than one responsible person, but our Supreme Ayatollas love kings just like Iran's Ayatollas love sultans, precisely what the Constitution and especially the Declaration of Independence railed against.

Property rights have also been "interpreted" as meaning that the state can indeed deprive people of their property by simply passing a law that allows the state to do exactly that. This is what allowed crooked politicians to steal hundreds of billions of dollars of valuable property from citizens in the '50s and '60s in a great criminal enterprise called "eminent domain" and "urban renewal". There is no judicial impediment whatsoever to this kind of massive government theft because any vampire can rule any theft as in the "public interest". This by itself shows the basic "Perfidy" of the kind of protoplasm that winds up in the Judiciary.

Lastly, the equal protection clause of the 14th amendment is an expression of the principle upon which the American Revolution occurred, which is that people cannot be taxed without being represented. This has again been "interpreted" as meaning that people *can* indeed be taxed without representation. This is exactly how we got such a monstrous national debt. Thomas Jefferson said specifically in letters that the government should not be allowed to accrue debts that could not be repaid during the lives of the people incurring the debt. Since these justices use the Constitution for toilet paper, this principle has totally disappeared. In order to pay for tax cuts for their idle, crooked rich friends, Reagan and Bush had to steal *trillions* from future generations, who will be taxed to pay interest on that debt but were never represented when these taxes were incurred. This is clearly taxation without representation, a fundamental pillar of our constitutional system.

It's bad enough that historically, presidents have chosen Supreme Court members with their inner brains, but along came Oliver Wendell Holmes to throw gasoline on the fire by enabling judges to rule as they dam well please simply by "interpreting" the Constitution. As a result, various Supreme Courts have been quite thorough in their total annihilation of the four foundational pillars of our Constitutional government on many occasions. They haven't missed a trick.   What we have now in effect is a country run by nine Ayatollahs, *exactly* the way Iran is run. They have absolutely no interest or knowledge of the Constitution. If they don't like a piece of legislation, they declare it unconstitutional. If they want a law the legislature hasn't passed, they simply pass it. They vote on the basis of their own distorted conception of what a country should be and absolutely nothing else.

23.5 THE POLITICAL SYSTEM ROLE OF GOVERNMENT

As we have mentioned, in an ideal society, the political system would be outside the economic system and so not part of a system mind. However, this principle has been difficult to maintain because the system mind emerging from the workings of the economic system mind is always trying to gobble up and digest the political system to make it part of a total system mind. It does this by trying to turn actors of the political system into important nodes of the economic system. But assuming an independent role for government, the governmental political system has 4 major roles to play. The first two are procedural, and the second two social. The first guarantees and supports rights and freedoms — if any. In the US, we have the right to a fair trial, and freedom of speech. Rights are the province of the *judicial* branch of government whose role is to protect the rights of *individuals*. The second and third roles are part of our *public ethics* and *morality*. *Economic* public ethics refers to the design and enforcement of contracts between parties in the economic system and to impose certain *rules that* guide contracts and other transactions between parties. There is *political* public morality which involves how we tax and distribute income to various levels of society. *Political* public morality should reflect fairness in taxing and distributing income. Both areas of public ethics and morality are the purview of the *legislative* branch of government. The role of the execute branch, which is the president and his or her administration is to carry out the wishes of the other two branches. The last role is to provide the public with knowledge on which to make political decisions. We can abbreviate these into *Rights, Rules, Fairness, and Knowledge.* The first is the purview of the judicial branch of government and the last three are the purview of the legislative branch.

Regarding rights and freedoms, the Constitution authorizes a Supreme Court whose main function is to protect the rights of minorities against the impositions of majorities. The Supreme Court is the *Judicial* branch of government and is not elected but appointed. This prevents a majority from suppressing the rights and freedoms of individuals, especially those in a minority.

The role of the judiciary and legislative branches mirrors the basic *Yin Yang* that pops up in all walks of life and all conceptual thinking. There is good and bad, right and wrong, positive and negative, on and off, plus and minus, up and down, top and bottom, in and out. There is a very important Yin Yang phenomenon that people often overlook in analyzing modern economic/political systems. It is the *opposition-cooperation* pair. There are basically only two ways one party can interact with another party, whether individuals, associations, clubs, institutions or government bodies. You can be in *opposition* to what other parties may want to do; this is *negative* interaction. Or, you may *cooperate* with another party to carry out certain activities or endeavors; this is *positive* interaction. These are basically the only two ways to transact with another party, no matter who or what it is.

The core concept involved in an *oppositional* interaction or transaction is called a *right* or *freedom*. Since rights and freedoms are *oppositional* transactions where the party claiming the right is an *individual in opposition* to the wishes of other parties who may be opposed to the individual's activities, all rights are *individual* rights. Only the judiciary can enforce *individual* rights which is their purview. All other rights must be extended to other parties or entities by the legislature. For example, in the US, we have a right of freedom of speech. This means you can speak your mind in spite of the *opposition* of other parties who may not agree with your views and might want to suppress your speech. We have the right of freedom of religion in the same way.

It is very clear in the writings of the founding fathers that rights are to be extended to individual flesh and blood human persons. This tenor appears over and over in the writings of the founding fathers where there is constant reference to *persons* or *people*. In the bill of rights, the first 10 amendments to the Constitution, the words 'person' or 'people' is mentioned in eight of them. In the 6th, there is reference to *him*, in the singular, in an amendment involving criminal prosecutions. The Constitution itself refers to "persons" many times. There are no *inherent* Constitutional rights for any kind of group of more than one, whether corporations, associations, or any other kind of group. *There are no Constitutional group rights.* The reason is that by its very nature, a right is inherent in the individual as part of what it is to be a human person. If these rights and privileges were to be extended to groups or any other kind of party, this would have to be done by the *legislature*. Thomas Jefferson and James Madison never came close to suggesting that corporations like the east India Company had freedom of religion or of speech.

Now historically, problems came up because as the 1800s progressed, various institutions came into being and questions arose as to the rights and freedoms of those institutions. For example, the Constitution guarantees freedom of the press. Well, at the time of writing the Constitution, the press consisted of small individual men who had a little print shop and turned out a little newspaper. Lots of times they were simply one sheet folded into 4 pages and the type all hand set. This was the way freedom of speech and the press were originally constituted. It was an *individual* proprietor who was exercising freedom of the press.

But newspapers grew into bigger and bigger businesses and finally into corporations. The question was, do these corporations also have freedom of the press? Well, through *legislation* designing the legal status of a corporation, laws were passed that since each person working for a newspaper had freedom of the press, it would be in this spirit that a *group* of individuals could unite into one entity that would allow the *individuals* in the group to enjoy their freedom of the press through one publication. Here, the purpose of the group organization would be to facilitate the freedom of speech of *individual* members. But it should be kept in mind that groups like corporations are the creation of the state and all rights and freedoms extended are done by *legislatures*.

But in order to pervert the specification that rights are assigned to *persons*, they've made corporations into *persons* in the famous *Citizen's United* case. A four-year-old would know the difference. As we explained in Sect. 16.10, a person is a human being with a mind and soul, with the cognitive ability to be rational and have a system of morality. But the latest Supreme Court has reversed the direction of derivation. Instead of companies or groups having rights assigned by legislatures being *derivative* on the rights of real persons, the Court has made corporations the persons involved; and *real* persons, who are viewed as merely wheels and gears of the corporate person, derive their rights from the rights of the corporate "person".

This even erases the basic concept of the person and the organization. When individual persons coalesce into a group, they are organizing around a concept that they all *already* share. The *New York Times* wasn't put together as an undifferentiated glob of people and then assigned freedom of the press. Individual people working for the *Times* already *had* freedom of the press, which was the concept they organized the *New York Times* around. This is why legislatures have given companies like *The New York Times* freedom of the press as *derivative* on the freedom of the press of all the individual people working for the paper. The rights of the *individual* come first, and the rights of groups of individuals are derivative on that. This is very important consideration. And you notice in quality publications, the editorial page is signed "the editors", indicating real flesh and blood persons are exercising their freedom of the press.

But the XYZ corporation is not organized around the concept that the court is assigning them personhood for. It is organized around the concept of producing a good or service. So when XYZ corporation is assigned personhood, not only are the freedoms coming to employees and stockholders *derived* from the freedoms of the corporation, but the mutilated derived freedoms coming to these individuals can be *assigned* views and opinions they personally disagree with. In *Citizen's United*, the court said that management of a corporation could actually *steal* financial assets of stockholders right out of their pockets and use it not for producing goods and services, but to promote political views in direct conflict with the views of the stockholder. This is a double humiliation.

The effect of allowing corporations as legal entities to exercise freedom of speech is to enable large corporations to dilute and crowd out not only the free speech of employees and stockholders in the corporation, but the speech of all other individuals as well. During the days the Constitutional was being written, wonder if every time someone got up on his little soap box to speak, the East India Company would have a loud speaker right there blaring a noise that drowned out the speaker on the soap box. Would he still have freedom of speech? This would be destroying the freedom of speech of the *individual*. This is exactly what our Supreme Court has done to *individual* freedom of speech in their latest droppings.

But *Citizens United* is just the latest attempt to snuff out freedom of speech of individual citizens. The Supreme Vampires have many times trampled on the right of free speech and free press of individuals. In a very important book on the history of free speech, historian David Rabban says: "No group of Americans was more hostile to free speech claims before World War I than the Judiciary, and no judges were more hostile than the Justices on the United States Supreme Court". [2] But they didn't stop at WWI. Inspired by the mother of all scumbags, Oliver Wendell Holmes, during the Palmer raids of the early '20s, and the McCarthy period after WWII, the Supreme Court continued its historical attack on freedom of speech. People were actually jailed and deported for nothing more than speech. And we're talking about real speech here, not inconsequential gossip. All the court had to do according to Holmes was show "clear and present danger", which any crooked court can "interpret" in any conceivable way. The clearest and most present danger we ever had to the Constitution was Oliver Wendell (fucking) Holmes. The Constitution gives no such exemptions from freedom of speech.

To show what a fraud the Supreme Court is, Ayatollah Scalia stated that Thomas Jefferson would have agreed with *Citizen United* when in Jefferson's own words, he feared that the rise of a "single and splendid government of an aristocracy, founded on banking institutions, and moneyed incorporations" could be "riding and ruling over the plundered ploughmen and beggared yeomanry". Of course, for this judgment, "originalism" is out and Holmes is in.

However, the framers of the Constitution were a little careless in defining speech, although you can glean the concept they had in mind by their various writings. The definition of *speech* should be: the concatenation of general words into sentences expressing abstract thoughts or concepts; and sentences into paragraphs to express a cogent argument, all of which involves or refers to knowledge, information and policy of groups or associations of any kind. This was suggested by the framers of the Constitution. Yelling "fire" in a crowded theatre is not speech. Talk referring to individuals and their private lives is not speech but *gossip*, which is not guaranteed at all by the Constitution.

Second, it is clear that the founders' concept of free speech was designed to protect especially *public* speech because it is wider audiences that could be antagonistic to what is being said. Also, any speech made in public should be available to anyone who is interested in what was said. But again various Supreme vampires have trashed the whole concept of free speech. When a lobbyist gets together in a dark room to *bribe* a crooked politician into passing some specific law he needs, these vampires have called it free speech. And if that isn't enough to cover any kind of crime they want to legalize, they call it "freedom of expression". Of course, when poor people get together to discuss *their* favorite crimes, the last thing on the minds of the Supreme Vampires is free speech. That stuff falls under *conspiracies* of various kinds, which carry enormous penalties.

Regarding broadcasting, the legislation giving them *permission* to engage in broadcast speech contained a proviso that they operate "in the public interest". After all, they are really invading our homes with their message. One of the motivations for the American Revolution was that in England, the king's men could invade your home at will and express his "freedom of speech", whether you wanted to hear it or not; and search your premises on top of it. Of course, there's nothing in the history of the world that has been more abused than this proviso of operating in the public interest.

But when it comes to our real *individual* rights that the courts are specifically empowered to protect, they flush the Constitution down the toilet time after time. They have enforced blatant discrimination against *individual* black people in the hiring of employees and enrollment in colleges. The Massachusetts Supreme Court allowed a blatant violation of the double jeopardy protection, which is the 5th amendment of the Bill of Rights. First they allow the state to give you a traffic ticket, which is fine. Then they turn around and let the state impose a *second* punishment for the same infraction, which allows the insurance company to tack on another two *thousand* dollar penalty. And this is for a traffic ticket. Recently this same supposedly liberal state has allowed municipal and state courts to add a charge just to go before a judge or get a hearing. It is clear from the spirit of the Constitution that dispensation of justice is not a commodity you have to pay for. Here again, where is the neoliberal Massachusetts Supreme Court to protect our basic *individual* rights and freedoms. They're in the back room figuring out what legislation they are going to impose on the American people and what rights they can manufacture for *groups*. The American judiciary is a national disgrace.

Regarding individual rights, people are often angry that a majority cannot prescribe what our rights should be. Well, the founding fathers realized that rights are often unpopular; but if we're to have a country that supports certain rights and freedoms, you can't have temporary majorities removing these rights. That's why they are specified in the Constitution and are the purview of the *judicial* branch of government where the parties involved are in *opposition*. Those of you who know some math will realize that rights specified in a constitution are like axioms of a mathematical system. They are the foundation and basic premises of the system.

Since our rights and freedoms are relatively small in number, they can be specified and enumerated in the Constitution as a finite state document. This means it can never cover every tiny detail of an infinite state system of interacting human beings. This is why we have a Supreme Court supposedly consisting of infinite state human minds to fill in the spaces between the finite state concepts of the Constitution to carry out the *spirit* of the Constitution. They are appointed instead of elected so that they can conduct their duties without having to appeal to majorities. But if you put finite state reptilian minds on the Court, they will impose whatever they please totally out of the spirit of the Constitution.

The *cooperative* half of the Yin-Yang contrast involves public ethics and morality, economic, political and social. This is the purview of the *legislative* branch of government. The founding fathers deemed that the ways and means parties will transact and cooperate should be determined by a majority of citizens which takes everyone's values and views into account. The way humans cooperatively transact should reflect the views, beliefs, perceptions and religion of all human citizens that can go back thousands of years and is really the culmination of what a culture is. To allow one person on a court to impose his values on millions of people and their historic culture is antithetical to the very idea of democracy. The ways and means the parties will cooperate is described in a *contract* which specifies the duties, obligations and responsibilities of the parties.

One of the major weaknesses of the structure of our government is that it is very tempting for the judiciary to encroach on the prerogatives of the legislature by, if effect, redesigning contracts themselves. This transgression of power has been executed many many times in our history. Since the Supreme Court also consists of a bunch of lawyers, they have been lenient on lower court judges who infringe on legislatures by designing contracts.

When various legislatures tried to weaken the institution of slavery by redesigning the basic labor contract, various Supreme Courts stepped in and created rights out of whole cloth. Since slaves were property, the Supreme Court was able to justify its decisions based on the *rights* of property. But of course, this is totally unconstitutional because property rights are *contract* rights and employment is clearly a contract matter; so it was completely within the legislatures' powers to *redesign* employment contracts so as to weaken slavery.

The only recourse we have to restrain the Supreme Court to its rightful powers is impeachment, which is very difficult to do because legislators are usually made up of the same shysters that are on the court. And because Supreme Courts have always used the Constitution for toilet paper, by the time Abe Lincoln became president, he had to engage in a civil war and pass a Constitutional amendment that redesigned employment contracts so as to *prohibit* the contractual buying and selling of slaves. We discussed this in Sect. 19.5. If the Supreme Court had stayed within its powers, various legislatures might have redesigned employment contracts so as to gradually weaken slavery and a totally ghastly and highly deadly civil war might have been avoided — a real catastrophe of history, for which the Supreme Court has never been sufficiently blamed.

We have discussed only a small part of *economic* ethics which is the design of contracts. But there are many other rules that constrain the economic game of producing, distributing, and selling goods and services. In order for transactions involved in these activities to go smoothly to the benefit of society as a whole, there has to be rules of the game that are enforced by independent referees. There are rules pertaining to preservation of the environment, rules that protect workers in the workplace and rules applicable to the financial services industry with its transactional paper instruments like stocks, bonds, loans, etc. There are many rules that constrain the economic system by the political system that involve how we interact in our economic lives. This is all part of the *economic morality* or *ethics* role of government of society. This is also the purview of the *legislative* branch.

We mentioned above that the political system is not really part of the system mind. But it is in the interests of the system mind to drag the political system into the bailiwick of the economic system. Then the impression can be communicated that what happens in our economic lives depends on immutable laws handed down on stone tablets to economists on mountaintops. There are "*laws*" of supply and demand, *law* of diminishing returns, *laws* of the money supply and interest rates. This gives the impression that the way goods and services are distributed depends on hard fast economic laws that nobody can do anything about. This saps the motivation from people who might want to change the system. When an oligopoly industry like oil raises their prices over the slightest pretext, blame is attributed to economic "laws", free markets, free enterprise, motherhood and apple pie.

The modern free enterprise system has become increasingly complex. As we have seen leading up to the crash of 2008, there has been a mountain of new paper financial instruments invented by economic players that could not possibly be anticipated by the founding fathers. This is why the Constitution is somewhat weak in talking about the rules of the economic game. At the time of the American Revolution, the legislative branch of government had about the same amount of power as the economic system, which consisted of small manufacturers and small farmers. So the rules they promulgated were sufficient to constrain the operations of the economic system in the best interests of society as a whole. However, the founding fathers could not anticipate the great nodes of wealth and power that would accumulate as a result of the Industrial Revolution after the Civil War. In modern times, we have seen large economic nodes able to buy and sell political actors like sacks of potatoes. This brings political actors into the economic system as important nodes. What is lost is an independent body that can act *outside* the system mind to oversee and regulate the workings of the economic system.

The third role of government is to provide for *political* morality, which is the political aspect of our public morality. This role concerns mostly how we tax and determine the *distribution of income*. Now you might say that protecting rights and freedoms is part of public morality. However, it seems to me that these concepts more appropriately fall under the concept of *justice* rather than morality. The view taken here is that public morality refers to how we interact in our economic and political lives. The most important consideration on the *political* side of public morality is the concept of *fairness* and the most consideration regarding society's fairness is reflected in the *distribution of income*. A society can produce a lot of goods and services, but it may allocate what they produce by too much *in*equality in the distribution of income.

Some think you need inequality to provide incentives for the most creative members of society to invent, invest and grow the economy. But there is a limit to this. In colonial times, a case could be made that the actual size of the economies of the North and South were comparable. Manufactured goods were made pretty much the same way by artisans in small shops. However, in the South, there was an aristocracy of planters who owned all agricultural means of production and lived pretty high on the hog while a third to half the population were slaves. In the North there was a more equal distribution of agricultural land. So even though the two societies might have been equal in terms of the *average* standard of living, we would certainly say that the South had a very immoral distribution of goods and services, to say nothing about rights. Thus, we can measure the *size* of the economy by the amount of their surplus that is produced, but the *morality* of society is measured by how goods and services are *distributed*.

But the North/South story shows something more. The argument about incentives is valid only up to a point. The great inequality in the American South did not inspire great technological and economic advances. It was in the more equal North that all the technological advances were made. And by the time the civil war rolled around, the North was able to win because of its greater economic and industrial strength based on the best technology of the day.

When we compare ancient Egyptian societies with those of the American Indians, because of technological differences, the Egyptians certainly produced a higher surplus, meaning a greater amount of economic wealth. However, there was an aristocracy around the Pharaohs who owned and controlled everything, while most everyone else was a total slave. This is why the famous pyramids, impressive as they are from a construction point of view, are examples of the worst of human *morality*. They were made totally by slave labor. We would certainly attribute a higher degree of *political* morality to the American Indians.

So what should society's political morality be regarding its distribution of income? This is where people's political views vary a great deal. Conservatives, (I'm talking about original real conservatives, not the brand of neoconservatives we've gotten in recent years) put the emphasis on economics where they can talk about *laws* and economic theory. They would say that society's wealth and standard of living depend mostly on people who invent new technology and on entrepreneurs who organize groups of workers into productive enterprises based on new technology. They would say that workers are a dime a dozen and that there would be no goods and services if it weren't for inventors and entrepreneurs, without whom we would all still be living in the stone age. After all, inventors *could* produce their own inventions. In fact, Thomas Edison hooked up with some investors and started the General Electric Company. As a result, conservatives would allot most of society's wealth in the form of income to those two categories of people. The emphasis in talking about free markets by conservatives is to shift the emphasis onto *economic* considerations.

Liberals on the other hand want to make the distribution of income depend on cultural and social values which involves some aspect of public morality and is the province of the political system. This is why many writers call the political system a political-cultural system because it depends on the *values* and practices of our culture and religion. Liberals also point out that markets aren't free at all, but rigged in favor of economic elites. Their say that without people at the lower income levels actually doing work in factories and shops, inventors would be living in little mud huts inventing light bulbs. They would say that children are helpless and unable to provide for themselves. Both the rich man and the poor man have children to feed, clothe and educate and income of their worker parents should reflect the fact that children's welfare and needs shouldn't depend solely on economics. This is a cultural/*social* concept, not an economic one.

Both sides in this dispute have legitimate arguments on their side. However, there are limits to how far you can go in the pursuit of the objectives of both sides. Briefly, if the conservative position is pushed too far, and too much income goes to entrepreneurs and professionals, you won't *clear markets*. This means that the consuming classes won't have enough money to buy all the goods and services businesses can produce. On the other hand, if income is distributed too equally, talented people who do the inventing and organizing of businesses won't have the incentive to provide society with a rich array of goods and services making up our standard of living. This is what happened under Communism. As a result, Communist countries were never able to make anything anyone wanted.

In practice, I think most people would approve of a distribution of income that would address both arguments. Given a choice, I think most people would opt for a system that rewards inventors and entrepreneurs more than others because of their greater contribution to our economic well-being, but would allow workers who actually produce goods and services an adequate share to be able to support their families. As shall see, if we want a real Capitalist economic system, our choices in the distribution of income are a lot more constrained than people think.

Our present system is designed so that about the only way society can affect the distribution of income is through a system of taxation, which is the purview of the legislative branch and is part of our political morality. Taxes are used not only to raise revenues for government operations, but are also used to affect our public morality by affecting the distribution of income. There are two concepts of importance in this regard. The first is *economic compensation*. Economic compensation is what a person receives in money in a market place of labor for his or her *economic* contribution to society's production of goods and services. This, of course, depends on a person's talents, education, motivation, etc. Economic compensation is based totally on market laws of supply and demand. People who have rare skills like a brain surgeon can command more economic compensation than an unskilled factory worker. Lots of people are indignant about the fact that a baseball player gets 20 million dollars a year to hit a ball with a stick. Well, what this shows is that very few people can hit a 95 miles per hour fastball with a stick.

Economic compensation is the value of any economic entity, like commodities and service. There is also economic compensation for labor determined in markets. However, with labor there is the concept of *earning*. This is a very *human* concept and refers to how much wealth or income society deems fair and just that should be awarded to each individual member on the basis of their total role in society as a human citizen. So *earnings* would depend not only on economic compensation as mentioned above, but also on the fact that this economic producer is also an infinite state *human being*, and that his labor is a manifestation of his thoughts, feelings, a soul, a moral compass and responsibilities for the well-being of children who should have certain economic rights. Someday there may be an anthropologist who decides to do something really useful. He or she would examine every population from any part of the world no matter how primitive, undeveloped or unsophisticated, and find that almost *every* society of people across the globe and across time has a concept of *earning* (along with a concept of the soul as we discussed in Ch. 2 of Vol. I.)

Also, since the most important relationship (outside of our family and relatives) between society's individuals is in terms of their *labor*, it should be rewarded on the basis that we are mind or soul driven human persons. One way to do this is to determine the value of labor in a democratic way by the value judgments of all members of society. A convenient way to determine earnings is through a progressive income tax. Even though nobody likes taxes, taxes really kill two birds with one stone. Any society needs taxes to pay for public goods. We want roads and bridges, we want an army to defend us, we want a system of courts to dispense justice and protect rights. Some think we should have health-care managed and paid for by the government as a right. So we have taxes. However, these very same taxes could also be used to adjust economic compensation to determine *earnings* for individuals. This is what a progressive income tax and minimum wage accomplishes. The fact that we vote for legislatures who have the power to tax and adjust compensation to arrive at *earnings* reflects a tiny bit that earnings are conceptually within the purview of citizens' *values*.

Of course, conservative don't like taxes and that taxes are a form of stealing. But on the face of it, the first question is, what is going to pay for their armies, their spies, their big brother government, their private wars, their secret police, and their corporate welfare, all of which is by far the biggest part of the federal budget? So do they want to admit that their favorite government roles, military, wars, secret police and corporate welfare are obtained through theft? The view here is simply that taxes and earnings should be determined politically on the basis of the democratic views of all our citizens. Labor is a very human thing and the value of labor, its *earnings*, should be determined by the views and values of other *humans*.

The irony is that these anti-tax neoconservatives call themselves Christians. And yet, when it comes to the most important transactions between human beings, our labor, neoconservatives want it to be determined in godless markets. Markets are for transacting non-human goods and services and the movements of money. When it comes to where we are preaching and praying and thinking about our souls and relations with God, and about our moral lives involving our relations with other human beings with souls — this is precisely where Jesus kicked the money-changers out of the picture. Yet these very same Christian neoconservative want to determine the value of transactions between *human beings with minds and souls, including their labor* — they want to determine all this in their godless marketplaces. These modern-day Christians better go to church and pray very hard that there's no God up there looking down on them.

Now I'm not a highly religious person, although a little bit. What does the Bible say on this issue? Well, this is one of the criticisms of Jesus the man. He wasn't very interested in my profession which is economics. The only allusion to labor I can find in the Bible is where Jesus paid the guy who came at the 11th hour the same as others. To me, this says that Jesus wasn't interested in the dictates of the market of supply and demand. As a *human being* while on earth and not a big corporation, *He* would determine the value of this person's labor. The implication here is that only *human beings* should determine the value of labor, and this could be better done in a democratic way. This province of political morality is the purview of the legislature.

The fourth major role of government is to provide facts and knowledge necessary for people to make decisions about the distribution of income, taxes, and rules of the economic game. This is the province of a *means of communication*. In my opinion, the most important role of government is the regulation of the dissemination of information, news and knowledge, i.e., the means of communication. One of the leading founding fathers, the second president of the United States, John Adams, said this about the dissemination of knowledge: "Liberty cannot be preserved without a general knowledge among the people, who have a right, from the frame of their nature, to knowledge…. The preservation of the means of knowledge among the lowest ranks is of more importance to the public than all the property of all the rich men in the country…." You can't say it any better than that. But as society evolved in the 1800s, this important aspect of the thinking and motivation of the founding fathers got lost in the shuffle.

Society cannot run without information and knowledge. This is why various levels of government are in charge of regulating education for young people. For adults who have voting rights to determine the course of public policy, we basically have nothing reliable. The biggest inadequacy in our Constitution is its negligence in the area of public information and knowledge. The founding fathers thought they could insure a free market in ideas and policies that the American people could make informed judgments on by insuring freedom of speech and a free press.

Of course, at the time of the Constitution, there were no large American corporations to interfere with the legitimate roles of government. This is why, except for the exclusion of black people and women, when it comes to the economy before the Civil War, we had a fair example of a Democratic Capitalist society. Information and education of adults was accomplished by a free press which was owned and sustained by very average Americans — small printers in very ordinary circumstances that probably reflected the interests of the majority of Americans.

When we come to modern times we find the press is no longer free at all. In fact, it is quite expensive. It takes millions of dollars to own a major radio or television station. Even newspapers require enormous capital. Democracy and especially Capitalism, unlike dictatorships, is an extremely fragile system. Although the founding fathers did take precautions to insure that laws would be enacted by representatives of the people, they were remiss in not insuring a means for the citizenry to have an *independent* source of information to maintain the integrity of the system. It is important to realize that *without an objective and independent means of communication* outside *the system mind to enable the public to be well-informed about the issues of the day, and especially their own economic and political interests, you are not going to have democracy or Capitalism.*

Now the legislature has the power to regulate the means of communication. We have an FCC, Federal Communications Commission, whose purpose is to license broadcasters to operate "in the public interest", as we mentioned. In this capacity, our means of communication should provide an accurate picture of reality upon which people can make intelligent decisions. It should be a transcendent entity *overseeing* the economic system describing it fully. But instead, our means of communication — our radio and television outlets — are owned by very large corporate nodes. Not only that, but the parties who pay for the programming are also very large corporate nodes.

So as opposed to being part of the political system that *oversees* the economic game, the economic system mind is constantly trying to pull the political system into its bailiwick so that the larger nodes will be better able to run society in its own interests. The means of communication has become the mouthpiece of the system mind and the "public interest" has long been forgotten. Thus it becomes *part* of the economic game as important economic nodes *included* in the system mind. This gets people's political lives to become part of the economic system mind to do the bidding for the larger nodes instead of allowing our political lives to operate *outside* of it so that we could be better able to look out for our own interests. The result is that the nightly news is a cesspool of statements that pass off *opinions* as fact, which is the very definition of propaganda. When it comes to information necessary for citizens to make informed decisions about their economic and political interests, they mislead about everything important. What they don't lie about they suppress. They suppressed all the fraudulent financial chicanery that led to the collapse of 2008. They suppress any economic news and opinion that is not beneficial to the system.

Some of you might be a little suspicious of the whole concept of a system mind. There is nothing tangible to see. There are no conspiracies, no backroom discussions, no agreements. The system mind is an emergent property of our gigantic system of information flows just as occurs in the human brain. But when we look at the reality of the modern media, we see them operating as players in the economic system like any other business node, instead of an independent purveyors of vital information. This is pretty good evidence of a system mind. I'm sure Thomas Jefferson and James Madison would turn over in their graves if they could see the public airwaves being used by the system mind to represent only the interests of the top levels of society.

The irony is that it is in the area of free exchange and exposition of ideas that we have a very legitimate place for the concept of free markets. The means of communication in a truly democratic society should be maintained as a *marketplace* of ideas in which the best ideas win out. Now when it comes to determining the distribution of income and the value of labor, neoconservatives run for markets, which are made for the exchange of *commodities*, not for *human* transactions. But when it comes to the means of communication, talking to most neoconservatives about a free marketplace of ideas is like showing a cross to Bella Lugosi. What they want here are very unfree markets, in which a certain segment of society, namely the corporate world, monopolizes the means of communication and there's less free exchange of ideas than you get in commodity markets in Communist countries.

But of course, you don't want the public to suspect any kind of bias in media communication. That would defeat the whole purpose. So what the system mind does to cover its tracks is to program an ultraliberal *social* agenda to cover up an ultraconservative *economic* agenda. You can see this on the soaps and the sitcoms. If you want to get your story into one of the soaps, you better make sure most of your characters are either illegal immigrants, gay, or having an abortion — preferably gay. There have been enough abortions on the soaps to kill off half the next generation of babies. A good question is, since most of the people in the soaps are gay, where do they get all the pregnancies needing so many abortions?

Commentators have said, well look at the internet. Anyone can get online with their point of view. But the internet has only made things worse. Once in a while, friends send me stuff from the internet. It is worse than the system mind mouthpieces. Bloggers on the internet don't inform the citizenry in any objective independent way that they are responsible for. The internet does nothing to guarantee an objective source of information. What it has done is to allow people to get their information from parties who tell them exactly what they want to hear reinforcing the very biases they already have. A proper role of government is to provide an *independent* and objective source of news and information for people to rely upon to make important political and economic decisions. The internet is not going to do any better job at this than the mouthpieces of the system mind.

Once in a while you get some really juicy evidence as to the how the means of communication has become part of the system mind. *The Economist* magazine quoted a couple of poles taken in 2009 right after the collapse. It turns out that the percentage of people who "believe that government over-regulates private businesses has risen from 38% to 45%.[3] This is one of the most astonishing results I have ever read. Here we had a meltdown where people lost a third of their 401Ks, the economy was hemorrhaging jobs, people still working were worried about losing their jobs, and the government was stealing trillions from the future to revive the economy — all because there was no viable independent rules governing the financial industry. And right in the middle of the mess, people say there's too much regulation. This shows the enormous power of the media propaganda machine in getting people distracted from real causes and real problems. When you read something like this, you realize that with the constant bombardment by the media system mind, we will wind up with a kind of Industrial Feudalism where the top 20% has everything and the rest basically a bunch of helpless peasants.

Before we describe and categorize modern economic/political systems. Let's first look at systems that don't really fall into modern categories because the ownership and production of goods and services is communal.

23.6 Traditional Economic/Political Systems

Because the means of production in premodern traditional systems are *communally* owned, these systems are difficult to categorize. Communally owned means that everyone has some control of the means of production which is mostly land and animals. Traditional societies didn't have a concept of ownership where you have title to a definite piece of real estate and have near total control over what you do with it. This is why, when Europeans came to the New World, they didn't feel guilty stealing the lands of the indigenous Indians. Why, they didn't even have fences and titles to the land.

There is a continuum of political organization depending on the degree of democracy on the political side that gives us a stack of systems we can briefly discuss. At the top of the stack are societies that are called *Utopian*. Many early religious groups in early America were Utopian, such as the Shakers, Mennonites, etc. The land was owned communally which means in practice that everyone has certain rights regarding the land and also certain obligations and duties. But the rules of the game were regulated by a political system that was very democratic. The people in a village of these early Utopians get together to vote on everything: how land for plowing would be allocated, how food products would be distributed, and the rights individuals would enjoy. There was some productivity and surplus which was shared by all members of society.

The next system down are *Communitarians* and are half-way between complete democracy and a dictatorship. Most American Indian tribes fall into this type. The land was communally owned with individuals having certain rights and obligations with respect to it. The Chief had most control of the political system, although this could be shared with certain elders in the tribe. All political considerations like the way farming was to be done, how animals were hunted, how goods would be distributed, and how religious and other rituals were to be enacted, was under the auspices of this group of elders. However, they acted mostly as *executives*. How society actually worked depended almost entirely on cultural and religious values and beliefs. Economic output was shared fairly equally.

At the bottom of the stack are dictatorships in which one person has control over all means of production. Examples are ancient Egypt with its Pharaohs, and Anglo-Saxon kings. It might be a bit unfair to call these early societies dictatorships because the ordinary lives of people were determined mostly by their traditions and religion that society had evolved over thousands of years, rather than by the whims of a dictator. Even though these societies could produce considerable wealth, most of it went to the very top of the economic pile and for wasteful projects like the great pyramids. About 100,000 slaves worked on the great pyramid of Cheops.

23.7 Some Basic Concepts.

Before we get into some of the characteristics of various modern systems, I would like to point out that we will be using as a definition of an economic or political concept, ideas as they were used by the writer who first introduced the term. For example, economic historians agree that Adam Smith was the father of Capitalism. At the time Smith wrote, the western world was coming to the end of a period of Capitalist development called *Commercial Capitalism*, and at the beginning of Industrial Capitalism called the Industrial Revolution. Smith wrote a famous book called *The Wealth of Nations* that details all the mechanisms of a Capitalist economy: money, banking, pricing, land use, manufacturing, etc. This book popularized the concept of Capitalism which was ironically called *Liberalism* at the time. Coincidentally, Smith wrote his book in 1776, the year of the American Revolution. At the opposite pole, Karl Marx was the father of Communism and Socialism. He popularized these terms and articulated their definitions.

As you know, when it comes to politics, people say and do anything to push their own political and economic agendas. If you don't like a kind of system, you try to make the word for that system into a dirty word, and then apply the dirty word to anything you don't like. This is why I am being very careful to use definitions of economic and political terms as they were originally defined by writers who explained, articulated and popularized the terms.

The last term we should define is the word *'propaganda'*. This is usually a derogatory term a writer uses to characterize what he doesn't like. 'Propaganda' is a word that characterizes statements. We have other words to characterize statements, like 'true' and 'false' or 'analytic' and 'synthetic', (I won't bother you with the last two). We know pretty much what true and false mean. A *true* statement is one that describes a state of affairs that happens to correspond to an actual state of affairs in the world, i.e., it corresponds to the facts. But what is a fact? Well, we have to start somewhere, and I will be using as a definition of a *factual* statement as one that more than 95% of people who have a reasonable amount of information about the statement would agree to or accept. The analytic philosopher, C.S. Peirce suggested this criterion. In contrast, we're going to define *propaganda* as a statement that purports to be a statement of fact, but is only an *opinion* because less than 95% of knowledgeable people would accept it. If something is *not* a fact, but you express it as a fact, then you have propaganda. Take for example the statement, "the Iraq war was the right war to be in". Now since *less* than 95% of people would agree or accept this statement, it is a propaganda statement. What should be said is, "in my *opinion*, the Iraq war was the right war to be in". This is not propaganda because you are letting your listener know this is only an opinion and you're not trying to pass it off as factual. You can make any statement at all no matter how outrageous, but as long as you say that it is your *opinion*, it would not be propaganda.

I'll admit that my definition of 'propaganda' is pretty tough. But I have never seen a better one. Some people have tried to define 'propaganda' as using emotion-laden words to push across a point of view. But who is to judge the use of emotions? Or you're using unfair means to convince people. But who is to judge unfairness. These sorts of definitions will be simply more matters of opinion and will quickly deteriorate into more propaganda. The definition I'm employing is one that can be easily decided upon because we can check the facts in any given situation. This is a very scientific, deterministic, and *decidable* way to proceed. (By the way, 'decidable' is a word in higher mathematics to describe a statement for which it can be determined in a finite amount of time whether true or not.)

Above, we spoke of commodities versus rights. Where do we draw the line between goods and services that are commodities and those that are rights? Well, this is where we hear a lot of propaganda. For example, in the system of courts we have in the US, we have a right to a fair trial. This is a service the government provides to guarantee and support a *right*. Rights and freedoms are not *products* that have prices and can be bought and sold in a marketplace. Our rights as individuals are guaranteed by the Constitution and so are not commodities.

We have mentioned that when you want to discredit a policy or a point of view, you simply characterize it with a bad word. And 'Socialism' has become a bad word because our means of production is mostly owned privately and Socialism is where the government partially owns or controls the means of production. Since rights are not products to be bought and sold in marketplaces, they have nothing to do with Capitalism or Socialism. Even the most rabid neoconservatives don't call the courts Socialism because even they would not consider a right as a commodity.

Healthcare is a great example of where it isn't clear as to whether healthcare is a commodity or a right. Of course, conservatives want it to be a commodity and so they have tried to characterize a government healthcare service as Socialism. They call it "socialized medicine". But is it? Well, we have to see what people say about this issue, and to my knowledge, this question hasn't been asked of Americans. But it should. If health care is a *right*, then it is no different than the court system: a service guaranteed and supported by the government. It would not be included in the commodity part of the means of production and would have nothing to do with Capitalism or Socialism. However, if you consider it *discretionary*, then it would be a *commodity* and if it were produced by the government, it could be considered Socialism. Well, without knowing how people view this issue, all we have is our own *opinions*. But I would bet my bottom dollar that 95% of American people would *not* consider healthcare a commodity. I would bet that certainly more than 5% would consider it a right. Of course, I don't think 95% of Americans would consider it a right either. This means that healthcare as a right is a matter of *opinion*, and therefore, calling it socialized medicine as though this were a fact, is pure propaganda. But we knew this all along.

I would like to take this opportunity to give my own opinion because it brings up an interesting issue. I think health care is a *quasi*-right, which means it is partly a right whereby each citizen has a right to a *minimal* level of healthcare. However, I think that health care is also a *partial* commodity in that it should depend partly on our ability to pay for it. People who contribute more to our economic output because of their skills and productivity deserve a higher level of healthcare. This might be hard to design in actual practice, however. But I think it could be enacted so that people who could afford to pay more for their healthcare because they earn more, would get the more experienced and better qualified doctors, and people who could not afford healthcare would get the less experienced. Of course, liberals would scream that this is unfair and that we should get *equal* health care.

(Liberals love distributing equal wealth to everyone since they never create any wealth to distribute.) Well, this is propaganda too, because I don't think you're going to get 95% of the American people to agree with equal healthcare.

Do individual Americans have the *right* to have a branch of government that owns and runs a military? Do individuals have a *right* to a defense department and a pentagon? The Constitution prescribes how the government would raise and pay for armies, but it doesn't say we have to have one. Even if it did, our army could consist of one lonely guy. Remember the pentagon didn't even exist before WWII. This means that it is perfectly possible and Constitutional for our congress to get rid of the Defense Department and Pentagon completely. They came into existence by the powers of the legislature, not the judiciary, and could be retired the same way.

If the legislature has complete control over whether and how much of a defense department we have, then obviously it isn't a right. No group of individuals can go to the courts and sue to have a defense department as a matter of *rights*. This means that defense is a *commodity* that we as a society can have as much or as little of as we want, exactly as is the case with cars and houses. To show that defense is a *commodity*, it definitely has a price and a very big one. And since the government produces, owns, and controls the service of providing military defense, this is really an example of Socialism. When it comes to killing people and spying on their private lives, it's perfectly okay to have a socialized pentagon and socialized spy agencies. But when it's time to *cure* people instead of killing them, then no matter what the government does it's automatically "socialized".

What about the post office? I've heard many conservatives howl about the post office — that it's Socialism and we ought to sell it into private hands. Well, if we think about this a bit, we can see that we certainly have more of a *right* to communicate freely with our fellow man, which involves a *means* to communicate via something like the Post Office, than a right to a Pentagon. There is a lot more Socialism in the Pentagon than in the Post Office; but that's not the way we hear it.

A difficult category is infrastructure. If the government hires people directly to build a sewer pipe, is the pipe a commodity which would make this an example of Socialism? In my opinion, infrastructure is a half-way category. It certainly isn't a right, and yet the sewer pipe is a necessary object as part of what we consider civilization. We could call things like this, *prerogatives*, which is a kind of quasi-right. It isn't going to be for sale, and would have value only to someone who is going to pump sewage through it. I would say the actual pipe is not a commodity and so building or controlling it would not be Socialistic. It is a prerogative the legislature would provide. However, the *service* of running sewage through it *is* a commodity, and when the local governments provide and control this service, that could be considered Socialism. But nobody, including conservatives calls it that probably because they create a lot sewage that has to be carried away.

There are many prerogatives in modern society and some of them have been totally abused. Social Security has a program called disability insurance. Well, as you can imagine, there's nothing with more abuse than this. I've seen videos of people playing football and jumping around like a frog claiming to be disabled. Here again is an abuse by the courts. People can sue for benefits in front a vampire who has no resources to judge the validity of claims. The government has a big bureaucracy with the knowledge and resources to judge claims. Disability is a *prerogative* not a right, and should be adjudicated by *legislative* agencies, not a totally uneducated and unprepared vampire. Let's go back to our categorization of economic/political systems.

23.8 MODERN ECONOMIC/POLITICAL SYSTEMS

Economic systems fall into a number of categories because there are lots of ways that the economic system can be organized. But most ways are on a continuum like the one from black to white with all shades of grey in between. At the right end of the continuum, the means of production is owned privately either by individual citizens as in a small business, or by a corporation with a number of stockholders, or a partnership composed of more than one individual like a law firm. You've heard of law firms with a bunch of names. For example, Mr. Peculation and Mr. Confabulation team up with Mr. Prevarication and Mr. Larceny to form the law firm of Peculation, Confabulation, Prevarication and Larceny. Systems where the means of production are owned privately are called *Free Enterprise* or *Market systems*. These are on the right on our continuum. Capitalism is an example.

At the left end of the continuum, the means of production is totally owned and controlled by the government. In this case, politicians in government become nodes of the economic system and become part of a system mind. What is important is the grey area in between. As we go from private ownership of the means of production on the right over to the left end where the government owns the means of production, the ties between the two grow closer. There are many different arrangements that can create ties between the two systems, so it is often difficult to describe these in-between systems. Sometimes it's just money influence, sometimes ownership ties and sometimes control ties.

Separate from the means of production is the *political* system, which is not usually part of the system mind the of the economy. We will categorize political systems on the basis of the degree of democracy. The definition of democracy is where people can vote for representatives. But there is a vertical continuum of the degree of representation. At the top, representatives truly represent the views and interests of the electorate. At the bottom end of the continuum, we have dictators, which are called *authoritarian* where there are no elections. In between, there are elections like congress in the US, but representatives represent partially the views and interests of a political class like in Russia or represent various economic interests, like in the US, instead of the real interests of the electorate.

Thus we have two variables. The horizontal *economic* continuum goes from government ownership of the means of production to private ownership. And we have a vertical political continuum based on how much democracy the system supports, from pure democracy on top, down to a dictatorship in which some autocrat has taken total control of the economic/

political system. These two continuums will give us a box of economic/political systems shown in fig. 23.8.

On the left end of the top row we have *Democratic Socialism* where a part of the government owns and controls the means of production, but another part is a democratic political system having the role of enforcing the rules of the economic game. This is really *Political Socialism*. It's the kind of system that old-line Socialists had in mind on the basis of their reading of Karl Marx. Even though there are fair elections, this kind of system can be quite unstable. The government has enormous power heading both the political and economic systems. Whenever Democratic Socialism has been initiated in a big industrial country like Russia or China, the system quickly degenerates into a Communist dictatorship.

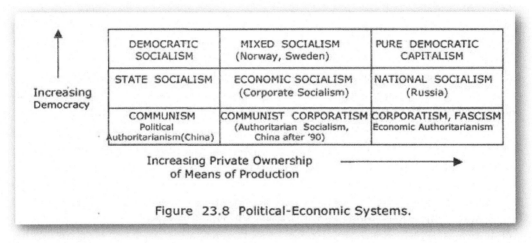

DEMOCRATIC SOCIALISM	MIXED SOCIALISM (Norway, Sweden)	PURE DEMOCRATIC CAPITALISM
STATE SOCIALISM	ECONOMIC SOCIALISM (Corporate Socialism)	NATIONAL SOCIALISM (Russia)
COMMUNISM Political Authoritarianism(China)	COMMUNIST CORPORATISM (Authoritarian Socialism, China after '90)	CORPORATISM, FASCISM Economic Authoritarianism

Increasing Democracy ↑

Increasing Private Ownership of Means of Production ⟶

Figure 23.8 Political-Economic Systems.

In the middle of the top row, we have Mixed Socialism in which the government owns or controls significant parts of the economic system. Even though the elected government can impose rules of the economic game in the interests of the electorate, there is the problem that by owning some of the means of production, it is in effect regulating itself, which is a glaring conflict of interest. This may be workable only in small countries where the political system is small enough to be viewed as a village get-together in a town hall just like in communal systems. Smaller business activity doesn't have the clout to pollute government rules that constrain activities of economic nodes. The strongly democratic political system with the approval of citizens can be independent enough to impose rules on most economic nodes. There are rules to keep the environment clean. There may be rules about safety for businesses. Scandinavian countries where the government owns and controls some of the larger means of production like steel or energy production or mining, etc. have Mixed Socialism. Of course, business sectors in these economies are always complaining that there are too many rules. But because economic nodes are relatively small, Scandinavian countries have been able to keep corruption out of the process of the government enforcing democratically chosen rules of the economic game. But this might not work in a large economy like the US, Russia, India and China.

It might also be the case that in order to avoid corruption from having so much power in the hands of the government because of its ownership of some of the means of production, the country in question must have a feudal past from which an ethic is derived. This is a very overlooked point. Whenever any kind of Socialism is introduced into a country without a feudal past, massive amounts of corruption emerges. Examples are some African countries, India, many Muslim countries, and most importantly, Russia.

At the right end of the top row continuum is pure *Democratic Capitalism*. As we mentioned above, the man credited for organizing the theory and practice of what Capitalism should be was Adam Smith as we mentioned above. The essence of pure Democratic Capitalism as Smith outlined it has three ingredients. 1) The economy consists of a number of industries comprised of firms owned privately by individuals or stockholders who *compete* to offer the best product for the least price and 2) who operate according to rules *independently* designed by society's representatives that truly reflect the interests of the electorate. These are the economic players. 3) There are consumers who have sufficient income to buy all the products that firms are able to make, i.e., to *clear markets*. Thus, a Democratic Capitalist system is an economic *game* with independently designed rules composed of privately owned producers *competing* in marketplaces and consumers with sufficient income to clear markets.

There were a few periods in history where we had something close to Democratic Capitalism: before the Civil War, the WWII years, and possibly in Holland in the 1600s. The government in Holland did a decent job of making rules of the economic game so as to create a growing economy with a reasonable benefit to all members of society. The financial sector was appropriately regulated so that trade and finance could be carried out in an orderly way. This was a period of great flowering of Dutch culture in the arts, architecture, and most importantly, political freedoms. The Dutch were engaging in trade all over the world which was made possible by their explorers. They got into the map-making business and Dutch maps from the 1600s are today worth thousands of dollars.

But it is almost impossible to hold onto Democratic Capitalism. As an economic system evolves more complexity, great pockets of economic power appear mostly in the form of large corporations. The modern corporation is a great invention. It takes the best technology and organizes human beings into productive units that produce goods and services in an optimal way. You organize a productive unit and try to "win", which means grabbing as much market share as possible, eliminating competition, and maximizing profits. It's a great game. However, the enormous amount of economic power that gets generated will always try to influence the political system into making rules that enable these same economic powerhouses to make money beyond the interests of society as a whole.

The only way to insure the continuation of this game for the benefit of the citizenry as a whole and reflect their interests, is for the rules of the game to be *independently* designed and enforced *as Adam Smith outlined*. This is the proper role of government in a Democratic Capitalist society, which is the only body with the power and resources to design and enforce the rules of the game, and which is democratically elected by the citizenry to represent their interests in carrying out this function. The political system is completely separate and independent from the economic system, and its role is really as a referee or umpire that enforces the rules of the economic game in exactly the same way that referees and umpires exist in the sports world to enforce the rules of the sports game.

The essence of any legitimate game is three components: players, rules, and independent referees. We can look at sports to see how a legitimate game is structured. The referees and umpires in professional sports are paid by the league, so that they are independent from the individual teams and can enforce the rules objectively without being influenced by the players and coaches. They do not hang out with, nor fraternize with players or owners, and aren't friendly to any of the players. Suppose the night before the super bowl, one of the referees in the game was caught having dinner with the coach of one of the teams in the game. He would probably lose his job, or at least be suspended. This is why you can see gigantic fights between the coaches or players and the referees. This shows that the referees are *independent* and not beholden to the coaches and players.

Baseball is an example of a flawed game. Of course, the umpires are independent and enforce the rules most of the time. But I am very suspicious of some of the play calling. Baseball is relatively easy to umpire, unlike football and especially basketball, which is extremely difficult to referee. And yet balls are routinely called strikes that are 6 inches outside. I think something is fishy.

But even in the structure of the game itself, the wealthier owners are able to rig the rules so that they can spend more money on players than other teams. The American league is basically a contest between the Red Sox and Yankees. 7 out of the last 10 years, one of these teams has won the American league championship. This is not sport. It reminds me of Roman days when a gladiator with a big spear would ride toward a poor helpless Christian and chuck a spear right through the guy and the crowd would roar. The other teams in the American league are just like the Christians in Roman times. Their purpose is to have somebody the Yankees and Red Sox can beat up on. Then in the middle of the year, both these teams scrounge around the league to see which players they can pluck from other teams just like a couple of vultures. There is great controversy as to whether or not to put asterisks next to the names and records achieved by players who used performance-enhancing drugs. There ought to be asterisks next to the names of teams who buy championships. But baseball however flawed, is a sterling example of a legitimate game compared to what goes on in Washington.

Another example of a legitimate game is the criminal justice system. Now I realize it is a very flawed system, but there is still a good deal of independence in the referees. Let's say there's a big lawsuit between two parties in a dispute. Suppose the judge in the case was caught having dinner with one of the disputants the night before the trial. He would have to recuse himself and possibly be disciplined in some way. This is the way real Democratic Capitalism would work.

Dropping down from Democratic Capitalism, as there is less and less democracy, you wind up with *Corporatism* on the bottom row right. This is where large economic units own and control the government. There aren't good examples of Corporatism in today's world. If such a system were to evolve whereby very large economic institutions were in control of the political system, some strongman would emerge as a dictator. *Feudalism* in the Middle Ages was a kind of Corporatism. Economic activity consisted of agriculture, livestock and small crafts on large tracts of land called manors controlled by an *aristocracy*. This was an upper class that had family names that were titles that got passed down. However, even though they controlled the political system of courts, culture, religion, and the distribution of wealth, economic output was really quite small and so the aristocracy was probably no more of an economic elite than a political/cultural elite.

Modern-day examples that resemble Corporatism is Nazism in WWII Germany and Fascism in Italy. At first, large economic players and industrialists in pre-war Germany thought that Hitler would be a nice puppet getting rid of liberals, labor unions and intellectuals that have always gotten in the way of large economic institutions. So they supported Hitler. Even as the Nazi party's popularity was dropping somewhat, it was German industrialists who propped up Hitler until his opening came. But it didn't last. Political systems are always quite hierarchical as opposed to large economic institutions that are organized horizontally. Thus it is much easier for a strongman to take over a political system than for some economic player to take over the entire economic system. And once the dictator has cemented his power, he can control the economic system even when it is still in private hands. This is what Hitler and Mussolini did before WWII.

But we shouldn't lose track of the fact that even though Mussolini and Hitler were political dictators, Mussolini's Fascism and Hitler's Nazism were market systems with privately owned corporations. This fact is very much suppressed by the American system mind as expressed by the mainstream media because American neoconservatives don't want anyone to suspect that our present day market system can easily degenerate into National Socialism. But this is exactly what happened in Germany in the 1930s.

Although Fascism and Communism look to be opposites, they have very much in common, starting with the fact that they are both dictatorships. What separates Fascism from Communism is the core beliefs of their ideologies. Both Nazi and Communist leaders got a lot of their support from the working class, but the theory for this appeal was different. Nazism is the result of glorifying a male super hero, der Fuhrer. Communism is supposedly based on people power. But this gets perverted into the dictator's power who claims to be representing "the people". And he does get some of their support by guaranteeing jobs, health care and education; also women and complying minorities do get some recognition in Communist countries. The Soviet Union referred to itself as the "Motherland". But just as under Nazism, there are no freedoms; and causing the deaths of millions is perfectly acceptable if the dictator decides they are against "the people". In contrast, Nazism is a male dominated system called "the Fatherland" that is partially built on racial and ethnic prejudices that turn into mass killings of certain minority groups. This difference is reflected in the difference between who the bad guys are. Under Nazism, the bad guys are usually racial groups, whereas under Communism they are the real or imagined "enemies of the people".

Moving leftward from Corporatism or Fascism, we get increasing control over the means of production by the political system. At the far left on the bottom in the diagram, we have *Communism* in which the political system owns and controls the economic system. The same question appears as under Democratic Socialism: too much power in too few hands. Every Communistic system that was ever put into practice turned out to have massive amounts of corruption or degenerated into an authoritarian dictatorship like in Russia and China with no democracy at all and none of the rights and freedoms we have in the US. They never allowed competing political or economic groups the freedom to compete for power. You simply cannot put the power of the political system *and* the power of the economic system into the same hands without some kind of strongman emerging with a small group of operatives who control everything and use their power to stay in power. Why Karl Marx and his followers didn't see this shows what a muddled thinker Marx was.

But in 1989, China introduced markets and private businesses into their economy, which puts China in the middle of the bottom row in a category of its own. It is a dictatorship with some of the means of production privately owned, although the most important parts of it are still in government hands. It is not quite Corporatism or National Socialism because the political system of the Communist Party is still in control. It is a Communist political system in bed with a corporate economic system. For these reasons, we are calling this system, *Communist Corporatism*. It is half way between Communism and National Socialism. So it is still a dictatorship, only by committee. As time goes on, China will attempt to create an illusion of democracy with fake elections just as in Russia. But economic players will have an increasing voice in running the economic game. As a result, China too will wind up with National Socialism or Corporatism, the exactly what the US system mind will lead us to.

Before the transition, China used to be called *Communist China*. In fact, in the media, books and articles, it was one word: Communistchina, without even a hyphen or a capital C for China. But during the Reagan administration, it was discovered that China would buy our paper that enabled Reagan to steal trillions from future generations. When our economic leaders discovered that we could drive down the value of labor by importing Chinese junk, the 'communist' word was dropped like a hot potato. It was now *China*, pure and simple. And instead of China being oppressed by a hateful Communist dictatorship, we were subsequently informed that China was "on the road to democracy". Yes sir — you could see it all over; business springing up, fortunes being made and money flowing like water. But of course, absolutely nothing has changed in the Chinese *political* system. This idea of progress to democracy is pure propaganda to justify propping up their government by giving them hoards of business and investing heavily in their economy. *The Economist* titled one of its issues "China's dash for freedom".[4] They're calling a turtle's method of backward locomotion, a "dash"? They ought to talk to the poet laureate, Liu Xiaobo, and learn something about China.

Events in '08 over the uprising in Tibet brought home the reality that China is every bit an authoritarian political system as it ever was. But because their *economic* system has become more privately owned, Americans can kid themselves as to what China is. Remember, in

Hitler's Germany, and Mussolini's Italy, the means of production were privately owned too. That didn't make them anything less than brutal Fascist dictatorships.

By the way, we're going to be quoting a lot from *The Economist* magazine which is probably the best-quality general news magazine in the world. All their departments are excellent: regional news, business news, finance, especially the science and technology sections. All but one: anything to do with economics is just warmed over and failed right-wing propaganda. Now if they renamed the magazine, *The Suidae*, everything would be fine.

In addition to the suppression of the reality of China's political system, the propaganda outlets have given us nice sweet-sounding names for their system. *The Economist* magazine tells us that commentators have offered all kinds of names for the Chinese system: "state-controlled, state-supported, quasi-state, parastatal, — without ever quite capturing what they are talking about".[5] Of course, the publication that knows the least "what they are talking about" is *The Economist* magazine. *The Economist* is going to outwit the competition in the west by coming up with the sweetest sounding name of all. Their name for the new system in China is "State Capitalism" to convey the impression that this is just another form of Capitalism that we can morally do business with. This is one of the most interesting examples of a Freudian slip you will find in modern times and very poignant evidence of a system mind. The reality, of course, is that their "State Capitalism" has as much to do with Adam Smith's Capitalism as rape has to do with sex. The rules are made by the Communist Party in bed with large economic players and there is virtually no middle class — only a large quite poor peasant working class. And now in 2012, all kinds of exposés are appearing showing that the families of leading party members have been making fortunes, confirming "...a nexus between wealth and power at the very top of the system".[6] This is the exact definition of Communist Corporatism.

The centerpiece of the new system is what is called a "hybrid" company. But in order to dull the impact of what this really is, they give it a sweet-sounding name like 'hybrid', which is the same word used for agricultural crops that have been bred for better qualities. It's also the name of a wonderful line of environmentally safer cars. We're not talking about mom and pop businesses here. We're talking about leading companies in leading industries. Presently, 54 out of the largest Chinese companies are "hybrids" making up *80%* of their stockmarket. This creates a nice bed for economic players and political actors in the Communist party to make their own rules. *The Economist's* lead for an article about China was, "China's business people are queuing up to become Communists".[7] In an issue discussing "State Capitalism", they say, "...the bosses of China's 50-odd leading companies all have a "red machine" ... "that provides in instant link to the Communist Party's high command."[8] That's just in work hours. After work they all hop in the same bed.

Of course, since these "hybrids" are in China and the developing world which can create competition with the west, *The Economist* views them with suspicion, characterizing them as enabling "inefficiency,...cronyism, inequality, and eventually discontent...."[9] However, when it comes to the west, they enthusiastically support policies that lead to something close to the same result.

It's what's happening on the second row that is the most interesting. Here we have democracy, but it is weaker than on the first row. Along the second row continuum there are varying degrees of ownership and control of the means of production. So we have varying degrees of Socialism along the way. And even though there are elections, representatives are somewhat beholden to the interests of a political class or economic elites. On the left side we have *State Socialism* where the government owns the means of commodity production, but the system is only partially guided by the views and interests of the electorate. Certain countries in Eastern Europe had systems like this during the age of Communism. But it is very easy for a system like this to degenerate into Communism.

It is in the middle of the second row that things are most important. We have what we are calling *Economic Socialism*. It could also be described as *Corporate Socialism*. This is probably the most prevalent system in the western world today. It includes the countries of Western Europe as well as Japan and most importantly, the United States. In Economic Socialism, the political system does not own the means of production, nor does the economic system control the political system. In the game of banking, investing, and producing goods and services, the referees and umpires of the game, who are government actors, are allowed to climb in bed with economic players even before important decisions have to be made directly affecting the economic game. They play golf with one another, go to lunch with one another, and exchange prostitutes amongst each other

Players from both systems are tied together in a wide variety of ways besides outright ownership. Sometimes individual people go back and forth between the economic and political systems. They start out in the economic system as officers of big corporations where they learn how to game the system. Then they get into government where they use their knowledge to fix the rules to the advantage of these very same large economic institutions. Armed with the intricate knowledge of how the government works, they return to the private economic system to further game the system to their advantage.

Maria Faccio of Vanderbuilt University did a study of political "connections" between government and the private sector. "These she defined as existing if a politician, former politician or someone cozy with the current governing party sits on a board of directors or is a big shareholder...." She found that "...broadly, connected companies enjoyed lower tax rates and higher market shares than otherwise similar firms." [10] There are lots of advantages when you're in on making your own rules.

Other ways people in both systems can be in bed with one another is through bribery of various kinds. It starts out with economic players paying huge bribes to political figures in government at election time. (As an aside, it's very easy to define what a bribe is. There are 4 points: party B has interests; party A know what those interests are; party B gives money to A; and A accommodates B's interests — 4 easy steps.) In congress, bribery is possible because this same congress, which is composed mostly of people who have gone to special schools where you learn to lie, cheat, and pervert the English language, passed *another* law saying that a bribe would be renamed. It would be called a "campaign contribution". Not only that, it is given the even loftier description as "free speech", even though when money flows, not a word is spoken. Then when real freedom of speech was greatly curtailed by the Supreme Vampires, it substituted "freedom of expression" for speech. Of course, since no words are spoken in these bribes, the Supreme Court could put them in the category of "freedom of expression".

"Freedom of expression" allows the courts to have total control over any type of behavior. Any crime the courts favor, is simply dubbed freedom of expression. In theory, they could allow muggings, assaults and robberies as freedom of expression too. A mugger is "freely expressing" his anger at society; a rapist is "freely expressing" is anger at women; and a robber is "freely expressing" his anger at the economy. At any time, the Supreme Court could legalize any of these crimes under the heading "freedom of expression". I'm sure that in the future, they will do just that. The Constitution doesn't say a word about "freedom of expression".

Of course, all of this is totally suppressed by system mind media propaganda outlets. Part of the role of the system's mouthpieces is to hide from the public the ties between the economic and political systems, which can be very strong. This is why it is a very subtle system and why it's hard to get a grip on it. This is partially why Economic Socialism is what Adam Smith warned against. System mind apologists sometimes call this "conflict of interest". There is no conflict of interest at all. As members of the Corporate Socialist camp, these economic players are operating in the interests of *themselves*, and there was no conflict at all. The only thing that keeps Corporate Socialism going is new technology which increases productivity so that the corruption of the system is papered over. Of course, there is still some democracy under Economic Socialism because we have the right to vote. But choices are greatly constrained by what the economic system dictates. Representatives often represent first the interests of economic elites, which is why a lot of people don't even bother to vote. We mentioned above the study showing that ordinary citizens have no influence on public policy at all.

Just as it is very easy for Democratic Socialism or even State Socialism to degenerate down to Communism, it is also very easy for Democratic Capitalism to slide down to Economic Socialism. Economic nodes grow in a Democratic Capitalist society to where they can greatly influence and control actors in the political system and make their own rules. This is exactly what happened in the US in the 2000s that led to the big meltdown of 2008.

Probably the most accurate measure of the degree of Economic Socialism in a given economy is the degree to which environment safety is enforced. This is one of the most important points to be made in this book. Keeping a safe environment does cost companies money. And of course, there is always a strong motivation in any company structure to minimize costs. This is why businesses in the US spend billions buying, selling, and climbing in bed with government politicos to rig the rules of the game to avoid environmental safety. And the more Corporate Socialism you have, the less resources, effort, and attention is going to be paid to environmental safety. Whenever the Republican party brings back Corporate Socialism, there's an uptick in genetic damage and birth defects due to relaxed environmental rules of the game. The current enormous uptick in auto-immune diseases, childhood cancer, gender ambiguity, etc. started with Ronald Reagan.

The tighter the bonds between economic players and political actors in Washington, with economic players really calling the shots, the more Economic Socialism you get. In the extreme, we have 'National Socialism' to denote a free-enterprise market system whereby powerful economic players totally control the political system. This is on the right of the middle row in our table. National Socialism resembles what we have called Communist Corporatism in China. Something like this has occurred in Russia. There is the slight difference in that there is a small degree of democracy in Russia, which is why we have them on the second row. Also economic players have more say in Russia than in China which is why we have put them on the right of the diagram.

After the breakdown of Communism, Russia was pretty much in the hands of an oligarchy of economic players who owned large economic sectors like the gas, oil, and mining industries. Soon power coalesced around Yeltsin and then Putin who has pretty much set himself up as a tsar. Putin ostensibly leads the political system. However, he has his hands on some of the means of production and the oligarchs who own major areas of the means of production have close ties with the Kremlin. Economic players are in bed with political actors at all levels and the result is a constant rigging of the rules to allow money to be made by certain groups at the expense of others that has nothing to do with the legitimate economic activity.

23.9 EVOLUTION OF ECONOMIC SOCIALISM

As we discussed above, Feudalism in the Middle Ages was a form of corporatism whereby the leading economic players, the feudal aristocracy together with the king, owned and controlled the political system. Feudal landowners had set themselves up as a god-given aristocracy with the divine right to own and control everything. Feudalism reached its peak in Europe in the Middle Ages between 1000 A.C. to about 1400 A.C.

The Commercial Revolution began in small ways in western Europe in the 1100's and 1200's with a new merchant class involved with trade between Europe and the near east.
As capitalism and trade developed, manufacturing became a bigger part of the economy. This picked up steam in the 1500's with the invention of spinning and weaving methods in Europe that led to the factory system of production and increasing amounts of trade between nations.

The increasing trade and small manufacturing carried out by the merchant class required money and capital. National currencies were needed, along with banks. But since the new class of people and new activities relied on individual initiative, they were looked down upon by the old feudal aristocracy. As a result, the new merchant was in a hurry to make money, which was their only means to acquire social status. However, they saw that trading was not going to make them enough money to achieve these goals. So they turned to technology as a means to make money and gain power at a more rapid pace. This produced a movement away from country manors and into cities where new developments in money, banking and technology would be taken up more energetically.

The merchant class was a very tiny class at first in the 1000s, but as trade grew and money became important, their power in society increased. Also, technology marches on. It's like a dam. You can hold it off for a while, but eventually it will flood the land. By using new means of trade and finance with a sprinkling of new technology in the way of weaving and spinning, the merchant class grew continuously after the 1100s. They were joined by a growing class of independent yeoman farmers, small manufacturers and professionals like doctors and lawyers. This was also an urban class because cities were located to facilitate trade. They wound up being about 15% of the population. They were called the middle class or bourgeoisie in feudal times, but in today's world we will be calling them the professional class. The growing wealth of the bourgeoisie enabled them to demand representative government and individual rights and freedoms like freedom of the press of speech and religion, because that is what they needed to achieve economic and political power to protect their interests. Contracts became important and this in turn requires an independent system of courts. Of course, this process took hundreds of years to complete.

As the bourgeoisie began to accumulate wealth and power themselves, they gradually got more and more of the lower orders in England on their side by preaching liberty, democracy and freedom. Also, increasing segments of the peasantry and even artisans began to identify with the wealth and power of this class instead of with the old aristocracy. This led to major revolutions. There was the English Revolution in the middle 1600s, in which the king lost his head. The French revolution saw the king, as well as the aristocracy, lose their heads.

The transition from the old feudal system into the Commercial Revolution and then the Colonial experience in the US took place along three different avenues of change. They correspond pretty much with the means the old feudal aristocracy was going to cope with the increase in trade and the production of goods and services, as well as the rise of a new class of merchants. One way can be called *resistive*. The old aristocracy could *resist* the rise of the new merchant class. This occurred mainly in England among a large segment of the aristocracy. Of course, it was a hopeless agenda, and by the late 1700s, some of them had lost land, income and wealth. They still had the upper class family name, but it wasn't worth much.

The second way was *transformative*. The old aristocracy could gradually transform themselves into bankers, businessmen and producers of goods and services. For hundreds of years, they had ownership and control over all agricultural land, and when resources were found under the land, they were in a position to take advantage of that too. Thus as merchant capitalism progressed, the old aristocracy could use their position as owners of agricultural production and natural resources to enter into new Capitalist transactions and exchanges and became part of the growing merchant Capitalist class.

The third way a transition occurred was through slavery. Even though peasants under the feudal system were the "lower orders", they were still considered human beings and had some rights. Of course, the aristocracy could justify different classes of people with different roles because even the bible recognized different roles in society. But the bible also said that we were all equal in the eyes of God.

As the centuries went by, it occurred to many in the aristocracy that more and more peasants and even the craft orders of the feudal system would be attracted to the values, ideas and institutions of the merchant class and other bourgeoisie. In order to have a class to replace the old peasantry, the aristocracy hit upon a very old idea left from Roman, Greek and Egyptian early times. You find people that you don't *have* to consider human beings with even a smidgen of basic human rights. They would continue doing the work of the old peasant class so that the aristocracy could continue their leisurely lifestyles. Not only that, but slavery allowed them to maintain total control over a class or workers by borrowing the concept of *property* from the merchant class: replaced peasants were property. It was a very immoral but clever idea. This is how slavery got started — or *re*started.

This kind of transformation is what occurred in the American south, where the second and third sons of the English aristocracy established a slave system. Because of the similarity between the agriculture of a feudal manor and the crops that could be raised in the south, it was quite natural to transform feudalism into southern slavery. With the clear distinction of skin color, it was easy for slavers to avoid any considerations of humanity for slaves.

These three stands of the transition between feudalism and Capitalism wound their ways through centuries between the 1100s and the 1800s. Sometimes the classes involved would be allied; other times they were at each other's throats. There were times when the merchants and aristocracy allied to get rid of the idea of a monarchy. However, some claim that a monarchy was a foundation for the nation state with national institutions like money and banking and other Capitalist structures. This is a very interesting period of western history, which was discussed in an excellent book review by George Fredrickson.[11]

These are the conditions that colonial American inherited from Feudalism and the Commercial Revolution in Europe. The colonies themselves were established as commercial ventures by the English. In order to escape from English feudalism and establish a more independent economic life, colonists came to America for economic *opportunity*. Since America consisted of colonies of England, the economic/political system transpiring in England was copied in the colonies. But as the colonies grew, sparks would flare up now and then as friction increased between the colonists and the English king (George III).

This is the climate under which the American Revolution transpired and the Constitution was written. The Declaration of Independence is one big blast at the king of England and everything he stood for: authoritarianism, aristocracy, religious intolerance, classes, etc. Our founding fathers wrote a Constitution that established Representative Liberal Democracy. The irony is that at the time, *Liberalism* was an *economic* term meaning pure Capitalism as Adam Smith described. By this time, all over Europe, the merchant class had accrued enough economic and political power to establish parliaments to represent them and to greatly influence the direction of the evolution of the American system of government and its Constitution.

People think of the founding fathers as political operatives, which is certainly true. But they were also economic players. We discussed them in Sect. 19.5. In fact, there are historians like Charles Beard who claimed the founding fathers and the Constitution were very much a counter-revolutionary period. It is true that all during the debates over the Constitution, many delegates were very worried that the new American experiment would unleash all sorts of radicalism and mobacracy. This is why the Constitution is a very conservative document.

Lots of books have been written in recent years putting down the founding fathers as liars, hypocrites, and covert feudalists. In my opinion, in view of the great influence the king of England had in determining the colonist's values and beliefs, we're very lucky to have the founding fathers we got. It's easy for today's liberals like Gore Vidal to nit-pick the founding fathers. These guys wouldn't get elected dog-catcher in those days. If I were born in Virginia in 1743, I would kiss the ground if I turned out as well as Jefferson with all his warts. It was he and Madison who sneaked in a Bill of Rights, which is the encapsulation of our rights and freedoms. There was absolutely zero chance of anyone elected removing or even mitigating slavery at the time of the Constitution. Even trying would have brought back monarchists. Even after 50 years of stable democracy and abolitionism, Lincoln couldn't do it without a horrible civil war.

As we discussed in Sect. 19.5, the reason the drafting of the Constitution appears such a schizophrenic process is that it is a conservative document in *essence*, but a very *existential* one at the same time.* Many of the founding fathers really were fast-buck operators, speculators and business sharpies, and most importantly, slave owners. But in spite of *essentialist* nature of their practices and behavior, they managed to write and pass a document that had a very *existential spirit*, providing for rights, freedoms, and participatory democracy that was as close to the people as possible. I realize that various groups like black people and women were not included in the political game. But they very subtly put language into the Constitution that *could* have enabled subsequent Supreme Courts to gradually wind down slavery and provide equal rights for women. What has dragged down our history is not the founding fathers at all. It's the fact for 200 years, inner-brain reptiles have been chosen for the Supreme Court who would look to the *essentiality* of the Constitution, whereas progressive legislators might have looked to the existential *spirit* of the document.

One of the major defects in the personalities of the main writers of the Constitution was their lack of foresight. Jefferson was very backward looking yearning for the good old

---

* The definition of 'Existential' is a pregnant example of a system mind. As we discussed in Sect. 21.2, the original concept as defined by Camus and Sartre after WWII was creating an essence by being, by becoming. The original connotations were that existential efforts were to accomplish, to reach up, to create a positive identity. But the system mind made quick work of that, turning a positive word into a negative one with *essentialist* connotations. So we hear of "existential threats, sanctions, force, power, aggressions, etc. — all a complete perversion of the original meaning — all the work of the system mind. Sartre and Camus would turn over in their graves.

days when the country consisted of small yeoman farmers, small businessmen and artisans making simple goods. He didn't seem to look forward to a time when the economic players would no longer be small people. James Madison was a present looking person along with other major political players like John Hancock, Benjamin Franklin, etc. As a result, the whole gang wrote a Constitution for a Democratic Capitalist system with a political government about equal in power to the economic system *at that time*. But this state of affairs didn't last long as we will see.

This contradiction inherent in the Constitution has sparked controversy as to how to categorize the southern system. Was slavery basically a new kind of feudalism because there were clear-cut highly unequal classes; or was it preCapitalism because the slaves were bought and sold in Capitalist markets? Since this is history, one of these views has to be "Marxist", but I don't care which one. Some historians claim that slavery *was* capitalism which shows that you really can't do western history without understanding a little economics. First, there was very little "capital" accumulated in the south until *after* the Civil War. Their cotton was sent north for processing. Second, there was only a miniscule middle class in the South. Plantation owners and kin were an aristocracy and poor whites and slaves were most of the rest. And last, all laws, courts, and rules were made by the aristocracy in bed with politicians making their own rules that legalized slavery in spite of the Constitution. That's strike three, called by Adam Smith, which is what happens when some of these historians step up to the economic plate. The reality is that slavery is in a category all it's own — an adaptation of feudalism to modern times by borrowing a few market mechanisms like property rights and markets.

In any event, when Capitalists in the North couldn't convince the South that their kind of slavery was more efficient and profitable than southern slavery, a horrible civil war was necessary to end southern slavery. Historians are still spatting about the economic benefits and profitability of southern slavery. Of course, southern slavery was profitable, but the question is, *how* profitable was it?

A southern slave was an investment. An owner had to make sure the slave had sufficient nutrition, housing and safety to keep the slave alive and working. These costs ate into profits. But these costs were not necessary for northern-style slaves. If a worker lost an arm, or got sick or didn't have enough to eat, he was thrown in the street and replaced by a newly-arrived immigrant. The proof of the pudding is in the eating. Wherever *northern* style slavery occurred like in England and the US north in the initial stages of the Industrial Revolution in the late 1700s, there were enough profits and economic benefits for Capitalists to accumulate huge amounts of capital to finance economic expansion. Obviously, profitability of southern style slavery did not accumulate sufficient capital for industrial Capitalism to occur. This is why the north (almost) won the Civil war.

Some say that the south could accommodate plantations, which were more advantageous than industrialization for profitability. But slavery was a cultural phenomenon that was a natural continuation of a feudal hierarchy as we have mentioned. It was never conceived as a profit-maximizing system. But the day the Civil War ended, the south immediately began to adopt northern slavery; and they did so quite proficiently considering all the momentum that southern slavery had accrued over the centuries. They were greatly aided in this regard by the Supreme Bloodsuckers who did everything they could to *bring back* slavery. In fact, they succeeded beyond all expectations. The South instituted what was called *peonage slavery*. Laws were passed against minor offenses like walking along a railroad track. There were vagrancy laws that were even more arbitrary. Offenders were put back into actual slavery which lasted into the 20th century. None of this was in my history books. But the new slavery was even worse because now the slave was no longer an investment the owner had to maintain. If the slave died, they threw him in a hole and brought in the next poor bastard walking along the tracks. The South was then able to accumulate capital for industrialization in textiles, mining, oil and coal, almost as efficiently as the north had done and with the same results.

23.10 TRANSITION TO ECONOMIC SOCIALISM

Let us repeat the very essence of pure Democratic Capitalism: *competing private property players, rules enforced by independent referees, and a middle class of consumers with sufficient income to clear markets.* Without each of these three components you don't have real Democratic Capitalism as described by the father of Capitalism, Adam Smith in his book *Wealth of Nations*. As mentioned, in 1776 the year of our Revolution when he wrote his book, his system was called *Liberalism*. The irony is that Adam Smith himself had many political views that are close to today's liberals. An explanation for this is that Smith was not merely an economist. He was also a renowned moral philosopher. So his economic views and his analysis of the essence of Capitalism are greatly informed by moral considerations. What I think motivated Smith was that by his day, the Commercial Revolution was already accruing abuses. The East India Company in Great Britain was already in bed with political actors in London to rig the rules in its favor at the expense of the rest of society, especially in countries it had invaded. At some level of his mind, I think Smith realized that Capitalism doesn't come with its own ethic. This is why Smith warned against monopolies, players making their own rules and larger economic nodes hogging too much wealth. So part of Smith's motivation in analyzing Capitalism and writing his book was to warn against possible abuses to Democratic Capitalism and outline a moral basis for a Capitalist economy.

There's a lot of detail in Smith's book about how the system works regarding prices, labor, money, etc. But he stressed in various places the three essential ingredients of a Capitalist system. First of all, Smith realized that the core of an economy is Consumption. He said, "Consumption is the sole end and purpose of all production; and the interest of the producer ought to be attended to only so far as it may be necessary for promoting that of the consumer".[12] The reason for this is that "...the real wealth or poverty of the country... would depend altogether upon the abundance or scarcity of those consumable goods".[13] And a corollary to this is that to realize this wealth, you need a consuming class with sufficient income to *purchase* the goods the system can produce.

Regarding labor as consumers, in Book I, Smith complements the system in Holland: "The province of Holland…is a richer country than England. … The wages of labour are said to be higher in Holland than in England, and the Dutch, it is well known, trade upon lower profits than any people in Europe".[14] I am quoting the man who historians attribute as the father of Capitalism just so you'll see how far we have drifted from Democratic Capitalism. Smith was very sympathetic to the ordinary workingman and thought he should make a decent living, not only for humanitarian reasons, but also for pure the economic reason that *Capitalists need consumers to buy their products.* He sums of both the humanitarian and practical aspects: "No society can surely be flourishing and happy, of which the greater part of the members are poor and miserable." [15]

In my opinion, the major motivation Smith had in describing in great detail the system of Liberal Capitalism was to introduce to the world the idea that with the coming of industrialization, a feudal aristocratic class could no longer be maintained by owning large tracks of land over which it had complete political and economic control. Even if your goal is a new economic aristocracy, it would have to gain its dominance, wealth, and power not by owning feudal manors, but by producing and *selling* something to those outside a feudal manor. This required that "labour" has sufficient income to buy what Capitalists are making, even at the sacrifice of profits. The modern neoconservative thinks you can maintain a modern economic aristocracy by grabbing ever-increasing shares of income, wealth, and power. A feudal aristocracy needed control over land; but a modern aristocracy needs *customers*. This simple fact is beyond the cognitive abilities of the modern-day neoconservative reptile.

Regarding competing firms in an industry, Smith was very much opposed to "combinations" that could take advantage of workers, fix prices and collude to keep prices high without corresponding improvements in the quality of goods produced. And most importantly, he realized that you're not going to have a viable Capitalist economic system if the economic players can make their own rules. Let's quote the last two sentences of Smith's first volume. Concerning the *order* of Capitalists and trader who he called "dealers", he said: "The proposal of any new law or regulation of commerce which comes from this order, ought always be listened to with great precaution, and ought not to be adopted till after having been long and carefully examined…with the most suspicious attention. It comes from an order of men, whose interest is never exactly the same with that of the public, who have generally an interest to deceive and even to oppress the public…."[16] These are the two most important sentences in his book. It very clearly shows in stark language that the man credited as the father of Capitalism saw the danger of economic players dominating the political system and making their own rules. He bemoaned the fact that "We have no acts of parliament against combining to lower the price of work, but many against combining to raise it". [17] This again is a reminder that Smith realized that the essence of a viable economy is a consuming class prosperous enough to buy the goods the Capitalist is making. And he was writing in 1776 before the Industrial Revolution and couldn't have foreseen the economic power the new "order" of industrial "dealers" were to accrue, and the power they would have to expropriate the political system and make their own rules.

Many of Smith's ideas of democratic Capitalism were incorporated into the American Constitution with its emphasis on private property, justice and the rule of law. And because of the Constitution and the right to vote for people even at the bottom of the economic ladder, there was somewhat of a balance between the economic system and the political system following the American Revolution. However, Capitalism is a very fragile system. Even at the time Adam Smith was writing, Economic Socialism was creeping into the English economic system. He didn't call it this because this was before Marx. But that's what it amounted to.

The idea of independent rules of the game enforced by the political system is the most important factor in a viable Capitalist economic system. The reason is that Capitalism is a very organic system with billions of transactions occurring every minute. The one characteristic of organic systems that is greatly misunderstood is that the secret of organic systems is not growth, but *inhibition*. We see babies in all living things grow into adults and we tend to think that the essence of organic systems is growth. But in spite of our perceptions, this is not the case. All organic systems tend to grow, even if uncontrollably. That's just what self-replicating systems do. The secret of viable organic systems is *inhibition*, where growth is stopped at an optimal time to create a viable functioning organic system. Recent research has shown that shorter men live longer than taller men. This is why when something goes wrong with a cell in the body, it tends to reproduce itself uncontrollably even if the growth is not viable, as we see in tumors and cancer. It was the genius of Adam Smith to realize this about Capitalism as an organic system. He said about the mercantile system that it is "…in its nature and essence a system of restraint and regulation…."[18] Without this sort of *inhibition* on the uncontrollable growth of the cells of the system, some cells will grow to where they are no longer functioning optimally but wind up distorting the priorities of a viable system. This is why Smith was so strongly opposed to monopolies.

The entity best equipped and best suited for designing and enforcing the rules of the economic game are the people's representatives because the government, by definition, is the only institution that represents the interests of the population as a whole. Not only that, but government in any country is the only entity that could conceivably accrue enough power to match the power of a modern Capitalist economic system with its huge international corporations and still represent the interests of the entire population. Thomas Paine, an important Constitutional advocate who supported commerce and business, promoted the government as the only available authority to enforce rules of the game.

This is why in modern times, representatives of the large economic nodes like big corporations, blare a constant drum-beat against "big government". And since our means of communication is in the hands of these very same economic units, this message is blasted at us almost every waking moment. They were able to take a grade D actor, Ronald Reagan, and make him into a superstar with the simple message that the government "is the problem". The motivation is clear. A small government does not have the power to independently make the rules of the game; and can easily be taken control of by large economic players who will make their own rules to the disadvantage of society as a whole, especially the ordinary citizen, as recent studies have shown. This is not Capitalism.

The concepts we are enumerating are the core concepts of Democratic Capitalism. And notice these do not include peripheral institutions. The modern neoconservative with the help of the media propaganda outlets carry on a continual drone calling anything they don't like Socialism because 'socialism' is a bad word. So they call health care socialism, along with unemployment compensation, welfare, minimum wage, pensions, Medicare, Medicaid, aid to education, and the hula-hoop. This is all pure crap. Whether or not an economy has a Capitalist system has nothing to do with these peripheral provisions. Capitalism consists only of a large number of competing privately owned firms producing goods and services, constrained by society's rules of the game, and a consuming class with enough income to buy this production. That's it. You can have Capitalism with or without a minimum wage, Social Security, healthcare or any other modern service the government provides. These are all peripheral services and have nothing to do with Capitalism. Adam Smith often referred to government public works programs, which in modern times can include any of our social programs.

Taxes are another issue we get a lot of propaganda about. Neoconservatives are fond of calling taxes socialism. Where do they think the government gets the money to run their trillion dollar wars and multi-billion dollar secret police agencies? Again, tax policy and spending policy has nothing to do with Capitalism. Adam Smith listed all kinds of revenue sources and spending measures in his mercantile Capitalist system. The government has some basic responsibilities, and taxes are necessary to finance these responsibilities.

Smith even anticipated the progressive income tax. He said, "It is not very unreasonable that the rich should contribute to the public expense, not only in proportion to their revenue, but something more than in that proportion."[19] A further motivation for a progressive income tax was that "The subjects of every state ought to contribute towards the support of the government, as nearly as possible,...in proportion to the revenue which they respectively enjoy under the protection of the state."[20] This is the exact opposite of the agenda of the modern neoconservative who pays for the government's "protection" of great pockets of wealth and "revenue" by stealing from the children of the country who can't defend their interests. Not only that, but this "protection" is maintained by armies made up of poor people who have very little "revenue". Even the feudal aristocracy in the Middle Ages had the honor and decency to "protect" their wealth and "revenues" using their own people, called *knights*, who were part of the aristocracy. Our modern-day aristocracy uses the peasants to do their "protection" and forces children of these peasants to pay for it.

Smith also saw the need for an estate tax on the "transference of all sorts of property from the dead to the living...." [21] Thomas Jefferson echoed these sentiments when he said the Earth belongs to the living. Compare this to our modern Bolshevik president, George Bush, who thought it was better to tax productive workers supporting children and families rather than tax dead people.

Regarding the fragility of Capitalist system Smith was promoting, he was very frank that "…as far as I know, [this system] has never been adopted by any nation, and at present exists only in the speculations of a few men of great learning and ingenuity in France".[22] The reason is that he already saw in his time, economic players were climbing in bed with political actors to rig the rules in their favor.

In the initial period after the American Revolution, there was still enough life left in concept of Democratic Capitalism to bring in a reformer, of sorts, Andrew Jackson in 1829. Jackson, as bad as he was towards black people, Indians and women, still maintained some semblance of Democratic Capitalism. He fought against the National bank and did what he could to help the workingman, especially creditors like farmers. Leading economic players at the time were still relatively small compared to the post-Civil War, and so the abuses were also relatively less. The government political system was almost an equal match for the power of the economic system during these years, and so could carry out its duties as referees and umpires of the economic game. This period is called Jacksonian Democracy and it was the last time there was any semblance of Democratic Capitalism for the next 90 years, until the crash of 1929 brought in Franklin Roosevelt.

Also, at that time the concept of honor was engrained in the culture of Western Europe. This was a holdover from feudal times. The founding fathers thought that people who would be attracted to government would be honorable men — umpires and referees, totally independent from the skirmishes and money-grubbing in the economic fray of competitive Capitalism. They set up a Supreme Court to guarantee basic individual rights and a legislature to design contracts that encapsulated the rules of the economic game. Little did they know.

What upset the equilibrium was the Civil War and the rapid explosion of technology. A number of entrepreneurs employed technological advances to build huge industrial empires and to amass huge fortunes. Great monopolies emerged like in oil and steel with enormous economic power. But as you might expect, this new great wealth was used partially to buy Washington political actors like sacks of potatoes, who would, in turn, rig the rules of the game so that robber barons could make even greater fortunes. This was Economic Socialism in its most virulent form.

Democratic Capitalism is a very fragile and unstable system. In physics they call it *unstable equilibrium*. An example is a ball perched on top of a pyramid. The slightest little push, even a breath of air, will topple the ball off the pyramid. Democratic Capitalism is like that. You might be able to hold it for a while, but the slightest nudge will send it down the road to Economic Socialism. No matter how strong the political system you devise, technological advances will promote the growth of large economic nodes that will enable the economic system to swamp the power of the political system. It is very difficult to maintain a balance of power.

After the Civil War, the economic system grew not only in wealth and power, but even more importantly in complexity. It truly became and infinite state system whereas a political system has rules encoded in finite language. As a result, in constraining the economic system, the political system is like a sieve that will always leak. No sooner had the ink dried on the Constitution, but leading economic players began to leak through the finite rules of the Constitution and rig the rules in their favor. It became impossible for the government to remain independent of the economic game and maintain fair and equitable rules for the benefit of all of society. The founders could not foresee modern day derivatives, interlocking corporate entities, and oligopolies. All of this creates an infinite state system that requires honorable human beings, also infinite state, to adjudicate. The purpose of a legislature and Supreme Court is to remedy this by creating infinite state institutions manned by infinite state human beings that might plug up the holes in a finite Constitution. What the founders didn't foresee is presidents choosing people for the court with their finite state reptilian brain, with the result that Economic Socialism is a constant threat.

23.11 Historians and the American Revolution.

There has always been a controversy as to whether the American Revolution was the existential end of the Renaissance, bringing together ideas of rights, freedoms, reform, virtue, and the public good into what is called *civic humanism* brought out by the historian J.G.A. Pocock; or was it the beginning of an *essentialist* Capitalism, called *liberalism* in those days, with its emphasis on the individual and his efforts to control the world around him, as claimed by Isaac Kramnick. [23] Even Aristotle recognized this dichotomy when he said that *citizens* "could not live a mechanical or commercial life". This dichotomy reflects a basic schizophrenia in the human mind as well as human historic evolution. There is the basic division of the brain into our existential humanistic virtuous nature, versus our essentialist selfish, exploitive and power-seeking nature. In my opinion, just as one brain holds both our existential and essential natures, so too the evolution of the America system has had both an existential and an essentialist aspect. We see this in the founding fathers who really meant what they said about rights, freedoms, virtue, and the public good, but practiced slavery and power-seeking at the same time. That's just the human condition.

In my opinion, Adam Smith was the most important practical thinker in all of history. You have a system of competing players that encourages technological progress, a higher standard of living free from the vicissitudes of nature, and a production and marketplace game that can unleash the human animal's *essentialist* need for self-interest and need for power and dominance. But you also have an *existential* political system that rises above the animalism of the markets and maintains rules of the game that channel human *essentialist* drives to constructive ends for benefit of all of society. This is what we're calling Democratic Capitalism. But with the enormous power developed in the economic system with the Industrial Revolution, the economic system began to overwhelm the power of the political system; so we're never again going to get it.

1   Gilens, Martin; Page, Benjamin, "Testing Theories of American Politics". Fall issue of *Perspectives on Politics*.

2   Rabban, David, *Free Speech in its Forgotten Years*. Cambridge Univ. Pr.

3   "A New Culture War", *The Economist*, Oct. 10, '09, p. 28

4   *The Economist*, Aug. 2, '08

5   "Too many companies…." *The Economist*, Dec. 5, '09.

6   "Riches Exposed". *The Economist*, Nov. 3, '12

7   "China's business people are queuing up to become Communists". *The Economist*, Oct. 6, '01.

8   "Theme and Variations". *The Economist*, Jan. 21, '12

9   "The Rise of State Capitalism". *The Economist*, Jan, 21, '12, p. 11

10   "Friends in High Places". *The Economist*, Nov. 1, '03, p. 63

11   "Class Act", New York Review of Books, Jan. 19, '84, p. 39

12   *The Wealth of Nations*, W. Lewis printer, London, 1811, printed for J. Maynard, Panton Street. Book IV, Chap. VIII.

13   Ibid. Book IV, Chap. I

14   Ibid. Book I, Chap. IX

15   Ibid. Book I, Chap. XIII

16   Ibid. Book I, Chap. XI

17   Ibid. Book I, Chap. XIII

18   Ibid. Book IV, Chap. IX

19   Ibid. Book V, Chap. II, Part II

20   Ibid. Book V, Chap. II

21   Ibid. Book V, Chap. II, Appendix

22   Ibid. Book IV, Chap. IX

23   "The Virtues and the Interests", Gordon Wood. *The New Republic*, Feb. 1, '91

CHAPTER 24

The Structure of the Modern Economy and the System Mind

———

24.1 THE ECONOMIC FLOW DIAGRAM

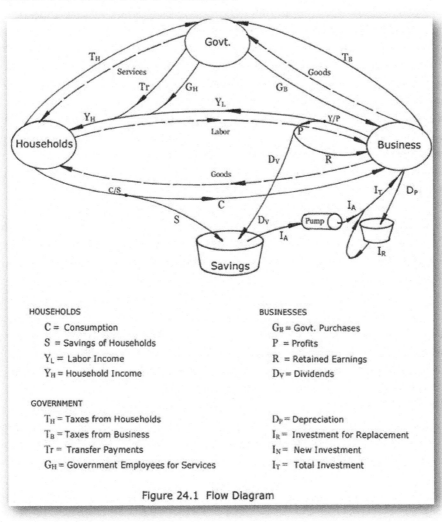

HOUSEHOLDS

    C = Consumption

    S = Savings of Households

    Y_L = Labor Income

    Y_H = Household Income

GOVERNMENT

    T_H = Taxes from Households

    T_B = Taxes from Business

    Tr = Transfer Payments

    G_H = Government Employees for Services

BUSINESSES

    G_B = Govt. Purchases

    P = Profits

    R = Retained Earnings

    D_V = Dividends

    D_P = Depreciation

    I_R = Investment for Replacement

    I_N = New Investment

    I_T = Total Investment

Figure 24.1 Flow Diagram

WE HAVE TAKEN A GENERAL view as to how the system mind of an economy works and what is its nature. Now let us look more closely at the various nodes in an economy and the various flows between them. It is on the basis of all the flows of information and goods and services that a system mind emerges. So we have to see what these flows are. This is pretty easy stuff. As shown in fig. 24.1, the basic structure of the economy consists mainly of a business sector that produces goods and services shown as the *Business* tank in the figure. Economic activity in any modern economy consists basically of making money by producing and selling goods and services. A person or group has an idea. They go into business by putting up cash of their own and borrowing from a bank. They hire a bunch of people to produce the good or service and try to sell what they produce. The object, of course, is to make a profit. The purpose of society allowing this game to go on is to provide the citizenry with goods and services that contribute to their standard of living. But the game can have costs to society that must be taken into account. Resources are degraded, energy is used, and waste products are emitted from production processes that can injure the population.

Then there is a *Household* tank which consists of all households in the country. The main streams of information between these two sectors are labor markets and product markets. In the upper flows, the business sector hires people from the Household sector and pays them to make goods and services. If you add up all the money firms are paying out for labor services throughout the economy, you get Labor Income, Y_L, shown as an income stream going to the household tank. Labor Income tells employees the value of the labor services they are providing, and it also tells firms what labor services are available and how much they might have to pay for them. In return, households provide labor services to firms, shown as a dotted line back to the Business tank. These flows also tell both parties how much labor in various categories is available.

Then people in the Household sector go into product marketplaces as *consumers* to buy goods and services. We see this as the lower stream of money flowing back to the business tank called Consumption, C. Along a dotted line we show a return flow of goods and services going from the Business sector to the Household tank. Again there is information passing back and forth between these two main sectors of the economy. The money Household consumers are willing to pay for particular goods and services tells businesses what to produce and in what quantities. Advertising is a way to inform consumers as to what is available in the marketplace. Of course, in modern times, advertising is also used to *induce* and psychologically *coerce* consumers to buy goods or services being advertised. But even in this capacity, advertising tells Households what is available and tells businesses what is selling. Whatever income consumers don't spend, they save, S.

There are two more tanks that make up the entire economy — a Government tank and a Savings tub at the bottom. And there are flows between these sectors as well. The major flows between Households and Government, including local state and federal governments, are taxes and transfer payments, and the services the government provides. Households pay taxes to the Government, which is the T_H flow in the diagram. Taxes are used by different levels of government to provide services like supporting the court system, building and maintaining infrastructure, schools, post office, maintaining a military, police at all levels of government, etc.

These services are shown with a dotted line and the money flows to government employees to render these services that all levels of government provide is G_H.

Transfer payments, Tr, are moneys the government tenders over to certain groups of citizens to keep the economy running smoothly. The major examples of transfer payments are unemployment payments to people out of work, and Social Security pensions. Transfer payments are the source of great controversy in the political realm. Basically conservatives say that it is unjust to dip into tax revenues to hand people money they didn't earn. Liberals counter saying that people do earn these payments in some way. Welfare was a way to pay single mothers for raising kids, until the system decided that motherhood was not a legitimate occupation. Adding Labor Income, Govt. Income and Transfers, we get Total Household Income, Y_H. When we use the term Income, we will be referring to Household Income.

I don't think that most people are against the *concept* of transfer payments as such. The problem is that the idea can be severely abused. Groups of people can organize themselves into blocks that simply vote to take money from the rest of society as a transfer payment. For example, today's retirees are getting massive amounts of money from the government in the form of Social Security and Medicare benefits and much of this money was never paid in by the parties receiving the benefits. Money is simply taken from younger members of society and from future generations to pay for it. Of course, this is unsustainable and sooner or later you will get a generation of people who will not receive the money they paid in. Conservatives have always been against the Social Security system and want to privatize it whereby working people would save for retirement on their own. On the other hand, liberals say the system is paying for itself, which, of course, is one of the biggest lies among the many lies you hear about how the economy works. It isn't even paying for itself now, let alone in the future when obligations pile up and baby boomers retire. A bank robber pays for himself too — until he gets caught. It isn't that the pensions retirees get are too generous. They're too stingy in my opinion. There simply has to be better ways to pay for it.

There are flows between the Government tank and the Business tank as well. Businesses also pay taxes, T_B. Some of these are spent on goods and services provided by the private sector of firms, businesses and corporations. For example, the government buys war goods from the business sector, such as guns, planes, tanks, ships, etc. The government also hires companies in the private sector to provide goods and services like roads and docks that government provides for the general population. In turn, firms pay employees through the Y_L pipe who work on these projects. The money flow from the Government to the Business tank to pay for goods services for the citizenry is labeled G_B, and the goods and services Businesses supply to the government is shown with a dotted line.

At this time, the federal government pays for medical care for the elderly (Medicare). In actuality, the government is really hiring *private* hospitals to provide health care and the government pays for it. People who want to make health care a right would have the government hire doctors and nurses directly to provide the same service. It would be a service in the same way as the VA provides health care for veterans and it would be a lot more efficient.

The last major sector of the economy is a tub, which consists of banks, investment houses, and other financial institutions, shown at the bottom of the diagram as the Savings tub. Households can do one of two things with their income. They can either spend it in the Consumption flow or they can save it by putting it into a bank or investing in stocks or bonds. This flow goes into the Savings tub and is denoted by S_H. Here again, the way households divide their income between Consumption and Savings provides information to the system. If consumers are saving more of their income, it might show that they are worried about the economy and want to have something for a rainy day.

The last flows are a little more difficult. Plant and equipment businesses use to make goods and services wear out. Money is set aside called Depreciation, D_p, to replace aging plant and equipment. This money is then *invested* in plant and equipment to replace the old. Of course, a business will buy replacement plant and equipment from other businesses. This is shown as I_R in the diagram which goes right back into the Business tank.

But a modern economy usually comes up with new ideas and inventions. If a firm likes a new piece of technology and they think they can sell new products derived from that technology, they will pump money up the Investment pipe and build *additional* plant and equipment to produce the new good or service. This is the I_A. They do this by selling stocks to households or borrowing from banks in the Savings tub. The household gets a piece of paper saying they own a piece of the firm and the firm gets money to use for expanding new plant and equipment to produce the new products. Thus the Investment flow provides information as to how firms feel about new technology and how they view their ability to sell products in the marketplace. The total amount of plant and equipment businesses buy each year from other businesses is total investment, I_T which is $I_R + I_A$.

Money coming out of the firms tank goes in two directions at a fork in the diagram called the Y/P fork. This money either goes for wages for labor to the Household tank, called Y_L, or it is in the form of profits, labeled P. Profits go either to the Savings tank in the form of dividends, D_V, or it is kept by firms for operating expenses, expansion, etc. This is called retained earnings, R.

The last flows are foreign trade. Households also buy goods made in other countries which is a flow going out of the Household tank and goods coming in. Also firms sell goods and services to foreign countries. This is called exports and is a flow coming into the business tank. For simplicity, we aren't showing these flows.

All of these flows — goods, services, labor and income — involve lots of information flowing back and forth between these four tanks. These flows of information between economic nodes in these tanks is what creates a *system mind*, just as the flow of information going back and forth between neurons in the brain creates the human mind. We will have a number of interesting questions in this regard. Can the system mind do propositional attitudes like beliefs? Before getting to these questions, we can learn about how an economy is doing from this diagram.

24.2 Deception in Measuring the Economy

You have heard about the size of the economy. The media and magazines tell us how much the economy expanded over the last quarter or past year. How do they measure the *economy*? Well, as you might guess, they measure the economy so as to make the system look as good as possible. They take all the goods and services flows and add them up to get what they call the GDP, Gross Domestic Product. Thus the GDP consists of C, the value of all goods and services purchased by households plus the value of goods and services provided to Households by the Government, G_H plus G_B, the money value of goods and services Businesses sell to the government, plus I_T, the money value of all plant and equipment Businesses sell to one another. (We are leaving out X, for simplicity.)

But does the GDP really measure the actual size of the economy, or is it nothing but a propaganda device? What people really want to know is, what are the goods and services the economy is producing and selling that actually contributes to their *Standard of Living*, which is how well we are living and the general quality of life. However, there are many factors that affect our standard of living that are not included in measurable goods and services. Clean air and water, safety on the job, environmental cleanliness, low commuting times, etc. certainly are part of our standard of living, but cannot be easily measured.

We will denote all the goods and services that contribute to our standard of living as the GEP, Gross *Effective* Product. It will turn out that the GEP is a lot less than the GDP, which is why the system never says peep about the GEP. Let's take an example, the Iraq war. After all the information came in, it turns out that Iraq had absolutely nothing to do with 9/ll. Also, Iraq didn't have anything close to weapons of mass destruction. The American people at first supported the war but when they slowly began to find out that it was based on a pack of lies, they turned against it. History will show that the whole adventure was totally unnecessary and actually destabilized a very volatile part of the world. So did the Iraq war contribute to our standard of living? However, all the money the government spent for war goods and armies, which people estimate was around a trillion dollars, was included in the G_H flow for army personnel and G_B flow for war goods the government buys from Businesses. When the trillion dollars spent is added in to the GDP, it makes the economy look pretty good. But if the war was totally unnecessary, the trillion dollars was a total waste. It would not be included in the *GEP* because it contributed nothing to our standard of living. It is a glaring waste when the majority of people want to get out of a war as happened in Vietnam.

I've heard neoconservatives say that conquering Iraq kept us safe from terrorist attacks. But the terrorists grew up in Saudi Arabia and were trained in tribal areas of Pakistan. Actually, by this logic you could claim that invading and conquering Norway would keep us safe too, just in case there's a Norwegian terrorist. Actually, using nuclear weapons to kill every human being in the rest of the world would keep us *very* safe. You'd get every terrorist. There is no end to this fraudulent argument. But nobody from Iraq had attacked anything about the US. As the CIA reported at times, Bush's invasion actually *created* terrorists.

And right along with the GDP, its partner in measuring the economy, productivity, is even worse. The definition of *productivity* is the amount of goods and services that can be produced in an hour of labor. Productivity numbers are twice as deceiving because there's no way to measure either variable. How can you measure labor hours when people are working all kinds of overtime hours that don't get recorded, in addition to tons of hours at home on computers and cellphones. And how do you measure goods and services when all you have is the dollar value? For example, if a factory turns out 10 chests per day, this becomes the output. In the 1800s, if a shop could turn out only 1 chest per day, then the numbers coming to the present would show a great increase in productivity. But the chest made in the 1800s is made from high quality solid hardwood, dovetailed construction, inlay, carving, and hand-rubbed finish, whereas the modern chest is junk made from crushed sawdust, stapled together and sprayed with acrylics. Productivity goes up, but what the consumer has is an orange crate held together with staples. There is no way some government bureaucrat can judge the quality of the goods we buy.

Now some products have improved, such as computers, chemicals, electronic devices, etc. So productivity in these areas might be underestimated. But the biggest part of the consumer goods basket consists of homes, all non-technology home products, clothing, and most food. (Where can you buy a tomato that tastes like a tomato?) Quality in these areas has plummeted. Homes now are made of piss, paint, plywood and plasterboard. So our measures of productivity, taking account of the whole shopping basket, is greatly overestimated.

This says nothing about the difficulty measuring productivity in the services area. Years ago you could call a company and talk to a human being and resolve your issue maybe in a few minutes. Now you spend hours trying to communicate with a long string of computer voices. The system says productivity has gone up, but what about the quality of the service?

The system makes a big deal about productivity. In one issue, *The Economist* gave productivity numbers for different quarters as .53, 3.91, 3.97, and 1.02.[1] This is absolutely ridiculous. They haven't the dimmest, faintest, foggiest idea what these productivity numbers really are. They show a bar graph with productivity going from 9 in one quarter down to 1 the next quarter.[2] This is impossible. For all these reasons, we haven't used productivity numbers in analyzing economies. Especially in the last 20 years, we haven't faintest idea what productivity we have.

The military in general is a prime example of fraudulent measures of the economy. We could call this a *productivity trap*. There have been enormous increases in military technology (If there had been as much progress keeping people alive as there has been making them dead, mankind would be in a lot better condition.) The government measures the productivity of the pentagon as the number of people they can kill per bomb. That might be okay if it were called the *Offense* Department. But it's called the *Defense* Department. Productivity appears to be going up because we are not measuring the actual service which is to *defend* the population and to make US citizens safe. That's what the service actually is.

But how safe are we compared to the immediate postwar period? Today, there are a number of nations who could land a nuclear weapon on a US city and some of them aren't friendly. WWII bombers could not reach the US, but today's bombers can reach anywhere in the world. And then there's terrorism which wasn't a problem years ago. So how much does it cost to perform the *decreased* service of keeping the population safe? Well, during WWII, an army tank cost about half a million in today's dollars and a fighter plane cost about a million. Today, a modern tank costs around *65 million* and today's fighter also costs over a *100* million. I was amazed when I looked up these numbers. *A tank: 65 million!* (And the government says that it can no longer afford to send us tax forms.) These costs prop up the GDP. We are all impressed with the technology but we lose sight of the fact that we are getting less and less of the actual *service* of keeping us safe in spite of all these costs. The service is not how many humans we can kill with a bomb, but how *safe* we are per dollar cost. And when we see that a fourth of the government's expenses are for the military which is about a *trillion* dollars, we can see that productivity numbers and the GDP as a measure of the economy is a total fraud.

Another productivity trap is in the area of housing and home accessories. There's a lot of impressive technology in building modern homes, but the final product is a home built out of piss, paint, plywood, and plasterboard. As hurricane Sandy showed, these houses blow away in a windstorm. Homes built in the 1800s were made of brick and stone and thick wood beams. So what is the productivity of home construction which is a major part of the economy? If the new home that blows away in a breeze can be built with less labor time, that would show up as an increase in productivity. But what about the sturdiness and quality of the new home? And what about accessories in the home? My very poor parents had hand-painted china, linens, tapestries, oriental rugs, and hardwood custom furniture. Now, you can go into up-scale million dollar homes and see nothing but junk.

What is the productivity of the criminal justice system? We measure the service in terms of how effectively we keep people in jail and we do get more efficient at catching and keeping people in jail. But the purpose of the criminal justice system is to *prevent* crime, which not only means better rehabilitation, but a more just, fully employed population who has less motivation to commit crimes in the first place. This is another productivity trap where the costs of police, courts, lawyers, jails, etc. have exploded in recent years, and productivity appears to increase. But these costs come out of taxes which lessens the money people have to support a decent standard of living. A certain number of people fall into poverty which increases the chances of turning to crime. As a result, the actual *service* of a crime-free society has not kept pace with costs at all. Crime rates have leveled off in recent years, but have not made up for the exploding increases in costs.

We have lots of complex production processes that result in very toxic waste materials being dumped into the environment, most of the time illegally. We have heard many horror stories and some noteworthy movies about environmental *pollution*. All toxic materials in our environment cause mutations in our genes, which results in many lamentable diseases and maladies. More than 4 thousand genetically based diseases have been identified, including childhood leukemia, immune system malfunctions, and brain circuitry miswiring. Some of this is due to environmentally induced genetic damage to germ cells that get passed on generation after generation. In the past 30 years, breast cancer has doubled and some of this was caused by inherited mutated genes that build backup systems that prevent cancer. Between 1950 and 1985, testicular cancer increased 300% in men who are only 25-34. When a person gets cancer this young, it's highly likely that he inherited mutated genes that guard against cancer.

We have heard of *genocide* at various times and places in history whereby whole peoples are wiped out. The most horrendous of these genocides was during WWII perpetrated by Adolph Hitler who murdered around 10 million people. Most of them were Jews of Europe who lost 6 million and was called the Holocaust. The word 'genocide' comes from two roots, genos, meaning race, and cide, meaning killing. But gen is the same phoneme as gene and if people knew about genes when these words were invented, genocide would most likely have meant killing *genes*. As a result, we don't have a word for killing or mutilating genes. Killing groups of people should more appropriately be called *anthropocide*, from the Greek root 'anthropos' meaning humankind. To be able to communicate our meanings, we will be using anthropocide to denote killing of *peoples*, reserving the word 'genocide' for killing and mutilating people's *genes*. This is the way it should be anyway, if we are to put Greek roots to their rightful use.

In many ways, mutilating genes is a worse crime than killing people. After WWII, Jews of Europe who survived and went to Israel had normal healthy babies. But because of the horrendous chemicals Johnson and Nixon dumped on Vietnam, enormous genetic damage was inflicted on the Vietnamese population. Their birth defect rate even today is 5 times higher than in the US. There will be babies born there a hundred years from now with birth defects who were no part of the war.

War has become a great source of genetic damage with the use of new and very toxic chemicals the body has no resistance to. "Epidemiological studies have shown that 26-32% of personnel who were deployed in the Persian Gulf [war] are ill", which means that "...175,000 to 210,000 veterans suffer from chronic ill health".[3] But at least these vets had some choice of going into this war. What about their kids who are showing up with above average genetic damage? They didn't have a choice in sustaining life-long impediments to a normal life.

"By EPAs count, one in four Americans lives within a few miles of a hazardous waste site." These sites contain "lead, arsenic, manganese, mercury, vinyl chloride, benzene and PCBs,"[4] all stuff that causes enormous genetic damage. And when they test kids growing up near these sites, they always test below average on any cognitive skill. A very alarming article by Barbara Koeppel details the health issues along a stretch of the Mississippi River in Louisiana called cancer alley, where there is a concentration of petro-chemical companies.[5] She says, "Clusters of asthma, stillbirths, miscarriages, neurological diseases and cancers have mushroomed". Most of these maladies are genetically based.

The three areas of the human body that are most susceptible to genetic damage are the central nervous system, and immune system and the sex system. The reason is that these systems are highly complex with very high information content. And so if there is damage to genes that build these systems, it will cause malfunctioning of some sort. Of course, some genetic damage and mutations are due to normal radiation from the sun. This is unavoidable. In what follows, we are going to be very conservative in our estimates. Our view here is that the incidence of genetic maladies that existed *before* 1976, the year we've chosen as the peak of civilization, was due to natural causes and unavoidable. But any increase in the incidences of genetic damage and birth defects *since* then can be safely attributed to our increasingly polluted environment. This is a very conservative criterion. And since 1976 is where we see alarming increases in malfunctioning. Speech defects (dyslexia, aphasia, etc.) have more than doubled since 1976. The same is true of immune system problems like autoimmune maladies — MS, rheumatoid arthritis, ALS, etc. I haven't seen studies about sex system malfunctioning, but doctors I've talked to say they are seeing more and more sexual dimorphism where the person has ambiguous genitalia. These numbers will continue to climb. Some genetically based maladies have grown at even faster rates. Asthma and autism have increased more than 300% since 1976.

Keep in mind, you don't cure or fix stem cell genes. Once they mutate, the mutation gets passed on forever. Anthropocide is an awful thing, but at least there is an end to it. WWII finally did end and with it the end of anthropocide. But genocide goes on forever. A hundred years from now, descendants of our war vets and people in places like cancer alley will be born with genetically based maladies.

With the way we have polluted our environment, we have been committing genocide in the US in alarming proportions especially since WWII. Incredible numbers of new chemicals not around during evolutionary times were invented after WWII that the human being simply has no resistance to and so are extremely toxic. Viruses and bacteria are alive and are very dangerous to other living things. But we've had millions of years to evolve an immune system that is designed to kill off these bugs when they invade our bodies. But we have absolutely no resistance to many of the chemicals that have been invented since WWII.

The really amazing thing is that when a company is trying to create a drug to help people and cure diseases, we put them through the ringer. They have to do lots of testing and then pass inspection by the FDA, which can take years and involves huge costs. The purpose, of course, is to make sure all our drugs and medicines are safe and effective. But you can start up a new production process that spits out an extremely dangerous toxic chemical into the environment and nobody exists anywhere in government to see how dangerous the chemical is and what its effects are on biological systems. This is a perfect example of Corporate Socialism. Companies that use these chemicals buy up congressmen and senators like sacks of potatoes. These political actors then turn a blind eye to industry players make their own rules. "Some legislators are even employed by the industry at the same time they hold office",[6] says Barbara Koeppel. The result is massive amounts of genetic damage to our gene pool. This is the real genocide. As we mentioned in the last chapter, *the most significant and accurate measure of the degree of Economic Socialism is the laxity of environmental protections.*

You might mention that we have an EPA which is supposed to keep the environment clean. Well, they enforce some rules about acceptable pollution levels. But you have to realize that the EPA can't make toxic substances disappear off the face of the earth. In fact, *every molecule of a mutagenic (gene killing) substance that was ever produced on the face of the earth, is still on the face of the earth — somewhere.* They try to bury the stuff in various places, but no matter what you do, some of these substances are going to leach out into the water and food supply. They find lead and other toxic materials in fish and animals on the North Pole.

Not only this but as the incidence of genetic maladies have risen alarmingly, the EPA seems to get less and less money. There were 1200 seriously contaminated hazardous waste sites that the EPA was supposed to clean up with a superfund. But funding for cleanups has actually dropped 38% since 1980, so the EPAs work of cleaning up these sites has been spotty, sometimes due to incompetence, but mostly just underfunding. It's amazing that when the defense Department wants money to go half-way around the world to kill people, they have no trouble getting hundreds of billions of dollars. But when it comes to keeping our own kids safe not just from illnesses, but genetic damage that goes on forever, the EPA has to beg, borrow, and plead. That's another trend started by Ronald Reagan. Even terrorists don't commit genocide as does our Economic Socialist system.

Obama threw a little money at the EPA in 2009 as part of the stimulus, but of course, this is like putting out a raging fire with a squirt gun. Our culture is so resistant to the idea of pollutants causing genetic damage that well-intentioned people like Barack Obama, whose only education was shyster school, doesn't seem aware of the problem at all. Instead of throwing money at corrupt state governments to be given to over-priced paper shufflers, a way to create *real* jobs doing *real* work for the nation's *real* health would be to first clean up the EPA of its incompetence and then hire people directly to clean up these sites. Toxins from these sites are causing genetic damage to your kids right as you read this.

And by the way, even the FDA is increasingly infected with Corporate Socialism. A former editor of *The New England Journal of Medicine* in a comprehensive article discusses problems with the FDA: conflicts of interest, internal squabbling, dealing with aggressive drug marketing to doctors, etc.[7] One of the worst problems is that there are members of their advisory committees who have financial ties to the drug companies: a perfect example of Corporate Socialism. This is to say nothing of the enormous bribes (i.e., campaign contributions) the industry makes to members of congress to get in on making their own rules. But Economic Socialism doesn't stop there. Often polluting industries use their massive profits to create chairs and departments at leading universities who proceed to hire scientists whose sole job is to pimp for the system. They just can't seem to see a link between very toxic pollutants and genetic maladies.

Devra Davis has written an incredible book (*The Secret History of the War on Cancer*) describing how the NCI, National Cancer Institute, ignored scientific evidence of cancer-causing mutagens in the environment. Listen to this: "early in its history, the NCI delayed and ultimately barred efforts by one of its most distinguished scientists —Wilhelm Hueper — to publish an uncompromising report on environment carcinogenesis".[8] Why do these abuses go on? "Partly, she claims, because of 'the revolving door of cancer researchers in and out of cancer-causing industries'." [9] There is little incentive to stop the incidence of cancer when billions in big salaries are paid looking for a cure that may be impossible to find. Part of the reason for this is that the medical research industry and the charities industry do not have an incentive to prevent environmental sources of genetic-based illnesses. They spend just about all their money on finding a cure, which is almost impossible when it comes to genetic damage. Finding a cure is not as important is *preventing* the disease in the first place. I keep promising myself that someday I'm going to stop giving money to these dam charities.

I don't totally blame companies and don't expect them to worry about pollution. They are in business to make a profit, not worry about the environment. But by this very same token, this is why the Business sector of an economy should not make its own rules, as Adam Smith stipulated. The worst polluter in the country is at least making a useful product that raises our standard of living. What do politicians in Washington make? It is neoconservatives, who have crushed real Capitalism and replacing it with Economic Socialism that is to blame. The neoconservative answer is free markets and "deregulation" which are really code words for Economic Socialism because to them, deregulation means companies free to make their own rules. Their solution is that if enough kids are born retarded, crippled and cancerous, they'll die and not pass on their genes. That's the attitude of our neoconservative rule makers.

But politicians have to get elected and they have to get bribe money to run campaigns. A prime source of money is from the corporate world. It all falls in the lap of the Supreme Vampires who are the archenemies of Democratic Capitalism. And now in 2010, these Bolsheviks have made rulings that allow politicians and corporate lobbyists to share smaller beds.

The media doesn't say a word about real genocide to our own kids it because their talking heads get their bloated paychecks from the very economic players that are doing the polluting. This was shown in the election of 2000 in which the environment wasn't even an issue. Al Gore's handlers obviously told him that there weren't enough votes for the environment to make it worthwhile running on the issue. This shows that the environment just isn't a priority for most Americans even though their children are increasingly born with genetic damage and birth defects. The reason is that the mouthpiece of the system mind, the corporate media, never says a word about genetic damage. Program after program features people wailing about various illnesses and diseases most of which have a genetic component. There is never a mention of genes. On Aug. 2, '07, Oprah Winfrey had a program about the alarming increases in autism. Conclusion: no known cause, no known cure. But Oprah isn't going to even hint that the causes of our toxic environment are the same corporations that pay her bloated salary.

What really amazes me is that the very people causing the genetic damage and the media people covering it up are also victims of pollutants. Their own kids are increasingly born with genetic problems. In the 2012 election, we had Sarah Palin and Rick Santorum as presidential candidates both of whom have children with massive genetic maladies. And there they are promoting economic animals in bed with political players making their own rules that allow them to pollute the environment resulting in more genetic damage. Power and money are more important than the health *of their own kids.*

Additionally, we really haven't seen all the ramifications to environmental degradation that are to come. Baby boomers most affected by the tremendous deterioration to the environment haven't yet retired. They will incur enormous health care costs in their later years. Our current health care costs to the elderly in the form of Medicare involve people born before WWII when the environment was relatively clean. The government estimates that by 2050, health care costs will be 20% of the GDP. I think they're genetically crazy. In my opinion, sometime this century, health care costs will reach 75% of GDP. Life for most people will consist of trying stay patched up because of the genetic damage they've sustained.

The important point for our discussion is that these increasing costs due to genetic damage do not show up as a negative in the GDP. They actually appear as a *positive* that adds to the GDP. This is a perfect example of the system mind at work. Now of course, costs of genetic damage before 1976 was due to natural causes and associated health costs should be added to the GDP because society is better off after treating these maladies that were unavoidable. But if the genetic damage was *avoidable* and due to our negligence as a society, costs of treatment are an indication of our negligence and should be *subtracted* from the GPD not added to it, to arrive at a true measure of our standard of living. This would be reflected in the GEP that would be less by the cost of treatment and would indicate that our standard of living had fallen giving us warning of these dangers to society.

When AIDS came into the US, you might think it was very unfortunate. Not so according to economists. Ronald Reagan thought it was God's punishment to gay people and didn't think it would affect the rest of the population. Large numbers of people got the disease totally unnecessarily because nothing was done about cleaning up the blood supply. But Reagan didn't have to worry about neglecting the blood supply. All the additional moneys that had to be spent fighting the resulting AIDS infections were celebrated by people who report on the economy by bragging about a rising GDP.

This is why GDP numbers we get from financial magazines and TV financial programs have absolutely nothing to do with reality. Even *The Economist* admits in one unobtrusive moment that the GDP "...is badly flawed as a guide to a nation's economic well-being". [10] But they never take their own advice and continue to use GDP fake numbers without ever mentioning the GEP. If you look at GDP increases reported by the system mouthpieces over the last 30 years, the average American should be living like a king. Instead, the standard of living of the bottom 80% of the population has been *dropping*.

24.3 CHARACTERIZING AN ECONOMY AND GOOD GOVERNMENT
We have discussed a lot of flows and there are a bunch of smaller ones we haven't mentioned. What we would like now is a way to characterize an economy that is simple

	Eisen-hower '53 – '60	Kennedy-Johnson '61 – '68	Nixon-Ford '69 – '76	Carter '73 – '80	Reagan '81 – ''88	Bush '89 – '92	Clinton '93 – '00	Bush '01 – '08	Obama '09 – '12
Unemploy-ment *	5.15%	4.62%	6.11%	6.4%	7.4%	6.6%	5.0%	5.6%	8.9%
GEP-Gross Effective Product †	$4.094 Tr.	$5.717 Tr.	$7.213 Tr.	$7.794 Tr.	$9.941 Tr.	$10.400 Tr	$13.305 Tr	$15.323 T	$15.448 T.
Growth of GEP ‡	3.15%	4.51%	2.34%	2.93%	2.88%	1.8%	3.7%	2.1%	1.12%
Deficits/ Yr Average	$4.24 Bil.	$7.5 Bil.	$25.0 Bil.	$56.9 Bil.	$167.3 Bil.	$233.5 Bil	$40.1 Bil.	$250.7 Bil.	$1,273 Bil
Deficits % of GDP §	.95%	1.00%	1.66%	2.37%	4.17%	3.92%	.76%	1.97%	8.8%
Personal Income †	$17,694	$23,512	$27,372	$28,314	$33,780	$34,153	$40,520	$43,466	$43,731
Personal Income Growth §	2.1%	3.6%	1.9%	.88%	2.24%	.29%	2.18%	.74%	-.71%
Median Household Income †			$51,328	$49,481	$52,982	$50,271	$56,138	$53,788	$51,371
Median Family Income †	$43,711	$57,105	$60,521	$58,751	$62,646	$60,013	$67,826	$65,784	$62,527
Inflation Rate §	1.37%	2.06%	6.38%	9.73%	4.65%	4.38%	2.60%	2.84%	1.60%
% Income Top 20% **		≈40%	41%	42%	44%	45%	49%	50%	51%
% Income to Bottom 80%		≈60%	59%	58%	56%	55%	51%	50%	49%
% Wealth Top 20% **					≈81%	84%	84%	89%	92%
% Wealth of Bot. 80%					≈19%	16%	16%	11%	8%

Figure 24.3 Economic Indicators

* Averaged over period
† End of period in 2012 Dollars. We have to use GDP in place of the GEP, Gross Effective Product, because the crooked Government does not make GEP numbers available.
‡ Average per year Growth
§ Average per Year over Period
** End of Period only approximately

and elegant so that the average person can relate to it. Well, there are 14 variables that I think completely characterize an economy and how well it is doing. Now this has nothing to do with freedoms, of course, which would be a different measure. These variables are the employment rate (which includes unemployment and *underemployment* rates); GEP, Gross Effective Product; growth of GEP; Deficits per year; yearly Deficit as a percent of GDP; Personal Income; growth of Personal Income; Median Family Income; Inflation rate; % Income to the top 20%; % Income to the bottom 80%; Wealth held by the top 20%; Wealth held by the bottom 80%. These are shown in Table 24.3. That's it — just 14 variables. The reason for the division between the top

20% and bottom 80% is that it pretty much reflects the breakdown in all of western civilization.

For hundreds of years under European feudalism, an approximate breakdown was the top 1% nobility, the next 4% aristocracy, the next 15% were Church, merchants, artisans and independent farmers, and the bottom 80% peasants. We have a similar breakdown now. We have the top 1% super-rich, the next 4% rich, the next 15% includes professionals like doctors, lawyers, engineers, scientists, etc.; and the bottom 80% includes the middle and working classes. This is a rough breakdown, but as mentioned, we're interested in concepts not precise numbers.

Now take a guess at how many of these 14 variables the government and its system mind media outlets report on. Only Personal Income, Median Family Income and deficits. Regarding unemployment, in a recession like in 2009, the media reported on the unemployment rate of around 10%. However, when you run out of unemployment benefits, you are not counted. The poor guy who has been desperately looking for a job every single day since he lost his job, but has run out of benefits, is labeled by the media as "given up on looking"; in other words, a lazy bastard who doesn't want to work. The unemployed guy is made to feel it's his fault, and he's in no psychological position to challenge the daily dose of propaganda from the system mind. And there's more. The computer programmer who is temporarily pumping gas because he has to pay his bills, is counted as *employed*, whereas he is really *under*employed. A very important category telling us how an economy is doing is the rate of *under*employment.

The Government produces a statistics book that has millions and millions of numbers that nobody in the history of the world will ever care about. But when it comes to the important numbers to characterize an economy, you get nothing. They can tell us that there was 1.8 million pounds of shellfish caught in 1977, and 3.4 million pounds of peanuts in 1973, but try and find the GEP in any given year, or the percent of income going to the bottom 80%, or the underemployment rate. Forget it. Here's an instance of where we can sympathize with conservatives and their dislike of government. Important statistics to measure how the economy is really doing is a national disgrace.

So what I've had to do for this volume is estimate, extrapolate, and interpolate to get some idea of these variables from the little the government gives. I used numbers from the official government statistical abstract which is an independent legitimate agency with no ax to grind. I avoided the internet as much as possible where the numbers can come from parties with no independence at all. But even my numbers are not 100% reliable. I simply don't have the wherewithal to get precise numbers. Besides this is only a book, not a phd thesis. I'm trying to bring out the *concepts* involved in understanding the economy. So the numbers here are only approximate — just accurate enough to bring out *concepts*.

In Table 24.3, I have substituted the GDP for the GEP because the government won't touch the GEP and there are no numbers available. As we mentioned it would be far less than the GDP. On the basis of these variables, let us come up with a way to determine an effective economy and good government *from the point of view of the average citizen.* Remember, the individual citizen doesn't see the GDP, or government finance, nor how income is distributed. He does see if he has a job and if his real pay is increasing and whether debt is being dumped on his kids. In my opinion, good government that would optimally serve the American people would have 4 major goals: minimize unemployment, sustainability, real growth in Personal Income, and minimize Inflation. We will present a formula for good government based on these variables. Now some of these variables are more important than others. So in the formula, we have a weighting factor for each variable. Thus growth of real income is more important than inflation because if a person's *real* income is growing sufficiently, any inflation would be compensated by a bigger paycheck leaving people better off on balance. Sustainability means low deficits which is more important than both growth and inflation. An economy that is stealing more from future generations than the economy is growing is a *failed* economy no matter what. Also, stealing from future generations of children to prop up an economy is not only unconstitutional, but the worst economic crime the government can commit.

Finally, if there is one role we could assign as the purpose of government it would be to maintain full employment. This variable is head and shoulders above the others. People without jobs cannot adequately support their children, nor even themselves. It's especially bad in these times when the system has made the almighty job the sole ingredient of our identities. Studies show that during recessions with high unemployment, depression and other mental illness increases, overall health diminishes, alcoholism and spousal abuse increase. I've seen people whose lives totally crumbled when they lost their job; and of course, the system mind doesn't give a crap about it. On these considerations, we have assigned weights, 5, 3, 2, and 1 to Unemployment, Deficits, Income growth and Inflation.

A very difficult factor to evaluate arises because an administration inherits numbers from the previous administration. If the previous administration was really bad, it will tend to bring down the performance of the present administration, no matter how good a job they are doing. So the performance of the current generation's negative variables like unemployment should be adjusted upward or downward depending on the performance of the previous administration; *but not by the whole amount.* The current generation should be able to overcome bad performance of the previous administration because it's in power just like Roosevelt immediately overcame the awful numbers left over from the Hoover administration. So the previous administration's performance should not count nearly as much. We have chosen a number of 30% as much. This is a bit arbitrary although I'm sure the coefficient should be somewhere around a third. Also, since the current administration is inheriting numbers for only the past few years of the previous administration, we will count only the last two years of the previous administration to calculate the effectiveness of the current administration.

Our formula for good government that we would like to adduce would be as follows. Good government Grade = $1.2\{5[10 - (U_C - .30\ U_P)] + 3[10 - (D_C - .30\ D_P)] + 2(\text{Growth of } Y) + 1[10 - (I_C - .30\ I_P)]\}$.

We have multiplied the whole formula by 1.2 to bring it up to a grade like you'd get in school. In the formula, U is unemployment rate, D is deficit as a % of GDP, Y is Personal Income, and I is Inflation rate. The subscript C refers to current numbers and P is previous administration's last two year's numbers. For example, D_C is current administration average deficits per year as a percent of GDP, and D_P is the deficit average over the preceding administration's last two years. The principle here is that *an administration is responsible for what happens on their watch.* This is to avoid the dishonesty of neoconservatives who blame anything bad during their watch on the previous administration, but take credit for anything good.

Let's compare the 1960s under Kennedy/Johnson with all the administrations since then using this formula. If you do the research and plug in the numbers, the Kennedy-Johnson years gets 95.4 good government points, an A grade. These are the numbers you get in a reasonable example of Democratic Capitalism. We have never duplicated these numbers since then — except for Clinton, who also gets an A; but that was because he inherited the most exciting bubble of the 20th century. Carter's good government grade is only 72.5, which is a C. But the real surprise is Reagan. His grade is only 67 which means he gets a D. This is stunning because it shows the power of propaganda. Reagan cut taxes for the talking heads of the system mind and they made him into an icon who most Americans still think was a great president. Carter did not cut taxes for these paid media whores and they made him into a goat. The facts are that Carter's domestic economic performance was almost 10% *better* than Reagan's. As we shall explain presently, once Ronald Reagan picked up the same system of Economic Socialism that left off in the 1930s, the system never again performed as well as the '50s and '60s.

Finally, we get to Baby Bush and Obama. Bush does better than I would have thought, getting 76.1 which is a C. However, he probably doesn't deserve this grade since the bubble which gave him his points was based on fraud and the whole problem got dumped on Obama. This is the only weakness of our formula: you can pump up your numbers with fraud. Of course, no matter what Obama inherited, he still flunks with a hopeless 38.22 points (Obama's numbers are a mess, but it's something near this). Bush is to blame for a little of this, but an effective stimulus program would have gotten him a passing grade. These numbers since Reagan show what a mess his Economic Socialism has imposed on the country. His agenda is good for getting elected, but requires ever increasing deficits to prop up the system.

Also, we should point out that we should be using after-tax income to make comparisons. But this is not available. But since top income tax rates have plummeted since Ronald Reagan, the share of income going to the bottom 80% since Reagan is overestimated in comparison. In other words, since top tax rates have fallen, the share of after-tax income going to the top 20% has risen even more than our table shows, which implies that the percentage of after-tax income to the bottom 80% is even lower than we show. We should keep this in mind.

24.4 Wasteful Transfers to Ideology and Leakage

When I taught economics, one of the first things I told the classes is that democracy has one major defect: you can form a group and vote to steal somebody else's money. It has been going on since democracy got started in Roman times. Now the Constitution tried to prevent this with an amendment guaranteeing the equal protection of the laws. But this has been no impediment at all to legalized stealing, especially when adjudicated by a Supreme Court who uses the Constitution for toilet paper.

As we shall see, most of the wasteful transfers are led by special interests and most of that is the result of ideology. We'll get into ideology in greater detail in Ch. 28 and 29. Suffice it to say here that ideology refers to strong political opinions based on a certain view of society. The major ideologies are liberal and conservative, which, in modern times have been replaced by neoliberalism and neoconservatism. Efforts to distribute the nation's income are based on these ideologies. However, they both have different ways to promote their agendas. The neoconservative uses the means of propaganda to distribute as much income as possible to the top 20%. One of our few real economists, Robert MacIntire, estimated that $170 *billion* would be given away in 2002 as corporate welfare, subsidies, tax loopholes, tax havens, etc.[11] As a result of their massive propaganda campaign since Ronald Reagan, virtually all new wealth and income generated during this period has gone to the top 20%. As a result, the top 20% now owns a full 92% of all wealth in the US, and the rest has virtually nothing except an orange crate shack they rent from the bank and a car they rent from a car agency.

The neoliberal has to get his due in a different way in effect by buying votes. We will discuss this in more detail in Ch. 29. This is why, even in the crucial years of 2009 and 2010, the Obama administration put buying votes at the top of the list of priorities, not the recovery of the economy. Of course, a side effect of buying votes was a somewhat anemic recovery, but it was at the expense of huge deficits dumped on future generations.

But probably the most important category of waste in the system is *leakage*. As our flow diagram shows, there are 4 major tanks in the economy, and as we have explained, these tanks should be filled as much as possible. Of course, the Government tank is usually empty, which is why the government is continuously stealing from the future to pay what it wants to spend on. The Business tank is usually full because in a free enterprise system, the corporate sector has enough political power to insure a full savings tub for Investment. It is the Household tank that is often empty.

These tanks are like the hot water heating system in many of your homes. The system of pipes and radiators is designed to be full at all times or you would be dangerously heating empty pipes. So in the basement, there's a little valve that lets in water to replace whatever may be leaking or evaporating. The economy works in a similar way. If an economic tank is leaking, there has to be a way to replace the leakage. And this is where we don't hear a peep for the system mind propaganda outlets. In truth, these tanks are leaking billions of dollars.

What is happening is that wealthier nodes of the economy are able to climb in bed with political actors in Washington and pass rules which allow them to take money out of the country to avoid taxes. The Government has tightened up some of the leakage from individual households, but the leakage from the Business sector has more than made up for this. Big corporations can create a maze of subsidiaries, offshoots, entanglements with foreign companies, foreign banks, façade foreign subsidiaries, etc. that enables them to sneak billions out of the country and avoid taxes. At least money going into the Savings tub can be made available for investment. But leakage out of the country is dead money. It doesn't hire people, it doesn't buy new plant and equipment, it doesn't invent anything, and it doesn't start new businesses. This is another example of the Economic Socialism picked up from the 1920s by Ronald Reagan and continuing for the next 35 years. Not only did the system mind steal trillions from the future in the last 35 years that wound up in the pockets of paid media whores and Wall Street financial wizards, but then they rig their own rules that allow them to sneak billions out of the system to tax havens. *They don't even want to pay taxes on money they stole.*

The only way the system has to keep the tanks full is by stealing from the future, which has created massive deficits under Bush, Reagan, and now Obama. Rather than going after these enormous leakages, it's easier for Obama to steal what he needs from the future with trillion dollar deficits. This is all unsustainable, and will result in permanent recession and eventually total collapse of the world-wide system with perhaps 30% unemployment.

Of course, the system mind propaganda outlets don't say peep about this racket for 35 years. After trillions were stolen from our children winding up in the pockets of the top 1% especially crooks in the financial services industry, and western world governments were going broke, finally in 2013, *The Economist* had a cover story called "The Missing 20 Trillion. [12] Nothing like on the spot reporting.

In other countries, this money has to be replaced by loans from the IMF who then enforces requirements that basically destroys middle class purchasing power. There is an attack on unions, social safety nets, minimum wages, government services etc., all to try to balance budgets. But these cuts in economic support for people drop their purchasing power and shrink the economy. With less Government revenues, there is very little alleviation of deficits which require more and more loans. Often these impositions of the neoliberal agenda result in massive collapses. Argentina had to default on its debt, and Russia has yet to recover from its "privatization" spree. Greece will be in debt to the IMF and Euro union for decades.

24.5 A Balanced Economy

Getting back to our flow diagram, we can see what a viable and optimal Democratic Capitalistic economy would require. We are defining an optimal economy as one that is prosperous and provides as high a standard of living to all citizens as possible; one that grows and one that is sustainable. Sustainable means that it can continue on the current path without threatening the optimality of the economy without deficits. We will call such an economy an *Optimal Equilibrium Economy*, OEE. In an OEE, all flows are as large as possible.

Now a high standard of living for the *average* citizen could come out in many ways. You could have a society where there's a layer on top who has everything — all wealth and power — while everyone else has very little. The *average* standard of living might be acceptable, but it would hide the fact that most people would have nothing. The system of Feudalism in the Middle Ages was like that. You could also have a society where everyone has about the same standard of living, but it is a low standard of living because it lacks technology and lacks means to expand the economy. This was the case with many of the American Indian tribes.

The real beauty of pure Democratic Capitalism is that if you maximize the standard of living of the average citizen, the distribution of income will not come out equal, but will come out to something most of us would find morally acceptable. What such an analysis would show is that with a given amount of technology, if you optimize the average standard of living sustainably you would have to reach a proper balance among the various flows.

The most important point in the flow diagram is the point labeled Y/P, which is where the flow coming out of the Business tank forks into two flows. A great deal of controversy over the running of the economy is a fight over what should happen at this key point in the flow diagram. At the Y/P fork, money from the Business tank can go either towards income to the Household tank as Labor Income, or kept as Profits. Profits go either to R, Retained Earnings that stays in the Business tank, or are paid out as Dividends to stockholders. This is shown in the diagram.

In an Optimal Equilibrium Economy, there is just the right balance between what goes to these two important flows. You would have the right amount going into the Savings tub so that businesses have available capital (money) to pump up the Investment pipe to replace aging plant and equipment, but most importantly to finance new businesses started on the basis of new ideas and new technology. And you should have the right amount going through the Labor Income pipe so that the Household tank will be full enough for consumers to buy the goods and services the Business sector can produce, i.e., to *clear markets*. An OEE clears markets. It would automatically insure a certain balance between these two flows.

If there is one important factor to stress about our economic system, it is that an *Optimal Equilibrium Economy* is extremely difficult to maintain. It is very easy to get unbalanced so that either Households cannot buy all the goods and services the system can produce; or Businesses cannot raise enough capital to replace plant and equipment or build new factories for an expanding economy. One of the main jobs of government is to enforce the rules of the Capitalist game so that a proper balance can be maintained and all flows are maximized. One of the sure signs of Economic Socialism is that it has a tendency to be out of balance — usually too much going to Capital and not enough to Households to clear markets.

Communism was a system that tried to send too much to the Household tank. The only way to do this is with an authoritarian government. But you can't have a viable economy if the Savings tub is empty. This is why Communism fails no matter where it is tried. It doesn't provide enough incentive, enough economic freedom and enough capital in the Savings tub for businesses to produce the best possible product for the least price. Nobody ever bought anything made in a Communist country. Communism is one side of a coin, the other side of which is where the economic system dominates the political system. This is the combination we are calling Economic Socialism where the economic system can rig the rules in its favor and you get abuses, imbalanced flows, and an under-performing economy.

This is why both extremes of National Socialism and Communism give you lines. In Economic Socialist systems, when you go to a mall at an odd hour, you see humungus piles of goods waiting in line for too few customers. In Communist countries, you have too many customers waiting in line in front of stores with too few goods. This shows pretty conclusively that you don't get an optimal economy when either the economic or the political system dominates.

We should remind ourselves that all the flows we have been discussing convey information between the major sectors of the economy. And it is these information flows that create a system mind, just as the impulses traveling between the neurons of the brain create the human mind. As explained in Sect. 23.2, the major difference is that the economic system mind is not determined equally by the nodes in the economy. The most powerful and important nodes have the most say in determining the wants and goals of the system mind. These are large corporations, businesses and wealthy individuals. As a result, it is a conservative system mind and it will always try to siphon off money away from the Y_L Income flow and towards high income people and then into the Savings tub as Dividends.

The most important way the system mind redistributes income away from the bottom 80% towards the top 20%, is to howl for "deregulation". This sounds good because nobody likes regulations. It is alleged that regulations impede economic growth, etc. Of course, this is another example of Economic Socialism. Forces pushing this idea really don't want to get rid of rules. All games have rules. They simply want to be in bed with political animals to make their *own* rules. Of course, there are many rules of the game in place that reduce productivity and entrepreneurship. However, it must be kept in mind that rules to protect the consumer are really rules to protect the consumer's *pocketbook*. When economic players make their own rules, it usually involves raiding their own customers' pocketbooks. This cuts Consumption, which will in turn cuts production resulting in layoffs and lower Household Income. To recapture some measure of balance, the system has to steal increasing amounts from the future to prop up demand.

Then to compensate for sluggish growth due to imbalances in the flows, the system comes up with another quack remedy that only makes it worse. Since Ronald Reagan, Europe has been cutting taxes for the top 20% and shifting them to middle class consumers in the form of sales taxes.[13] It's called a VAT (very asinine tax). In the US, corporate tax rates have been slashed. The reason-box diarrhea given for this is that it would spur the economy, "unleash" the private sector, pay for the loss in revenue, and they would reach the pot of gold at the end of the rainbow. And what have been the results? Massive deficits *every single year* of Republican administrations since Reagan, and almost total collapse of a number of European economies who need big bail-outs, and another layer of fake paper.

The answer to the resulting massive deficits under 20 years of Republican administrations is to "cut government spending". Of course, some government spending is wasteful, but what the system mind won't tell you is that *government spending is somebody's income.* Neoconservative propagandists, which you hear everywhere, push the impression that government spending is like a turd on the Christmas tree: you just cut off the turd, and you have a beautiful Christmas tree in all its glory. When the government spends money even if a little wasteful, it buys health care, or military equipment, or roads, or infrastructure, or pensions. This puts money in the pockets of the lower 80%, who can then buy goods and services. The only way to avoid government spending is for the private sector to create enough demand on its own to keep up production and employment. But when neoconservatives keep sending income *away* from households and into profits in the Savings tank, the government has to step in with spending to prop up demand which incurs deficits. If the Government doesn't step in this way, reduced Household income will cut Consumption, jobs and income, which also reduces taxes. With less government revenue, the deficit will stay right where it is.

Of course, liberals being what they are have gotten into act with an intelligencia promoting various abstruse theories trying to convince everyone that their theory of income distribution is best. Intellectuals like Richard Rorty, Ronald Dworkin, Bruce Ackerman, and many others have written learned scholarly treatises, and then reviews of each others' learned scholarly treatises arguing for some theory or other as to how income should be distributed and what "economic rights" citizens have.[14] Most of these theorists have no understanding of economics. They think we must have an abstruse philosophical *theory* that distributes income in *opposition* to what they think are the dictates of Capitalism, which they basically view as the enemy, continually robbing their heroes on the bottom of the economic pile. You would think that the fact that Capitalism was initially called '*liberalism*' would give them a clue. Not the slightest, which shows how much the great fraud, Karl Marx, gums up the minds of many thinkers.

The reality is that *pure Capitalism is the liberal's very best friend.* If we start from an assumption of low unemployment and a maximally expanding economy with no theft from the future, the system *itself* will determine an optimal distribution of income. If we look at periods in history when we had something close to pure Capitalism, we find a distribution of income that was balanced and morally acceptable to any reasonable liberal or *legitimate* conservative. Such was the case in the 1950s and '60s when the economy was averaging a growth of more than 4% over the period, and 4 ½% in the '60s. Not only that, but there were almost no deficits. The reason for this was there were high taxes on the larger nodes, and strong unions to keep worker wages and Consumption up. And there was still enough money going to corporations, businesses and the rich to maintain a full Savings tub. Keep in mind, the top tax rate for the rich in the 1950s was 90%, which shows that taxes have nothing to do with growth.

In the last 30 years, a viscous circle has emerged. As more and more income has been redistributed away from the bottom 80% to the top 20%, including the very rich, they have increasing amounts of money to buy up and control the major means of propaganda and to climb in bed with political actors to rig the rules of the game so even more income is diverted to the top 20%. This coalescing of the political and economic systems is what we are calling Economic Socialism. In the past 20 years, the share of National Income going to the top 1% has doubled from about 11% to about 22%, while their share of taxes has dropped by a third. Of course, these great imbalances require continual stealing from the future to prop up demand. In the next chapter we will look at the forces that have prevented a balanced economy, some sinister and some accidental.

24.6 ECONOMICS OF POST CIVIL WAR ECONOMIC SOCIALISM

After the Civil War, there was a great explosion of technological advances. Now it is probably a moot point as to how much of the new technology and industry was due to the Civil War and how much to the coincidence that this would have been a time of great strides in technological development even without a war. The new technology consisted of means to mine resources like coal, iron and oil, inventions of new mechanical devices in agriculture and machinery and new production methods. Another important development was the invention of new roller printing presses that could turn out many copies very quickly. Also very importantly, this was the age of the spread of the great railroads crisscrossing the entire country that greatly stimulated trade between regions.

In my opinion, it is no accident that Karl Marx wrote his famous book Das Kapital right at the end of the Civil War, just in time for a new direction in western economies. After the Civil War, there was an enormous growth of industrial and financial corporations. It was quite natural for these huge agglomerations of economic power to try to use their financial power to influence the direction of government. Karl Marx led the way by showing that enormous overall power could be achieved by *combining* economic players with political actors. Of course, he would have them as the same people. New large economic nodes took their cue from Karl Marx with the slight variation that instead of political animals dominating the pair, *economic* players with their enormous fortunes could dominate the combination. If they weren't the same people, the next best thing was to have them in the same beds making their own rules. And this is exactly the blueprint *in reality* for American government for the next 65 years directed mostly by Republican administrations. With inspiration from Marx, the Republican Party spun on a dime from the party of Capitalism and anti-slavery to the party of Economic Socialism of big business. As we will explain, this form of government was interrupted briefly by the Roosevelt administration in the 1930s, but was taken up again by Ronald Reagan and has continued unabated to the present day where we find a new movement called neoconservativism leading the way putting economic and political players in the same beds just as Karl Marx's droppings suggest.

There are stories after the Civil War of the big industrialists dumping paper bags of cash money on the desks of congressmen. All of our national resources were stolen from the American people by the large economic nodes in bed with politicians. The settling of the west was probably the most egregious example of Corporate Socialism in all our history. Railroad magnets in bed with Washington politicos were able to steal hundreds of millions of dollars of public assets and given to economic players who were able to make their own rules. If you want to read some of the details of this racket, read Richard White's book.[15] Their rules were such that "on the Illinois Central between 1874 and 1884, one of out every 20 trainmen died or was disabled; among brakemen...one in seven".[16] We know who made these rules. The government at this time had nothing to do with Adam Smith's Democratic Capitalism but was simply a slight variation of Karl Marx.

With players making their own rules, oligopolies mushroomed after the Civil War. Sometimes, actual monopolies formed like around John D. Rockefeller. He had a little oil company along with many others. But he was a very smart, aggressive, with a merciless drive for power. He would go into an area and lower his prices until he drove the competition out of business. Then he would raise prices to pay to pay for lowering prices in the next area he wanted to dominate and would then drive competitors out of business in the new area. After a number of years, he controlled most of the oil business in the US. Similar things happened in other industries. There was Andrew Carnegie in steel, Vanderbilt, Gould, and Harriman in railroads, and J.P. Morgan in banking. This was a 35-year period of Republican party dominance, which had become the party of Economic Socialism.

I had a similar experience with two kittens. While in grad school, somehow I wound up with two very small kittens who would feed in the same dish. One day I noticed that one kitten was growing twice as fast as the other. I couldn't figure out why. What had happened is that, maybe because of genes, one of them got a tiny bit bigger. Being a bit more intimidating, he could grab a slightly bigger share of the food. This was a perfect example of unstable equilibrium. The bigger the big one got, the more food he could hog, which would enable him to grow even bigger and hog even more food. The little one might not ever grow up. So I changed the eating scenario. I would put the big one in the bathroom and feed the little one separately, so that they both got the same amount of food. And wouldn't you know, the little one caught up to the big one and wound up about the same size.

But the reason I was able to get the kittens back to equilibrium and equal growth rates, is because I was there to change the rules to be fair. But after the Civil War, there was no institution that would keep the game fair. This is why Democratic Capitalism is almost impossible to maintain in equilibrium. Once nodes are established that have great economic power, monopolists like Rockefeller, or a bunch of oligopolists like the railroad industry, would go to Washington and start buying up congressmen like sacks of potatoes.

The Republican Party had become the party of Economic Socialist big business, and the Democratic Party was dominated by Southerners whose main goal was to recoup some form of slavery. The ordinary worker really had nowhere to go and all through Victorian times never made significant economic progress. The robber barons and other oligopolists had total control of the government and they owned the major means of propaganda. In fact, it is hard to find one tiny piece of legislation after the Civil War that would benefit the lower 80%. Even into the 20th century, unions were suppressed and wages were kept low. Workers had to work 12 or more hours a day 6 or 7 days a week for a dollar a day. Factories became dirty, unsafe and unsanitary sweatshops. These were probably the worst working conditions outside of outright slavery that ever existed in human history. If a worker got injured, he would be thrown in the street and replaced by another newly-arrived immigrant. Even in the 1920s, my grandfather was working 12 hours a day, 6 days a week for peanuts. My father couldn't even go to high school because the family was too poor and he had to go to work instead.

Because working conditions for labor were so atrocious, there was never enough income and demand among the bottom 80% to buy what could be produced. All during the Victorian period up to WWII, the system could never clear markets. Consumption is the engine of an economy as Adam Smith stressed. Without it, there will be little growth no matter what ideas come on line.

Poverty and desperate lives of the bottom 80% became so rampant and the abuses and corruption of the robber barons got so egregious that people rebelled and elected Teddy Roosevelt who was able to initiate a period of reform at the turn of the century. Roosevelt ran and won on a platform of "trust-busting" whereby many of the great monopoly industries like oil and banking were broken up into smaller units. Standard oil was broken up into a number of smaller oil companies that would have to pretend to compete.

There were financial reforms as well. *Teddy Roosevelt was the first real semi-Capitalist of the 20th century.* The most important quote he made, which is totally suppressed by economic history books was, "Labor is the superior of capital and deserves much the higher consideration".[17] This is exactly the sentiments of Adam Smith and anyone else who understands the essence of Capitalism. Of course, he's not saying that the worker should make more money than the Capitalist. What he is saying is that if you want a viable Capitalism, you can't disregard the consuming working classes. You have to make sure they have sufficient income to buy what the capitalist is making.

But Teddy Roosevelt had an enormous ego, which explains why he was the first real imperialist president sending the great white fleet around the world showing off his muscle. Roosevelt loved war; actually, he loved any kind of killing including defenseless animals. You have to wonder, was Roosevelt killing elephants because they resembled big corporate trusts; or was he after big corporate trusts because he saw them as big elephants to kill. In view of his invading the Philippines and murdering thousands of totally innocent underdeveloped people, I think his going after big bigness was just corollary to wanting to kill big things.

But he was also the first real conservationist as well, starting a whole movement for setting aside a number of public lands for national parks. Because of his totally unusual mix of political policies, he split from the Republican party and lost the election of 1912. Woodrow Wilson became president followed by WWI. After the war, conservatism again took control of the public discourse mainly because they owned the major means of propaganda, especially the new medium of radio. And there followed 12 years of conservative Republican presidents, and the usual massive dose of Economic Socialism leading to the Great Depression.

Throughout the whole post-civil war period of 65 years, there was never even a hint of a middle class which Adam Smith said was the essence of Democratic Capitalism. Even though the GDP went up in this period, all the gains in the GDP from new technology and productivity after the Civil War went to the top 20% who gained 95% of all new wealth and income, while and the share of income to the bottom 80% fell steadily. This created huge fortunes which were able to finance the purchase of political actors at every level so that they could make even bigger profits without sharing any of it with their workers. This was a period of rampant Economic Socialism and the lack of improvement of the great working class has some economists calling the period after the Civil War our first great depression.

Some conservatives would claim that the great inequality during Victorian times enabled investment in research and technology, which would pay off later on. This is the standard line used by conservatives for hundreds of years. As we have mentioned, a full Savings tank is necessary to provide capital for investment in new technology. But the Civil War with great fortunes being made was the last period in history where you would expect a lack of capital available for expansion. Whenever a new invention came on the scene, there was plenty of capital available. Isaac Singer invented the sewing machine around 1850, and went into business in 1851. He had no trouble getting capital and by 1855 was the largest sewing machine company in the world. The great inventors and competitors, Thomas Edison and George Westinghouse had no trouble starting businesses and getting capital to expand rapidly into General Electric and Westinghouse Companies.

Lithography companies had no trouble finding capital to incorporate all the improvements in printing methods and lithography into production processes. In fact, this was the golden age of lithography. I am very familiar with printing methods after the Civil War, and every single improvement in lithography and printing that came on line during this period was eagerly pounced upon by new and old companies. When photo-offset printing was invented, again there was plenty of capital for new businesses to start up using the new methods and for old businesses to incorporate them.

I'm sure someone can find some invention somewhere that had trouble attracting capital back then, just as now when there is plenty of capital. As I remember, Xerox once had trouble attracting capital. Often investors just don't see the potential in a new invention. But the vast majority of inventions throughout the Victorian period had no trouble attracting capital, which there was plenty of.

Historians have shown that what enabled Europe to take off in the 1400s and 1500s was that the great plagues of Europe had wiped out a third of the peasant class. This was mainly due to very poor sanitation. And because of the scarcity of ordinary factory and farm labor, the value of labor went up. This allowed the lower 80% to buy the goods the new merchants and capitalists were making. This is what impelled the great economic expansion in this period and enabled Europe to surge past the rest of the world in economic development.

In the same way, if real Capitalism was in place after the Civil War, there is no doubt that the economy would have increased at a far faster growth rate, and a reasonable middle class could have been created. This is just what happened after WWII due to Roosevelt bringing back a reasonable semblance of Capitalism. Of course, in its usual neglect of real economic history, you won't find anything useful in this area on the internet. That internet even has antiseptic discussions of slavery itself, making it sound like just another kind of labor agreement.

Even if it could be shown that the great inequality and an overfilled Savings tank during Victorian times created slightly faster technological improvements than would have occurred with more equality, there was a great price to pay, which is rarely taken into account in this debate. For 65 years after the Civil War, there were hundreds of millions of workers in the bottom 80% who led miserable, poverty-stricken, degraded lives. Their babies died like flies and adults *died young*, often from industrial accidents that were totally unprotected. Our antiseptic history books and the major means of propaganda never tell us of the real story of the misery and poverty during this period while great fortunes were made. And our latest propaganda outlet, Wikapedia, won't tell you about it either. But dead people can't complain. We can now observe some of the *benefits* that accrued to today's world because of the investment made in new technology during the Industrial Revolution, but nobody is ever going to add in the price millions of workers paid in the form of a miserable standard of living including crippling injuries and death.

With plenty of money at the top, there were times during this period like the 1920s, where the value of stocks and other assets would skyrocket, and the economic building would rise into the sky. But the working class was left with stagnant wages, and so couldn't clear markets. There would be increasing weakness in the foundation of the economy and eventually the economic building would come crashing down. Stocks would plummet, unemployment would increase and there would be great misery throughout the land.

This phenomenon is called the *business cycle*. Because Consumption was constantly starved among the lower 80%, there were crashes about every 10 years all through the Victorian period. The 7 crashes of 1873, 1884, 1893, 1901, 1907, the really big one of 1929, and 2008 *all* occurred at the end of *Republican* administrations. After each crash, new politicians would be elected who promised "reform". Sometimes this would involve temporary gains among the lower 80%. But *immediately*, agents of the corporate world went right back to work climbing in bed with political figures to rig rules to the benefit of these very same corporations. The process would start all over again with income and wealth going increasingly to the top 20%. Markets would not clear and sooner or later the whole system would collapse again. This is exactly what happened after the 2008 meltdown. Even Republicans were talking reform, which lasted exactly 2 months, after which they were back to "deregulation", which is code for Economic Socialism where economic players whose bribes they take, make their own rules.

Of course, economists are the modern version of the witch doctor whose job is to support the current culture and value system. They give the impression that the business cycle is just a natural phenomenon whose causes come from the cosmos and we can't do anything about it. But the real cause of the business cycle is really a natural outcome of Economic Socialism that doesn't allow Consumption to keep up with production.

What economic history since the Civil War shows is that *the foundation of a real Capitalist economy is the ability of the middle and working classes to clear markets and buy the goods and services the Capitalist is able to make.* The basic problem is that *real* Capitalism is a very delicate unstable system as we mentioned in Sect. 23.10. It is almost impossible to sustain a political system that has the power and the independence to match the complexity and power of a modern economic system of big corporate institutions and great pockets of wealth. They have infinite money and endless time to work over government representatives, with bribery, lobbying and control. The infinite complexity of a modern economic system is impossible to patch up with finite rules, unless there are independent rule-makers designed by human legislatures and enforced by a *human* Supreme Court. But with legislators for sale like sacks of potatoes and the Supreme Court chosen by presidents' reptilian brain on the basis of their total venality and corruption, we're not going to get very much Democratic Capitalism any time soon.

Of course, you could ask, why can't we strengthen the political system so that it could match the power and complexity of the economic system? Well, you would have to rewrite the Constitution to provide for an independent legislature and an existentially chosen Supreme Court; and the only way that could be done is by the very politicians who are already in the pockets of powerful economic players. So nothing is going to change until the whole system collapses.

Getting back to our topic of balanced, we can get a better idea of how balance can be achieved by looking what can be done to get out of recessions. One way would be for the government to either buying more goods from the Business tank, or by directly employing unemployed people. Let's look at this path.

24.7 STIMULATING A RECESSIONARY ECONOMY VIA GOVERNMENT

When the economy is in recession, there is a vicious circle. Businesses aren't employing enough people implying lower Household Consumption. And so businesses are not prone to hire people because their sales are low and they aren't going to produce more stuff they can't sell. How is it possible to get out of this dilenema? Probably the only sure way is to have the government step in and start sending money any way it can into the Household tank so that people can start spending money for goods and services. This is what Franklin Roosevelt did in the 1930s to get the economy going again. Let's look at this history.

After WWI, in the 1920s, there were three consecutive Republican administrations who had almost total control of government where they often had massive majorities. They used their political power to return to the usual massive doses of Economic Socialism with its usual shredding of the core ingredients of Democratic Capitalism. Instead of using the war as a foundation for independent rule-making and support for increases in Household income, Republicans in the 1920s used the post-war period to actually *attack* the working class among the lower 80%, and allowed the biggest nodes of the economy to write their own rules. There were the Palmer raids where the FBI rounded up thousands of union advocates and either put them in jail or kicked them out of the country. Of course, some of these people were either communists or sympathetic to Communism. But all they were doing was organizing unions and trying to get a decent share of the pie. Of course, the Supreme Court did nothing to protect their rights of free speech. In fact, the message sent out from various Supreme Courts throughout most of our history is that in the US, *the only time you have real incisive freedom of speech is when nobody is around to listen.* There was also an attack on the small farmer who often could barely survive. There were actual instances of malnutrition and starvation among some of the poorer farmers. Huge numbers of farmers in the Midwest went to California to get a new start. The final result in 1929 was the most massive economic crash in the history of the country.

In 1921 when the first of these "conservative" Republican presidents was elected, the top 10% was getting about 45% of all income. By the time of the crash in 1929, the top 10% were getting almost *half* of all income. This is reflected in wealth figures. In 1921, the top 1% had about 35% of all wealth in the country. By 1929, their share of wealth increased to about 45% which means that the lower 99% had only 55% of wealth. By the way, is this 1% figure familiar to you? Wages for the lower 80% did not budge all through the 1920s and in fact actually decreased after 1925. It even amazed me to learn that during the '20s, the majority of Americans didn't even have running water nor electricity. A middle class never emerged because all new income and wealth went to the top 20%.

The 1920s is another blatant example of Economic Socialism at work. What led to the Great Depression was the same old story that had been occurring periodically all through the years after the civil war. Income to the bottom 80% flags, Consumption doesn't keep up with supply, which keeps a lid on employment and wages. According to neoconservative propaganda, income to the top is supposed to create jobs and grow the economy. But it never does. All it did was to give the top 20% more money to put into the stock market, which climbed steadily during the '20s. But it was all built on a rotting foundation of a starved out middle class. Finally, we got a massive Depression that crippled the economy for 10 years with 25% unemployment and trillions of dollars of losses (today's dollars). This pattern is being repeated under Barack Obama: high profits, rising stock market, but stifled demand, retarded Consumption, and little job creation. This is what we got from the usual conservative supply-side quackery of throwing billions at the crooked and idle rich, "unleashing the private sector" by allowing business to make their own rules. This shows that if you let the large nodes in the economy run the system, they will eventually foul their own nest.

It isn't that the people involved are evil any more than a football coach like Bill Belichick is evil when he disagrees with the referees. Belichick is supposed to win and wanting to win results in violently disagreeing with some of the calls. The game restrains the coaches and players from rigging the rules which is why the game has umpires and referees paid by the league instead of by coaches and players. That's why football is a great game. Capitalism is a great game too and can provide a society with a high standard of living, basic freedoms and rights, and the freedom of the citizenry to determine the rules of the game for everyone's benefit. But as long as we have a neoconservative system mind, we're not going to get it. In the words of the great 20th century architect, Frank Lloyd Wright: "I believe totally in a Capitalist System, I only wish that someone would try it." As we can see, with the Republican Party hijacked by the new neoconservative, we aren't going to try it any time in the near future either.

This is the situation Roosevelt faced when he took office in 1933 and the situation Obama faced when he took office in 2009. But the world had changed by '09. The system mind had so penetrated the minds of the citizenry that even Obama was swept along the usual Economic Socialist way. What makes matters worse during a recession is that when the economy is slow, the government is taking in less money than usual in taxes and doesn't have the revenue to pay for increased spending on goods and services. So how can they stimulate the economy? Well, it simply steals from the future, to be very frank about it. This is called the *Federal Deficit* mentioned above, which allows the government to keep spending so that money can flow into the Household tank for Consumption.

With tax revenue down, Roosevelt had some small deficits, but only about 3% of GPD a year. But in 3 years, Roosevelt reduced unemployment from an incredible 25% down to about 12%. This works out to a cost of about a billion dollars for each 1% drop in unemployment. Obama hemmed in by a Corporate Socialist culture had deficits of *10*% of GDP costing about *3 trillion* dollars for every 1% drop in unemployment. This is about a three *thousand* times more costly than Roosevelt's efforts. But comparing Obama's pace of economic improvement with the Republicans is like comparing a turtle to a snail.

In order for Roosevelt to have gotten out of the Depression, he would have had to incur deficits proportional to the size of the country. But conservatives will allow deficits only for wars or tax cuts for their idle crooked rich friends. You can have deficits, but only if they are used to create jobs in the lower 80% because their increased purchasing power will increase Consumption, which induces greater production of goods and services and more hiring of people to make those goods and services. This is exactly Adam Smith's perception. The increase in business activity, employment and income gives the government enough additional tax revenue to pay back the money borrowed and the deficit can be paid back. But if deficits are used to throw money at the top 20%, all it will do is bid up the price of assets like the stock market. The debt incurred by Reagan, Bush and now Obama will continue to grow until there will be permanent recession or eventually collapse.

What Roosevelt basically did to get the economy out of the depression was to pass legislation that would put money directly into the Household tank. The great economist John Maynard Keynes wrote his famous book in 1936, which basically said that the way to get the economy out of a recession is to put money in the pockets of the great working class. Roosevelt passed the Wagner Act, which gave unions the right to bargain collectively. All larger industries were unionized: coal, steel, oil, trucking, autos, chemicals, large electronics, etc. One of the reasons he was able to unionize mass unions was that immigration was halted in the 1920s which gave workers a better bargaining position. Unions after WWII, especially the strong ones like the Teamsters and the UAW (United Auto Workers), set the standards for factory and medium skilled labor all over the country. Minimum wage laws were passed; companies were forced by competition to offer health care to workers. He started unemployment compensation, which enables unemployed people to keep up Consumption. Also, Roosevelt passed Social Security which enables senior citizens to keep spending even if the economy takes a drop.

But the most important measure Roosevelt took to spur the economy was the creation of new government agencies that would directly put people to work. The WPA (Works Projects Administration) hired people to work on infrastructure. Some of the parks, roads and bridges we have today were built with WPA labor. Government contracts out these projects to firms, shown as the flow G_B in our diagram. Then firms hire people to build infrastructure which shows up as income, Y_L to the household tank.

In the area of rule-keeping, for the first time in decades, Roosevelt tried his best to return to Democratic Capitalism by getting new rules passed that would keep the game sound. These are discussed in an article by Michael Greenberger.[18] He passed the Securities Acts of 1933 and '34 to regulate securities. He passed the "Commodity Exchange Act of 1936 to regulate futures transactions". He created the Security and Exchange Commission to prevent insider manipulation of the stock market. This is the government agency that neoconservatives fought tooth and nail in the 2000s, and by starving it of funds, led to the collapse of 2008 because there was no one looking over the transactions of fraudulent paper.

Roosevelt's legislation had the effect of enforcing transparency in financial markets, "record-keeping, capital adequacy, full disclosure, anti-fraud and anti-manipulation prohibitions", etc. He passed the Glass-Steagall act that created the Federal Deposit Insurance Corp. that insured deposits of ordinary people against mismanagement by bankers. He also separated commercial banks from investment banks. (This latter was repealed in 1999 with the urging of the very people Obama rehired to mismanage his own economic policies.) There were stricter rules on the stock market, and laws were passed to prevent abuses in banking and investment businesses. Of course, Corporate Socialists fought these measures tooth and nail with every disgusting propaganda trick that the evil mind of man could concoct. But they didn't have an articulate army of system mind econowhores promoting their policies like after the collapse of 2008. So Roosevelt was able recover *some* measure of Democratic Capitalism as outlined by Adam Smith. Roosevelt did what is essential for a *Capitalist economy: rules of the economic game that were independent of economic players, and a consuming middle class prosperous enough to clear markets* just as Smith emphasized. (Roosevelt was even smart enough to see that even though the south was soaked in racism and segregation, there was still some populism in the southern Democratic party and he used their votes to pass his liberal Capitalist legislation. He realized that a good way to remedy the racism problem was to create a strong economy with jobs)

All of these measures should have gotten the economy going again. And Roosevelt's economic policies did work. He inherited an unemployment rate of about 25%, and gradually reduced it to only about 12% by 1337. But there was legislation that sabotaged the measures we have mentioned. The Economy Act of 1933 actually cut spending. And even though the Business tank did nothing to help, they do not deserve all of the blame. Businesses are not going to hire people and increase income to make goods and services they can't sell. Also, the country was between bubbles — the auto bubble had petered out as it became a mature industry and the WWII electronics and chemicals bubble was yet to come.

In my opinion, Roosevelt's policies would have ended the Depression if he could have gotten just a little more into the pockets of the lower 80%, as WWII showed. However, as in the '20s, conservatives controlled the means of propaganda and mounted a sustained attack on Roosevelt's policies. They wanted him out of power and the good of the country was of secondary importance. They didn't care if half the country was unemployed. The same scenario repeated under Obama in 2011 where the first Republican priority was defeating Obama in 2012.

Even though Roosevelt had gotten unemployment down to 12% and the economy was improving, in 1937 and '38 Republicans mustered enough political power to completely sabotage the economy. All during the Depression conservative pundits and in congress were screaming about Roosevelt's spending. They complained about deficits and loose money. When they saw that Roosevelt's spending was successful in creating jobs and encouraging Consumption, they attacked the *source* of this success, which was government spending. They insisted that he balance the budget and stop coddling the working class. Their motives were clearly to sabotage Roosevelt's success in bringing back Democratic Capitalism. Having control over the major means of propaganda, they got some Republicans elected in the '36 election, who immediately went to work sabotaging the economy. Starting in 1937, government spending for jobs was cut. Also, conservatives were worried about deficits and inflation which they never worry about when they're in office. So they forced a tightening of the money supply in '37 and '38, and unemployment increased. This put Roosevelt on the hot seat.

Also it is important to note that all during the 1930s, Republicans in Congress wouldn't let Roosevelt prepare militarily in any way to counteract Hitler, which would have created jobs and allowed us to have some preparations for WWII. The same stance was taken by the Conservative party in Great Britain. They were isolationists by some coincidence just when Hitler needed a clear path to arming for war. But Roosevelt knew that conservatives never see a war they don't like. So seeing that he might not ever get the economy out of the depression, Roosevelt decided that his only remedy would be to get us into a war. Not that this was wrong. Certainly Hitler had to be stopped. In the Pacific, the system mind at the time created a "surprise" attack on Pearl Harbor, which allowed Roosevelt to get into a bigger war. However, he was lucky in that the wars he needed were just wars. George Bush needed a war too, but since he didn't have a just war handy, he had to get us into an unjust and unnecessary one.

All of these measures led to a post-war economy in which the lower 80% rose from a working class of poor 12 hour-a-day work slaves to a new and relatively prosperous *middle class* getting about 60% of National Income. This is an essential ingredient of Adam Smith's Democratic Capitalism. And what's most important, the increase in tax revenue from the huge expansion of the economy enabled the war deficits to be almost eliminated. We even had small government. This was as close to pure Democratic Capitalism as might be possible.

Even now, as I write this, sewer radio has been trumpeting some yokel who has written a book saying that Roosevelt's spending didn't get us out of the Great Depression, *World War II* got us out of the depression. And we hear the usual horseshit that has been drummed into the public mind for 200 hundred years during and after every Republican-caused depression: throw money at the Business tank, stop coddling the working man, get rid of rules on business, and "unleash" the private sector. This never works. It is simply propaganda to get the government to steal from the future to throw at the people pushing these ideas.

In 2010, and 2011, Businesses were sitting on trillions in cash because of neoconservative economic policies for 30 years has been keeping the price of labor down, and *redistributing* income to the top 20%. Where was the promised new hiring? Of course, the mainstream propaganda outlets came up with some reason box diarrhea to explain this. The stark facts are that no matter how much you cut taxes on firms, no matter how much money you throw at the rich and fill the firms tank, no matter how many incentives you give them, no matter how much you bribe, cajole, plead and beg, *they are not going to hire one single worker to make goods and services they can't sell*. If the Household tank is empty, households will not be able to buy more through Consumption, *no matter how full the Business and Savings tanks are*. Any money you throw at them will simply be stuffed in their pockets. This has been illustrated time after time in history and has been shown in study after study. It happened under Reagan and Bush, and happened under most of Obama's term with his hundreds of billions in bail-outs.

The reason why WWII got us out of the Depression was because congress allowed Roosevelt to *spend* huge amounts of money for production of war goods, racking up huge deficits in the process — *the very thing he was criticized for doing during the Depression*. During the war, no durable goods were made like home appliances; even cars companies were making only tanks and other military vehicles. The war required massive government spending that conservatives howled against all through the 1930's. After the war, great numbers of businesses started up making goods based on new technology and many large old corporations greatly expanded production of existing goods like home appliances and most importantly cars. This enormous jump in employment and income resulted in a growing economy after the war, which enabled the government to erase the deficits incurred for the war. The moral of the story is if conservatives would have allowed Roosevelt to spend the same amount of money to *build* bridges and buildings as they allowed him to spend during WWII to *destroy* bridges and buildings, the Depression would have ended many years earlier.

And did sharing of some the new wealth to the lower 80% retard investment, or prevent the introduction of new technology or prevent the expansion of the economy, all of which is given as an excuse by these pathetic econowhores doing economic history, for the harsh conditions the working class had to endure during the Industrial Revolution? The truth of the matter is that Economic Socialism during the Industrial Revolution actually *retarded* economic expansion and created major depressions every 10 years which robbed people of their jobs and savings. All you have to do is compare the late 1800s with the period after WWII when we had a degree of pure Capitalism when you got maximum technological innovation, maximum improvements in working conditions, the appearance of a real middle class and maximum economic expansion.

But in honesty, some of Roosevelt's reforms can lead to abuses too. As the UAW gained more power being supported mostly by Democrats in Washington needing votes, they actually created an extortion racket in the auto industry. I remember some of their strikes. Ford, GM and Chrysler had no choice but to give in because strikes would lose them customers. But the UAW wasn't smart enough to see that American car companies were losing customers to foreign car makers. So their membership began to shrink. The reason is found in the very weakness of union theory, which is to attend to the interests of their older core members. This is *core unionism*. The union movement can be successful in the long run only if it promotes *mass unionism* that, instead of maximizing pay, maximizes the number of members. But for some reason, unionism is what we could call a *system vector trap*, which leads to *core* unionism. (This is something that a systems dynamics professor ought to tackle. It's probably caused by what mathematicians call climbing the *local* optima.)

The UAW was getting bigger pay and benefits for a shrinking union. In order to avoid strikes, the American car companies had to rack up increasing debts to meet union demands. It was all unsustainable. Finally, GM declared bankruptcy and had to be bailed out. And the very same union had to accept concessions that discontinued some of the very benefits that shrunk their membership in the first place. The only reason they didn't lose all their benefits is that Obama personally stepped in and stole money from bondholders to give to the UAW. This was really illegal, but with current Supreme Courts, all laws are up for grabs.

What this shows is that any economic entity is going to try to grab more by abusing their power and that you have to have independent rules to keep them in check. Corporations create thousands of abuses of economic power too. Does this mean we should get rid of corporations who are the most efficient way to produce goods and services with the latest technology? Unions are fine but must be held in check by independent rules just like corporations. But by legalizing and supporting unions, Roosevelt created a balance of power as between capital and labor which resulted in a prosperous middle class for the first time in the history of the world.

We have been stressing Roosevelt's economic accomplishments. There is no room here for Roosevelt's political accomplishments, which are also greatly underrated. Remember this was the Great Depression. Democracy and Capitalism was being threatened all over the world. On his left, Roosevelt was being pulled towards Stalin's "worker's paradise" by delusional liberals with their heads in their butts not seeing reality and who wanted to believe that Stalin was the great wave of the future. On his right, he was being pressured by conservatives who were having wet dreams over the things Hitler was getting away with on his National Socialist trip through history. Roosevelt not only made his way through this political minefield, but bought back Adam Smith's Liberal Democratic Capitalism after 75 years of rampant Economic Socialism and a new prosperous middle class at the same time. He wasn't perfect, but he was a deity compared to the Bolsheviks, dummies, draft dodgers, war criminals and bunglers we've had since then.

24.8 STIMULATING A RECESSIONARY ECONOMY VIA THE PRIVATE SECTOR

The first point to make about the successful working of the economy is that what drives an economy is flow in the Consumption pipe as Adam Smith wrote. But except for the use of credit cards, people can't spend more on Consumption than what they get in the form of wages through the income pipe, Y_L. So even though everything depends on Consumption, this flow is dependent on other factors. We have a vicious circle going here. Businesses can only make money on how much they can sell. And this determines how much their wage bill will be. But how much they can sell depends on how much households are buying, which in turn is determined by their wages are. Where do we get on this merry-go-round?

As we mentioned, the starting point is the Consumption pipe, which is the driving force in the economy. This determines how much firms can produce and sell. In normal circumstances, firms will produce only what consumers are willing to buy. This amount of production of goods and services will determine how many people firms will keep employed. We mentioned the OEE above, the Optimal Equilibrium Economy. But Feudalism, which we are calling Corporatism, was a stable economy that wasn't optimal. Feudal systems lasted hundreds of years and were in equilibrium because the aristocracy owned all the means of production. And they also totally controlled the political system of courts and laws. They were able to make their own rules of the economic game. There is nothing unstable about this to get it off course as long as technology doesn't change.

But it must be kept in mind that feudalism was not a market system. The people on manors were like children in a family. They produced the goods and services that only the manor needed and didn't have to sell goods to the outside world. That's why there really wasn't a system of national money during feudal times. Also, there could be enormous inequality in the standard of living on manors. Even though the aristocracy could make their own rules, it didn't destabilize their economies because there were no markets and the aristocracy didn't derive its wealth by selling goods and services. Also, there was very little technology, which is why feudalism was so stable for so long.

But the economic nodes of a modern market economy derive their wealth by *selling* stuff. This is a very important difference. The best way to make money quickly is to make a new product on the basis of new technology. This is how a modern economy changes and grows. So we must also ask, what are the requirements of a growing economy. We can answer this question and kill two birds with one stone by looking at how an economy gets out of a recession. Whether you want an economy to grow from equilibrium or to get it going from a recession requires the same measures. There's two major ways to get out of a recession, the first is the government spurring the economy, which we've discussed above. The second is for firms to hire more workers to increase Labor Income.

Whenever the economy gets in trouble for whatever reason, it is because Consumption starts to fall. This occurred in 1929 and also in 2008. In 1929, the stock market crashed. People panicked and ran to the bank to get their money out. Well, as some of you may know, the banks aren't like they were a thousand years ago. The money you think you have in the bank is only on paper. The bank lends your money to businesses and consumers often in the form of mortgages. So if suddenly people want their money like happened in 1929, and the bank doesn't have it, people panic, and there's a "run" on the banks. This wipes out people's savings so they have no money to spend. Firms sell less goods and services so there are layoffs. The system spirals down to very high unemployment, which reached 25% in 1932 at the end of 12 years of Republican presidents.

A similar thing happened in 2008 at the end of George Bush. When the mortgage market crashed, people homes went down in value. So they couldn't borrow against their homes as before. When people's wealth decreases, they are less inclined to spend money. So the flow in the Consumption pipe started to fall, and a vicious circle sets in. With less money flowing through the Consumption pipe, there is less production and more layoffs. The economy spirals down.

The question is, under what circumstances will the Business tank be able to get an economy going again? Well one circumstance is where a new technological breakthrough occurs that gets people very excited. This creates what is called a *bubble*. What happens during a technological bubble is that an idea comes on the scene that attracts the interest of investors and firms who consider ways to make money on the new idea. Now it is important to understand what a bubble is. *The definition of an economic bubble is where more money is pulled up the Investment pipe for the idea than it really deserves.* And this won't happen with just any old technological idea. It has to be a very special idea. Let's explain this.

In any given industry producing some good or service, there will be a certain amount that consumers are willing to buy. This is true of cars, refrigerators, fast foods, any product at all. This amount of sales will require a certain amount of plant and equipment needed to produce the output and a certain number of workers to make the product. We can call this the *EPR, Equilibrium Production Requirement.* Thus the EPR is labor income, Y_L, to produce what is being sold, plus I_T, money to pay for the plant and equipment making goods and services being sold. For example, the automobile is not a new idea, so there will not be much *additional* plant and equipment to make more cars than can be sold. So there will be very little *new* Investment, I_A.

Now let's say a new idea pops up that excites people like the personal computer in the '80s or the internet in the late '90s. Well, businesses will suck money up the investment pipe, I_A, to buy *additional* plant and equipment needed to make the new product and they will hire additional workers. Now if the amount of money flowing up the Investment pipe and the amount of income going to new workers making the product, is *greater* than the EPR, you have a *bubble.* To put this in another way, if businesses are so excited about a new product that they buy *more* plant and equipment and hire *more* workers than is really needed to make the amount of product consumers are willing to buy, then you have a bubble.

At the beginning of a bubble, firms and businesses are frantically buying plant and equipment, setting up production processes and hiring lots of people to make the product. This creates income and increases Consumption. Also, firms going into business are buying new plant and equipment from other firms. Those firms, in turn, hire more workers, which also spurs Consumption. The economy spirals up and up. After the smoke clears away, the whole economy is operating at a higher level of output and income than before the bubble.

What really drives all this is the *idea.* It has to be an idea that excites firms and businesses into going into production no matter what is in the Household tank. If the idea is exciting enough, businesses will believe they can sell product even if the Household tank is not full. And *they will do this no matter how good or bad the economy is and no matter what their taxes are.* This is because they will deem that if the idea is exciting enough, consumers will simply substitute the new product for other things in their consumer basket.

In recent times, the computer-software and internet bubbles occurred under Ronald Reagan and Bill Clinton respectively. The economy was slow when Reagan got elected and he made it worse. In spite of Reagan not helping the PC sector in any way, there was still a PC bubble. The money Reagan was stealing from our children was thrown at companies from *older* industries who did nothing to expand or hire people. All of the economic activity produced by the PC revolution under Reagan took place without one iota of help from Ronald Reagan. On top of this, the internet bubble under Clinton occurred after he actually *raised* taxes on the larger nodes of the economy, including the companies that were making the bubble. This bubble enabled Clinton to balance the budget for the first time in 30 years.

But the industry that starts the bubble slowly comes back down to earth. With too much production capacity and too many firms making the product, there is a period of "shaking out" in the industry. Some firms will go bankrupt. Some will merge and buy each other out. Finally, the production capability in the industry will be equal to the amount of the product that can be sold. A new equilibrium and a new EPR will be reached where the amount of replacement plant and equipment stays pretty much the same. Even though there is a shaking out period, the bubble leaves the whole economy operating at a higher level of Income and Consumption.

But our history shows that between bubbles, there is always a period of economic stagnation. A very interesting question we will want to address is, can a Capitalist system sustain itself without bubbles? As we will explain, I think so, but only if there is the proper balance between Income going to capital as Profits and Income going to labor and households. This is what we have called a *balanced* economy. But events in the last 30 years make this state of affairs impossible. As we explained in the last chapter, ever since the Civil War, there have been periodic business cycles and the system collapses, basically caused by Economic Socialism. But what is interesting about our economic history is that every time the system collapses into a recession or depression, along comes a bubble that gets the system going again. There was a time when I thought I had originated this idea. But there seems never to be an original idea. An economist names Joseph Schumpeter thought of this in the beginning of the last century.

The first bubble was the steam engine bubble in the early 1800s. Lots of firms went into business making steam engines that could power the machines of industry. Up till then the major source of power in factories was the waterwheel. That's why the old mills you see all over the east coast are always located on rivers. But the original steam engine bubble began to die down in the 1840s which was a recessionary decade. After the civil war, the railroad bubble appeared that lasted about 30 years. Railroad companies sprung up everywhere. In New England, if you drive around you see where lots of old tracks have been removed and the channel used as a hiking or bicycle path. Trunk lines were built that extended across the whole country. But then there was the usual shaking out period when railroads were consolidated. By the 1890s the railroad bubble was petering out and the 1890s were again recessionary. Then came the auto bubble.

Around 1900, the automobile was a new product. It was so revolutionary that they called it a horseless carriage. In Vermont, you had to have a guy walking in front of the car waving a red flag to let people know that the machine was propelling itself. For the next 30 years, lots of people went into the auto business. Henry Ford was a leading carmaker along with R. E. Olds and Walter Chrysler. By 1920 there were around 2 *thousand* businesses making cars. Of course, most of them were little garages making custom cars, which is the way Henry Ford got started. But then there was a massive shaking out period where most of these little car businesses folded or were bought out or merged. Alfred P. Sloan organized and consolidated General Motors with its 5 major brands. By the 1930s, the money needed to produce the amount of cars sold was down to the EPR and the bubble was over. There wouldn't be a time again when more money was thrown at the car industry than it needed to make the cars that could be sold. In fact, there has never been a time since then when the industry was operating at full capacity.

World War II created quite a postwar bubble in two industries, chemicals, including plastics, and electronics with television and what was called hi-fi. In the 1950's, there were hundreds of new plastics and chemical companies. Because of this bubble and because

Roosevelt reintroduced real Capitalism, there was more economic expansion in the 1950s and '60s than had ever occurred before.

Poor Jimmie Carter wound up *between* bubbles which is why the economy was slow during the 1970s. But then came the PC bubble in the mid 1980s, which bailed out Ronald Reagan's failing economic policies. This petered out and there was again a recession in 1989 which hurt papa Bush. Bill Clinton inherited the internet bubble. Everyone went into the internet business, making sites, web pages, sales venues and software companies. The economy expanded so much that the stock market more than doubled between 1995 and 2000. Many more businesses were initiated than could possibly be sustained. Again there was a shaking out period, but now it's a mature industry.

24.9 RONALD REAGAN AND ECONOMIC SOCIALISM

As we have mentioned, the '70s was a period between bubbles as the economy had slowed down after the expansive '50s and '60s. Not only that, but inequalities began to appear that made it difficult for middle class households to maintain the required level of consumption. The '70s decade was really a warning sign that Capitalism is simply not sustainable with the kind of economic inequality prescribed by the neoconservative agenda. So instead of attempting to put the system in balance as was the case in the '50s and '60s, the stagnating economy of the '70 created a political vacuum, into which a new political movement began to germinate. By the '80s, conservative thinking had been able to recover from the bad reputation it had accrued because of the disaster it caused in 1929. A new breed of conservative came on the scene and a new political movement called *neo*conservatism. Leading nodes of the economy, especially the idle and crooked rich, *began to complain that the Capitalism reintroduced by Roosevelt's reforms of the '30s, was simply not allowing them to hog as big a share of the pie as they thought they deserved.* It's really as simple as that.

The neoconservative had a simple agenda: attack middle class income and wealth and redesign the rules of the game so as to send all new income and wealth to the top 20%. Even if this cripples the economy, they will gain a bigger share of it, which is more important. They took advantage of the slow-down in the economy in the 1970s after the post-war bubble and began a long cultural/political agenda that would sweep them into power for the next 35 years.

Of course, this agenda had to be rigidly concealed from the middle class. This involved a two-pronged initiative. First, they put all their political efforts into creating the perfect puppet that would sell the new agenda to the American people. This was not difficult since the major means of propaganda were already in the hands of these same large economic nodes. So out of whole cloth, a hank of hair and a Boris Karloff crooked smile, came Ronald Reagan — the most perfect puppet ever to be invented by the system mind and the most dedicated enemy of Democratic Capitalism in our history. The Reagan election marked the most important fork in the road of our economic history. In 1980, the question was, would we take the fork that would continue on a path of perfecting and grounding a system of pure Democratic Capitalism reintroduced by Roosevelt, or would we take the Economic Socialist fork towards the ultimate goal of National Socialism?

Neoconservatives realized that modern means of communication, especially television and talk radio, could be used as a powerful propaganda tool to sell their agenda. They pushed aside the old conservatives and we never again heard much from them. The neoconservative movement had plenty of time and money to perfect a new line of propaganda, which was used to cover up the drive towards Economic Socialism even more destructive than had ever occurred before.

In creating a positive image of Reagan, the system mind propaganda outlets took advantage of the essentialist thinking that been growing for the previous 20 years. Recall, in Sect. 21.3, we discussed how the shift to the individual as the unit of production enabled the system to greatly encourage essentialist thinking. Keeping energy in the bottom of the brain is what enabled the system to shift to essentialist thinking that revolves around aggression, conquest, control and greed.

To conceal the new Economic Socialist agenda, the system mind divides the neoconservative movement into two groups. The first group gets elected to office and proceeds to put economic players in bed with political animals rigging the rules so as to send all new income and wealth away from the middle class and towards their idle crooked friends — all in direct opposition to Adam Smith's Capitalism. Meanwhile the other half buys up propaganda outlets and hires whole strings of paid whores who preach the *exact opposite* of what the elected half is doing. In this regard, they have the complete cooperation of the system mind media outlets through which favorite political actors were not defined by what they *did*, but by what they and their paid whores *said*. What neoconservatives *said*, led by Ronald Reagan, was to praise Capitalism to the hilt. They championed fiscal responsibility, small government. Totally lost in the shuffle and suppressed by the corporate media is what Reagan actually *did*, which was to increase the size of government every single year he was in office and to design, sign and submit budgets with deficits averaging over 165 billion dollars each year. What he was in *essence*, what he existentially *did*, was to promote big government as he racked up more national debt than all presidents before him combined. But by this time, existentialism was dead, to be replaced by an essentialism that could define a person in terms of a soul, which is as squeaky clean as the media wants us believe. Reality is now defined by words, and this is why we have thousands of talking heads on television and sewer radio belching out words, words, and more words to define people's essences regardless of what they are doing.

What the neoconservative movement led by Reagan *did* was to pick up right where 1920s Republicans left off with massive doses of Economic Socialism. They mounted a vicious attack on the two core principles of democratic Capitalism as outlined by Adam Smith: a prosperous middle class and independent rule makers enforced by the political system. The attack on the middle class consisted of big tax increases, downward pressure on the minimum wage and a vicious attack on middle class unions so that private union membership began its long slow decline.

It was under Reagan that the flow of illegal immigrants surged which decreases the value of labor among at the lower end of the middle class. He let in about 3 million illegal immigrants all to provide cheap labor for business, which is why conservatives, regardless of what they say, *in practice*, have allowed a steady flow of illegal immigrants ever since. Finally, he started up the idea of free trade which puts downward pressure on the wages of ordinary people. To increase profits for the system nodes that created him, Reagan chased away 10 million well-paid productive jobs overseas to be replaced only partially by lesser paying service jobs. Now I would like to know what minute detail was left off the list of measures Reagan took to make *class war* on the middle class? *An attack on the middle class as Reagan promoted is an attack on Democratic Capitalism.*

The second prong of Reagan's attack on Capitalism was in breaking down the barrier between the government rule-keepers and the economic game in the private sector. Money started flowing like water from the economic system into the political system in Washington to allow the corporate world to make their own rules. Reviewing a book about lobbying, Michael Tomasky says: "But the really big money didn't start infiltrating the system until the mid-1980s".[19] Of course, corporations in the private sector have interests, mainly to make money. However, they can make more money in the short run if they can rig the rules of the game in their favor. Under Reagan, great scandals arose in almost all his government agencies. "By the end of Reagan's terms, administration officials had been convicted, indicted, and/or subjected to official investigations for official misconduct and/or criminal violation — more than in any other prior administration." [20] You'll never hear this from the paid whores who infest our propaganda outlets. Every one of these scandals involved the same thing: economic players in bed with politicians in Washington to rig their own rules, a corollary to the system outlined by Karl Marx.

One of the first things Reagan did in '81 was to overthrow an anti-trust law. Whereas the '60s was a highpoint of anti-trust enforcement that helped support a prosperous middle class as Adam Smith outlined, Reagan began a period of massive collectivization in industry which created oligopolies and monopolies everywhere. The power and bigness in all aspects of society from the war-making pentagon to huge financial institutions is what made him a hero of neoconservative mentality. Reagan's anti-trust division of the Justice Department swept away rules to prevent mergers, takeovers and collectivization in industry. Thousands of small farms were driven out of business as agriculture was increasingly collectivized into huge corporate-government farms. Then billions are stolen from taxpayers to prop up profits for these totally unnecessary large agricultural units. This suppression of competition directly contradicts Adam Smith who said, "But the cruelest of our revenue laws, I will venture to affirm are mild and gentle, in comparison of some of those which the clamour of our merchants and manufacturers has extorted from the legislature, for the support of their own absurd and oppressive monopolies".[21] Smith, who was a very austere and proper person, almost never uses language this strong. But it shows how strongly he felt about the monopoly threat that was starting to happen even in his time against the mercantile

Capitalist system he was defending. It also shows what the father of Capitalism would have thought of Ronald Reagan, America's leading Bolshevik.

This is why regardless of what their paid whores say, the neoconservative in *power* is basically a collectivist. He will invariably vote for big everything — big brother government invasion of our private lives, big theft, big corporations, big farms, big banks, big bombs, big wars, big torture, big killings, big, big, big. He achieves identity by identifying with nodes of massive economic, political and government power. This is why no matter what aspect of the economy he considers, it's a rush to collectivize small nodes into larger more powerful nodes. The result is not free markets, but *bully* markets where the biggies can push everyone else around by making their own rules.

Reagan next passed the Garn-St. Germain Act of 1982, which allowed the Savings and Loan crooks to make their own rules, the exact definition of Economic Socialism. This led to the collapse of the S&L industry under papa Bush, and the recession of '90-'91. Cleaning up the mess required the theft of 150 *billion* dollars from our children. As more economic players especially on Wall St. climbed into smaller beds with the rule-keepers in Washington in a huge socialist gang-bang, they passed the Secondary Mortgage Market Enhancement Act in 1984 that ended state restrictions on the sale of mortgage-backed securities. This act started a derivatives scam that picked up speed under Bush and led to the '08 meltdown.

To continue the gradual takeover of the economy by the financial services industry in bed with political actors, they passed the Commodities Futures Modernization Act in 2000. This allowed the financial services industry to write their own rules as to how derivatives would be printed up, traded, sold and gambled on. Thomas Jefferson wrote in 1802 to the treasury secretary, Albert Gallatin, "If the American people ever allow private banks to control the issue of currency…the banks and corporations that will grow up around them will deprive people of all property…". Jefferson, with all his warts, is my favorite American. This guy had real insight, and this was back in 1802 before later corruption took place.

The Commodities Act began a whole historic trend of allowing private institutions print up their own money. And this wasn't the kind of money like Abe Lincoln's "greenbacks" which, if kept within bounds, only allows for transactions in a growing economy. Conservatives all over the world decried Lincoln's greenbacks as a threat to monarchy government. But the new monarchs, Reagan and Bush had better ideas. The new money Reagan and Bush printed up wasn't just paper. It was illegal and unconstitutional paper, called derivatives that could reproduce itself exponentially. Derivatives are the most ingenious scam ever invented by the evil mind of man. It provides a semi-legal means for financial wizards to buy, sell, and bet on fraudulent paper *they themselves print up*, extracting billions in bonuses, commissions, and fees from the system in perpetuity from all future generations. This explosion of unregulated and unconstitutional derivatives is what finally led to the collapse of 2008, requiring *trillions* to be stolen from our children to prop back up the stack of illegal paper. After the crash, players like Alan Greenspan go before congress and claim like Sergeant Klink in Hogan's Heroes: "I know nuhthink".

The effect on people's economic lives of the Reagan agenda was that median household income for the lower 80% actually decreased under Reagan and continued to decrease ever since. The share of income going to the bottom 80% *decreased* from about 60% in the '50s and '60s to 55% during the Reagan years, and to less than half when Bush left office. Reagan's attack on the middle class by raising their taxes, attacking their unions, and stealing from their future, caused Business Investment as a percent of GDP to *plummet* during his term.[22] As income to the bottom 80% declined, Consumption lagged, as would production, which caused unemployment to average 7.4% during Reagan's eight years. With this economic climate, of course businesses aren't going to invest in new workers.

Now in the past, there used to be real conservatives who understood this. A major leader in this regard was Henry Ford who was a staunch conservative. Ford was smart enough to realize that if his workers didn't get decent pay, they couldn't buy his cars. So he paid them 5 dollars a day, which was above average for factory work at the time in the 1920s. Ford today would never make it in the ranks of the modern neoconservative who *is so cognitively impaired that he thinks the way you make money is by emptying the pockets of your customers.*

When the ties between economic players and government actors gets tighter that is the very definition of *Economic Socialism*. When they become the *same* people, as in Russia today and China tomorrow, you have National Socialism or Communism depending on whether the economic or the political system dominates. After a 50-year hiatus where we had some semblance of Capitalism, Economic Socialism was back in the saddle with Ronald Reagan. As had happened many times before in our history, the system finally collapsed in 2008.

Of course, in order to completely hide what was really going on, our propaganda outlets, corporate media, newspapers, etc. were going to have to label all this in a way that it would be acceptable to the average citizen. So they revived the term "laissez-faire". Laissez-faire is a French term meaning, to leave alone, to not interfere. Ronald Reagan preached that we have to get "the government off our backs", and this meant laissez-faire capitalism.

Reagan peasants hate the government because it collects taxes while the services they get from the government conflicts with their self-image as self-sufficient rugged individualists. But the psychology is interesting in this regard. Whenever the average person receives a service, he really doesn't want to see himself getting something for nothing. It detracts from his self-image as a proud self-sustaining American. So he takes the service and quickly runs away. Wild animals do something like this. If you offer food to a wild animal, it will come and snatch the food quickly and run like hell as though he doesn't want to admit he's getting something for nothing. In the same way, when a citizen gets a service from the government, he suppresses any thoughts of where it came from, how he got it, or whether he deserved it. This is simple psychology. Like the Tea Party guy who blared out that he didn't want government interfering with his Social Security. What this means is that even though the government is viewed negatively because it collects taxes, there are no counterbalancing positive effects due to the services it dispenses. So when Reagan preached that he was going to get "the government off our backs" by "deregulation", this was received very positively by Americans with cognitive deficits because, again, people build reality out of words. This has been a clever theme of neoconservatives since then. The reality, of course, is that besides taxes, the only contact 90% of the American people have with the government is through getting services, not the government on anyone's back.

Of course, since 'regulation' is a bad word, *de*regulation must be a good word. Most people don't like the word "regulation" from their childhood when they were regulated by parents. However, what regulation really amounts to is, instead of economic players in bed with the government making their own rules, rule-making is conducted *independent* of economic players. But since most people would clearly support independent rule-making, the system propaganda outlets have to hide this practice with the word 'regulation'.

Our economic system had rules since the earliest New England towns. Free-enterprise systems are games involving productive private players acting according to *rules*. Without rules of some sort, there is no game — it simply evaporates. The game of economics has to have rules involving contracts, money, banking, labor, investments, trade, and the rest of the factors and instruments needed for transactions and business. There were rules in place all through the modern period just like any other period of western free-enterprise economies.

There is no such thing as deregulation and there has never been Laissez-faire Capitalism in the US since the Civil War. Reagan had no intention of "*de*regulating" anything, or there would be no game. Even with his Alzheimer, he knew that much. It's only a question of who's making the rules. What gets passed off as laissez-faire doesn't consist of the government staying out of rule-making business at all. It really consists of the corporate world in bed with political actors in government *re*regulating *new* rules held in utter secret by the system mind propaganda outlets for the benefit of the corporate world, neglecting the needs of ordinary consumers.

This fraudulent Laissez-faire description of Corporate Socialism reached epidemic proportions under Bush. And it infects the descriptions of everything. In 2004, a bunch of investment bankers twisted arms in the SEC to change the rules for debt limits and capital reserves needed for a rainy day. This was kept such a secret by the system mind media outlets that I learned about it in the *Scientific American* magazine no less. [23] But even in this prestigious 160-year old *science* magazine, we find them saying that the SEC "...lifted a rule specifying debt limits...etc.", making it sound like the government got out of the rule business in a Laissez-fair way. That simply is not the case. What the SEC really did was to *change* the rules so that debt limits were raised and capital requirements lowered. This shows how massive propaganda efforts by the system mind can hide reality even from the minds of scientists. They did get the results right, however: the new rules "...freed billions to invest in complex mortgage-backed securities and derivatives that helped to bring about the financial meltdown ...".

What we should learn from this history is that *de*regulation and Laissez-faire Capitalism are really *code* words for blatant Economic Socialism. What really went on under Reagan's clichés of "deregulation" and Laissez-faire, was "the government getting off the backs" of his crooked friends, fast-buck operators, fraudulent money managers, and money changers — all the people Jesus kicked out of the temple — so that they could rig *new* rules that allowed industry to be collectivized into bigger and bigger units that are "too big to fail". The tremendous increase in buy-outs, mergers, and takeovers resulted in massive waste and the loss of productive jobs among the lower 80% costing the taxpayer and future generations trillions of dollars. This is why Reagan had such high unemployment numbers. This is not Adam Smith's Capitalism at all, but Economic Socialism.

Of all the research I've done for this book, one fact is at the top of the list of surprises. A *Fortune* survey in 1970 found 53% percent of Fortune 500 executives in favor of a national regulatory agency and 57 percent believing that the federal government should "step up regulatory activities".[24] This shows that even high-power executives are human beings like the rest of us. With constant pressure to make money, corporate executives are right on the knife edge between right and wrong. With proper leadership setting the example and a period of real Capitalism of the Roosevelt era, executives and CEOs realized that any viable economic game needs independent rules, devised and enforced by the political system. However, with a little push in the opposite direction by a crooked system mind puppet like Ronald Reagan, they are firmly in the Corporate Socialist camp where the object is get rich quick, be a pig, and corrupt the system for personal gain.

Of course, a major part of the new rules under Reagan's fraudulent "deregulation" was to cut taxes, especially at the top of the economic pile. This was payback for all the campaign money he took in to get a grade D actor elected. This was trumpeted as a cure for the slow-down in the last year of the Carter administration. But as we mentioned in the last section, taxes have almost nothing to do with economic expansions and bubbles. Reaganites pointed to Kennedy's tax cuts in the 1960s. But the post-war period of expansion began right after WWII in the 1950s *before* Kennedy thought about being president. But what they won't tell you is what he reduced them *to*. The top tax rate in the '50s was a full 90%. Kennedy only reduced them to about 80%. This is not a significant tax cut. Objectively however, 90% is pretty confiscatory and it is quite likely that the 90% top tax rate was too much for an optimal economy and optimal growth. Kennedy's tax cut was accompanied by an uptick in growth from about 3.7% in the '50s to about 4.5% in the '60s, so perhaps this tax-cut did put the economy in a more optimal balance. However, perhaps this growth in GDP in the '60s was due to the Vietnam war which was a total waste. There's no way to tell.

But Reagan cut taxes on the rich and other special interests *in less than half*. The results were absolutely no stimulatory effect on the economy at all which underperformed in every important way for *8 straight years*. To this day, paid whores in the propaganda business on sewer radio and other venues tell us Reagan inherited a "terrible recession" from Carter and turned it into an unprecedented economic "boom". Here are the *facts* from official statistical abstracts.

The so-called Carter "recession" was no growth in his last year — not good but certainly not recessionary, which is defined as minus growth. Unemployment was 7.2%, again not good, but better than Reagan averaged. What did Reagan's economic "boom" consist of on the basis of his tax cuts? In Reagan's first year, the economy grew at an anemic 2.3% and unemployment shot up to 8.5%. But the "boom" was just getting started. In his second year the economy actually *shrunk* by 2.5% and he drove up unemployment to *10.8%*. This is the economic "boom" these neoconservative paid whores brag about. The only reason unemployment came down a bit afterwards was because of the PC bubble, which created one good year of growth under Reagan. After that, growth was back down to less than 3.2%, and in his 8 years, he still averaged less growth and averaged 7.4% unemployment over 8 years. If a liberal had this number, the systems propaganda outlets would call it a *recession*. Under Reagan, it was a "boom". But the most important factor was Reagan averaged a half *trillion* in debt per year in today's dollars in his 8 years to prop up his failing economic policies, more in one year than Carter had in his whole term. Reagan's good government grade is a smashing *D*. In reality, Reagan oversaw an eight-year recession but you'll never hear that from the system.

On top of this, Reagan threw all kids of money at the Business tank in the form of tax cuts, massive changes in depreciation allowances, and other forms of corporate welfare. But what was interesting is that he threw the money at the *older* more mature industries. Guess what? These industries did not expand one bit relative to the population. In fact, overall, investment in new plant and equipment as a percent of GDP actually plummeted under Reagan. The historian Gary Wills says, Reagan's "Supply-side economics was supposed to promote savings, investment, and entrepreneurial creativity. It failed at all three".[25]

Behind the scenes, within months of Reagan taking office, the system mind took him into an office and turned him into a system zombie. So when he concocted tax cuts for the rich and corporations, the system mind informed him that if he tried to compensate with cuts in spending to the Household tank, there would be less demand, less jobs, a recession, he wouldn't get reelected and nobody would have wanted to carve his crooked face in the side of a straight mountain.

The last thing a megalomaniac like Reagan was going to do was endanger reelection. So government spending stayed right up there and with the massive tax cuts Reagan enacted, there was enormous stealing from the future. Of course, the corporate media and their paid propagandists, which is the mouthpiece of the system mind, never said one word about the dangers of an ever-increasing national debt. In fact, as payback for cutting their taxes, they proceeded to fabricate Reagan into a God-like Santa Claus handing out goodies to everyone.

What slightly bailed out his failed economic policy was that Reagan was lucky enough to inherit a bubble for his second term — the personal computer-software bubble, something poor Jimmie Carter didn't have. IBM came out with the first PC in '81, and touched off a flurry of economic activity resulting in a classic bubble. Hewlett-Packard got into the PC business; Apple came out with its Macintosh in '84, followed by Michael Dell making a PC in '85. This created a whole software industry. Even though this industry got no favors from Reagan, no tax cuts, no generous depreciation allowances, the industry expanded greatly and produced *one good year* of growth under Reagan. But this success had nothing to do with Reagan's failed economic policies. As history shows, a good bubble will make Mortimer Snurd look brilliant. Bubbles depend on technology and have nothing to do with how crooked politicians are mismanaging the economy. They also have nothing to do with how the Federal Reserve is tinkering with the money supply.

But even with the bubble Reagan inherited, and the theft of trillions from the future, the economy still underperformed over the Reagan years. As Table 24.4 shows, in the '60s, the economy expanded over 4 ½ % a year and median family income increased 50% in the '50s and '60s. Unemployment averaged only about 5% the whole period and, most importantly, *there were virtually no deficits.* Compare this with Reagan and Bush where the economy slowed to only 3.2% a year under Reagan and 2.1% under Bush.[26] Unemployment went up to averaging a very high 7.4% under Reagan and 5% under Bush. While the genius of American inventiveness was expanding the economy in the information technology industry, Reagan was actually sabotaging the very things that were expanding the economy.

But a very important and totally suppressed fact about the '80s was that even the growth numbers at about 3.2% a year under Reagan is a fake number because it was mainly due to military spending to try to maintain the king's empire. This has nothing to do with the standard of living of the average citizen. Here again, the system mind's mouthpiece isn't going to report the GEP. Many studies show that it was under Reagan that the actual standard of living for the lower 80% of Americans began a slow decline that continued for the next 35 years.

The bottom line is that in spite of cutting taxes and doing all kinds of favors for investors and the corporate world, not enough money was pumped up from the Savings tub to maintain employment and Labor Income to households. The stock market went up because the wealthy were gaining wealth and income just as in the 1920s. But this was built on a crumbling foundation of starved Household income and strangled consumer demand. In the 1920s, this led to the great crash of 1929. But there was one difference in those days. At least conservatives back then had enough of a sense of honor and decency to take it on the chin and lose elections. But by the time Reagan took office, the system mind had discovered that you could prop up an unbalanced economy by stealing from the future, exactly what Reagan did and what Bush and Obama have done. In fact, deficits are a direct measure of the degree of imbalance in the major flows in the economy. If the system is balanced there is no need for deficits as the post-war years show. But with Reagans tax cuts, the deficit *doubled* to 128 billion in his second year from Carter's average 56 billion dollar deficit.* In the third year, it almost doubled again to *208* billion. Reagan never even *hinted* at submitting a balanced budget. *He designed, signed, and promulgated 8 straight years of about*

---

* In fact, Robert McIntyre calculated that in the '91-'93 period, "the relationship is almost exact: the deficit is up by 2.6 percent of the GDP and the tax cuts for wealthy cost 2.6 percent of the GDP. McIntyre, Robert; "Borrow 'n Squander". *The New Republic*, Sept. 30, '91, p. 12

a third of a trillion in today's dollars of deficits every single year he was in office stolen from the children of this country to prop up demand. Compare this to Carter's average of 56 billion. The US was "...transformed from global creditor to the world's greatest debtor nation".[27] This point cannot be stressed enough: *if you have to steal a third trillion dollars every single year you're in office to keep the economy stumbling along, this is palpable proof that your economic policy is a failure.* But you won't hear a word of it from the system mouthpieces and their hand-picked econowhores.

It reminds of my mother telling me that in the old Italian neighborhood, the mafia would hold parties for people in the neighborhood to spruce up their image. There was free food, free drinks and free entertainment. Of course, many of the neighbors didn't know the money to pay for all this was coming from various kinds crime. This is exactly the phenomenon under Reagan. With the economy stumbling along acceptably and the media keeping it a deep secret as to where the economy was coming from, they were able to anoint Reagan as the great masturbator (or was it communicator?) and the harbinger of a new prosperity.

Of course, these massive deficits are all very unconstitutional because one the main principles of our Constitutional government is no taxation without representation. This was the main concept that inspired the American Revolution and was reflected in the equal protection clause of the Constitution. The major complaint the founding fathers had against the British king was that he was taxing Americans without representation in parliament. Reagan greatly increased taxes on the children of the country who were not represented when these taxes were incurred. After Reagan and Bush's administrations, with normal interest rates, each child in this country will pay an additional *quarter million* dollars of taxes over their working lives for interest on the debt these two racked up. This is equivalent to a house. This is a blatant violation of the Constitution and a complete renunciation of one of the pillars of our government. But he didn't have to worry about the Supreme Court because reptiles had already stacked the court with people who use the Constitution for toilet paper.

In fact, because of the constant media propaganda all my life about how wonderful Reagan was, I thought that there ought to be *some* economic measure that came in better under Reagan and Bush than the post-war II years; but not so. The economy underperformed under Reagan and Bush *in every single measure* — unemployment, deficits, growth, and median family income, compared to the post-war II years. We've been bombarded all our lives from system mind about how bad a president Carter was. In the important measures of an economy, employment deficits and growth, Reagan's economy wasn't even as good as Carters.

When you see the real numbers, you have to be a complete intellectual prostitute not to change your views on how to run an economy, which is exactly what these neoconservatives are. They will squirm, wriggle, shift, deflect, bob and weave, and hurl avalanches of irrelevancies — butterflies on the White House lawn increased, government revenues went up, the number of toilets in the US increased (to accommodate Reagan's speeches) — but they won't look at the stark facts of the important measures of an economy. They even manage to get their pathetic apologies into Wikipedia. (When it comes to Economics, in my opinion, Wikipedia is just another propaganda outlet.)

The corporate media created a popular political animal out of a bumbling, stumbling grade D actor, who probably had the beginnings of Alzheimer's the whole time he was president. In fact, recently one of his sons suggested just that. Media propaganda outlets pasted tapes and cut out all the bumbling, stumbling and factual errors during his press conferences until he looked normal. Even when he was speaking normally, the only words out of his head were a bunch of clichés left over from his days as a WWII grade D actor.

Ronald Reagan started all the economic, social, and political trends that ensued. The system collapsed in '08 because of a dominant culture began by Ronald Reagan to "deregulate" and get the government "off our backs", which translates into letting companies, and especially the financial services industry to write their own rules so that billions can be made gaming the system. Of course, the real culprits are the media, who glorified Reagan in the first place because many of their advertisers were the ones wanting to get rid of rules that protect people. This propaganda campaign continues right to the present.

The result of 35 years of Economic Socialism since Reagan is over 95% of new wealth created went to the top 20%. The middle class got virtually nothing. The share of wealth of the top 1% went from 25% to a full 35% during Reagan's term. When Reagan took office, the bottom 80% had only about 20% of financial wealth. That is enough of a disgrace. By Obama's presidency, the share of wealth of the bottom 80% had been sunk to only 8%, while the top 20% had a full *92%*. On the social level, 35 years of the new neoconservatism has given us gigantic oil spills, alarming increases in birth defects among newborns, collectivization in all industries, various Wall Street scams that led finally to the meltdown of 2008, and to top it off, massive deficits and an ever-exploding national debt.

By '08, Economic Socialism get-rich-quick culture started by Ronald Reagan was entrenched so powerfully that the collapse and perfunctory liberal who got elected never got a chance to create a period of pure Capitalism like under Roosevelt. The first thing Obama did was to prop up the very economic institutions that had caused the crash in the first place. Economic Socialism was pretty much back in the saddle laying the groundwork for the next crash. This whole period of Economic Socialism was started by Ronald Reagan, which is why I would nominate him as the most destructive president in all US history.

On Reagan's 100th birthday, the media (ABC) rounded up the usual gang of intellectual prostitutes to heap praise on Reagan. It was one of the most disgusting displays of dishonesty you will ever see. They brought up Reagan's "principles", which were small government, balanced budgets, and honest government. These media whores realize that people create their realities on the basis of *words*, not *perceptions*. This is why they can belch up massive lies with a straight face. The reality is Reagan increased the size of government every year he was in office; he never even *attempted* to submit a balanced budget, and he okayed the Iran-Contra scandal that broke US laws as well as international laws as well as presiding over numerous government scandals. There was his enthusiastic support of a

Hitler-type killer in Guatamala who murdered 200 thousand South American Indians [28]; and very importantly, all the deaths from AIDS he could have prevented, which is estimated at around a quarter million people. Of course, our massive media propaganda machine basking in Reagan's tax cuts did almost nothing to point this negligence of the blood supply and proceeded to create a totally fraudulent image of Ronald Reagan who most Americans still like. I've seen ratings by historians that put Reagan at number 11 of presidents, which is another indication of the deterioration of the history profession. Even if they considered just the growing corruption of the blood supply because of blatant prejudice, how could they even consider Reagan as among great presidents? He should be at the bottom of the list.

Even if Bill Clinton and Barack Obama had been strong leaders, the Reagan culture was so engrained into the American psyche, that they wouldn't have been able to change much even if they tried, which they were too weak-minded to do. We've had bad presidents who damaged the system, but it was never *permanent* damage. When the system collapsed, reformers were able to crank up the economy with a combination of technology, government borrowing and new rules. But there's no way to get out from under the massive national debt initiated by Ronald Reagan which will continue to grow on the way towards National Socialism.

[1]   *The Economist*, Oct. 14, '00, p. 70

[2]   *The Economist*, Aug. 17, '02, p. 7

[3]   "War of nerves", *The Economist*, Mar. 15, '08, p. 96

[4]   Kaplan, S.& Snell, M, "Sapping the Superfunds Strength". *The Nation*, May 3, 2010, p. 23

[5]   Koeppel, Barbara; "Cancer Alley Louisiana". *The Nation*, Nov. 8, '99, p. 16

[6]   Ibid. p. 20

[7]   Angell, Marcia, "FDA, This Agency Can Be Dangerous". *The New York Review of Books*, Sept. 30, '10

[8]   Horton, Richard, "Cancers Malignant Maneuvers". *The New York Review of Books*, Mar. 6, '08, p. 25

[9]   Ibid. p. 25.

[10] "It's high time economists look at more than just JDP". *The Economist*, Feb. 11, '06, p. 72

[11]   McIntire, Robert; "Your Federal Tax Dollars at Work". *The American Prospect*, May 20, '02, p. 17

[12] "The Missiing $20 Trillion", *The Economist*, Feb. 165, '13.

[13] Stancil, Jordan, "Europe's Vodoo Economics". *The Nation*, June 28, '10, p. 20

[14]   Dworkin, Ronald, *New York Review of Books*, Jan. 20, '83, p. 47, Feb. 3. '83, p. 32

[15] White, Richard; *The Transcontinentals and the Making of Modern America*. Norton.

[16] *The Nation*, Nov. 30, '09. P. 31

[17] Chase, James, "The Road not Taken", *The New York Review of Books*, July, 17, '03, p.   38

[18] Greenberger, Machael, *The American Prospect*, June, '10, p. A8.

[19] Tomasky, Michael, "Washington: Will the Lobbyists Win" reviewing Robert Kaiser's book, *So Damn Much Money;* Knopf. *The New York Review of Books*, Apr. 9, '09, p. 18

[20] Borosage, R. Op. Cit. p. 23

21 Ibid. Book IV, Chap. VIII

22 *The Economist*, May 8, '10, p. 59

23 "After the Crash". *Scientific American*, Dec. '08, p. 45

24 Judis, John, The Spirit of '68. *The New Republic*, Aug. 31, '98

25 Wills, Gary, "The Politics of Grievance", *The New York Review of Books*, July 19, '90, p. 3

26 Graph in *The Economist*, Feb. 27, '10, p. 36

27 Borosage, Robert; "Conservatism Itself". *The American Prospect*, July, '07, p. 22

28 Alterman, Eric, "Where the Rest of Him?" *The Nation*, Mar. 27, p. 12

CHAPTER 25

The System Key Forks

───

WE SAW IN THE LAST chapter how the flow of money and goods and services circulates around the economy. All these flows carry with them information, just as electrical impulses between neurons of the brain carry information. And whenever you get a system in which there are an enormous number of nodes connected together in a huge net, like the neurons in the brain, you get a mind. Of course the brain has a hundred billion neurons, and a hundred *trillion* connections, which is why the brain can create consciousness. The economy has fewer nodes. If you add up all the people and all the groups of people and all the firms and all the government agencies in the country, you probably don't have a hundred billion nodes. But it will be a very large number — not enough to create consciousness perhaps, but certainly enough to create a mind.

In Ch. 23, we looked at the nature of the system mind and we alluded to its having interests, wants, and goals. So the first group of questions we must investigate are what kind of an economic system does the system mind want?

25.1 ECONOMIC GOALS OF THE SYSTEM MIND

We have seen why it is important for optimal growth and prosperity for the system to be balanced. But we have also seen why it is impossible to be balanced under our Economic Socialist system. Because businesses and the wealthy are the most powerful nodes of the system mind, these interests will always attempt to send as much income and wealth as possible to the top 20%, especially the top 5%. This implies sending as much national income as possible to the Savings tank and less to the Household tank. This is why, especially in the last 35 years, the system mind has mounted a sustained attack on the essence of Capitalism and a constant drive to promote what we are calling Economic Socialism. Sending all new wealth and income to the top 20% is not consistent with democratic Capitalism.

This has two very important ramifications. First, since more money is going to the Savings tub than would be the case in a balanced economy, there will always be money to expand the capacity of the system to produce goods and services. This is one of the sure signs of Economic Socialism: it has a tendency to *overproduce* — to be able to produce many

more goods and services than can possibly be sold. This creates the need for each producing node to compete with other nodes to attract customers to their product and away from
products of other nodes. This is why the advertising industry is so huge in the US.

We should also mention that a powerful system mind is a relatively new phenomenon.
Before WWII, the system mind was much weaker. Before radio and television, there were
not the enormous flows of information we have today. There were markets, of course and
there were small newspapers. But they were often local markets and very small local newspapers. But WWII was a milestone in the evolution of the system mind. Television became
a staple in every home. National news magazines sprouted up and the old ones expanded
greatly and incredible propaganda venues sprung up like weeds.

Of course, there are many more ordinary workers and households than there are
large corporations and wealthy individuals. But even the number of ordinary citizens is
no match for the enormous strength of the new system mind since WWII and the force
of its propaganda outlets. As we saw in the last chapter, the new system mind was able to
elect a total system puppet who sent the economy down the road of Economic Socialism.
But as we shall explain in this chapter, if the middle class votes itself to receiving an ever-
decreasing share of income, that's their choice. If the Tea Party votes to steal trillions
from their own children to fill the pockets of Wall Streeters, why should we care? The
problem is that it is all unsustainable and sooner or later leads to a total breakdown of the
system.

In this chapter, we will look at the many ways the system has to send ever-increasing
income to the top 20%. But first let us look at evidence of how the system can monitor the
citizenry to clip in the wings any attempt to deviate from the values and goals of the system;
and how the system can redirect social movements it doesn't like towards support for the
goals of the system.

25.2 DISPERSING DISSENT AND DISTRACTING THE POPULATION

A very powerful way to distract the general population from their economic interests while
sending most new income and wealth to the top is by having continuous war. Wars incite
basic emotions, and attention to the process of war keeps people from understanding their
economic interests. The perfect war to accomplish this is *perpetual* war and the war on terror has been an enormous boon to the system mind because it enables continuous, perpetual
war. We will devote a whole chapter to this phenomenon.

One of the most impressive accomplishments of the system mind, especially in the west
after WWII has been the degree to which it has been able to disperse, disarm and nullify
any sources of dissent towards of the goals of the system mind. The reason dissent is an
important enemy of the system mind is that dissent can involve lots of people. And even
though they may not be important nodes in the economy, their numbers and political activity may create sufficient information flows to redirect the goals of the system mind towards
alternative paths not acceptable to the major nodes.

If anyone doubts the existence of a system mind, this is the area to look at. Any flicker of a movement springing to life that might thwart the wants and needs of the system are either snuffed out or resculptured and redirected towards its needs. Even individuals who might be able to provide some leadership in the direction of improving society in any way are neutralized and often made into system mind zombies who go off promoting the system.

The Civil rights movement of the '60s was a major social movement that was really initiated by Eleanor Roosevelt and her attempts during WWII to integrate the armed forces. Of course, Martin Luther King was a very capable leader who picked up these fragile beginnings and developed a major social movement for equal rights for minorities, especially African Americans. Of course, King was not part of the system mind mainly because black people had never been part of the system. King usually gets the credit for the success of the civil rights movement. However, even though King's efforts may have been necessary, they were not sufficient. It also took the efforts of fiery leaders of the movement, like Skokely Carmichael and H. Rapp Brown who were doing physical damage to the system.

In any event, the civil rights movement took the system by surprise and initial means to thwart the movement by the system were so incompetent that they were actually counterproductive. The system actually took a beating during this period. When people saw cops smashing water from high-pressure fire hoses into crowds of people who were simply demonstrating, most people became sympathetic with the demonstrators. When some KKK loonies actually killed some civil rights workers, again the majority of Americans were repulsed. When the system saw its buildings being burnt down, markets being disturbed, and profits dented, it was paralyzed from action. This is a partial answer to how Johnson and civil rights leaders were able to pass historic civil rights legislation right under the system's nose. All of this created an uptick of economic well-being of black people, who, for the first time since the Civil war made significant economic progress.

But it didn't last long. As we mentioned in the last section, the very powerful system mind we have today was only in its infancy in the immediate post-war years and it didn't take long before the system was able to regroup and counterattack. The response of the system mind was one of the most clever, ingenious and resourceful responses that no individual mind could ever have conjured up. What it did was to pluck the Stokely Carmichaels, H. Rapp Browns and other fiery leaders from their poor neighborhoods, their demonstrations, their destruction of the system hardware and the system's jails, and stuff them into suits and ties and give them fancy titles paying big bucks. Every major corporation, bank and business had a black guy in the store window. That was the end of the civil rights movement. Ever since, the economic well-being of average black people has continuously deteriorated. When Clarence Thomas was nominated for the Supreme Court, there was some routine mumbling from system black leaders stuffed into their shirts and strangling ties. What would Carmichael and Brown have done? I'll tell you exactly what they would have done. They would have shut down the city of Washington until the hypocrisy was ended by nominating either a *white* Ku Klux Klanner or a real black man. But these kind of leaders were no longer around.

In 2013 on the 50th anniversary of the famous march on Washington in which King made his famous speech, all the propaganda outlets brought on a myriad of black faces to harken back to the march to paid homage. The conclusion was the same in every venue: we've made progress but have a long way to go. Yes, the progress they made is for *leaders* of black people to be stuffed into collars choking them to death telling us about progress, which, of course, is only progress *they* made being on TV. These very same potential black leaders are now part of the system led by a trying-hard-to-be-black president, resulting in the majority of black people going backwards. The system mind conquers all.

When the system saw the success of the 150-year old feminist movement resulting in the right to vote and equal rights legislation of the 1960s, it had an immediate response. Out of whole cloth it created a "Women's Liberation" movement whose job it was to engineer the final resculpturing of the human citizen to meet the needs of the system mind. We will explain this in a later chapter.

An article in *The Nation* magazine bemoans the fact that even though the middle and working classes are getting screwed, they don't complain: "Working people are losing their homes and their pensions while robber baron CEOs report renewed profits and windfall bonuses. Shouldn't the unemployed be on the march…demanding big initiatives to gener-ate jobs?"[1] He's looking for the good old days like the 1930s and the 1960s when masses of people demonstrated for jobs or civil rights or the 8-hour day. But the system mind back then was nothing compared to today. This guy doesn't realize that the system mind has evolved to control a network of media propaganda outlets that keep people totally in the dark as to their real economic interests. Even if a spontaneous grass-roots movement were to emerge, the system would immediately take hold of it and redirect it to its own interests. A perfect example is the Tea Party.

Here was a grass-roots spontaneous coagulation of ordinary people who feel in their bones that the system is heading towards disaster. Immediately, a bunch of billionaires took control of the movement and turned it into just another force to keep all new income and new wealth going to the top 20%, to cut off services to the bottom 80% including some of these very same people, and dumping trillions of debt on future generations and especially their own children that will eventually collapse the system. The Tea Party is part and par-cel of the system.

Some people have thought that the democracy of the internet will be a force for the interests of ordinary people. I can assure you that if it were, it would be transmogrophied into a force in the interests of the system. As we discussed in Sect. 23.5, what we find on the internet is nothing even remotely resembling an objective point of view. Politically motivated people now have a public media outlet that reinforces the opinions they already have. I have a friend who sends me neoconservative blogs and another friend sending me neoliberal blogs. Neoliberals lie through their teeth about the viability of Social Security and Medicare, they constantly push unconstitutional means to stuff the country with illegal immigrants and of course, push for gay everything. Neoconservatives are even worse. They lie about every conceivable thing. You'd have to be a total jellyfish to plug into this crap.

This is not a force for improvement but only a way for the extremes of both sides to waste their energies fighting each other while the *"moderate"* views of the system mind walks off with increased profits, bonuses, and commissions betting on fake paper money and sending all new income and wealth to the top 5%. What the country needs is an *independent* point of view just like we need an independent source of rules for the economic game; and we're probably not going to get it.

25.3 THE SYSTEM MIND AND FOREIGN POLICY

An interesting question we could ask at this point is, does the system mind include other countries as nodes? If we were to include other countries and nodes within those countries, we might have a world system mind. This would be a very complex system to analyze beyond our scope here. Recall in Sect. 23.3, we discussed the problem that our political lives do not form a system mind. Most of what our political lives consist in is the right to vote once in a while. This is not enough for a mind. The economic system mind is constantly trying to force our entire lives into the bailiwick of the *economic* system mind. And this is why we see people voting against their own interests. Since the means of communication are part of the system, people are constantly being pulled into the system mind, hook, line, and sinker. They then have no political life *outside* of it that could help them look out for their interests. In Ch. 27, we will discuss the lack of information flows regarding our foreign policy that negate the development of a system mind.

As we described in Sect. 24.5, a viable Capitalist economy has to be in balance. To maintain balance, there would have to be proper divisions of flows at key forks in the flow diagram. They are the important decision points, and as you might expect, these points are the source of major controversy in how the system should be managed. They are both forks in major pipes.

25.4 KEY FORKS IN THE FLOW DIAGRAM — THE C/S FORK

A very important key point in the flow diagram is the C/S_H fork shown in fig. 25.1. It's really a simple fork. Total Household Income, Y_T, can go towards either spending for Consumption, C, or it saves its income, S_H. And this is where a major contradiction arises for the system. On the one hand, the system needs to send as much flow through the Consumption pipe to buy the goods and services businesses are making. This is why advertising is such big business in the US. On the other hand, the system tries to send as much money as possible to the top 20%. This actually hurts Consumption. The reason is that households at higher income levels make enough money to be able to save a good deal of their income which they use to buy stocks, bonds and other investment vehicles. At the lower levels of the income pile, however, households have to spend all of their income just to survive. So any force that gives more to the top 20% and less to the bottom 80% will cut Consumption and so less production of goods and services and less jobs.

However, there have been many forces at work to shift income to the top 20% that are not the result of sinister forces, but just bad luck like the high tech bubble under Bill Clinton. The IT industry needs an array of brains, talent, and education which increases the demand for higher skilled workers and reduces it for lower skilled. The system needs educated engineers, designers, and highly intelligent managers. This increases the value of labor at the top and decreases it at the bottom. Again the result has been shifting of income upwards.

In the past, the breakthroughs in technology were beneficial to all layers of society. The car industry in the early 20th century and the chemical and electronics industries after WWII, needed labor at all levels of sophistication from the janitors cleaning up factory floors up through factory assembly line workers, or chemical workers up through engineers and scientists, and finally to management. These kinds of industries are best at creating a balanced economy. Since all levels of society are needed, demand for all levels of labor is maintained which creates and maintains a proper distribution of income so that there is enough income to the bottom 80% to clear markets.

What the IT industry has done relative to other bubbles is, *in effect*, to put a tax on the lower 80% and a boon to the income of people with the needed skills and education. We could call this a *technology tax*, which in effect sends income towards savers and away from consumers. The result is that the lower 80%, who spend most of their income, hasn't received sufficient income to clear markets. This requires massive theft from the future to prop up demand.

Some mouthpieces of the system mind have tried to paper over the effects of high technology by showing that the *demand* for labor at the bottom end has also increased. *The Economist*, in reviewing some economics papers, explained that because of the IT industry, demand for labor at the *bottom* end as well as the top end has increased.[2] We can understand the increase in demand at the top end, of course, but *Economist* writers were pleasantly surprised (pretending to be real humanitarians) to find that demand for labor at the bottom end had also increased.

Let's go back to another time in history when demand for labor at the bottom end mushroomed. In the 1600's in the American South, a few plantation owners discovered that they could get their labor done very cheaply by importing slaves from Africa. The idea spread like wildfire and *demand* for labor in the new field of labor skyrocketed. Thousands of positions in this exciting new labor field were opening up every day in the South. Importers of the new labor category could hardly keep up with demand. Well, a similar thing has been happening in the last 35 years because of Reaganomics. With the constant drumbeat by system mind propaganda outlets like *The Economist* for free trade and "labor flexibility" (this is code word for watering down the rights of labor to organize), the value of labor in the bottom half, especially the bottom 20%, has been crumbling. So just as in the South, demand for labor at slave labor wages has been increasing, and we can all rejoice with mouthpieces like *The Economist* over this happy state of affairs.

But there is another factor that has made this problem even worse. Starting in the late '70s, we had a women's movement that stressed education and careers. Women began to go to college in large numbers and eventually surpassed men in college graduates. The brighter, more educated and more talented among them began to get good white collar jobs in all industries, and this had the effect of reducing the number of babies they would have. The birthrate among professional women began to plummet and even went below 2. (It takes a birthrate of 2 to keep a population at a constant number because each woman has to replace herself as well as a man who can't make a baby.) The sad effect of this is that as the relatively smaller number of babies being born at the upper end of the career scale, and demand for people with *more* talent and more education increasing, the income going to the professionals in the top 20% started to climb dramatically.

In the meantime, women at the bottom end of the education/career scale continued having babies about the usual rate. But because of automation and a growing high technology economy, the demand for labor at the bottom end of the career scale began to drop. What this did was to actually reduce the bargaining power of ordinary labor. And without the protection of unions or some other means to keep income up, income going to the lower 80% of the population did not increase at all for the next 35 years. In fact, if we really had a measure of the GEP, the standard of living of the lower 80% actually fell during this period. Over the next 35 years, about 98% of all new wealth and income generated by the economy went to professionals in the upper 20%. Nobody is to blame for this. It's simply the bad luck of the draw and something we can't do much about, although discouraging women in the top 20% from having babies is a disaster for an economy.

Another very important factor that shifts income from the *consuming* bottom 80% to the *saving* top 20% is the National Debt. Neoconservatives have their own reasons for wanting a high national debt. But liberals are guilty too, and it's because they just don't understand economics, especially the big picture. When the government has a deficit, it prints up bonds and sells them to investors. But investors are mostly the wealthiest nodes of the economy (or foreign investors). These bonds pay interest and in the future, the interest on outstanding bonds must come out of government revenues. The trap is that even if the economy rebounds, there is a threat of inflation and this puts pressure to raise interest rates. The result is that down the line, money must be taken from people who tend to spend for goods and services, especially the lower 80%, and tendered to people holding the bonds, who tend to save and invest instead of buying goods and services. This again starves Consumption and keeps the economy out of balance.

Starting with Reagan the share of income going to the bottom 80% has decreased from about 60% to less than half currently, which simply not enough to clear markets. A result of this enormous inequality, it has been necessary to prop up Consumption over the last 35 years since Ronald Reagan by stealing from the future in the form of massive deficits. Neoliberals think you can go on forever like this but you can't. Neoconservatives, as shall explain, want massive deficits in spite of what they say because it pushes us towards the kind of society they want.

25.5 Key Forks in the Flow Diagram - Y/P Fork

As we discussed in Sect. 24.1, a key point in the economic flow diagram is the Y/P fork. At this fork, money from the Business tank can go either towards income to the Household tank as Labor Income, or kept as Profits. In Sect. 24.5, we explained that an Optimal Equilibrium Economy is where the standard of living of the citizens is as high as possible and the economy was expanding as fast as possible given the current level of technology. This requires proper balance. The amount of income that goes to the large nodes of the economy through the P pipe as Profits, Retained earnings, Dividends, and high pay for people at the top of the economic ladder, has to balance with how much goes to the Y_H pipe as Household income. In modern times we probably came close to an OEE in the 1950s and '60s. The economy grew an average of over 4% a year over these decades. Real median family income increased 50%, and unemployment was relatively low. This is why for the first time in our history, we had a viable and prosperous middle class. And most importantly, there were virtually no deficits. So we can use this period of our history as a yardstick to measure the effectiveness of the economy since then.

But in the past 35 years, the system has not been in balance. The share of national income to the bottom 80% has continued to fall. This brings up a point that is never mentioned in any media. We really have two kinds of taxes, nominal taxes, which are monies people actually send to the government. But we also have in place, *in effect*, a tax on the bottom 80% that has had its share of national income suppressed to below half. We could call this an *effective* tax. This is not a tax in the usual sense. It is a tax that workers are *effectively* paying because their income is artificially low relative to an optimal economy. Let's explain.

Regarding the distribution of income, we see in Table 24.3 that during the '50s and '60s, the bottom 80% of households was receiving about 60% of National Income. The first thing to notice in this regard is that all along, we've had pretty much the same distribution of job categories. We still have managers and entrepreneurs all the way down to janitors. However, compared to the '50s and '60s, income has been redistributed to the top 20% and away from the lower 80%. This is what we are calling an *effective tax.* Compared to an optimal, sustainable economy, the lower 80% is being deprived of the income it had in an optimal economy and the amount it is being deprived of resembles a tax, which we are calling an *effective tax.* Under George Bush, the effective tax on the lower 80% was about 32% because that's how much less they were getting compared to when the economy was optimal. And the top 20% of Households are paying an *effective* tax of only about 8%. The result is that the distribution of income has become much more unequal, something that you have heard about. Too much is going to the P pipe, and not enough to the Y_H pipe.

Now Bill Clinton tried to neutralize these effects by raising taxes on upper income groups. This has the effect of lowering the relative taxes on the lower 80%, and for the first time in about 20 years, median family increased. It also had the effect of allowing the lower 80% to get a share of the pie that would be more in line with what the average citizen would think is fair. This allowed Clinton to even balance the budget for a few years. But neoconservatives squealed to high heaven that he was "redistributing income". Of course ever since Reagan, we've had a constant shift of income "redistributed" upward to the top 20%. But in 35 years, not one peep was ever spoken to this effect by the paid whores of the system mind. Let's look at some of the ways an effective tax comes about.

One way firms try to maximize income going to Profits and away from Households is to be able to charge high prices. High prices send income to the top 20% who invest more than they spend. With reduced Consumption, there will be less jobs and lower pay because Businesses would have leverage over labor. However, in a real Capitalist economy, there are supposed to be many other firms to compete with. This is the beauty of real Capitalism. By having a number of competing businesses all trying to get the consumer's dollar, competition will assure that the consumer will get the best product for the least price.

However, if profits are squeezed by competition, this interferes with businesses' overall goal of maximizing profits. One way out of this dilemma is for firms to collude and fix prices artificially high or to simply reduce the number of competitors in an industry. This is why firms are always trying to combine, to buy each other out and to collectivize into a small number of large firms. This is how we get oligopoly industries. 'Oligopoly' is from the Greek root *oligos*, meaning small number. Often this led to *monopolies* in many industries, which is where you have only one firm in the industry that Adam Smith decried. Even *The Economist* warned that "... collusion among producers to rig prices and carve up markets is thriving, with cartels growing ever more intricate and global in scope." [3]

In oligopoly industries, there are many subtle ways to collude and fix prices artificially high. What usually happens is that one company is recognized as the industry leader. When it raises prices, the other companies in the industry simply follow suit and copy the same price rise. Have you noticed that when the price of gas goes up, the price at every single gas station goes up and by about the same amount? This is oligopoly in action. In industry after industry, we find *de*creasing numbers of producers. The purpose is to enable oligopolies to impose higher prices and send a larger share of Income to profits and to investors and managers most of whom are all in the top 20% and less to ordinary Households.

Of course, part of the rules of a pure Capitalist economy would be to prevent the agglomeration of companies in an industry, as Adam Smith prescribed. However, with the reintroduction of Economic Socialism under Ronald Reagan and continuing under George Bush, the Anti-trust Division of the Justice Department was given huge amounts of Unisom to keep them sound asleep. When they're awake, they have masturbation parties and give out prizes. As we will explain in Ch. 29, the neoconservative system mind is a *collectivist* mind. As a result, since Ronald Reagan, there has been enormous collectivization in all industries. In banking, collectivization continued unabated under Reagan-Bush so that we wound up with banks that were "too big to fail". When the crash occurred, the government had to steal *trillions* from our children to prop them back up. To rub salt in the wound, the propaganda outlets lie that they paid back all the bailout money.

Another development over the last 35 years has been the increasing use of *credit cards*. Credit cards allow consumers to buy things today even if they don't have the money. This allows Consumption to continue and prevents firms from having to lay workers off who are producing goods and services. For 35 years, consumers were able to keep their Consumption up by maintaining the amount of goods and services they would buy; the interest they were paying would simply be added to the credit card debt. By 2007, the average credit card had over 5 thousand dollars of debt.

But credit cards are really a regressive tax. Over time, the real effect of credit cards is to transfer money away from consumers. The interest that consumers pay is going to banks and their stockholders in the top 20% who tend to save, and away from households in the lower 80% who tend to consume and keep up income, spending and jobs. This is why you get a credit card invitation every month. This is part of the problem in the collapse of 2008. Consumers were so laden with debt that they couldn't maintain Consumption levels.

Credit cards are especially bad for kids who don't understand the long run. In fact, it becomes an addiction. There is absolutely no difference between getting kids addicted to cocaine or even cigarettes and getting them addicted to credit cards. The only reason the system can't entice kids into drug addiction (except for alcohol) is because of health issues. The damage from credit card addictions is more psychological than physical.

An issue that came up in the 2012 election was *corporate raiding* that occupied Mitt Romney much of his career. What happens is that a bunch of investors combine their moneys and borrow heavily from banks that they use to buy out companies. They are called "private equity firms". They claim to save companies, but studies show they mostly buy out profitable companies. They proceed to milk these companies of billions of dollars which, of course, they stuff into their pockets. As a result, a full *half* of the time, the company files for bankruptcy with the loss of thousands of jobs.

But let's look at the best case scenario. There are instances where the equity firm reorganizes a troubled company, makes it more efficient, and enables it to continue on. Romney claimed he save thousands of jobs in this way, and he gave Staples as an example. For a citizen like me, this is a very personal example. In my town, there was a cozy, intimate little office supply shop called Bob Slate. He had 3 shops in town and I used them. But Slate was finally forced to close most his stores. Are we better off? First of all, in a Bob Slate store, you could get advice and help from a number of knowledgeable reasonably paid employees. Also, I could buy one red flair pen and one mechanical pencil. After Slate was gone, I went into Staples. It was difficult to find anyone to ask a question, and if I did find someone, it was a low-paid employee probably working near the minimum wage. But the worst of it is that I couldn't buy one felt pen — I had to buy a package of 10 and it's the same with everything they have. This might be fine for large offices, but it is of no use to many people in the community.

Romney bragged about making companies efficient. *Romney didn't produce anything.* He simply rearranged the chips. Most of the reason for the increase in efficiency is due to replacing reasonably paid jobs in a nice working environment with lower paid jobs in a big corporation. But the savings from efficiency didn't go into the company. It went into the pockets of people like Romney who extract million-day paychecks. All of this amounts to transferring income from the lower 80% of middle class workers and consumers to profits of high-flying corporate raiders. And by the way, an ABC investigation showed that Romney hid some of his loot in the Caiman Islands, where it isn't doing a thing to make funds available for American banks to lend.

It's because of corporate raiding that all businesses have been stripped down to bare essentials and often by people like Mitt Romney. Services are minimal. You can't find anyone in stores to ask a question. On the phone, you get computer voices. People have to wait hours in airports and then they don't even get a nice meal like they used to. Mitt Romney is a national icon representing the slow replacement of decent paying jobs by low paying jobs and poorer service. The difference fills the pockets of the Mitt Romneys of the world, which is why these CEO's make millions. This again is a gigantic transfer of wealth from the bottom 80% to the top 20% and requires increasing deficits to prop up demand. In the recessionary times we'll have in this century, we need a full Household tank — corporate raiders are the last things we need.

Another development that was an impediment to the economy in the last 35 years was *free trade*. We sell the Chinese government paper that we print up and they give us money to buy their junk. The real purpose of free trade is to enable Chinese businesses to keep their wages low because by dumping their tires on us, they don't have to rely on their own people, especially their lower 80%, to buy their tires. Also, it puts our tire workers out of a good union job and forces them to flip hamburgers at the minimum wage. Millions of good paying manufacturing jobs have been sent out of the country and replaced by low-paying service jobs because large corporations have been given incentives to move operations overseas for cheap labor. "In 1993, Caterpillar's workforce was 74 percent domestic; by 2008, it was just 46 percent domestic." [4] System mind propaganda outlets like the network media blame the lack of hiring by American corporations on "uncertainty". What is totally suppressed by these outlets is that there is *plenty* of hiring. Only it's at low wage labor in faraway countries.

The Nation reported that "The trade deficits accumulated during the Bush administration — a whopping $4.8 trillion — were a major cause of the loss overseas of 5.3 million manufacturing jobs and over 2 million service jobs...." [5] The end result of the lack of money in the Household tank is massive theft from the future to prop up demand. But the US can't keep printing up money to buy Chinese junk forever. And when our imports from China level off to world levels, China will sink into economic stagnation just like in the west.

And we haven't even taken account the costs of shipping stuff halfway around the world especially with high fuel prices. And what about global warming due to fuel usage, which even *The Economist* gets interested in once in a while? The reality is that the US is perfectly capable of making tires as efficiently as the Chinese and we can certainly make all of the junk we import from China. And the Chinese are perfectly capable of making computers.

These are not stone-age people we're talking about. The comparative advantage of trading is almost nil and when you throw in transportation costs and fuel usage getting tires and computers back and forth over large distances, there is no savings at all.

But what is hidden by the free trade racket is the fact that financial ties it engenders enables all kinds of fraud. WTO (World Trade Organization) rules broke down barriers to cross-border trades in money instruments. A number of countries of Europe, Ireland, Portugal, Greece, Spain are under severe financial difficulties because the crooked governments in those countries, especially Ireland, allowed their financial services people to get in the game of buying, selling and gambling on fake paper with even less oversight than in the country where the paper was printed up. And who is doing to bail out all of this? The bankers and finance wizards in Ireland won't have to pay back one penny of all the loot they stole from future generations by dealing in fake paper. The children or Ireland will have to pay to clean up the mess. As described in an insightful article in *The Nation*,[6] the people who led the way to enable financial institutions to peddle their paper all over the world are now Barack Obama's team of economic experts. The economist Jeff Faux (one of our few real economists) said, "banking integration under NAFTA made money laundering much easier".[7] That is whole purpose of "free" trade.

Of course, there are situations where free trade would help everyone. In developing countries who can't make computers and who have some resource we lack like metals or oil, free trade does benefit both countries. But a lot of what the US exports is high-tech goods which helps professionals who produce those goods. So publications like the *Wall Street Journal* and *The Economist* magazine *claim* that society as a whole is better off because "Trade hurts some people but helps many more".[8] This is a bald-faced lie. It's the exact opposite: it helps some people but hurts many more, as is proven by the steady lowering of *real* wages to the bottom 80% since free trade took off under Ronald Reagan. The slightly lower price of some of the junk they buy is wiped out by shifting to jobs with half the paycheck. All the benefits of free trade have gone to the top 20% and they clearly do not comprise "the many more". But from the point of view of the system mind as expressed by its propaganda media outlets, only the larger nodes count. They don't care how the smaller nodes are doing because they do not determine the interests and goals of the system mind.

Free trade will help the majority of people only when there is great disparity in production capabilities between two countries and only when there is sufficient democracy to insure that the benefits from free trade will be spread over the population. How many developing countries are like that? Most of the trade that occurs among the advanced countries and China and India is pure waste and only makes the distribution of income less than optimal.

But there's no stopping the free trade bandwagon because all the benefits go to the top 20% in both trading countries. With the economy in crisis, there was some talk of protecting American jobs. *The Economist*[9] went ballistic when Obama put a tariff on "tyres" from China (when are these Limies going to learn how to spell?). A header article was titled "Economic Vandalism", no less.[10] Obama was committing "vandalism" by nicking the increasingly over-paid top 20% to help American workers in the lower 80% keep their jobs. But when *The Economist*, expressing the neoconservative system mind, cheerleads the transfer of hundreds of billions from the 80% to the top 20% with free trade crap, there's no vandalism here — that's just economics.

The Economist calls the era before free trade, "economic nationalism", which comes from "…the darkest period of modern history…and is threatening the world with depression".[11] Those medieval times in the '50s and '60s when the bottom 80% got a reasonable share of Household income and could clear markets is "the darkest period of modern history". As our Table 24.3 shows, the economy performed better in every single important way during these "dark" ages — faster growth in GDP and median family income, low unemployment and most importantly, virtually no deficits. Continuing, if this "economic nationalism" isn't snuffed out quickly, "… the consequences will be dire".[12] The "dire consequences" would be that the bottom 80% would get a reasonable share of national income. *That's* what has these reptiles all bent out of shape.

They even try to equate free trade with Capitalism itself: "…*The Economist* has argued that governments are failing to defend globalization — that is, Capitalism…."[13] This is pure unadulterated crap. The essence of Capitalism is the means of production in private hands, operating under independent rules. Trade was fine according to Adam Smith, but it wasn't a *necessary* ingredient of Capitalism. Capitalism can have as much or as little as can be justified. When Adam Smith wrote, there were probably great differences in natural resources available and what different countries could make efficiently.

In my opinion, to put it in frank language, *free trade is slave trade*. The fact that the means of propaganda have been pushing free trade should tell us that it is benefiting the larger nodes in the system mind in the top 20% at the expense of the bottom 80%. But *The Economist* is not interested in the bottom 80%. It's the same old story. It is beyond the cognitive abilities of these system apologists to see the simple fact that if you starve out the lower 80% who buys most of the goods and services an economy produces, who is going to buy what the Capitalist is making? The fact that *trillions* of dollars had to be stolen from the children of this country to prop up demand since the great advent of free trade in the '80s should tell *The Economist* something. But all the brain energy in these inner brain reptiles is in the bottom creating emotional blocks that prevent them from seeing reality. It's only the glorious *theory* in their books that counts, a theory with just the right assumptions to come to the desired conclusions.

But the propaganda campaign marches on sweeping along everyone. Even Bill Clinton, who sometimes pretended to be a liberal, pushed free trade and got the WTO started. Suppression of Consumption under Clinton due to free trade may have exacerbated the slowdown in 2001. The reality, of course, is that since the rapid growth of free trade under Ronald Reagan, we have never had the kind of performance in the economy as before the tremendous increase in free trade.

We have enumerated all the forces in our economic system in the past 35 year period that have shifted income away from the bottom 80% to the top 20% to where the share of income to the bottom 80% is less than half down from 60% when the economy was optimal. I have never seen one single economist from either the left or right who brings out this important fact. They will gas on about every conceivable aspect of the economy except the most important point that income to the lower 80% has been constantly redistributed upward. When you combine this with the enormous tax cuts to corporations and the top 20%, the only way the system has been able to do a half-assed job of enabling the Consumption pipe to keep flowing is with massive deficit spending year after year. Reagan and the Bushes stole over 8 trillion dollars from the children of this country for this very purpose. And with Obama's supply side stimulus, he's doing more of the same. These deficits are all unsustainable. But as we will explain in Ch. 30, a large national debt is part of the neoconservative political agenda. The reason is that both a crippled economy and even meltdowns give the top 20% a bigger share of the pie. This is why propaganda from the system mind media outlets keeps a constant blare to snuff out any attempt to put the system in balance.

By encouraging collectivization in industry, credit cards, corporate raiding and free trade and shipping good-paying jobs overseas, the bottom 80% is getting 14% less Household Income and the top 20% is getting 14% *more* than when the economy was operating in an optimal way in the '50s and '60s. As we will discuss in Ch. 28, all of this was accompanied by increasing working hours, suppressing the minimum wage and a constant attack on unions. As we calculated above, if we compare to an optimal economy, the *effective* tax rate for the top 20% is only about 8% and the effective tax rate for the bottom 80% is about 32%! This inequality has enabled the top 20% to accumulate over *90%* of all wealth in the US, leaving the bottom 80% with almost nothing. Now, I want to warn nit-pickers, these are not very accurate numbers mainly because the crooked government won't supply accurate numbers. But we are only interested in *concepts*, and rough numbers are adequate for that.

In criticizing the new DPJ party in Japan for attempting a "redistribution of wealth", *The Economist* advises the party to "kick that foolish notion..." out.[14] This piece of "redistribution" propaganda is repeated ad nauseum by system mind propagandists, as expressed by John McCain during the 2008 election. Now I can assure you, you can go back 35 years in *The Economist* magazine and scour every sentence in every issue of that magazine and you won't find one single sentence about Republicans having constantly voted to 'redistribute' income away from the bottom 80% *upward* to their favorite top 20% class.

But after the crash when the system desperately needed a more prosperous consuming class, and the Obama administration darkly hinted that maybe we ought to put the economy back in balance, neoconservative propaganda outlets started screaming about "class war". And *The Economist* was squealing and whining about "redistribution of wealth". The reality it that the neoconservative propaganda machine has been waging class war against the middle class in the bottom 80% for 35 years. When *The Economist* pontificated about "what went wrong with the economy", not one small word was mentioned how far the system had gotten out of financial balance, and there's not one allusion to what real Capitalism requires. [15]

These media outlets that pimp for the system mind *say* that they support Capitalism. However, when it comes time to support specific policy, they sabotage the core of a Capitalist economy, which is a consuming middle class prosperous enough to clear markets. Although Adam Smith was writing during a very early period of industrial Capitalism, even he saw the need for balance in the system. We mentioned above his complement of Holland for paying higher wages than England. This shows how little these modern neoconservative Bolsheviks care about real Capitalism: they constantly ignore the important words of the father of Capitalism, and give us constant massive doses of system mind propaganda to con people into giving up on real Capitalism. You would think that after 35 years of reality under a wide variety of circumstances, during which there was an enormous redistribution of income *upwards* from the bottom 80% to the top 20%, and the system had to continuously steal *trillions* from the future to prop up demand and prevent recessions, that they would finally perceive the need for a balanced economy. The fact that they don't shows how little energy is getting out of the bottom of the brains of these neoconservative reptiles.

But we have a democracy. Why can't democratic institutions with ordinary middle class people voting and the bottom 80% in a clear majority, keep these powers about equal. With less flowing through the Labor Income pipe to ordinary households, why would they vote for this state of affairs? The only way they would vote for this outcome is with a very special brand of propaganda. And of course, the larger nodes of the economy have the means to maintain these imbalances because they own and control all means of propaganda, the newspapers, magazines, TV and radio outlets. As a result, we have a constant drumbeat telling us that we must cut taxes at the top and on corporations so that more will go into the Savings tub, which will goose the economy to greater heights.

Now, you do have to maintain a full Savings tank so that any ideas or new technology that comes on line will be able to pump investment money up the I_A pipe for new plant equipment and new workers. But what the system mind won't tell you — and this is the rub — *there has never been one minute since WWII when the Savings tub has not been overflowing.* There were a few times in the 1700s and 1800s when the Savings tub was not sufficiently full. But that was before people knew much about economics. Even now in 2013 when people have lost tons of money, there are *trillions* of dollars sloshing around in the world's Savings tubs. When the computer revolution occurred in 1981, and the internet in the early '90s, investment money came out of the woodwork to be thrown at these new ideas.

Not only is a full Savings tub not going to give us economic growth, but in my opinion an overflowing Savings tub is actually a danger. There was so much money available that when the internet bubble appeared, *too* much money was thrown at the idea which lead to a letdown in 2001. Then George Bush cut taxes at the top along with new rules. This put so much money in the Savings tub that it enabled the top 1% to print up trillions of fake money in the form of derivatives thrown on top of the fake mortgage market. This lead to the crash of 2008. And on top of it, while we're in the midst of a deep recession, we learned that there was a "savings glut" as expressed by the Ayatollah of the Federal Reserve, Ben Bernanke. Of course the propaganda outlets totally suppress this major contradiction. But even if the Savings tub were empty, throwing money at the top and filling it wouldn't do any good. It would just sit there stagnating.

The moral of the story is the same no matter when: *overfilling the Savings tub does absolutely nothing to spur the economy* because it does nothing to create *customers* for businesses. Without a bubble or without customers, money isn't going to be pumped up the Investment pipe for new plant and equipment and new hiring. Unless we get a new technological bubble, which seems unlikely, only Consumption will stimulate the economy, which requires more money to the bottom 80%. The only way this can be solved is for the tax code to distribute income so as to create a balanced economy.

Even with huge deficits, the economy under Reagan and the Bushes just crept along. And if they hadn't stolen trillions from our children there would have been no expansion at all, but major recessions, which is finally what we got. (By the way, this is another example of the God-is-a-dummy Christian: the bible says the sons shall not inherit the sins of the father. Well, Reagan and the Bushes dumped over 8 *trillion* dollars worth of sins onto the sons.)

In conclusion, the Y/P fork is really the key to a stable, prosperous and sustainable economy. The flow out of the Business tank has to be divided in a reasonably balanced way at the Y/P fork. This is not rocket science. It's Econ 101. In fact, it's Econ 99 for kindergarten. But because of the enormous influence at this fork by the larger nodes of the economic system mind, it is almost impossible to maintain the proper balance between Y_{H}, household income, and P, profits. As we shall explain in Ch. 30, it is only due to a brain malfunction that neoconservatives are unable to see this very simple point. All the fighting and bickering and political maneuvering by various ideologues, both conservative and liberal, is totally beside the point. *It is pure Capitalism itself that determines the proper balance between what goes to Household income for labor and what goes to corporations and the wealthy into the Savings tub as profits.* If the system gets out of balance, it will automatically underperform and collapse periodically.

Of course, in my opinion, the closer you get to pure Capitalism, the less imbalance there will be. But we have rarely experienced pure Capitalism and the Economic Socialism that has existed during most of the history of the western world always over-produces. This is what causes most of the social problems that have plagued the west for hundreds of years. Reagan's and Bush's deficits will only grow until we get a national debt that totally cripples the economy leading to the big one.

25.6 Tax Policy

Today's neoconservative doesn't even understand something as simple as *inflation*, which is truly astounding. Inflation means simply that prices are going up. So what causes inflation? Well, a third grader would say that what *causes* inflation is people raising prices. Duh!

But this is beyond the cognitive abilities of *The Economist*. They think, "In the long term, inflation is a primarily a monetary phenomenon".[16] This means that you get inflation when the government prints up too much money. Again, reality has no effect on these inner brain reptiles. Jimmie Carter had relatively low deficits (not printing up money), and inflation over 10%. Reagan *quadrupled* deficits and printed up more money than all presidents before him *combined*, and inflation went down. George Bush stole around 5 *trillion* dollars, and inflation was relatively low.

In reality, inflation has nothing to do with monetary policy. There can be inflation when the government prints up money but only if it sends the money to the consuming classes who may bid up the prices of goods and services. But you can also have inflation with no new money, if there are monopolies. And you can have low inflation while printing up lots of money, if the money doesn't go to the consuming class. The reason there was no inflation under Reagan and the Bushes is that the money these presidents printed up went mostly to the top 20%. The fact that the Fed hasn't had to fight inflation in the last 35 years is just another sign of the failure of supply-side economics: none of the added income and wealth went to the bottom 80%, so there was no consumer power to drive up prices. There may be no inflation, but there is an unbalanced economy and ever-increasing deficits. *Inflation is a bad thing, but a good sign — a sign that the lower 80% is getting a decent share of income, enough to make purchases in markets and drive up prices.*

If you look at the share of national income that would go to the lower 80% in a balanced and expanding economy, what we have done in effect, to impose a technology tax, a fertility tax, a free trade tax, and national debt tax on the lower 80%. Sect. 25.5 shows that the lower 80% is paying an *effective* tax of about 32% and the top 20% is paying a rate of only 8%. Of course, propaganda outlets are constantly reminded us how much the top 5% are paying in taxes.[17] They smother us with numbers. What they won't do is tell us what their *effective* taxes are. The reality is that *pre-tax* income to the top 20% has exploded while their taxes have been slashed. This is why the economy is not balanced and requires huge deficits.

Of course, high income Households are not going to accept the fact that they have been the beneficiaries of enormous *effective* tax cuts. They think they've earned their enormous increases in wealth and income. These CEOs who get 15 or 20 million would have to see their after tax income down to only 3 or 4 million, which is impossible for them to live on. But if we're going to be objective about it, the value of the labor of the top 20% is really no different from what it was in the '50s and '60s when we had a balanced economy. The array of labor in the economy is pretty much the same. Because of increases in technology, all levels of labor require more education and training than they did in those decades. Even a lathe operator on the factory floor has to understand the use of computer driven production methods. Of course a case could be made that the increase in skills needed for the jobs in the top 20% is more than in the lower 80%. However, not so much as to put every penny of new wealth and income generated in the last 35 years in the hands of only the top 20%.

Even though we remain in continuous recessionary conditions, the system mind keeps plugging away on their propaganda outlets for more of what got us into the mess in the first place. For example, *The Economist* very starkly comes right out and asserts (as though they understand economics), "American taxes income and investment too much and consumption too little." [18] They did a big spread called "Time to Balance".[19] I initially thought, they finally caught on to the need for a balanced economy. My hopes were quickly dashed. What they wanted to "balance" was to shift from consumption to savings, exactly what the economy does *not* need to get out of a recession. We must realize that their idea of "balance" is code for class war against the middle class.

Probably the most ubiquitous piece of propaganda the system mind drums into the heads of the citizenry is that cutting taxes will "unleash" the private sector to great heights of economic activity by spurring firms to pump more money up the Investment pipe and hire more workers. As recently as the 2008 election, *The Economist* was cheerleading McCain's proposed tax cuts: "Lower taxes on capital gains, dividends, and corporate profits…encouraging firms to invest more".[20] Also, "Higher taxes at the top…will make a weak growth rate". [21] In 2011 they said, "Japan urgently needs cuts in business taxes".[22] Notice the word, 'urgently', as though they have some facts. After a while they start believing this crap and so they don't mind lying: "history suggests that low taxes on the rich encourage investment and growth".[23] This is a bold-faced lie: history shows no such thing. If we stick with the facts, every economic study that has ever been done shows that there is absolutely *no relation* between taxes and when firms are inspired to pump money up the investment pipe. *If Businesses see an idea that will sell in the market, they will invest no matter what their taxes are.* As we mentioned, in the industries Reagan threw the most money at, there was almost no new job creation and investment. The money Reagan threw at these older industries was simply stuffed into their pockets and wound up stagnating in the Savings tub. It was the IT industry that almost no money was thrown at, who pumped money up the Investment pipe and created the new jobs. Even recessions don't discourage investing in a good new idea. Major companies like General Motors, AT&T, Disney and MTV were all founded during recessions. "A 2009 study found that over half of Fortune 500 companies got their start during a downturn or a bear market." [24] I'll bet the reporter who found this got fired.

When the economy expanded the most in our history in the '60s at 4½%, the top tax rate was 80% and corporate taxes were over 50%. When Reagan cut taxes on the wealthy and corporations, investment as a percent of GDP fell and growth rates averaged 3.2% over his term. Clinton raised taxes on the rich and corporations, and investment in the internet industry exploded. Some studies show that for the first time in 10 years the lower 80% improved slightly under Clinton. Consumption was up and the unemployment rate decreased every year Clinton was in office and went below 4% as he left office. The stock market more than doubled. With an expanded economy, Clinton was able to balance the budget and had some surpluses. Now Clinton doesn't deserve credit for this. Clinton *inherited* one of the biggest bubbles in history. But we can give him credit for not sabotaging his bubble as Reagan did. By raising taxes on the top, he was effectively lowering taxes on the bottom 80% and lowering taxes that our children will have to pay. Also, by avoiding deficits, he avoided what in economics is called *"crowding out"*. When you run deficits, the government has to steal from the future which it does by selling bonds. But this attracts people into buying government bonds instead of investing in businesses. When Bush cut the same taxes, investment did nothing and growth averaged only 2½% in his years, and required massive deficits to prop up demand.

Currently, studies show that the tax rate paid by the S&P 500 corporations is down to only 16%, only *one third* of what it once was when we had an optimal economy. This money that corporations don't pay in taxes will be paid in dividends to stockholders the majority of whom are in the top 20%. Back in the '50s and '60s when we had an optimal economy, the corporate tax rate was a full 50%. Cutting taxes at the top deprives the government of revenue that could be spent on services like health care for the elderly and veterans, research, school, roads, etc., which creates middle class jobs. What's worse, the loss of revenue incurs ever-increasing deficits. The "history" *The Economist* talks about is the history in their wet dreams. Reality, facts, studies — it all means nothing to these inner-brain supply-side reptiles, because their *faith-based* economics is motivated solely to hog all wealth and income for the nodes they identify with. The constant propaganda you hear about cutting taxes to spur the economy is simply bald-faced lies. Its only purpose is to steal money from ordinary people and future generations to fill the pockets of the people behind the propaganda. It shows that when emotions are pushing in a certain direction, here, to pimp for the system, you can get anything imaginable from the reason box. If someone has a better explanation of the mind of these reality-squelching neoconservatives than I've given, I'd like to hear it.

But cutting taxes on the middle class and raising them at the top isn't going to happen, because when it comes to cutting taxes on the middle class, all of a sudden the neoconservative system mind starts screaming about deficits. Obama is raising taxes on income over 250 thousand a few percentages to up around 39% or whatever it is. This is like pissing in the ocean to create a flood. And he's taking a lot of heat for that. Besides, the middle class is easy to tax. They're working too hard to keep track of their interests and don't pay much attention to the taxes they are paying, especially their *effective* taxes.

Another example of the system mind's obsession with passing off taxes from the top 20% to the bottom 80% is the issue of double taxation. When discussing taxation of the top 20%, system mind mouthpieces invariable call it "double taxation". *The Economist* says, "Equity capital [dividends] is subject to double taxation". Well this is another bold-faced lie — a *double* total lie — and I don't believe they don't know it. First, a flow of money is defined by its source and its destination and a tax can be at the beginning or the end of a flow. Corporations get taxed on their revenue (minus their expenses, of course), which is at the end of a first flow between customers for their product and the corporation. Dividends are a *separate* flow between the corporation and its stockholders and are taxed at the *end* of this flow which is on the stockholder. So what we have are *two* separate flows involving two *different* legal entities — the corporation for the first flow and the stockholder in the second; and two *separate* taxes at the end of these two *separate* flows on these two *separate* legal entities. These are perfectly reasonable taxes and there is nothing "double" about it. I'm talking to first graders here.

But in the scores of issues of *The Economist* where they're cheering for higher consumer taxes to balance budgets, you will never hear a peep about double taxation on the bottom 80%. Sales or consumer taxes are a prime example of double taxation and doubly bad for the economy. Here we have *one* flow going between a company and an employee as pay. The one legal entity, the employee, gets taxed at the *beginning* of this flow as income when she gets paid. Then she gets taxed at the beginning of a flow from her to a store, but this is also the *end* of the same income flow. Here we have one flow, and one relevant legal entity, the employee, who gets taxed *twice* both at the beginning and the end of this *one* flow — clearly double taxation. But you'll never hear a word of this from these neoconservative reptiles.

Looking at the matter very practically, what causes a business to hire people is when there is more work. And there is more work only if there are more customers. You can increase, decrease, stomp on, mutilate, push up, push down taxes on a restaurant all you want, but this will not create customers who want something to eat. Taxes have nothing to do with it, and study after study shows this. The restaurant owner will only hire more people if she has more customers waiting to eat; and this means putting money into the pockets of his customers. But of course, taking money *out* of the pockets of middle class customers is exactly what the neoconservative system mind is constantly trying to do: by cutting wages, destroying unions, increasing working hours and massive theft from future generations. In fact, you could define a neoconservative as someone who is dumb enough to think he's going to get rich by starving out his customers.

What is totally hypocritical about this stance is that if taxes are cut at the upper end, how do we pay for their armies, their wars, their war toys, their secret police, and their corporate welfare, favorite government expenses of the neoconservative system mind used to prop up some semblance of a sexlife. The real irony is that besides entitlements, the biggest expenses the government incurs are for wars and the secret police. If corporations don't want to pay taxes for these expenses, they will be passed on to the middle class, which cuts into consumption.

Projections now are for half trillion dollar deficits each year as far as the eye can see. If congress were 100% Republican or 100% Democratic, or even 100% Tea Party, we will get the same massive deficits because Reagan laid down the Economic Socialist tracks that will take the US economy train far into the future.

25.7 GEORGE BUSH AND ECONOMIC SOCIALISM

In any event, Economic Socialism picked up steam under papa Bush, baby Bush and even Bill Clinton. The middle class in the lower 80% was receiving less and less percentage of national income and the only way demand could be propped up was to steal increasing amounts from the future. This explains the steady increase in deficits as time went on. There was a respite during Clinton's years, but that was due to one of the biggest bubbles in our economic history. But Economic Socialism again picked up right where it left off under George W. Bush.

As you may remember, the internet bubble died down around 2000 when Bush was (almost) elected and the economy began to slow down. The economy continued to be sluggish and with Bush's ratings falling, something had to be done. 9/11 enabled Bush to start the Iraq war and just as under Reagan, this allowed him to greatly increase military spending, which had the effect of spurring the economy. But it was done with stolen money, only at even higher levels than under Reagan.

Again the system mind propaganda machine goes to work. They were going to cut taxes on the wealthy and corporations and this would "unleash" American entrepreneurs to great heights of economic dazzle, or so said everyone on sewer radio. We didn't have to worry about the deficits that would result because the tax cuts would so spur the economy that government revenues would mushroom and erase the deficit. And just as happened in the 10 other times in American history when this was tried, it didn't happen. If fact, it never happens — *unless* there's a bubble, in which case taxes don't matter. Throwing money at large businesses and financial firms went into the Savings tub and wound up as seed money for a whole swindle in fraudulent derivatives. It did absolutely nothing to spur the economy. The economy struggled along, growing at only around 2 ½ % a year, which was "about $1.5 *trillion* less than it would otherwise have been".[25] Without the wasteful war in Iraq, the GDP was probably dropping. The GEP was clearly dropping — although nobody is going to give us statistics on the real measure of the economy. One piece of evidence for this is that medium family income for the bottom 80% dropped about 7% during the Bush administration. In an age of high-technology and increases in productivity, this is a national disgrace.

Not only was there no spur to the economy from Bush's tax cut, but over 40 thousand factories closed costing the country about 5 *million* good-paying manufacturing jobs.[26] With a truncated amount going to the Household tank, in order to clear markets, consumer spending had to be propped up by credit card debt, borrowing on the basis of artificially rising house prices, and most importantly, huge theft from the future.

The forces that eroded relative income going to the lower 80% of households continued all through the Bush years. Union membership continued to drop and free trade continued to erode the wages of the lower 80% who do most of the consuming. But just as under Reagan, this was compensated for by the government running massive deficits. Bush had to steal almost 4 *trillion* from future generations to pay for another dose of failed supply-side economics. And as usual when it comes to flushing the Constitution down the toilet, the Supreme Court did nothing to prevent this massive violation of the principle of taxation without representation. Of course, the mouthpiece of the system mind *at no time even for one second* ever pointed out that when you have to steal trillions from future generations that is palpable proof of the failure of your economic policies.

This theft from the future enabled the Bush administration to pay for his tax cuts and to pay for an Iraq war that wound up costing about a trillion dollars. But unlike Reagan, whose failed economic policies were somewhat mitigated by the personal computer bubble, there was no bubble under Bush to partially bail out the usual supply-side quackery. There was a bubble, of sorts, but it was a totally artificial bubble. But it's even worse than this.

Instead of this stolen money being spread out evenly in the population, much of it went to the top 20% where it was used not to invest and hire workers, but to bid up the price of assets like stocks, property and most importantly fraudulent paper money in the form of derivatives. It even bid up the price of buying senators and congressmen. Of course, the corporate media mouthpiece of the system mind sold Bush's tax bill as a tax *cut*. Everyone likes tax cuts. This was one of the most blatant lies ever told by the media. We must keep in mind that interest has to be paid on this debt as far as the eye can see into the future. This interest must come from future taxpayers — and not just a minority of them. The interest on this debt must be paid by *every single taxpayer* into the indefinite future. People who are children now will be paying increased taxes for this interest *the rest of their lives*. Now any human being with one ounce of intellectual honesty would say that a tax bill that increases taxes on hundreds of millions in order to cut taxes on a few should be labeled a tax *increase*. But because the tax bill cut the taxes on the bloated paychecks of these media whores, it was trumpeted as a tax *cut*.

Neoconservatives in congress and on sewer radio were perfectly happy with Bush racking up humungus deficits to pay for Bush's private war in Iraq, all based on blatant lies. At the time, they, and their corporate media propagandists were telling us that deficits don't matter. But when the system collapsed, and it was again necessary to get people back to work, Obama started to hire people to *build* buildings and bridges — guess what? Neoconservatives in congress, sewer radio, and the corporate media started squealing to high heaven about spending and deficits. It's always the same story from these neoconservatives: if you want to *destroy* bridges and buildings, deficits are fine and dandy; but if you want to *build* bridges and buildings, deficits are a great evil.

A lot of this underperformance of the economy was due to another massive dose of Economic Socialism. An article in the *American Prospect* details how *every single* agency of the government under George Bush was infected by economic players in bed with government actors making their own rules. Public Citizen released a study in 2009 of public finance showing that Wall St. spent about $5 *billion* in campaign financing and lobbying. Similar things happened in all other industries. Our newest Supreme Court justice called these, bribes, which in my opinion also is exactly what they are *by definition*. But the same Supreme Court calls it "freedom of expression". There is not one word in the Constitution about "freedom of expression" which, as we mentioned, can legalize any crime.

In the history of the United States, there has never been a time of greater "freedom of expression". The corporate world, especially the financial services sector, "expressed" their wishes with massive bribes (i.e., campaign contributions), and "expressed" their desires to rig the rules so they could spend the next eight years gaming the system. And congress "expressed" their total disdain for the public good by being in bed with economic players, exchanging whores, playing golf, vacationing, wining and dining together — all in order to facilitate making their own rules. Authors of an important book say, "America's big banks act as an oligarchy, a group that has gained political power because of its economic power and then uses that political power for its own benefit".[27] This is the exact definition of Economic Socialism and the exact opposite of Adam Smith's Capitalism.

You would think that in the areas of science where truth is more highly prized than any other field, scientific enquiry would be immune from interference from economic players. Not so at all. The Departments of Commerce, Agriculture, Health and Human Services, and Interior all had egregious examples of where scientific work and research was reworked, manipulated, and squelched by lobbyists and other players of the economic system. And a lot of this involved not just money but the health of American citizens.

As we have mentioned, one of the most accurate measures of the degree of Economic Socialism is how environmental safety is addressed. Much of the efforts of lobbyists for businesses climbing in bed with political operatives is directed towards making their own rules about environmental safety. And it is noteworthy that as Economic Socialism took off under George Bush, environmental safety was relaxed in as many ways as they could. Under Bush, "superfund cleanups decreased by 52%,… and civil citations to polluters fell 57%." [28] We will never know the increased incidences of cancer and other genetically based illnesses that were caused by Bush's lax environmental enforcement. I can assure you, we aren't going to find out from the media propaganda outlets whose advertisers are among the very people causing the pollution. You would think that aside from all the lies and suppression of important news that they indulge in, that these talking heads would have the common decency to look after the genetic health of our children who don't ask to be born. But money trumps decency every time to these media whores. Even increasing birth defects doesn't impede one iota the almost total cover-up by system mind media outlets of the degree to which environmental hazards are destroying the genes of newborns — *even their own kids.*

One particular swindle will bring out the effects of blatant Corporate Socialism, that of Enron. As a *Nation* article details, after Ken Lay created Enron, "…he lavished millions on lobbyists and campaign contributions to free Enron from regulation…",[29] mostly to so-called conservative politico's including George Bush, who was caught on camera once going to lunch with Lay. Enron had "set up a staggering 2,832 subsidiaries, with almost a third in the Cayman Islands". When Bush took office, his Secretary of Treasury announced "that the administration will not 'interfere with…sovereign nations' ". For the next few years, "No-account accountants, see-no-evil stock analysts, subservient 'independent' board members, gelded regulators, purchased politicians" — all were in place for Enron to print up tons of fraudulent derivatives and every other kind of Wall St. wheeling and dealing. "Enron's twenty-nine top executives cashed in a staggering $1.1 *billion* in stock in the three years before the firm went belly up. Small investors got soaked, and faithful employees got stiffed".[30] Then Enron's bought and paid for political actors in Washington who proceeded to cut their taxes.

Remember our flow diagram in Ch. 24? Just like a hot water heating system, all these tax shelters, fake subsidiaries, off-shore accounts, drug money-laundering, are schemes to sneak money out of the country to avoid taxes. The way it's replaced is by stealing from the future. This impediment to government revenues resulted in Bush having to steal a quarter *trillion* dollars from the future each year he was in office to replace money being skimmed off the system. Enron was the tip of the iceberg. There were a few democrats involved too, which is why there was never an investigation. Most of the sordid mess was totally papered over by the media outlets of the system mind.

But of course, these paper instruments that financial institutions like Enron print up and bet on, don't represent anything economically tangible. But they appear on the asset side of balance sheets. This appearance of money assets meant there was plenty of monopoly money sloshing around. This is what created the housing bubble. We must first admit, however, that the seeds of the housing bubble were liberals in government with *supposed* good intentions of putting more Americans into their own homes. Believing they have God on their side, and with the holiest of motives, they believed you can get something for nothing. So they spurred on Fannie May and Freddie Mac to insure increasingly dubious mortgages. This created the *appearance* of a bubble, but it was a fake bubble.

Throughout history, bubbles are caused by a new revolutionary idea that firms can herd into. We explained bubbles in Sect. 24.8. Previous bubbles always involved products that could be bought and paid for almost immediately. So the money firms get for their sales can be put into expanding plant and equipment and hiring new workers. That's what makes a bubble. But the housing bubble was not like this. It was a bubble in the short run because a house is a big purchase that can be paid for only over a period of time. So it is possible to sell more houses than people can legitimately afford and create a bubble with fraudulent mortgages. This created employment for construction workers, which increased Income to Households and more Consumption. This allowed the economy to grow a bit. The stock market went up and the Dow Jones reached around 14,000 in 2007.

But it will be an artificial bubble. But this was only a small part of the cause of the collapse of 2008. If rules had been in place when these mortgages began to default, even the housing bubble would probably not have caused a meltdown of the economy as occurred in 2008. It would have resulted in a mild recession at worst. The government would have had to come in and prop up fraudulent mortgages, in the exact same way that the government had to clean up the Savings and Loan scandal in the late 1980's. It would have cost about the same amount, around 150 billion. This isn't chump change but certainly not enough to cause the meltdown that occurred.

But fraudulent mortgages were only the beginnings of the story. What really caused the meltdown was that the system mind ever since Reagan was working constantly, night and day to rig the rules of the game so that their crooked friends could game the system and walk off with billions in fraudulently obtained profits. This is a perfect example of what happens when you "deregulate". But as we discussed, what gets passed off as deregulation is that the old rules that constrained the game to protect the ordinary citizen were "*re*regulated". During the Bush years, the financial services industry invested about 300 million dollars in bribing various members of congress, mostly those God-fearing neoconservatives. Quietly behind the scenes, *new* rules were passed into law by economic players in bed with these very same congressmen; and practices that had been illegal for decades were suddenly made legal. They don't *de*regulate, they *re*regulate. This is a perfect example of Economic Socialism in action.

As *The Nation* reported, "… in 1998 powerful voices close to the Clinton administration — Robert Rubin, Larry Summers and Alan Greenspan — argued that the derivatives market was just fine." [31] (These are the very same guys Obama hired to get us out of the mess they got us into). As Michael Greenberger describes, "…a Republican controlled congress… on the recommendation of … Larry Summers, and Fed Chair Alan Greenspan, rushed through a 262-page rider to an 11,000 page omnibus appropriations bill on Dec. 15, 2000." "The rider, the Commodity Futures Modernization Act (CFMA), removed what was by then the $94 trillion OTC-derivative market from all federal regulation,…including capital adequacy requirements, reporting and disclosure…and bars on fraud and manipulation." [32] The only thing we can disagree with in this description is the word "deregulate". This act didn't "*de*regulate" anything. It didn't eliminate rules. What it did was *re*regulate by creating *new* rules that made it legal to, buy, sell and bet on fraudulent paper that big financial institutions could unconstitutionally print up.

And how did this fraud-making law get passed? This same article reports that "one of the men charged with shepherding the bill through Congress was none other than the Treasury's undersecretary for domestic finance…". And where did he come from? Well, he had "…spent eighteen years at Goldman Sachs…". [33] This is the exact definition of Corporate Socialism. You have people working in the private sector playing the economic game. But they aren't making enough money. So they go to work for the government where they learn the intricacies of the rules and how they should be rerigged. Then they're back to the private sector to bribe Congress into passing the very rules they're going to live under. Then they make fortunes under the new rules. This is the exact definition of Economic Socialism.

On the basis of this rerigging of the rules, when mortgages began handed out like free candy samples, the financial services industry was elegantly poised to jump into this sea of fraudulent paper like a hungry lion on a pot roast. With CFMA opening the door to the safe, the financial services industry proceeded to invent and issue all kinds of phony paper instruments on the basis of fraudulent mortgages that they proceeded to sell to one another. Along with Chairman Alan Greenspan, they got interest rates to be lowered so that the whole gang could borrow at no cost to jump into the fraudulent paper racket. As Tim Fernholz says in his description of the Fed, "While monetary policy requires independence from politics, regulation requires independence from industry — but at the Fed, banks have essentially been picking their own supervisors". [34] You couldn't say it better.

Not only were mortgages bought and sold like kids playing with baseball cards, but they were packaged up and formed the basis for more paper. Banks would package up their paper instruments, print up a derivative of some sort, and sell it to another financial firm, where it would again appear as an asset on their books. They in turn would package up more such paper and sell it to the next bank; all based on fraudulent mortgages. Hundreds of *trillions* of dollars of fake money were printed up and passed around. It takes the forms of an alphabet soup of derivatives, MBSs, mortgage backed securities; CLOs, Collateralized-Loan Obligations; CDOs, Collateralized Debt Obligations; CDSs, Credit Default Swaps, and CMBSs, Commercial Mortgage-backed Securities; SIVs, Structured Investment Vehicles. All this in addition to legitimate paper like stocks and bonds.

But, as we mentioned this was only a seed. The beanstalk that grew from it to the sky was hundreds of trillions of dollars of fraudulent paper which was nurtured by Corporate Socialists in the financial services sector in bed with crooks in Washington making their own rules. This is why you will never hear economists or talking heads in the media talk about this stack of paper. This totally unsupported paper will poison the books of many banks for years to come.

This new paper is a form of money because it is paper on the asset side of a company's balance sheets. This is totally illegal since the power to print money according to the Constitution is with the US Treasury. Of course, with our current Supreme Courts, we don't have a Constitution anymore. On the basis of only a 14 billion dollar GDP at the time, floating around the financial sector is about 300 *trillion* dollars of fake paper. I'm not even sure of this figure because recently a congressman stated on TV that the stack of paper was *500* trillion.

It has taken many years for economists and others to finally realize that what backs money is not gold, but the *production of goods and services*. This humungus stack of monopoly money is not backed by anything tangible at all. And in all the discussions among the mainstream economists, is it only a coincidence that the core of the issue is consistently avoided? Nobody will ever mention the real problem, which is that *the stack of financial paper instruments that created by Corporate Socialists is totally unsupported and totally unconstitutional.* And with all the talk of regulation going on now and new laws being passed affecting financial transactions, absolutely nothing is being done to put this humungus stack of fake money piled to the moon into some reasonable proportion to the actual economy.

What this enormous stack of over 300 *trillion* dollars of fraudulent paper accomplishes is that it allows a whole financial services industry to can buy, sell, trade and bet on this stack of paper right under the noses of agencies like the SEC who got paid to keep an eye out for this kind of thing. It is nothing but a vehicle for the biggest swindle that has ever occurred in the history of the world. On the left, we have future generations of children who, after the meltdown were 8 trillion dollars lighter. And on the right we have an army of Wall St. money-changers who wind up with much of the 8 trillion in their pockets. In between we have a black box producing fake money, a meltdown and a contraction of the economy. If this isn't a gigantic swindle, what is? The players who made millions simply had to wait under the black box spout, and the system mind on its own devices would send down hundreds of billions in payouts with nobody responsible.

Many of the transactions involving derivatives went on in what is called the "shadow banking system", consisting of hedge funds, private equity firms, investment banks, etc. that is very lightly regulated. On the basis of this activity, they pay themselves huge salaries, and billions in bonuses, transaction fees and commissions. In 2009, Wall St. paid out 145 *billion* dollars in this way. The proportion of GDP going to the financial sector has *doubled* in the last 30 years. And keep in mind all this ill-gotten loot taken by individuals in the financial services industry doesn't have to be paid back.

For example, Merrill Lynch earned record profits in 2006. In October 2007, when "Merrill reported a $2.3 billion loss, Stanley O'Neal, the chief executive, was forced to take leave, ...But O'Neal took with him a $160 million severance package"... In the same way, Citigroup's leader, Charles Prince "...walked away rich from Citigroup...".[35] The bonuses, commissions, fat paychecks were going right into their pockets each and every month, topped off by a golden parachute at the end.

Since there is no real economic activity going on to underpin this fraudulent paper blizzard over a 20 year period, where does the hundreds of billions of profits, bonuses and commissions come from? Well, it came from two places. One was from the future in the form of huge budget deficits, and the other took place later in the form of just about every household losing a fourth of their 401Ks. This theft was led by the very people who snuffed out people like Brooksley Born who was trying to mitigate this massive fraud. If you want to see a prime example of the system mind at work, there's no better place to look than at these events leading up the to the 2008 crash. And if you don't believe in a system mind, you're stuck with the conclusion that the billions in profits, bonuses, and commissions are just a complete coincidence, extracted on the basis of "mistakes".

Beneath all the commotion of housing prices and the stockmarket booming, and all the money being made on Wall St., the foundation was crumbling as we have described. Finally, in 2007, the housing market started to weaken because higher interest rates on mortgages began to kick in. This started a chain reaction. With the housing market weakening, households began to weaken Consumption. This sent out the first signals just like slight vibrations in the earth can be detected by some animals as signals of an impending earthquake. Finally, in 2008, the whole stack of fake paper money derivatives started to topple over. Banks around the world were stuck with hundreds of *trillions* of dollars of fake assets that had almost no value at all. And where were those neoconservatives who worship market mechanisms to determine values? When the value of their derivatives went to near zero in the *marketplace*, they did what any good socialist does: he *intrudes* into the market to prop up his crooked artificial creations, *exactly* the way the old Communists would *assign* values to their corrupt and worthless production facilities.

But what happened to the oversight institutions of the government who are supposed to prevent these abuses? We have a Commodity Futures Trading Commission (CFTC) that should have overseen this alphabet soup of derivatives. *The Nation* reported that CFTC "...efforts to impose regulatory oversight on derivatives were stymied by Fed chair Alan Greenspan, Treasury Secretary Robert Rubin and SEC chair Arthur Levitt in 1997".

These three "very publicly kneecapped commission chair Brooksley Born and effectively drove her from government. They staged a brutal dressing-down and urged Congress to prevent her from acting", accusing her of "…threatening a financial crisis".[36] Get that? A financial crisis.

Also, we have credit-rating agencies like Moody, etc. They're supposed to rate the creditworthiness of various kinds of paper that get unconstitutionally printed up. Well guess what. They are paid by the very people who they are supposed to rate — another blatant example of Economic Socialism. Again we have to refer to the father of Capitalism, Adam Smith, who warned against players making their own rules. Sure enough, "In 2004 and 2005, Standard & Poor's and Moody's lowered the standards again and again, as each sought to avoid the perception that it might be even marginally less accommodating".[37]

Finally, we have the Federal Reserve which everyone thinks is our national bank. There is no greater blatant example of Economic Socialism than the Federal Reserve. I'll bet most of you don't know that the Federal Reserve is owned by a number of *private* banks. Instead of being an independent national bank for clearing paper transactions, enforcing rules for capital requirements, overseeing the creation of money instruments, and all the other rules necessary for the smooth and sustainable functioning of the banking industry, the Fed is simply a tool of the *private* banking system. They pass their own rules, and of course, they give themselves the privilege of printing up their own money, totally unregulated, and then gambling on it. It was a corrupt operation from the day it was cooked up by the system mind. Not only did the Federal Reserve institute policy that caused the Great Depression of 1929, but it did everything it could to sabotage Roosevelt's efforts to get out of the Depression in the early 1930s. It actually encouraged printing up of unconstitutional fake money in the run-up to the 2008 meltdown.

When tons of derivative paper were exposed as being fraudulent and worthless after the crash of 2008, the Fed stepped in and used good taxpayer money to buy worthless derivative paper. You know it's a scam because it always gets nice acronyms. Here it was TARP, Troubled Asset Relief Program. The Fed bought "some $1.25 trillion in purchases of toxic mortgage-backed securities from private financial institutions, including banks with ownership interests in the regional Federal Reserve Banks".[38] See, the *member banks who are supposed to be regulated get to vote for the Fed buying their own fraudulent paper.* All with money stolen from our children. But there's more. Under another racket called TALE, The "Federal Reserve has lent more than $1.5 trillion to those same private financial institutions in exchange for more toxic assets as collateral". Not only that, but the Fed charges only 1% interest on these loans, and the banks turn around and use the money to buy government treasury bonds paying 3% — a massive profit. Of course, nothing is being produced and there is no economic output from this racket. So where do the profits come from? They come from future generations who will pay the interest on the government paper being held by the very banks who are sitting on them. The Fed is a completely crooked institution. Its job is to make money for its member banks when money is to be made, and to pass off losses to future generations when their economic policies fail. The operation of the Fed mirrors precisely the operations of the Cosa Nostra.

The excuse the government gave for the hundreds of billions of money stolen and given to the banks and other financial firms was that it was needed to lend money to businesses to get the economy going. Guess what? Over the following months, lending to businesses actually *decreased*. This again is one more proof that filling Savings tub is not the problem. Firms are not going to pump money up the Investment pipe to expand business and increase employment when they can't sell the output they are currently making.

This bail-out was the greatest investment payoff in the history of the United States. And who was there arranging for buy-outs, mergers, and the further collectivization of the financial services industry so as to better coordinate all the fraud going on including further collectivization in the industry? You guessed it: our dear old Federal Reserve controlled by the very people it is supposed to oversee. This was detailed in a really excellent article by Robert Kuttner about the whole racket, discussing "...mergers to create even bigger banks, thus redoubling the too-big-to-fail problem". [39] This is a blatant example of Corporate Socialism.

We should point out that much of these ill-gained profits and bail-out money was in private hands by the time of the crash. The financial institutions that paid out all these profits were now in dire straights. But instead of the Obama administration putting a tax on all this ill-gotten money, they began stealing over half a *trillion* from future generations to prop up the very financial institutions who had been stripped bare by their high-flying top executives. Wealth accumulated by bankers and money managers during the whole fraudulent period was allowed to remain with these managers, and sometime reconstituted. [40] Of course, when legitimate productive companies like GM go bankrupt *in the process* of trying to make a legitimate product with legitimate productive employees, they are treated as parasites. In fact, every reading I've seen pimping for the system mind told us that bail-outs to the financial services industry were "necessary", but companies that are the real core of a productive economy like GM were called "socialism".

Part of the Capitalist game of investing capital to make something to sell is that you incur risk. If you're not successful, you can lose your capital. If you are successful, you can make lots of money. That's what makes Capitalism a great game that can benefit all levels of society. But in this fraudulent derivatives game, there was no risk whatsoever for the people perpetuating the fraud. The risk was with their stockholders and future generations. When you look at the incredible propaganda blitz spewed forth by the system to paper over all the details leading up to this meltdown, I want someone to explain to me the cleverness, the comprehensiveness, the coordination of it all without postulating a system mind. Even ardent critics of everything that happened including writers quoted here, have no explanation at all, except fairytales coughed up by the system itself. What is very interesting is that the Attorney General of New York is looking into this whole racket of fraudulent mortgages and fraudulent foreclosure practices. [41] No matter what he comes up with, I can assure you if anyone pays for all this, it will be investors in banks who engaged in shady practices, investors who naively bought fraudulent paper, and taxpayers whose money was stolen to prop the system back up. It will not cost the real people who *authorized* this swindle one penny from the huge bonuses, commissions and paychecks they received to carry it off.

Finally, eight years after the collapse, CBS on 60 minutes did an exposé as to what had happened eight years before. And we're all supposed to be grateful for their wonderful investigative reporting. When it was time to impeach Clinton for raising their taxes, these same TV networks had bevies of investigative reporters sniffing around in every nook and cranny (actually every cran and nookie) to find dirt on Clinton. In the process, they were even able to determine the exact number of pimples on Bill Clinton's ubiquitous pecker. Hundreds of media outlets, not only TV but newspapers and magazines as well, were offering outright bribes to women of up to ten thousand bucks, who would come forth with a lurid story involving Bill Clinton's sex life. I was extremely impressed by the inherent honesty of women in general. Out of the millions of women, only a very few came forward and a few of them were probably telling the truth. Of course, these stories were greeted by the system media mouthpieces with the most serious credulity.

But when *trillions* of dollars were at stake in the big gambling casino created by congress in bed with the financial services industry, absolutely nobody in the media anywhere managed to get the story. Where was 60 minutes then? Where was ABC's bevy of Clinton era crotch-sniffers? But of course, this is understandable because the media is just part of the same system mind that created the scandals in the first place.

As far as explaining the meltdown, thousands of articles appear in the propaganda outlets and hundreds of books are written to explain what happened. Every article, every book, every talk, every review comes from the system mind with the exact same phrases. *The Economist* [42] in Sept. '09 reviewed two books explaining the meltdown, and as you can see, the books, the reviewers, the reviewees, the whole gang spouts the same system mind crap. This was "underestimated", "undervalued", and "underrated"; that was "overlooked", "over-extended", and "overrated". There was "misjudgment" of this and "misexamination" of that; "misperception" of this and "maladjustment" of that. Just like Schultz used to say in Hogan's heroes, "I know nuhthink". They were just "mistakes" of one kind of another and nobody had any idea of the consequences. Even an old hand player as Paul Volcker says, "… all the new complicated products, including the explosion of derivatives, that were intended to diffuse and minimize risk, did not work as had been claimed." [43] Shows how something as subtle as a system mind can fool the best of them. Volcker and other system players are telling us that all those billions of profits, commissions and bonuses are just coincidences based on "mistakes". This kind of flood of system mind propaganda is pumped out of the system mind 24 hours a day 7 days a week. Don't waste your time reading any of this crap. Read a good history book instead and learn something.

For one thing, the word 'mistake' entails that there is a penalty. If you make a *mistake* cutting up your vegetables, you cut yourself. If you make a driving *mistake*, you damage your car. If you make a *mistake* on ice, you slip and fall. If you make a *mistake* and buy the wrong paint, you ruin your walls. But not the "*mistakes*" Alan Greenspan's crooked friends in the financial services industry make. When they make "mistakes", they wind up making hundreds of billions of dollars that has to be stolen from our children. These are very special "mistakes".

In front of me now is a review of Alan Greenspan's book by Benjamin Freedman in the very reputable *New York Review of Books*, showing that they desperately need an economics editor.[44] Greenspan was one of the supply-siders who cheered Reagan's tax cuts that were going to spur the economy to great heights and balance the budget too. It didn't happen. Did he learn anything? These inner brain neoconservatives not only know nothing, perceive nothing, and understand nothing, but learn nothing on top of it. When Bush wanted to do the same thing, Greenspan was again right there pimping for the system predicting the same thing as before; and just as before, we wound up with massive deficits. Alan Greenspan oversaw the theft of over 8 *trillion* dollars from the children of this country to prop up the very system he was cheering *for the previous 20 years*. And this went on year after year after year for his whole term. Once in a while, he would make a Sarah Palin exclamation, gee, the defishits are kinda high.

Greenspan, in my opinion, is the heart and soul of Economic Socialism. He was among the leading enablers who made the arrangements for economic players, especially in the financial services industry, to climb in bed with the political actors in Washington to rig the rules of the very game they were playing. And by some coincidence, they just happened to make rules that enabled the financial services to print up over 300 *trillion* dollars of fake money all based on a GDP of only about 14 trillion, and then to extract billions in bonuses and commissions by betting on this fake paper. He and his cronies now tell us that nobody understood the printed-up paper or knew how to evaluate risk. They sure knew how to evaluate their own *personal* risk, which is like no risk at all. As they create the paper, they tell us it's to *spread* risk. After it collapses, they then tell us it *hid* risk.

Are we to believe Greenspan doesn't understand all of this? Greenspan is an old guy. He was around in the '50s and '60s when the economy expanded at 4½% a year, no deficits and median family income *mushroomed*. How did the economy do all this without these fake derivatives that supposedly grease the wheels of the economy? Where did he think all the profits, bonuses, salaries, and commissions were coming from? These players weren't producing anything. When we had the great unprecedented economic expansion in the two decades after WWII, there was none of this fake money, and even Wall Streeters then made a tenth of what they do now. And the few people who did understand all this and warned about it, like Brooksley Born, were snuffed out like a spark under an avalanche; and guess by whom? *By the very people led by Greenspan who Obama later hired as his economics team.* And when he saw that finally the whole swindle was going to collapse, he quietly snuck out of the picture just in the nick of time and later claimed like Schultz: "I know nuhthink". And here is this pathetic review by a major con artist talking about a few *mistakes* "…in an otherwise laudable public service".[45] It's enough to turn the stomach of a billy-goat. As I said, the *NYR* desperately needs an economics editor.

If Greenspan had one ounce of integrity, when he saw that his economic policies required the continuous theft of trillions, year after year after year, an honorable man would have resigned. When I was young, I found myself working in top-secret statistical analysis for the military, which, after a while, I suspected was biological warfare. I never really found out for sure. But I quit the job and went back to starving in grad school. But Greenspan wallowed in all the stolen money with his finger in his butt as it wound up in the hands of his crooked friends in the financial services industry.

The reality, of course, is that the whole scam worked like a well-oiled machine. The structure was complex but the result was simple: a gigantic swindle. These financial wizards very correctly and very accurately estimated that there was no *personal* risk at all. There were no mistakes or misjudgments at all. *In fact, Wall Street's calculations were extremely accurate and on-target.* It is impossible to know exactly how *conscious* the players in this whole crooked game were. I believe vague strands of the scam were conscious. It is a *system mind* that clearly sees the potential for great profits, bonuses, and commissions by rigging the rules that allow trillions of fake money to be printed up in conjunction with these rules.

To show how little risk there really was to the players, even after the collapse when trillions were lost in people's 401ks, more billions lost in the value of their homes, millions of jobs lost, more millions getting kicked out their homes destroying families — even after all this and right in the middle of a recession, "Wall Street paid $140 *billion*" in commissions and bonuses "in 2009, a near record, when the rest of America was mired in the worst recession since the 1930s".[46] These paychecks and bonuses are 10 times what any CEO of any productive company in the history of the country ever made.

In a good Wall St. book, Doug Henwood explains that Wall St. has very little to do with allocation of funds for productive investment, because 90% of all stockmarket trades involve nothing more than speculation and shuffling pieces of paper.[47] Not only that, but much corporate debt and stock issuance is not used to build new plant and equipment and to hire people, but to simply underwrite mergers, buy-outs and acquisitions. And since he's probably not a company historian, Henwood doesn't even mention that a lot of these buy-outs are of historical firms who for a hundred years have made an excellent product. The mother company uses the high quality brand name to hide the cheapening of the product to create big profits in the short run, until the public finally figures it out that it's a crap product. And down the drain goes a hundred year reputation of a quality product. I'd love to mention names for you to sleep on, but I can't afford a lawyer. This is not Capitalism, but a perfect example of Economic Socialism. But Henwood does understand that the purpose of this whole non-productive game is to push all wealth and income to the top 5%.

Another consistent characteristic of mainstream economists is that every point these economists make are *effects*; the never talk about causes. And when they infrequently talk about causes, they confuse them with effects. For example, they reverse cause and effect regarding Savings and Investment. There's a law in economics that says Savings equal Investment. But which is the horse and which the cart? Very conveniently, they make Savings the horse, and Investment the cart. So in order to get Investment to create jobs and consumption, all you have to do is increase Savings and Investment will be dragged up to it. Very conveniently, you increase Savings by throwing money at the wealthy and companies with subsidies, tax cuts and corporate welfare. These guys aren't stupid. The reality, of course, is that Investment is the horse, and Income will be adjusted so that Savings will tag along and meet the level of Investment. Except for technology bubbles, investment depends on new ideas and what consumers are able to buy.

Typical of this cause-effect reversal is a book by Martin Wolf reviewed by Robert Skidelsky in *The New York Review of Books*, again showing the *NYR* desperately needs an economics editor.[48] He says the Fed "used low interest rates to keep money too cheap for too long". That is not a cause, but an effect — an effect whose cause is the financial services industry needing low interest rates to borrow even more money to make billions in commissions and bonuses by "investing" in the racket of betting on fraudulently derivatives.

Then Sidelsky says that "Chinese savings made it possible for the US consumer to go on a spending spree". Again, this is an effect. For one thing, Americans have been on a "spending spree" for the last 35 years. The cause of an *additional* spending spree came from borrowing on houses valued artificially high with fraudulent mortgages created by a fraudulent financial services industry. All of this is the product of a system mind that understands everything even though individual nodes of the economy, like Schultz, understand nuhthink.

But in case you think this whole affair is too abstract to draw specific conclusions, let's look at a very concrete example of Corporate Socialism, the BP oil spill. The BP oil spill was the greatest disaster to ever hit the country. The talk will die down and we will never hear another word even though the costs and the effects of the spill will be felt for a hundred years. Not only are there reports of massive liver, bladder, kidney disease and cancers attributed to the spill, but the worst of it is the genetic damage that causes birth defects that will go on for hundreds of years and will show up in kids having no say in the rules. *

In order to understand the oil spill, we have to go back to the last major government blueprint for energy policy, which was the National Energy Policy of May 17, 2001, better known as the Cheney plan. In a *Nation* article, Michael Klare, describes the plan that "... wholeheartedly embraced wider exploitation of the deepwater gulf. To speed these efforts, the Bush administration encouraged the Minerals Management Service to streamline the issuing of permits to giant oil firms like BP.... BP clearly took shortcuts when drilling offshore — thus inviting the blowout on April 20. ...The 2001 energy plan was devised with substantial input from the energy industry... and was widely viewed as a payoff to Bush/Cheney supporters in the oil industry." [49] This was probably accompanied by millions of dollars of "campaign contributions", which our new Supreme Court justice calls "bribes". This is a perfect example of what Adam Smith warned against: *"traders" making*

---

* In July, '12, a final report on the Japanese nuclear disaster came out. The media had lots of fluffy words (cozy, conflict, influence, etc.) to describe the fact that the regulators and power plant owners were in bed together, sometimes the very same people, making their own rules. Another example of Economic Socialism leading to an incredible disaster, exactly what Adam Smith warned against.

their own rules, by being in bed with Washington politicos. This is the precise definition of Corporate or Economic Socialism. [50]

Anyone with half a brain and has taken Physics 101 knows that at the very *minimum*, all deepwater drilling should be done in pairs. In case anything goes wrong with one drill hole, the other one could relieve the pressure and prevent oil from actually being *pushed* out of the seafloor. But you might ask, why weren't executives for BP more careful? After all, BP will take a tremendous hit from this disaster, which is going to cost their executives as well as stockholders plenty of money. The answer is simply that there is enormous pressure on all executives to make big profits any way they can. This causes them to hide from reality. BP is not an evil company. They are in business to make a profit by procuring oil, not to devise safety rules, nor even to look out for the environment. The job of making the rules of the game to prevent these kinds of disasters and keep the environment clean is the *government's* job, not BP's. What do we pay these crooks in Washington for? They don't drill for oil, nor do anything else useful.

To top it off, there was Barack Obama getting on his high horse balling out BP. This was all public relations to polish up a good guy image. Of course, he knew there were plenty of people in his own party that allowed the oil industry to make their own rules. As a senator on the way up, Obama favored campaign finance reform. But as we will discuss in the next section, the day he became president, he became part of a system mind that completely papers over problems like disasters and his efforts so far to insure oil drilling safety are half-assed at best.

25.8 BARACK OBAMA AND THE SYSTEM MIND

Preceding Obama, George Bush, with the help of a bunch corrupt shysters on the Supreme Court, had single-handedly created a king with unconstitutionally kingly powers. In fact, no other president and Supreme Court in the history of the country had violated each and every concept pillar that this country was built upon. Recall in Sect. 23.4, we discussed these 4 pillars. They invaded our privacy spying on Americans without a court order. They had a court ruling that clearly stole somebody's property for the sole benefit of another party. They stole trillions from the children of this country in the form of massive deficits. This is clearly taxation without representation. And finally, Bush started a private war in Iraq with no mandate from the people and no congressional initiation. This cost a *trillion* by itself. All this was done by breaking laws, breaking treaties and making their own laws and *interpretations* of the Constitution, exactly the "Injuries and Usurpations" the Declaration of Independence railed about the British king.

So Obama runs on a platform of "change". He was going to clean up the mess created by Bush. But as usual with most of our elections, the mouthpieces of the system mind keep the race close to hold onto people's attention so their ratings are high and they can sell more stomach fizz. Then at the last minute, they come up with some dirty trick that derails the candidate who is most likely to increase their taxes. This happened in both the 2000 and

2004 elections. The system was all set to do the same to Barack Obama. The only regret is we never got a chance to see the dirty tricks they had prepared to derail Obama at the last minute.

But then surprise! As we have detailed, the Bush financial corruption finally led to the crash of 2008. Immediately after the crash, the SEG (shit-eatin' grin) on George Stephanopoulos's face disappeared. He turned pale. The very next day, Obama began getting high grades for his debate performances. The dirty tricks that the networks had been preparing to crash Obama's campaign at the last minute were stuffed into drawers for another day. Stephanopoulos started giving Obama A's and B's for his performances in debates. So on the scene comes Barack Obama — Mr. Clean himself.

The system mind had calculated all the variables. It calculated that the important nodes in the economy like the TV network bigwigs were losing more money on their stock portfolios than they would lose with Obama's tiny tax increase. But it could kill other birds with the same stone — actually three. First, the system knew that the swindle initiated by Bush could best be continued and covered up under a supposed liberal. And the system mind could look like good guys, saviors, by giving us a real Mr. Clean. Then with the passage of time, it could gradually dump the blame on that very same liberal. Finally, it could use this blame to get right back in the saddle. So Obama was elected — no surprise to me.

Since there is no way out of the mess without a major overhaul of the system to put it in balance, the system mind decided to set a trap for Obama. The system mind seemed to know that Obama has a very weak mind and that his own *personal* mind would get taken over by the system just like happened in that famous movie, *The Invasion of the Body Snatchers*. Of course, Reagan and Bush were total creations of the system mind too. But Obama seemed to be an independent thinking guy before he took office.

In any event, after getting elected, Obama woke up the next morning, probably pretty scared. He was facing the full brunt of the system mind. In the first few days of his administration, he was corralled by system people in his office who proceeded to beat the livin' crap out of him to soften him up so that the system mind could turn him into a total zombie and an important node in the flows of system information. Down the drain were all his childhood dreams of how, when he got to the top, he was going to really reform the system.

This is one of the great examples that illustrate how a system mind works which we should be very careful to delineate. The first thing that must be emphasized is that there is no conspiracy. There were no back room meetings of network players discussing how they were going to get Obama elected. It works exactly the same as the brain. Neurons of the brain do not have thoughts, nor beliefs, nor any other mentality. Thoughts and beliefs are the result of billions of impulses flowing back and forth between neurons of the brain. It's called *emergence*. The mind *emerges* from billions of neurons sending impulses between each other. The system mind works the same way. The nodes don't have explicit thoughts about what the system mind wants or thinks or believes. Of course, sometimes individual nodes may have the same thoughts and wants as the system mind, but the thoughts of individuals are just accidental and not necessary for mentality to emerge from the system. It is the enormous flows of information *between* the nodes of the system that creates its mentality just as in the brain.

In fact, while viewing the networks after the stock market crash, it was very obvious that none of the talking heads, including smiley-face George, had the faintest idea what the system mind had decided. They all thought they were being very objective in their treatment of the candidates. Of course, you could say that you'd have to be semi-conscious to get big bucks from the networks to continuously pimp for the system. However, the individual mentality of network actors is not relevant. The system mind is created by the flows of information between the many nodes of the system, with a direction mostly determined by the larger nodes.

Now there were still small parts of his own mind that hadn't been absorbed. But as we shall explain later, the personal proclivities of the president are just as important in determining his foreign policy than being part of a system mind. This is why our foreign policy is schizophrenic. There aren't enough flows of information back and forth in our foreign dealings to create a complete system mind. And this is why Obama's foreign policy was somewhat under control of his own values and thinking. But many of his initiative were just window-dressing that are peripheral to the major part of his mind that got absorbed by the system. He started out ordering the cessation of torture at Guantanamo and he began to make friendly overtures towards the Muslim world. But when we look a little deeper, torture was continuing only in countries not in the spotlight. (Foreign countries without a free press are better able to cover up torture.) And in some ways the friendly words to the Muslim world were belied by an escalation in Afghanistan, an uptick in drone strikes and nodding approval towards Israel taking more land.

The historian Gary Wills details the many ways Obama has continued with the kingly powers of the president that George Bush initiated.[51] The NYR article says, "A former CIA official told the *Washington Post*, 'Leon Panetta has been captured by the people who were the ideological drivers for the interrogation program in the first place' ". I love the word 'captured'. Remember, before being turned into a zombie by the system mind, Leon Panetta himself was also a good guy. This describes exactly the way the system mind takes over the personal minds that are inserted as important nodes in the system. The article goes on to enumerate the many special powers the president now has in effect to run a secret government beyond the auspices of congress or anyone else.

On the domestic scene, because of all the flows of information he was involved in, Obama became part and parcel of the system mind. The system looks out for itself and perpetuates itself, but I wouldn't have thought it could judge the detail of how weak-minded a leader is. But we saw it right before our eyes. The system knew it needed a liberal to continue the swindle, but liberals often have strong minds. If you are looking for reasons to reject the idea of a system mind, a good question is, how did it know Obama would have such a weak mind?

First of all, the response to the crisis was the most incisive example of a system mind that you will ever see. The system hunkered down into survival mode in which in every detail of the system, in every propaganda venue, coming from the mouths of every paid system whore was the same message: to prevent the sky from falling and the world coming to an end, it was absolutely essential to prop back up the very financial institutions that got us into the mess in the first place. Within months after the meltdown and without the slightest shame on their faces, the neoconservative propagandists and the system mouthpieces started cranking up the same one-liners left over from Ronald Reagan. "Reduce government", "unleash" the private sector by cutting taxes, and "deregulate". This is after it was plain as night and day that the cause of the crash was no regulation at all on the fraudulent paper the system had been printing up under Bush.

Obama had a trillion dollar seed money to stimulate the economy and get unemployment down. But as a result of the propaganda blitz and Obama's inherently weak mind, what we got from Obama was basically the Republican philosophy of throwing money at the top, and seeing if any trickles down. He proceeded to prop back up all the fraudulent practices and institutions that led to the meltdown so as to pay back all the bribes democrats in Congress had received from Wall Street. He threw money at the *top* of state governments who proceeded to stuff most of it into their pockets; he threw money at the *top* of the health care industry, big insurance companies, drug companies and hospitals; and most importantly he threw money at the *top* financial institutions that got us into the mess in the first place. And he stole trillions from the future to do it. This created only vestigial improvements in the economy and fell right into the neoconservative agenda of racking up more debt. A high-powered think tank couldn't devise a better way to incur the greatest deficits for the least results.

First, the stimulus package included throwing money at the top of state and local governments on the theory that they would hire people to do infrastructure. Some money did go for that purpose, but most of it got absorbed into these paper-shuffling bureaucracies just like a glass of water thrown into a sand box. Of course, this would buy votes which is mostly what Obama's stimulus was all about.

In the area of healthcare, neoconservatives had just enough votes to squelch any reasonable plan that would accomplish anything worthwhile. We got a health care bill designed and implemented by a *Republican* that gives a blank check to doctors and drug companies at the top of the health care field and then creates a big government bureaucracy to try to keep them from charging too much. Already healthcare costs are rising. And while Obama is getting blamed, insurance companies who have been sending tens of millions in bribes (I mean campaign contributions) to congress, would get record profits behind the scenes. You have to be unconscious to think this is going to cut costs. But of course, Republicans have no intention of cutting costs, because high costs will increase the national debt, which is part of the neoconservative political agenda as we will explain in Ch. 30. The new system mind under Obama left no stone unturned. Regarding the financial rules of the game, as part of the system mind, he immediately surrounded himself with a neoconservative crowd who for 30 years promoted "deregulation". Their experience to a man and woman, was not in the area of devising rules that guide a pure Capitalist economy successfully. Their experience was in how to *game* the system. Obama hired them on the same theory that the way to fight the mafia is to hire people who were formerly *in* the mafia because they understand it.

Even in less instrumental government functions, Obama fell right in place as one of the nodes of the system mind. *The American Prospect* reported that Obama's "...Security and Exchange Commission chair, Mary Schapiro, used to head the financial industry's self-regulatory body, FINRA, which missed the major abuses that led to the financial collapse".[52] Also, Obama's "chair of the...(CFTC), Gray Gensler, while Treasury undersecretary in the Clinton administration personally instructed then — CFTC Chair Brooksley Born to cease her efforts to intensify regulation of derivatives".[53] I want someone to explain to me how people who engineered the country into a financial collapse can be right back in the saddle under Mr. Change without adducing a system mind.

These moves itself graphically illustrate the distorted view of economics of the new neo-conservative system mind that will sink this country. Just as a cockroach sees the world from the point of view of a cockroach, an investment banker sees the world through the eyes of an investment banker. In this view, financial services are the *core* of the economy. This was the exact same view as happened in southern Europe during the counter-reformation. To these new Economic Socialists, the core of the economy is not the production of legitimate goods and services by reasonably paid middle class workers as Adam Smith outlined. The core now consists of financial institutions that don't produce anything but spend most of their time buying, selling and betting on fraudulent paper money that their bribed members of congress allow them to unconstitutionally print up. This requires stealing trillions from taxpayers to prop up huge financial companies that are "too big to fail". *This* is the system that's at stake, not companies like GM who are actually producing something tangible with real productive employees.

Just to rub it in, these financial institutions began giving out bonuses with taxpayer money as a reward for the executives in these institutions having stolen hundreds of billions from people's 401Ks. Well, to our great surprise, there were a few liberal politicians who raised a fuss about this and wanted to tax the bonuses in some way. You wouldn't believe the reaction on sewer radio. When I tell you about this, it will blow your mind. They claimed that the government had no business telling corporations how to spend "their" money. You see, before the money had even been stolen from the taxpayer, it had become the *corporation's* money. And it was gross interference in the free enterprise system for the government to be meddling in the affairs of the private sector. The money stolen from the taxpayer, you see, was never really theirs in the first place. This is because in the neoconservative spinal chord, all power, all wealth, all money is rightfully owned by the biggies. It is "their" money, and the ordinary taxpayer has no business telling these executives what to do with "their" money. If there is the slightest hint of a threat to the nodes of wealth and power, the neoconservative becomes alarmed like somebody is cutting off his privates. He begins to rant and rave until the threat is removed and he can go right on identifying with big money, big power, big wars and big brother government.

Of course, as Roosevelt showed, there is only one way to revive an economy after a collapse, which is by sending money to the *bottom* where the real consumers are. The best policy to get out of recessions is to hire people who have lost jobs. Getting a job after not having one for a while results in the highest percentage of the new income going for Consumption because out-of-work people build up needs while unemployed. Now Obama is doing some of this, but not nearly enough. I haven't had the time to analyze the stimulus package in responsible detail. But just off the top, I would say that only about a third of a dollar of stimulus resulted in creating more than 33 cents in wealth. The other 66 cents are pure waste of which a third went to buying votes with no new hiring.

Of course, when the stimulus proved mostly ineffective, there were the liberals moaning that he didn't steal enough from our children. Paul Krugman complained that Obama's stimulus was too small to do the job.[54] This is complete horsecrap. As we calculated in Sect. 24.7, where Roosevelt spent a billion to drop unemployment a percentage point, Obama is spending 3 *trillion* to drop unemployment by the same amount. This means that Obama's economic policies were 3 *thousand* times less effective.

Clearly, Obama is no Roosevelt. He was putty in the hands of the Economic Socialist policy makers of the past 35 years. Roosevelt didn't waste taxpayer money propping up crooked banks; he used his deficits to cut unemployment and grow the economy. But with the financial services industry now the core of the economy, Obama is wasting trillions to prop up basically corrupt banks who unconstitutionally print up their own money. When it all failed, neoconservatives put the blame on a Democrat. It was a perfect trap and Obama fell right into it.

The simple and effective Keynsian idea of injecting money into the *bottom* of the economic pile was long buried under the avalanche of Reagan Economic Socialism. What we got instead was a 24/7 pounding from the system mouthpieces that we can't let these big financial institutions fail. It was perfectly okay to let General Motors with productive employees go bankrupt after only about a 15 billion dollar loan. In an article entitled "Saving Detroit", *The Economist* said, "Bailing out Detroit would be bad use of public money".[55] But it was perfectly all right to let the backbone of the economy (households) fail with jobs hemorrhaging and housing values plummeting. But when the government made available $900 *billion* to prop up banks who had been involved in massive fraud that caused the meltdown, *The Economist* titled their article, "saving the system", saying this "...is not enough".[56] The Wall Street Urinal "...editorial approved of the $700 billion bank bailout." [57] In my opinion, most of these paid system whores have absolutely no sense of shame.

There was total disregard of the pain and suffering experienced by the unemployed, the foreclosed housing owners and of small businesses failing. The number one priority was bailing out big financial institutions that had been spending billions on bribes (freedom of expression) between economic players in bed with political animals in Washington to rig their own rules so they could make billions. This is as good an example of Economic Socialism as you'll ever find.

However, somewhere along the way, a few legitimate liberals in congress probably reminded Obama that he is a Democrat and that at least he ought to *pretend* to make some rules of the game to prevent future meltdowns. So the Obama administration together with a few honest politicians in Washington tried to take rule-making away from Corporate Socialists and put it in the hands of independent factors that represent the population as a whole. So we got the Dodd-Frank reforms, and a new consumer protection agency that would try to install independent rules of the game to create stability and prevent abuses as detailed in a *Nation* article. [58] But crooked economic players, especially from Wall Street led by the Chamber of Commerce are climbing in bed with every neoconservative bribe-taking politician in Washington in one big Socialist gang-bang to turn this legislation into a sieve. And this is only a few years after a meltdown caused by these same people. Within a few years, the banking system will wind up getting rid of the Volker rule so that banks can use depositor's money to gamble with. If they win, they will stuff the money in their pockets and secret bank accounts. If they lose, they will immediately run under the skirts of big tit, big mama government for more bail-outs. What we're doing is creating incentives for young people coming up to jump into the Wall St./government Corporate Socialist bed and concoct more rules to steal from the system instead of becoming an engineer who might be able to make something to compete with the Chinese.

Of course, this vestigial attempt to pretend to reform the system completely overlooks the real reason for the meltdown, which is that there was over 300 *trillion* dollars worth of monopoly money permeating the system based on only a 14 trillion dollar economy. This fraudulent and unconstitutional paper is poisoning the books of every bank in the world. Real reform would have stopped the continuous printing up of this fraudulent paper in the first place. But it's not going to happen with this bribe-taking congress. Periodically the stack of paper will topple over and require trillions to be stolen from the future to prop it back up as happened in 2008.

But neoconservative have no problem with meltdowns. Meltdowns always result in a greater percent of wealth going to the top 20%. So when the system mind saw Obama's efforts to put in place a few new rules of the game, a new line of propaganda arose. In March '10, the *Economist* whined, "the president has gained a reputation for being hostile to business".[59] *The president is not there to be friendly, unfriendly, mildly friendly, or massively unfriendly to business.* As part of the government, his job is to objectively design and enforce the rules of the game, not look for bedfellows playing the game. Why doesn't *The Economist* complain about the referees in football not being "friendly" to the players and coaches? They bring up the Chamber of Commerce complaining that Obama has "vilified industries", and was "anti-business". Economic Socialism has been in place so long that propagandists on *The Economist* have no idea what Capitalism really is.

If we look at the real definition of *business* as described by the father of Capitalism, Adam Smith, *business consists of the producing, buying and selling goods and services. That's what business is.* When you ask your friend who has a car dealership, "how's business", you're asking if he's selling cars. When you ask another friend who owns a restaurant, "how's business", you're asking if he's got people coming in to eat. Obama was really trying to keep money in the pockets of consumers so they can do more *business* by enabling them to buy more legitimate goods and services in the marketplace. When the Chamber of Commerce wants Obama to lay off the banks and their shady practices, they are really enabling banks to climb in bed with political actors in Washington to make rules that allows credit card banks to steal money from consumers lessening their ability to do real *business*. You do *business* only when you have a prosperous middle class which the economic socialists in the Chamber encourage millions of ways to steal from. The reality is that the US Chamber of Commerce is the most *anti*-business organization in the country next to the Communist party. What the country desperately needs a *Capitalist* business organization to promote real *business*.

And we also have to keep in mind that all this diaper-filling whining we get from Economic Socialist organizations like the Chamber of Commerce is at a time when the middle class has been gradually and inexorably eroded by the "laws" of supply and demand in godless markets to where they now get less than half of national income. In the past, there might have been some reason for complaint like when top tax rates were 90%. In modern times, the top 20%, which includes these diaper-fillers, is getting a larger share of income than ever before. But that's the nature of a hog: there's no amount he can hog without wanting more.

But of course the system media had to pay some lip-service to the massive deficits carried over from Bush and made worse by Obama. *The Economist* had all kinds of ideas to raise revenue and reduce deficits. And guess where the revenue is going to come from? As usual, from the lower 80%. They suggest a VAT (Very Asinine Tax), sales tax, gas tax, carbon tax, foreskin tax, and any other tax their evil minds can think of to tax the lower 80%. A grammar school kid can see that you can't *pull* your way out of a recession — the only way to get out of a recession is to *push* your way out, which even the most dim-witted economist would know. And this can only happen by stimulating demand that *pushes* the economy forward.

But once in a while there's a moment of truth coming out of these propaganda outlets. In a discussion of the massive deficits world economies are racking up, and how taxes may be necessary, *The Economist* suddenly announces: "A premature increase in Japan's consumption tax in 1997 may have aborted that country's recovery".[60] Well, I'll be. Of course, this was part of a very long article that probably put the editor temporarily to sleep because a few months later they're back at it: Japan now needs "a gradually higher spending tax."[61] "Compared with other countries, American taxes consumption too little and income too much".[62] "That suggests that the route to continued recovery lies where it has long been: through the consumer's pocket". [63] Right. When you need to sell more goods and services to a group of people, you do it by first emptying their pockets. This is what you learn when you get a Phd in economics.

But of course, when Obama saw that there was no chance of reducing the deficit and when he threatened to tax the only people who have benefited from any economic expansion that has occurred over the last 35 years, he was vilified. The cover headline in *The Economist's* Sept. 24, '11 issue in blaring letters was "HUNTING THE RICH". Of course, over the last 35 years during which time, in every single year, the system "hunted" the middle class, deprived them of every penny of new wealth that was created, shipped their good jobs overseas, created a meltdown that robbed their savings, reduced the value of their homes and stole trillions from their children, not a peep of complaint did you hear from these inner brain reptiles. A street-walking prostitute has more of a sense of shame.

As you might expect, even though taxes are fine for the middle class, when it comes to corporations, the neoconservative line to get the economy going is to lower taxes on corporations and the top 20%. But that's exactly what George Bush did, and where were the jobs and explosion of the economy? The reality is that upper-income tax cuts under Reagan and Bush resulted only in massive deficits, and high effective taxes on the bottom 80% led to an economy that crawled along at 2 ½ % growth during Bush's term, and led to a climactic meltdown. But the neoconservative never learns. One-cell paramecia learn, neoconservatives don't.

If we cut taxes on GM and Chrysler, are they going to borrow money or invest in new car production facilities, when they can't sell the cars they are making now? Unless Household income begins to flow to consumers, companies are not going to borrow to expand plant and equipment, buy capital goods, nor hire people no matter how much money you throw at them. Regarding the largest banks, "… just before the crisis hit, American's largest banks…had outstanding…loans totaling $962 billion. By the end of 2010, that had dropped more than 28%, to $693 billion". [64] These large financial institutions simply stuffed the money in their pockets and continued on with no accounting. On the other hand, between '07 and '10, loans to *small* business "…fell from $329.2 billion to $179.6 billion" due to lower deposits from unemployment and business failures. But where was the bailout here? A measly "…3% of Tarp funds went to the community banks that do 60% of America's small business lending". [65] Then the government proceeded to rig the rules so that the big banks could *claim* they paid the money back; and of course, the media propaganda outlets didn't spend one minute looking into this. I have to give Geithner credit though. When he told Charlie Rose that the banks had paid back all the money, at least his face showed he was lying. Yes, they paid it back with profits obtained by borrowing at 1% from the Fed to buy treasuries paying 3%. This "payback" was obtained by stealing the money from our children.

If the Feds saw that the reason for shrinking bank lending was uncertainty or hesitancy to accept risk, the Roosevelt way would have been to hire retired bank loan officers, stick them in each social security office in big cities and allow them to make loans directly to businesses from the government; private banks would sit in on these loan interviews and could take over a loan at any time. You would avoid the enormous waste like fraudulent bonuses that resulted from throwing money indiscriminatingly at big banks.

But by 2010, it was obvious that the economic theory that has been pushed for 35 years was unraveling. Free trade and trillions of dollars of tax cuts and loopholes had been thrown at the business sector under Reagan and especially Bush to where they were stuffed with cash. So when it became obvious that this supply-side crap wasn't producing the economic activity as advertised, and the only effect of the Bush tax cuts were corporations stuffing the money in their pockets, *The Economist* had to act surprised: "For the economy to proceed smoothly, firms must stop hoarding cash".[66] Naughty, Naughty.

Of course, system mind propaganda outlets aren't going to tell us where they got all this cash to hoard and why it wasn't being put to use in making investments and hiring. With companies hiring workers in cheap labor countries, the value of American labor stagnates. With no increases in pay and firms able to get more work for the same pay, profits are going to increase too. Even *The Economist* mentioned in passing that [in 2009] "...firms are now able to wring more productivity out of their workers. ... "...the Bureau of Labour Statistics reported a fourth-quarter labour productivity growth of 6.9%, after increases of 7.6 and 7.8 in the previous two quarters".[67] Now why should productivity suddenly jump to these record-breaking numbers out of the clear blue sky after low productivity all through the Bush years? It's easy to put the pieces together, which the semi-conscious writers for this magazine are completely incapable of. The productivity numbers, of course, are pure lies. When you can get 12 hours of work from an employee for 8 hours pay and 8 hours reported work time, of course, productivity, *as reported*, is going to shoot to the moon. Why should an employer hire another worker to add to two workers putting in 8 hour days, when he can get two *12* hour days from his present two employees? Quite naturally, firms are going to simply stuff the increased profits into their profits. And here are these guys complaining about hoarding cash. What else do they expect them to do with it?

Investment and the accompanying hiring depend on ideas and nothing more; and is totally independent from tax policy. With the business sector doing nothing productive with their ill-gotten "hoarded cash", they got a scolding from *The Economist:* Firms should, "...loosen their purse-strings to hire workers and to invest...".[68] They're even surprised that "Big companies are still refusing to hire, despite sitting on piles of cash". [69] This is a pregnant example of how the bottom of the brain works. The limbic system is like a Bunsen burner, generating a continuous stream of energy directed towards certain beliefs. Energy never gets to the existential brain which sees reality. And the reality here is as simple as any reality can get: *firms are not going to invest in more equipment and hire more workers to produce goods and services they can't sell.* As we have stressed, there's only one relevant number. As long as the bottom 80% is getting less than half of national income, there will not be enough flowing to the Household tank to clear markets. This creates a climate of continuous recession and requires ever increasing theft from the future to prop up demand. Japan illustrates this.

In spite of the Japanese being very inventive and very productive as a people, their economy has been mostly recessionary for 35 years now. In the 2001 recession, *The Economist* had a 3 page spread about the recession in Japan;[70] in Jan. '09, they had another.[71] Since Japan wasn't much involved in the toxic securities and fraudulent paper rackets, these writers just couldn't figure out why Japan should be hit by recession. In spite their brilliance, when it's convenient, they suddenly go dumb on us. Among a highly productive people, there is only one reason for this: their national debt is almost twice the size of their economy.

The LPD, Liberal Democratic Party, has had the continuous policy for over 50 years of naked Corporate Socialism. They don't even try to hide it. They are the Republican party of Japan. They have overt institutions where industrialists and party members climb in bed with each other to rig the rules of the economic game. That's what led to their nuclear disaster. In recent years, corporations have made record profits, while at the same time wages to the bottom 80% have been eroding. This is exactly what Adam Smith warned about comparing England and Holland. As inequality in Japan grew in the '70s, '80s, and '90s, the only way markets could clear was to steal from the future to prop up demand until they now have a current crippling national debt. In 2014, Abe wants to increase consumption taxes. The theory is when you're in a hole, you dig deeper. The result is that Japan is in a permanent state of recurrent recessions and it will only get worse. And with a neoconservative system mind, we are heading in exactly the same direction.

With the economy faltering, *The Economist* had an issue (June, 2010) about the economy. In truth, they don't have the dimmest, faintest, foggiest idea as to what the economy needs. They totally ignore the post-war expansion when WWII debts were *paid off*, maximum expansion of the economy, growth of real income and low unemployment. A year later they're still in the dark (June, 2011), talking about "repressed savings", capital flows, interest rates and other chickenshit issues. Following their Bolshevik hero Freidman and not knowing a thing about Adam Smith, these neoconservative reptiles think economics is about tinkering with paper and fake paper at that. Where do they think the middle class got its "repressed savings"? They got it from good paying union jobs during the war.

These econowhores never mention one word that the top tax rates after WWII were 80%, the corporate tax was almost three times what it is now, and that Roosevelt, by encouraging unions, the minimum wage, and labor benefits, had created a middle class prosperous enough to clear markets and create full employment, exactly as Adam Smith prescribed. And most importantly, the bottom 80% was getting more than 60% of after-tax national income. The fact that these people think we're going to get out of this recessionary period by tinkering with trillions of dollars of fake paper they've printed up shows their lack of basic understanding of simple economics is profound, it is deep, it is unremitting.

In any event, with Obama's neoconservatively designed stimulus failing, Republicans were able to counterattack and won the midterm elections in 2010 and Corporate Socialism was immediately back in place. Their total goal was crippling the economy any way they could and then, with the help of the system mind propaganda outlets, blaming it on Obama for the 2012 elections. The next day after the midterm elections, Obama got up in front of the nation and took credit for bipartisanship for extending Bush's tax cuts. But where were those tea partiers who had been screaming about Obama's deficits? They hopped in bed with the financial services industry, Obama's liberals, and the rest of the neoconservative crowd with a bipartisan show of unity as they perpetuated one big theft gang-bang which will steal about a *trillion* from our children over the next 10 years to add to the ballooning national debt. Democrats, being dumber than a cardboard box, simply went right along, thus shredding their main argument against Republicans.

And what will this stolen new loot be used for? To prop up Fannie Mae to keep housing prices at levels younger people can't afford; to keep billions flowing to Wall St.; to further collectivize agribusiness; to raise tuitions for college entrants; and to continue to send jobs overseas so that young people won't even be able to get jobs to pay back loans they needed for outrageous tuitions. Nice work. In fact, as I write this, the system mind is favoring Obama in the 2012 election. The reason is obvious. He's a fake liberal to keep his peasants happy, but will guide the system to the required real 8% unemployment and keep the top 20% with over half of national income and huge amounts of money gobbled up by the financial services industry. His health care legislation will give doctors and hospitals a blank check. And more importantly, billions will leak out of the system into a maze of corporate Frankenstein companies around the world. He will continue to send all new wealth and income to the top 20% and he will continue massive deficits that will keep us in permanent recession as National Socialism gradually takes hold. And most important, if there are any complaints from the peasants, blame can be put on a liberal. Why take a chance with Romney. He might crash the system before the people who own the country can steal more trillions from future generations.

[1]   Piven, Francis; "Mobilizing the Jobless". *The Nation*, Jan. 10, '11, p. 7

[2]   "Automatic Reaction", *The Economist*, Sept. 11, '10, p. 95.

[3]   "Boring can Still be Bad". *The Economist*, Mar. 29, '14, p. 16

[4]   Myerson, Harold; "Business is Booming". *The American Prospect*, Mar. '11

[5]   "Complementary Trade Policies", *The Nation*, Jan. 13, '09, p. 23

[6]   Palast, Greg, "Confronting Globalcrat, *The Nation*, Dec. 21, '09

[7]   Faux, Jeff; "So Far From God, So Close to Wall St. *The Nation*, Aug. 3, '09, p. 18

[8]   *The Economist*, Mar. 31, '08, p. 31

[9]   "The return of economic nationalism", *The Economist*, Feb. 7, '09, p. 9

[10]   "Economic Vandalism", *The Economist*, Sept. 19, '09, p. 13

[11]   "The return... op. cit.

[12]   "The Return of Economic Nationalism", *The Economist*, Feb. 7, '09.

[13]   "Anti-liberalism old and new". *The Economist*, Oct. 21, '00. P. 92

[14]   "Out with the old", *The Economist*, Aug. 22, '09, p. 10

[15]   "What went wrong with economics". *The Economist*, July 18, '09, p.11
       Also, "The Great Stabilization". *The Economist*, Dec. 19, '09, p. 15

[16]   "Is Inflation Dead". *The Economist*, Sept. 28, '96, p. 39

[17]   "Diving into the Rich Pool". *The Economist*, Jan. 24, '11, p. 83

[18]   "Hope at Last", *The Economist*, Apr. 3, '10, p. 13.

[19]   "Time to Balance". *The Economist*, Apr. 3, '10, p. 3 of a special report.

[20]   *The Economist*, Oct. 4, '08, p. 7 inside.

[21]   "Are we there yet?". *The Economist*, Sept. 18, '10, p. 13

[22]   "Sleepwalking Towards Disaster". *The Economist*, Apr. 10, '10, p. 14

[23]   "Diving into the Rich Pool". *The Economist*, Sept. 24, '11, p.83

[24] *The Economist*, Jan. 7, '12, p. 70

[25] *The Nation*, July 13, '09, p. 23

[26] McCormack, R., "The Plight of American Manufacturing". *The American Prospect*, Jan. '10, p. A2

[27] Review of book by S. Johnson & J. Kwak, *Bankers: The Wall Street takeover and the Next Financial Meltdown*, Pantheon. *The Economist*, Mar. 20, '10, p. 91

[28] Goozner, Merrill, "Can We Housebreak Capitalism". *The American Prospect*, May, '05, p. A15

[29] "Enron Conservatives". *The Nation*, Feb. 4, '02, p. 4

[30] Ibid. p. 4

[31] "Never Say You're Sorry", *The Nation*, Feb. 16, '09, p. 8

[32] Greenberger, Machael, *The American Prospect*, June, '10, p. A8.

[33] "Never Say You're Sorry", p. 8

[34] Tim Fernholz, "Cleansing the Temple". *The America Prospect*, June, '10, p. A20

[35] Madrick, Jeff, "How We Were Ruined & What we can do". *The New York Review*, Feb. 12, '09, p. 16

[36] Greider, William, "Establishment Disorder", *The Nation*, Nov. 17, '08

[37] "Watching the Watchers", James Lardner. *The American Prospect*, June, '10, p. A10.

[38] Canova, Timothy; "The Federal Reserve We Need". *The New York Review*, Nov. '10, p. A17

[39] Kuttner, Robert, "Betting the Fed". *The America Prospect*, June, '09, p. 33

[40] Grafstein, Lawrence, "The Real Banker Boondoggle". *The New Republic*, Sept. 23, '09, p. 22

[41] Greider, William, "New York AG Takes on the Banks". *The Nation*, July 18, '11

[42] "A year on". *The Economist*, Sept. 12, '09, p. 91.

[43] Volcker, Paul, "Financial Reform", *The New York Review of Books*, Nov. 24, '11

[44] Freedman, B., "Chairman Greenspan's Legacy". *The New York Review of Books*, Mar. 20, '10.

[45] Freedman, B. Op. Cit.

[46] Madrick, Jeff; *The Nation*, July 10, '10, p. 21

[47] Henwook, Doug, *Wall Street: How it Works and for Whom*. Verso Pr.

[48] Skidelsky, Robert, "The World Finance Crisis & the American Mission". *The New York Review of Books*, July 16, '10, p. 31.

[49] Michael, Klare, "Freedom from Oil". *The Nation*, Apr. 2, '10, p. 12

[51] Wills, Gary; Entangled Giant, *New York Review of Books*, Oct. 8, '09.

[52] Kuttner, R., "The Radical Minimalist", *The American Prospect*, Apr. '09, p. 30

[53] Ibid. p. 30

[54] Krugman, Paul; Wells, Robin; "Where Do We Go From Here?". *New York Review of Books*, Jan. 13, 2011.

[55] "Saving Detroit", *The Economist*, Nov. 15, '08, p. 17.

[56] "Saving the system", *The Economist*, Oct. 11, '08, p. 15

[57] *Wall Street Journal*, Sept. 27, '08,

[58] Berman, Ari, "Disarming the Consumer Cop". *The Nation*, June 20, '11, p. 20

[59] "The Wages of Negligence". *The Economist*, Sept. 25, '10, p. 18

[60] *The Economist*, Oct. 3, '09, p. 13 inside.

[61] "Japans debt problem, *The Economist*, Apr. 10, '10, p. 15

[62] *The Economist*, Nov. 21, '09, p. 13.

[63] *The Economist*, Aug. 3, '02, p. 23

[64] Kuttner, Robert; "The Cost of Financial Favoritism". *The American Prospect*, Mar. '12, p. 26

[65] *The Economist*, Aug. 3, '02, p. 28

[66] *The Economist*, July 3, '10, p. 68

[67] *The Economist*, Mar. 13, '10, p. 36

[68] *The Economist*, July 3, p. 68

[69] The Economist, Sept. 8, '12, p. 67

[70] "Chronic Sickness". *The Economist*, June 2, '01, p. 71

[71] "Early in, early out", *The Economist*, Jan. 24, '09, p. 80.

CHAPTER 26

Economic Development

———

THERE IS NO HOTTER TOPIC among economists than economic development. Why do some economies grow and some not, and what is responsible for growth?

In an article on the subject, William Easterly says, "Yet hundreds of research articles later, we wound up with a surprising end point. We just don't know."[1] Well, I don't have the magic answer either. But we might make a few remarks.

26.1 HISTORY OF WESTERN ECONOMIC DEVELOPMENT

We have a very interesting question to ponder in looking at the evolution of Christianity vs. Islam. From what we read in the Bible, Jesus was a very other-worldly man, a total ascetic. He often said that His was not of this world, but of the Kingdom of God. He spent a good deal of time praying and interacting with ordinary people to provide inspiration to enter the Kingdom of God. It has always been frustrating to me that Jesus of the Bible was very little interested in economics. All we get from the Bible are wispy allusions and indeterminate conclusions on economics. Jesus obviously didn't think that this world was very important. It was salvation and the next world that He was most concerned with.

On the other hand, Muhammad, the prophet who started Islam in the 600s A.C. *was* concerned with earthly matters. At various times he was a businessman, believed in trade, money exchange and other business concepts. Of course, Muhammad was also a deeply religious man and originated religious doctrines that became Islam. And yet, when we come back 1400 years later, we find that the religion started by a total ascetic became the underpinning of the most extensive economic development in the history of the world, and the religion started by a partial businessman extends across the Muslim world and includes many countries that are considered only "developing".

Well, the first thing we have to notice is that these two founder-prophets *did* greatly influence the directions their respective religions took in the first hundreds of years after their inception. Since Jesus was an evangelist, Christianity spread by evangelism and conversion as opposed to conquest. A very interesting question has puzzled religious historians is why did Christianity spread so quickly? For the first hundred years, Christians spread the gospel but remained a relatively small sect in a basically pagan world. However, by 312 A.C., the emperor of the eastern empire, Constantine, declared Christianity the official religion of the Roman Empire.

Another interesting question is, how did the ancient Greek civilization ever get started among a bunch of barbarians in Europe? The Greeks discovered many scientific and mathematical laws. The Romans constructed great marvels of building construction, roads, aqueducts, and various styles of architecture. Even the early civilizations in the Americas and Middle East never evolved modern institutions like democracy, rule of law, property rights, freedoms, etc. that the Greeks created and the later Roman Empire continued. Now, as has often happens in history, religion spreads because an elite segment of society like a king assumes the religion in question. This is top-down spread of religion as Constantine did as well as the later King Henry VIII and others. But in most of the Roman Empire in the first few hundred years A.C., the Roman political and military hierarchy had little interest in Christianity. Nevertheless, Christianity spread like wildfire.

One of the characteristics that both the Greek and Roman empires had in common was that they appealed to all levels of society and recognized that there was some value and some recognition of humanity in each individual. They did have a rather sophisticated democracy for the times. Of course, this concept didn't apply to slaves. But they were never considered citizens. But for citizens, even the lower levels of society were given some semblance of human dignity and value. It was their simple concept of dignity and value of each individual human citizen that may have inspired Jesus himself.

Whether or not Christianity borrowed the concept of universal human dignity from Judaism or from the Roman Empire or both is a moot point. However it came about, Jesus and Christianity amplified this concept. There are many allusions all through the Bible that we are all equal in the eyes of God, and that we all have an equal shot at getting into heaven. Somewhere it says the first shall be last and the last shall be first (if I remember right). Our view is that it is these allusions to *equality* in the eyes of God towards all human beings that made Christianity acceptable and even desirable among the lower levels of the later Roman Empire.

And this may have been why Christianity spread so quickly.

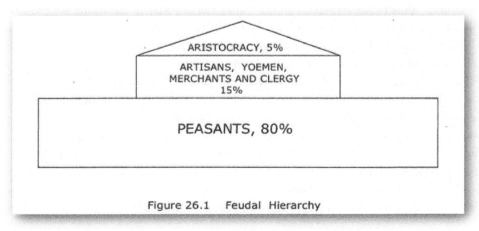

Figure 26.1   Feudal Hierarchy

In fig. 26.1 we have a simple looking house-shaped figure illustrating a very basic structure of European economies after the fall of Rome. The pyramid on top consists of an aristocracy of large landowners. As we go to the larger tracks of land, the numbers get smaller until perched at the top is an incipient nobleman, who in Medieval times was often a local fighting king. The clergy could be considered part of this aristocracy since Church lands were pretty much like the lands of the landowning aristocracy. The middle part of the house is a rectangle of about 15% showing that there was quite a bit of equality among the professionals of the day who were mostly artisans, small farmers, and small traders. The bottom 80% rectangle represents peasants.

Now it is true that for a religion to become completely entrenched in society, it must be acceptable to the elites of that society. Acceptance and adoption of the lower levels of society may be necessary for a religion to spread, but probably not sufficient. A second necessary condition may be acceptance by the most powerful elements of society. Even though the Roman Empire fell around 400 A.C., some of the threads of the political and economic system of the Empire did survive with much variation in different parts of the Empire. The basic economic structure of large landowners presiding over a large population of peasants and artisans was in place, which formed the basis for the subsequent feudal manorial system. However, the shift towards militarism in the medieval period caused a deterioration of the great Roman cities and trade between them. Even the professional classes, merchants, lawyers, builders, artisans, etc. shrunk. With a deterioration of the economic structure of the Roman Empire and its city life, was a slowing of technological progress, which is why the medieval period between about 400 and 1000 is called the *Dark Ages*. Even the Church was loosely organized both hierarchically and doctrinally during these times with many cults appearing with differing views of the trinity and status of Jesus. But it did mirror the basic hierarchically organized economic structure of Roman society that continued and gradually morphed into the later feudal manorial system.

Now even though a necessary condition for a society to adopt a religion is for elites to embrace the religion, it must to taken account that elites in medieval times from 400 to 1000 A.C. were mostly *military* elites. They were not religiously nor economically inspired conquerors. Some became military kings. They were mostly in the business of killing and conquest and not economic development or the spread of religion. The result is that lower levels of medieval society, the top rectangle of artisans, merchants and yeomen and the bottom level of peasantry were able to adopt Christianity fairly much unopposed.

The Dark Age medieval period is difficult to characterize. Francis Fukuyama says there was a period of tribalism for a few hundred years after the fall the Roman Empire.[2] This reflects his focus on political systems to the neglect of economic systems. In my opinion, economic development most often pushes the political system in corresponding directions. Although there were local kings in the period after the Romans, this was not true tribalism. Tribalism as practiced all over the world consists of a population headed by a king or chief and a group of elders who presided over not only social values and practices, but also the political system of laws and morays. Most importantly, instead of private property, it was a primitive *communitarian* system. This was not the case in Europe after 400. There were still large landowners left over from the old Roman Empire who gradually morphed into a feudal system. No tribal people ever made this transition — a fact with enormous ramifications in developing nations to this day.

Some have suggested that the feudal system evolved to mirror the hierarchy of the church. I think this is backwards because the early founders of Church doctrine realized that the appeal of Christianity would be greatly enhanced if the Church mirrored the economic and political hierarchy of existing society and the coalescing feudal system. Because Christianity was monotheistic and its God was called a Lord of the world, it was easy for the early founders of Christian doctrine to mirror the structure of the late Roman Empire and subsequent feudal system with an earthly lord at the top who was the Pope. (Of course, hierarchies were probably the last thing on Jesus' mind.) followed by a thin layer of aristocracy: cardinals and bishops. They were followed by the analog of artisans, vassals, and small farmers which were the local priests. Nuns were analogous to peasants under feudalism. (Nuns also made sure that none of the other nuns got none.) By conveniently stressing the tone of the Bible, which was to put all the emphasis on the *next* world as Jesus preached, the medieval system led by the nobility in tandem with the Church, could discourage change as being a threat to the hierarchical structure of the economy and a distraction from life's purpose, which was to enter the Kingdom of God. This tandem was able to keep itself solidly in power for hundreds of years.

Of course, Judaism also had the concept of one God. If Jesus had never lived, Judaism might have become the religion of the later Roman Empire. However, Judaism was weak in the one area that the Roman Empire and feudalism needed, which was a strong concept of hierarchy with a king perched on top. The early Jews were monotheistic and equality conscious, but they lacked a strong and *universal* concept of a king. They had kings, of course, but they were kings of the Jews, not kings of the universe. Jesus very insightfully saw that if he was going to start a religion, even if after he died, He'd better have some appeal to the concept of a Roman Emperor. This might be why He stressed the *universal* Kingdom of God.

Starting around 1000, trade, cities, professionals and economic structure picked up again mirroring the economic structure of the Roman Empire. The period between about 1000 A.C. to about 1400 is called the Middle Ages. Kings, large landowners and knights seemed to have come to the conclusion that fighting and conquest weren't all that it was cracked up to be. The emphasis shifted from military prowess to *economic* prowess. The large landowners began to see themselves more as a class both economically and culturally as opposed to a feuding bunch of fighters and conquerors. But the feudal economic system that evolved still mirrored the economic structure of the Roman Empire wherein large landowners from the Roman Empire increasingly marked themselves off as a hereditary aristocratic class. Their land areas were called *manors*. I don't know why historians don't see more of a similarity between the Roman Empire and the later Feudal system. Both had an aristocracy that controlled land and agriculture. The artisans, builders and small farmers who were the professionals of the day remained at the same level in society under feudalism as under the Romans. Finally, the bottom 80% were peasants who had been the daily workers and slaves under the Romans. An important difference was that manors were more self-contained financially and economically, whereas cities of the Roman Empire engaged in considerable trade. Without large cities, there wasn't as important a modern-day professional class on manors as in Roman cities.

The owners of manors were called *nobility*, who gave themselves titles like Lord, Duke, Baron, etc. The lord of the manor was basically a king of his little fief. They were less than 1% of the population. Although you could say manor lands were partially communally owned, the lord of the manor controlled and, in effect, owned the land of his manor. They built large manor houses and castles. If you visit the countryside in Europe, you can visit many of the old manor houses and castles, some of which have been turned into museums. Since they were intact self-sufficient production units, most of them were isolated in the countryside.

The next 4% could be called the *gentry* who had titles and sometimes had smaller manors. The segment of the gentry that did the fighting were called Knights. We will call the combined nobility, gentry, and clergy, the *aristocracy*, which might have been about 5% of the population. The clergy had approximately the same social and economic status as the lower aristocracy. The manor system shifted the core of the economy from large cities during the Roman Empire to manor life. But although manors were large tracks of agricultural and livestock land, they also had small villages that resembled small cities with a semi-independent group of artisans, yeoman farmers, villains and vassals and a small group of professionals of the day. They were about 15% of the population. The remaining 80% were peasants and laborers who did agricultural and construction work on the manors. The hierarchy on a manor cooperated and mutually supported the hierarchy of the medieval Church.

Along with the coalescing of a manorial feudal system around 1000, a small merchant class started up around the same time although much of the trade was local and manufacturing involved building construction and small farm and home accessories. Merchants at this time were mostly itinerant peddlers. Now even though cities went into decline with the fall of the Roman Empire, they began a slow rise after 1000 A.C. Because of the head start southern European cities had during the Roman Empire, mercantilism (Commercial Capitalism) thrived best in southern Europe for a while near the heart of the Catholic Church. A long period of urbanization created what is called a *Bourgeoisie* consisting of artisans, merchants, professionals, and small manufacturers, mostly in textiles, and eventually became the *Commercial Revolution* of the 1400s. This was a very tiny class at first and their cities were not much more than complex villages. Trade and commerce, especially in Southern Europe, created wealth which the Church was in line to get in on. But as bad as some of the things the Church did like crusades, they at least used a good deal of its wealth to build architectural marvels, the great cathedrals all ever Europe. In my opinion, a measure of civilization is its architecture.

An important factor was the great plagues of the 1300s. This wiped out a third of the populations of Europe. Because there was a resulting dearth of labor, the value of labor went up, which meant that ordinary people could buy more goods and services. Some economic historians give credit to the plagues and resulting labor shortage for the great expansion of the economy of the 1400s and subsequent centuries of the Commercial Revolution. A lesson should be learned from this, but of course, the modern system mind has no interest in learning anything. It's the mind of a dinosaur that simply self-seeks in the short run.

As time went on, many merchants became stationary organizers of business in general. The merchant class was slowly evolving a Capitalist model that in addition to commerce and trade was slowly adding small manufacturing to its economic activity. This is a more solid basis of an economy because it requires stationary physical plant. Even physical Church buildings were located on Feudal manors who could provide protection and support. In turn, the Church's ties to the economy of the manor system enabled the ethic of the Church to inform economic development. The ties between the Church and the Feudal system provided a foundation for economic development and a feudal ethic to support it.

As international commerce increased in the 1200s and 1300s based to a great extent on small manufacturing, more sophisticated means of finance, money and credit were required. This would involve high finance Capitalism that needs large financial institutions hierarchically organized, which can be accommodated best by the hierarchical aspect of the Catholic Church. It was in *Southern* Europe, mostly Italy that the great commercial banks evolved in the 1200s and 1300s.

Even though the institutions like money, banking and contractual trade left over from the Roman Empire were quite skeletal, Italy had a head start when the expansion of city life took off in the 1300s. Great trading cities of Florence, Genoa, and Venice flourished and became intact city-states. As time went on, technology and manufacturing became an increasing role in merchant capitalism.

To protect themselves from antagonism with the manorial system and its armed aristocracy, walls were built around most commercial cities parts of which can be seen today. The aristocracy was forced to turn from a paternalistic family model of the old feudalism to a money/rent/wages capitalist model. By providing an alternative to feudal life for Southern European peasants, the feudal aristocracy had to lighten up its domination of the peasant class. Peasants were able to hook their wagon to the political progress carried forward by the merchant class who provided even peasants some degree of rights and some recognition of dignified humanity.

Also, what enabled the merchant class to get a foothold in a basically feudal world order was that it was really operating in the interstices of feudal society. Trading bases were located near rivers and seas. Feudalism, which consisted of agriculture and small crafts, was mostly located in the countryside over large areas of agricultural land. So as cities grew along waterways after 1100, Commercialism could develop without being in direct conflict with the feudal system, at least with regards to land use, property and occupation.

The merchant class and Bourgeoisie class grew in importance in the 1200s and 1300s and attracted people from the old feudal manors. We are estimating that by 1400, the economic output of the economic units operating with a capitalist model in both rural and urban economies might have equaled the output of the manor system, which is why we have settled on about 1400 as the beginnings of the Commercial Revolution. I'm not sure of this date, but since I'm not a historian, I have more leeway in picking dates easy to remember.

The Catholic Church who by feudal times had allied themselves with the feudal aristocracy became manors within manors. It mirrored the feudal hierarchy and together produced a relatively strong political/cultural/religious unit as well as an economic unit. But here again, we find what seems like coincidence because the Church was making some of its own rumblings. If society was going to undergo a slight reorganization centering around cities and a merchant class and trade involving contracts and even laws, perhaps the Church might take this opportunity to clean up its act and get into the spirit of the times as well. With the threat of a new order looming, perhaps the Church also saw an opportunity to assert a little more power in the Medieval relationship between the Church and the secular.

The moral tenor the Church had deteriorated during the Dark Ages with all kinds of clerical abuses. But because the Church was a hierarchy with a Pope on top, a very strong-willed Pope Gregory VII was able to reform the Church in the 1000s and codify a system of laws so as to assert its position as a moral guide to society. He turned to Justinian Law from the Roman Empire for guidance. He was able to establish dominance and independence in certain areas over the feudal hierarchy. After his reforms, the Church had the power of investiture (appointing bishops and cardinals), not present during the Dark Ages. And very cleverly, he stopped the practice of priests marrying and having children so as to direct peoples' allegiance from kin to Church. The new Church doctrine specified celibacy.[*]

In accordance with his emphasis on political development, Fukuyama says, "the rule of law … was the product not of economic forces but of religious ones".[3] Well, yes, but the only reason the Church was able to establish this rule of law and other political powers is that it had adapted to the feudal *economic* system from which it obtained economic support and to which it owed some self-interested doctrine like the divine right of kings. And the feudal economic system still had remnants of a rule of law left over from the Roman Empire. The church, being in the morality business could use these vestiges of Roman law to take the lead in public morality, which is the rule of law, and establish a bridgehead leading the

---

[*] F. Fukayama (*The Origins of Political Order*) says the Church was able to establish a rule of law because of celibacy instituted by Pope Gregory VII. This is pretty funny actually. The reality is that all through the Dark Ages, priests had gotten into the habit of getting more action than the rest of menfolk who were not in as good a position to dispense a seat in Heaven. This resulted in an uptick in the IQ of Europeans relative to the rest of the world, and may be responsible for the explosion of science and technology among Europeans in the Middle Ages. Priests were still doing pretty well in the old Italian neighborhood my parents grew up in. Their mistake was not sticking with girls.

feudal/Church tandem. Evidence for this is that without a feudal system as a means of guidance and support, Muslim Caliphs and Sultans were never able to establish a universal and national rule of law.

Just as in families, there was continuous squabbling between the Church and the feudal aristocracy and kings all through history till the modern era. But the Concordat of Worms in 1122 sorted out the respective powers of the feudal kings and the Church. Since the Church was a partial creation of the feudal system, differences were papered over. They were never important enough to disrupt or destroy the tight cultural, political, and economic tandem of the feudal system and the Church. In fact, when technological progress picked up later in the Reformation, the tandem was strong enough to be able to resist technological and consequently economic progress in Southern Europe.

Islam was a very different story. A small local merchant class did evolve in Muslim countries after the 600s A.C., consisting of merchants, traders and money-handlers. The lack of a feudal system in the Muslim world at first gave their merchant class equal opportunity and free rein to expand. Since Muhammad had a great interest in business and trade, Islam's evolution did mirror the trade and business aspect of their societies. The equality of opportunity in the Muslim world unimpeded by an entrenched aristocracy led to economic progress in money and trade and a flowering of technological advancement, which led the Islamic countries dominance in the western world by the 1100s and 1200s. This is in contrast to European feudalism that was stuck in the Dark Ages. Muslims excelled in mathematics and we have inherited their number system. They led the advance of technology with the invention of various navigational instruments like the astrolabe. Through their superior navigational abilities, they pretty much dominated trade throughout the Mediterranean world, especially near the end of their first 500 hundred years. In fact, Muslim boats were often able to subdue English boats and enslave English crews during this period, a fact that might have influenced the English system mind to join in on the invasion of Iraq a thousand years later.

Leaders in the new system of business and trade did not have to fight for the rights against a feudal order because there was no feudal order to oppose. Also, religion in Muslim societies did not have a feudal *economic* system from which to obtain support. A possible explanation for this is that in the Middle Ages between 1000 and 1400 A.C., economies in Muslim countries consisted mostly of itinerant trade which is a more peripatetic endeavor. There was less development of manufacturing and so less development of a physical basis for economic activity.

Thus, Islam did not form a tight bond with economic and political hierarchies as occurred in Europe, and economic ethics may not have had to develop in coordination with a religious doctrine. To this day we see that much of the strict laws of Islam like Sharia law are out of sync with modern life and modern economic institutions. They never had to slowly evolve in lock-step with economic developments as Christianity did. Additionally, without a pope to converge religious thinking, nor strong ties to economic development and economic hierarchies over the centuries, Islam has splintered into any number of groups all having their own versions of Islam. There is Shiism, Sunniism, Sufism, Salafism, Wahhabism, etc.

Various Caliph/Sultan administrations did try to establish strong central governments that are essential in creating a national rule of law. They realized that you have to wean people away from tribalism and kinship that was so extensive in the world of the day. So they tried to establish a religion-based political system just as in the Holy Roman Empire. But there was no Muslim Pope with sufficient power to establish a uniform national rule of law or national institutions.

Thus, instead of a religion and a feudal society marching in lock-step into the future, Muslim authoritarians turned to expansion through conquest. This required effective armies. They solved this problem by instituting soldier-slaves. The very best of young boys, the brightest and most fit were stolen from their parents around the empire and indoctrinated into the hierarchical administrations and great conquering armies. What this meant, however, is that instead of an aristocracy evolving in the Muslim countries being composed of *economic* elites, their aristocracy was more composed of *military* elites and garrison controllers rather than economic landowners. This has important ramifications.

When an aristocracy is composed of *economic* elites, a more organic society evolves with a system mind. And a system mind will look out for its interests and power in sustainable economic stability. This is how the feudal economic system grew in Western Europe as the aristocracy worked hand-in-glove with the church to expand power and control over all of society. From this evolved the nation state.

Another important development is that starting around 1000 and picking up speed with the Commercial Revolution was the emergence of a strong monarch in Europe. A king is a national institution and can organize armies, collect taxes, support a stable currency, and coordinate a system of courts — all things a merchant class needs. So there was a natural alliance between the merchant class and the monarchy that was often at odds with the aristocracy. That's why kings grew in importance and power as the Commercial Revolution progressed. The competition between the monarchy and the aristocracy benefited all layers of society especially the merchant class. However, with national armies at their disposal, kings were able to start and engage in larger and larger wars that benefited nobody. They also brought about the long period of colonialism that extended into the 20th century. But monarchs being national institutions opened the way for parliaments to evolve all over Europe which mostly represented the interests of the merchant class. But eventually kings began to abuse their powers and wound up losing their heads in the English and French Revolutions.

In the later Middle Ages, the constant striving for status and success among the rising Merchant Class climaxed in the *Renaissance* of the 1500s and 1600s mostly in Italy, when culture, art and music greatly blossomed. The Renaissance was supported and financed by the merchant class who were trying to earn social status through support of the arts. Sometimes as in England, money could be used to basically buy oneself into the aristocracy. But even though the core of the Commercial Revolution in Southern Europe was high finance conducted by large banks, after a while technology began to become the foundation for economic expansion. And because Northern Europe was farther away from the core of the Church, technology could better gain a foothold there. Where the Church was strong in southern Europe, it had the power to squelch progress. We know the story of poor Galileo. After the 1500s, Northern Europe took the lead in technology which led to faster economic progress. The merchant class in the north along with a small manufacturing base also urbanized just as it had in the south.

As the Commercial Revolution proceeded, a Bourgeoisie class grew in numbers and strength. It included not only the merchant class, but artisans, small manufacturers and a small professional class like doctors and lawyers — people of the "lesser sort" as they would say, not from the feudal aristocracy. The Bourgeoisie economic system had little in common with the old Feudal manorial system and began to diverge from the dominant Catholic political/cultural system. The old nobility was gradually forced into the Capitalist model. Traditional feudalism's days were numbered. As the Bourgeoisie became more conscious of their class, they saw that it was in their interests to establish political institutions and practices that would allow upward mobility in economic and political power. They needed rights to property and an independent court system to enforce contracts and equality before the law as well as freedoms of speech and assembly. If we were equal in the eyes of God, we ought to be equal in the eyes of the law. As we pointed out in Ch. 21, all of this progress was greatly aided by the existential thinking that the Reformation encouraged. These developments required a whole new ethic and system of values. The ground was laid for a change in direction of the old Church by two events that weakened the hold on the cultural/religious doctrine of the old Church. King Phillip IV of France had a run-in with the Pope in 1302, and Marsilium of Padua elaborated a new political theory proclaiming the state as the source of political legitimacy as opposed to the divine right of kings.

The old Church simply could not change fast enough to meet the needs of the growing Capitalist system. In fact, the Church viewed the new merchant class with suspicion and the system of money, banking and finance with antagonism. But this is the beauty and success of Christianity. All through western civilization since Roman times, there had always been a symbiotic relationship between the economic system and some version of Christianity. During the Middle Ages when the feudal system was supreme, there was an emphasis on the *essential* differences in classes, with the aristocracy given its essential place of dominance in society, and the peasants essentially of a "lower sort". The Church reflected this essentialism with the use of Platonic categories and Aristotelian forms. Church doctrine emphasized essentialist spirituality, the soul, and abstract places like the kingdom of God, heaven and hell. But with the tiny beginnings of the Commercial Revolution in the 1100s, Church doctrine and practices became more materially and physically oriented to reflect the introduction of money, produced goods, and trade of the new economic system. The physical body and blood of Christ was emphasized, along with the Resurrection. Body parts of saints were copied into icons, and there were rituals involving the bones of dead saints. Author Carolyn Bynum has written extensively on this phenomenon.[4] This put increasing emphasis on the physical world and this included behavior especially commercial behavior. This led finally to the existentialism of the Reformation which we'll get to presently.

Also, even though Muhammad got Islam off to a good start and encouraged business and trade, the lack of a code of honor and a feudal ethic began to show through after a while. Trade between Europe and the Middle East often entailed dealing with strangers. With the long distances involved, there has to be a certain amount of trust in business dealings and a reliance on contracts and some form of agreed upon money or the system would collapse and trade would become impossible. The Merchant class that arose from a feudal system had a code of honor and the concept of *trust*. It wasn't so much laws that lubricated the wheels of commerce the merchant class was engaged in, but the moral tenor of Christian doctrine it inherited stressing a sense of honor and trust in *contracts* like the famous Italian *commenda* that enabled them to conduct long distance trade. Even though western Europeans were still barbarians during the great civilizations all over the world, what enabled them to forge ahead of the rest of the world was one basic instrument: the *contract.* The ever increasing trade over longer distances was a hallmark of the Commercial Revolution.

But in the Muslim empire, without a preceding Roman Empire, a feudal-based economic system did not evolve that would encompass the majority of people into an organic economic system with a system mind. Too much of their aristocracy was in the hands of military elites. People might accept the prevailing religion because religion explains people's worlds, but not so much the hierarchical central governments that Caliphs and Sultans were trying to establish. This leaves the majority of people identifying not with a central government or even a feudal aristocracy based on economics, but with their tribe and kin. This prevented the consolidation of the rule of law based on a national moral system.

Also, the loose ties between Islam and economic elites and no feudal system to inject a moral code, meant that when trade and business got more complicated the 1300s and 1400s involving long distances, Muslim peoples did not have as strong a moral code with its concept of trust to conduct advanced business, contractual trade and banking in accordance with a code of honor as the Christian merchants had. Rules of the game remained local which often results in corruption and mistrust. And so with the beginnings of the Commercial Revolution, Western economies expanded and flourished while countries of Islam remained pretty much arrested in place for the next 800 years to the present day where we see less economic development in the Muslim world than you might expect from a very intelligent and energetic people. Without central governments based on the economic progress of an organic system involving all levels of society, Sultanates and Caliphates were eventually conquered themselves by the Ottoman Empire, which in turn was easily subdued by European powers in the age of colonialism.

Even the consolidation that occurred in the Ottoman Empire starting in the 1500s was not enough to overcome the momentum build up over that past thousand years of a lack of an economic base to prevent the splintering of religious doctrine with a number of sects. The Ottoman Empire was based on finding the "best and the brightest" for administration and important economic nodes as opposed to a hereditary aristocracy in Europe, especially England. This should have enabled more economic and technological development than actually happened. In my opinion, what kept the Ottoman Empire back was the lack of an economic order like feudalism working in tandem with the Muslim religion that could lead to a coherent national system of laws and institutions, as was the case all along in Europe. Without such an order, a strong ethic based on trust and honor did not evolve as under feudalism. To this day, corruption is always greater in Muslim countries than in the West. This greatly impedes economic growth and progress.

Even in modern day 21th century Islam, we see a divergence between economic and religious/cultural developments. Instead of people like our founding fathers leading the way towards modernity, who were very aware of economic considerations and drew up a constitution accordingly, leading Muslim thinkers were able to maintain religiosity as the center of attention independent from economic considerations. The most important thinker in this regard was Sayyid Qutb.[5] He emphasized establishing extreme Islam in Muslim countries without regard for economic development. He suggested that the details of the structure of society would fall into place. That's why people have deemed Communism as a kind of religion. Marx did the same thing. Once the "dictatorship of the Proletariat" was established, he didn't bother with the details. It would all fall into place. Compare this with Adam Smith, the father of Capitalism, who wrote very boring books going into every minute detail as to how Liberal Capitalism would be structured.

In the present day, even after the Arab spring, we see things evolving in Muslim countries based on tribalism and religion. It will be very difficult in these circumstances to evolve a strong central government capable of establishing a rule of law and liberal rules of the economic game. This is going to be the most severe social and political problem facing the world this century. The Bush administration and even Obama exacerbated these problems by using *conquest* just as early Islam did to supposedly spread our system into Iraq and Afghanistan. This has set the example to the Muslim world that you solve problems with violence and killing. And just on schedule, there has been no legitimate economic aristocracy based on a viable political system and a national system mind. They write constitutions which their Ayatollahs and secular leaders will ignore just like in China and Russia, all following the example set by the US where 9 Ayatollahs make decisions without the slightest regards to the meaning of the Constitution. Consequently, when we leave those countries, they will revert right back to tribalism and sectarian violence following the example Bush and Obama set. Even British imperialism was better than this. Alongside their armies of conquest, they at least set up responsible government administrations on which their former colonies patterned their own institutions when the British got thrown out.

Muslim countries have a double challenge to not only converge religious doctrine of their various sects, but to coordinate this convergence with the needs of viable economic development. If they make no progress in this regard, they will fall into sectarian violence, political chaos, and retarded economic development.

In Europe, with the growth of the merchant class and the spread of market economic systems, the Catholic Church in trying to maintain its traditional doctrine and beliefs was losing touch with economic developments. A growing gap developed between the values and doctrine of the old Church, and the needs of the new economic system. This opened the door to a new brand of Christianity that would meet the needs of a growing and increasingly important Bourgeoisie class. And sure enough, whenever a gap opens because of economic developments, some cultural, social, or religious movement will emerge to fill it. Here again, Christianity had devices in its little bag of tricks that could meet the needs of the growing merchant class and its Capitalist economic system. As a reaction to what was perceived as corruption and apostasy in the Catholic Church, various Protestant religions sprung up led by various reformers like Martin Luther and John Calvin in the early 1500's, and later, John Wesley in the 1700's. This is the source of the Protestant *Reformation*, which gathered momentum in the 1600s. Even though the Renaissance was the culmination of southern Europe's economic success, its existential thinking was running headlong against the essentialist thinking of the old Church. And because there was greater opportunity for technological progress in northern Europe, it was here where the existential thinking of the Renaissance would take root. This was the foundation for the Protestant Reformation.

Protestants put the emphasis on change and progress achieved through business and technology. By tweaking the doctrines of early Christian doctrine with its *equality* aspect, early Protestants were able to use long established Christianity for their own use in going into the religion business with the support of the rising Bourgeoisie. Protestants came up with an extremely successful PR campaign that the way to tell who God preferred was to look at how much worldly success a person achieved. This was called the *Protestant Ethic*. It was a great departure from the old Church, where going into business to make money had no meaning. There had been reformers all through Christian history from the very beginnings. However, most of them wound up being toasted, like Joan of Arc. Protestant religions were able to get a foothold in the Christian community because they now had the economic backing of the capitalistic Commercial Revolution.

The Protestant movement was gradually molding itself to fit hand-in-glove with the evolving Capitalist system just as the early Church molded itself to work in tandem with the feudal system. By accommodating the professional class and rising industrial class where production was the core of an economy, the Protestant movement was able to grow the economies of northern Europe at a faster rate than in Southern Europe which was stuck in the view that banking and finance were the core of the economy. Over the next four hundred years, western society progressed politically and economically to the present day where western Christian societies lead the world in economic, political and social progress.

It is interesting to contrast the mode of thinking of the old feudal/Church system with the new thinking of the growing merchant class supported by the Protestant religion. The feudal/Church system employed the somewhat essentialist thinking of Aquinas of Aristotilian forms, whereas the Reformation involved the *existential* thinking led by Marcilius and William of Occam.

ESSENTIALIST THOMAST VIEW	EXISTENTIAL SECULAR VIEW
Catholic Church	Protestantism
Nobility/Aristocracy	State/Parliaments
Natural Law	Secular Law
Communal Property	Private Property
Social Obligations	Contracts

Feudalism relied on the essentialism of classes in society willed by God and supported by the Church. The natural law enforced by the nobility of the feudal system was replaced by the existential thinking necessary to pass secular laws in accordance with the growing needs of the Commercial Capitalist system. Of course, the social obligations that accompanied natural law were replaced by the formal contract to describe relations and transactions between individuals and institutions. This had a definite downside. Even though the divine right of kings inherent in natural law put the lower orders to a definite disadvantage, there were still social obligations that provided a floor on the rights of even the peasant class. These mutual obligations were part of the *essential* structure of society. This was possible partly because property of the feudal system was somewhat communally owned.

Now, the existential secular laws of parliaments involving contracts and private property did benefit the merchant class and made possible the rapid growth of Commercial Capitalism with its accompanying technological progress. Also, many of our basic rights and freedoms came as a result of ordinary citizens led by the merchant class petitioning parliaments. However, the old aristocracy took advantage of these trends to water down the social responsibilities of the old feudal ethic. What resulted could be called *neofeudalism*. Many concepts of the secular ethic were adopted which led to the enclosure movement. The old feudal manor gradually morphed into the plantation concept with a return to the slavery of the Greeks and Romans. It got worse with the Industrial Revolution of the 1800s. Horrible factory conditions appeared with no economic rights at all for the working class because there were no longer any *essential* social obligations between classes. But for a while, society did seem to be better off in general with the rise of the Merchant class and the existential mode of thinking of the Reformation.

Although Southern Europe took off first with its large banks and a national money base, when Commercial Capitalism began to thrive in Northern Europe, there was a reaction to the new Protestant cultural system. This was called the *Counter*-reformation in which the Catholic church fought back the inroads of Protestantism and maintained the dominance of the Catholic Church in Southern Europe. But because economic development in Southern Europe was arrested at the stage in which only finance, money and banking were dominant, this part of Europe went into slow decline relative to the north where Commercial Capitalism gradually merged into Industrial Capitalism of the 19th century.

26.2 THE NEW CHRISTIANITY

In my opinion, not enough credit is given by historians to the Roman Empire and Christianity for the economic and political progress experienced by western societies. It had some bad times, and some bad practices like the crusades. But when all is said and done, it had tools in its conceptual arsenal to meet the needs of whatever developments were occurring in the economic and political systems of the western world. Our house illustration with its triangular top and rectangular bases has been able to appeal to both hierarchical and equality-oriented needs of societies. When Christianity needed equality to appeal to ordinary people in order to win them over to Christianity, there was the equality aspect of the Bible wherein we're all equal in the eyes of God. When it needed to appeal to hierarchies as during feudalism, it took the concept of an all-powerful Lord and barons down to yeomen, artisans, and finally peasants to match the hierarchical structure from the Pope down through priests and nuns. When a hierarchical system of high finance and banking was needed, it supported the initial Commercial Revolution in Southern Europe. Subsequently, when it needed to accommodate the merchant and Bourgeoisie classes in the 1500s and 1600s, it again relied on the equality aspects of Christ's teachings in the Protestant Reformation. Finally, when Industrial Capitalism began its rise after 1800, the Protestant ethic gave every person an equal shot at economic success and relied on the ethic of the old church that was conducive to capital and technological progress. As frosting on the cake, Christianity had the concept of the trinity. So they always had a Godly entity waiting in the wings who could be given specific assignments in support of various specific economic initiatives.

But things didn't stop there. When Ronald Reagan was elected who proceeded to attack the very core of a Democratic Capitalist society with large hierarchical corporations in bed with political animals in Washington, there was Christianity marching right in step with the reintroduction of Economic Socialism. Essentialist thinking was back in vogue after the post-war decades, which energized the emotions of aggression, acquisitiveness and greed. There is nothing that more graphically shows the change in our economic system under Reagan than the changes that occurred in Christianity that fit hand in glove with Economic Socialism.

The new Christians were again evangelists who used the new medium of television to spread their message. Their message was exactly what was needed to support the new economic system consisting of an economy of large corporate nodes and a practice of sending most wealth and power to the top 20%, which is covered up by continuous war. The new religion is now power and money, which takes precedence over the values and lifestyles of the old traditional religions of bygone days. Churches of the traditional religions began to close down in droves. Christianity was back again using its hierarchical structure to support an all-powerful king atop an economic hierarchy and an ever-increasing *un*equal society that Economic Socialism strives for. It even appeals to peasants who love the one-liners served up by neoconservative propaganda outlets. We are once again in a feudal period, one that encompasses not only modern business and trade practices but the Industrial Revolution as well. Let's look at the new Christianity.

If we look at words ending in 'ian', you would think it means having the values and policies of the person in question. A Jeffersonian democrat is someone who has the political values of Thomas Jefferson. A Kantian philosopher is someone who believes in the philosophical theories of Emmanuel Kant. So you would think a Christian would be someone who has the values and beliefs of *Christ*. Wrong. I recently made friends with a preacher who got me to reread the Bible, which, since I'm not an overly religious person, I hadn't done since I was a kid. It basically relates many stories of Christ's life on earth: what He did, what He believed, and the examples He set. It's an amazing comparison with the modern so-called Christian leader. In fact, no matter what the story in the Bible is, the modern Christian leader preaches the exact *opposite* and sets an exact *opposite* example.

Where Christ went around in simple robes, the modern Christian leader wears 5 thousand dollar suits. Where Christ went around on foot or a simple donkey, the Christian leader rides around in 100 thousand dollar limousines. Where Christ ministered medical attention to the poor, especially children of the poor, the neoChristian leader votes to deny medical attention to people, especially children. Where Christ's favorite people were children who he protected by saying that the sins of the father shall not be bequeathed to the sons, the neoChristian leader supports politicians who steal *trillions* from the children of this country. Where the Bible deems the greatest of God's creation is the human being whose blueprints are our DNA, the neoChristian leader supports politicians who pollute the environment causing enormous genetic damage to the DNA blueprints of God's greatest creation. Where Christ chased the money-changers out of the temple, the neoChristian leader makes money into the new God, supporting political policies that make grabbing more and more money. Finally, whenever the emperor makes a private war in some faraway land where thousands die, the neoChristian *joins* the emperor in Washington and cheers on his invasion and conquest; whereas Christ was put to death by the Roman emperor for being too peace-loving. When the Bush administration invaded and conquered Iraq, killing tens of thousands in the process, the new evangelical "Christian" cheered the whole bloody mess on, exactly the opposite of what Christ taught. We have to realize that modern neoChristianity has absolutely nothing to do with Christianity. We could call them God-is-a-dummy Christians. They think God is too stupid to see the contradictions between the teachings and examples set by Christ and that of the modern neoChristian leader.

What has happened in the modern period is that religion and in particular, the new Christianity led by the modern-day evangelical has been molded and warped into a new religion tailor-made to the modern Economic Socialist system. Money is the new God, and the agglomeration of raw *power*, economically, politically and militarily, the example that is set and worshipped. When the unit of production was the family, the Church was needed to maintain values, beliefs, and lifestyles that were conducive to the maintenance of the intact family. But in modern times, it is great sport on TV programming to *diminish* the status of Christian churches, especially the old Catholic Church. The old Christian religions and their old traditions and values are under constant attack by the corporate media because it is those religions that preached values and lifestyles that supported the maintenance of the intact family.

Without the need of our modern day economic system to maintain the family as the unit of production, Christianity, especially evangelical Christianity, does not have an anchor to all the traditional medieval values and is free to wander all over the place in their doctrine and practices. And where they wind up is practices that have as an end result the destruction of the family, which is exactly the way you make the lone individual the unit of production; this is what the economic system wanted all along. Marriage and family are no longer needed, and are actually a distraction from the all-mighty job. And the new Christian churches have been reworked and redesigned to support the whole game by promoting identification with money, power and conquest, which keeps energy in the bottom of the brain.

26.3 ECONOMIC DEVELOPMENT IN DEVELOPING COUNTRIES

From what we have seen in the development of the west, it may be possible for a Capitalist economy to evolve a system of laws to guide economic transactions. *But it does not come with its own ethic.* One can wonder if a system of rules of law could ever evolve in an economy that was not informed by an economic system like feudalism supported by a religious moral code. If we look around the world, what we mostly see are countries without a feudal past having great trouble getting Capitalism going. And this is the case all over the underdeveloped world, in Africa, the Muslim countries, to some extent India, all of which never had a feudal past. And where is all the economic expansion going on? Mostly in Asia where there is a strong feudal past. Not being a historian, I don't know a great deal about Chinese and Japanese feudalism. The real mystery of Chinese feudalism is that it seems to have organized itself almost spontaneously without a Roman Empire in the Zhou and Qin dynasties, BC. We have all heard about the famous Japanese feudalism as exemplified by the Samurai with its strong sense of moral duty and code of honor.

Russia is a special case which we'll devote a chapter to. Russia had a form of feudalism but it didn't have the same strict codes of honor and morality as European feudalism. It was unfettered gangster feudalism. This why the Russian economy in the present day is stumbling along, greatly impeded by massive amounts of corruption.

Now a great question would be whether any economic system could be devised that wasn't kept upright by a strong religious system of moral values. What we do know is that feudalism was the economic foundation upon which Capitalist economic development was built. And feudalism was kept intact by a very strong Christian religion which kept a moral code alive. Even when you try to introduce an economic system of money, trade, and industrial production into non-feudal countries, it is shredded to pieces by massive amount of corruption.

Capitalism is a wonderful economic system, constantly introducing new technology and new products into marketplaces for high standard of living. But its weakness is that it lacks its own system of morality and ethics. Adam Smith who was a *moral* philosopher, was probably motivated by a desire to attach a moral element to the Capitalist economic system that he was explaining. Without something like a feudal foundation from the past, Capitalism introduced in countries of the modern world degenerates into corruption, waste and tremendous inequality and eventually leads to National Socialism. This is what we see in all over the developing world.

In an important review, Jared Diamond reviews a book called *Why Nations Fail* by two authors who, along with Diamond are among world's experts in development.[6] But every time they come up with a factor that explains the widely varying pace of development, you think of counterexamples. They say that civilization started in the fertile crescent in the Middle East because there were domesticatable plants and animals. But why did they fall behind later. Diamond maintains that temperate zones are good for development because there is less year around pests and less communicable diseases. But then why didn't the countries in the Middle East temperate zone forge ahead. The authors bring up the need for economic and political institutions. Well China had made considerable progress in forming institutions based on merit no less. But where did they go after the Ming dynasty.

I think there is a very overlooked factor that sent Europe ahead of the rest of the world. What really creates economic expansion as we have explained are technological bubbles based on breakthrough technology, which are created by a rare combination of genius ability, the right emotional makeup and a culture that encourages people to think outside the box. Except for basics, education has little to do with it. Many of the leaders of our IT revolution never graduated from college. The great robber barons of the 1800s who build huge industrial empires had almost no education beyond grade school.

And where does genius ability come from? It comes from a small number of people like the Steve Jobs of the world who have the exceptional talent necessary to create technological breakthroughs. You could write the names of the people who created the Information Technology bubble in the last 30 years on a postage stamp. England seems to have produced an abundance of such people all through the Commercial Revolution. What explains this kind of genius ability?

An overlooked factor in this regard is the concept of *assortive mating*. This is a biological concept which basically means that people of like abilities will mate. At the top end, this entails that people with lots of talent or intelligence will find each other and have children. But because of the way statistics works, this has the effect of producing some offspring with even more talent than the parents; and once in a while a child prodigy is born. These are the people who have the genius ability to create technological breakthroughs.

If this is the case, we might be able to explain why Europeans especially produced this kind of talent. I'll give my crazy theory. I think that the European aristocracy always felt threatened because their lives were enormously better than the majority of people. And the threat grew with the Commercial Revolution starting in the 1400s and the growing merchant class. As a response to this situation, males in the aristocracy might have sought out talented and bright women to marry and have children with so that their children would have the brains to hold on to their economic position in society. This is a very incisive example of assortive mating and the results are very apparent in English history.

If we look at the men who created the major scientific and technological breakthroughs all through the Reformation, they most often came from the aristocracy. Sir Isaac Newton, Sir Robert Boyle, Lord Kelvin, James Clerk Maxwell, Bertrand Russell come to mind. And even when they didn't, they usually came from the Bourgeoisie who were also motivated to maintain their economic position in society. As an aside, the US inherited this practice from the English, which is why Americans have invented new scientific and technological breakthroughs way out of proportion to our population.

Assortive mating might have been a factor in the glory days of the Muslim world. But the lack of a Roman Empire and its subsequent evolution prevented economic and technological advancement, which has created an incendiary situation in the Muslim world. The combination of intelligence and talent with a lack of economic development creates a very angry world view. And with the continual rubbing it in the faces of the Muslim world by the west over centuries of imperialism, it is easy to see why terrorism would emerge among young Muslim men. The answer, of course, would be to leave them alone and allow them to develop at their own pace, which is what China is doing. But as we shall explain later, it is in the interests of Economic Socialism in the west to have continual war.

But there may be a worse causal element in the slow pace of development in many parts of the world. The suggestion here is that the system mind in the west wanting to send economies eventually towards National Socialism, may actually be sabotaging efforts to further development. There are many commentators in the west who try to fashion a foreign policy towards economic development. But the system mind overwhelms any such attempts because it has a strong motivation to establish National Socialism wherever it can to pave its own way. An issue of the *American Prospect* was devoted to attempts in various countries to get development going in a sustainable way.[7] Authors, including Joseph Stiglits, Amartya Sen, etc. show how important the "Washington Consensus" is in influencing development policy in other countries. These policies include free enterprise, free markets, free trade, and free flows of capital, all in the name of efficiency. You ought to get very suspicious when there's so much free stuff. These policies are introduced with a massive dose of lending by the IMF and foreign investors. Of course most of this winds up in the hands of people who use it to maintain their elite positions in society. Immediately unstable conditions arise. Drawn by all the talk of "free" this and that, investors pile in, buying up national assets that have been "privatized". There is a frenzy of financial activity that feeds on itself. But when there's the inevitable letdown, capital begins to gush out in torrents. What's left in the wake is lots of unemployment, dead companies, and billions of debt that future generations will be enslaved by.

The irony is that the US itself did not develop with this much "free" stuff. For one thing, in the old days, there weren't trillions of international capital sloshing around the world looking for opportunities. Home industries were often protected by tariffs and import restrictions, etc. Democracy in the US insured some measure of purchasing power in the growing middle class. Most importantly, even though Corporate Socialism was in place after the Civil War for the next 65 years, there was still a degree of independent rule-making and finally a Constitution.

Getting economic progress going in most developing countries is like walking with a tray full of water. The water starts to slosh back and forth by increasing amounts until it all winds up on the floor. This is why there are buffers on insides of waterbeds. Many developing countries have very little of this. After an initial phase, economic factors like capital, labor, trade, banking, financing began sloshing around uncontrollably until some important sector of the economy is hit with a tsunami and the system collapses. With all this so-called "liberalization" and free everything, there were collapses in southeast Asia, Africa, Latin America, Indonesia, Malaysia, etc. Argentina had to default on its sovereign debt in the '90s and Russia collapsed in the same period.

My claim is that this is no accident. Policies pushed on these countries have one motivation, which is to allow large economic interests in the west to go in and milk big profits from the unstable economic conditions created by these very same policies. There should be protections of home industries, restrictions on trade, controls on capital, and most importantly protections for labor and small businesses. And above all, means for independent enforcing of rules, all of the factors Adam Smith outlined for a Capitalist economy.

26.4 THE SYSTEM MIND AND MOMENTUM

But the situation is even worse in countries that the west invades and conquers, like Iraq and Afghanistan. There will be even less economists, political theorists, entrepreneurs, etc. and more paid killers in the countries the US invades. This is why, when these neoconservatives with their total ignorance of Capitalism or history, try to plant markets and puppetocracy into countries like Iraq and Afghanistan, they are pissing into the wind. Our policy makers cannot grasp the most important lesson of history, which is that cultures have enormous *momentum*. Those of you who know some physics know that the definition of momentum is simple: Momentum equals mass times velocity. Momentum is a vector and is denoted by an arrow pointing in a particular direction that a mass is moving in. Momentum is the most important key concept in discussing economic development. Momentum takes thousands of years to gather steam that you don't change easily.

You have heard of a collision course. Ocean liners that weigh thousands of tons, have enormous *momentum*. Even though their speed is slow, their mass is enormous, which creates a large momentum vector in a certain direction that cannot be changed easily. If two ocean liners even 20 miles apart have momentum vectors pointing towards each other will collide no matter what they try to do to steer away. The earth weighing trillions of tons, has so much momentum going around the sun that it slows down only a fraction of a second every *century!*

A nation's economy has the same kind of momentum. A slight movement in a particular direction in the codes and morays of a society will still not change a large momentum vector because nations are huge masses, and momentum is mass times velocity. The momentum of a country takes hundreds of years to change direction. What carried the west to modern economic development was 2 thousand years of *momentum* left from the direction the Roman Empire had established.

If you want a really incisive example of momentum, look into the history of Vermont. I had always wondered why Vermont was such a liberal state and New Hampshire a conservative state. Driving around these states, you don't see much difference. They are small states studded with many small colonial villages, some farms and a few small cities. Why the difference in politics? This is discussed in an excellent article in the NYR.[8] Well, back in colonial times, the crooked governor of New Hampshire was making lots of money selling farmland to unwary farmers and settlers in Vermont. The state of New York disputed these claims and sent in their own Corporate Socialist land speculators in bed with the political animals in Albany to grab land in Vermont. Well, a guy named Ethan Allen organized the Green Mountain Boys to defend small Vermont farmers against both sides. He was a radical at the time and sent Vermont in the direction of defending the rights and freedoms of the little guy. This was reflected in their state constitution which is among the most liberal in the country. This started a *momentum* vector that has come down to us over 200 years that sent these two very similar states in opposite directions politically. Vermont even has a socialist senator, Bernie Sanders.

Marx stressed the economic determinants of momentum vectors. However, the force component is more important than the direction component in economics. If fact, the force component can greatly change the direction as happened in the west with the Commercial revolution. However, in the area of ideas, it is the *direction* component that dominates a momentum vector. In the 1800s, Great Britain and Germany were pretty much on a par intellectually, with Germany possibly leading the way in psychology and math, and Great Britain leading in philosophy and history. However only a few men in each country started a *direction* in the ideas vector that sent these two countries in very different directions especially politically and then internationally. With G. E. Moore and Bertrand Russell leading the way with their very readable and original writing, they determined a vector that enabled England to lead the world intellectually in the 20th century in many areas. However, the Germans were saddled with Hegel, Heidegger and Marx whose obscure verbiage covered up a barrenness of important beneficial ideas that enabled German leaders to do anything they wanted while maintaining concordance with these thinkers. When the force components of these vectors grew in the 20th century with economic development and technology, the English wound up with Churchill and the Germans wound up with Hitler.

What enabled most of the Asian countries, especially China, to take a market direction, was thousands of years of feudalism and a moral code and rule of law. Communism with its total lack of a moral code introduced massive doses of corruption because Communism does not come with its own moral code any more than Capitalism. But when China's leaders introduced markets around 1990, it had thousands of years of momentum under a feudal system that was a foundation. Of course, the corruption introduced by 60 years of Communism still throttles Chinese development. This is why China presents a very interesting confluence of trends.

You could view today's China as a long tube of water. At the top of the tube, 20% of the water is boiling hot and building up steam pressure. This layer contains most of the talent, intelligence, inventiveness, emotional and creativity energy in society. As you go down the tube the water gets cooler. What the Communist party did in the early '90s was to take the lid off the top of the tube. The built-up pressure exploded in a gusher of hot water and steam. This is the economic miracle of China. The Communist party had absolutely nothing to do with this. It was simply the result of taking the oppressive and constraining lid off of the tube of the Chinese people's inherent abilities, especially the top 20%. But as you might expect, more than 90% of the new wealth, income and property has gone to this top 20% layer of Chinese society. They're in worse shape than we are.

Of course, these same industrialists and oligarchs use their new-found wealth to climb in bed with the Communist Party and make their own rules that keep income going to themselves. As a NYR article details, "Few Chinese companies call themselves private — *siying* in Chinese — preferring instead the more nebulous term *minying*, or 'run by the people'. What this means is that ...the manager is often a former official or close to party circles" ,[9] and often a member of the party itself. In China and many countries of the Muslim world, the *army* actually owns hundreds of companies and industries. This is a very dangerous kind of National Socialism because the army has guns to enforce its hand-made rules.

This is why the rules of the game in China are among the worst in the world. In spite of old Communism supposedly championing the worker and the little guy, Chinese industry has been able to treat China like one big pigsty. Pollution in China especially in the cities is among the worst in the world and it's affecting their genes where we see dramatic rises in birth defects, genetic damage and all-around health problems. A similar thing is happening in Russia. This is a clear indication of National Socialism with industry making its own rules.

The Communist Party's reason box answer is they need quick development to catch up to the west. Well, it is true that this state of affairs does lead to quick accumulation of Capital and technological development. What these guys don't understand and are certainly not going to be informed by western propagandists is that once you enable leading economic players to become part of the government, using their capital to influence the rules of the game, you create a vector that is very difficult to change. They may get fake democracy like Bush installed in Iraq and Afghanistan, but the ordinary guy in China will never be represented.

In the short run, the explosion of business and money-making among the top 20% in will impress the world. Remember with a population of 1.34 trillion, this top class is more than a third of a billion people which is close to the population of US. So this economic explosion had an enormous international impact. By having a basic slave labor force below them, this top 20% will probably pass the US in wealth and income very soon. But by the time this top 20% reaches its potential in wealth and income, leading economic players will be firmly in bed with the Communist party and a very repressive form of National Socialism. By the way, a similar thing is happening all over the developing world. The top 20% in all these countries has been freed for a variety of reasons to expand their economies. However, with the help of the "Washington Consensus", they are all taking the National Socialist road and none of them is creating real middle classes including China and India. Without a prosperous middle class all over the world, the top 20% have no customers to sell to. Trade, which is a zero sum game at best, will accomplish nothing in this regard. This is why growth and trade is slowing down all over the world, especially in the BRIC countries of Brazil, Russia, India and China.

Leading political actors in Washington say they are trying to introduce Democratic Capitalism in Iraq and Afghanistan after a thousand years of momentum in the direction of tribalism with no sound foundation of a moral code. When the Bushies went into Iraq and Afghanistan, they did not hire economists, anthropologists, political scientists, technologists, or development experts. They hired paid killers. That's what they do: they kill, just like the Terminator in the movie. They kill because that's all they know. And when they don't succeed, they throw a temper tantrum, fill their diapers just like an enraged baby and start killing more people. But of course, what Bush introduced into Iraq and Afghanistan has nothing to do with Democratic Capitalism. Not only that but while we talk about Democratic Capitalism in these developing countries, inner brain neoconservatives are slowly dismantling Democratic Capitalism right here in the US.

But there is an even worse aspect of the US approach to development in countries like Iraq and Afghanistan. Bush and Obama are pouring billions of dollars into these countries to change their momentum vectors towards economic development. *But money only makes things worse.* The political structure of these countries basically consists of warlords who attract tough young men on the basis of their display of violence. But our volunteer army was attracted to George Bush the same way the so-called insurgents are attracted to their warlords: on the basis of a display of power and violence. Young men in other countries are no different from our young men. The difference is that the US has a history of civilized economic and political institutions and a momentum vector that keep people like Dick Cheney from becoming a Joseph Goebbels. The violent leaders that attract their tough young men are not constitutional presidents, but leaders of tribalism thousands of years old. So when money is thrown into these countries, all it does is reinforce the very corrupt practices that prevent development in the first place. Let's give a good analogy.

Depending on topology, there is a system of rivers running through most countries. Our most important river is the Mississippi. Important rivers in the west are the Colorado and Columbia. We also have the Allegheny, Missouri and Ohio Rivers in the Midwest and the Hudson and Potomac rivers in the east. There are hundreds of smaller rivers and thousands of streams. When it rains, rainwater doesn't flow in new ways, but flows along the rivers and streams that are already there and simply makes them wider. There were great floods along our rivers. Remember the Mississippi flood of 1993 and the Susquehanna flood of 1996? You would never create a *new* system of rivers simply by dumping more water on the country. More water would only deepen and widen the rivers that are already there.

This is the way cultures work. When tons of money are sent into Iraq and Afghanistan, it simply flows along channels that have been in place for hundreds of years in the form of bribes, pay-offs, political associations, militia groups taking money for protection etc. It doesn't create *new* channels but simply reinforces the channels that are already there. The results are massive amounts of corruption right under the noses of our armies. Billions of dollars of taxpayer money wind up in Swiss bank accounts held by people in the puppet governments we installed. The *Nation* details how USAID money sent to employ people to do infrastructure jobs, often disappears, and actually winds up in the hands of insurgents themselves.[10]

It's even worse in Afghanistan, and if it weren't so sad, would be a real joke. Another *Nation* article discusses how in order to provide safe passage for military personnel and equipment being shipped by various trucking companies, the military has to pay extortion fees to area warlords.[11] The title of this article is "US Funds the Talaban, II". These kinds of expenditures by the US government simply reinforces and strengthens the very channels of illegal money flows that are supposed to be replaced, often winding up in the hands of our supposed enemies.

The cultural and economic momentum vectors in most developing countries are thousands of years old. No amount of killing is going to change the momentum vector built up over this long history. It would take hundreds of years of very guided momentum change to get them going in the direction of Democratic Capitalism; and that's with the aid of our best people. Putting our foreign policy for development in the hands of inner brain paid killers will do nothing to change these momentum vectors. It will do only what paid killers do; they kill.

But even in the developed world, as our feudal past recedes, corruption is starting to appear. When I first came to New England, I was impressed by the way the old Yankees did business. I went to my first auction in NE and the auctioneer would sell a piece and after the hammer went down, the runner would bring the object right to the seat of the winner in the audience with no payment at all. The auctioneer trusted that when the auction was over, the purchaser would come over and pay his or her bill. But as time went on and new people began to appear from other parts of the country and other parts of the world, this practice had to stop. But it gave me an on-the-spot observation of why the US developed so impressively in the early 1800s and after WWII. American Capitalism had its impressive explosion of economic development because it was built upon a foundation of a feudal past of Europeans, especially the English, who came here and set the tone. It was the

Yankee culture of honorable business practices that set the stage for economic development throughout the country. This code of ethics is the remnants of a thousand-year momentum vector of feudalism in conjunction with the Church.

But as we take in increasing numbers of people from failed states and failed cultures, the feudal code recedes into the past, the moral code of honor that it brought with it is beginning to fray and we see ever increasing amounts of Economic Socialism with its massive fraud and corruption. The courts are getting increasing numbers of suits mostly involving people not keeping their word. The internet is seeing fraud of all conceivable kinds. And con artists are coming out of the woodwork to bilk especially older Americans out of life savings with various kinds of investment fraud which the FBI says has doubled recently. You would never see this kind of fraud and corruption among the early New England Yankees. Economic Socialism and National Socialism is exactly what you get when you plant Capitalism in a society without a feudal past. The only exception might be most of the IT industry led by geeky scientific types who are too engrossed to be thinking about corruption. But with the IT bubble, we might have seen the last surge of uncorrupted economic development.

When we come to the Bush era, the old feudal code had been sufficiently washed away that the financial bubble that occurred was based on total fraud. The core of the economy had shifted to financial services which, starting with Ronald Reagan, had been in bed with political actors for many years. The result was the usual collapse that had occurred many times in the history of Economic Socialism.

[1] William Easterly, "The Anarchy of Success", *The New York Review of Books*, Oct. 8, '09

[2] Fukuyama, Francis, 2011. *The Origins of Political Order*, Farrar, Strauss and Giroux

[3] Ibid. p. 275

[4] See review of Bynum by Eamon Duffy, "Sacred Bones & Blood. *New York Review of Books*, Aug. 18, '11, p. 66

[5] Rodenbeck, Max, "The Father of Violent Islamism". *The New York Review of Books*, May 9, '13

[6] Acemoglu, D.; Robinson, J. *Why Nations Fail: The Origins of Power, Prosperity, and Poverty*; Crown

[7] *The American Prospect*, Winter '02.

[8] Breen, T.H.; "The Vigilantes of Vermont". Review of W. S. Randall's book, *Ethan Allen: His life and Times*, *The New York Review of Books*, Apr. 5, '12, p. 64.

[9] Johnson, Ian; "The Party: Impenetrable, All Powerful. *The New York Review of Books*, Sept. 30, '10

[10] Mogelson, Luke, "Aiding the Insurgency", *The Nation*, May 31, '10, p. 14

[11] Roston, Aram, "US Funds the Talaban, II", *The Nation*, July, 12, '10. P. 4.

CHAPTER 27

International Relations

____

27.1 THE SYSTEM MIND AND LAWS OF INTERNATIONAL RELATIONS.

AS WE HAVE STRESSED, THE system mind is controlled mostly by the most powerful and wealthiest nodes of the economy. And their constant goal is to send as much power and wealth to the top 20% as possible, especially the top 5%. But in spite of the constant drone of media propaganda, there is a small chance that the average American will see through this agenda and rebel. And so it is in the interests of the most powerful nodes of the economy to distract citizenry as much as possible from economic considerations. The system mind cannot allow the average American to see that he is being left out of growing wealth, 98% if which is going to the top 20%. And one very important way to distract people from the quality of their own lives is by keeping the country in a permanent state of war.

In order to have an easy transition to wars of various kinds, the system mind usually lays the groundwork in different parts of the world that can act as a foundation for wars. We would find that they follow six major laws, which we'll call Wells' Laws of International Relations.

Law I Whenever possible, like in developing countries, push foreign governments into one of two categories: puppet or enemy. The purpose of puppet governments is to be able to buy raw materials cheaply and have markets to sell into; and the purpose of an enemy government is that it can become a vehicle for making war.

Law II. Strive through economic, political, and international means to have weak neighbors. Weak neighbors decrease the chances of being invaded, conquered and occupied by an aggressive neighbor.

Law III. A nation's allies should be the first countries *out* from immediate neighbors; in other words, neighbors of its immediate neighbors. This puts a squeeze on immediate neighbors. France has often been on hostile terms with Germany as in WWI and WWII. However, France's natural ally has been Russia. Japan's two neighbors are China and the US, both of which have been either at war with Japan or on belligerent terms during many periods of history. However, the next neighbor on the other side of Japan from the US is China, which has been a natural ally of the US. Pakistan and India have been at each other's throats since Pakistan's inception, but Pakistan seems on reasonable terms with Bangladesh, one country over. Iran and Iraq had a horrible war, but Iran is on good terms with both Pakistan and Palestine one country over on each side. There are exceptions like the US and Canada, which is a suburb of Detroit. But the US had big wars with Mexico.

Law IV Whenever a nation leaves a region after conquest or colonial occupation, it should leave things in as much of a mess as possible so as to be able to exert influence in the region at later times. When England left its colonial possessions in Africa, it drew lines for new countries that maximized the antagonism between all historical tribes in the region. When England left India, is set up a bloody war between India and what became Pakistan.

LAW V Whenever a nation of people is invaded or occupied by a foreign nation, the people in the invaded country, especially the tough young men, will be attracted to the most violent, aggressive and fierce leader they can find, which gives them their best chance to expel the invader. A brutal occupation brings about a brutal resistance. Bush's brutal invasion and occupation of Iraq eventuated in ISIS. The mild occupation of the British in the colonies led to a mild resistance and a good guy leader and first president.

LAW VI Whenever a tribe, population or nation organizes an army, a war will usually be concocted for that army to fight. Hitler remarked to an adjutant viewing a military parade that he didn't build this army to march down the streets of Berlin.

These are the basis for most foreign relations policies in most countries in most periods of time. But there are two categories that must be delineated regarding the total foreign policy of a nation. The first consists of aspect of foreign policy that is motivated by domestic economic and political considerations. That aspect of foreign policy is very much the product of the system mind. The second are foreign policy initiatives that are confined to economic and political relations with other countries, having peripheral repercussions at home. As we shall explain, this latter aspect of foreign policy is carried out by a very tenuous and sketchy system mind. A very incisive example of this has been American foreign policy in the Middle East since WWII, which is a great example of Law IV.

After the Holocaust, to many Jews, Europe was like a hot stove: you don't touch it again. This is why it was easy for the UN to create a newly reconstituted "homeland". With UN approval, remaining European Jews went to Palestine as Zionists had wanted all along. If you look at events of this important period, you would find that every decision, every resolution, every recognition that occurred in Palestine at this time created a situation that was as indeterminate and ambiguous as you could possibly design so that the US and Great Britain would be in a position to exert maximal influence in the region for years to come. Not only that, but the US system mind was laying the groundwork for the perfect war vis a vis the domestic situation in the US.

Most of the observers and writers about Palestinian view it as a Jewish-Palestinian problem probably because many Jews who survived the Holocaust went to Palestine after the war. But I don't think this is a Jewish problem at all. It's a *European* problem. Before that, Arabs and Jews lived in Palestine relatively peacefully as equals. No leader on either side wanting to drive the other side out. There might have been individual skirmishes now and then like among any neighbors, but as *peoples*, they got along reasonably. It was *Christians* who persecuted Jews in history, not Muslims. Often it was *Muslim* countries that took Jews in. They might have been second-class citizens — they put a tax on Jews, but they protected them from Christians and at least let them live.

But starting with the Zionist movement in the 1890s, Palestinians could see that Jews coming to Palestine now were not the same people as they had been living with peacefully for 4 thousand years. The problem, in my opinion, was that European Jews coming to Palestine were not coming as *Jews*; they were coming as *Europeans*. Being Jewish had nothing to do with it. Palestinians could see that the new Zionist model was not so much a Jewish model, but a *European* model that had been in place for 400 years. In this model, you *conceptualize* indigenous people so that you can go to their far away land as invaders and conquerors *wavin' a book* and cherry-picking history to justify destroying their crops, killing their animals and ethnically cleansing to make room for settlers. It's that simple. You might call this terrorism. Not so. The official definition of a 'terrorist' is any indigenous individual who responds in any way to invasion and conquest. Even if all he does is complain, he's a "terrorist *suspect*". His job is simply to disappear. This is the exact model used on the American Indians. A leading historian of Palestine, Rashid Khalidi, quotes a Hebrew writer Josef Chaim Brenner in the early 1900s describing the "degeneracy and savagery of the Arabs…" (Khalidi, '06, 68). They were "natives", "savages", "barbarians", "terrorists", not totally human — *untermenchen* as the Nazis called Jews — to be pushed aside or preferably snuffed out.

Of course, with a modern world looking on, European Jews couldn't do what Europeans of all stripes did to indigenous people all over the world. But the point is not what you can get away with. The point is the *concept* you have of the indigenous people. This is what creates the sore spot in the Middle East, not so much what people do, but what they *think*. Europeans never viewed the American Indians as real human beings either. At the height of WWII against the most murderous regime in the modern history, Americans never viewed Germans in a racist way. Our popular culture made fun of Hitler — we called Germans "krauts", but this was a far cry from racism. However, the original American Indians weren't even recognized as human beings; they were part of the flora and fauna like bushes and trees to be chopped down to make room for European settlers.

When Europeans arrived in the New World, there were about 12 million Indians in North America. As more European setters arrived, more Indians were killed, more land stolen, more Buffalo killed and more treaties signed and broken. Their numbers reached a low of about a quarter million around 1900. This means over 95% of the American Indians living in North America when the Europeans arrived were either killed or kept from reproducing by drastic measures. It was about the same percentage as Hitler did to the Jews. They were cooped up in home-made Bantustans of worthless land, euphemistically called "reservations". A leading historian, Barnard Bailyn has an excellent history of the initial stages of ethnically cleansing North American Indians by European settlers.[1]

Nothing was ever said about all this because Europeans had arrived wavin' a book which had awarded the New World to the Europeans. It was just a matter of time before the "natives" would learn about this infinite scheme of things. Of course, there were a small coterie of Christian ministers who thought that being a Christian meant following the life and values of *Christ* — a very unpopular view at the time. Finally, in total frustration, an Indian posse would attack a village and scalp some Europeans. The European settlers would go ballistic. The presses rolled, the ministers and preachers screamed from every pulpit, and the politicians went apoplectic. The indigenous population became "savages", "murderers", "barbarians", "terrorists", which justified their total annihilation.

The US government signed over 800 treaties with Indians and broke every one of them. You don't have to keep your promise to an Indian anymore than you have to keep your promise to the local skunk or coyote. The American press never reported Europeans' stealing Indian land. The reason is that there's no such thing as Indian land any more than there is buffalo land, wild horse's land or rattlesnake land. In the same way there's no such thing as Palestinian land. And you don't have to worry about laws, or agreements, or treaties when dealing with "natives, savages" and now "terrorists". There was one quote I found that was pretty funny because of the way Indians express themselves. Ogdala Chief Red Cloud in his old age said to congress: "They made us many promises, more than I can remember, but they never kept but one; they promised to take our land, and they took it".[2] If Israel were a major power in the Middle East, that's exactly what Jewish *Europeans* would have done to the Palestinians. They couldn't bring it off because they're a small country and the whole world was looking on.

In my opinion, the adoption of the European model by European jews started a momentum vector trap that has carried things right to the present day. It was formally expressed in 1948 with the creation of the state of Israel. Alan Pappe's book discusses a plan by an army of the new state of Israel in 1948 called the Haganah that had a plan called Dalet, "a plan for the ethnic cleansing of Palestine".[3] We all know what ethnic cleansing means don't we? It means get rid of them and snuff them out any way you can exactly what Europeans did to the American Indians. And some of this was actually carried out by the Irgun and Haganah.

Israeli propaganda outlets only talk about what has happened since 1948. Yes, Palestinians have probably done a lot more bad things since 1948 than the Israelis. It's just like the American Indians. *After* Europeans settlers stole all the Indian's land and killed their animals, then yes, Indians scalped more Europeans than Europeans scalped Indians. But the problem is how it all got started. Since Britain, the US and Israel totally controlled the rhetoric coming out of the region, they dug out from the Palestinian population a few street gangsters who hated Jews and assigned them as "leaders". As Khalidi points out, the British only recognized and granted for the Palestinians "...a religious leadership, authorized, encouraged, legitimated, subsidized, and always in the end controlled by the British" (Khalidi, '06, 63). Right on schedule, when these "leaders" refused to recognize this totally racist, international lawless, and blatantly unjust drawing of national boundaries, Israel was awarded the right to call it "war" and proceed to kill people and take more land.

After all, if it's a war you're in, anything goes. Official state-sponsored terrorist groups like the Irgun and Haganah went into Palestinian villages and killed everything that moved. This reign of terror caused three quarters of a million Palestinians to flee their villagers and became refugees in other countries.

And now there's a Jewish propaganda operation called FLAME rewriting history for people who don't know any better. It turns out that the three quarters of a million Palestinians who got terrorized out of their homes and villages and went as refugees to other places, had children. In various peace talks, the Palestinians want what is called "right of return" to where they were originally from and had been living for 6 thousand years. FLAME calls them "fake refugees" because they are only *children* of refugees. This means that children of Holocaust survivors are "fake" victims of the Holocaust. Of course, the reason they're "fake refugees" is that the Palestinian people themselves are fake people. Of course, European Jews, who ignored Palestine for 2 thousand years, are *real* people. Nothing fake about them. Reason? They're Europeans who God awarded lands to all over the world.

But all the finger-pointing and propagandizing as to what this or that leader or groups of young men were saying and doing, whether terrorizing, or sabotaging or fighting has nothing to do with real *people* — plain folks, women, children, 99% of men, etc., who want to live peaceful lives. But of course, Britain, the US and Israel had no intention for any kind of permanent solution. By creating a sore spot in Palestine, they could exert influence in the region at any future time to their benefit as Law IV says. What the system mind did was use the situation in Palestine as a foundation to build what later became the "war on terror". The closest the US and Britain came to a Palestinian state was a Partition Plan in 1947 assigning some of the land to the Palestinians. A *Nation* article stated about negotiations to achieve peace, "Netanyahu has never offered to concede even one inch of territory to the Palestinians — not even from Palestinian territories Israel acquired in 1948..., which the 1947 Partition Plan had assigned to the Palestinian Arab population".[4] Of course, in 1948, the US, Great Britain and Israel pulled every trick in the trade to stop the UN from declaring a Palestinian state based on this Partition Plan. And that is for a people who had been living there for 6 thousand years. But don't think for one minute that the US and Great Britain had humane attitudes towards European Jews. Their motivation for a Jewish state was to avoid having to take in hundreds of thousands of European Jewish war refugees.

A Jewish historian, Benny Morris, admits that Palestinians owned three times as much privately owned land as Jews. In 1948, the original Palestinian Jews owned about 30% of the land and Palestinians owned 70% of the land. These figures are from *Jewish* historians. The Jews wound up with 70% of the land *and a country;* whereas the Palestinians wound up with only 30% of the land and no country. That was blatant injustice right from the start, exactly as happened to American Indians.

Now I don't *ever* remember hearing anyone say that the Jews of the Middle East didn't deserve a nation because the coming state of Israel had a terrorist element. Israel was created as a nation for 99.9% of every-day peaceful Jewish *people*, not a handful of Jewish terrorists.

But of course, when it comes to non-Europeans, it's an entirely different story. Everything that happened in Palestine was arranged by European Jews in combination with the US and Britain because they both had significant and influential Jewish populations. You find just the right "leaders" to give you the end result you want. These trumped up "leaders" were no more leaders of the Palestinian people than Al Capone was a leader of Chicago. The 99.9% of real Palestinian *people* were never asked anything. There was no referendum, nor election nor even a pole to make even a vestigial attempt to ask them. Britain, the US and Israel chose convenient leaders, drew the lines, and arranged for the end result which was a Jewish state. This continued a momentum vector that had been going for over 50 years whereby land is continually taken from Palestinians with the end result that Palestinians will wind up in a number of bantustans totally isolated from each other just like the American Indian tribes.

When you're creating new states out of tribal lands, if you really consider the inhabitants of these lands as equal human beings, you don't draw boundaries on the basis of what war criminals, gangsters, terrorists or tribal chiefs are saying and doing. You draw them on the basis of where the 99.9% of real flesh and blood ordinary people have been living for a reasonable period of time, which is what they did in Yugoslavia. In Yugoslavia, they didn't draw boundaries around Serbia, Bosnia and Kosovo on the basis of what Milosevic and other war criminals were saying and doing. The UN didn't cherry-pick history going back to ancient hatreds and injustices. But that was because they're Europeans — real people. But since the European model doesn't consider indigenous people as equal human beings, the US, Great Britain and Israel found all kinds of clever ways to avoid drawing national borders for the Palestinians. You don't have to take a principled solution for a bunch of "natives", "savages" and "terrorists". What they did instead was to ask some local tribal gangsters for their views of Israel, who were carefully chosen by the Israelis. And where was the Palestinian state? Regardless of fairness, it would show some vestigial indication that Palestinians were human beings too. But there was no more of an effort for a Palestinian state than for an American Indian state. In fact, the British deliberately kept a UN commission *out* of Palestine, just in case it might threaten to restore order.

And now Benny Morris gets into big pissing contests as to who said what, and plays this infantile game of "my pop can beat up your pop", and "my terrorists aren't as bad as your terrorists". He reviews books by historians of the region in various propaganda magazines. When an author says that a Jewish terrorist group killed everyone in a particular village, Morris jumps on them like a lion on a pot roast, hurling epithets that the guy is a liar, a cheat, and a scoundrel. Morris gives the real facts: the Jewish terrorist group killed only *half* the people in the village. When an author says that a bunch of Palestinian terrorists went in and killed 19 Jews in a particular village, Morris again blasts the author hurling the same epithets. Why? Because the Palestinians killed *26* Jews, not 19 as reported.

And now there's a new pissing contest as to who is a "people" and who is a "nation". This crap about who is a "people" and who is "nation" is just more propaganda to keep the area a sorespot and to justify more land grabs and more openings for big powers like the US to use for some political purpose like the war on terror. The US, Great Britain and European Jews knew that there were two kinds of real people living in Palestine in 1948: Jews and Muslim Arabs. But they were never considered equals by anyone. It was with this mindset that the early "...League of Nations mandate for Palestine, constituting the entire legal basis for the British regime...explicitly refrained from mentioning either the Palestinians as a people or their national self-determination. By contrast, the Jewish minority of the population was so recognized" (Khalidi, '06, 32).

Recently a guy wrote a book saying in effect that the Jews of Europe were never really a people.[5] They had so integrated and intermarried with people in other countries they immigrated into that after two thousand years of assimilation, they really were no longer a people even though they had the same religion. After all, we don't consider Catholics of Ireland, Poland and Italy a "people". The book was reviewed by Hillel Halkin who wants to determine the fate of flesh and blood humans with goals and on-going lives, not on the basis of where they're now alive and living but on the basis of thousand-year old DNA. With the usual cherry-picking of history, what Halkins winds up giving us is that light-skinned people from England, along with swarthies from the middle east, blue-eyed blonds from Russia, tutsoons from Spain, albinos from Sweden, and jungle-bunnies from Africa — this menagerie constitutes a "people", you see. Blond haired, blue-eyed Goldie Meir from Milwaukee Wisconsin, who was the Prime Minister of Israel in the early '70s, said not only that, but that there was no such thing as Palestinian people even though the very homogeneous dark-skinned, dark-eyed, swarthy Palestinians are real Semites and have been living there for 6 thousand years. The Nazis said Jews weren't real people either. *The end result was that this motley assortment of Jews from the far reaches of Europe and Russia of all colors and nationalities was assigned to the land of Palestine, whereas Arab Palestinians who had been living in the same place for 6 thousand years were assigned to the far corners of the Arab world. Jews get gathered, Palestinians get scattered.*

It doesn't make a dam bit of difference whether flesh and blood human beings are a "people" or what they're called. If you don't like "Palestinian" or "Muslim Arabs", call them non-Jews. Call them fucking Martians. The only relevant point is there were two different groups of flesh and blood *people*. And they had been living there for thousands of years. And when lines were drawn after WWII establishing nations, it should be these real *people*, both Jewish and non-Jewish *who had been living there for reasonable periods of time*, that should determine national lines, not the names we give them nor two thousand-year-old history. European Jews claim Palestine was their original homeland going back two thousand years. But at that time, the Jewish people didn't have a nation with national boundaries and titles to land either. They were a tribe of people like thousands of tribes of people all over the old world. But tribal occupation thousands of years ago is good enough grounds to award the Jews of Europe a modern nation with national boundaries and all. But this wasn't good enough to give tribal Palestinians a similar claim who never moved for thousands of years.

Now I am not Jewish and I have no ax to grind. In fact, if I have any biases, they would favor Jews, since I've had lots of Jewish girlfriends, Jewish men friends and Jewish business associates. I've only known one Palestinian in my life — a Palestinian woman I got fixed up with by a dating service. But she was too pretty, and rejected me. But every single history book and review I have ever come across on the history of Palestine, in mountains of detail, they quibble about as to who did what, who was promised what, what documents exist, who were the terrorists, who were the leaders, and on and on going back thousands of years. Real flesh and blood alive people have nothing to do with all this and took no part in these details. In my opinion, there is only one relevant fact: *how many of each people were living in the area at the time of drawing national boundaries.* That's it.

In a review of Tom Segev's book by Anita Shapira, amongst *reams* of irrelevant detail she accepts the British mandate made in 1922 like it came down from a mountaintop on a stone tablet. [6] What I want to know is, what kind of modern-day international law do we have that allows imperial countries like Great Britain to go to faraway lands and lawlessly invade, conquer and kill people who have been living there for thousands of years? And establish a *"mandate"*, no less, whatever the hell that is. Both these authors mention Jewish opinion and factions who felt betrayed by the British for not *"giving"* European Jews the whole enchilada. Listen to this logic. Benny Morris claims that since a Palestinian state wasn't established, "Israel was mandate Palestine's successor state and heir to the state lands".[7] *"Heirs"*, no less. Now how did the British come to own this land so as to *"bequeath"* it to anyone? How does Israel come to "inherit" land that was obtained through British invasion, conquest and killing? And if some international posse gives England this right what kind of an authority is it. It's the same racism over and over again. *Europeans* own land and can dispense with it as they please — "natives" don't own land any more than the local rattlesnakes own land. Europeans went around "claiming" land all over North America as though the Indians were no different from the trees and coyotes.

Now if the UN, being directed totally by the West after WWII, had established nations on the basis of real people living there like they did in Yugoslavia, you would get an Israel and a Palestine nation having land somewhat proportional to their actual numbers *at the time of drawing the borders. Then*, if the Arabs attacked Israel, Israel might have to right to take land from the Palestinians as a cost of making war. (For this same reason, I think Israel has a perfect right to keep the Golan Heights. Syria had no business attacking Israel and if they lost land, it should be just like the land Germany lost in WWII.)

When he was young and honest, Morris wrote history books that exposed the first Israeli governments as implicitly (or explicitly) supporting terrorist groups who terrorized thousands of Palestinians from their homes and destroyed their villages. But he now revises his own history and these expulsions have been miraculously transformed into a "war". Morris's "war" is the usual ethnic cleansing that has been perpetrated by Europeans for hundreds of years. Hitler claimed to be at "war" with the Jews of Europe too. Does Morris accept the results of that "war"? Europeans were at "war" with the American Indians too. (However, there are some sensitive Jewish historians who understand the situation, for example, Gideon Levy.)

Benny Morris, who should apply for a patent in the patent office for all the history he invents, talks "about the Jewish people's three-thousand-year-old connection to the Land of Israel...; and that for the next two millennia, after going into exile, they aspired and longed for repatriation." [8] This is a perfect example of what the lower intestine reason box can spew forth regardless of reality. If Italians had new WMDs, maybe they could invade England to reclaim their "connection" to England left over from the Roman Empire. Maybe Christians ought to raise an army and reclaim our 2 thousand year old "connection" to the whole Middle East which was once entirely Christian. In fact, this is *exactly* what the crusades were: an attempt by European (so-called) Christians to reestablish their thousand-year-old "connection" to this very same area using the same methods.

Jerusalem and other parts of Palestine were controlled, at some time or other, by Babylonians, Israelites, Jews, Philistines, Jebusites, Assyrians, Persians, Greeks, Macedonians, Maccabees and Romans. Are we supposed to let peoples with some ancient ties to an area start killing one another over whose claims are the most legitimate? The answer is, when it comes to people who didn't write history like the American Indians, Europeans start cherry-picking history. But for real people like Europeans in Yugoslavia, nobody quibbled about history. You draw lines *now* on the basis of where real people are living *now*.

Even under the nose of a Hitler who had warned of his hatred of Jews, the few Jews who left went mostly to the US and other European countries. Most real flesh and blood *individual* Jews of Europe were *voting with their feet* to renounce a "connection" to Palestine. That's what they *did*, regardless of what anyone like Halkin and Morris now *say* with their history rewrite bedtime stories. This idea that they "aspired and longed for repatriation" is total inner brain reason box crap. The vast majority didn't acknowledge a connection even under the nose of Hitler and while exposed to the intense preaching and prodding by Zionists for 50 years before WWII. Even during the Spanish Inquisition in which thousands of Jews were killed, the remaining Jews went to *Holland* who was nice enough to take them in, instead of Palestine to establish Morris's magic "connection".

European Jews were not a separate people first, but were Frenchmen or Germans *first*, and Jews after, *just like any other religion or ethnic group*. But of the ones that did leave Germany that Istvan Deak estimates was about 300 thousand,[9] did they go to reclaim their "connection" to Palestine? Only a trickle did. Most came to the US, claiming that those *other* Jews had a connection to Israel.

Oh, but I forgot. Anita Shapira tells us that a White Paper prevented Jews from going to Palestine, of which "they would have departed in the thousands".[10] Guess when this was? 1881? 1905? 1932? Absolutely not. *It was 1939.* She makes a dam fool of herself even mentioning this embarrassing White Paper. After 2 thousand years that European Jews had to "reclaim" their Benny Morris "connection" to Palestine, but instead remained as European nationals even under Hitler's nose, we finally learn from Shapira that, in effect, at the last minute, European Jews would rather have gone to Palestine than Auschwitz.

And where's the White Paper to cover those 2 thousand years? And what about enforcement? Well, we finally get an explanation here as to why England so desperately needed our help in fighting WWII. During the 1930s, instead of the English army being organized to face an obvious madman preparing for a looming war in Europe, it was lined up shoulder to shoulder to a man along every foot of Palestine border preventing one single European Jew from entering Palestine.

What European Jews "aspired and longed for" was to be accepted as equal German and French and Russian citizens, like any immigrant group in history; and we have a whole Jewish-American history of Jews "aspiring and longing" for acceptance to become part of the *American* people, even fighting off prejudice and discrimination in the process. And even with a state of Israel, American Jews, even the worst of them in the propaganda business, are "aspiring" to becoming leaders of *American* Jews right here in the US, not to be a bunch of desert rug dealers in Palestine. The same trickle of American Jews has gone to live in Israel from the US as the trickle that left Europe to go live in Palestine.

Of course, these "historians" conveniently erase 50 years of *relevant* history, which is what any propagandist does. When Theodor Herzl started the Zionist movement, their job was to convince European Jews that they have a 3 thousand-year-old "connection" to Palestine and that they should return to their original homeland. This small group of Zionists, traveled all over Europe, writing, lecturing, begging, pleading and imploring Jews to go to Palestine. (I am very sympathetic to pre-war Zionism.) But major Jewish leaders in Europe, *including* important Rabbis said that God didn't want the Jews to have a homeland because it would be the end of the world. And on the practical side, historian Gordon Craig says, Jews "could not as Germans imagine starting a new life in a strange land".[11]

Zionists did convince a small number who went and bought land, settled and formed a community *that had a legitimate claim on parts of the land of Palestine when national lines were drawn*. But all of their efforts produced only a trickle —the *same* trickle that left the US to pick up stakes and go live in Israel, *even after Israel was an established state*. In fact, the estimates are that only 40% of Jewish European refugees went to Palestine to establish Morris's imaginary "connection" and this was *after* 6 million deaths in the holocaust.[12]

What is even more remarkable about this history is that much of it went on right under the nose of Adolph Hitler and the Nazi third Reich. Here was a madman in speech after speech starting in the 1920s, blaming Jews for all evil and bellowing that he was going to rid Europe of its Jews. And yet even Rabbis advised Jews to stay. As Gordon Craig says, "… Jews found it difficult to believe that the Fuhrer's threats were really directed at themselves because they regarded themselves as Germans." [13] They might be parked for a while during a temporary Nazi period, but would live happily ever afterwards. This is why the deportation of Jews to death camps took them so much by surprise. They didn't believe it until they got there.

Jewish historians led by Hannah Arendt have been severely embarrassed and then angered by the fact that Jewish Rabbis and other leaders actually made lists that aided the Nazis in keeping track of Jews and in rounding them up for death camps. They propose treacherous self-serving motives to these leaders. Well it's hard to judge people's innermost motives. In my opinion, these seeming traitorous Jewish leaders really did believe that Jews were an organic part of European civilization and that cooperating with the governments they were living under was the historically lawful thing to do, even if it was a government led by Hitler. If there is even a small germ of truth in this view, it would show that European Jews couldn't conceive of themselves as anything but *Europeans*. And many of them believed this even as they were boarding trains to death camps.

Morris ought to read a new book by historian Niall Ferguson about the famous Jewish German banker, Siegmund Warburg.[14] When Warburg saw the first signs of the rise of Hitler, he left Germany, which is exactly what anyone with a morsel of historic understanding would do. But did he go to Palestine to reestablish a "connection" to Palestine? Absolutely not. He went to England and established a very important bank that led the way in modern banking. Not only that, but he called Zionist talk of a nation as being infected with "that worst modern epidemic of folly called nationalism". This is a very typical reaction by European Jews, even important ones, to the idea of a Jewish state: "folly".

And what about the famous diaries of a very average Jewish German, Victor Klemperer? Repeatedly, Klemperer makes no bones about the claim that he is a Jewish *German* and not a German *Jew*. He kept refusing to believe that real Germans could be imposing humiliations on the Jews of Germany. He wrote in his diary, "I am a German, and I am waiting for the Germans to return".[15] Of course, these real Jews of Germany are not going to enter into Morris' fantasy world.

Of course, when WWII ended and found 6 million Jews dead, the remaining European Jews fired their old God on the spot who had gotten them into so much trouble and hired a new God who had been out of work since the early American settlers. The new God claimed that the Jews of Europe really were a people all along in spite of their two thousand-year history as various European nationals. Not only that, but He dredged up from the dustbin of history, a "connection" to Palestine, which had been well-concealed, well-renounced, and well-shredded for two thousand years. But there was more the new God bestowed upon European Jews. He gave them an inherent *right* to push aside the "natives" and set up an exclusively Jewish state, making it a *God-given* right.

So the land was claimed by blond-haired, blue-eyed Vikings invading Palestine from the north country claiming to be Jews. Most of them have less Semitic blood than I do. They got together with the US and Britain and got the UN to carve out a state of Israel — just another move the UN made that destroys its credibility. This agreement seemed to allow European Jews to not only push aside people who had been living there for 6 thousand years, but the real clincher was *they also pushed aside dark-complexioned original Semitic Jews who had also been living there for 6 thousand years as well* and made them second-class citizens who couldn't even hold important political office. This is the most important fact, frequently overlooked, about the whole history of Israel.

To show how European Jews conceived the Palestinians, they had racist views about their own coreligionists who, if anybody among Jews, had a legitimate claim on Palestinian land. You would think the *first* thing these Jewish Vikings would do would be to make truly Semitic, original, and native Palestine-area Jews into the *centerpiece* of their new state, with *super*-legal status. They should have built monuments of them for maintaining a *real* and long-lived connection to Palestine, a difficult corner of the world. Quite the opposite: they were given *sub*-legal status. They too were pushed aside and demoted as just more unenlightened natives, not much more important than the Palestinians themselves. It was only after a lot of embarrassment and legal wrangling that Israel's Supreme Court finally gave the *native* Jews of the region their basic civil rights. This shows the basic mindset that all Europeans have exhibited for 400 years.

In my opinion, if it hadn't been for Hitler, the Jews of Europe would have continued living for the thousands of years the same way they had been living for the past 2 thousand years just as Catholics and Protestants have been living for hundreds of years in Europe, namely, as *European nationals*. And there would have been no manufactured "connection" to Palestine. History books by Benny Morris, Anita Shapira, and other Jewish revisionists would be telling us to renounce anti-Semitism by showing us how totally assimilated and loyal European Jewish nationals are, and how they had "aspired and longed for" being an integral part of European civilization for two thousand years and how they actually *led* European civilization during this time. And we should be proud of their leadership in this regard. That is *precisely* what they would be writing right now, instead of millions of pages of totally irrelevant reason-box diarrhea about ancient history. If the emergence of the Third Reich couldn't get the Jews of Europe to immigrate to Palestine, it is certain that a peaceful, prosperous, and very advanced post-war Europe certainly wouldn't have done it. Palestine might have become a country at some point and the original Jews living in the area would have been citizens of this country, along with many others like Palestinians, Bedouins, some Christians, some Persians, and a few others. And they would probably be getting along.

But there was a Hitler and a Holocaust and a consequential rush for a Jewish homeland. And by the way, what ever happened to the thousands of Nazis who had actually killed European Jews? There was a Nuremberg trial where a big deal was made out of executing a handful of Nazis. The rest were never even questioned let alone identified or punished. The US and Britain basically told the Jews of the new state of Israel that they needed all those Nazis as a bulwark against the rising threat of Communism. The implicit message was, if you're angry over the Holocaust, go pick on the Palestinians — nobody cares about them anyway.

This is where we find ourselves in the early 21st century. And it's the European model all over again. When Palestinians are committing terrorism acts, the Israelis say you got to stop terrorism before we can negotiate, and proceed to take more land. When Palestinians stop terrorist attacks. Guess what? The Israelis announce more settlements. Most of the time taking of this land is even against Israel's own laws. "In 2006, Peace Now used data collected by the [Israeli] government itself to calculate that some 40% of land allocated to settlements is actually Palestinian private property, not state land as the settlers claim."[16]

There were no terrorist attacks in the first half of 2010. Hilary Clinton conveyed the *message* that taking more Palestinian land was fine. When Obama saw his popularity falling because of his failed economy and needed to crank up the war on terrorism, in July, 2010, he had a heart-warming, hand-wringing, huggy-bear meeting with Netanyahu to congratulate him on his newly-taken Palestinian land. Obama looked like he was pumping for well water. Henry Siegman details the fraudulent efforts of the Obama administration to get a settlement in Palestine.[17]

And now in 2013, and '14, in order to keep the war on terrorism moving right along, we have John Kerry starting up a "peace process", another graphic illustration of the system mind. But, while Kerry was trying restart peace talks, Natanyahu was taking more land for settlements exactly in line with their hundred year-old vector. It's no accident that this is exactly at a time when the NSA is under scrutiny for spying on the American people and is very much in need of justifying their existence. The purpose of this "peace process" is clearly to inspire another layer of terrorists for the NSA to keep track of and chase down.

The plan for Palestine is exactly the plan carried out for the American Indians. The American Indians would have wound up either dead or in "reservations" *no matter what they did*. In fact, the only event they're now proud of is Little Big Horn. And the Palestinians will wind up the same way, *no matter what they do*: in a bunch of isolated and disconnected bantustans totally disarmed and surrounded by Israeli military. In the US, we called them "reservations". I'm sure they'll come up with some nice term for Palestinian reservations.

But there may be a difference in Palestinian. American Indians lost because they had no friends except the French for only a little while. American Indians were humiliated into not reproducing because they had no friends. But the European model isn't working for Israel. The reason is that the Palestinians have a billion and a half Muslim sympathizers, just as the Vietnamese had over a billion Chinese supporters. And they are reproducing even faster. But Israel is on a hundred-year-old momentum vector trap and can't change direction. Every time there's a new confrontation like in July, 2014, Palestinians do a little better. Israel only loses world support by killing innocents even if justified in some way. In my opinion, Israel is on a vector leading right to another holocaust exactly the way Jewish leaders ran European Jews into the last one: *not seeing reality*. And influential Jewish opinion in the US makes it worse.

There's a Jewish News Agency (JNS) that complains about lack of "objective coverage". Here we have many leading propagandists in the system media outlets are Jewish. Jews are one of the earliest immigration groups in colonial times. Many have been very successful using financial resource to support their cause. Congress and government agencies have Jewish employees out of proportion to their numbers in the population. There is a sizable and very influential Jewish vote in the US. And yet, the JNS claims Israel "generally receives inaccurate, harsh, even hostile coverage from the world's press".[18] This outrageous statement is in the midst of a system media agenda in which, in all these years, I have never *once* heard a Palestinian point of view. How many Palestinians are in ABC's news department, or any other US propaganda outlet? The reason, of course, is that Palestinians don't have a point of view, because they really aren't people. They're just part of the flora and fauna to be chopped down to make room for settlers. Even new Israeli "historians" are saying that the Palestinians were "forgotten", "overlooked", and "ignored". This is how being deliberately and violently driven from lands is described. This kind of pro-Israel propaganda only makes it less likely that Israel will see reality and change course. Of course, these propagandists aren't going to die in the next holocaust and if Israel is eventually gone, they'll make millions bitching about how bad it all was. And the only reason it will happen later instead of sooner is because of the economic and political disarray in the Muslim world. This is a solid way to base your national existence.

Israelis have hunkered down into an inner brain survival mode. As Law V describes, when a people is threatened, they gravitate to their fiercest leaders. This creates a feedback loop: the more besieged they are, the more they turn to their fiercest leaders who only intensify Arab animosity. But Muslim countries are undergoing drastic changes. Israeli and Jewish leaders won't be able to get the US to bribe new governments into being friendly with Israel because they won't be one-man shows. Countries of the Muslim world have no momentum vector for historical institutions that can form the basis for stable government and prosperous economies. They will be in disarray for a long time. And who is sitting there to take the blame for their problems? *Israel*, that's who. Even now, Israel and head-in-the-butt American Jewish leaders greatly underestimate the latent anti-Semitism in Muslim countries. And bitching about it won't change a thing. Netanyahu's mole view of the world sees Israel surrounding Palestinian incapacitated reservations. He *doesn't* see the bigger Muslim world surrounding *him*.

Myself, and probably most of you do not want to read any more holocaust books. Maybe Jews in the US and Israel ought to get a little more interested in surviving than in being right, by seeing some reality and prodding the Israeli government to make a reasonable settlement while they still have an advantage in doing so. And with the uprisings in 2011 in many Arab countries, they may not even have the advantage anymore.

27.2 ATTRACTION TO VIOLENCE IN INVADED COUNTRIES.

Whenever a country is invaded, it causes a tremendous increase in gossip about the invasion among the invaded population. It is all the native population thinks about and talks about. This tremendous increase in flows of information among all members of the population creates a system mind that is not the usual kind we have been mostly concerned with. It is a rather simple system mind that has a single goal — expel the invader. And this is where bad luck comes in. The most effective way to expel the invader is for their system mind to gather around a leader that is best able to expel the invader. It must be a government or leader who attracts the most violent, aggressive and toughest members of their society, which are their tough young men. So we must ask, what best attracts such men? The answer is simple. It would be a leader or government that projects the most violence and the most raw power himself. Throughout evolutionary history, this is the kind of leader who can best protect the group against foreign aggressors or vanquish outside threats and attacks. This is exactly the situation Israel is in.

This is how the Bush administration took advantage of 9/11. This attack, which many critics believe was invited, caused many Americans to shift their support to the most aggressive and violent leaders we have. This is why when the Bushies invaded Iraq with a dazzling display of destruction and killing, most Americans gave their full support, even though Iraq had nothing to do with 9/11.

I don't think Communism is a viable economic system. However, it has suffered the historical disadvantage of coming about in countries that were engaged in expelling an invader. This is best accomplished with the most violent and brutal leaders society can produce that tough young men can identify with. This creates a feedback loop. The more fierce and brutal the leader who emerges, the more the population of the *invading* country will support equally fierce leadership to go get the bad guys. This not only perpetuates the violence, but prevents real economic and political progress in the invaded country. *It is only when a country is* not *under attack that progress towards civilization, rights and freedoms can be made.*

But even if the invader is expelled, the kind of leader who has engaged in the most violence in expelling the invader, is not going to be competent at nation-building. We read about Mao Zedong in China and Lenin and Stalin in Russia. These guys had absolutely no qualms about killing people. But Lenin was expelling the Germans in WWI; and Mao was kicking out the historic invaders of China, especially Great Britain and the Japanese. But this kind of brutal mass murderer is not going to have the dimmest idea how to build a nation. The model these leaders established sets the standard for Communist revolutions in other countries. If Communism had been established by society's peepees (Pacifists, poets and peaceniks), it might have been a mild modern-day Communalism.

On Oct. 11, 2010, Diane Sawyer of ABC snooze had on an Afghan woman whose face had been mutilated by her Talaban husband. Sawyer, of course, was whipping up murderous impulses in her audience to go get the bad guys, which is exactly what the system mind is paying her to do. But we have to ask, where was she when it was time to invade Afghanistan? Her network was passing on bold-faced lies to get us to invade Iraq and Afghanistan to spruce up their ratings. As a response, these countries are attracted to very brutal regimes and networks like the Talaban and Al Qaeda to ward off the invader. The Talaban was set up by our own CIA as a strong government capable of kicking out the Russians. Why should they think any differently about the US? And how does the Talaban attract recruits? By displaying ruthless violence, the raw power of which is an attraction for young men who are looking for an identity and are hard-wired through millions of years of evolution to follow the violent strongman who can lead them to victory over the invader. The Bush administration used the very same strategy to attract our own tough young men: by a spectacular display of killing, torture, and destruction.

Sawyer was shedding tears because her young protége's face was mutilated by a Talaban husband. This is exactly kind of violence that attracts Afghan young men to their side. And where did this strong but brutal leadership come from? It came from Afghans hunkering down on a strong authoritarianism which Sawyer helped bring about by working for a system propaganda outlet that passed on the blatant lies that enabled the illegal invasion in the first place. It's all a totally circular feedback racket. If her network didn't have to pay her bloated 8 million dollar a year salary, it might be able to keep from passing on bald-faced lies that gets us into these wars, which leads to brutal leadership and winds up causing violence to Sawyer's girl. If Sawyer wants these developing countries to treat women equally and decently, the way to do it is to use her network position to influence the US to leave them alone so that they can take a natural course towards modernity. Of course, she wouldn't get paid 8 million dollars a year to do that.

27.3 No Foreign Policy System Mind

In Sect. 25.5, we alluded to the fact that our political lives do not form an articulate system mind. But it's ever worse regarding foreign policy. It is because the flows of information between the administration in Washington and the outside world are so intermittent, distorted, inconsistent, and choppy, that there is no coherent system mind in forming foreign policy. This allows the president to run our foreign policy on the basis of ideology, whim and needs of the domestic economy. Since the intelligence agencies have no more of a system mind that the presidency, they aren't going to be of much help.

This is why foreign policy of the US all throughout our history has been a patchwork, from the really humanitarianism like saving Europe in two world wars, all the way to invading foreign countries, killing people, and replacing elected governments with basically fascist dictatorships like in Iran and Chile. Our foreign policy depends entirely on the whims of the president (and advisors) who the Supreme Court has anointed as king. It is absolutely no different from the powers of the kings of Europe in medieval times.

One minute the president is supporting true democratic forces and the next minute this very same president is invading and conquering small countries. Sometimes a president is giving billions in foreign aid to third world countries, the next minute he's overthrowing elected governments and replacing them with brutal dictatorships. We found Bill Clinton cranking up the war on terrorism while at the same time organizing the UN to prevent genocide in the former Yugoslavia. There had been no overall general philosophy in American foreign policy since WWII. The basic reason is that there is no system mind directing American foreign policy in our best interests because there are not sufficient information flows between the US and other nations of the world.

We have a CIA whose primary job is to provide information about other countries, but this agency is constantly sabotaged by politicians wanting to hear and believe descriptions of the world that have nothing to do with reality. Even within the CIA, truncated information flows are chosen on the basis of ideology. The Bay of Pigs invasion under JFK is an example. Each layer of CIA hierarchy would pick and choose information coming from below and at each layer the views of the Cuban people would drift towards hatred of Castro.

By the time one-way information flows got to the top of the CIA, it had the Cuban people just itching to oust the Castro government. This was all fantasy. It is one thing to complain about your government and even bitterly oppose it, and quite another thing to invite in a foreign invader, especially one who had been supporting brutal right-wing dictators for over 50 years in Cuba. If Martians were to poll Americans during the Bush or Obama administrations, they would find lots of complaints about the government. Does this mean that Americans would join an invasion by Martians to overthrow our government?

This is why the CIA is clearly the most troublesome institution in all of society. When the CIA tried to tell the Bush administration that Saddam Hussein did not have weapons of mass destruction, the Bush administration told the CIA what to say and believe until they finally gave grudging support for Bush's invasion. The first impulse would be to make them more independent so they could evolve a more efficient system mind. The trouble is that the CIA has been a magnet for neoconservative ideologues who turn it into a country within a country with their own foreign policy, starting wars, assassinating world leaders and doing all kinds of things detrimental to our national interests. This is exactly what happened in the past in Iran, Chile, Guatemala, etc. On the other hand, if they have a short leash totally under civilian control, it is easy to become just a rubber stamp for the king as was the case under Bush in the Iraq situation. The best solution would be to completely sever the ties between the president and the CIA. The CIA should be controlled by a congressional committee which would insure many more flows of information and a more cogent system mind. We are not going to have a rational foreign policy if the king can twist the arm of the CIA for the whims of his murderous personal foreign policy.

27.4 PSYCHOLOGY OF A LAWLESS WORLD

Now the system mind has other reasons for making the president into a king. It is to create a node of power and aggression for powerless peasants to identify with. And in order to facilitate this gradual transition from president to king, the system mind must promote just the right kind of propaganda. What this mostly consists of is convincing the American people that we don't want our "hands tied" by international agreements, treaties and laws. This allows the king to do what he dam well pleases, thus creating the image of a real king with unlimited powers.

This is why the system mind propaganda outlets rarely talk about international law. During the run-up to the Iraq invasion, for every sentence about international law and treaties discussed by the system mind, there were a *hundred* statements from the Bush administration about the "coalition" and weapons of mass destruction. Of course, this coalition was nothing but an ad hoc ratpack of countries like England, who wanted to get in on the theft of Iraq's oil. The system media can make more money reporting on wars than any other topic, so the last thing they are going to promote is international law.

Without a foreign policy system mind, the door is open for any president with too much energy in the bottom of his brain to make himself into a king and invade, conquer and kill anywhere he pleases just like the European kings in the Middle Ages. This is not only possible but probable with a modern army at his disposal. Often it leads to disaster. What did the American Revolution do for England? 200 years later, another King George did the same thing with the same results.

There is a substantial segment of the American population who, having become increasingly powerless over their economic lives, is ripe fruit for the opportunity to identify with someone who projects massive amounts of power. The Boston Globe reported that at various times, Bush claimed he had the right to ignore 750 laws. The fault, as most problems, lies with the reptiles on the Supreme Court who have a dedicated and decisive agenda to make the president into a king with unlimited powers in direct violation of the Constitution.

The Bush administration has flaunted every kind of international law. These include the Geneva Conventions, the Convention Against Torture, the International Convent on Civil and Political Rights, and the Foreign Intelligence Surveillance Act. This is in addition to violating important tenets of international law and not just once but repeatedly. Like any bully, it's not in the president's interests to have laws and international rules constraining what he feels like doing. This is also promoted by the kind of people that worm their way into powerful foreign policy positions. With no foreign policy system mind, there is a vacuum which is an open invitation to people who want the power to invade, conquer and kill. And they have a modern army at their disposal to do it just as Law VI states. These kinds of people like under Johnson and Bush have all the energy in the bottom of their brains. The result is that the energy-starved parts of the brain that see reality, don't get used. Bush's people thought Iraqis were going to have tickertape parades welcoming the US invaders. They can't see the reality that young men in other countries also have undeveloped existential brains, which means they are going to be motivated by the same inner brain emotion of territorial aggression as our young men. They will fight forever to expel the invader. Even under Obama, this weakness in our foreign policy is still in place whereby policymakers think they're going to wean young men of Afghanistan from their primary motivation by calling them names — terrorists, insurgents, etc.

In my opinion, what a lawless foreign policy overlooks is that 5 out of 6 people in the world live in the Afro-Eurasian mega-continent. This is where the action is. And this is where the other superpowers, China, Russia, and India are located. It would seem to me that a lawless world is in the interests of *these* strategically located superpowers. It's no advantage to have a free hand in the western hemisphere where only 1 in 6 of the world's population lives, while the other world powers have a free hand where the vast majority of people live. It seems to me that a law-*abiding* world would be more in our national interests.

There is probably no solution to this. The corporate media system mouthpieces are going to allow only information to the American people that is in the interests of the neoconservative major nodes. They love wars because they're corporate sponsors make money on them and they keep people distracted from the fact that they are getting screwed in their economic lives.

The founding fathers had insight into this, which is why they gave the power to make wars to Congress. Because there are more people in Congress, there would be more nodes and many more flows of information between our government and events in foreign countries and between our ambassadors and Congress. This would create a more consistent and even-handed political system mind promoting a foreign policy more in line with the needs as well as the ideals of the country.

What the founding fathers *didn't* understand and provide for was that the president, having the power to pick Supreme Court injustices, would use their *inner* brains to make choices who identify with raw naked power and have made the president into an all-powerful king. And the king attracts people who are also motivated by raw, naked power who fill our foreign policy vacuum and can close their eyes, ignore important information flows, and follow their reptilian brains to invade, conquer, and kill. It's not so much an evil system, but no system at all.

[1] Bailyn, Bernard, *The Barbarous Years: The Peopling of British North American*. Knopf Pr.

[2] "Proken Promises", *The New York Review*, Oct, 23, '07, p. 14

[3] Pappe, Alan, *The Ethnic Cleansing of Palestine*. Oneworld.

[4] Siegman, Henry, "Netanyahu's Freeze Scam". *The Nation*, Oct. 18, '10

[5] Sand, Shlomo, *The Invention of the Jewish People*. Verso Press

[6] Shapira, Anita, "Eyeless in Zion". *The New Republic*, Dec. 11, '00

[7] Morris, Benny, "Details and Lies". *The New Republic*, Oct. 31, '05, p. 31

[8] Morris, Benny, "Derisionist history". *The New Republic*, Nov. 18, '09, p. 45

[9] Istvan Deak. *The New York Review of Books*, May 31, '84. p. 39.

[10] Shapira, Anita, "Eyeless in Zion". *The New Republic*, Dec. 11, '00

[11] Craig, Gordon,"How Hell Worked". *The New York Review of Books*, Apr. 18, '96, p. 8

[12] Kimmerling, Baruch, "Israel's Cult of Martyrdom". *The Nation*, Jan. 10. '05

[13] Craig, Gordon,"How Hell Worked". *The New York Review of Books*, Apr. 18, '96, p. 8

[14] Ferguson, Niall, *High Financier: The Life and Times of Siegmund Warburg*, Penguin Press. Reviewed by   Anthony Julius in *The New Republic*, Sept. 2, 2010, p. 25.

[15] Bartov, Omer; "The Last German". *The New Republic*, Dec. 28, '98, p. 34

[16] "The battle for the territories", *The Economist*, July, 12, '08, p. 59

[17] Siegman, Henry, "Netanyahu's Freeze Scam". *The Nation*, Oct. 18, '10

[18] JNS, *The New Republic*, May 27, '13, p, 57.

CHAPTER 28

The System Mind - Social Ramifications

——

IN THE CH. 25, WE looked at some of the economic ramifications of the system mind. In this chapter we will look at some of the *social* ramifications which fall into two groups: those that are the result of the actual *needs* of the system mind; and those that just happen to *result* from meeting these needs. Regarding the former, we have to ask what kind of a society does the system mind want and need? Its needs are the interests of the major nodes of the system and what is good for the self-perpetuation of the whole system. Since the major nodes in the American economic system are major corporations and wealthy individuals in the top 5% of the income and wealth ladder, the desires and goals of the system mind are going to be policies and practices that accommodates those nodes.

28.1 PRESSURE ON LABOR

First of all, since the bottom 80% spend most of their money on Consumption, the less income they have, the less will be spent to buying goods and services the system produces. This forces businesses to compete for reduced consumer income by advertising and by offering a cheaper or better product. This can be accomplished by lower operating costs. The most important component of business costs is labor costs, especially in labor-intensive industries. The price of materials to make products depends on international forces of supply and demand. Businesses cannot control these costs effectively. However, if a firm can minimize its labor costs, it can offer its products at a lower cost and increase profits. This is why throughout the history of market systems, businesses have always done what they can to reduce labor costs. This in turn can be best achieved by getting the most labor from workers for the least pay. This in turn involves coercing workers to put in as many hours as possible, which can be best achieved by a work force consisting of people whose lives revolve solely around their jobs.

The ultimate goal of the system mind is to create the perfect worker, which is a mindless 12-hour day, 6 day-a-week work slave whose personal life has shriveled away. His identity, his waking hours and most of his thoughts will concern this almighty job. The life of the ideal citizen will have no human connections and associations, no love, no romance, no marriage, no friends, no roots, no involvement with others at a deep emotional level — nothing that could distract from the almighty job. This takes work. Human beings have a natural inclination for more meaning in their lives than what an almighty job can provide. Males and females have a natural attraction to each other. Studies show that intimate relationships, such as marriages, are the most important sources of happiness and satisfaction. The system mind tries to sever all these human connections.

The perfect citizen will have a few hours a week to go out and buy the junk the system is making. This is why advertising is a multi-billion dollar industry. The reason advertising is so important is that with a 70-hour week, the worker's brain is so fried that he will have little discriminating powers to judge the quality of what he is buying. He will be a sitting duck for junk that he may not even need. This is why many firms spend more money on advertising and less on the quality of what they're selling.

The ideal citizen will not be a member of any group like a union that could inform him of his real economic and political interests. He will be plugged into the major means of propaganda which will instill in him values, beliefs, opinions and an ideology that are conducive to the wants and needs of the system. As we have said, this will be a neoconservative ideology. Even if he thinks he's a liberal, his criticisms of the system will be exactly what the system has programmed into him.

There are many examples of businesses trying to minimize labor costs. One of them is in the area of healthcare. Our current system of healthcare started during WWII. There were so many workers in the armed forces that there was a shortage of labor. This would normally put pressure to increase wages. This combined with all the money Roosevelt was printing up to pay for the war would create inflationary pressure. So the government put a freeze on prices and wages. To get around this, many firms began to offer healthcare to new employees. After the war, there was so much economic expansion that firms continued to offer healthcare benefits to attract employees. This was done through insurance companies. This is how we came to the health care system we had.

But again with the sophistication of the system mind gradually improving all the time, by the '80s, it had figured out that maybe we don't have to offer health insurance with a job. And this began a slow process that really picked up steam under George Bush so that by the end of Bush's term, there were around 40 million families without health insurance. Obama tried to reform the system and offer a public healthcare option but what we got was a blank check to doctors and hospitals. This is just one more way that labor costs have been dropping for the lower 80% of income earners. If a family has to buy their own plan and the employer doesn't, that effectively shifts costs to wage earners.

Now there are a few institutions left over from Roosevelt's New Deal that try to maintain income to the bottom 80%. One of these is the *minimum wage*. The minimum wage is the most efficient way to keep up demand among the bottom 80% because workers at this level have such low income that they spend every penny they earn to survive. If you want to spur Consumption, the quickest way is raise the minimum wage. But of course, the system mind mouthpieces come up with all kinds of disaster scenarios to suppress the minimum wage. It kills jobs, kills businesses, causes the sky to fall and even kills the goldfish. It is an example of how conservatives think they're going to get rich starving out their customers.

But I want to say something in defense of small businesses. I remember in 2009, I was talking to a woman struggling to run a little sandwich shop who had the usual complaints about taxes and wages. I began to realize why small businesses tend to have conservative political views. The only things she could control were her taxes and wage costs. It is only natural she would try to minimize these, which conservative politicians propagandize about. I told that if she had lots of people coming in the door for a sandwich, her tax and wage bill wouldn't be so important. But she didn't see how she could control that. That's the problem. She was concerned with taxes and wages because that is all she had some *control* over.

But in reality, the success of her business relied much more on who came in the door to buy a sandwich than on her taxes. Due to the downturn, she wasn't paying taxes anyway because she wasn't making any money. What this woman needed most was not a tax cut or a low minimum wage. *What she needed most were customers,* plain and simple, who were just middle class neighborhood people coming in for a sandwich. But they would only come in if they had decent paying jobs which requires a reasonable minimum wage.

So it's a vicious circle and it's hard to get out of. Bush's tax cuts led to huge deficits and his fake deregulation led to people at the top of the economic game to orchestrate a gigantic swindle. So the whole system collapsed and people didn't have the money to come into my friend's shop for a sandwich. In 2009, we had thousands of small businesses failing because their profits were right at the margin; and when income to the middle class faltered, they didn't have enough customers to keep their businesses going. Bush's tax cuts did them very little good. The moral of the story is that *small businesses will succeed only if their ordinary middle class customers have enough income to come into their shops.* This means a balanced economy, which real Democratic Capitalism will provide. The shop owner will probably continue to vote for a conservative agenda even though it starves out the very customers she needs to do business.

This amplifies to the larger economy where we find businesses of all sizes attempting to keep wages down even though this reduces the flow to the Household tank. The paradox is that even though it is in the interests of each firm taken *individually* to minimize its labor costs, if all firms do this, there won't be enough Income to the Household tank and those very businesses won't be able to sell all they can make. So what each firm is hoping for is that *it* can lower its labor costs, while other firms can't, so that *other* firms in the economy are providing the purchasing power to buy the products the wage-cutting firm is selling.

That's why I don't have sympathy for large companies who pay below average wages. Back in the '60s, Sam Walton who started Walmart was enraged when Kennedy raised the minimum wage to $1.15 an hour. The facts of the matter, however, is that if everyone was paid the minimum wage, the Consumption pipe would slow down to a trickle, production and sales would fall, unemployment would increase, and we would have a recession. What allowed Walton to expand stores was that most *other* workers in the economy earned more than the minimum wage. A lot of this was due to unions, which Walton fought to keep out. In my opinion, people like Walton are simply economic parasites: they rely on someone *else* to pay wages to keep Consumption up and his stores going. I am proud to say the only thing I ever did in a Walmart store was take a whizz.

Walmart bragged that it created jobs and Walton did improve the efficiency of retail selling with many new methods. But many economists have opined that by driving local businesses out, he also had the effect of replacing better paying jobs with low paying jobs. The improvement in efficiency was probably not enough to compensate for the fact that his company tended to *decrease* wages to the lower 80% who spend most of their income. This causes an imbalance in the economy which requires big deficits to prop up demand.

The desire to keep labor costs down is the main reason why corporations and businesses throughout the history of free enterprise systems have always pushed for unlimited immigration. Throughout our history, people have come to the US for two basic reasons: *opportunity* and *deprivation*. Those coming for opportunity were usually from the more educated and talented members of society in the old country. They are usually able to contribute their fair share of economic output. People coming from *deprivation* were usually from the less uneducated and least talented levels of society. Often they were actually starving in their native land.

Of course, the business community would brag about how they were letting in these poor immigrants and giving them a new life. But the real reason for continually pushing for immigration was to reduce the value of labor. Immigrants in the 1800s couldn't even speak English. The very precarious position of newly arrived immigrants prevented them from ever bucking the system to petition for labor rights. By having a fresh supply of labor, there would always be enough unemployment to force labor into accepting terms businesses set. By this method, the corporate community was able to keep wages and working conditions at deplorable levels for 65 years after the Civil War. The system mind made sure we were never given the real history of Victorian times in high school. Big business would brag about how wonderful they were bringing in immigrants for a bright new future. However, what our history books never told us is how many of them went back because conditions were worse here. The only answer was to have unions who would fight for labor rights, decent pay, reasonable working hours, safety, etc. However, the history of the union movement is very sad.

The start of the union movement was in New York in the early 1800's. There's a great book written about the early stages of unionism called *Democratic Chants* by Seal Wilentz, a great historian. All through the 1800s, unionism was fought tooth and nail by the business sector. Businesses would hire a special police called Pinkertons who would actually use violence to prevent unions from forming or striking. Unions would have to compete with newly arrived immigrants who were so deprived that they would work under horrible labor conditions. This prevented the system from expanding as much as it could from new technology coming out.

Finally, in the late 1800's unions were able to establish themselves but only in certain highly skilled craft industries, like machine tools etc. There was a federation of unions called the American Federation of Labor, the AFL. But the vast majority of factory and mining workers had to wait for the total collapse of the system in 1929 for Roosevelt to legalize big industrial unions who were poised to petition for better wages and working conditions. In 1935, they formed a federation called the Congress of Industrial Organizations, the CIO. In 1955, the AFL and the CIO merged to form one union organization and at the height of their growth had about a third of all private sector employees in one of their unions. All the larger industries were unionized: coal, steel, oil, trucking, autos, chemicals, etc.

The union movement during the Depression set the standard for all labor. After WWII, the great increase in the relative flow through the Household Income pipe at the Y/P fork due to unions is what greatly surged the economy in the '50s and '60s. Consumption rose, more goods and services were sold, which meant more hiring of workers to supply expanding markets. Union membership (mostly *mass* unions) in the private sector rose to where the lower 80% was getting 60% of national Income. The economy expanded at rates we haven't seen since, and unemployment remained low through this period. And they paid off WWII debt.

But corporations and businesses have never let up their propaganda against unionism and for unlimited immigration. So once the Roosevelt era ended and the age of television began, the system mind had a new tool to reestablish Economic Socialism. Ronald Reagan in 1980 was the perfect cardboard man for the job of reducing income to the bottom 80%, which is best accomplished by attacking unions. This is why the percentage of income to the lower 80% of households at the Y/P fork has come down to less than half by the time of George Bush.

But with the loss of unions and the purchasing power they represented, there was only a few ways to replace their purchasing power: steal from the future and push credit cards, both of which really picked up steam under Reagan. But this was unsustainable and led finally to the collapse of 2008. The problem under Obama is that even though he is trying to make union organizing easier, I doubt if he will be able to buck the trends of the past 35 years. What is worse is that the little union membership we do have is in public sectors like police, public works, teachers, etc.

I am not totally enraptured by unions for the simple reason that they are not very democratic. The wages a union can extract from an industry does not depend on skill, or the difficulty of the work, or even how society values the work involved. It depends on force. If a union has big tough guys like in the coal and trucking industries, it can strong-arm more wages out of the industry. The Lady's Garment Workers Union never had this kind of muscle and they get paid accordingly.

In my opinion, the entire justification for the concept of a union is to balance the power of the employer whoever it is. In the private sector where we have huge international corporations, workers need to have strong unions to balance the enormous economic and political power of corporate employers. However, in the public sector, the employer is basically the unorganized individual citizen. He has no economic power and is not organized into a self-seeking political unit. Therefore, a public sector union can overwhelm the power of individual citizens of a political unit. What we see is public sector unions extorting paychecks and pensions that are not democratically determined. Lots of times these benefits are financed by stealing from the future which is blatantly unconstitutional.

A lot of public sector employees become campaign workers when it's time to reelect the crooked politicians in office. So in return for their support, the politicians hand out benefits and high pay to *core* unionized public sector workers. These crooked politicians are, in effect, promising people somebody else's money. There are instances in city and state governments where "cops and firefighters can retire in their 40s and draw defined-benefit pensions for life. ...Including benefits, the average employee of New York City makes more than $100,000, according to Forbes, which some California prison guards 'sock away $300,000 a year' ". [1] There are thousands of examples like this. Trillions of dollars in taxes are being passed on to younger people who were not represented and never participated in legislating these taxes, another example of unconstitutionally violating the equal protection clause, a prime motive for the American Revolution. And remember, the taxpayer *paying* these benefits makes, on the average, about $45,000 per year and often retires on a Social Security pension of a measly $15,000 a year.

As we saw in Sect. 24.7, it wasn't the *core* unionism of the old AFL that created the post-war boom, but the *mass* unionism of the CIO under Roosevelt that lead to the post-war prosperous middle class. But by the time Obama came on the scene, *mass* unionism was dead. As a result, when Obama threw *billions* at state governments in his fraudulent stimulus program, *core* unionism stepped in and grabbed the money for bigger paychecks and pensions, while *mass* unionism was ignored and millions of public sector employees were actually laid off. This fit like a hand in a glove with spending cuts promoted by the Republican Party.

I think public sector employees of a community, whether local, county or state, should be paid what the citizens of that community offer because it is their taxes that are paying the bills. This is one place for pure democracy. If a community doesn't want to pay enough, their services would suffer and they would have to offer more pay. But it should be up to them. The only way this will come about is when the deficits at the state and local level get to a point where all tax revenue goes to paying interest on outstanding bonds, which is stolen money; and there will be no money for current services. The only way out is for government units to declare bankruptcy and start from scratch, paying public service employees what citizens want to pay. They should be paid well because they are middle class people too. But as Mason said to Dixon, "you got to draw the line somewhere".

But *private* sector unions are a different matter. What we have done in effect since Reagan is to replace unions in the private sector where they *should* be, by strong unions in the public sector. People are working in the *private* sector 12 hours a day for 8 hours of minimum wage pay, compared to some public sector employees working 6 hours a day for

8 hours pay at a level beyond taxpayer wishes. As we explained, Capitalism does not come with its own ethic.

The neoconservative culture we have had since Ronald Reagan has mounted a sustained attack on the wages and benefits of ordinary labor among the lower 80%. The system mind's media outlets waxed eloquently over Reagan and covered up his shrinking mind by broadcasting only times during his press conferences when he happened to be coherent. Reagan attacked unions and began a trend that lasted 35 years of gradually reducing union membership to where unions are only about 7% of the private workforce. Additionally, it was under Reagan that illegal immigration took off. Reagan thus initiated a double-pronged attack on the rights of labor. That's the real class warfare. Steven Greenhouse details much of this in his book, *The Big Squeeze*, which is a perfect title.[2] There are violations of the minimum wage laws, relaxed safety recognition, tons of extra work hours per week, and the latest racket is temporary workers to do full-time jobs so that companies can avoid health-care benefits and pensions.

Neoconservatives supported their attack on labor with a very ironic theory. They believe that the value of everything depends on supply and demand in a Godless market-place by Godless forces run by the kind of people God threw out of the temple. And they call themselves Christians no less. They think God is so stupid that He just doesn't see the reality that these neoconservatives are turning human beings and human labor into Godless commodities.

But as we mentioned in Sect. 23.5, labor is a very human consideration. Labor involves the way human beings interact in the production of goods and services. All through the Middle Ages, the skills a man had were held in great esteem. In fact, one of the reasons why historical objects are valued so highly is that these feudal artisans believed they were producing things in the eyes of God. Therefore, they couldn't cheat or cut corners on the materials and methods they used. Labor was part of their religion — a God-given glue that held society together and enabled even strangers to interact.

A whole book could be written about this but it would take an author with knowledge of religion, economics, sociology, history, and even anthropology. We don't have people like that anymore. Not being a historian, I can't do justice to the topic myself, except to point out some bottom lines. Labor is an important component of being a human being and a vehicle for human interaction. This is why, even though I'm not overly religious, in my opinion, labor is not a godless, soulless commodity in a marketplace. *The value of labor should be decided by conscious, morally informed human beings, who have human perceptions and human values — not in Godless dehumanizing marketplaces.*

One of the cleverest ideas the system mind has come up with to prevent unionization is to con workers into thinking that they are not part of labor at all, but part of management and management has to work many hours. This has some very funny repercussions. For example, there are no longer secretaries, but "office managers". Also many categories of work are called "professional" which again puts people into a special category *above* the blue color working class by making them appear more like management. And since management often work 12 hours, so do their "management" employees. Of course, there's the slight detail that the CEO is paid in millions whereas these artificial professionals are still paid in thousands.

Of course, this was made easier to bring about because less and less jobs are blue-collar. But this isn't because there are more white-collar jobs in the sense of a professional job. What we have are *pale*-color jobs. These are jobs in retailing, hotel services, various office work like data processors, restaurant services, etc. These jobs are between professional jobs and traditional factory blue-collar jobs. Many of these jobs are in the bottom two quintiles (40%), some actually at the minimum wage. Mostly, they wear pale colored clothes, which is why we're calling them *pale*-collar. The psychology is obvious: if the pale-collar worker can be convinced that he or she is part of a management team, they will be less inclined to form unions to butt heads with management who can take advantage of them by keeping wages as low as possible. This is one more reason why the share of income going to the lower 80% has been in steady decline.

The opposite side of the coin of keeping pay levels low has been to increase hours of work. The industrial revolution after the civil war saw the emergence of large factories and powerful industries like mining, manufacturing and agriculture. The system made sure there would never be a dearth of labor, which might enable working class people to demand more wages and better working conditions. This could be accomplished with a continuous supply of immigrant labor who would work long hours for very little. This is why labor conditions were deplorable after the Civil War when the factory system really picked up speed. People were working 12 and 14 hour days 6 or 7 days a week for subsistence wages and no benefits or safety protections. Every man you met had a finger or two missing from some accident with a machine and many women too worked in those horrible factories.

But after the Roosevelt revolution, one of the main purposes of bringing in a cardboard man in Ronald Reagan was to dismantle the accomplishments of post-war unionism, which was good wages, benefits, safe working conditions and above all, the 8-hour day. Reagan's attack on the middle class was supplemented by a women's movement that not only washed away the 8-hour day, but would also cover up the fact that real *personal* income was actually dropping. The system mind could give the *impression* of increasing family incomes by getting married women to get out into the workforce. In the 21st century, the lower 80% has the same standard of living, probably even lower, with two thirds of housewives working as they had in the '50s with only perhaps a fourth of housewives working.

One of the major thrusts of the woman's movement was to encourage "careers". This was supplemented by telling women they were smarter than men and the way women convinced themselves of this was to put in a few more hours of work and, of course, a few more hours of output. Men, not wanting to look inferior, responded by putting in extra hours themselves to try to stay ahead of women. It was an arms race until everyone is a total work slave. It took the union movement 150 years up against great resistance from the Economic Socialist world to achieve the 8-hour day. In one generation it is gone. It exists only in certain very powerful private sector unions who are only 7% of the workforce. As soon as the system gets rid of those unions, the 8-hour day will be like the model T.

The system doesn't often admit the long hours people are forced to work just to keep up. In Sect. 23.3 we defined *productivity*, which is the amount of goods or services a worker can make in an hour of labor. But how is productivity measured? The system has the cunning to measure the working day by calling in sociologists. They can give you any number you want. This is why when publications like *The Economist* magazine report that people are putting in an extra 10 hours a *week*, these numbers are as worthless as most of the numbers the system's mouthpieces report. Here's how I got a tentative idea of the hours people put in.

I lived near a road that a lot of professional commuters took from work each day. Now in the '70s, the rush hour would start about 3:00 in the afternoon, it would peak around 5 and be all over by about 7. It really was an example of a bell-shaped curve with an average at about 5. Now in the 2000s, you can drive pretty much at the same pace all day until about 4:30, when the rush hour seems to start. It peaks at around 6:30, and isn't all over until about 8:30. Of course, this is not a controlled study but it convinced me that we have no idea how many extra hours of work people put in. Since the collapse, the situation has got worse. *The Nation* details the additional working hours for many employees.[3] And we are leaving out hours people put in at home on computers and cell phones because people wouldn't admit to it. Among most workers, the 8-hour day is gone like the dinosaurs.

The interesting thing about the system mind is that as the means of communication became more sophisticated, so did the sophistication and effectiveness of the system mind. This shows that it is the flows of information that create a mind in any complex system. We have had massive increases in the flows of information in the last 40 years. First it was television, mass marketing and advertising. Then came the computer and now the internet and the cell phone. Right in step, there have been a number of new developments that show the increased sophistication of the system mind especially with regards to promoting its interests and evolving the means to achieve those interests. Regarding our present analysis, this has been manifested in the steps taken to reduce labor costs.

Only pure Capitalism maintaining strict rules to keep the system in balance can avoid this. But with a very sophisticated system mind, it becomes almost impossible to maintain Capitalism. All free enterprise systems wind up as Economic Socialism. Firms climb in bed with political players in Washington through social interaction, bribes and lobbying, and rig the rules. When firms are successful in their drive towards Economic Socialism, they are able to squelch unions, depress wages by having unlimited immigration working for low wages, and in the short run, increase profits. The stockmarket goes up and it all looks good. But this is not sustainable because all other firms are doing the same thing. With less and less relative Income going to the Household tank, there is less for Consumption, business flags, and the system eventually collapses. Reformers are elected but Economic Socialism never goes to sleep and the process starts all over.

28.2 Pressure on Families

Another trend we have observed in the last 30 years since Reagan is the loss of job security. At present, the average length of a job in the US is about 4 years. It is in the interests of the system mind to have continual job insecurity by forcing people to relocate often. The other factor that reduces job security is a high unemployment rate. High unemployment keeps people scared enough of losing their jobs that employers can milk 12 hours a day out of them. However, this gets tricky. If unemployment gets too high like in 1929, the people might wake up and vote in a Roosevelt who could threaten the whole Economic Socialist scam. In my opinion, the optimal level of *real* unemployment for the system mind is about 8%. Less than that removes fears of losing a job, and more than that could cause the natives to get restless. 8% is about right for keeping workers in tow. Reagan unemployment numbers averaged 7.4% over his 8 years, which is about right.

The high unemployment rate accompanied by job insecurity and long working hours lessens the connections working people have with other people in their private lives, especially family. Home life deteriorates as antagonism grows between spouses, the house is a mess and the kids are out of control. For many spouses, being at work is a better deal than being home in a totally dysfunctional household. This enables employers to extract longer hours the purpose of which is to reduce labor costs. In addition, these trends cause frustration among men who are often likely to take it out on their wives. Reagan's attack on job security and relative wages of middle class earners was also a cause of the increase in domestic violence in the 1980s. This also has the effect of keeping wives at work where they are probably safer.

But the system mind had other tricks up its sleeve to get people to work more hours. And this was to make a direct assault on the whole idea of marriage and families. In the eyes of the system, families are a distraction from the almighty job. A normal person is usually anxious to get home at the end of a working day to interact with their spouses and play with their kids. But if families can be destroyed by various means, people would more likely spend their time at work. The two most important ways to attack the family are to attack traditional religion and the institution of marriage.

28.3 Traditional Religion

I think it is fairly well established that traditional religion, whether or not it is really true is a support and a facilitator of the family concept. Remember the old saying that "families who pray together, stay together"? I remember as a little kid being dragged to Church every Sunday morning. We had to get up, put on some decent clothes with super clean itchy underwear and all go to church together. It didn't matter if the religion is true, or even if there really is a God. The process of getting the family together and going to a solemn place to hear God's message was a binding force for marriage and family.

(By the way, when I was a kid, I would take a quarter every Sunday for the collection basket. But I was smart enough to outwit the priests when there was more than one collection. I took my quarter in nickels and dimes, so if there was more than one collection, I would divide my quarter into portions and contribute to each collection, thus insuring never having to give up more than one quarter. And the priests weren't smart enough to keep quiet about additional collections. In fact, they would apologize for them. This gave me time to divide up my contribution into the right number of portions. If priests were smart, they wouldn't announce more than one collection. Then if I put my whole quarter in the first collection, I would be embarrassed as hell not having money for later collections. I would have had to take *three* quarters every Sunday to have something for additional collections. But that's why priests are priests: they would never make it in business.)

But the system mind has no sense of humor. Since religion and marriage are binding forces for families, religion and marriage have become prime targets of attack by the major media mouthpieces of the system mind. Often you see movies and television programs with nuns as prostitutes and priests as drug-dealers and other criminals. A really remarkable example of the working of the system mind regarding the system's view of religion was the sex scandals among Catholic priests in the early 2000s. First of all, without a conspiracy, without prior agreements, without meetings behind closed doors, the media system mouthpieces had to cover up who the real criminals were and what the crimes really were. What seemed like total coordination, every media outlet had the exact same approach to the scandals. It looked like a complete conspiracy, except there was no conspiracy. It was simply the working of a system mind.

First of all, the crimes had to be shifted away from the people perpetuating them to the Church itself. So the first stage in the process was to recategorize the crimes. In reality, of course, these sex acts were molestations of young boys by gay men impostoring as priests. They had lied threw their teeth about believing in God just to have access to young boys. That is the barebones accurate description of the crimes. But the system was not about to focus attention on gay priests, since glorification of the gay lifestyle was so important to the establishment of gay marriage. The reason of course, is that the system mind is a dedicated enemy of religion, whereas, gay anything is its bosom buddy. So instead of the perpetrators being gay *child molesters*, which was the case in *reality*, these priests were given a cleaner identity as *pedophiles*. Now what is a pedophile? Well, if you look it up in the dictionary, you'll find that it has Greek language root meaning "lover of children". Isn't that sweet. These criminals were miraculously transformed from gay *child molesters* into Godly lovers of children. How cheerful.

Now when a guy rapes a girl, the media mouthpieces of the system mind are very quick to call it RAPE, in loud tones and bold print. No question about what this crime is. When a black guy commits a crime, he is identified as *black* in the media when the color of his skin had nothing to do with the crime. But the system mind is dedicated to keeping gayness as pure as the driven snow, even though the *essence* of the crime is homosexuality. So they were transformed into "pedophiles": lovers of children. It's really heartwarming. If the system didn't want to identify these priests as gay, they should have at least identified them as child molesters. What prevented this, of course, is that they were gay. But they *were* identified as *priests* with the implication that these crimes didn't occur because the perpetrators were gay impostors, which is the reality, but because they were *priests*.

But there was double barrel action to all this. Not only were the crimes shifted from gay impostors to *priests*, but the entire Catholic Church was also miraculously transformed into a criminal enterprise. Now I'm not saying this as a Catholic because I'm not much of a Catholic anymore. But historically, religious institutions started out as *congregations* of people meeting in a particular building who held certain religious beliefs and practices. I realize that many religions, especially the Catholic Church has grown in power and status as an institution. But individual churches are *congregations*. They could be considered like franchises of a mother church. When a movie was made on the basis of a Boston Globe spotlight team investigation, there is actually a line in the movie saying that their job was not to go after the real perpetrators of the crimes but to go after the *Church*. But the *Church* is a congregation of ordinary people like you and me who had nothing to do with these crimes. The system loved this fraudulent movie so much, it gave it an academy award. And by the way, how did the Church of ordinary people get transformed from congregations to businesses like corporations. I don't know the history, but I'll bet my bottom dollar that somewhere along the way, in the process of the system wanting to rid society of religion altogether, a bunch of vampires ganged up on society and made them into businesses that could be sued.

But as a congregation, the money it collects is really the *congregation's* money held in *trust* by Church officials, to be used according to the wishes of the *congregation*. When a member of a congregation gives money to be used for things like spreading the word of God, or nunneries or orphanages or schools for children, that's where the money should go. *It is their money*. And the Church does use their moneys mostly for these purposes. Priests and nuns don't exactly live high on the hog like people who run corporations. Parishioners do not intend their money to wind up in the pockets of a bunch of atheistic vampires who went to work transforming a religious institution, which is a *congregation*, into a business that could be sued with their money going right into the pockets of the vampires running these suits. And I have to say, as unreligious as I am, it was very painful to watch the Church closing down orphanages and schools for children because the money intended for these uses had been stolen.

And what did all those Irish and Italian Catholics in the Massachusetts statehouse do about it? Well, they are all vampires themselves. To a vampire, the interests of other vampires comes much before religion and God. They were not going to get in the way of other vampires grabbing huge chunks of Church moneys. The net result was exactly as the system mind had intended: to close orphanages and schools that the church ran to get religion out of children's lives. The new religion is not values and lifestyle of Christ, but money and power.

And by the way, to cap it all off, what ever became of the gay priests? Or the church officials who covered up the scandal? Did they go to jail? Did they get fined? I have no idea what became of them, and we were never told by the system mind mouthpieces. It was all pushed under the rug. Their fate was unimportant to the system. Once tens of millions were stolen from the Church, the system mind totally lost interest in the crimes committed and the perpetrators of those crimes.

28.4 TRADITIONAL MARRIAGE

The second means the system used to attack the concept of the family was to attack the institution of marriage. As we have mentioned, in the eyes of the system mind, marriage is a distraction — a distraction from the almighty 12-hour day job. Married people want to get home to their spouses and children, not stay all hours at the office. But starting in the '80s, the system mind realized that a major means to weaken the institution of marriage is to water it down and lessen it as a source of identity.

Recall in Sect. 20.5, we talked about identity. Our identities are the most important facets of our existences, especially for men. Women have a built in identity as mothers. Even if they don't have a baby, the wiring is still in women as *potential* mothers. First, there's the Freudian problem of establishing an identity. All babies are little girl babies and it's a smooth transition going from a baby girl to a teenage girl, to a young woman to an older woman. There are no abrupt jumps in identity. But at some point, a baby boy has to make the transition from an identity of what is basically a baby girl to a young boy and then a man. Freud thought this was a very problematic jump from identifying with a mother to identifying with a male father. Some people think that the inability to make this transition leads poorly formed identities in young men.

Add to this the fact that in evolutionary history men had to make another important transition. Human males had to go from promiscuous males competing to be the alpha male who is wired to get 'em all, to the last stages of evolution where males were needed to protect their own families. This is not an easy transition as most men understand and most women don't. The suggestion we are making here is that *human culture, religion, and morays evolved over thousands of years to turn men from promiscuous hunters into stable, reliable family men.*

Historically, marriage was invented by almost every population of people that was discovered on the face of the earth, from New Guinea headhunters to Stone Age tribes in the Amazon jungle. Among most of these peoples, marriage was the most important milestone in a man's life and a component of male *identity* — a measure of real manhood. It relied on the only good basic emotion men have: the tendency to protect. In this regard, marriage was able to guide males into supporting their kids and being faithful loving husbands and companions for their wives; and to inhibit them from behavior that is destructive to families.

When the Industrial Revolution arrived in the early 1800s, reliance on marriage as a source of identity became even more important. One of the most important effects of the market economy during the Industrial Revolution was the gradual alienation of the worker from his work. Karl Marx made a big deal out of this idea as did the sociology profession.

Most of today's antiques were made before the Civil War in small shops consisting of a handful of workers, who had an intimate relation to what they were fashioning. Objects are reality and the history of objects is evidence of past human executed skills. Men could point to the houses they built, the furniture they made or any other lasting objects that exhibited skill in making. A cabinetmaker made the entire piece of furniture that he could claim as his own. One woodcarver would carve the whole carousel animal. It is by executing skills in manipulating, creating, and fashioning real objects that there would be tangible evidence of a man's existence and a strong contributor to his identity. Compare that with today's world with its myriad of meaningless office jobs.

But as Industrial Revolution progressed, objects were increasingly made in large factories employing hundreds of workers. This was the basis of the great mills you see all over New England that sprung up after the Civil War. This gradually evolved into assembly line production which took off after Henry Ford developed a very efficient assembly line for making cars. This is what is referred to by the sociologist's concept of *alienation*. In modern life, we see a vacuum in male *identity* that was once filled by human artifacts and human skills that is now filled by the almighty computer-pecking job which seems remote from the final product.

In reaction to this loss of identity, male workers may have turned to their families as a means of identification. In Sect. 21.1, we explained the increase in romantic love during the Industrial Revolution as a reaction to the fact that the Industrial Revolution was changing the unit production from the family to the individual. Since the family would no longer be necessary, the Church and the culture stepped in to try to prop up the family with romantic love.

During WWII and immediately afterwards, men very energetically identified with their families. I remember even as a kid, going to my father's warehouse, the center of conversation was the married men with children. They would stick their chests out to announce, "I'm a family man". This was probably the most important part of their identity. They were the real men. A lot of the talk was about their wives and kids. The single guys were still only *boys* at the periphery of conversations. Now it's reversed. Among a group of working men, it is the single guys running the conversation about all their girlfriends and sexual adventures, and the married guys are on the periphery jealously observing the conversation.

In fact, one of the major motivations for finding someone to marry that was so prevalent in my generation and my father's, was to get a family going that would be a rich source of *identity*. This is why there was so much courtship and marriage even at young ages. I grew up in a social milieu that stressed the idea that to become a real man, you should look for a girl to marry and start a family. But all this was bad news for the system. In fact, in the post-war years, the system looked with great alarm at the fact that especially men were increasingly getting large contributions to their identities from their families instead of the almighty job. So starting with the Reagan administration, the system mind had an important new job, which was to remove marriage from being the most important component of a man's identity. Without the support of the economic system, forces keeping marriages intact gradually eroded. And once identity through marriage disintegrates, it greases the skids towards enabling the system to get men to work 12 hours a day at their jobs to establish an identity. And as our job identity grows, our personal identity and our home identity shrinks, until there is very little identity left other than the job. This is the goal of the system mind.

However, as we have emphasized, the values and practices of the system are mostly determined by the wealthier and more powerful nodes of the economy. And their politics has become neoconservative. But conservatives throughout history resisted change and maintained traditional values, which includes marriages and families. However, economic considerations often trump social values. So in the face of a history of traditional values including families, the system has to invent ways to destroy families while at the same time looking like they support traditional values. The system picked the perfect man for the job in Ronald Reagan.

As we remember, Reagan ran campaigns and attracted political support by constantly trumpeting "family values". Now of course, the system mind understands that people, especially women, create their views of reality not on the basis of *perceptions* but on the basis of *words*. That's why it was important for Reagan to go around preaching "family values". The reality of course, is that Reagan was the most anti-family president in the history of the country as is proven by the fact that the divorce rate increased in the 1980s, the marriage rate started to drop and violence against women increased steadily.

Now of course, Ronald Reagan certainly thought he was a great supporter of the family. Well, this is a good place to stop and examine what the system mind is. It is not a conspiracy. People don't gather behind closed doors and agree to get a president who will get rid of the family concept. Well, how does this happen? Our suggestion is that the system is exactly analogous to the human brain. Individual neurons in the brain are not thinking, I want a new car. They are not thinking at all. But by sending enormous amounts of information back and forth between them, you get a mind. The system mind comes about in the exact same way.

But what about the individual minds of economic and political players? Don't they have their own views? Well, yes. In his own mind, Reagan thought he was very pro-family. Of course, Reagan had a very weak mind which is why the system chose him in the first place. I think he had the beginnings of Alzheimer's the whole time he was president. This made it all the more easy for his own values and his own thinking to be quickly taken over by the system mind just like in the *Invasion of the Body Snatchers*. As such he mounted an enormous attack on the family with economic policies that attacked the economic interests of the middle class.

Another way to attack the institution of marriage is to constantly dangle temptations in front of men's noses that would pull men away from their marriages. So Reagan and his conservative political allies in congress passed laws that *de*regulated television. This gave the major networks a blank check as to what they could program. And since sexual interest is a very old emotion at the bottom of our brains, people would always be tempted to watch programming with sexual overtones. This is why you get a constant stream of sex and violence on TV. TV is a very graphic medium, and it has been put to great use in creating all kinds of means to tempt men away from loyal marriages. My father, who was raised before WWII and before television, once remarked to me that you could see more pretty faces and sexy bodies in one hour of television, than he saw the whole time he was growing up. This trend was greatly amplified by the introduction of tape recording and computers that have put pornography at everyone's fingertips. How men are supposed to stay interested in their wives with the constant bombardment of sexy bodies and sexy practices from television and the computer, is a gigantic mystery.

What we have is what we could call the family values merry-go-round. It starts out with political leaders like Reagan favoring marriages and family values. This gets conservatives elected. Then they deregulate television and other media. Then even though leaders of big corporations are supposed to be conservative politically, what they actually do is hire a bunch of Hollywood *liberals* to make programs with as much sex and violence as possible. Of course, these same economic leaders blame those Hollywood liberals in the "liberal" media for all the sex and violence. They rely on the fact that the average voter doesn't see that the people running this programming, sponsoring it, and hiring the people to create it, is the *corporate* media. They can blame liberals and hide the fact that these liberals *are nothing but hired hands in the whole process* — hired by a very economically *ultraconservative* corporate media. But people don't see through this. This is especially true of the Christian right that votes for fake conservatives who deregulate the media who are then free to stuff a constant dose of sex and violence into their lives. This gives those very same conservative leaders grist for the mill, who proceed to complain bitterly about all the sex and violence in our society and the loss of family values in order to get elected and continue around the circle. They proceed to prop up Reagan's "family values" shpeel where we got on the merry-go-round. It's a racket that makes the mafia look benign.

To top off the whole system agenda, we had a woman's movement that had a two-pronged agenda of encouraging working careers for women and of attacking the whole idea of marriage. Women were told that marriage was a form of slavery and exploitation and that it was careers that should make a woman's identity. One of the results of this is that almost half of children are now born out of wedlock. This is a double prize for the system. First is the fact that without fathers, young boys are put at a disadvantage in many ways. One of most important pieces of evidence for fatherhood was a *Mind* article describing how fatherhood actually improves brain development and that in animals experimented on, "…pups raised without a father had deficits in the orbitofrontal cortex and the somatosensory cortex". [4] Of course, this evidence was squashed by the system mind propaganda outlets like a steamroller over an anthill. Since females make the babies in the first place, it is difficult to make them irrelevant to child-raising. But men are a different story. It's just a matter of enough propaganda to get them out of the child-rearing business entirely. Without father figures to identify with, the avenue is paved for a young man to achieve identity by joining the king's current war, or at least by identifying with the almighty job.

There's no question that the Economic Socialist system mind is very much anti-friend, anti-marriage, anti-family and anti-all human connection. These human aspects of our lives simply detract from extra hours of work. We tend to think of the destruction of families as reflected in divorce rates. But an equally important factor is the marriage rate, which has been plummeting in the last 40 years to half what it was in the '60s. Around big cities, it's a third. The reason the divorce rate hasn't gone even higher is because people aren't getting married in the first place. But the system mind has one more trick up its sleeve to fade away the marriage institution.

28.5 GAY MARRIAGE

In my opinion, the last nail in the coffin of the marriage institution is gay marriage. And in order to promote gay marriage, the system also had to tirelessly promote the gay lifestyle. In fact, if Martians visited the earth, their first impressions from television would be, how do these people reproduce themselves? There's nothing wrong with the gay lifestyle, but to constantly promote it indicates that the system mind had a lot more in mind than the gay lifestyle. But it wasn't always this way. As we discussed in Sect. 24.9, Ronald Reagan neglected the blood supply in the 1980s while it continued to be contaminated by the AIDS virus. Up to a quarter million people, mostly gay, might have died totally unnecessarily. But Reagan didn't have to worry one iota about his image in this regard. For hundreds of years, gays were considered deviants by mainstream society, which is why they were in the closet. So it didn't matter at all to society that gays were dying like flies from the spread of AIDS. They simply didn't count. The system mind propaganda outlets could continue propping up Reagan's image unabated without having to worry about the gay predicament and gays dying of AIDS.

However, picking up steam in the '90s, the system mind realized that great use could be made of the gay phenomenon in pursuing its goals of ridding society of the marriage institution. All of a sudden, portrayal of the gay lifestyle turned on a dime and was promoted to the moon. Gays were popping up everywhere, in books, articles, movies, and most importantly, TV, as a glorious lifestyle that all right-thinking people would recognize. Leading characters on the soaps and sitcoms were all of a sudden gay. Gays gradually became the heroes of society. The reason is obvious. The gay lifestyle was only a means to an end, which was to promote gay marriage as the ultimate goal of the system mind. The system mind understands that the best way to weaken the marriage institution is to reduce its meaning and status, and gay marriage is one great way to do it. Let's see why.

Recall back in Sect. 3.3, we discussed the concept of meaning. The meaning of a symbol or event is measured by its information content. Information content depends on how special the symbol or event is in its Universe of Discourse. For the marriage concept, the Universe of Discourse is all possible pairs of people who could be included in the marriage contract: brothers and sisters, fathers and daughters, males and females, gay couples, etc. What makes traditional marriage *special* in this Universe of Discourse is that it eliminates all other pairs. This then gives traditional marriage high information content, which in turn, gives it meaning.

Now gay marriage advocates will trumpet that gay marriage has meaning to them. But we are not talking about *personal* meaning which we explained in Ch. 16. We are talking about the *public* concept of marriage and its *public* meaning, which is what young people face when considering marriage. It would be almost impossible to have a quantitative measure of personal meaning. However, public meaning is a finite state thing and it is simple information theory that gives a quantitative measure of public meaning. Measured in this way, a marriage contract that includes gay couples would make the contract less special because you are eliminating less pairs. With less specialness, there is less information content and less public meaning. This reduces its status and contribution to male identity. And the way you achieve specialness is to create *exclusivity*. Exclusivity eliminates most items in a Universe of Discourse leaving items that are then special and meaningful. What is most important is: *when you dilute the exclusivity of an organization, club, or association, you reduce its status and meaning, which lessens its contribution to a person's identity.* This fact occurred to me on a few occasions.

One time I signed up for a class that was to be held in a Masonic hall. Well, I didn't know where the class was, so I entered the magnificent building and went bounding up the steps. I got to the top and was immediately confronted by two elderly men. They didn't say a word, but just stared vacantly at me like a couple of zombies. I was an intruder who had invaded their inner sanctum. What was so important to them was that a good deal of their *identities* was wrapped up in having the status and associated exclusivity of being Masons, which is a very old association going back hundreds of years. To end the story, without saying a word, I retreated down the steps and found the class in the basement.

I have a similar story. I took another class — this one to be held in a VFW hall. Having learned my lesson, I went for the basement. As luck would have it, this time the class was upstairs. But I went into the basement and all conversation stopped; all eyes were pinned on me standing there like I had no clothes on. No words were spoken, there were just grim incensed stares until I turned and hightailed it out of there. What gives these vets the identity of being vets is its *exclusivity*. Not everyone is a vet and not everyone can become a vet. Its restricted membership provides the *exclusivity* that gives this organization its status, its meaning and its importance in the identities of its members.

Suppose I were to tell you that I'm starting a new club. It will be called the AAAB, the American Association of Air Breathers. Now how much status would this club have? How much would being a member of this club contribute to your identity? You see the point. *When you reduce the exclusivity of an association, you reduce its meaning and its status.* This is an iron law of associations.

When I first heard of gay marriage, I pretty much approved. I'm mostly a liberal guy and it seemed that since gay people can love each other just as much as straight people, why not let them into the marriage club just as any other loving couple? But when I began to see this enormous push for gay marriage by the system media mouthpieces, I got a little suspicious. We should point out one very salient fact about this issue for those of you who might be sympathetic to gay marriage. Advocates claim that it is good for marriage and good for society. But ask yourself — *has the system mind media mouthpieces ever pushed* one thing *that was good for people's private lives and for society?* They lie to get us into wars, they lie about the economy, they lie about employment, they lie about tax policy, they suppress discussing genetically based diseases, they suppressed fraudulent derivatives that led to the last economic collapse, and they present us with massive doses of sex and violence on TV some of which rubs off on human behavior. If gay marriage is good for society, it will be the first time in the history of the world that the system has promoted something good for people's private lives and society.

Another interesting piece of evidence is that to the surprise of many, a majority of black women are against gay marriage. They realize that the disintegration of marriage is raising havoc with their private lives and ruining the lives of their children. Not to worry though. On Mar. 2, 2014, a bunch of system neoliberals were promoting Obama's "my brother's keeper" initiative to counteract the fact that young black boys have no role models because of the breakdown of the family. This is showing up in falling school performance of boys relative to young girls. The black neoliberal guy on the show will go home, wipe the black paint off his face and jump on Obama's gay marriage bandwagon to reduce the exclusivity of the marriage institution so as to squeeze what little meaning is left in marriage right out of it. This results in less and less contribution to male identity from marriage and increasing numbers of young black boys in broken families with no father figure role model and increasing numbers of black children born out of wedlock with no father at all. Then the system can bring together a bunch of talking liberal heads on TV to pretend to be concerned. This is 1984 to a tee.

The major reason the marriage institution evolved in all societies as part of their culture, however primitive, was to get males to attend to their own children as opposed to being wandering hunters as they were for millions of years. This point can't be stressed enough. It is of the *essence* of the marriage institution that it is a symbol of the procreation of the human species and a means to keep parents, especially males, attending to and protecting children *that a couple creates*, who had become increasingly helpless as evolution progressed. Marriage became a ritual and a symbol of this essence. In this regard, it was important for all societies to augment and extol the status of marriage so as to make it an important part of a man's identity. That's why, historically, western society and the church made marriage a unique holy sacrament of God and the most important event in a man's life. Marriage added status and identity to men because it made them feel manly, important and very special in the eyes of God. We mentioned above my father's generation, where real men got married and started families. The purpose of the gay marriage bandwagon was to change the very *essence* of marriage from one of mutual procreation and *protection* and masculine identity to one whose essence is sexual orientation and display.

Now, I can see men favoring gay marriage. By reducing the status and meaning of marriage, men have more freedom to wander away from marriage responsibilities without feeling guilty. But no matter what is said about women's careers, still, the core of a woman's *personal private* life is her marriage and family. And yet we find many *women* voting for gay marriage that reduces the exclusivity and meaning of marriage especially in the eyes of men. This is in the face of lower marriage rates, high divorce rates, increasing incidences of abuse, neglect, cheating and abandonment by husbands. And they say women are smarter than men.

On Jan. 22, '15, the son of Cyrus Vance was on Charlie Rose mentioning the growing incidences of domestic violence. People don't value their marriages because marriage is simply no longer a part of a strong male identity. Around major American cities, the marriage rate is a third of what it was in the 60s, which is the exact goal of the system mind. *This* is what women are voting for. On top of it, there are millions of young women wanting a family and unable to find a like-minded man because the marriage institution no longer has the *public* status and meaning for young men to create a masculine identity by marrying and attending to their families. They wander around just like in Neanderthal times totally oblivious to the needs and desires of young women around them. But I can't feel too sorry for these women either who proceed to vote for gay marriage making it less likely to find a partner. In my opinion, if we want to strengthen the family in the interests of children, the marriage institution should be *tightened*, not loosened. We should try to make it *more* exclusive, not less, if we want it to have status and meaning and contribute to the identity of men especially. It should be reserved for a man and woman *who intend to make babies.*

The most important fact about the marriage debate is that the legal *essence* of the marriage institution is that marriage is a *contract*. This has been part of English common law for hundreds of years. This isn't fighting over a word, but the name of a *specific* document. Thousands of law case books for the various states do not refer to *"a"* marriage contract, but to *"the"* marriage contract which is a specific document with a specific title and specific wording. We're not talking about a generic contract like *a* car contract or a roofing contract where there can be many variations. 'The' is a definite noun meaning one and only one. You can't have two contracts with the same name that essentially conflict. If you did, the traditional marriage contract would no longer be exclusive. Traditional marriage vows, which expresses *the* marriage contract, state: do you take this *husband*, etc., and do you take this *wife*, etc. This refers to a man and a woman by my dictionary. That's *the* contract that millions of couples entered into. This contract doesn't say this is part B or that it can be amended in any way.

One of the disgusting shysters pushing gay marriage says gays want a marriage oriented family for their kids because they want the solemnity and authority that marriage confers. And how did it accrue such solemnity? The solemnity, legitimacy and status of the marriage contract accrued over thousands of years by *hetero* couples because it was kept exclusive, special, meaningful and virtuous in the eyes of God. Gay couple want to steal the solemnity and status of the traditional marriage contract while throwing away it's specialness and virtue in the eyes of the major religions. They should have to build up their own solemnity and legitimacy over the years for *their own* contract. And what about the thousands of unmarried cohabiting couples raising a baby often their own. In my day, if you got a girl pregnant, you married her. Not now. Why? In my opinion, the reason a guy won't marry these girls and create a marriage-oriented family for their kids is because marriage adds nothing to his identity and no additional meaning to his life. Why doesn't the system have sympathy for those kids?

Of course, gay people have the right to a cooperative family contract just like straights. But they should have *their own* contract designed specifically for their needs. Let's say we combine 'gay' and 'marriage' to get a contract named *gayriage*. Gay couples would be getting *gayried*. Now what would the courts do if a movement of straight people arose to change the gayriage contract so that the pair would have to be the same weight, or height or financial capacity, for example. Why, the courts would snuff out such a movement as homophobic, discriminatory, bigotted and otherwise unfair. And we'd never hear from it again. What does this tell you about the motivation for gay marriage.

We discussed the distinction between rights and contracts in Sect. 23.5. Individual rights are the bailiwick of the judiciary because only the judiciary has the power to hold in check majorities who might want to infringe on rights. Commerce and its primary instrument, the contract, are under the purview of the *legislature* which is the direct representative of the people. In Sect. 23.5, we explained how the core of a historic culture is its system of contracts. Most of what a culture consists of is the ways its citizens cooperate and transact which reflects the values, beliefs, and perceptions of all citizens going back hundreds of years and involving hundreds of millions of people and their values. If you don't have procedures and rules for individuals to *transact*, you don't have a culture. You can't have one uneducated shyster determining how millions of people will interact, cooperate and transact. Sect. 8 of Article I of the Constitution says, "Congress shall have the power To regulate Commerce with Foreign Nations, and among the several states...." If you look up 'commerce' in the dictionary, one of the definitions refers to any kind of transaction among a number of individuals and groups. My dictionary, in addition to business intercourse, also lists *social* intercourse in the definition of commerce. And of course, this was the common use at the time of the Constitution. Now even though the judiciary has the power to insure that parties *adhere* to contracts, the founding fathers put regulation of commerce in the hands of the *legislature* the means of which is to design contracts.

It should be kept in mind that designing contracts is the most important job the legislature has. Yes, they have the dirty work of extracting taxes. But if they cannot design contracts, in theory, they would have no power to even spend the taxes taken in. All labor, all commercial transactions, all business dealings, involve contracts. If the judiciary has the last word on the design of contracts, what powers would the legislature have? This is why the Constitution is very clear that the *legislature* has the powers to regulate commerce, which entails the power to design contracts that convey all commercial transactions including social transactions.

But even the legislature doesn't have the power to fiddle with contracts because contracts are private agreements to cooperate among two or more parties. Even the king in the Middle Ages couldn't change contracts which is why the west's economic system went ahead of the rest of the world. This is why the US Constitution is very specific about this: it specifically *prohibits* laws that are "impairing the obligation of contracts". The reason for this is that *when you change a contract, you abrogate and nullify the contract.* The main obligation of the marriage contract is that a man is *obligated* to marry a woman. Allowing one crooked shyster to change, and so nullify, a specific contract that hetero people have lived under for thousands of years is the most blatant violation of the equal protection clause ever occurred? By the way, by nullifying and abrogating the traditional marriage contract, one shyster has really ended the marriages millions California couples because they no longer have a contract. And by the way, where was the ACLU when it came to defending the contract clause in the Constitution?

The leading feminist of the 1800s, E. C. Stanton, led the fight to stress the *contract* aspect of the marriage institution. It was by stressing *rights* that the institution was able to allow the *rights* of husbands to abuse and dominate their wives like it suggests in the Bible, and that forced bad marriages to continue regardless of how onerous they were to a woman. Stanton insisted on marriage as a contract which is a *cooperative* endeavor implying *equality* entering the contract. If two people are no longer *cooperating* but are in opposition, that would be grounds for allowing abused wives to get a divorce. What would she think of today's fake feminists in the libber movement who support gay marriage as a right?

Current Courts are gradually replacing *cooperation* with *opposition* in human commerce that you get from rights. Making marriage a right implicitly endorses marriage not for binding people in a *cooperative* venture, but to lay the groundwork for *opposition*, discord and enmity between parents. This should tell right away that the mind system has no use for marriage as a binding force in human commerce but it wants married couples to be in *opposition* right out of the gate.

But don't think for one minute that the courts care one iota about gay marriage. What the gay marriage issue did for the courts was to provide an *opportunity* to continue their 200 year-old agenda of nullifying legislatures. The courts hate contracts because it is legislatures that design them; and historically they have done everything they can to nullify contracts. But in many allusions to the Constitution, the founding fathers intimated that if any branch was going to be superior, it would be the *legislature* because the legislature was the direct representatives of the people. This is why it is doubly unworthy for the judiciary to usurp the powers of the legislature.

This is why people don't vote. What difference does it make? If the courts don't like a law, they declare it unconstitutional with some reason-box diarrhea. If they want to pass a law, they simply take a case that allows them to write an opinion that gives them the law they want. The judiciary imposing gay marriage is just another power-grab by the judiciary to gradually nullify the Constitution and the direct representatives of the people and install a king.

Divorce is nothing but the rearrangement of the marriage *contract*. It should be in the legislative purview like all aspects of commerce. How did divorce wind up in the courts? Its purpose is again to squeeze the legislature right out of the picture. Shysters have a vested interest in destroying the marriage institution. And like any complex system, when you want to find the motivation, look at the result. By turning divorce proceedings into an *adversarial* contest, the result is not only a lower marriage rate but these shysters can extract billions from emotionally distraught parents by getting them to hate one another and divorce. That's the result, and that's the motivation. And kids wind up the victims of this sordid mess.

If you ever needed evidence of a system mind, simply look at the massive propaganda campaign the system has mounted in the last few years for gay marriage. Every media outlet, every newspaper article, even politicians got on the gay marriage bandwagon. And you notice, in all the thousands of hours of pro-gay marriage propaganda, not one single shyster in the entire Unites State of American and not one single media whore came forward to explain the legal *essence* of the marriage institution, which is that it is a specific *contract*. The blatant avoidance of this core concept in media discussions was as predictable as night and day — a very poignant example of a system mind. But wherever it has been nationally legalized like Belgium, the marriage rate plummets and within a generation or two, there won't be marriages (except among gays). The ultimate goal of the system is to eliminate marriage entirely from society and it is right on schedule. Marriage is a distraction from the almighty job and the system mind fully intends to get rid of it.

There are three obstacles to legalizing gay marriage, and advocates including shysters on various courts stampede over each one of them. The first is that there are no group rights in the Constitution. Nor are there rights of any kind involving *contracts*. In Sect. 23.3, we discussed the Yin Yang of transactions. They are either positive or negative. The core essence of a negative transaction consists of an *individual* in question enacting behavior that can be *opposed* by all other parties, whether groups, individuals, institutions, or government entities. These are our basic *rights*. The core of our basic rights and freedoms is contained in the Bill of Rights, which are the first ten amendments to the Constitution. In these amendments, the word 'people', indicating individual people, is mentioned five times; the word 'person' is mentioned twice, and words for individuals, 'him' and 'owner', mentioned once each. In sum, *individual* persons are referred to nine times in the ten amendments. The implication is that all rights are *individual* rights. They are prerogatives the *individual* has in possible *opposition* to other parties. *Nowhere* in the Constitution is there reference whatsoever or even an allusion to any kind of group right. This is because groups do not come together to oppose. Groups come together in *positive* transactions to *cooperate* in a world of their own. In fact, the entire reason for creating a group in the first place is to *cooperate* in carrying out some endeavor independent of other parties. This is the *essence* of the group concept. There may be opposition to what a group is doing, but that is peripheral, not part of the core essence, which is *cooperation*. Positive group transactions are called *commerce*. The terms of what they will accomplish and the responsibilities each party has in their cooperative venture is described in a *contract*. Contracts and commerce are two sides of the same coin. A contract is an indication that a number of parties are cooperating, not asserting a right.

The purpose of newly created group rights, of course, is to push legislative contracts right out of the picture. Various courts have also given *rights* to artificial creations like corporations, banks, cities, even states. Individuals no longer have freedom of speech; it is now *derived* from the freedom of speech of the company they work for which is now the new "person" entitled to speak for them. Citizens now exist to serve the interests of *cities* who have the *right* to steal people's property and to blatantly invade individual citizen's legitimate right to privacy.

Propaganda outlets have droned on about "discrimination" and "marriage equality". Legally, the word 'discrimination' only applies to *individual rights*. The only application the word has to contracts concerns *entering* the contract. A contract is like a house. There may be discrimination against *entering* the house, but once in, the concept of discrimination becomes meaningless and inapplicable. Racist labor laws discriminated against *individual* black people because a white guy could *enter* a labor contract with an employer, but a black guy couldn't. There was discrimination against women because there were jobs a man could get that a woman couldn't. But there is nothing in *entering* the marriage contract that treats any *individual* different from any other *individual*. Upon entering the marriage contract, the gay *individual* has the *same* prerogatives and privileges and restrictions as a straight individual. Neither can marry another guy. It is a completely *equal* contract vis a vis prospective *individuals*.

And far from marriage equality, gay marriage is marriage *in*equality. If a guy couple has a contract to buy a house, or enter into a business or whatever, we wouldn't allow a straight person to break into their private life and tear up their contract. However, for a straight couple living under a living marriage contract and continuing civilization having children, we allow gay people to break down their doors, invade their private lives and tear up the contract they've been living under for 50 years. Talk of marriage discrimination and "marriage equality" in the propaganda outlets is pure blatant lies, which might tell you something about the motivation of the system mind.

Additionally, all contracts *"discriminate"* against groups who don't qualify for the contract. The marriage contract also "discriminates" against fathers and daughters, brothers and sisters, polygamists, mafia families and chain gangs, all of whom could marry if it were a "right". If a plumber wants to do electrical work, the electrical contract "discriminates" against the plumber even entering an electrical contract (he doesn't have an electrician license). The plumber doesn't have equal rights with the electrician to sign an electrician contract. This is just one among millions of contracts designed by legislatures to regulate commerce. (By the way, since marriage is a *right*, polygamy is now perfectly legal.) Talk of discrimination involving contracts is a total misapplication of the word and is simply another propaganda tool by the system to rid society of marriage altogether.

A parent, child and employer cannot sign a work contract, no matter how much they agree. They are "discriminated" against because they do not have "equal rights" with other workers to sign labor contracts. Work contracts in the US *preclude* child labor. This was a legislative mandate. Of course, in the late 1800s, the Supreme Vampires struck down Ohio's laws against child labor saying that they interfered with property *rights*. They gave companies, which are artificial creations of the state, *rights*.

In another case, the state of New York legislature had passed a law limiting working hours. This was part of a legislatively designed work contract. In a famous case, *Lochner vrs. New York* in 1905, here again the Supreme Vampires gave "rights" to companies, squelching the law and forcing twelve hour workdays on working people. On the basis of these decisions, eight year-old children were forced to work in coalmines 12 to 14 hours a day. They never saw sunlight. That's the kind inner brain reptile we get on the Supreme Court. Of course, neoliberals, being the intellectual prostitutes that they are, would be all on the side of legislatures in these cases. In fact, when a recent Supreme Vampire ruling gave freedom of speech to *groups* like corporations, liberals came out of the woodwork like termites from a burning building howling against this newly created group "right". But when it comes to the marriage contract, all of a sudden, group "rights" are loudly back on the table. 'Rights' is *exactly* the word the courts used to maintain slavery before the Civil War and to impose child labor on our social fabric. Historically, the concept of rights has been used more often than not as a means to establish *in*equalities.

People point out that a girl can marry a guy, but a guy can't. By extension, this argument would show that members of all possible pairs in the marriage contract are discriminated against in some way. Within a cooperating group, there are asymmetries in roles and obligations under the contract, which can be used to manufacture talk of discrimination. In the doctor contract, the doctor can cut open the patient but the patient can't cut open the doctor. So the doctor contract "discriminates" against the patient. But the patient has to pay the doctor real cash money and the doctor doesn't. So the medical contract also 'discriminates' against the patient. Since the medical contract discriminates against everyone, we ought to throw out the whole contract. This shows that the concept of discrimination simply doesn't apply to contracts once you're in the contract house.

But some of these "discriminations" are worse than others. Miscegenation laws were a legislative abuse that the courts jumped into. Even though the courts probably overstepped their powers even in this case, at least their interference was on the basis of race. But there is no such thing as discrimination on the basis of gender. Once in the contract house, the marriage contract can preclude our gay guy signing up with another guy even though a woman can, just as a labor contract of an all-male wrestling team can preclude signing a contract with a girl, or the Dallas Cowboy cheerleaders can preclude a contract with a guy and the boobytube brassiere company can discriminate against male models. This is why we have all-girl colleges and woman's restrooms.

Certainly miscegenation laws seem unfair to us. But legislatures have to get elected and sometimes have to appeal to popular moods and prejudices. What we don't hear about is the 200 year history of various *courts* who are insulated from popular prejudices, giving plantation owners the *right* to buy and sell people, and employers the *right* to inflict child labor on kids among many other abuses. Even in modern times, a corporation now has the *right* to drown out the free speech of individuals with money-powered loudspeakers. When you consider that legislatures have to get elected and the judiciary doesn't, it is even more of a disgrace to compare legislative abuses with the most important government abuses in our history that were imposed by the *judiciary* like slavery and child labor.

There's an ultraliberal named Ronald Dworkin who, every time conservatives flush the Constitution down the toilet, gets on his high horse and writes a big fat article of righteous indignation usually in the *NYR*. He passes himself off as a constitutional expert. But when it's his turn to flush the Constitution down the toilet, he's right there pulling the lever.[5] Dworkin's article is dripping with mushy stuff about how wonderful gay marriage is: "...people of the same sex often love one another with the same passion as people of different sexes...." "...marriage has a spiritual dimension that civil union does not." (Now that a man can marry his pet sheep, we have a new "spiritual dimension" for marriage.) This sweet talk has nothing to do with crisp rules concerning contracts. Talk about discrimination and equality are bald-faced lies. Marriage is about contracts and if Dworkin doesn't know this, he's just another neoliberal intellectual prostitute flushing the Constitution down the toilet just like the people he's always criticizing. The same goes for the ACL (Screw) U.

The system even allows gay marriage advocates to determine *everyone's* motives. Professor Martha Nussbaum claims that opponents of gay marriage are motivated by a "disgust" of homosexuality, so their opinions shouldn't count. Do advocates of traditional marriage then get to determine the motives of gay marriage advocates, which is to destroy the institution? Absolutely not. Their motives are love of mankind. I want to tell Ms. Mind Peeping Tom, when it comes to *value* and aesthetics, it's none of her god dam business why people have their views. Citizens of this country have a right to design contracts through legislatures any way they please as long as they don't discriminate against *individuals* entering a contract, which the marriage contract certainly does not. What is really disgusting is the intellectual dishonesty of these neoliberals to squelch the Constitution and stuff their glandular views down our throats.

The gay marriage debate is just another clash of prerogatives and privileges. The question is, does maintaining the exclusivity and status of marriage enhance the marriage institution *enough* to compensate for preventing gay people from enjoying a privilege that straight people have. My opinion is based on the needs of children who are the most vulnerable to abusive marriages and divorces. We have piled enough crap on the heads of our children: we have depreciated marriage to the point where *half* babies born to women under 30 born out of wedlock; we have stolen their money, destroyed their jobs, polluted their environment, endangered their climate, committed genocide on their genes, and piled trillions of debt on their heads. In spite of a myriad of fraudulent sociology studies, we don't really know how much gay marriage hurts traditional marriage. However, for thousands of years, society *did the best it possible could* to enhance the solemnity, exclusivity and status of marriage to maintain its stability and quality and a component of people's identities, especially men. This includes maintaining the special-ness, exclusivity and meaning of the marriage *contract*.

28.6 SOCIAL CAPITAL

There is one more area to bring out regarding identity, especially male identity. As many of you know, in the past 20 years or so, there has been increasing interest in what sociologists and political scientists call *social capital*. What this term refers to are the endeavors members of society embark on to create motivational resources through social networks, personal connections, volunteer groups, clubs, associations, etc. Of course, most discussions of the term involve showing social capital used to create entrepreneurship, business ventures, and inventiveness. But an interesting question is, do people need a strong identity to create social capital, or does social capital create an identity? I think it's a feedback loop going both ways. But what gets the process started? In my opinion, it is skills and existential love lead-ing to families. We were homo habilis for a few million years and it left its mark. Skills are really unique special body actions. As such they have high information content and there-fore a lot of meaning. And of course, existential love and the associated communication also involve high information content behaviors and so meaningful as well.

Before the industrial revolution, it was easy to create social capital because the unit of production was the family and work involved skills in making whole objects. Much of the population lived in villages; and families with children form more meaning-laden connections to other families. Families were more engaged with church congregations and leisure-time activities. There is also division of labor in families that allows time for members to engage in volunteer groups, clubs and associations. With identity formed by meaningful skills, place of residence, religious affiliation, ethnicity, and most important, family, in the past, men espe-cially had more secure identities. This led to stable families, better parenthood, more com-munity involvement and better all-around citizenship as well as social capital.

But when the unit of production became the lone individual especially after WWII, jobs became more specialized, routine and automated. This decreases information content and so meaning. People can't form leagues and associations as *individuals* in the same way they do their jobs. Leagues and associations are better formed when there are intact and integrated *families*, which are encouraged by the family as the unit of production. But when identity is made up almost entirely of the almighty job and the average length of a job is down to 4 years, identity is very tenuous, especially in men who can't create an identity by making babies.

And even though the church tried mightily to maintain the family as recently as WWII, it was a losing battle. A woman's movement arose preaching the marriage was oppression and slavery. The great emphasis on sex along with other sociological variables led to a decline in existential love and a slow disintegration of the family. With less meaning coming from routine jobs and less meaning coming from marriage and family, identities, especially male identity weakened. When you don't know who you are, your self-awareness lessens and your sense of self lurches into all sorts of anti-social behavior — drugs, crime, unsteady support, wife abuse, cheating, abandonment, and poor parenting. It also leads to poor citizenship, as shown by the great increase in the need for lawyers and police. In turn, the disintegration of the family again has the feedback loop of forcing identity to be composed solely of the almighty job, leaving less resources to create social capital.

This sets up another merry-go-round as in Sect. 18.4. Neoliberals promote people like the Clintons and Obama. They proceed to puff up the free trade racket, which sends millions of skilled jobs overseas to be replaced by unskilled meaningless service jobs with less pay. Then these neoliberals bring in millions of illegal immigrants that destroy the value of what little labor is left. With lower pay, the middle class guy can't keep up his identity as a bread winner, nor his identity as a skilled worker. Then they top it off with gay marriage taking what little meaning there is in the marriage institution right out of it. This again reduces the contribution to identity from marriage and family. With reduced identity and disintegrating families, middle class people, especially men, are in no position to create social capital. Then these neoliberal social scientists can come along and create big university chairs and make lots of money bitching about the loss of social capital.

Also, we should add that poor citizenship leads to tremendous increases in political antagonism. Because of lack of identity, people are not motivated to be involved in political life by the need to have a functioning economic system and a viable society. They get involved in political life as a means to achieve *identity*. This fact has been taken advantage of by the neoconservative system mind that attracts people to globs of raw naked power in the form of big corporations, big brother government, big wars, big bombs, big killings, big everything. Politics has become a way to direct energy towards creating *identity*, not to solve problems

This was very incisively brought out by the tea party movement, which consisted of a bunch of infants meeting to cheer on bigness and power and filling their diapers when they can't have everything. They want a new bike and a new doll and have no idea how to pay for it. When Sarah Palin shouts for a bigger army and bigger wars, the crowd roars. When the speaker calls for more spies to go after terrorists, the crowd roars. When the speaker screams about deficits and spending, again the crowd roars, even though things they just got through cheering for are by far the biggest sources of spending. The last roar comes when the speaker announces tax cuts. So what they want is more spending on things that take up most of the budget, but less spending; smaller deficits alongside lower taxes. It is impossible to do all this. This is about identity, not solving problems.

[1] *The Economist*, Oct. 10, '09, p. 38

[2] Greenhouse, Steven, *The Big Squeeze: Tough Times for the American Worker*. Knopf Press.

[3] Kaplan, Esther, "American Speedup". *The Nation*, Nov. 17, '14, p. 28

[4] Bai, Nina, "Evolution of Fatherhood". *Scientific American Mind*, July, '11

[5] Dworkin, Ronald, "Three Questions for America". *The New York Review of Books*, Sept. 21, '06

CHAPTER 29

Ideology - Dem Liberals

―――

FIRST WE HAVE TO DEFINE ideology. It basically means the kind of political views a person has. However, it is usually reserved for more dogmatic kinds of political views like Liberal and Conservative, or even more extreme forms like Communism and Fascism. What makes discussing politics messy business is that people with strong political views are always trying to win over converts. So what they say about themselves is usually never what they really are because what they really are might not be acceptable to the average American. Well, in the next two chapters, I'm going to be very frank and pretty tough and calls it like I sees it. I am going to describe the political views of people with different ideologies exactly the way a Martian who didn't understand earthly languages would do it: completely existentially. He would rely what people are actually *doing*, and not what they're *saying* about themselves. For example, neoconservatives would swear up and down that they believe in democracy and Capitalism. But when it comes to actually supporting candidates, they wax eloquently over politicians whose actual practice and voting records show a clear-cut case of Economic Socialism.

Not only is there much misrepresentation among ideologues as to what they really are, but one of the purposes of the next two chapters is to show that most people with strong ideologies promote political views that are basically incompatible with pure Democratic Capitalism, which everyone says they like. We will see that unlike some of the sociologists and political scientists that predicted the end of ideology, in recent years, ideology has become even more extreme than ever before. The Ronald Reagan presidency was a fork in the road which enabled the old ideologies to be highjacked by the new breed of ideology: neoliberism and neoconservatism, both of which are incompatible with Democratic Capitalism. We want to explore why these trends have occurred and why traditional Liberalism and Conservatism have been pushed off the political stage.

29.1 CAUSES OF IDEOLOGY

In order to explain ideology, we should first characterize the extremes. This might give us a clue as to why some people are so ideological — why they are such ardent neoconservative and passionate neoliberals. We are going to explain these extreme ideologies by reference to the way the brain is wired and where most the energy is expended in the brain. Briefly, we will explore the fact that the frontal cortex of the brain where our sense of self and identity mostly lie is the key to understanding differences in ideology especially extreme ideology.

As we discussed in Sect. 15.1, the frontal cortex is relatively new in evolutionary history, perhaps only a few million years old compared to the age of mammals themselves which is probably 150 million years. For this very reason, the circuitry in the frontal cortex might not have all the chinks worked out. This is also true of the visual cortex in the back of the head. Genes for the visual cortex haven't had time to spread out into the whole population. This is why there is a great deal of variation between people, from great artists with prodigious abilities to visualize and draw to people who are visually dead.

The same holds for the frontal cortex. It is so relatively new that the genes for building this circuitry haven't had time to spread out evenly in the population and why there are enormous differences between people. The newness of the frontal cortex is also why it lacks redundancy. This means that it is very prone to malfunctioning if there are small mistakes in the genes that lay out the basic circuitry. Since our sense of self is located in this area of the brain, circuitry problems here are most often going to affect our sense of self, which explains the many variations in autism, discussed in Sect. 15.1. Research should be done to find differences in people's time and space concepts as well as the self concept.

One category of malfunction is the amount of energy expended in the frontal cortex. If too much energy is expended in the frontal cortex you will get one kind of malfunction, and if too little is expended, another kind. The view taken here is that these two kinds of deviation correspond to extreme differences in people's ideology. What got me onto this idea is that when you look at the heroes of extreme ideologues, you have to conclude that there is basically something wrong with these people. What follows is just a theory as to what might be wrong.

The hero on the extreme left, of course, was Karl Marx. One of the heroes of the far right was Ayn Rand. Well, I'll relate my experiences with these two. I was pretty much a normal average kid: I played sports, chased the girls, hot-rodded cars and got kicked out of school a few times. Then I got to an age in college where you start hearing about liberals and conservatives, so I thought I'd check this out. Well, especially in those days, you heard a lot about Karl Marx and how he got Communism started in the 1800s, and inspired the Russian Revolution. And you heard about how thousands of intellectuals and writers around the world were attracted to Communism.

A similar thing happened on the right, where hundreds of thousands had gotten "inspired" by the works of Ayn Rand. So I was ready to read Rand with a pretty open mind. Although not being a highly educated person at the time, what I found was the most pathetic, infantile, unenlightened crap I had ever read in my lifetime. How could this stuff ever be the inspiration for any normal, healthy human being was beyond my comprehension. Well, after thinking about this many years, we'll attempt to explain these important sources of ideology. Let's look at neoliberalism first, which in many ways is just the opposite of liberalism.

29.2 Neoliberalism

For centuries, liberals main thrust was the support of labor: the 8-hour day, safety on the job and decent pay. They supported unions. Their second major thrust was to reduce the amount of misery and human deprivation in the world and to stick up for the little guy. They supported a long list of social programs to these ends, many of which are meritorious. This strand of liberalism is really a continuation of Adam Smith's Democratic Capitalism, which was actually called Liberalism in its day.

Liberals have always had the general reputation of having enormous egos. And the more extreme the liberal, the greater the ego. During the Vietnam war, ultraliberal protestors had trouble organizing into coherent groups. A radical group called the SDS had so many chiefs and so few Indians that they could never coalesce into a really effective force. Modern neoliberalism has an inner brain emotion to get in people's faces, to offend in some way, to attack things that are important and meaningful to people's core values and to crush the system in the process. Neoliberals are always pushing something, shoving something else, often with policies that offend many people's basic values and lifestyles. Now, why? The view here is that *this enormous sense of self and ego is due to an above average amount of energy being expended in the frontal cortex.* Of course, since liberals are able to get energy out of the bottom of their brains, they do have some existential qualities like a desire for justice. But often, ultraliberals promote policies that have a more sinister cause. They are just clever at coming up with reason box explanations for what they are promoting.

The neoliberal offends so many categories of voters that they rarely get elected to public office. Their response in recent years, is to cooperate with neoconservative political animals in crippling the economy and then manufacture government "benefits" to buy the votes of the casualties. Let's first try to figure out Marx's real motives and why he "inspired" so many liberals all over the world.

29.3 Karl Marx and Communism

The most important thing to realize about Karl Marx was that he never said one word about the structure of the economic system he was promoting. Once the "dictatorship of the proletariat" was established, it would all fall into place. All of his book is devoted to attacking what he thought was Capitalism. The core of his criticism centered around the only piece of theoretical work he did which was his value theory of labor.

This theory had a way to value labor and *prove* what the workers share of the pie should be. But Marx had such an infantile concept of economics that he thought the guy who invents something, saves his money, risks his capital, devises a production scheme, designs the machines he needs, arranges his production facility, actually produces something, and then figures a way to sell it — this guy doesn't seem to deserve anything at all for his trouble. There wasn't even a passing mention of the contribution of the Capitalist.

After Adam Smith, a whole bunch of economists called "marginalists" like C. Menger and W.S. Jevons, claimed that the only true source of value was labor. However, there were two ways to go with this idea. The leftish interpretation was exposed to the idea that even if labor is the source of value, how does this value get determined except in marketplaces which puts them in a trap set by the right. Literary elites quickly responded to this opening with the idea that value could properly be fought over among elites, experts, and Nietzsche supermen in an intellectual marketplace, which they, of course, ran. This led to the coalescence of *economic* marginalists on the right. They took the obvious path of putting social and aesthetic realms, along with human labor, into *economic* marketplaces to be valued as commodities. This led to the strand of economic theory later called the Chicago school led by people like von Mises and Frederick Hayek, whose cognitive disabilities prevented them from seeing the most obvious and profound differences among the various categories of economic activity. But they coated their infantile theories with inscrutable high-minded talk involving everything under the sun including aesthetics, art, and morality of all things. This brought them a whole army of self-serving econowhores we see to this day.

It never seems to have occurred to any of these word-mongerers to look at the *essence* of an economic phenomenon to determine value. Part of the *essence* of being human includes skills and the expression of those skills, which is labor. The first hominid considered on the line to the human species was *homo habilis*, as we explained in Sect. 15.1. You value *human* skills and labor simply by the political choices of other *humans*. This is how we determined *earnings* in Sect. 23.5. Things that humans *use*, which are commodities, are not part of the essence of humanness, and so can be valued in marketplaces. Matters of aesthetics, art, literature, etc. are also human skills, but because they do not require *quantitative* value, can best be judged by expert opinion. Michael Jackson got millions more dollars in the market than Jimmy Rushing but nobody who knows anything about music is going to rate him as the better singer.

Getting back to Marx, he criticized the most minute detail of free-enterprise systems. But when it came to his own system, where was the brilliance, where was the insight, where was the erudition? There was no articulation, no detail, no analysis no nothing of any intellectual merit. Adam Smith went into excruciating detail about the workings of what he defined as Capitalism (Liberalism in his day) — about value, about production and distribution of goods and services, the money supply, the banking system, interest rates, taxes, role of government, etc. Marx's droppings about his communist system had nothing of the sort. It was simply a blueprint for murder symbolized by infantile clichés like "dictatorship of the proletariat". This is why when various war criminals took over countries in the name of Marxism they hadn't the faintest idea how to proceed. How would prices be determined? How would industry be organized? What would the banking system be like? None of this was ever considered by Marx.

He did mention democracy, but was careful not to articulate what kind of democracy he had in mind. But his anger at the what he saw as Capitalists and the viciousness of his attacks left no doubt that he intended more than quiet peaceful things like voting in what we would consider democratic elections. This wasn't like parliamentarianism in Europe that was preaching liberty and democracy and was having a terrible time struggling to get instituted in society against the overwhelming power of the king and aristocracy. It wasn't like the early unions composed of very ordinary workers who simply wanted reasonable pay and working conditions but who were being beat up and shot at by huge corporate giants and their police. Marx, on the other hand, had his eye on killing — mostly anyone who might have anything. And of course, it was easy to interpret his writings that the way to go about this was through revolution led by strongmen who would take matters into their hands, wipe out the "ruling class" and create the so-called "worker's paradise".

He had murder on the mind to such an extent that even his criticisms were a total muddle. Marx wasn't criticizing Capitalism because Marx wasn't *looking* at Capitalism. What he was looking at was Economic Socialism — a system *that was the exact opposite side of the very coin he was promoting*. It had the slight variation that instead of economic and political players being the same *people* as Marx demanded, they were only in the same beds. So instead of the economic players being able to own, control and manipulate the political system as was occurring in his time, he would have *political* animals owning and controlling the economic system. This is the "genius" of Karl Marx. Economic players as bad as they can be, still produce goods and services that society needs. What do political animals produce? Absolutely nothing of value. Just look at Washington. When *political* actors are in charge as in Communist countries, it's even worse than Economic Socialism. Instead of a producer, you get a brutal dictator from whom you get less advances in technology, and less organization of people into productive units. Nobody ever buys anything made in a Communist country.

For a hundred years after Marx, liberals all over the world read his droppings and this created a fork in the road for historical Liberalism. One fork led to a path of improving and perfecting the old Liberalism of Adam Smith. This was a very thin strand for quite a while, but culminated in the presidency of Franklin Roosevelt. The other was a take-off from Karl Marx who as this fork grew, became the standard bearer of all intellectual activity. Because of Marx's extremism, this is the fork that took off and led to modern day neoliberalism. In academia, there were Marxist historians, Marxist sociologists, Marxist anthropologists, Marxist economists, even Marxist circus performers and dog-catchers. It was hailed as the greatest intellectual breakthrough in the history of the world. Thousands of books were written articulating Marxist views. Professors and big intellectuals were joining the cause. Since historians often get together for history conferences, there is great opportunity to transmit communicable diseases. The most insidious communicable disease of the mind, of course, is Marxism.

So what was motivating this historical steamroller? It wasn't an articulated system like Adam Smith described. In my opinion, Marx had no need to articulate a coherent economic system because he was appealing to one of the oldest inner brain emotions in human history: the emotion to annihilate, to destroy, to *crush*. On the basis of this basic emotion, he was able to attract and energize millions of liberals all over the world and for a couple hundred years. If Karl Marx hadn't invented a clever way to play on this strong emotion in all of us but especially in the liberal mind, he would have remained an obscure sociologist trying desperately to get his flimsy value theory of labor published.

There's a little of this emotion in all of us. In its worst form, it's behind holocausts and pogroms and ethnic cleansing. It's the emotion some Europeans had towards the American Indians. In milder forms, it motivates sports fans. I'm not a very good sports fan because I want the Patriots to completely crush and annihilate the opposition. It's awful; I don't even want to see a close game. This is a harmless outlet for this emotion. It would be nice if the neoliberal had such a harmless outlet. But he doesn't. He wants to crush the system.

Apologists for Marxism try to pass off this unholy alliance between economic and political actors as an "organic" system where everybody works together. They use the organic idea for the rest of society too. Yes, you can be an individual as long as you're part of this great "organic" whole: the dictatorship of the proletariat. What is organic in a market system is the flow of money, goods and services. But the various *nodes* of the economy do not have the same DNA like the cells of the body that cooperate to form functioning organs. Even in a pure Democratic Capitalist system, there is natural tension between capital and labor and between sellers and consumers because they all have different DNA *not* designed to cooperate as in a body organ. Real Capitalism recognizes this and attempts to resolve differences with an independent body democratically elected that maintains rules that take account everyone's interests. Talk of "organic" society under Socialism is just reason box crap the party uses to shoehorn everyone into the same mold destroying everyone's freedoms in the process.

Finally, all that fancy Marxist talk had a chance to be put into practice. The Russian Revolution occurred in 1917 in which Lenin established Communism in Russia. There was immediate mass killing. Not only did the wealthy get killed, but many ordinary Russians as well. After Stalin wormed his way to the top of the pile, he not only killed capitalists but he killed ordinary farmers who committed the crime of owning a little piece of land. Then he starved out 35 *million* peasants because they weren't overjoyed having their crops stolen to provide food for industrialization. You would think that the poorest of the poor would be the first beneficiaries of any kind of a reasonable liberal revolution. Not under Stalin. The poorest of the poor were starved to death for "collectivization". But he wasn't through. He killed off scientists and intellectuals in case they were not overjoyed with Stalin's grand plan. Then he killed off his best generals because they had guns. When Hitler invaded the Soviet Union in WWII, millions of people and soldiers died unnecessarily because so many of its best generals had been killed.

And what did those big-brained professors, writers and intellectuals all over the world think of all this? Well, they proceeded to idolize Stalin's Russia as the "wave of the future". And keep in mind, this acclaim didn't occur during Marx's time on the basis of abstract angry writings. This idolatry occurred right during the very times when Communism was being put into practice in Russia with Stalin as a brutal dictator killing anyone who owned anything including 35 million peasants.

But maybe the academics were just temporarily on the wrong track with all the glitz of Marxism. But then the system collapsed in 1929 and Roosevelt was elected in 1932 and proceeded to bring back Capitalism after a 70 year hiatus. He reintroduced sensible rules of the game — rules promulgated *independent* of the economic game just as Adam Smith prescribed. *If liberals understood Capitalism, they would realize that Democratic Capitalism is their best friend and would be praising Roosevelt for saving Capitalism instead of following the party line laid down by that dumkoff Karl Marx.*

After WWII, the rules Roosevelt introduced led to the greatest economic expansion in our history for the first time anywhere. But instead of neoliberal historians giving Roosevelt *credit* for bringing back a semblance of Democratic Capitalism, *including a middle class*, they actually blamed him for it. Roosevelt was impeding Marx's historical march towards the great worker's paradise. Marxist historians ascribed negative motives to Roosevelt, saying that instead of being a liberal, Roosevelt was saving Capitalism no less, as though a real traitor. The human animal really is addicted to words, and the words of one diaper-filling dummy still prevents even many of today's liberals from seeing reality.

All through this period, in every single country where Communism took over, it turned into a brutal dictatorship in which millions were outright killed. And the purpose of this was not to create liberty and democracy, but only to keep the dictator in power and to destroy anybody who owned anything usually by murder. They were the most homicidal dictators society could come up with who worked their way to the top by the worst of means — intrigue, crime, murder, betrayal, the lowest of human behavior. Until the late 1980's when Mikhail Gorbachev miraculously came to power in Russia, there was never one single guy in all those years of Communist history who wasn't a brutal tyrant.

By the 1970s, liberalism's agenda had been fulfilled by the Roosevelt revolution. There was a prosperous middle class, strong unions and protections for labor. But bad luck hit. Jimmy Carter was caught between bubbles and the economy slowed. But modern means of information flows created a system mind that enabled neoconservatism to have a revival after the disaster of 1929 with the presidency of Ronald Reagan. But instead of liberalism attempting to hold on to their historical mission, a major strand of liberalism forked off to actually climb in bed with the system. This was today's neoliberalism. The fork of traditional liberalism simply died on the vine and we don't hear much from them anymore.

But guess what? After all this history and all the killing and destruction of society that retarded progress all over the world for a hundred years, now that our economic system has had a crisis, they are back again. Neoliberal writers, academics, political analysts and their monkey-see-monkey-do book reviews are once again falling into line imitating Karl Marx and stuck in the same categorical ruts, trying with the usual intellectual prostitution to revive Marx.[1] These extreme neoliberals are just like neoconservatives. They learn nothing. Just reading a handful of sentences in Adam Smith's book would tell these people that what they are criticizing has very little to do with Capitalism. For example, one of our leading lawyers has titled his book about the 2008 meltdown, *"A Failure of Capitalism"*. [2] What led up to the meltdown had absolutely nothing to do with Adam Smith's Capitalism. Now this guy is only a lawyer so we maybe we can't expect him to know anything about economics. But what about Joseph Stiglitz, the renowned international economist who, in his book has all kinds of criticism of late 20th century "capitalism".[3] Then there's the leading economic historian, Sean Wilentz, who talks about "laissez-faire pro-business conservatism" of the 1920s.[4] This is a complete contradiction in terms, like hot ice. If the government was really laissez-faire, they would have their hands off the rules; and the game without rules would collapse. Just like in Victorian times, if you went to Washington, you wouldn't see politicians off to one side doing nothing. They were in the same offices as the players, at the same lunches, in the same country clubs, exchanging the same whores, in addition to bribes flowing like water. They were pro-business not because of hands-off, but because they were actively passing *new* rules that were the direct result of being in bed with the players so that they could walk off with huge profits while workers were near starvation. They passed rules against unions, against free speech, and for lax rules that allowed all kinds of fraud on Wall St. Every single federal law for 12 years under Republican administrations in the 20s favored the corporate world. Not one law was ever passed that protected labor, and innumerable laws that clearly opposed labor. *This is not laissez-faire.*

Not only that, but people who rose to the top of the economic ladder were not always the ones with the best ideas, as would occur in a real Capitalism economy, but the ones who did the most to own and control the political system and arrange the rules of the game. Even the improvements of technology brought about by various inventors never improved the lot of the lower 80%. As usual, the results were a massive meltdown of the system in 1929. If real Capitalism had been allowed to gain a foothold in the economy after the Civil War, technology would have progressed faster, but most importantly the system would have grown faster, and the working class would get a reasonable share of Income. This is exactly what happened when a real liberal, Roosevelt, brought back a semblance of Democratic Capitalism in the 1930s.

All this shows is that when all the energy in the brain is in the frontal cortex, all mental activity is directed towards crushing the system, not in seeing reality. They still can't see the difference between the democratic Capitalism we had after WWII when we created a prosperous middle class, and the Economic Socialism of the Industrial Revolution, the 1920s, and reintroduced again by Ronald Reagan in the 1980s that retards and impedes economic progress.

Karl Marx was a total fraud, and an above average high school student can see it very easily (as I was). He didn't know what he was really talking about because he never got past the emotional development of a five-year-old, and his very shackled mind and telescoped view couldn't comprehend the simplest of economic concepts and relationships. He saw injustice and exploitation among the working class and without the slightest understanding of its causes, filled his diapers, and screamed out infantile formulas that could be used by any brutal dictator that needed some new slogans to attain raw naked power and use it to kill.

Now you look at all these facts, and ask yourself a simple question. Were these liberals all over the world beating the drums for Communism and idolizing the really pathetic Karl Marx, while at the same time bemoaning the exact opposite side of his coin in Economic Socialism, really motivated first and foremost by a desire to improve the lot the average worker? Or was their real motivation to annihilate, to crush and to get in people's faces? Let's look at some of the more egregious ways the modern day neoliberal has concocted to get in people's faces and to buy the votes of the economic casualties that results.

29.4 HOUSING

One of the insidious schemes ever concocted by the evil mind of the neoliberal to buy votes has been in the area of housing. Of course, the stated motives were pure as the driven snow. They would try to help lower income families to own their own houses. But of course, the concocted scheme does no such thing. The neoliberal community has a system mind of sorts itself, and it figured a way to look like they were helping the little guy, when the real motive of this system mind was simply buying votes.

First of all, young people starting families are too busy working and paying bills to bother much with politics and voting. They are a perfect group to steal from. On the other hand, the neoliberal system mind knows that seniors tend to vote in large numbers because they have plenty of time to think about their interests. To get their votes, neoliberals would want the prices they get from selling their homes and retiring to Florida to be as high as possible. The way mostly liberals chose to accomplish this end was to create out of whole cloth two semi-government agencies back in the '60s whose job was to insure mortgages, Fanny Mae and Freddie Mac.

The immediate effect of loans and insuring mortgages is to raise the price of houses. Every time one of these agencies increased their fake benefits to new home-buyers, up went the price of housing. Not only that but money needed to prop up these agencies had to be stolen from renters who may want to buy someday and future taxpayers. The motive for the whole scam was not to help new home-buyers at all, but to simply buy votes of retirees. Fannie Mae has about *tripled* the real prices that today's retirees can get for their homes making it impossible for many younger workers to buy a home. So the new home-buyer or renter is twice clobbered. First his taxes are stolen to prop up another fraudulent government scam that pays bonuses and commissions to financial services parasites. Then he's clobbered a second time when he goes to buy a home and has to pay triple its real value because of Fannie Mae's intrusions into the market.

Two liberals comment about Fannie Mae: "For roughly 50 years Fannie Mae did its job".[5] It certainly did. Its job was to steal money from new home-buyers to buy the votes of seniors selling their houses for outrageous prices. Not only are these retirees getting social security pensions far more than they ever paid in, but now they get to cash in on selling homes they paid nothing for in the '40s and '50s for big bucks that younger working class people also have to pay. And most of the benefits to retirees was to not to the poorest among them, but mostly the upper half of them who could initially afford a house in a good area in the first place. This was the cause of the big run-up in housing costs in the 2000s.

On top of that, mortgages were handed out to new home-buyers in the 2000s at exorbitant prices that could never be repaid. They became the basis for a Wall St. derivatives ponzi scheme. Of course, since absolutely nothing tangible is produced to correspond to this stack of fraudulent paper, it led to the meltdown of 2008 and the enormous loss of savings of renters and other young people *ironically* intending to buy a home. Then future potential home-buyers had trillions stolen from their future earnings to prop the whole crooked system back up.

Here's something to try. Go to Google and look up Fannie Mae. They have a website titled "MakingHomeAffordable.gov". This is most in-your-face-lie you will ever see, which shows that the human animal creates his realities not on the basis of perceptions but on the basis of words. Right before our eyes, we saw the tripling in *real* dollars of housing prices over the last 50 years and here is the government telling us that Fannie Mae "makes homes affordable". Google passes on this lie. No wonder they call it "google". (They'll probably change it when they read this.)

The results of allowing easier mortgages and to guarantee them on top of it will be the same as before: to interfere with markets and keep up prices for senior sellers whose votes they're after, which keeps prices out of the range of sincere new home-buyers. There ought to be a constitutional amendment that prevents segments of populations from stealing from one another, which would prevent bureaucracies like Fannie Mae from ever coming into existence in the first place.

29.5 HIGHER EDUCATION

The exact same thing has happened in education. The purpose of aid to higher education is certainly not to make education more affordable to most middle class people. "The cost of attending a private college has increased by a factor of more than 13 in the past 40 years; and tuitions for even state college have increased by a factor of 15.[6] And this is during a period when the family income for the bottom 80% has actually gone down. I put myself through 4 years of college and 11 years of grad school with part-time jobs. But those days are long gone. Now students coming out of college have a *trillion* dollars worth of debt for their educations. Kids are graduating from Mickey Mouse colleges with BS degrees with a $100,000 dollar debt. Not only that, but "a federal survey showed that literacy of college-educated citizens declined between 1992 and 2003.[7] To add salt to the wound, they can't even get jobs to pay back these loans even if they were qualified.

Andrew Hacker and Claudia Dreifus have a really super book, *Higher Education? How Colleges are Wasting our Money and Failing Our Kids*. They mention all the abuses in American colleges that push up tuition, from professors increasingly "on leave", to bloated administrations, to larger class size to fat paychecks for professors who often don't even have classes. Students don't complain because in return they get easy grading, or no classes at all. Grade point averages have risen from about 2.52 in the 1950s up to 3.11 in 2006, even as literacy was declining. What is pumping up these costs is government aid to education. Every time the government throws money at higher education in the form of scholarships, loans, transfers, etc., up goes tuitions. There are estimates that about 400 *thousand* qualified high school graduates don't go to college each year because of the costs of higher education. And yet, many articles in liberal magazines are still beating the drums for aid to education and more student loans.[8]

The neoliberal system mind knows that school employees, professors and college bureaucrats vote in large numbers, whereas kids going to college have a low voter turnout. Again the working class family gets hit three times. First his taxes are stolen to pay for "aid to education". Then he gets clobbered again when it's time to pay tuitions. Then, "bright" brats going to Harvard learn fancy economic theories as to how to steal even more from working class families and their children whose education they paid for. Sure enough, when Obama was elected, one of his first initiatives was more aid to education. This is one of the worst rackets in all history. *There is only one purpose of aid to higher education: to buy votes of education bureaucracies, paper-shufflers and professors getting 200K to teach sociology,* all of which is the core constituencies of neoliberals. And when a very liberal article in a very liberal magazine complained about the rising costs of higher education, not a word was mentioned of the burgeoning army of paper shufflers, deans, and professors getting outrageous pay-checks to teach a few courses in sociology.[9] "Aid to education" has nothing to do with aiding education; it's about buying the votes of these neoliberal higher ed bureaucrats.

29.6 SOCIAL SECURITY

Let's look at another example of suspicious motivations of the modern day neoliberal. Probably the most egregious example of using the vote to steal money from the rest of society is the Social Security system. Of course, a pension to senior citizens is an absolute must in a civilized society. Before Social Security, older people could find themselves living close to animal existence, sometimes dying of starvation. So retiree pensions were necessary and the program was finally put in place by Roosevelt in the 1930s. But the Social Security system that emerged was part of a pattern that has been going on for 150 years.

A serious problem emerges in society that needs addressing. For example, after the civil war, there was a great number of widows with children and very little means of support. So a program was needed to provide support for widows with families. The same problem appeared after WWII when there were increases in the divorce rate which left many women with children and no means of support because the husband disappeared or was a dead-beat. Also, with advances in medical care, there were means available to keep older people alive, but which they could not afford. Even until recently we had a healthcare system in which over 45 million families had no health insurance.

In just about every single instance, liberals would try to address the problem in some way. But also, in just about every case, conservatives would fight like tigers to prevent any *workable* program that was being proposed by liberals from being enacted. They never had a program of their own. In the 1930s, Social Security was portrayed by conservative opinion as part of a communist takeover. The same with the minimum wage. Medicare was called socialized medicine and was vigorously resisted by conservative forces.

And what results in just about every single case is that after spending all their energy fighting conservatives, and not being very smart to begin with, neoliberals give us a program that is a total mess. If conservatives would have sat down and tried to address society's problems in a rational way, perhaps workable solutions would have emerged. But their stance was always being *against*.

Social Security and Medicare as it is constituted presently are probably the most unfair, most unconstitutional, most unbiblical schemes ever devised by the evil mind of man. And it will lead to eventual disaster for the country. It continues because seniors are a block vote. They care little about the abortion issue, or the current king's war, or the unemployment rate, or the GDP, or the latest IUD. Their main concern is that monthly check and health benefits. They simply vote to keep taking money from younger workers at an ever increasing rate, which is not sustainable. As we have mentioned, right now retirees get all the money they paid in to the system over their working lives back in pension checks in only about 3 years. After that they are simply transferring money from younger workers trying to support families. As the population of seniors over 65 continues to increase relative the rest of the population, it will require ever increasing amounts of theft to pay for pensions. Social Security and Medicare as they are presently constituted are just big Ponzi schemes, which are simply not sustainable.

But of course, this Ponzi scheme must come to an end like all Ponzi schemes and that is being planned right now. In 2011, both Democrats and Republicans are planning in their own way to cut the benefits for younger generations. Young people don't vote as much nor keep track of their interests. So both party's plans to cut the deficit are to cut benefits on *young* people. *The Economist* criticizes other countries like Hungary and Argentina who have stolen or "nationalized" people's pension money. These are the good guys. In the US, Social Security taxes from young people are taken before they even get into the pot.

So the story goes that Bush got drunk one night, and woke up the next morning as a liberal and remained that way until Dick Cheney came in and threw cold water in his face. He wanted to privatize Social Security. So instead of the government stealing money from younger workers to pay pensions, individuals would be able to put their own money aside for their pensions. Under the Bush plan, you would have a period of time when retirees could not steal from younger workers for their pensions but would have no time to save up for the own. Thus there would be a short-fall in the immediate future until enough time had passed for retirees to have saved for their own pensions. The only way remaining to pay today's retirees pensions would have been through something like an estate tax.

But neoliberals saw a chance to make some political hay on the idea. So they embarked on a massive propaganda campaign that the Republicans were going to "destroy Social Security". I remember distinctly Senator John Kerry of Massachusetts coming right out on television: "we saved Social Security". That is a blatant lie and he ought to know it. What he saved was a gigantic Ponzi scheme based on unsustainable *theft*.

The very liberal *American Prospect* magazine devoted a full issue on propaganda to support the current Social Security program. One article said that the program "...ran a surplus of $122 billion last year and had accumulated a reserve of $2.54 trillion...".[10] This is probably as big a bold-face lie as you will ever see. The truth of course, is that there is *zero* reserve and *zero* surplus. The reason these people can belch out a lie like this is that system had been taking in more than it was paying out. But even this artificial surplus has been wiped out in 2011. But this imaginary surplus and imaginary "reserve" has been stolen to pay for the king's war to create terrorists and on spy agencies to track down the resulting terrorists. It doesn't exist. In its place is a piece of paper that says the government has temporarily stolen 2.54 trillion dollars. That's a neoliberal's idea of a "surplus".

The only reason the program took in more than it paid out before now is because the senior cohort was born before WWII when the birthrate was very low. So there aren't a lot of them. And the people paying in are the boomer generation when the birthrate more than doubled. So there is a big and very successful cohort paying in. But this has already reversed. When the boomers retire and are promised high payments because they paid in a lot, whose money will be stolen to pay for them? Illegal immigrants, that's who — and they don't pay in anything because they work at the minimum wage.

And add to this the fact that after WWII, we had an enormous increase in the production of toxic chemicals causing many genetic anomalies. Today's retirees were born into a relative clean environment, and still their health care costs are over half a trillion dollars. But many more boomers were born than earlier cohorts, and in a very toxic environment, causing enormous genetic damage. This will balloon Medicare costs to where by the middle of the century, Medicare will probably be *half* the GPD, and by the end, it will be three fourths of GDP. And who will pay for it? More illegal immigrants.

This is why, when the crooked politicians saw that young people didn't vote in the 2010 midterm elections, the very crooked commission to address the deficit jumped on this fact like a vulture over a dead cow, and suggested raising the retirement age to 70. This shows how democracy in the US works. If you turn you back for one moment, or don't send in your bribes to congress just once, you will be hijacked in some way and your money will be immediately stolen and given to some group paying attention.

What will happen, of course, is that when people under 35 get to retirement, they will find there is no money for their pensions. It will all have been stolen. And the retirement age will be 88, and most of them will not get a cent after paying in all their lives. But even in the short run, neoliberals "saved" a system of Social Security that violates the core principle of liberalism. It is stealing money from working class citizens needing to support real families and real children to give to retirees some of whom are millionaires who never paid into the system what they are getting back. But what it *does* accomplish is to get in the faces of Republicans who have been pushing for reform and in the faces of the children of the country and all future generations. Again the neoliberal motivation seems not to be justice, fairness or constitutionality. It is to continue getting in people's faces and stealing ever-increasing amounts of money in a gigantic Ponzi scheme.

Now I'm going to give you a morality or ethics test so you can judge whether or not you have any moral sensitivity. In my opinion, the absolutely *fairest* way to pay for social security pensions is to get the money out of an inheritance tax, so that each generation would be paying for their own Social Security. Retirees to be the sole judge through a vote as to how much their pensions would be. If a generation of retirees wants a higher social security pension, they would have to accept a higher inheritance tax. If they didn't want a high inheritance tax, they would have to get by on a lower social security pension. Now if you can't accept this simple principle, you have a real problem with basic moral turpitude. To keep stealing from the future at increasing rates is not only unfair, unconstitutional and unethical, but against the Bible as well, where it says the sins of the father should not be passed on to the sons.

To rub salt in the wound, when the voting block of senior citizens wanted higher Social Security pensions and trillion dollar Medicare benefits, they didn't get the money from an inheritance tax so that the money would come from the top 20% *of their own generation*. In fact, they had the inheritance tax actually *cut* under George Bush so that Social Security and the new drug benefit will be stolen from children who had no representation when this Ponzi scheme was concocted.

To sum up, there has not been a single law, not a single program not a single bureaucracy promoted by neoliberals that had any other purpose but to buy votes. We saw this in immigration, housing, aid to higher education and Social Security.

29.7 IN YOUR FACE WITH SOCIAL AND ECONOMIC BENEFITS.

Even when the neoliberal has an initiative with beneficial consequences to society, they will invariably do in a way that most gets in people's faces. For example, most rational people know that global warming will eventually cost trillions in flooded lowlands on the coasts of countries all over the world. Half of Florida will be under water. It will increase the chances of violent weather events like floods and tornadoes with tremendous loss of life and property. Of course, the conservative answer to all this is just denial, not because the science supports them, but because if liberals have a certain view, they must be wrong somehow.

Scientists have shown that global warming is caused by burning fossil fuels. So if we can get our energy in other ways, we will save future generations trillions in lost lives and property. There are many very attractive ways to do this, such as wind and solar power. However, because of the physical plant involved, they are not highly cost effective, barely paying for themselves. However, any source of non-carbon energy is welcome and would greatly benefit society, especially future generations. So we have wind turbines and solar panels being installed everywhere. But these turbines are not like road signs or guardrails. They are gigantic pieces of equipment 4 stories high that are pretty scary to be near. You would think that promoters of these turbines would be quite apologetic and humble in their approach to ordinary people in small communities. But oh no. Because they have a good cause, they feel justified in very arrogantly getting right in people's faces with their turbines to maximize their offensiveness. So instead of putting the turbines first in isolated and sparsely populated areas of the country, they love to invade small towns and stick their turbines right in people's faces. There is no excuse for this, and it actually sends people in a political direction that actually impedes progress in eliminating carbon-based energy.

29.8 The National Debt

One of the most baffling of neoliberal ideology is its total disregard for future generations. They have never even *considered* the ramifications of a large national debt. At first glance we could say that the national debt is not an *objective* of the neoliberal agenda. It is mostly a side effect of promising social programs that the neoconservative agenda won't allow taxes for and to buy votes. But when we examine these social programs in detail, we find that there is absolutely no care given to the waste involved, just as we discussed with the social security program.

One of the main motivations for the American Revolution was to put an end to taxation without representation, which European countries had been engaged in for centuries. This is expressed in the equal protection clause, which doesn't really do a very good job of protecting this fundamental right. Stealing from future generations not only violates this basic American principle, but it does so against the most defenseless class in all of society, who are children. I would think that the head and shoulders example of the "little guy" would be children. Stealing from them is not only the most unfair thing the country does, but it is a direct violation of the Constitution and against the Bible to boot. As we shall explain in the next chapter, a growing national debt is one of the core impositions of the neoconservative political agenda in *reality*. But why would the liberal agenda be so dismissive of a growing national debt?

While Ronald Reagan and George Bush shamelessly racked up over 8 *trillion* of national debt, liberals never said peep about it all. As Dr. Phil would say, what are they thinking? This was amply illustrated with Obama's economic plan. There was absolutely no concern for the amount they would be stealing from the future. Of course, some deficit spending was necessary to get the economy going. But the vast majority of money stolen from the future had nothing to do with creating jobs. Even when the motivation was buying votes like throwing money indiscriminately at crooked state governments to be used for more wasteful public service jobs and pensions, there was absolutely no concern for the debt being incurred.

You can search with a fine-tooth comb in liberal publications and you will never find a word about the dangers of deficits. For example, in an issue of *The Nation*, there was an in-your-face blast at people trying to limit deficits. The more they talk, the angrier they get at the deficit hawks: "…the drumbeat of deficit hysteria thumping in self-righteous panic grows louder by the day." [11]

One liberal no-nothing referred to deficit reduction as a "fetish".[12] The *American Prospect* said "…paying close attention to the deficit right now is bad politics, bad economics, and flatly undemocratic".[13] Hear that? — undemocratic, no less. Of course, "democratic" to these authors means stealing *trillions* from our children — children who cannot defend themselves, cannot vote and have no representation in Congress. That's the new neoliberal version of democracy.

In an angry article against deficit worriers, William Mitchell in *The Nation* said the government is not like a household because "it can consistently spend more than its revenue because it creates the currency".[14] In economics just as in physics, there's a second law of thermodynamics that says basically that you never get something for nothing. Deficits are *not* currency. Currency is the transactional *representation* of the production of goods and services, which is why there is no interest on the money in your pocket. Interest-bearing bonds are a kind of money, but it is fraudulent money because it represents nothing except a stream of money future generations are stuck with paying out.

Peter Galbraith says that for major sovereigns like the US, "bankruptcy is an irrelevant concept",…"nor is public debt a burden on future generations".[15] Galbraith gives his lies in pairs, just for reinforcement. National debts are *huge* burdens on future generations who have to pay interest on the debt. Also, sovereign debt is even more dangerous in larger economies and clearly not "irrelevant". You could get to where you get a negative feed-back loop. As the debt grows, you have to pay increasing interest rates to sell more bonds to pay the growing interest payments. This is exactly the situation Greece found itself in 2011. But Greece is a very small country the size of one American city and was able to be bailed out temporarily by the rest of Europe. And who bails out the US if it gets into the same position? There is an analysis showing that after a certain level of debt, collapse is inevitable like a collision course with ocean liners because the dollar would lose its international currency status. We don't know exactly where that point is, but we may be approaching it soon.

Another consideration is that liberals are not supposed to be in the business of stealing from the middle class to give to the rich. In Sect. 25.4 above, we said that the national debt does this very thing at a time when it is Consumption among the bottom 80% that needs to be increased. The people who now hold the bonds are mostly in the top 20% around the world. In the future, hundreds of billions of dollars will be extracted from government revenues, not to pay for health care, or infrastructure, or medical research or any of a number of things society needs, but to pay interest on the total debt. You could get to where so much government revenue would go to paying interest on the debt that services would have to be drastically cut, costing jobs, income, and consumption. Not only that, but the top 20% often doesn't consume with its growing wealth, but simply bids up the price of fixed assets, which just increases rents to households. The debt held by foreign countries is a total loss to the system. Not to worry, says Galbraith; "we will pay interest on it, not with real effort, buy by typing numbers into computers".[16] Government revenues sent to China for interest are not typing numbers, but real money that is a total drain on the economy. These are the reasons large national debts really cripple an economy for many years into the future. This is the experience Japan has had in the last 30 years.

You would think these neoliberal propagandists would have the decency to give an accurate description of deficits while having to incur them. Of course, the only way to get out of recession is deficit spending to get demand up and get the economy spiraling up. Roosevelt incurred deficits too. But they should be viewed not as a wonderful panacea that gives us something for nothing, but as a necessary evil. It's like getting a shot before a bad tooth is drilled. Pain is necessary to cure the problem, but that doesn't make pain a good thing. If deficits were viewed realistically, people would allow deficits but only if a dollar of deficit will create more than a dollar's worth of wealth and subsequent revenue increases to pay back the deficit. But you will never hear this from the modern neoliberal.

As a result of this thinking, Obama's deficits mushroomed and it still had little effect in getting the economy going. What happened to the theories of these deficit cheerleaders? The reason is pretty obvious. Their main goal was buying votes, and the economy was of secondary importance. He didn't have to worry about creating wealth to pay for deficits because it's all free money according to these neoliberal "economists" — nothing to worry about: "just typing numbers into computers". Also, Obama listened to the people who got us into the mess and stole trillions from the future to prop up hundreds of *trillions* of fraudulent derivatives. His place in history will be a failed president. And he had a chance to bring back Capitalism and create a whole era for the Democratic Party just as Roosevelt did.

29.9 THE IRAQ WAR

As people grew weary of the Iraq war which was based on media mouthpieces of the system mind perpetuating massive amounts of propaganda and lies, they began to turn against the war. In the 2006 midterm elections, neoliberals led by fancy Nancy Pelosi ran on a campaign promise to get out of Iraq. And the democrats won over Congress on the basis of this promise. But when it was time for George Bush to steal more hundreds of billions from the future to pay for the war, Nancy Pelosi and the rest of the democrats went right along and approved of this massive theft. Now let us assume that it was politically or militarily impossible for liberal democrats to keep their campaign promise to get out of Iraq. We should to give them the benefit of the doubt. But Pelosi's democrats had a chance to at least not compound the injustice. They could have attached an amendment to the bill to pay for the war by raising taxes on Bush's idle and crooked rich friends. Then they would have had Bush in a real trap. If he didn't sign the bill, he would have had to give up on his private little war of invasion and conquest. And if he signed it, he would have to get money from the very people who put him in office. This could have been a great squeeze play. So why didn't Pelosi and the democrats take this obvious tack?

At the top of Pelosi's neoliberal democrats' list of priorities was not the war in Iraq. It wasn't the kids coming home with arms and legs blown off. It wasn't the 20 thousand innocent Iraqi children killed in the war. It wasn't the hundreds of billions of waste that could have provided health care, a cleaner environment or any other of the nation's needs. None of this was at the top of neoliberal Nancy Pelosi's list of priorities. What was at the very *top* of fancy Nancy's list was the *theft* pipe. Her neoliberal friends in Congress had seen Bush steal *trillions* from the children of this country and they wanted to make sure that when it was their turn, they could steal too by turning on the theft faucet even more. And that's exactly what happened. When Obama took office, the theft pipe was clean and clear because of Bush stealing a third of a trillion *every year he was in office*. This gave the democrats a blank check to get into future taxpayers faces by opening up the theft faucet even more as Obama began stealing over a *trillion* dollars a year. All of this was possible because neoliberals never said a word about Reagan or Bush's deficits. And what did they do with the stolen money. You guessed it. They used a good part of it to buy votes with more "benefits" — and not even votes of Republicans or undecideds, but votes they already had. You will never out-stupid a neoliberal.

29.10 ILLEGAL IMMIGRATION

As we are illustrating, neoliberalism has clearly shifted the priorities from sticking up for the little guy to getting in his face any way they can. But in order to push the neoliberal agenda, there has to be some political power to do the necessary legislation. So the second priority of the neoliberal has been to puff up their political muscle by simply buying votes, and *then* getting in people's faces. Let's look at an issue whose neoliberal position is both to buy votes and to stick it in our faces: illegal immigration.

We all know the history of the Industrial Revolution after the Civil War. It created factory conditions that were as bad as anyone could imagine, almost as bad as slavery in the south. Workers worked 12 and 14 hours a day 6 or 7 days a week for peanuts. The vast majority of people, especially in the cities where the new immigrants usually went, were desperately poor. We could call it Northern slavery. This was a period of intense Economic Socialism as we have described.

The 1920's big spurt in the stock market never benefited the working class who remained poor all through the '20s. The paycheck for the average worker actually *decreased*. All the new wealth and income was going to the top 20%. This led finally to a big meltdown called the Great Depression. But immigration was greatly curtailed in the 1920s, which is important to notice.

Well along came WWII and the creation of millions of jobs for the war. And they were decent paying jobs because there was a great shortage of labor and the curtailment of immigration gave workers enough leverage to form mass unions. Not only that, but it was a relatively equal expansion with the working class benefiting as much as the top 20%, perhaps even more so. By the 1970, there really wasn't a poor working class anymore. The working class had become a middle class with decent paying jobs and their own homes, as median family income of the bottom 80% went up 50% in real dollars.

But by the 1980s, the greatly increased flows of information made for a powerful enough system mind that it was able to create a neoconservative juggernaught in the Reagan presidency who proceeded to revive the Economic Socialism of the 1920s. This scattered historic liberal opinion like kicking an ant hill. The ants run around in disarray until they can reorganize into a new viable society. Besides, the historic mission of liberalism had been accomplished. All that was left was to bring up the bottom 20% of poor into the middle class. But it became obvious that this would be impossible in the face of the Reagan juggernaught.

What led to the forking off of historic liberalism into neoliberalism was that liberals had gotten used to winning over a long period of time during the Roosevelt revolution. Winning becomes addictive. And besides, newer liberals coming up were a bunch of spoiled kids from middle class backgrounds. They had run out of intellectual and theoretical gas and were too spoiled and too lazy to get in the trenches and come up with new ideas that might enable them to buck the system and continue liberalism's historic mission. What emerged was a system mind motto that if you can't beat 'em, join 'em. This is how neoliberalism got started. By jumping in bed with the system, they could continue winning and be comfortable in the process. So whereas historic liberalism wanted restricted immigration and championed the 8-hour day and worker protections in order for workers to get home to *traditional* families, neoliberalism climbed right in bed with the system as it began attacking religion and traditional families with initiatives like gay marriage and all means for ordinary people to put meaning into their lives.

For the last 20 years, in neoliberal magazines like *The Nation*, we have one intellectual prostitute after another claiming great victories with gay marriage and illegal immigration. They are too stupid to see that these great "victories" have come as a result *not* of bucking the system as they had done for hundreds of years, but by climbing in *bed* with the system. They pay lip service to the working conditions of the slave class, to a shrinking middle class and lip service to the establishment of an above-the-law nobility on Wall St. down to an immigrant slave class on the bottom. Eight years of absolutely nothing done about these problems by the neoliberal Barack Obama, has meant nothing to these word-mongerers. The system throws crumbs at these problems just to buy votes.

Regarding immigration, I'm not against immigration per se. I'm for democracy and the Constitution. We should have the amount of immigration that the American people want, no more and no less. But instead, what the system has done is another of the most clever scams in our history and could only be done with a system mind. The system came up with the phrase, "immigration reform" and you hear it every election cycles for 35 years now. What this amounts to is that neoliberal leaders in the democratic party teamed up with neoconservative leaders in the Republican Party to bring off the scam — all done behind closed doors and without the slightest regard for the wishes of the American people. Here's how it works. Neoconservative Republicans blame Democrats for sneaking in millions of illegals, and Democrats blame Republicans for not making them citizens. Together they have kept the scam going for 35 years and it will continue for another 35 years. This gives both sides just what they want while the army of illegals gradually coalesces into a slave class.

Neoliberals also want a basically slave class whose votes they can buy with benefits. But an aristocracy on top of a slave class doesn't seem to accord with historic liberal ideals which was to reduce poverty and misery and protect labor. But the new neoliberal with his reenergized emotion is so intent on crushing the system, that what comes afterwards is of little concern. Younger neoliberals don't even know about Marx's worker's paradise.

But the aristocracy has it all figured out. They get neoliberals to vote for the Clintons and the Obamas of the world who have continued right along towards a hierarchical society with an aristocracy on top of a shrinking middle class becoming a helpless peasant class on top of a slave class on the bottom. They know exactly how to keep a slave class in tow. Just look at the south before the Civil War with an aristocracy owning all land and resources and wealth. (They've been replaced by Wall St.) They would hire poor whites to "oversee" the huge class of slaves who were close to half the population in some states. Life went on. This is why they were so pissed when Lincoln came along to upset this very stable state of affairs.

But in the process of having hordes of poor people overrunning the country, labor especially at lower levels of income has no leverage at all. The May 2013 issue of the *American Prospect* droned on page after page with dozens of charts and graphs to show how much poverty there is in the country and how much worse it has gotten. The numbers show that since illegal immigration took off under Ronald Reagan, the real income of the bottom 80% has been continuously dropping, with the real income of the bottom 20% falling off a cliff.

The working conditions of actual illegals are even worse. They have no unions, no labor protections, no safety requirements, no minimum wage and can't even vote. This creates a whole cottage industry of neoliberals in magazines and books, writing horror stories about working conditions of illegal immigrants, especially the food growing and packing industry.[17] In one article, we hear about "...noticeable body modifications, such as permanently hunched backs, crooked fingers, and hands so swollen that they look as if someone has attached a valve to a finger and pumped vigorously".[18] They really are the beginnings of a bottom slave class. But in all these years of immigration, even when Democrats had total control of the government, almost nothing was done to improve the lives of illegal immigrants. But why should they. You can't steal from the rest of society and buy votes if there's no misery, poverty and human degradation among the people you're supposedly stealing for.

None of this will affect the the top 20% including the media aristocracy. With lower and lower labor costs and protections, company profits continue to soar, giving the top 20% and the corporate world unlimited profits to be used to buy and sell politicians like sacks of potatoes. This will result in making their own rules which means less worker protection and more illegal immigration to maintain a class of slave labor resulting in more "hunched backs" and "crooked fingers". The hard facts are that if you want to alleviate poverty, you increase wages; and the only *real* way to do that is to restrict the numbers. It was only because immigration was stopped in the 1920s that Roosevelt was finally able to create a prosperous middle class after 65 years of stagnating miserable working conditions among the working class.

But we haven't gotten to the worst of it. If all we were doing was emptying out Mexico by bringing in poverty-stricken people for a better life, you could justify immigration. I'm an old style liberal. In the '80s, when Ronald Reagan let in 3 million illegal immigrants, I supported it. I thought, we can bring them here, find them housing and jobs and they'll have a better life. But I'm also a realist. A few years later, I happen to run across some population statistics, and lo and behold, I found that Mexico had replaced the 3 million and had actually doubled down and *added* 3 million more poor Mexicans. Now we have 6 million poor Mexicans instead of only 3 million. Mexico City now has 21 *million* people more than any city in the Western Hemisphere. That's more than New York city and we know what an ant hill that is. The poverty in some of their barrios is unbelievable. There are millions of children running around with no clothes. They don't even get enough nutrition for their brains to grow normally. Of course, this fits right in with a slave class the American aristocracy is creating. You don't want slaves to have too much intelligence or they might cause trouble.

The motivation of neoconservatives is clear. They want to drag down the value of labor in the middle class and to provide of slave class of cheap labor to puff up profits for big business. But liberals are supposed to be in the business of *reducing* poverty and misery not adding to it. But that kind of old-style liberal has been pushed right off the political stage. Illegal immigration actually *increases* the amount of misery and poverty in the world. And the reason is that it creates an *incentive* for the poorest of people in Latin American and the rest of the world to have as many babies as possible to send to the US and western Europe, because the more babies a woman has, the better the chances that one of them will sneak in and send money home. Not only that but neoliberal politicians are actually *bribing* starving people from failed states (with entry into the US) to have more babies so they can bring them into the US to vote for people like them. As a result, even though developing countries will continue to send hundreds of millions of poor people into the advanced economies, the populations in these poorer countries will continue to increase and the absolute number of people living on 2 dollars a day will not decrease one iota. (And parenthetically, another indication of the neoliberal motivation is the push for gay marriage. Why didn't they run their gay marriage bandwagon in Mexico City or Bangladesh or Mumbai, India or parts of Africa where populations of deprived miserable people are exploding. Oh no. They run their gay marriage bandwagon in the very places, western Europe and the US, where native populations are actually *shrinking.* Now what does that tell you about motivation.)

Neoliberals claim that the birthrate is falling in Latin America. If the birthrate among Hispanics is very high in affluent US, it is certainly not going to be lower south of the border where they're in survival mode. In 1980, the population of Mexico was 70 million.

After 35 years of about 25 million illegals, the population of Mexico is now 130 million and growing. And they're probably lying about that. In 2016, in one of their publications, *The Economist* reported a population of 122 million in Mexico. In another publication *of the very same magazine at the very same time*, they report a population of 128 million. [19] This shows that nobody has any idea how many babies in little poverty stricken villages in the third world are producing and they don't care. It's in the interests of the Mexican government and all pro-immigrant groups to increase their numbers while lying about population and birthrates. In fact, because of our past history, Mexico is probably still angry that we stole Texas from them. The goal of Mexican leaders is to take over the US and merge the US with Mexico. And someday they'll have the votes to do it.

Illegal immigration has absolutely nothing to do with eliminating poverty, misery and human degradation in the world. It's all about buying votes and crushing the system. Just look at reality. There's been improvement in the standard of living of the professional class in Mexico due to natural increases in technology and productivity. But liberals are supposed to be interested in the bottom where destitution lies. And the bottom 20% is every bit as poor and destitute as it ever was, probably more so. An '01 *Nation* article admits, "According to data from the 2000 census, fully 75 percent of the population of Mexico lives in poverty today,…as compared with 49 percent in 1981, …." [20] They blame free trade which average poor people know nothing about. And this is a magazine with constant doses of propaganda pushing for illegal immigration. But the professional neoliberal couldn't care less about human poverty and misery. "Hunched backs" and "crooked fingers" are down their list of priorities along with any other economic considerations relevant to the bottom 80%. Their number one priority is to crush Capitalism. If this requires great amounts of misery and poverty to get there, so be it.

Also, the numbers that are available to measure all this are from a century of unlimited natural resources, lots of land, advanced agricultural methods, and in producing goods and services without regard to the environment. When these costs start appearing in this century, the growing populations of developing countries will insure increasing amounts of poverty, misery and human degradation. But poverty and human degradation are the life-support system of the professional neoliberal. The end goal of the neoliberal is a billion people in the US, 20% of whom are dirt poor. That's a lot of votes to get in the faces of the dwindling rest of Americans.

An article by Katha Pollitt in *the Nation*, shows the intellectual dishonesty of these pro-immigrant neoliberals.[21] She starts complaining about Europeans trying to raise their fertility rates because they are all below the rate required for the population to be maintained. Of course, what she is really upset about is that these countries have too many *white* people. She ascribes the motives as a desire "…to breed the next generation of workers — ethnically correct workers, too, not the troublesome immigrant kind". Yes, these home-grown white workers don't cause enough trouble: they pay their own way and create a prosperous enough economy that stealing from others isn't necessary. That is not the society Pollitt wants.

She adds to this argument against increasing fertility among white people the idea that it's "…weird to promote population growth while we wring our hands over global warming, environment damage…", since "…it's the developed world that's doing the Earth in". I take it we should encourage the poverty-stricken peoples of the world to do the reproducing. They will cause less global warming and they're not white, which is their most valuable quality. And we can encourage more of them by letting them sneak into richer countries. But if global warming is as bad as Pollitt suggests, why do we let them come into the US and raise their standard of living to where they cause more global warming? Logic is not Pollitt's strong point.

Speaking of global warming, what about the deterioration of the environment? One weekend, neoliberals are marching for immigration "rights" and the next weekend they're marching against global warming. An article in the same *Nation* magazine by Andrew Ross shows the intellectual prostitution of this "immigrant rights" crowd.[22] The author had FAIR in his sights (Federation for American Immigration Reform). FAIR is an environmental group who sees the dangers to the environment from too much immigration and a growing world population. Ross does the usual bobbing and weaving when you have a dishonest argument. He says things like, "how we produce and consume energy is a much more important determinant of pollution than our numbers." Right off the bat, this is a bald-faced lie. This guy doesn't know squat about science. He doesn't even know what pollution is. Energy use and efficiency affects global warming, but it is not the source of the real dangers to the health of human beings, which is why this is the only consideration Ross drones on about. Even if we got all our energy from nuclear, tides, solar, farts, or any other kind of wind power, this does nothing to stop the most dangerous pollution. What is causing the genocide to our gene pool *are the toxins and waste products emanating from production processes.* We discussed this in detail in Sect. 24.3. *Every additional human being on the face of the earth uses some amount of goods and services thereby adding to the toxic pollutants that causes the alarming rates of genetic-related diseases.* And they expect another 4 *billion* people this century.

The reality is that if the almost 7 *billion* human beings on this earth were to have the standard of living of the poorest of Americans, the planet would choke to death. Much of the world's land mass would be under water, and there would be enough pollutants in the environment and resulting mutations in the gene pool to devolve us all back to the monkeys. The addition to our own population of one single human being is one more source of environmental degradation, regardless of the degree of environmental safety we have.

But there's another important factor that illustrates the new concept of a "tipping point". Immigrants coming to the US before Reagan were coming from countries and cultures that were very similar to the people who originally came to the US from Great Britain. They were mostly Christians and they were coming from the most advanced states in the world of the day in terms of technology and economic development. Even though some of them were still stumbling politically, all the countries they were coming from like Germany, Poland, Ireland, Italy, etc. had tasted freedoms and representative democracy. These were not failed states. Even Hitler's Germany could not be characterized as a failed state. His economic and technological development enabled him to take on the whole world. As a result of these similarities, people from these countries were able to assimilate very quickly. Today, in terms of appearance and lifestyle and values, you can't tell someone of Irish ancestry from someone of German ancestry (both sometimes have red hair).

But if immigrants are coming from cultures and states that are sufficiently *different* from the native population, you get a tipping point. This is especially the case if they're coming from the *bottom* levels of the economic ladder. They are in the lowest 10% of unskilled workers who probably require more wealth to maintain a reasonable standard of living than they create. They are coming to the US out of *deprivation*. This sets up a feedback loop. In order to maintain a reasonable standard of living for immigrants and provide services they will need, money will have to be *taken* from the more affluent layers of affluent countries, which will be done by the solid voting block of new immigrants. This, combined with the larger difference in culture immediately creates some antipathy towards immigrants. This in turn causes the immigrants to hunker down into survival mode which causes them to cling even closer to their own culture and lifestyles. And what is worse, they start to survive through *quantity* instead of *quality*. This is true of all forms of life from lowly bugs all the way up to humans. They all fill the ecological niche until there is starvation. And the process speeds up if survival is threatened. This results in immigrants multiplying twice as fast as the native population. And now we see where Pollitt's argument is going. The more productive layers in affluent countries, being the target of Pollitt's theft, are exactly the people who Pollitt is castigating for wanting to increase their numbers. See how it all hangs together? By *decreasing* the numbers who create most of the wealth, and by *increasing* the voting block numbers who *need* services, you get to steal more and more from less and less, until you're stealing a great deal from nobody. That's the neoliberal logic of the situation.

Recently, neoliberals have started to brag about the fact that non-whites made up 48% of the newborns in 2008. In fact, they come right out and threaten the rest of society with huge numbers of illegals whose voting block will be enough to run the country. So in the present state of affairs, the really important question is, in a hundred years from now when immigrant populations have completely taken over both the US and Europe, what will these countries look like. Will Germany look like it does today or will it look like Iraq and Syria? Will the US look like it does today or like Mexico? Well, to be honest, nobody knows for sure. However, when we look at all the countries of the world, only about one in ten human beings on this earth is living in a country with a reasonable amount of freedoms and standard of living and democracy. Nine out ten of the earth's inhabitants are living in dictatorships or oligopolies like in Russia or states that are failing in one way or another with miserable poverty-stricken people. Africa and Central America are a mess, there is enormous poverty in South America and India, and civil strife all over the Muslim world. I think we should do more to help these countries by lending them our institutions. But do we want to play Russian roulette with the few countries in the world that are doing okay. It's just an opinion, but, we may be entering another dark age just like the six hundred years after the fall of the Roman Empire when there was another invasion of peoples from failed states.

The big picture question that remains is what has current immigration done for Europe and the US? It hasn't curtailed population growth especially at the bottom. It hasn't reduced the civil wars, sectarian violence, terrorism, starvation and strife in the failed states immigrants are coming from, nor has it reduced their destitute populations. It *has* reduced the value of middle class labor in countries taking in immigrants to where they are having to steal *trillions* from their own children to prop up their economies. It *has* increased the population of the world and consequently the amount of environmental hazards that threaten the gene pool and life in general. And from now on, every time a French family goes to a restaurant or movie or sporting event, the thought will pop into their heads that they could be blown apart in a terrorist attack at any moment. That is no way to live.

But the pro-immigrant forces have taken the lead since the aristocracy owns the means of propaganda. They have charged forth like the ACLU assigning thoughts to everyone. Anti-immigrants are "nativists", "xenophobes", "white supremacists", bigots, and many other names; while they are lovers of mankind. But when you look at the sum total of effects on world human conditions, what is the motivation of pro-immigrant groups except for the business class to have a source of cheap labor, for the neoliberal to crush western civilization and for the aristocracy to have a slave class to clean up their shit.

29.11 Sex Education

The concept of sex education presents one of the most interesting phenomenon from the point of view of plain logic. And because of the glitch in the logic, the issue again provides a means for liberals to squeeze through a crack in the door. We don't need to get into the details about how much sex education children should get. I realize that it is possible for parents to teach their kids to be racists or Ku Klux Klanners. However, once you allow the government to interject itself into the private lives of families, where does it stop? And whose opinions are we to use? The irony in this issue is that while neoliberals are always championing "diversity", when it comes to the education of children, they have a completely uniform, government-enforced curriculum to be imposed on every family throughout the country. Diversity only counts when it can be used to again stick it in the faces of average people. When getting in the faces of people requires total *lack* of diversity, down the drain goes diversity.

My own opinion is that I would be willing to allow a few cases of parents inculcating despicable doctrines into their kid's minds in order to preserve the freedom of parents to create the kind of moral environment for their kids that they deem desirable. If parents are prevented from this, it interferes with the cohesiveness of families and prevents the teaching of any kind of parentally approved norms and values.

Now liberals claim that sex education is just another form of education that children should be exposed to along with reading, writing and 'rithmetic. This seems reasonable at first glance. But sexual practices essentially involve people's moral values. And the question is, should the state be in the business of tinkering with the moral values of a family? And here is where the logic presents an interesting glitch, which, of course, liberals have exploited to the hilt.

Liberals claim that they are not introducing values because they say their sex education is value-neutral. An article in the ultraliberal *Nation* magazine gets very indignant about conservative parent groups having the nerve to put value terms into sex education such as decrying premarital sex. [23] This totally hypocritical article decries local parents making decisions on their children's sex education: "The extreme decentralization in the United States not only makes possible but invites local culture-war battles over curriculum...". Yes, and this writer is going to put a stop to all that local bickering by a big brother government coming in and squelching them all with a liberally designed national curriculum imposed uniformly on everybody. There are no more wars once you've defeated and crushed the opposition. I don't think it's anybody's business including this writer and certainly not the state, what values, especially about sex, parents want for their kids. But how value-neutral are these liberal programs anyway?

For example, suppose you simply describe a particular sexual practice, like, for example, gay sex with no connotations or suggestions of value whether approval or disapproval. But if we look closely at this claim, it is very disingenuous to say the least, as are many liberal claims. Let's put approval and disapproval on a scale from minus 10 to plus 10, and ask, where does a neutral presentation of an issue lie. Of course, liberals would claim that a neutral position would be at zero. But is this the case? In my opinion, describing a sexual practice in totally neutral terms is not at zero at all, but actually in the positive side of the scale. Suppose the teacher describes gay sex in very unemotional, neutral words, saying, well the man gets in this position and the other man gets in that position; then the first man puts this thing into this position and the second man puts that thing in that position and on and on. Value-neutral words do not create value-neutral *meaning*. In fact, value-neutral words create value-*laden* meaning: one of tacit approval and belongs on the positive side of the scale, maybe a plus 2 or 3. As such, there *is* a moral value which is really interjecting itself into the moral environment of the family. This is why many groups of parents have balked at sex education. And of course, this is why neoliberals are so much in favor of it. It provides a perfect opportunity to get in the faces of average people and clobber them over the head with their very *non*-neutral version of neutrality.

But how would a teacher describe a sexual practice that would lie exactly at zero on the approval scale? This is where more conservative parents are somewhat in a bind. It would appear that if there is any suggestion of the undesirability or negativity of a sexual practice, that would immediately put the instruction in the negative side of the scale and that might not accord with a value-free education, as well as being unfair to people who engage in the particular practice. It may be near impossible to describe a sexual practice with a value-free meaning.

The only solution to the dilemma, in my opinion, is to allow only parents to create the moral and value environment of their kids. This is a very simple and decidable principle to go on. I realize there are costs to this principle and liberals have pointed them out. Lack of sex education can lead to dangerous practices among kids and ruined lives. But the undesirable consequences are often easy to see. However, we can't measure the lack of moral values in kids because the state has so greatly interfered with parents having the job of inculcating moral values, that they simply give up and abjure any responsibility for their kids' moral education. This might be a bigger factor than omitting sex education.

In modern day society we certainly don't see an *increase* in morally informed behavior. Scams are popping up everywhere. The moral climate in the US is certainly not improving in any area including sexual practices. And this is in direct proportion to the degree that the state has interjected itself into the value education of children. Maybe we ought to get back to parents through their PTAs having sole responsibility for the sex education and moral education of their children and see if this helps. A system of values a parent believes in, however inadequate, will be more effective than values a parent doesn't believe in, however superior it may be.

In other areas of education, the decisions are a lot more difficult. In some school districts, parents don't want their kids to hear about slavery in history courses. This is a very tough call. I would still come out on the side of parents, although barely. But they should never teach anything that is false.

29.12 CRIME AND PUNISHMENT

If there is one issue that very incisively illustrates the neoliberal agenda of getting into people's faces it's in the area of crime and punishment, especially over the death penalty. I want to be very upfront in my opinion on the issue, so that you can take account of my biases. *I don't give the tiniest crap about the death penalty.* I don't care if we have it or don't have it or anything in between. Liberals have made a big deal about the death penalty. They write enormous books and an unending flow of articles about the death penalty to get in our faces about how uncivilized it is and on and on. I'm sure you've heard all this. My question is simply, how can any sane, normal person get excited about the death penalty.

First of all, we have an environment policy that winds up causing an alarming increase in birth defects. Then we have a health care system that neglects the health of millions of children many of whom will have truncated lives because of lack of health care. Then, because these liberals piss away any support they might get in the population on stupid issues like the death penalty and gay marriage, when it's time to vote, we get a bunch of paid killers who go to far away lands to invade, conquer and kill hundreds of thousands including tens of thousands of children. In this moral climate, we're supposed to get excited about *one isolated* guy who raped some random woman and chopped her up into little pieces. I just don't see it. *I don't give a crap about this lone murderer* when it's embedded in a world of death, destruction and anthropocide.

And what about the system that puts people on death row in the first place? If we're ever going to revive the Constitution, one of the first things on the agenda should be the establishment of fair trials in the criminal justice system. But of course, you never hear these liberals promoting fair trials because most the shysters who make money off this ridiculous system are neoliberals. When some poor black guy gets accused of a crime, his case is given over to some old, drunk, down-and-out lawyer who cheated his way through some Mickey Mouse law school and has a hundred cases just like it. He has neither the time nor resources nor often even the inclination to properly defend his client. Often he's up against a bunch of brilliant, sharp, crisp Harvard law school shysters in the prosecution office.

Then we see the exact opposite. The defendant is a Wall Street crook who has just stolen hundred of billions of dollars from the economy and who can afford a whole army of 2 thousand-dollar an hour Philadelphia shysters. Meanwhile the prosecution has a couple of kids fresh out of some Mickey Mouse law school who have no idea how to prosecute the case. All this passes for fair trials in the US.

There is only one way to insure a uniform fair trial for all defendants. After a trial, the judge would give a grade as to the overall performance of the lawyers in the case on both sides. The grades would be the usual F through A, and we could go to double A and triple A, just to give these shysters better grades. The grade for a lawyer in a particular trial would be added in and averaged over the career of the lawyer in question, perhaps with a weighting factor that gives more weight to more recent trials. Then if a defendant showed up with grade double A (AA) lawyers, the state would have to provide double A lawyers to prosecute. If the defendant could afford only grade C lawyers, the prosecution would be required to consist only of grade C lawyers. This very simple program would take the constitution seriously and insure fair trails. But we're not going to get it with a uniform army of venal shysters running the country and especially the criminal justice system.

And we should point out that because of the total lack of fair trails in the US system, innocent people are routinely put on death row. When DNA analysis became possible, over 80 people were discovered on death row who were completely innocent. Convicting innocent people, which is clearly outlawed by the Constitution, is a much worse crime than anything you can do to a guilty guy.

The only proviso we should note about the death penalty is this. The death penalty is a pre-planned killing by the state. Conforming to the principle that the punishment should never exceed the crime, the death penalty should never apply to anything less than pre-planned killings. This is an easy principle to implement.

29.13 Welfare and the Social Safety Net

One of the biggest surprises of my life came when I began to learn about practices in the welfare system. In just about single instance of a welfare system in any state, the story was the same: lots of welfare fraud. The systems actually went about trying to find people who under the most remote criteria of qualifications could be put on the rolls. This amazed me.

I would have thought that people working for the system would realize that moneys for welfare was coming from working taxpayers and that it would be of the *utmost* necessity to make sure that every penny used would be absolutely needed and justified and incorruptibly dispensed. Not at all, as we shall see.

The modern welfare system really started after the Civil War when many mothers had lost husbands and had little means to support their children. The American people voted to expand this system in the 20th century. Of course, conservatives, having only a vestigial trace of humanity, fought against these programs every step of the way, even though it was mainly a children's program — children who didn't ask to be born in a system controlled by a neoconservative system mind. But the majority of Americans, most of whom are decent people, maintained family support programs for a long time in our history.

But with the emergence of the neoliberal in the 1980s, the situation began to deteriorate. Welfare fraud started to pop up in every state, some worse than others. Here again, welfare systems were infested with neoliberals who probably got great joy out of getting in the faces of the taxpayer. The goal of the neoliberal seemed to be to have in place a big fat mama sitting on the porch at the corner of every street with a joint in one hand and a beer in the other, surrounded by a flock of out-of-wedlock kids on full display for every real taxpaying, working person to see as they turned the corner on the way home.

A whole issue of the ultra liberal *American Prospect* was devoted to how many states were cutting services to the poor and elderly like pre-school education, public transit, visits to the elderly sick by nurses and helpers, etc.[24] They drone on with righteous indignation. But not one word in the whole issue about the abuses and fraud, which is the wedge neoconservatives use to cut many of these very much-needed services. Are these neoliberals really concerned with people's needs or getting into the faces of average Americans?

As a result of massive abuses in every corner of society for many years, the whole system was dismantled under Bill Clinton in 1996. Of course, out with the bath water went the baby. We should keep in mind that the Constitution guarantees the right to "life, liberty, and the pursuit of happiness". There's no way to insure anything close to this if a child gets off to the kind of start many kids do. The whole thrust of the Constitution was equal dignity, equal rights, and most important, an equal chance at a decent life. In my opinion, the opportunity to be raised by a willing parent is a necessity for a child to have an equal chance at a decent life. Welfare reform completely trashed this right. Now, even willing parents are forced to throw their kids in child abandonment centers so they can keep jobs. This is putting all the abuses of the welfare system on the backs of children who did not ask to be born in the kind of unequal world we live in.

On the other hand, if we allow a willing parent to raise their kids at the expense of society, how do we prevent abuses like we saw before '96, where teenagers were having babies to get their own apartments on welfare? I have an idea which would never be put into practice, but would solve the problem in an equitable way. In my opinion, it should be against the law to have a baby with no means to support. So how could we penalize the parents without hurting the interests of the baby? The idea here is to have special cities erected just like any other city with street shops, schools, theatres, bars, houses, cars, rapid transit and the rest of it. The only difference would be that there would be a wall down the middle of this city; male parents would live on one side, and female parents on the other. This would prevent more out-of-wedlock children. Together they would take turns working to provide support. The rest would come from the state. But this would allow a combination of parents to make up one full-time parent to raise children. Of course, nothing like this will happen because it infringes on the freedom of parents who vote. So we will continue to impose a no-parent penalty on children whose only crime was to be born in the wrong circumstances.

But even the cheating we get on welfare is peanuts compared to what we waste for the military, spy agencies, corporate welfare, etc. But people identify with the latter nodes. The explanation is simple. The average American doesn't like poor people. And the reason is that they don't want to be poor themselves and they are repulsed by anything close to what they do not want to be. They want to be rich themselves and imagine they would be doing the same thing the crooked rich are doing if they were rich. This is why peasant juries will give some poor black guy 20 years for stealing 35 bucks from a candy store. But Wall Street crooks who steal *billions* are often let off Scott free. The peasants *identify* with nodes of power and wealth, which is how we get these far away wars of invasion and conquest.

What this means is that if we are going to really insure a decent start for the children of this country it is absolutely necessary that any support from society to the poor and needy must be squeaky clean and above reproach. However, this conflicts with the neoliberal's basic need to get in the faces of average people. These neoliberals *want* to show that they can steal people's money and use it for fancy underwear and liquor and there's absolutely nothing we can do about it. That's why there is never effort to keep any form of welfare, income supplements, and other benefits to the needy above reproach. The major motivation for these neoliberals isn't really to help people, to but to get in the faces of everyone else by stealing their money, wasting it, and showing they are helpless to do anything about it. This is why huge numbers of children do not get the necessary support to start a fulfilling life.

Welfare agencies should be manned (and womaned) by *conservatives*. But these agencies will continue to attract neoliberals whose main motivation is to get in the faces the average American. There will be continued waste and fraud, which conservatives use to starve out these programs mostly at the expense of children who are the real victims of the whole sordid mess.

29.14 GAY MARRIAGE

One of the ripest areas for attack on the social fabric of the country is in the area of social institutions. This is an area that is just mushy for an attack by neoliberals. It allows them to put all that extra energy in the frontal cortex into an identity bursting with aggression to really get in people's faces. We just have to look at social institutions and social practices that provide a means of identity and allows them to put meaning into their lives. Two major areas in this regard are religion and religious institutions like marriage.

We saw in Sect. 28.5, how the system mind acting through its media mouthpieces has taken many measures to reduce the importance of family and friends in people's private lives so as to free them up for more hours on the almighty job. We discussed the enormous efforts taken to promote gay marriage and to attack religion of any kind in the all media outlets.

In Sect. 28.4, we discussed the identity aspect of marriage and how marriage used to be a way to support identity formation especially in men. Without this avenue to achieve identity in men, there is a subtle coercion in favor of making the almighty job the only source of identity. The way to weaken the status of marriage as a source of identity is to simply water it down. And the best way to do that is to allow anyone to marry including gay couples.

When the liberal community heard about gay marriage, it was an epiphany. There has never in history been a more energetic reaction to a social movement than the neoliberal reaction to gay marriage. They jumped on the idea like a lion on a pot roast and have held a death grip ever since. Here was a perfect way to get in people's faces and destroy an important means for ordinary people to put meaning in their lives. Of course, liberals will always claim they are for human interaction and meaning. But when it comes to what they actually *do*, it is the exact opposite. The gay marriage bandwagon is a perfect example.

After the Nov., 2008 elections, one article was bemoaning the rejection of gay marriage in "…the passage of four heart-breaking bigoted ballot measures…" in four different states. [25] Get that: *bigoted*. When ordinary people are trying to salvage an institution that has been the core of their private lives for thousands of years and the basis of family life that defenseless children have always relied on, they are "bigoted". You would think that after years of massive propaganda by the system mind media outlets pushing gay marriage, and still a majority of average people in most states tried to defend their most cherished institution, that these neoliberal intellectual prostitutes would back down. Instead they throw a temper tantrum, fill their diapers, and start calling whole populations of people any name in the books like "bigot" even in the public dialog. But traditional marriage advocates have to keep their language squeaky clean. It's really hard to decide who is more disgusting, neoliberals or neoconservatives.

Of course, neoliberals are too semi-conscious to realize that it was the *system* that did in traditional marriage: liberals only hopped onto the back end of a moving bandwagon. Fifty years from now, the only people marrying will be gays. Children will be raised by clumps of women in condo complexes with no men, no marriages, and no traditional family life. Being raised without a father figure to identify with will insure that young men will eagerly sign up to the current king's private murderous war to muster some sense of identity.

29.15 CREATIONISM

One of the most egregious examples of the misuse of science came in a very controversial suit involving what is currently called Intelligent Design. As you might expect, when it's time to destroy elements of society that have meaning for people, the ultraliberal ACL(screw) U would be right at the forefront sticking it in people's faces. I won't go into the details of the suit, just its important ramifications and the concepts involved. The Intelligent Design people had wanted to put something in the science curriculum to the effect that it is possible that the earth and the universe came into existence by an intelligent designer. We discussed creationism in Sect. 9.3. The anti people led by the ACLU claimed that Intelligent Design was just a back-door way to sneak religion into the curriculum and sought to remove any mention of intelligent design. Of course, large numbers of Americans believe in Intelligent Design as part of their system of values and beliefs. This was a ripe fruit if there ever was one and a perfect chance for these ultraliberals to stick it in the face of a large segment of the American population and they did just that.

Now the concept of intelligent design simply means that there is some force, entity or being who designed the enormous intricacies of the physical world around us — its elements and its laws. Now what does this have to do with God? Well, some people believe that the intelligent designer is God. But does the concept of intelligent design logically entail anything at all about God? This gets into the definition of God. Throughout the ages, if we look at the concept of God among hundreds of societies and populations all over the world, we find that a common ingredient of the GOD concept is *morality*, the good and the bad, the right and the wrong. He judges people's actions and has a system of rewards and punishments that will be meted out at some future time. In other words, God is a *moral* being.

A minimal intelligent designer, on the other hand, is not concerned with morality at all. The definition of an intelligent designer is simply a grand and universal *engineer*. He designs the universe and the laws of physics and steps out of the picture. The logical definition of an intelligent designer has no necessary ingredient of the God concept whatsoever. Now he *may* also be a God concerned with moral concepts. But this is not *necessary* to the concept of intelligent design.

Now the first question we should ask is, is intelligent design a *scientific* theory? Well that is a matter of opinion. On the one hand, when you're talking about physical matter and the laws of physics, this is certainly about science. On the other hand, intelligent design cannot be proven in any scientific way and does not point to any scientific experiments that could confirm or refute it. But of course, the same is true of the theory of human evolution as we explained in detail in Sect. 9.3. There are no scientific experiments that could conclusively confirm or refute the evolution of human beings either. There is only *supporting* evidence for the theory of human evolution. They find bones in the ground of primates that appear to be on a linear scale gradually leading to humans. It is highly likely that most primate bones found are *not* on our evolutionary line, but are evolutionary dead-ends: species of primates that became extinct along the way.

One of the reasons Einstein believed in God was that he could not believe the enormous complexity of the laws of physics could just pop into existence without something designing it all. Even though an intelligent designer doesn't have to be a God, the enormous complexity of the universe can be viewed as supporting scientific evidence of an intelligent designer. Of course, this is not conclusive evidence either. Whether this supporting evidence is more substantial than the bones in the ground evidence for human evolution is again a matter of opinion. Neither is *conclusive* evidence. From the point of view of real science, there is not a strong case for making any *conclusive* difference in scientific status between intelligent design and evolution theory. It is possible that God put bones in the ground to test our faith as some creationists say. And where do the anti-intelligent designers think the complexity of the universe comes from? They have no answer. They don't think it's important to know where complexity comes from, just as creationists don't think the bones in the ground are important.

The irony, however, when these very same liberals as paleontologists find complex tools or any other device in the ground, they immediately look for a *designer*, no less. This allows them to get in the faces of people who might dare to think there is something better about modern society over early headhunters. But the whole universe with infinitely more complexity doesn't seem to need a designer. Given a choice, the modern neoliberal will always take the road that maximizes the amount they can get in people's faces and destroy their cherished values. Anyway, the only thing the ID people wanted was put a small paragraph in biology books that the universe could have been created by an intelligent designer, a perfectly reasonable request. I would want my own kids to be aware of that possibility.

Well, the ACLU rounded up a bunch of in-your-face neoliberal scientists, rushed to the trial and got there before the rest. They proceeded to *assign* thoughts to the intelligent design people. By the time the latter got to the trial, it was too late for them to make any claims about their *thinking*. The ACL(screw)U had smoked out these detestable believers who were *assigned* thoughts that the intelligent designer is really God dressed up as an engineer. You can't fool the ACL(screw)U. As such they were trying to bring God into the classroom, which is unconstitutional.

It's a good thing I didn't go to the trial myself or my thoughts would have been assigned as well. And there's no way I could deny it, because once you get your thoughts assigned by the thought police of the ACL(screw)U, you're stuck with them for life. Now since I didn't go to the trial and I am proud to say the ACLU never got a penny out of me, I can tell you about my thoughts. I'm a perfect example of someone who *does* believe in an intelligent designer. My beliefs in intelligent design are totally separate from my beliefs about God. To show that they are separate beliefs, I believe quite strongly that there was intelligent design. However, my belief in God and whether it was a God who designed the universe is a great deal weaker. These are two separate and independent beliefs. In fact, you can believe in intelligent design and be a total atheist.

But it was too late for the ID people to make any such claim. Their thoughts had already been assigned. Not wanting to appear ignorant in the eyes of all these high-fallutin scientists, the judge ruled against the intelligent designers. Now, I don't have much against the judge. He's just another uneducated shyster who has no competence to rule on matters he has absolutely no understanding of. But that's the way our system works. And nowhere in the near future is anyone going to require lawyers to get any kind of real education, especially scientific education, in a modern world that is replete with science issues. Their curriculum is already filled, and filled with learning how to lie, cheat, and pervert the English language.

But I *do* blame the scientists who were part of this tawdry mess. They were a total disgrace. I think it's abhorrent that scientists were allowed to make an example in front of a whole nation of kids that science is not going to allow a perfectly reasonable and possible explanation of anything. This is exactly what the Church did in the middle ages. Back then, when scientists wanted people to learn of the *possibility* that we don't have souls or that the earth revolves around the sun, the church conducted a cook-out with them. Today's *scientists* are the Dark Ages authority. They don't want to admit a perfectly reasonable and possible scenario for the existence of the universe because their religion says that we have a closed universe and no unearthly entity has a role to play in it.

These court cases have emboldened the anti-religious community. There is now a group of them led by people like Richard Dawkins who have started their own brand of faith-based science. They are no longer satisfied that the theory of human evolution is a scientifically supported *theory*. They are striving to make the theory of human evolution a *fact* — "as incontrovertible fact as any in science", as Dawkins put it. This is pure unadulterated horseshit. There are no "*facts*" about human evolution. There is supporting evidence, of course, but it does not rise to the level of *conclusive* evidence giving us *facts*. I don't know how many people Dawkins thinks he's going to bulldoze, but he isn't going to con any objective observer who knows anything about science.

Most "facts" in science can be confirmed by on the spot experiments right before our eyes. We can look through telescopes and see light rays from Mercury bending in the sun's gravity field *today* and confirm Einstein's theory. We don't claim people saw this a thousand years ago, but we can't do it now like the miracles at Lourdes. What is an incontrovertible *fact* is that, as Bertrand Russell said, the world *could* have been created 5 minutes ago "complete with memories and records". If this is a possibility, then human evolution is not a "fact". The only *facts* about evolution are what can be shown in the short run. Viruses like AIDS evolve and breeders evolve animals. This says that the theory of human evolution as a *theory* has a great deal of *supporting* scientific evidence which is good enough for me and maybe you too, but not *fact* because the evidence is not *conclusive*.

There was some scientific evidence at times in the past that everything revolved around the earth. Heavenly objects were seen to move relative to the earth, the moon being the most important example. Of course, it wasn't very good evidence; certainly not conclusive evidence. But it was good enough for the Church to claim as "fact" the theory of an earth-centered universe and to persecute anyone who disagreed. This is what Dawkins and his faith-based "scientists" are doing now. They are taking some *supporting* evidence and turning it into "incontrovertible fact". At least the Church was using faith and religion, which have always been matters of emotion, faith and opinion. These scientists are using the concept of *scientific*, no less, to steam roll over the rest of society. It's a dam disgrace.

I very well believe that if these in-your-face neoliberals could get away with it, they would be persecuting non-believers in pretty much the same way as the Church did in the middle ages. They would be cast out of the schools and made into social outcasts. Their books would be banned from public libraries and classrooms. Of course, these neoliberals would emphatically deny this, but we all know what power does to the human mind. And we all saw what these in-your-face liberals did in the 1930s right after Stalin's Communism starved 35 million peasants to death. They hooked up with Communism in the same way.

29.16 Religious and Social Symbolism

An even more ripe possibility of getting in the face of ordinary folk and their cherished beliefs occurred in a very similar case. You remember in the old days, town squares might have had a nativity scene at Christmas. Have you noticed that it doesn't appear anymore? Well, you can thank the ACLU for that one too. Now I don't know how to find the exact court cases but it's the concepts that are important for this discussion.

Here again before anyone had a chance to make claims about their thinking regarding the Nativity scene, the ACLU, ever vigilant for ways to get in people's faces over matters that go to the heart of people's values and beliefs, had again smoked out these covert believers and assigned thoughts to people viewing the Nativity scene. And what was the assignment in this case? People who put up the Nativity scene and viewing it were thinking about God, you see. And there was no use denying it. And once assigned and approved by in-your-face liberal judges who have no understanding of the logic of these cases, these assignments are forever.

I remember when I was working in California as a young man, I worked with a guy who was interested in ideas concerning conceptual thinking. Even though he was a lefty, on one occasion he said that he liked the Nativity scene because he was tired of the media constantly bombarding us with depictions of wealth and power. In the vast majority of soap operas, dramas, etc., stories feature affluent characters in upscale clothes and upscale surroundings. He thought the Nativity scene was a refreshing depiction of a very poor and simple couple getting together with family and friends to celebrate the birth of a baby, a real sin in the eyes of the in-your-face neoliberal ACL(screw)U. What was interesting about his views, however, was that he was totally unreligious. He had no strong beliefs about God whatsoever. He just enjoyed a scene of ordinary people to remind us that there is more to life than wealth and power. And Christmas was a good time to think about other values and different meanings to life than the usual hustle and bustle of monkey-climbing power seekers. I personally feel the same way about the Nativity scene. I have very weak beliefs about God and I do not care whether the Nativity scene depicts God or not.

Now were my friend's thoughts about the Nativity scene allowable? Absolutely not. The ACLU had once again beat him to the punch. The thought police of the ACLU had *assigned* him thoughts that when he passes by a Nativity scene, he is thinking about God, by God. And they had a troupe of scientists to help smoke out these detestable believers. Once this assignment is made of course, there would be no way for him to squirm out of it. It was then easy pudding squelching the Nativity scene because it intruded God into the public sphere. Now if there was a sign above the cradle pointing to the baby saying, "this here is baby Jesus, son of God", well that would clearly be unconstitutional. But the nativity scene doesn't say anything. Viewers are *free*, and I stress the word '*free*', to put any interpretation they want into the scene. But the ACL(screw)U, has no interest in freedom. What they did, of course, was to stuff God into the Nativity scene and then proceed to snuff out the Nativity scene for having God in it.

In due time, of course, they'll go after the Christmas tree, which has the absolutely same logical status as a symbol of Christmas as the Nativity scene: to celebrate the birth of Christ. The verbal police of the ACLU have already attacked the mention of 'Christmas' in public. Their barnacles in the media are insisting that we should not say "Merry Christmas", because Christmas has the word Christ in it, who lots of people think was God. We're supposed to say "Happy Holiday". Well, which holiday? Christmas, of course, but you're not allowed to say it. Christmas simply has too much meaning in ordinary people's lives and the ultimate goal of the ACLU and the like-minded is to get into people's faces and snuff it out of the public domain and eventually out of our lives. And it's working. Every year there are less and less people who do anything to celebrate Christmas. No gift giving, no home decorations, no activity at all.

We can look forward into the future and see where this leads. Someday, you will be eating supper with your family and there will be a loud knock on the door. The ACLU will appear with a bevy of big brother, big government neoconservatives claiming that their newly installed thought monitors had determined that you were thinking about a terrorist attack. You are assigned these thoughts and there would be no use denying them. You will be hauled off to the police station for questioning.

What is really disgusting about these issues is that by constantly getting in people's faces — by constantly trying to remove any source of value and meaning in people's lives, people rebel in many instances and refuse to vote for liberal candidates in elections. So we wind up with a bunch of Economic Socialists. In the 2000 election, the race was pretty close. During the campaign I was wondering what the media mouthpieces of the system had in store in the way of dirty tricks to get Bush elected. Sure enough, for two weeks before the election, the media got right in people's faces showing gays playing grab-ass in the marriage line, cheered on by their neoliberal supporters. I saw this scenario every single night on the 6:30 news for two straight weeks. Sure enough, Bush almost won the election until Ayatollah Scalia and Ayatollah Alito on the Supreme Court invaded state matters, directly prohibited by the Constitution, to stuff neoconservative George Bush into office. (Eight years later when the Ayotollahs of Iran did the very same thing stuffing conservative Ahmadinejad into office, these same neoconservatives were outraged). By the way, the very next day after the election, we never again saw gays playing grab-ass in the marriage line.

Down came the props, the lines, and liberal banners and cheerleaders. All to be put away for another day when the system mind needs another dirty trick.

When it was a matter of a bunch of small folks wanting their kids to hear about another perfectly reasonable possibility as to the creation of the universe, here comes the big brave ACLU with their army of high-falutin' shysters and science intellectual prostitutes, coming down like the wolf on the fold like the Syrians in the Bible, to squash this simple request. Big brave ACLU. Bit when Bush started breaking laws, breaking treaties, and trampling over the most important pillars of our constitutional government, where was the ACLU for 8 years under Bush? I'll tell you where. They were huddled in the corner with their balls cut off looking helplessly on in holy terror at the neoconservative onslaught for big brother government, big wars, big torture, big invasion of our privacy. By constantly getting into people's faces over minor issues like in Arkansas, there wasn't enough liberal support in government including the judiciary to defend basic safeguards to keep the president from making himself into a king who proceeded to snuff out the lives of a hundred thousand people. That's what we get from neoliberalism.

29.17 CULTURAL DIVERSITY

We have mentioned some of the more important ways that the neoliberal has in his arsenal to stomp out any means for ordinary people to put meaning into their lives. Whether its religion, social institutions like marriage, values and morality, the neoliberal is going to get in our faces. A very stark illustration of this fact was a book review by Timothy Ash concerning the growing immigration problem in Europe. [26] A German guy named Thilo Sarrazin wrote a book showing concern over the fact that the immigrant Muslim population of Germany was growing at a great rate, much due to high fertility, whereas the indigenous Germans are not having enough babies to replace themselves; and that sometime this century, the indigenous German people would become a minority and eventually disappear altogether. Of course, the neoliberal Timothy Ash gives this book a scathing review calling it an "indigestible pot of goulash" poured forth by this "intemperate, illiberal, and inaccurate" miscreant. What is really going on here is that the German people have a long history of culture, religion, and especially economic progress that the German people can be proud of and use to put meaning into their lives. As we explained in Sect. 16.9, being human entails the ability to have the time concept which enables us to entertain propositional attitudes, the most important of which are beliefs. This is a great deal of what a culture amounts to: having religious and social beliefs about the world and the human being's place in it. Of course, being human also involves knowing about the past containing the evolution of the arts, sciences, literature, and economics making up the culture. And just as with any other population the German population has a long history of cultural evolution going back a few thousand years.

In my opinion, cultural diversity is not the top priority of these neoliberals at all. What they have in their sights is *anything* that enables average people to put meaning into their lives and getting in their faces to stomp it out. And the perfect way to do this is to overwhelm a culture with another very different and faster growing culture that simply outnumbers the first and establishes itself as the dominant culture, especially if it's snuffing out a white culture. And remember, we're not talking about some beleaguered little culture fighting for its very existence like, ironically the German culture. The Muslim world extends from the far west tip of Africa to the far eastern tip of Asia in a swath of land at very optimal latitudes and a population of one and a half *billion* people whose numbers are increasing faster than any European population. This culture is clearly not in any danger of extinction. However, the German culture *is* in such danger along with other cultures of Europe. Why isn't Ash concerned about them? The answer, of course, is that noeliberal Ash has no interest at all in cultural diversity. His motivation is to get in the faces of any culture that might excel in some way especially one that is white. It makes the conquest all the more sweet.

By the way, the European Christian culture came to the new world in increasing numbers, just like immigrants coming to Germany now, and proceeded to snuff out indigenous American Indian cultures. Does Ash approve of that? Probably not — after all, Europeans were white. In addition, the American Indians were too economically behind to make getting in their faces a jubilant conquest. So what is Ash's motivation. It can't be to reduce poverty-stricken people or victims of strife in failed states. Their populations are increasing. I don't see any other motivation except that he sees a long-lived culture that a population of people can use to put pride and meaning into their lives and he fully intends to snuff it out.

This is just another example of neoliberals getting into people's faces. This enormous push comes from too much brain energy going into the frontal cortex. When I as a kid, liberalism meant supporting the rights of labor, basic freedoms and economic justice. *Neo*liberalism supports immigration that not only destroys the value of labor, but enables them to get in the faces of average taxpayers to pay for "benefits"; and again getting in the faces or ordinary people by looking into every nook and cranny of society for meaning like traditional marriage or religion that he can snuff out. They have offended so many people along the way, real liberalism is dead in the political arena. This has allowed neoconservatives to totally dominate politics in the US for 35 years bringing us closer and closer to National Socialism and all that goes with it. We have lost the 8-hour day, a right to privacy, representative taxation, and a constitutionally bound president. What we have gained is a large illegal immigrant population to provide a basic slave labor force enabling the top 20% to make bigger profits and to ripen the possibility of crushing the dreaded Capitalist system and traditional American culture.

To top it all off, these same neoliberals get themselves stuffed into university chairs and proceed to write great learned books about how we've become too materialistic, too culturally barren, too conservative — there is no social glue, no care for others, no morality, no meaning in people's lives. They are all for humanitarianism as long as it's very abstract and academic. But when it comes time to destroy these very means for people to put some humanity and meaning into their lives, there is the neoliberal, including all those meaning-obsessed professors, ready and waiting to get into people's faces to stomp it out and to snuff out western civilization in the process.

At least liberals from the past built upon their germ of existential justice using inner brain motivation to attack the goliaths of the day. Building on what might have been a small existential desire for justice, Roosevelt's and LBJ's inner brain energy was at least directed towards getting in the faces of the biggies, which was conservatism in Roosevelt's time and the southern political machine in LBJ's time. Today's neoliberal goes after little people in Arkansas.

If we had to assign blame for the country going down the tubes, you would have to put most of the blame on these neoliberals. As we shall next explain, neoconservatives are hard-wired reptiles. All their brain energy is in the bottom of their brains, which means their response to anything is hard-wired, deterministic, and mechanical just like the robot in the Terminator movie. They can't help themselves even if they wanted to. But the professional neoliberal does get a little brain energy up from the bottom of the brain. But instead of using it to see reality, to solve problems in an intelligent way, it all goes to the frontal cortex where it is used to get in people's faces — to assert, to aggress, to offend, to push people around and to stomp out the slightest morsel of meaning in their lives and finally to crush western civilization.

[1] Gray, John; "The Rreturn of an Illusion". Book reviews in *The New Republic*; July 14, '11

[2] Posner, Richard; '08. *A Failure of Capitalism: The Crisis of '08 and the Descent into Depression*, Harvard Univ. Pr.

[3] Stiglitz, Joseph, *Freefall America*, Norton Press

[4] Wilentz, Sean, "The Mirage". *The New Republic*, Nov. 17, '11, p. 31

[5] Madrick, J; Partnow, F. "Did Fannie Cause the Disaster". *The New York Review of Books*, Oct. 27, '12, p. 48

[6] "Declining by Degree". *The Economist*, Sept. 4, '10. p. 74

[7] "Not what it Used to Be". *The Economist*, Dec. 1, ;12, p. 30

[8] "A Better Third Way", *The Nation*, Mar. 5, '01

[9] Anya Kamenetz, "The Virtual University". *The American Prospect*, May, '10, p. 22

[10] Altman & Kingston, "Social Security and the Deficit". *The American Prospect*, Nov. '10, p. A22

[11] Hayes, Christopher, "Deficits of Mass Destruction". *The Nation*, Aug. 29, '10.

[12] "Change you can Believe In". *The American Prospect*, May '10, p. 37

[13] "Deficit Attention Disorder". *The American Prospect*, Nov. '10, p. A8

[14] Mitchell, William, "Beyond Austerity". *The Nation*, Apr. 4, '11, p. 14

[15] Galbraith, Peter; "In Defense of Deficits". *The Nation*, Mar. 22, '10, p. 23

[16] Ibid. p. 23

[17] Cooper, Mark, "The Heartlands Raw Deal". *The Nation*, Feb. 3. '97   Also, Franklin, Stephen, "The Hands that Feed Us". *The American Prospect*, Oct. '10. p. A14

[18] Sarah Abramsky, "Today's Other American. *The American Prospect*, May, '10, p. 49

[19]   Pocket World in Figures *2016* edition, p. 180 and The World in 2016, p. 123.   *The Economist publications*

[20]   Sanders, Jerry, "Two Mexicos and Fox's Quandry". *The Nation*, Feb. 26, '01

[21]   Pollitt, Katha, "Europeans Do It Better". *The Nation*, Apr. 2, '07, p. 10

[22]   Ross, Andrew, "Greenwashing Nativism". *The Nation*, Aug. 16, '10, p. 18

[23]   Heins, Marjorie, "Sex, Lies, and Politics". *The Nation*, May 7, '01

[24]   *American Prospect*, Mar. '10.

[25]   Friedman, Ann; "Don't Call it a Culture War". *The American Prospect*, Dec. '08, p. 11

[26]   Ash, Tomothy Garton; "Germans, More or Less". *The New York Review of Books*, Feb. 24, '11

CHAPTER 30

Ideology - Neoconservatism

———

WHAT DOES AN IDEOLOGICAL NEOCONSERVATIVE want to conserve? Absolutely nothing. And the reason is that to achieve identity, he is addicted to power, mostly the power to destroy. The neoconservative gets no joy from building because building does not involve enough power. Now people who create wealth like entrepreneurs and businesspeople are often conservative in many of their views. But very interestingly, they often have many liberal views as well. But ideological neoconservatives are addicted to power and never create anything.

In the last chapter, we saw the effects of too much energy going to the frontal cortex of the brain. It produces a strong urge for aggression, assertion and getting into the faces of ordinary people who are trying to put little meaning in their lives. But now we want to look at what happens when *not enough* brain energy gets to the frontal cortex. Insufficient energy in this area of the brain probably causes difficulty in forming an identity and a sense of self. Damage to the frontal cortex has been shown to disrupt mental activity that involves the self. There is curtailed ability to plan. People with such damage "are bereft of a theory of their own mind and the mind of those with whom they interact" (Damasio, '84, 58+).

The neoconservative all through his life tries to pump energy out of the bottom of their brains into the frontal cortex to try to form some semblance of an identity. They do this by a constant search for agglomerations of *power* to identify with, which creates a bit of limbic system energy. Some if this energy gets up to the frontal cortex and a semblance of identity is formed. Thus the neoconservative will always be attracted to and idolize anything big and powerful. They like big power, big brother government, big corporations, big farms, big business, big wars, big bombs, big killing, big, big, big. And he goes apoplectic if there is any threat to the sources of power he identifies with.

They want their leader to be all-powerful a king just like in the Middle Ages with no impediments to the exercise of power. No matter how much the king may fail and bring disaster to the country, the identification continues. The slightest impediments to the king's exercise of raw, naked power is met with intense hatred and a burning desire to snuff it out.

Insufficient energy to the frontal cortex also accounts for the lack of a theory of mind in the neoconservative. He cannot imagine the plight of the less fortunate. With all energy in the bottom of his brain, the only emotions that get fed are the primitive ones of greed, selfishness and intolerance. The neoconservative wants a simple world his inner brain can comprehend; understanding others is too complex to be handled by the bottom of his brain. This is why the neoconservative is extremely intolerant of the interests, practices and values of others.

In the field of economics and public policy, a certain body of doctrine has evolved over the years. With a constant need for identification, this body of doctrine gets hard-wired into the neoconservative's brain and nothing will change it. In Ch. 17, we discussed in length the concept of *free will*. We don't have as much of it as we think, but the neoconservative has none of it. He is like a boa constrictor who is really an organic machine. In the 1920s, after 12 years of Republicans running us into the greatest depression in the history of the country, there was not one tiny bit of doctrine that changed. There is no contingency, no disaster, no failure, no calamity they bring about that would change one strand of hard-wiring in these reptiles. There is no creativity, no ability to plan and no adapting to the current problems. The reason is that their followers don't care about the meaning of the doctrine, they don't care what it is, and they don't care about its effectiveness. Once it coalesces into a lump standing for raw, naked power, that's the end of the game. They fall in line like an army of robots worshipping the current king and his coterie of acolytes.

In 2011, with corporations and businesses flush with money and still very little hiring, what was the remedy of the Republican candidates? Cut their taxes and "deregulate". This was after the 1920s spree of "deregulation" where all new income and wealth went to the top 20% and led to the greatest Depression in our history; and after Reagan's tax cuts to the rich and corporations which resulted in nothing more than massive deficits. Bush did the same thing with more Economic Socialism's economic players making their own rules, which required even larger deficits, finally leading to another meltdown. Within one year, neoconservatives were right back with the same policies that led to the meltdown and with the same policies of Hoover, Reagan and Bush that created slow growth and finally a massive meltdown. The labels may change but never the doctrine.

Many historians have theorized that whereas conservatism is past oriented, liberalism is future oriented. The reason is that the past is fixed, solid and immutable. This is the rock of Gibraltar that the essentialist neoconservative mentality needs to latch onto as a source of strength and identity. Hitler's Nazis were mesmerized by a mythical past of ancient Germanic heroes, Teutonic warriors and ethnic symbols. A favorite Hitler portrait had him in full medieval armor.

The future is fluid and provides an opportunity for the liberal mentality to imagine, invent, and experiment, all of which provides an outlet for the brain energy that is pulled out of the bottom of the liberal brain. This is why liberals are more existential and more creative than conservatives. What is interesting about this dichotomy is that the intersection of the past and the future is the present, which is the end of the past and the beginning of the future. And when we come to extreme conservatism like Nazism and extreme liberalism like Communism, they have one thing in common: they destroy the present, but for different reasons. The ultraconservative destroys the present so as to wall off the pure immutable past and isolate it from the future which is then destroyed by destroying its beginnings in the present. He is then free to replace the annihilated future with a future that really consists of the past. What he is really after is constancy, groundedness and immutability that can only be found in the past. The ultraliberal destroys the present in order to wall it off from the past which can then be isolated, ignored or destroyed thus bringing about the possibility of a new future of the worker's paradise, millennialism, and the promised land.

There is no better example of conservative tendencies than the droppings of a major hero of the far right, Ayn Rand. As mentioned, I read Ayn Rand when I was only a kid and didn't know all the intricacies of liberalism and conservatism, nor their histories and detailed ideology. I just read what was on the page without an adult's amount of meaning to project to the words. But I did know that Rand was a big hero of conservatives, and had "inspired" thousands to her viewpoint. So I looked into it, as a fairly unbiased open-minded kid just to see what was the source of this thing called conservatism. Well, it was a major milestone in my life. What I read in Ayn Rand was the most pathetic, simple-minded, pecker-idolizing infantilism I have ever read. At least Karl Marx had a small brain — this pathetic woman didn't have that. Ayn Rand provided the model for all neoconservative women coming afterwards right down to the present day: show them the big cahuna and they immediately fall to their knees and idolize. Admiring, emulating or studying is one thing — but unquestioning idolatry is quite another. There has to be something fundamentally wrong in the brain of anyone who gets "inspired" by Ayn Rand.

Let's look at the ways the neoconservative identifies with raw naked power.

30.1 Seeing Reality and Belief Idolizing

Since 'Capitalism' is a good word and it was the system the country started out with under our Constitution, they slap 'Capitalism' onto their favorite Economic Socialism. *Despite what these neoconservatives say, in actual practice, there is absolutely nothing they like about* real *Adam Smith Capitalism* — not its freedoms, not it's prosperous middle class, not its sustainability, not its lack of need for continuous war, not dispersion of powers, not its competition among businesses, not its independent rules, not its balance in the distribution of income — *nothing*.

The reason the neoconservative's words trump reality is that with all the energy in the bottom of his brain, reality is simply a wispy indistinct cloud in the distance. As we pointed out, the existential parts of the neoconservative brain are starved of energy. This is where meaning lies and with insufficient energy in these parts of the brain, the neoconservative does not see reality. George Orwell famously said, "to see what is in front of one's nose needs a constant struggle"; to the neoconservative, it's more than a struggle — it's impossible. But this enables him to rewrite history and to eschew principles. That's why when he says something untrue, there is no reality before his mind to compare with what he's saying. This includes the reality that his own political bedfellows are creating. They have no interest in facts or logic. It's all about identifying with raw, naked power.

There is no better way to see this than to check out readers and listeners to neoconservative propaganda outlets. What you find is absolutely no interest in reality. Their readers and listeners are there to identify with people who point to nodes of power: big brother government, big corporations, big wars, big killings, big, big, big big; and a big king on top of the pile.

I had a chance to test this out in 2009. I decided to hold my nose and listen to sewer radio for a while to see the reaction to Obama's winning the presidency. As I listened for a few hours every day, I began to see that there were no calls to disagree with anything, no calls with new facts, nor alternative theories, no calls with any kind of criticism. What I heard was a long string of *idolizers* — not a single listener ever called. They call and to a person, give a eulogy to the host. "Oh Lance, my life was nothing until I discovered you on the radio." "Oh Lance, you've completely changed my life. Now I see everything." "Listen Lance, get dem dam liberals." "Lance, I'm 100% behind you. You're saving this country." And it goes on and on, idolizer after idolizer. The brown-nosing is enough to turn the stomach of a billy-goat. Finally, after about 3 months, a listener who was probably a black guy called and tried to defend Obama. He was charged at like an angry bull. This was the enemy and you simply squelch the enemy.

Neoconservatives were *guaranteeing* that Saddam had weapons of mass destruction. They were betting their lives on it. As late as 2012, fully 63% of Republican respondents to a survey believed "that Iraq had weapons of mass destruction…".[1] This is really scary. How will democracy ever survive with this kind of self-delusion? Of course, it was pretty obvious he had no such thing. The UN inspectors had been in the country for over a year and had found nothing. CIA spy planes can detect a mouse on the ground and they found nothing. Nuclear installations require huge buildings, numbers of huge centrifuges and other massive equipment. The CIA knows exactly who is building what, which is what enabled Israel to knock out Syria's attempts at nuclear development. So it was puzzling as to why these war-lovers would risk embarrassing themselves by being so wrong. But it was an interesting lesson in hero-worship. When it turned out that the closest thing Saddam had to a nuclear weapon was a used bathtub, were the neoconservatives who had bet their lives and reputations on it, embarrassed? Did they lose support? They did not lose one single idolizer? None. This shows that facts are irrelevant, promises are irrelevant, predictions are irrelevant, and principles are irrelevant. It's all about identifying with big power. The king was invading, conquering, and killing people with a massive projection of power, and that is all these idolizers need for identification and some semblance of a sex life.

Another issue that appears to be a set-up for embarrassment and being blatantly wrong is global warming. Now they have been aided somewhat in this regard by climate change proponents. We have used the term 'global warming' ourselves. In truth, there may not be "global" warming. Climate change skeptics have *averaged* temperature readings from all over this world. But the danger from climate change does not come from temperature changes over most of the earth's surface. The danger comes from temperature increases *at the poles.* That's where the ice is melting which will eventually raise ocean levels and flood huge areas of not only urban centers but prime agricultural land as well. There's no ice to melt over most of the earth's surface. The only *relevant* temperatures are those at the poles and they have been rising alarmingly. Talk of global warming only weakens arguments to do something about the real culprit, which is *polar* warming.

This is why neoconservatives have assured us there's nothing to worry about. It's all a conspiracy by the "liberal" media to scare us into interfering with what their heroes in the corporate world want to do. But do these guys have to worry about the truth? Absolutely not. In 2013, they were telling us that polar ice was actually *growing*. This didn't sound right, so I checked Google and found that photos of the North Pole in 1979 and then in 2003 showing a shrinking ice cap. You have to ask yourself, aren't they worried about being wrong? Not at all. These neoconservatives know from past experience that they will not lose one single idolizer no matter the facts and no matter how much of a fool they make of themselves. When half of Florida is under water, they will blame it on God or the "liberal" media. The explanation is that facts and truth have absolutely no part to play in the views of the neoconservative idolizer. It's about identity. The king and his men say there's no melting ice, and that's the end of discussion. They are identifying with the *power* of the king's men — the power to invade, to conquer, and to kill. These idolizers have a big hole in their brains where an identity and sense of self is supposed to be. Identifying with power of any kind is a way to fill the void with brain energy that can create some semblance of an identity.

30.2 NEOCONSERVATIVE LACK OF PRINCIPLES

We have said that one of the ramifications of the neoconservative's need to identify with bigness and power is that they don't see reality that might interfere with such identification and no sense of self-awareness that they are doing so. This also results in the most important characteristic of the neoconservative mind: he has *no* principles — none. Zero, zip, zilch, nada, nunca, nyet.

Having principles interferes with identifying with bigness and power. And so principles are always sacrificed in the neoconservative reptilian brain. Also, so little energy gets to the existential parts of their brains that there is not enough *meaning* attached to what they say to enable a comparison with reality, as we discussed in the last section. That's why their propagandists talk about principles — *core* principles, no less, and they can raffle off what they are. In the meantime, their elected politicians to a man and woman exhibit actual behavior that blatantly violates every one of their imaginary principles. A perfect example was George Bush who violated every core principle conservatives are supposed to have.

In terms of the economy and their practices, neoconservatives have a simple formula for giving credit and ascribing blame that keeps their failed doctrines intact. It really is very funny, but also in another sense alarming because it shows the results of energy not getting out of the bottom of the brain. Here's the formula. When a conservative administration is in power and something good happens, credit is immediately given to the administration.

If something bad happens, blame is assigned to the *last* liberal president. If a liberal administration is in power and something good happens, credit is immediately given to the *last* conservative administration, no matter how far back you have to go. However, if something bad happens, of course, you blame it on the current administration.

There has never an exception to this rule in all the post-WWII history of neoconservatism. Reagan was given credit for bringing down communism, but in his first year when the economy shrunk, unemployment shot up and the deficit tripled, blame, of course was put on Carter. In his second year, when unemployment shot up again, it was still Carter's fault. But after *one* year of Obama and unemployment increased, sewer radio put the full blame not on Bush but Obama. Neoconservatives waxed eloquently about the success of Bush's economics. But when the whole thing collapsed and was found to be based on fraud and theft, blame was immediately pinned on Bill Clinton. When the Economic Socialism inaugurated by Ronald Reagan resulted in companies like Enron in bed with Washington politicos able to write their own rules of the game, this, of course, was blamed on Clinton. And guess why. The Wall Street Journal blamed Enron on Bill Clinton's envious sex-life.[2] Of course, to a neoconservative capon, Bill Clinton's very normal sex-life *was* criminal. Credit for no major terrorist attack was awarded to George Bush and his torture program, unless there was one, in which case Obama is right in line for the blame. This is why, in our good government formula in Sect. 24.3, we held each president responsible for events on his watch regardless of party the president was from.

Listen to this. A supply-side neoconservative named Lawrence Kudlow said about Clinton: "There's no question that President Clinton's across the board tax increases on labor, capital and energy will throw a wet blanket over the recovery and depress the economy's long-term potential growth".[3] Hear that? *"No question"*. Actually, there was no tax increase on labor, only on capital, corporations and the wealthy. Of course, as happened every time these neoconservatives make a prediction, they turn out to be dead wrong. The economy expanded and Clinton actually wound up with surpluses for the first time in 40 years. And whom did Kudlow give credit to? You guessed it: Reaganomics — *12 years earlier.* Then on Feb. 8, '14, this same guy tells us of the three "recessions" in the 1950s. In the *worst* of these so-called "recessions", unemployment hit 6.2% in 1958. This is compared to the Reagan "boom", where unemployment never got *below* 6.6% during his first 6 years, and averaged 7.4% over 8 years. Now I'm not saying you should be a liberal, especially those of you who grew up as Republicans. Liberals are pretty bad too. But how anyone with *one ounce of integrity* can identify with this kind of propaganda is the 8th wonder of the world.

Now some of these credits and blames may be true. But truth is not driving the conclusions. It's an inner brain formula that is applied regardless of how ridiculous. With no energy in the existential brain and not seeing reality, neoconservative beliefs are determined by the inner brain driving the primitive emotions towards identifying with raw naked power. This is why neoconservatives never have to worry about lying, dissembling, being dead wrong or intellectual dishonesty. Their idolizers will stay glued no matter what the facts.

30.3 THE NEW KING

The need in the neoconservative to identify with bigness and power means that he will support any all-mighty leader that he can identify with. You could see an incisive example of this in the national conventions for presidential elections in the old days. When the Democrats got together for their convention, there was mass confusion. Everyone was running around trying to be a chief. There were more candidates than supporters of candidates. There were more ideas than supporters of ideas and more factions than members of factions. Sometimes it would take days of infighting, each candidate trying to destroy his competitors, all to the advantage of the Republicans. Finally, a party leader would emerge, bruised and battered and in no condition to compete with the Republican candidate.

Conservatives had an entirely different looking convention. All delegates would arrive at the Republican convention in a zombie-like trance — looking, searching, grasping, seeking, wondering. What they were looking for, of course, was der fuehrer and were lost without one. But once a fuehrer was found, there would be roars of approval, fits of ecstasy and a chiliastic display of jubilation. There was no disagreement with der fuehrer's ideas, his policies, nor his agenda. When the excitement finally died down, everyone went home and prepared to get behind der new fuehrer. It was total and complete identification. And nothing he promoted would lose one single idolizer, because it is only through der fuehrer that the neoconservative gains identity and sense of self.

But even those old-line conservatives were nothing compared to today's neoconservative. Historically, Roosevelt assumed many powers to the presidency during WWII not really mandated by the constitution. Nobody complained because WWII was really a fight for the survival of the free world. However, right after Pearl Harbor, congress did meet that afternoon and declared war on Japan. But then Harry Truman continued these powers and unilaterally without congressional permission committed an act of war by invading Korea. So the Democrats are no angels in this regard. And where were the Supreme Bloodsuckers? However, during this period, conservatives were outraged at the usurpation of powers by the president. The leading conservative at the time, Senator Robert Taft, said in 1951 that Truman had "simply usurped authority in violation of the laws and the Constitution when he sent troops to Korea".[4]

Liberal Democrats continued to support extraordinary presidential powers in the Korean war, Kennedy's Bay of Pigs in Cuba and the Tonkin Gulf resolution that Johnson used to crank up the war in Vietnam. Arthur Schlesinger excused Truman saying presidents "have repeatedly committed American armed forces abroad without prior congressional consultation".[5] Henry Steel Commager agreed. Every Democrat in the House voted for the Tonkin gulf resolution which was based on complete lies. As we have seen, liberals are not very smart. They can't imagine the shoe on the other foot. But with the disaster in Vietnam, leading liberals began to question presidential war-making powers, denouncing the "imperial presidency". Commager complained about the abuse of presidential powers, and Schlesinger became the leading critic of the "imperial presidency".

After Taft's death in '53, William Buckley took over the conservative mantra of the anti-presidential viewpoint. His conservative colleague, James Burnham howled to the moon about a "Caesarist" president that "looms like a colossus" over congress.[6] William Rusher, publisher of the conservative *National Review*, opined that "a presidency whose steadily growing power has for forty years been the most serious danger facing the American society". Tough stuff. This is when there were real conservatives who took the Constitution seriously. It's really an eye-opener to read the strong conservative opposition to an all-powerful president back then when we compare them with these no-identity neoconservatives now.

But don't be fooled by a temporary display of principle. When the Vietnam war turned sour and conservatives wanted to make more and bigger war, their "principle" shifted in line with their war aims, which is like no principle at all. Barry Goldwater turned on a dime from being against presidential powers in the '60s to saying that he would "put more faith in the judgment of the office of the president in the matter of war-making than I would of Congress". These ideologues are the worst intellectual prostitutes you'll find on the planet and really a disgusting lot. There is not a speck of principle in them. They are infant dinosaurs having only an inner brain. They know what they want at the moment, and if they can't get it, they respond by filling their diapers and running off to invade, conquer and kill.

The explanation for the changes that occurred to replace the old conservative who might have an ounce of principle, was a change in psychology from *principle* to *identity*. Recall in Sect. 20.5, we discussed the loss of identity especially in males in modern life. Because males do not have the most important source of identity that of creating more life, societies from the beginning of history, has had to invent ways to provide males with identity. In my opinion, this is the whole explanation for culture itself: to keep a bunch of wandering hunters focused on protecting the integrity of families. But after WWII and the rise of mass media, cultural means for males to achieve identity began to wash away. It was in the interests of the system mind for the only source of identity in males to be the almighty job. One by one, we have seen traditional means for male identity disappearing. Family name, birthplace, religion, village, friendships, parenting, marriage, special skills and talents — all this has been washed away, leaving only one source of identity, especially in males.

By the time Bush came into office, the process of converting a president into a king was well along the way. And this trend fell right into the laps of the new neoconservative who proceeded to discard en toto every major principle that conservatism had championed for hundreds of years. Neoconservatives do not rely on principles, but rely instead on having a presidential monarch who projects raw naked power all over the world, while his castrated followers slavishly follow every aggressive thrust without question. Bush knew he had a Supreme Court that uses the Constitution for toilet paper and would "interpret" the Constitution in direct opposition to the letter *and the spirit* of the Constitution. Where the Constitution clearly specifies that Congress shall declare wars and to "make rules concerning Captures on Land and Water", the people around Bush and the Supreme Court "interpreted" this as saying that the *president* has the power to declare wars. Even Abe

Lincoln, a Republican no less, wouldn't have gone this far. When Lincoln's law partner thought the president should be able to invade other countries, "...Lincoln sent a devastating reply. Herndon, Lincoln said, would allow a president 'to make war at pleasure'. The Constitution, he went on, gave the 'war-making power' to Congress precisely to prevent Presidents from starting wars while 'pretending...that the good of the people was the object.' " [7] You'll never hear a neoconservative quote Lincoln in this regard, a Republican. And Lincoln was facing the very life of the country, not some faraway adventure for the inner brain purpose of killing. Of course, the founding fathers, Lincoln, the Constitution and history itself means nothing to the neoconservative reptilian power seeker. Without a king who can invade, conquer and kill, neoconservatives have nothing to identity with and no sex life. Of course, in all these years of many kinds of wars, neoconservative Supreme Shysters *never once* stepped up to prevent the complete usurpation of war powers from congress to the king.

Nightmares of neoconservatives often consists of falling down, losing the grip, being swept away by a flood, lost in the jungle, searching for familiarity. It is all due to lack of brain energy in the frontal cortex. This is why neoconservatives will take any means, adopt any theory and believe any ideas that enable identification with something big and powerful. And the most intense projections of power and aggression are in wars, which can only be brought off by big government. The next level of nodes of power to identify with is big corporations, and next down is big agriculture. The last level to identify with is the local police.

As we explained above, the neoconservative has no free will just like a boa constrictor. He will gobble up anything within a certain size in a totally mechanical, deterministic way. Without free will, his response to anything small is to attack and snuff out. Also, smallness reminds them of their flimsy identities and their ever-shrinking sex lives. And the smaller the entity, the greater the hatred and aggression. In the early 2000s, people in the Bush administration saw small countries like Iraq and Afghanistan the same way a boa constrictor sees a rabbit: something to attack and swallow. There was no more thought to their invasions than a boa constrictor gives to the rabbit he is going to swallow.

Among people, the ones they hate the most are the poor because they're small. But there's a group of even smaller people they hate: children. In the 2012 debates about balancing budgets, the first aim among neoconservatives was to attack the interests of children who can't defend themselves. All over the country, neoconservative state governments have slashed spending on nutrition programs for kids, they cut teachers and other aids to education, they cut health services to children, they cut environmental safety for the genetic health of kids.[8] They're laying off teachers and packing more and more kids into uncontrollable classrooms.

When it comes to standing up to the *big* crooks on Wall Street whose financial fraud led to the meltdown taking billions of profits to do so, the neoconservative is grabbing his withered genitalia and hiding under the bed scared shitless. But when it comes to stealing from children who are small and can't even defend themselves with the vote, out pops the neoconservative from under the bed, chest forward, eyes bulging, mouth bellowing, swords drawn, guns loaded and spears cocked to attack kids. First they engineer a financial meltdown. The resulting unemployment greatly affects not only the physical well-being of children but their psychology as well. Then, kids coming out of college can't even get a job to pay for their extorted tuitions. Because so many trillions have to be stolen to prop the crooked system back up, children are the easiest target. Right now, a kid reaching 18 owes the government half a *house* (about 150 thousand) in taxes he will have to pay over his working life for interest on the national debt — a classic case of taxation without representation. To top it all off, they dump enormous increases in birth defects on children coming up so that their big business idols can make more money ignoring the environment.

What is very alarming about this is that in developing countries where even jobs are not secure amidst high unemployment, what is left is religious affiliation for identity. This is why we're seeing a steady increase in sectarian violence in developing nations. And it will continue throughout this century. We see this in stark relief in Muslim countries that Bush invaded and conquered. But it's going on all over the world — Buddhists vs. Muslims in Myanmar, Hindus vs. Muslims in India, Shias vs. Sunnis in the Muslim world, among many other examples. In every case, the modern male all over the world is a sitting duck for a need to *identify* with something big and powerful like a powerful group or strong-man religious leader who can threaten, invade, conquer, and kill.

30.4 War

As we discussed in Sect. 25.3, since the system mind is mostly controlled by the larger neoconservative nodes of the economy, their attitude towards wars is reflected in US foreign policy. And one of the most consistent things about neoconservatives is that they love wars of conquest. A neoconservative never sees a war he doesn't like. They love any kind of war; big wars and little wars; wars you can win and wars you're sure to lose; legal wars and illegal wars. No matter what kind of war it is, they are fervently for it. The reason is that war involves power — power to conquer and power to kill. Wars are big: big bombs, big armies, big brother government, big killings, big torture, big destruction. It's *bigness* and *power* of it all that attracts the neoconservative like flies attracted to a pile of crap.

Big wars are massive aggressions that induce the production of energy in the limbic system at the bottom of the brain. A pinch of energy is then able to get pumped to the frontal cortex to create an identity. This is why der fuhrer can achieve great power by enabling his subjects to identify with wars. In the words of a leading American historian, "Behind... all the lofty rhetoric about civilization and progress was a primal emotion — a yearning to assert control, a masculine will to power...".[9] This guy doesn't know what masculinity is. Real masculinity is *protective*, not to *look* masculine by controlling, killing and conquering.

Neoconservatives aren't even interested in whether they are winning or losing a war. That's why they don't care how many of either side are dying. Of course, they would rather that more of the other guys are dying. But that's not the top priority. The top priority is bigness, power and destruction. The new neoconservative would rather be in a big war he's losing than a small war he's winning. It's the use of massive amounts of raw, naked power that's the turn-on.

But there is a little neoconservatism in all of us, and it comes out in certain times. During WWII, two German armies had been defeated and surrendered to the Russians by early 1943 in the battle of Stalingrad. Another large German army was bogged down in Leningrad. This was obviously the beginning of the end. Historians like Tom Segev wonder how and why such a large percentage of German people still supported Hitler for the next several years, even after it was apparent to anyone with half a brain that the war was effectively over.[10] As we expressed in Law V, in Sect. 27.1, after millions of years of evolution, the human animal is wired to be attracted to the fiercest leader who could best protect the group from predators and human enemies. This is true even in the middle of defeat.

What is even more interesting was the complete about-face after the war. The very next day after Hitler's death, word got around and immediately energy began to flow upwards in the brains of the German people. They began to see reality and even active Nazis shed their uniforms and went back home to peaceful idyllic lives. If you go to Germany now, everyone is very nice, polite, (a little stiff though), friendly and very liberal politically. How is that, since they have the same genes that were in the Nazis and their supporters. It's where the energy in the brain is being expended. The aftermath of the war turned the German people into a very existential lot. And seeing reality and getting energy into the top of their brains explains why they have been so inventive, productive and successful in a very competitive world economy.

The same thing occurred during the Vietnam war. People are attracted to the guy who can conquer and kill. At an instinctive level, Johnson understood this and why he knew that a big war displaying lots of power could give him the political muscle he needed to pass his liberal political agenda. It's a pretty sad commentary on the human animal. But his display of conquest and killing so captured the minds of most Americans that they were unable to see that the war in Vietnam was a proxy war with China as we have described. The Chinese army was bigger than our entire population. With their population, we would run out of young men long before they ran out of circus performers. Did this matter to neoconservatives? Not at all. They went apoplectic when we left Vietnam — the opposition was accused of giving up, traitorism and a stab in the back. Without a big war to identify with, where would their sex lives go? They care very little about who is dying. They are attracted to the *power* of it all — something really big they can identify with.

This is also why neoconservatives vote for ever-increasing amounts of military power. No superiority can ever be enough to make them satisfied that they are safe, because throughout all evolutionary history, mammals could never be sure of their safety. So there is a constant drive for more control, more military power, and more scripting of the larger world. During the cold war, conservatives in power in Washington voted to spend billions on a bigger and bigger pile of nuclear peckers which reached about 30,000. The Russians have about 6,000. With obsolescence, we have 7,200 left which is still enough to kill every single human being on the face of the earth 12 times over. But that is still not enough. These inner brain reptiles want it to be 20 times over, then 40 times over. And if they are threatened with policies that might level off or retire some of these killer peckers, they squeal to high heaven that we are "disarming". What they really feel is castration. As a result, we live in a world where there are more and more nuclear weapons. But keep this in mind: hydrogen bombs create enormous amounts of atmospheric radioactivity. If you set off only a few hundred hydrogen bombs, most life on the planet would come to an end. And not a nice quick end. It would be a slow, painful death due to biological damage like cancer, radiation burning, etc.

In the future, we will see a world where country after country have gangs of neoconservatives who also want nuclear weapons, especially young men looking to identity with power. Iran and North Korea are only the beginning. And anti-Iran propaganda based on blatant hypocrisy and racism only increases their motivation to get a nuclear weapon. In an April, '09 article, *The Economist* referred to "…*rogue* regimes such as North Korea and Iran" (Italics mine). Now this magazine comes from Great Britain. Recently I learned that in the past, the British had invaded and conquered more than *150* countries in every corner of the world. They have murdered thousands of innocent peoples all over the world. British gunboats used to cruise up and down Chinese rivers in the old days, machine-gunning down anything alive on the banks. They killed men, women, children, even dogs with the same abandon as you would chop down trees. There was the massacre of thousands of MauMau tribesmen in Kenya as recently as the 1950s.[11] The British in India went into a neighborhood of Delhi and murdered 1,400 unarmed citizens.[12]

You might say that this was the old days. But as recently as the early 2000s, there were the British joining Bush, invading, conquering and killing in a sovereign state of Iraq for the sole purpose of killing people, setting up a puppet government and stealing their oil. The British have been playing this game for hundreds of years. *Iran*, on the other hand, in spite of its rhetoric, hasn't invaded another country in over one *thousand* years. And yet, to these Brits, Iran is the "rogue" country. This is a prime example of a total lack of self-awareness of these inner brain reptiles. *The Economist* did publish a letter from a Tom O'brien who needled them about their use of the word 'meddling'.[13] But O'brien is wrong. England never "*meddled*" in other countries at all. What they did was invade, conquer, and *kill*, (not meddle) hundreds of thousands of "natives", bringing them to civilization.

Of course, this blatant hypocrisy and racism is only going to spur on nuclear ambitions all over the third world. Not only that, but it's another source of terrorist recruitment. What the west has done is to crank up a big pecker contest between the young men of all countries looking for power to identify with. If Iran gets them, Turkey might want to join in as well. Saudi Arabia and Egypt might follow. Every few months, *The Economist* had an article about how evil Iran is. Never once is it even hinted that maybe the best way to stop Iran and anyone else with nuclear ambitions is to at least *pretend* to reduce the stockpile in the west.

This leads to the question as to why big countries even have nuclear weapons. Numerous reports have indicated many close calls where a near accident at a nuclear site could have been cataclysmic. But most importantly, the reality is that no nation, could ever actually *use* these weapons. *There is only one entity that can use a nuclear weapon: a terrorist cell.* Big countries like Russia and China couldn't use them against each other or it would be the end of life on Earth as we know it. A small country can't use them against a major power because that would be suicide. Large nations couldn't use them on smaller nations or there would be world outrage. Russia didn't use them in Chechnya, the French didn't use them in Algeria, the British didn't use them in India, and we never used them in Korea, Vietnam, Iraq or Afghanistan. No matter how safe the arsenals of the world are, there is still a small probability that a terrorist cell will one day get a hold of one and set it off in some western city. We should be trying to rid the world of them altogether. This may not be possible. But to continue sprucing up the arsenals of the west while telling everyone else they can't have them, will only bring about more nuclear ambitions and more terrorists enraged by the enormous hypocrisy.

The very least the US should do is get together with Russia and *pretend* to reduce our arsenals to set some sort of half-assed example to the rest of the world. China may not be interested because the megalomaniacs running China probably think they could afford to lose a few hundred million people in a nuclear exchange. But Russia has a lot more at stake. In 2010, Obama made an attempt to crank up the START treaty with Russia. And guess who balked at this effort? Those same neoconservatives whose sex lives are seriously threatened by any hint of reducing the pile of nuclear peckers they identify with. So the US provides no leadership and no example for the rest of the world. If our leaders got energy out of the bottom of their brains and rationally perceived reality, they would realize that huge numbers of WMD's is not in our national interests nor the interests of other nuclear powers.

Getting back to their love of wars, as we explained in Sect. 29.10, when you want to find the motivation for an action of a complex system, you simply look at the result. So what was the *result* in Iraq and Afghanistan? Dead Iraqis and Afghans, puppet governments and a training ground for terrorists. So what was the core motivation for invading these countries? *To kill Iraqis and Afghans, to set up puppet governments and establish training grounds for terrorists.* This is not rocket science. The training ground for terrorists finally led to ISIS. If you could turn off the propaganda machine for a few months, you'd see it. Once the motive was achieved, the system cobbled together a policy based on reason box justifications with all kinds of noble ideas like elections, nation-building, freedom and economic development. But when you look closely at these reason box justifications, they were all cobbled together *after* the invasion. There was certainly no Marshall plan like after WWII. If economic development, nation-building and democracy were the core motivation for these invasions, most of the money spent would have gone towards extensive *planning, study, and preparedness* to achieve these goals. Violence and killing would have been peripheral. But the exact opposite was the case. Any planning that occurred was about invasion, conquest and killing. Reason box rationalizations were slapped together willy-nilly in an ad hoc amateur-ish manner especially for a great country.

A headline in an issue of *The Economist* was, "Why the Afghanistan war deserves more resources, commitment and political will".[14] Remember, the neoconservative has all his energy in the bottom of his brain. This is why they perceive nothing, know nothing, and learn nothing. Perceiving and learning are existential mentalities that are beyond the cognitive abilities of the neoconservative inner brain, which is why the writers of this headline were unable to perceive that there is absolutely no difference between tough young Afghan men and tough young British and American men. We are the invaders even if we were coming from the North Pole behind a bunch of reindeer. They are going to expel the invader even if it takes hundreds of years. Even if Obama's and McChrystal's motivations were pure, to believe that the tough young men of these countries are going to see things our way is a pipe dream. George Washington's army didn't care about the fact that all our democratic institutions in the colonies were created by the British. They were the occupiers who had to be expelled — end of story.

After 300 years of continuous British colonialism costing millions of lives and finally another killing spree when they finally get kicked out, these Brits have learned absolutely nothing. Now they have a new one: leaving Afghanistan "...would amount to a terrible betrayal of the Afghan people...".[15] Are they talking about the ones they've already killed or the ones they'll kill on the way out?

On the other hand, the British occupation of the colonies was not totally bad. They had set up representative government, courts, contracts, and all other institutions of Democratic Capitalism. They were not here to steal our resources and set up a fake puppet government. They were not bad occupiers like the Bushies in Iraq. Without Washington, life under the British would have been pretty much as before. Life under the puppet governments in Iraq and Afghanistan might even be better than under what they'll wind up with. But that's irrelevant to the motivation of the tough young men of an occupied country. Washington was able to raise an army to kick out the British and the young men of Afghanistan are doing the same regardless of how good life would be under the Americans. The reason US policy doesn't see this is a deep and unconscious racism. We're the great white hope, they're the Pickininnies, and it's just a matter of time and killing before they recognize this picture. All it takes is a little more "resources, commitment and political will", as *The Economist* preaches. They probably said the very same thing while getting kicked out of over a hundred countries, killing millions in the process.

The only reason Bush and Obama remotely appear like a great white hope is because the Muslim world is in such disarray. They just as soon kill each other as the invader. What if they had an organized and effective opponent like the Americans under Washington? Obama and *The Economist* would have no credibility at all. By giving the appearance of disunity and incompetence, Muslim insurgents give some credence that the west is going to make it all better.

The escalation in Afghanistan very graphically illustrates the neoconservative system mind. The additional 30 thousand troops and supporting bureaucracy are *government* employees. This will cost up to another hundred billion. But not a word was said by Obama to indicate how he will pay for it. Where were the neoconservatives then to complain about big government, big spending and big deficits for this escalation? And this is right in the middle of a healthcare debate, where neoconservatives have been nitpicking for months about government spending. See, when it's time to identify with the king who is raising a *big government* army of men trained to *kill* people, there is no limit to the amount of spending and deficits these neoconservatives will object to. But when Obama wanted to raise a government army of *doctors* whose job is to *cure* people, these same neoconservatives are squealing about big government, spending, and deficits. This shows exactly where the energy is in the neoconservative reptilian brain.

But every once in a while, the real motives of these neoconservatives comes poking through their blanket of propaganda. An important piece of evidence of this was contained in probably the most important headline I've seen in the last 10 years. The May 7, 2011 issue of *The Economist* had this as it's cover headline after the killing of Osama bin Laden: "Now kill his dream". I think this one little sentence shows the mindset of the neoconservative, which, being as unself-conscious as they are, didn't take real notice of what they were saying.

Osama bin Laden's *dream* was to get western armies out of Muslim countries, the exact *same* dream George Washington had about the British. Of course, using terrorism to accomplish any dream is total pathology and criminality and getting bin Laden was a legitimate goal of US foreign policy since 9/11. It was his *methods* that were criminal, not the dream which was exactly the same as George Washington's: get the occupier out. And by the way, what was the Bushie's dream while invading Iraq and Afghanistan killing not 3 thousand as bin Laden did, but *tens* of thousands? And what was the Brit's dream invading and conquering Iraq, killing thousands in the process who can't complain now that they're dead? The methods *The Economist* and like-minded want to use to kill bin Laden's dream is, of course, to invade, conquer and kill Muslim people. And they want to smother anyone who might resist US and Britain's prerogative to conquer and kill anyone wherever they please. This, of course, has the additional motivation to keep the war on terrorism going by creating more terrorists. It was really enlightening to see their motives come through during one of their few moments of semi-consciousness.

30.5 ADOLF HITLER AND THE SYSTEM MIND

A very incisive example of identifying with power and bigness came in Hitler's Germany in the 1930s. I had trouble figuring out where to put this section. Unless a book is definitively about Hitler or the Holocaust, this period is so monstrously out of proportion compared to any other topic as to seem out of place. But it has to go somewhere because this period of history illustrates two very important topics: the natural inclination among all humans to be attracted to power. And second, the Nazi period is an excellent illustration of the operation of a system mind.

There is not room here to go into the enormous detail that characterizes the Nazi period under Hitler. This is the job of historians. But it is important to bring out that the Nazi period combined two key factors that can lead to a very powerful system mind. Germany even under Hitler was a free-enterprise system. Of course it didn't take long for Hitler to turn it into National Socialism where leading industrialists became members of the Nazi party deeply in bed with Hitler's political system. But the system already had all the information flows that characterize a free-enterprise system. Then you add the enormous information flows due to a gigantic Nazi propaganda campaign in newspapers, radio, movies and especially Nazi rallies where emotion-laden speeches were made, many by Hitler himself. The bottom line is you had a very sophisticated, intrusive and expansive system mind in place all during the Nazi period. And it continued and amplified the anti-Semitism that was initiated by a number of German intellectuals back in the 1800s.

This is why when historians examine the documents of the period, they find very little overt evidence that the Nazis were going to and finally did kill the Jews of Europe. There were very few specific orders given or documents to be found. The reason, in my opinion, was that the final solution of killing Europe's Jews was the result of an every-growing, intense and self-fed *system mind*. Of course Hitler and leading Nazis had to give it direction, but they never had to specifically give the overt orders to do anything. The system mind they supported did all the dirty work for them. This is also why the whole enterprise was so difficult for Europe's Jews to comprehend. The final solution for their deaths crept up on them slowly and almost imperceptibly. There was no sudden jump in anti-Semitic activity, no sudden orders given, no sudden swerve in policy. And this is why even after it was all over, it was difficult to know where and how to look for explanations.

Another interesting factor was that immediately after the war, the enormity of what had happened totally fractured the Jewish system mind that had been in place for thousands of years. Jewish intellectuals went in all directions like kicking an ant hill destroying their whole structure. They scurry around for a while before starting to reorganize and rebuild their social and physical structure again. This is what happened to Jewish thought, and, in my opinion, is why they still haven't evolved a consistent system mind that could be effective in perpetuating their existence. The only thing holding together Jewish opinion even to this day is the threat from Arab countries against the state of Israel and it doesn't always do a good job of that. My question for Netanyahu is, *what is your endgame?*

In any event, there were a number of factions that evolved who were quite acidic in attacking one another. The two leading historians after the war were Raul Hilberg and Hannah Arendt. Hilberg dedicated his life to the study of the Holocaust and personally found many documents covering the war period. Arendt emerged with her book about the Eichmann trial. Interestingly, neither of these intellectuals were high-profile Jewish leaders. Their participation in normal Jewish life was minimal, which might explain the antipathy many Jewish leaders had towards them over succeeding years. However, they were both dedicated Zionists especially in their early days and to me that is the most important distinction that marks off those who were most interested in the perpetuation and survival of

Jewish culture. Arendt was among the greatest human beings of the 20th century. Although not perfect, she was a Zionist when that position would have *saved* European Jews (Arendt was important in Jewish relief organizations in the 1930s helping Jews flee Europe). After the war, she was a critic of Israeli policies towards the Palestinians because, in my opinion, she saw the beginnings of a path to another Holocaust.

As we mentioned, Jewish opinion splintered all over because of the Holocaust. One focus of opinion blamed everything on Hitler depicted as a total madman. Then there are those who blamed world opinion, which, it was claimed, did nothing to save European Jews. In a really super review of this history by Nathaniel Popper, he quotes Hilberg's views on the Holocaust: "The destruction of the Jews was an administrative process, and ... required the implementation of systematic administrative measures in successive steps".[16]

There is one point of view which I favor most says that for thousands of years, Jews survived as a people and usually as a minority by initiating, supporting and promulgating the *Law*. The idea of law goes back to the very beginnings of Jewish culture. When you're a minority and always under threat from the majority, your only protection is the *law*. Hilberg suggested this view: "Jews had a centuries-old tradition of complying with violent anti-Semitic rulers".[17] Because of thousands of years of this culture, when the Nazis starting passing *laws* circumscribing Jewish life, major Jewish leaders, including many important Rabbis, advised their people to obey the law because that is what saved them in the past. However, Arendt's response to many Rabbis' cooperation in providing lists of Jews for the Nazis, was to underplay this historic tendency and instead to criticize European Jews for not resisting and fighting back. For this she took lots of flak from Jewish organizations. Since WWII, Israelis think they can make up for the lack of spine claimed by Arendt by picking on the Palestinians. I don't think there's anything to make up for: Jewish reaction to the Nazi machine was understandable in view of their history.

This is the context in which Arendt went to Israel to cover the Eichmann trial in 1961. We have very little idea what she was looking for specifically or what she was thinking. My own opinion was she went to look for explanations, to see how the bad guys operated and to learn the history of the period. But she ran into a brick wall. There was nothing to see, nothing to grab onto, nothing to get one's teeth into. There was no specific evidence as to who was giving orders and who was responsible. In my opinion, Arendt started out energetically looking for answers, and wound up being intellectually *paralyzed* when there were no answers. Her rather bland and boring conclusion was that Germans like Eichmann "... were neither perverted nor sadistic, they were, and still are terribly and terrifyingly normal".[18] This really raised the hackles of most Jewish intellectual opinion. But if one doesn't understand the workings of a system mind, this is all one could say.

Our explanation for the whole episode including Arendt's response was that the Holocaust was the result of a very powerful Nazi system mind in which Eichmann was a powerful node. As such, most of his thinking process in this role was mostly sub-conscious. However, some of it, or most of it could have popped through to consciousness at various times. We'll never know how much. My criticism of Arendt is that she didn't see even a smidgeon of this possibility. And with so little tangible evidence as to the exact sequence of events, the best explanations people like Hilberg and Arendt came up with stressed the "banality" of it all, and how it was an "administrative" process. As we shall see in upcoming chapters on the Kennedy assassination, 9/11, and the Russian transition, when a system mind brings about an event, there are no smoking guns, no one to pin the blame on, no conspiracies, but, most importantly, no usual answers.

Any population of people is capable of becoming part of a system mind, cooperating with any event imaginable. All it takes is propaganda to wear away a few layers of existential brain leaving all the energy in the bottom and a leader projecting raw naked power. He will immediately make 20% of the population into total intellectual slaves. Hitler achieved the support he did by projecting raw, naked power, which galvanized the worst 20% into effective action, and a good percentage of the rest into supporters of varying degrees, except for the top 20% who were determinedly anti-Hitler but who were disarmed and often killed.

When Bush invaded Iraq, he had the immediate support of 20% of the population who had no questions, no hesitancy and complete attachment like a barnacle on a sea rock. On sewer radio, hard-ons that had been dormant for months began popping up like springs in a worn out mattress. When Obama was elected, his total lack of understanding of the neoconservative mind led him to think he might win over some of their support by an escalation of the war in Afghanistan. What he didn't understand is that all he has to do is show one split second of hesitancy and he would lose the support of that hard-core capon 20% who are addicted to killing, destruction and the all-around naked power.

30.6 CONSERVATIVE SYSTEM MIND AND HISTORY

One of the really sad facts about modern life is that the system mind invades just about every aspect of our lives, including academic disciplines. This is especially true of economics which is why you have never heard of an out-or-work economist. He can always find work somewhere pimping for the system. A major exception to this general rule *sometimes*, is history. The system does not care about the past. It is future oriented because it is in the future that money will be made and power accumulated. So the history profession is free to be objective and get the facts straight although it sometimes takes a hundred years. Historians have pretty much straightened out the colonial period, but there is still controversy about Lincoln's real motives and goals. But as we closer to the present, we can see how the system mind penetrates the history profession more and more, until in the immediate past, there is almost no difference between what historians are saying and what the system mind is saying. The 1930s are a perfect example.

The history books are still telling us that the Prime Minister of Great Britain *appeased* Hitler. In my opinion, this is a perfect example of the system mind talking. To appease is to acquiesce or accommodate another point of view out of *fear* of what the other might do otherwise. Appeasement requires an element of fear. You oppose you neighbor in some way and you appease your neighbor out of *fear* of what he may do if you don't accommodate.

There is no evidence of fear or even opposition among conservatives in the US and Britain, as is shown by the fact that they did nothing to prepare for hostilities with Hitler. Without fear, there is no "appeasement". It was simply *accommodation* and sometimes *facilitation*.

In a very important review of the 1930s, historian Gordon Craig discusses a number of books detailing the degree of cooperation between US industrialists and Hitler's Germany.[19] Many British and American corporations including General Motors and Ford were doing a brisk business with Hitler's Nazism. IBM, headed at the time by Thomas Watson, an arch conservative, actually made punch cards that enabled the Nazis to keep track of Jews making it easier to round them up during the Holocaust.[20] The author, Edwin Black says, "Without IBM's machinery, Hitler's camps could have never managed the numbers they did". Watson warned that we shouldn't interfere with the internal affairs of countries we are doing business with. Of course, if there's not *enough* "business" like in Iraq, you can "interfere" with the internal affairs of a country with no limit by invading, conquering and killing.

When you have some of the largest companies playing ball with Hitler, it's no wonder the politicos in Washington who are bought and sold like sacks of potatoes by these same companies, would be pressing to give Hitler the green light. But when Hitler attacked the west, Churchill made his famous speech, blaring that we were "stabbed in the back". That, to me, is a dead giveaway. He thought Hitler was a fellow soul who he was facilitating, and when Hitler attacked the west, it *was* a real stab in the back. When you *appease* out of fear and apprehension, you are never "stabbed in the back" afterwards. You expect it.

Conservatives in both countries mounted a massive propaganda campaign preaching peace, isolationism, and conciliation; and that we shouldn't interfere with the internal affairs of other countries. In my opinion, what explains the behavior of conservatives at this time was that they were green with envy over what Hitler was able to do in Germany. Hitler was squelching Jews, liberals, and anyone suspected of being a communist or socialist, all of whom were objects of hatred among conservatives. This was everything American and British conservatives were wishing they could do in their own countries. If we ever get a real historian of the period and he were to go back and read actual statements and speeches made by conservatives in both the US congress and parliament, especially the latter, he would find all kinds of excuses to allow Hitler to carry out his agenda. Some of them actually supported Hitler. During the war, thousands of allied lives were lost because of the total lack of preparedness. This, in my opinion, is an egregious example of distorting history to placate the current neoconservative culture.

Conservative elements in both France and England were so enamored by Hitler's political agenda that their navies were scattered all over the world guarding their "natives" in far-away colonies, instead of putting them in safe British harbors to guard against a possible Nazi attack. Of course, a fellow soul like Hitler would never do such a thing. When war surprised both countries, Churchill said it was necessary to sink half the French fleet killing hundreds of French sailors. The French were coerced into sinking the other half to prevent it from falling into the hands of the Nazis. Because of these losses and lack of preparedness, Hitler's u-boats were able to sink hundreds of British ships *and* US supply ships. Anyone with half a brain could see that there should have been even the tiniest measures taken to protect these assets *before* war arrived.

But if support for Hitler is a bit too subtle to convince historians of these conservative motives, there is *overt* evidence of their motives. The Spanish Civil War was raging through the late 1930s, pitting an elected Popular Front government against a Fascist dictator, Francisco Franco. During the war, Franco received military aid and money from Hitler which allowed him to win this civil war. Conservatives in both the US and Great Britain would not allow one cent to help the forces of democracy. After his victory, in the ensuing years, Franco put tens of thousands in jail and murdered many more tens of thousands, news of which was suppressed the western media system mind.

After the war, a bunch of conservative Republicans centered around Senator Joseph McCarthy cranked up a government-sponsored witch hunt to accuse, weed out and criminalize anyone who they could tie in with sympathy for Communism. People lost jobs, reputations and resources. Where were the Supreme *Vampires* who are supposed to protect freedom of speech. Since most of them were chosen by the reptilian brains of Republican presidents in the 1920s, they watched the whole sordid mess and did nothing. In my opinion, the whole McCarthy episode was a system mind reaction to distract the American people from finding out about how these same conservative Republicans had been facilitating Hitler all through the 1930s. And where is the history of the tie-in between McCarthy and sympathy for Hitler in the 1930s? We could expect a cover-up by the system mind propaganda outlets, but where are the historians? A great movie, *Good Night and Good Luck*, told how Edward R. Murrow and CBS did their best to resist McCarthy's witch hunt. Murrow wouldn't last one week on today's Columbia Bullshit System.

And because of the neoconservative economic agenda of the system's mouthpieces, and to smother their tacit support of Hitler during the '30s, anti-communism was blown up to monumental proportions to the extent that the only way Johnson could pass his liberal anti-poverty program was to get into the war in Vietnam causing millions of casualties. Of course, when the system saw that the Chinese system could be used as a magnet pulling us in the same direction, down came the "communist" banners and we were assured that China was "on the road to democracy". Since then conservatives have been propping up China with trade, selling our paper and importing their junk while China allows North Korea to develop missiles that could reach the San Francisco with a nuclear weapon. So much for the safety of the American people.

History is the most important component of a nation's culture. As we showed in Sect. 16.9, the essence of human personhood is the ability to *plan* on the basis of comparing propositional memory with moral judgments encapsulated in symbolic (language) representations of the past. History is a very important ingredient of this process and consequently an essential component of the *human* condition. But the modern neoconservative culture is starting to infect even the history profession which really is in crisis. Post Civil War history is a total misrepresentation and the history of the 1930s and the resulting McCarthy period after WWII is a national disgrace. What will the history of the Iraq war and 9/11 look like? I'm betting for the next 50 years, it will be the same reason box diarrhea that we've been getting from the system mind. The history profession is going to have to make up its mind as to whether it is going to do history, or just another gear in the system mind propaganda machine.

30.7 RELATIVE WEALTH AND POWER

What we are going to see in this section is that the enormous debt that neoconservatives have piled on in the last 35 years is no accident. This is not simply letting principles slide or getting careless and lax about core principles. Neoconservative propagandists blast forth 24/7 about "core principles". But invariably, their other half actually in government is doing the exact opposite.

The ultimate psychological needs of the neoconservative are to identify with massive nodes of raw naked power, dominance and control. The way to achieve this is for larger nodes of the economy to have as much *relative* amounts of wealth and power as possible. The key here is *relative*. This fact was observed by the great 19th century economist and philosopher, John Stuart Mill who said, "Men do not desire merely to be rich, but to be richer than other men". This is one of the most important quotes in all history. This is why neoconservative psychology derives its sense of superiority and power by maintaining high degrees of inequality. This has been the case all throughout history. The perfect example to illustrate this is the feudal system in the Middle Ages.

The feudal system in Europe created a thousand years of stability whereby the aristocracy in the top 5% of the population was in total control. They owned all the means of production which was mainly agriculture, animals and crafts. The lower 80% of peasants had nothing. This aristocracy was able to control and dominate the rest of society by having a maximum amount of *relative* wealth and power. The feudal system mind was not very effective at that time due to the lack of information flows that we have in modern society. However, it was coherent enough to realize that technology and economic progress was a threat to their dominance and control, *even though it would have benefited them.*

Their lack of technology actually resulted in a low standard of living. There are stories of castles and manor houses stinking to high heaven because there was no indoor plumbing or means of sanitation. They didn't even have soap. You would think that they would welcome new technology that would raise their standard of living. But they saw that additional wealth and power from technology might go to other classes like the merchant and professional classes — or, God forbid, the peasant class. Technological advancement, by improving the economic welfare of other classes, would jeopardize the aristocracy's *relative* position as top dogs who controlled all economic wealth and activity.

The paradox is that just as in today's society, there was a large segment of the peasant class, perhaps a majority, who supported the aristocracy and especially the king, because it gave them something big and powerful to identify with. It was the merchant class in Europe who eventually brought down the feudal system, not the peasants who were the most oppressed by it. But the aristocracy resisted and fought back every step of the way because even though their wealth was not decreasing appreciably, what they were losing was *relative* wealth and power. The important lesson we should learn from this history is that the conservative system mind does not care about their *absolute* wealth and standard of living. What they want is *relative* wealth and power because it enables them to dominate and control society and establish themselves as nodes of raw power for people to identify with. We can make a tie-in with our present situation.

The Great Depression brought in Franklin Roosevelt who allowed the establishment of large industrial unions, a minimum wage, the 8-hour day, unemployment compensation and Social Security pensions. All of this in addition to the new technology introduced from WWII, created a balanced economy. The wealth of the lower 80% rose to over 33% as compared to only about 15% during the 1920s; and the income of the lower 80% rose to about 60% of National Income compared to only 40% in the 1920s.* This is probably as close to pure Capitalism as the country has ever got, as we have stressed. And the citizenry voted for a series of presidents who believed in democratic Capitalism: Truman, Eisenhower, Kennedy and Johnson. This degree of balance produced the fastest expanding economy in our history and brought most of the lower 80% who had been pretty poor since the Civil War into a middle class. But this was all totally unacceptable to the neoconservative system mind. The reason is that this equality lessened the *relative* wealth and power of the modern aristocracy in the top 5%.

When Reagan took office, the lower 80% had about 22% of all wealth and was getting about almost 60% of national income. But there has been a constant redistribution of wealth and income ever since brought off by the neoconservative agenda introduced by Reagan. Of course, this was totally suppressed by the system mind propaganda outlets, so that when Bush left office, the bottom 80% had only 13% of all wealth and was getting only 48% of national income. When Obama suggested that maybe we should balance the economy, neoconservative politicians and their paid media whores began screaming about Obama "redistributing income" and "class warfare". But for 30 years, as income was redistributed *upward* to the top 20%, not a peep from the system mind.

This also explains why system mind leaders have absolutely no concern about the viability of their policies because they can't lose. The rat-pack gang of economists, fast-buck operators and financial money-changers led by Alan Greenspan had absolutely nothing to lose in the explosion of Economic Socialism under George Bush. They printed up their own money in the form of derivatives by the hundreds of *trillions* and made rules that allowed them to buy, sell, and gamble on their own paper. While the swindle went on, they extracted hundreds of billions in pay, bonuses and commissions from taxpayers and especially the children of the country who can't defend themselves. But even if the game

---

* These numbers are very rough, but the best I can do. Our crooked government refuses to give even the simplest measures of the economy, while they keep detailed numbers for how many cans of sardines sold in Idaho in 1973.

crashed, they had even more to gain in terms of the long-term goals of the system mind, which is to garner a greater share of *relative* wealth. And this exactly what in fact happened.

Since the neoconservative system mind for 200 years has had absolutely nothing in their bag of tricks that could conceivably get an economy going again, it chose Barack Obama to do the dirty work, who fit into the neoconservative agenda like a hand in a glove. There is a measure called the Gini index which measures the degree of inequality. Inequality has been increasing since Ronald Reagan and actually increased during the current recession. This is the exact goal of the neoconservative system mind.

But Economic Socialism cannot be sustained with this kind of inequality. As the share of National Income going to the bottom 80% began to fall under Reagan, markets could not clear. This started a 30-year trend of massive deficits. But this was a boon to the neoconservative system mind for two reasons. First, the money stolen went mostly to the top 20%, especially the aristocracy in the top 5%. But even more fortuitously, a huge national debt eventually cripples the economy and prevents growth. With a crippled economy, the top 5% can again grab a larger share of national income and wealth just as in Feudal times. This will enable the aristocracy to once again have the wealth and power to dominate and control the citizenry and to stay in power by giving a good segment of society who have a weak frontal cortex, a means to create an identity by identifying with the big nodes in the economy or the current king's war.

This explains why the top priority of neoconservatives *actually in power* has been huge deficits. And remember, we are talking about *reality* here, not what their paid propagandists say in words when they lie through their teeth to the citizenry through the system mind mouthpieces. They would swear on their mother's graves that they want growth and Capitalism and the rest of it. But the system mind that emerges from the tremendous flows of information creates a mind designed to meet the psychological needs of people who need to identify with something strong and powerful. Its purpose is to facilitate as much wealth and power going mostly to the top 5% which in turn enables them to have total control over society's values, institutions and lifestyles.

Just to give an idea of how far our culture has absorbed the flagrant misrepresentation of the motives of the neoconservative system mind, on July 7, 2010, a new guy just hired by the so-called *liberal* PBS is talking about Republicans getting back to "core principles". This jerk didn't even get his first paycheck and already he's lying through his teeth about the neoconservative agenda. And taxpayers have to *pay* for crap coming out of PBS. The "core principles" of the neoconservative-dominated Republican party *for the past 35 years IN PRACTICE*, has been ever-increasing size of government especially the parts of government that invades our privacy and makes the king's private wars, ever increasing deficits, and a constant attack on the middle class so that almost every penny of new income and wealth has gone to the top 20%. That's the reality.

The attack on the middle class leaves no stone unturned. The attack against unions goes unabated. Of course, unions have their share of misdeeds and I certainly don't support many of their practices. But the *concept* of unionization is to provide a counterbalance to the power of employers. Remember, union members are middle class people. Sewer radio talks of union members like they're a small invasion party from Mars. Union people whether good or bad *are* the American people. They are not a small rat-pack of media whores. There are 15 *million* of them about 10% of the working population. They cause many abuses just like any other group. Big corporate nodes that give these neoconservatives their sex lives also incur abuses. They pollute, make their own rules, and buy politicians like sacks of potatoes. That doesn't mean we should get rid of private corporations. They are the most efficient means to make goods and services that create our standard of living. They have interests just like unions, and they do what they can to pursue their interests. We simply have to enforce *independent* rules to keep them honest. We have to keep unions in line as well and prevent them from abuses. But that doesn't mean a vicious attack as Reagan did.

There is nothing more Reagan could have done to attack the middle class than what he did, and it's been going on since the 1920s. The motivation is again for their nodes of economic power they identify with to have greater *relative* wealth and power. Listen to this. In Jan. '13, House Majority Leader Eric Cantor (R-Virginia) assailed fiscal cliff legislation, calling it "a classic example of putting the 98.5 per cent of the American people ahead of the rest of the country". This seems pretty funny but it shows the incredible psychopathology of neoconservatives. The 98.5% really don't count — it's the 1.5% with all the power and wealth that this neoconservative derives his identity.

Japan is farther along in this process than we are. One of their political parties, a party of neoconservatives, was in power for over 50 years. Starting 30 years ago about the same time Reagan was elected in the US, this party began allowing the redistribution of income upward to their aristocracy. The resulting inability for their middle classes to clear markets forced them to steal from the future with huge budget deficits. Japan has been recurrently recessionary for the past 20 years and now have a national debt *twice* their GDP. With the downturn, they are increasing their national debt even more.

But Japanese conservatives have one big disadvantage. Since WWII, Japan was prevented from having a military. This means that they haven't been able to invade and conquer other countries like they once did. This makes it is difficult for them to invite a terrorist attack ala George Bush. So, not being able to jump into the war on terrorism or any other war, their conservative party was unable to distract the population with patriotic war fever. So after 50 years, they were voted out of office in 2009. But it's really too late. There is nothing that can be done to recapture a vibrant growing Japanese economy. Their economy will be crippled for as far as the eye can see. Their aristocracy doesn't care one wit about this because they have the lion's share of National Income and wealth. And they can stay dominant in their society because they have the money to control the means of propaganda of their system mind. We are headed in the exact same direction.

The first thing neoconservative Republicans did after winning the 2010 midterm elections was to pass a bill adding *1 trillion* dollars to the national debt over the next 10 years. They were able to do this knowing full well that the system mind media whores would totally suppress this most important fact of the year. Then they got into a pissing contest with Democrats fighting over 50 billion in spending cuts, which included a vicious attack on services for children. This is after dumping a trillion dollars of debt on their heads. Thus, for every hundred dollars they *added* to the debt, they were subtracting 50 cents from spending. The propaganda outlets went rapturous mentioning Republican spending cuts at every possible opportunity, but not peep about the addition of a *trillion* to the debt.

There is one fly in the ointment however and this involves the lack of a time concept in the system mind. As the national debt increases in the coming years, it will eventually become impossible for neoconservatives to run around the world invading and conquering countries and propping up puppet governments. It costs the US hundreds of billions for governments in Iraq and Afghanistan to *pretend* to have democracy and huge armies. In other countries, our government has to spend billions bribing governments to *pretend* to be allies and to help in the war on terrorism. Now that there are uprisings of people all over the Muslim world, the new governments that evolve will require even bigger bribes to pretend they're on our side and to help with the war on terrorism while at the same time harboring terrorists. We will get to a point where we simply don't have the money for this kind of foreign policy and its invasions and conquests. It will be interesting to see what these neoconservatives do for a sex life at that point.

In the remaining sections, we will look at the various manifestations of the neoconservative search for bigness in any shape or form.

30.8 COLLECTIVIZATION

Before the Civil War, this country had a fairly decent system of democracy and Capitalism. The nation consisted of small farmers, small craftsmen and merchants of various kinds. Of course, as we have described, the Industrial Revolution changed all that and we started on the road to Economic Socialism that, except for a brief period during the Roosevelt era, has lasted to the present day. But during this time, the situation in agriculture remained pretty much what it had been in the beginning: a nation of relatively small farms.

Again, starting with Ronald Reagan, the small farmer slowly got driven out of business to be replaced by big corporate farms. Reagan himself drove a quarter *million* small and medium sized farms out of business to be replaced by collectives, which are nothing by government/business partnerships — the centerpiece of Economic Socialism. A collective is nothing but a bed holding both political actors and economic players together rigging the rules so they get more and more subsidies, which is corporate welfare. Money is stolen from taxpayers and the future to give to the biggest collectives as bribes for not growing anything or to pay for price supports. These price supports, of course, are rigged so that the small farmer can't make a go of it and he sells his land to the nearest collective. Collectivization has been going on now for 35 years and although the number of tiny specialized farms have increased in recent years, the number of medium and small farms continues to fall. And the basic reason is the neoconservative hates smallness. It's a reminder of himself and his non-existent identity. He must have bigness. Not only big wars and big government, but even big collective farms.

A similar phenomenon occurs in ordinary industry. One of the pieces of raw propaganda the neoconservative spews forth is the idea of "rugged individualism". This is taken from the old Capitalist notion going back to Adam Smith that what best serves society is a number of competing firms all trying to get the consumer dollar with the best product for the lowest price. The leaders of these firms must be "rugged individualists" who, without government help and all on their own, build successful companies in a highly competitive world. But of course, the reality is the exact opposite. What the neoconservative mind needs is identification with *bigness, power, and might*. This is best accomplished by having very large *monopoly* companies who don't compete at all. An avalanche of collectivization also began with Reagan's economic socialism. Financial wizards on Wall St. concocted dozens of ways to finance collectivization in all industries. There were mergers, LBOs, (leveraged buyouts), takeovers, junk bonds and more. Often collectivization meant job losses, inferior products and bankruptcies to pay the exorbitant fees of the economic parasites who concocted these schemes — all with the blessing of Ronald Reagan. It got totally out of hand under Bush and led to the meltdown.

Of course, in order to maintain one of the basic assumptions of Capitalism, there must be laws preventing the agglomeration and collectivization of companies in an industry to insure a number of competing companies. Thus, the basic psychology of the neoconservative mind is in direct contradiction with this core principle of Capitalism. So while preaching for competition and rugged individualism in their propaganda outlets, the neoconservative *other* half in political office is supporting measures that facilitate companies to merge and collectivize. In fact, in actual practice, regardless of what they say, *the neoconservative is a collectivist.*

The first thing Ronald Reagan did upon being elected was to get rid of an anti-trust law in 1982. George Bush did the same putting the anti-trust division of the Justice Department to sleep for 8 years, while in industry after industry we find a stampede towards mergers, takeovers, and buyouts. This resulted in companies "too big to fail". In order to achieve an identity in a brain with no frontal cortex, he must have bigness to identify with, which includes big corporations. When the system mind took over Obama's mind, he threw taxpayer money at the collectives that Bush had created during his term in office. As a newly minted zombie, he put up no resistance at all to the idea that if we let the collectives fail, the sky will fall, the world will end and dogs will stop barking. Down the drain went trillions of dollars stolen unconstitutionally from future generations. Stealing *trillions* from our children most of which wound up in the pockets of people who caused the meltdown, was the biggest swindle in the history of the world.

30.9 ENVIRONMENT
Maintaining a clean environment requires rules of the game to minimize pollution. We discussed the concept of genocide in Sect. 24.2. Pollution and toxins in the environment

kill genes and cause birth defects. However, minimizing pollution costs money and eats into profits. As we have stressed, anything that detracts from the bigness and power of things like corporations, farms, armies, wars, etc., will be smothered and fought by the neoconservative agenda. So they are constantly putting roadblocks against any efforts to pass legislation that tries to keep the environment clean. We discussed the problem of polar warming above.

But these urges and itches in the neoconservative brain can reach really pathological proportions. They see growing numbers of birth defects just as the rest of us see. And yet, when it comes to a choice between identification with bigness and power or the health and happiness of their owns kids, it's identification that wins out. They will wriggle and shift, bob and weave to avoid blaming their big business gods and the pollution they cause for the health problems of their own kids. They demand that you have to take a picture of an atom of toxin going into DNA and chopping it up right before our eyes before they will accept any causal relation between pollution and birth defects. Of course, there's no way to take a picture of atoms and molecules at work in a person's body. So they have an out. As a result, we see continuous increases in genetic maladies even in their own kids.

A very poignant example is Sarah Palin. Because Alaska is such a desolate place, lots of toxins and pollutants have been dumped up there over the years. This has resulted in an Alaskan "...birth-defect rate that's *twice* the national average...".[21] Now here's Sarah Palin with a child with a severe genetic mental handicap and she's poking fun at environmental-ists: "Drill baby drill". And there's *her own dam kid*. Thousands of children are born each year with similar handicaps due to environmental toxins that mutate genes. And right in her own state.

I have to say, of all the unbelievable astounding phenomena that can be observed about people's politics, this one takes the cake. I can see having many neoconservative views, hating the poor, loving the rich and powerful, cutting taxes on crooked rich friends, loving wars — all of it. But this environment issue tops the list. Her own kid has a severe handicap that will drastically impede his entire life. But bigness and power and profits of soulless corporations come first. Of course, with all the brain energy in the bottom of her brain, there's no way she can abstract the possibility that she could have been born with the same handicap.

Government agencies are predicting health care costs to reach 20% of GDP by 2050. *They are crazy.* In my opinion, by the end of the century, three fourths of the economy will be health care much of it due to genetic damage. And by then there will be no way to steal from the future to pay for it all.

30.10 Immigration

One of the most effective ways to achieve collectivization in farms and industry is to allow businesses to make as much profits as possible. In this way, they can merge, buy each other out, and takeover. And one way to increase profits is to have a cheap supply of labor. This is why, with the ascendancy of Ronald Reagan, the influx of illegal immigrants started its upward climb. Illegal immigration provides cheap labor especially for large economic units, which allows greater profits and more economic power to drive smaller competitors out of business. Small businesses can't make use of illegal immigration like the biggies can. This is exactly what we have observed in the last 35 years.

Apologists for illegal immigration have all kinds of reason box crap to rationalize bringing in low wage labor. They say that the illegals will do jobs regular Americans won't do. The question is, *won't do for what pay?* If the pay is high enough, there will be people who will do just about anything. What they don't tell us is that *Americans won't work for slave labor wages and conditions.*

Once I was at a convention and we noticed outside there was a line two blocks long in front of the hotel. Well it turned out that the hotel needed people to do regular room cleaning etc. So they put an ad in the paper, but they made a mistake on pay. Instead of 5 dollars an hour, (minimum wage at the time) by mistake, they put a 1 in front of the 5 and were advertising pay of *15* dollars an hour. The line was two blocks long waiting to get a job at 15 dollars an hour and they didn't seem to care what they would be doing.

The Economist says that immigrants "…are often vilified, but they are increasingly necessary".[22] These are exactly the words of the southern plantation owners who also said that more slaves were absolutely "necessary". *Everyone* wants slave labor, including these media whores who constantly push for more illegal immigration to clean up their shit. And since normal citizens won't work for slave labor wages, modern-day work slaves are absolutely "necessary".

30.11 BIG GOVERNMENT

Remember, the main motivation in the neoconservative mind is identity. To achieve a semblance of identity requires identification with bigness — big banks, big corporations, big farms, and most importantly big brother government: one big and powerful enough to not only suppress and control the home population, but big enough to go anywhere in the world to invade, conquer, and kill people of its choosing. Yes, they want small government when it comes to ways to help people like health care, drug safety, anti-trust, the environment, etc. But when it comes to parts of the government that are engaged in killing people, creating enormous war machines, spying on people, and propping up Economic Socialism, there is no limit to how big they want the government to be. Aside from Social Security and Medicare entitlements, these are the largest parts of government spending.

And of course, the system mind propaganda media outlets aren't going to tell us what the numbers are. It turns out that armies, war-making, spy agencies, the Pentagon — all institutions neoconservatives hold dear, in addition to entitlements like Social Security and Medicare — are almost all of government expenditures, about 85%. What's left is called discretionary spending. Even if we cut out every penny of discretionary spending in recent budgets, no EPA, no drug-testing by the FDA, no health research, no money for vets, no courts, which is impossible to do, we would still have a big deficit. Bush's last budget was about half trillion dollars in deficit. Let's say we give these neoconservatives a real knife and let them cut out *half* of all discretionary spending. We would still have a fifth trillion dollar deficit. If one of your principles is small government, you are not going to cheerlead increases in the parts of the government that are the largest components.

I want to bring out an important historical point about size of government. During colonial times and before the Civil War, the size of government at all levels was miniscule. Ironically it was *conservatives* like Alexander Hamilton who were worried that the government had too little power to govern a growing country. After WWII and the economic expansion of the '50s and '60s, again there was very little growth in government. What periods of stability in the size of government have in common is that there was some semblance of Democratic Capitalism. What got the Federal government to grow were *abuses* due to Economic Socialism. This began right after the Civil War when great fortunes were used to buy and sell political actors like sacks of potatoes. This led to massive abuses: lack of education and nutrition for children, starvation wages, unsafe working conditions, health problems. This motivated ordinary people to join liberal causes to remedy these growing problems, which could be remedied only through stronger government.

As the postwar period shows, *you don't need big government to enforce the rules of the game.* You need big government to remedy *abuses* stemming from Economic Socialism having economic players in bed with the government. The EPA is a perfect example. It takes far less manpower and money for the EPA to *enforce* rules for the environment than it does to *clean* up sites once they are poisoned by polluters making their own rules. It would have taken very little resources to get after the blood supply when AIDS first hit the US in the 1980s. But Reagan, doing nothing about it for almost two years, incurred hundreds of millions of dollars of *big government* costs to treat the many cases of AIDS that had unnecessarily spread because of a contaminated public blood supply.

The basic reason neoconservatives are always howling against big government is not they are against big government per se. What they want is for the parts of the government that maintain and enforce the rules of the economic game to be miniscule. And the motivation for this is so that with no constraints on large economic nodes, they can collectivize to their hearts content, providing the bigness and power the neoconservative needs for his identity. Historically the size of government increased most under Reagan and then baby Bush, not only to make unnecessary and unconstitutional wars but to protect against the terrorism that these wars inspired.

Another role of big brother government is monitoring the people to make sure their thinking is in line with the system's needs. The way to assure that is to watch everyone. But this requires big brother government leading to National Socialism exactly the way it is in China, the neoconservative's ideal society. In July, 2010, the Washington Post tried to do a study of the ever-growing government agencies involved in so-called intelligence. They found hundreds of different intelligence agencies, employing thousands of people, spending billions of dollars. But the reporters could find very little detail as to exactly what these agencies are doing. This is exactly Big Brother George Orwell was talking about in his famous book, *1984*. Neoconservatives love this because it creates more entities with power and control to identify with and the spending that goes with it.

Conservatives like to brag about their principles, which are supposed to be honest government, balanced budgets and *small government* no less. But we had Ronald Reagan who was up to his neck in government malfeasance with the Iran-contra scandal. There wasn't one year out of Reagan's 8 years in office that he didn't increase the size of government with massive deficits. Then along comes Bush who engages in massive government lying to get us into Iraq who also increased the size of government every year he was in office and stepped up the deficits to a *third* of a trillion a year as compared to Reagan's fifth of a trillion.

The bottom line is while neoconservative propagandists howl about big government, their buddies in power will invariably vote for the biggest possible Economic Socialist government. The reason is that the only way the neoconservative can drum up big wars, big bombs, big killings, big invasions, and big control of our private lives is through big brother government.

30.12 NEOCONSERVATISM AND ANTI-CAPITALISM

We can tie together many of the facts and events we have discussed into a general theme. The neoconservative system mind is the arch enemy of Democratic Capitalism because this form of government is antithetical to the needs of the neoconservative mental makeup, which needs power and bigness to identify with. In order to enable a middle class able to clear markets, Capitalism demands a reasonable share of income to the middle class. And in order to maintain competition in the marketplace to insure the best products for the least price, Capitalism needs a political system designing the rules of the economic game that prevents the collectivization and agglomeration of businesses into these huge mega-conglomerates that are "too big to fail". Without the power and bigness of such collectives, the neoconservative has nothing with sufficient power and bigness to identify with and down the drain goes his sex life.

These facts are amply illustrated in the reaction to both Roosevelt and Ronald Reagan by the neoconservative mind. Conservatives all through the Roosevelt years mounted the most insidious attack on Roosevelt in the history of the presidency. They called him every name in the books — 'communist', 'socialist', 'traitor', etc. And yet the core of the Roosevelt agenda was the essence of Democratic Capitalism. However, when Ronald Reagan brought back the same Economic Socialism that had prevailed since the Civil War, neoconservatives wanted to carve his face into the side of a mountain. Now, Reagan wasn't any worse than the Republicans who held the White House for most of the years after the Civil War until Roosevelt. However, during this period, the country's political system was unprepared for the power and money accumulated by the Robber Barons. So the Economic Socialism they engendered took the political system by surprise.

However, Reagan was a different story. He was in a position to see that for the first time since the Civil War, Roosevelt had created a middle class prosperous enough to sustain viable Capitalism with low unemployment, rapidly rising living standards, and no deficits. But Reagan's Economic Socialism deliberately took all means to destroy the Capitalism Roosevelt had brought back. He mounted a massive attack on the middle class by raising their taxes and suppressing their wages. He put the anti-trust division to sleep and encouraged the collectivization in industry. He drove a quarter million small farms out of business, and he began the takeover of the economy by the financial services industry in bed with political actors. And yet neoconservatives ignore Dwight Eisenhower and lionize their hero Ronald Reagan. Eisenhower was part of the post-war blossoming of Democratic Capitalism that had proven itself capable of a growing prosperous economy. Not only do they not like Eisenhower, but they labeled him a Communist sympathizer. Capitalism requires a balanced economy. This is unacceptable to the neoconservative inner brain. He needs massive power and dominance. And this is why he turned his back on Democratic Capitalism and created Ronald Reagan out of a block of wood just like Pinocchio, who proceeded to promote Economic Socialism that gave the neoconservative the power and wealth he needs to identify with.

30.13 The New Imperialism

The neoconservative system mind never goes to sleep and it prepares a future that meets all of its needs, which means continuous war. In fact, there's a neoconservative think-tank called The Project for the New American Century. The new century is going to be an American one, you see. They churned out a paper called *Rebuilding America's Defenses*, which presses for more military bases from which to project more *power*, (they don't even bother to hide the fact that it's power they're idolizing) in case we need to bring about more "regime change". 'Regime change' is the new code work for 'invade, conquer and kill'. This whole game plan is a recipe for a lawless world as we discussed in Sect. 27.4. Even in the old days of British imperialism, what good did it do for the vast majority of the English people? Of course, you might say that a percentage of them got some psychological gratification identifying with an all-powerful king who could send armies all over the world to invade, conquer, and kill. But what about their economic lives? Even Adam Smith in the late 1700s saw that imperialism was overall a losing proposition: "Such colonies, therefore, have been a source of expenses, not of revenue, to their respective mother countries." This is why the neoconservative hates everything Adam Smith stood for.

What most people don't realize is that on the eve of WWII and after 300 years of imperialism and the killing of millions and theft of huge quantities of natural resources, the vast majority of the English people were still dirt poor. All the death and destruction in countries conquered by the British in their long age of imperialism benefited perhaps a few at the top. The rest got nothing but dead and maimed relatives from these conquests and an impoverished economic life.

And what will the new imperialism envisioned by the neoconservative system mind do for the vast majority of Americans? We can see already, Iraq has cost 4 thousand dead young men, another 40 thousand severely wounded, many with handicaps the rest of their lives, and about a trillion dollars in treasure. All this destruction, all the wasted lives, and all the wasted resources, all to supply about 10% of the population who desperately needs an all-powerful king to identify with. At least the British aristocracy was able to conquer and control many countries they invaded. They got some slave labor out of it. The new imperialism envisioned by the neoconservative system mind won't get this much.

The Chinese are smart. They watch the US invade developing countries to keep up the war on terrorism, waste hundreds of thousands of lives, trillions in costs, and when we're done, they send in a little Chinese guy with a ballpoint pen who signs a contract to develop their resources that enables them to benefit billions — all without costing a single Chinese life nor one cent of their money. This is happening already. The American people will be stuck with lots of dead young men, lots of mentally handicapped vets, lots of national debt and no oil. But these results are of no concern to the neoconservative agenda which is to establish National Socialism in the US before considering rational foreign policy.

[1] Alterman, E., The Washington Post Problem. *Tha Nation*, July 16, '12, p. 15

[2] TRB, "Backward". *The New Republic*, July 22, p. 6

[3] Chait, J.; "Formula one". *The New Republic*, Jan. 22, '01.

[4] Goldsmith, Jack; "The Accountable Presidency". *The New Republic*, Feb. 18, '10. p.33

[5] Ibid. p. 34

[6] Ibid. p. 35

[7] Foner, Iric; "Lincoln's anti-war Record". *The Nation*, Mar. 12, '07

[8] Rapoport, Any, "No Funds Left Behind". *The American Prospect*, Mar. '12

[9] Leras, Jackson. *Rebirth of a Nation*, Harpers.

[10] "The Day of the Hunter", Louis Begley, Review of *Simon Weisenthal* by Tom Segev; *The New York Review of Books NTR*, Dec. 8, '11

[11] Eviatar, Daphne; "In Cold Blood". *The Nation*, Feb. 21, '05

[12] Dalryimple, William, "Plain Tales from British India"., Apr. 26. '10. p. 47McC

[13] *The Economist*, Aug. 21, '10, p. 14

[14] *The Economist*, Oct. 17, '09, p. 15

[15] Ibid. p. 15

[16] Nathanel Popper, "A conscious Pariah", *The Nation*, Apr. 19, '10, p. 25

[17] Ibid. p. 32.

[18] Ibid. p. 30.

[19] Craig, Gordon; "Keeping Germany Fat". *New York Review of Books*, Sept. 20, '01, p. 78

[20] Black, Edwin; *IBM and the Holocaust*. Crown Press

[21] "Northern Exposure", *The New Republic*, Oct. 22, '08, p. 10

[22] "A continent on the Move". *The Economist*, May 6, '00, p. 25

CHAPTER 31

Russia And The System Mind

——

When you look over history, if there's one country that you have to feel most sorry for, it might be Russia. It's not that the worst things in the world have happened in Russia, but from the point of view of *potential*, Russia is a pretty sad country. Russia accrued an enormous land mass, unlimited resources, an intelligent population, and an exposure to the thinking and culture of both east and west. Why has their history been so depressing?

The first question to ask is why did Russia evolve a form of feudalism that was so severe as compared to both the feudal systems in the west and the east? We sketched a brief history of Muslim economic development in Ch. 26. The rest of the world in Africa and the Americas remained pretty much tribal throughout most of its history. This leaves only one major area to account for — Russia and Eastern Europe. Russia, because of its geography, basically fell between the cracks. In terms of the needs of a developing economy, Russia was just in an unlucky geographic position. Asian feudalism didn't spread into Russia probably because of the Himalaya mountains. But most importantly, European feudalism never spread into Russia because the Holy Roman Empire went in a north*west* direction towards England and bypassed Russia. This had important ramifications.

Now in the 1300s and 1400s, a small merchant class emerged in both Russia and Europe. But it was pretty much a local merchant class in all regions, trading mostly through barter. The upward mobility made possible by this new class insured some degree of dignity to the peasant classes even in Eastern Europe and Russia. In Southern Europe, the brisk increase in trade and the rise of a vibrant merchant class caused a good deal of urbanization. By providing an alternative to feudal life for Southern European peasants, the feudal aristocracy had to loosen its domination of the peasant class.

Before the Commercial Revolution in the 1300s, there had been some serfdom even in Western Europe. But because Russia was less populated and less organized, Russian peasants might have not been in any worse status than in Western Europe. The start of Commercial Revolution involved mostly local trade all over Europe in the 1300s. But as we discussed in Sect. 23.9, when trade over longer distances evolved in the 1400s, the Western European merchant class had tools inherited from the Feudal ethic supported by the Church, like the concept of honor and trust that enabled them to flourish. They began to push for rights and freedoms. They were joined by other classes of the Bourgeoisie in the growing cities of Europe. Peasants were able to derive some benefits from this movement and escape from the surfdom of the Dark Ages.

Also, Western Europe had a higher density of people and their kings had a bigger population of people to make wars with. The kings needed finance for their wars and had to rely on the merchant class and their bankers. Also, needing the allegiance of the peasant class to do their fighting, kings often sided with the merchant class or the peasants to keep the aristocracy in check.

However, the lack of moral code along with the fact that Eastern Europe and Russia are more land-locked meant that Russia did not evolve an important international merchant class who would petition for national institutions like property rights, a national system of money and banking, basic rights and freedoms, and parliaments as occurred in Western Europe. However, Russia was close enough to developments in Europe, Asia and the Muslim world to absorb some degree of technological advancement, commercialism and nation building which created a quite well organized and articulated hierarchy.

So when local trade started in the 1300s, the economic development that ensued enabled the nobility in Russia to organize a hierarchy with no guiding ethos of the rule of law and the feudal ethic. As the Commercial Revolution continued in the 1400s with trade over longer distances, there wasn't a feudal ethic that would create a vibrant international merchant class. And without a flourishing merchant class and growing urban trade centers, the Eastern Church was never nudged in the direction of greater human rights and dignity as in the Western Church. As a result, peasants in Eastern Europe and Russia had neither a powerful Church nor a growing economic force in society to hook their wagon to. Thus, without the strong moral code of Western European feudalism, and without a countervailing force of economically stronger tsars who might have defended the peasantry, the aristocracy in Russia was able to organize and impose a more brutal form of feudalism called serfdom. And to top it off, the merchant class in Russia never achieved the economic or political power to bring off a Reformation or Renaissance that might have helped the lower orders.

So whereas peasants in Western Europe were gaining some status and privileges, peasants in Eastern Europe were being enserfed. English peasants might even appear in court which, even though totally rigged in favor of the "better" classes, was still an institution with some degree of recognition of humanity of all individuals. Arbitrary violence against the peasants could reduce the status and esteem of the lord of the manor. This was not the case in Russia. A Russian nobleman could kill a serf almost at will with no repercussions at all. Without a feudal ethic and with a weak Church, the tsars and nobility were able to maintain a tight control over society and prevented the evolution of modern institutions and were able to keep the serf class leading miserable depraved lives pretty close to slavery. One Russian nobleman owned 300,000 serfs, and some Russian tsars were the worst tyrants in all of Europe. This explains modern horror stories. We've all seen vampire and wolf-man movies. These stories usually have their source in eastern European folklore. There would be a lord or some aristocrat who would go crazy and start killing people in a secret way. Nothing could be done about it. It was the terrorism of the times. The Dracula story probably originated around some Count in eastern Europe who extracted people's blood.

Their total dominance and lack of constraints created a basically lawless aristocracy in Russia. Courts dispensed very little justice. When a small amount of economic advancement occurred after the Commercial Revolution, lawlessness turned into corruption at all levels of society, including at the national level with totally tyrannical tsars. In fact, the status of serfs even worsened in later centuries until as late as the 1800s, Alexander II finally abolished serfdom.

Russia, especially is vulnerable to authoritarianism because that is pretty much all it has ever seen. Putin is gradually establishing himself as a new tsar, and yet he has the overwhelming support of the Russian people. Some of the former Soviet satellites are having similar problems. This momentum vector has continued to the present day. *The Economist*, commenting on Russian society in the '90s, says: "The rich and powerful are above the law". [1] One index of corruption puts Russia at 147 out of 180 countries, worse than Bangladesh.

There were reformers at times in Russian history like Peter the Great and Catherine the Great, but this was not enough to change the *momentum* vector that Russian society had built up over hundreds of years. Then, just as modern economic developments might have pushed Russia in a European direction, along came another piece of bad luck. Lenin brought off his Communist Revolution in 1917, which cleared the way for a new tsar to emerge that was just as oppressive and absolute as previous tsars. And he had the intellectual backing of Karl Marx in forming an even more brutal dictatorship.

But the important point we must stress is that neither Capitalism nor Communism comes with its own ethic. In Western Europe, Capitalism was built on the moral and ethical foundation it inherited from its feudal past. Communism in Russia, even if by some miracle was a workable economic system, had no feudal foundation to build on. The result was that the momentum of corruption and lawlessness at the top built up over hundreds of years of serfdom continued right into the communist period. If communism had a chance of success anywhere in the world, the last place for it would be Russia. The Protestant countries in Northern Europe with a strong ethic are able to absorb a small degree of socialism. It can work there only because of their feudal past and its strong moral code.

The purpose of this chapter is to provide another illustration of the working of the system mind both in Russia and the US as illustrated by events in Russia starting after WWII until the final the Russian transition of the 1990s. The reason we are pointing out Russia as an example of a system mind is that the transition to a market economy in Russia created a system mind.

After Stalin died, there was renewed optimism that perhaps Communism could work in the Soviet Union especially with new leaders like Krushchev. This renewed optimism enabled the Soviet Union to stumble along with a certain degree of economic expansion. They even thought they were going to surpass the west. And interesting phenomenon was that it was in the interest of the American system mind to greatly exaggerate the power, especially the economic power, of the Soviet Union after WWII. In fact, what might have kept the Soviet system going was that they were hearing from the US how powerful they were. This might have helped paper over the great cracks in their Communist economic system as time went along. Also, the Marxist program of free health care, free education and a job for everyone probably took the revolutionary fervor out of the Russian population.

Just when their system might have collapsed, there was the oil shortage of the 1970s which greatly benefited them. However, two things happened in the '80s that doomed the Communist system. The price of oil dropped, and they got into a calamitous war in Afghanistan. The dent in the Russian economy caused by loss of oil revenues, and the total inability to control their war in Afghanistan exposed their economy as basically weak. And just like many animals, dogs for example, when they sense weakness, they attack. With a weakened Russia, eastern European countries accelerated their moves away from Soviet dominance. This started with the Solidarity movement in Poland and spread to the rest of Eastern Europe. Even though they maintained Communist systems, they all went their own way in its application. Some of them introduced liberal reforms and market mechanisms. A weak Soviet economy was powerless to do anything about it, and Mikhail Gorbachev gradually melded from an emperor over an East European empire to pretty much a political consultant.

Neoconservatives give Ronald Reagan credit for ending Communism in the Soviet Union and Eastern Europe by a military build in the US. Neoconservatives love to think their murderous impulses bring about wonderful results. This is simply part of the glorification of Reagan by the system mind for cutting their taxes. This is clearly not the case, because while Reagan was building up arms and saber rattling, there was no reform in the Soviet Union. They had been able to keep up their end of the nuclear threat every step of the way for 35 years after WWII.

It was in Reagan's *second* term that his Alzheimer's began to bottle up energy in the bottom of his brain, and fortunately for mankind, in the fear areas. Reagan grew increasingly fearful of a nuclear exchange. He grew warmer towards Gorbachev and talks grew more frequent. For all we know, they might have talked on the phone every other night like a new girlfriend. It was then that Gorbachev was able to take his mind off military matters and turn attention towards reforming the Communist system. But things got out of hand and Yeltzin sent Russia in a new direction. It was Reagan's *withdrawal* of military threats that enabled Gorbachev to initiate measures that led to the end of Communism, *not* Reagan's militarism or belligerence. Because he cut taxes on these media whores who bring us reality, there are more lies surrounding Reagan than any other American in history.

On the other hand, Reagan provided a very spirited leadership for dissidents and reformers all over the Communist block and inspiration to continue their work towards either reforming Communism or preferably getting rid of it altogether. Reagan had the perfect mix of subtle threats, sympathy for the people of the Soviet empire, inspiration that things could change, while yet maintaining a cordial and sympathetic relationship with Gorbachev. Reagan was confident he could bring about the end of Communism with these talents without directly intervening militarily anywhere in Europe. And he was right. This was probably Reagan's finest initiative. Reagan probably saved hundreds of thousand lives in the transition from Communism all over the Communist block. Can you imagine the carnage that would have ensued if the Bush-Cheney team had been in power at this time?

By the late 1980s, the situation in the Soviet Union was dire. Of course, many in the west give Gorbachev credit for dismantling Communism in Russia. This was not the case at all. What he tried to do with perestroika (restructuring) and glasnost (transparency) was to *reform* the Communist system so that it would work more effectively. The story of Gorbachev is one of the most interesting in history. It never happens that a man who worms his way up a power ladder in a tribal or developing nation ever has any idea as to how to bring about modern civil society and a working economy. Gorbachev was a lonely figure in history with a small degree of decency who managed to change course for the better.

But he was in effect trying to change a thousand-year momentum vector that had completely institutionalized massive corruption. What is important to point out is that *Communism does not create an effective system mind.* And this is why it cannot work anywhere but in a tiny society. All information flows are downward from central planners. There are no markets and this precludes any flows of information between important nodes of the economy. In effect, Gorbachev was trying to create an effective Communist system mind by adding flows of information between nodes. But it was too late. He couldn't buck the thousand-year momentum vector of corruption that precluded such a course.

What is really interesting in studying this period is that while Gorbachev was trying to dismantle the top-down system of information flows under the Communist system, there wasn't any structure in the economy for new flows to be encouraged. With the weakening of Communist authoritarian flows, numerous groups coalesced that were isolated economically and politically from the rest of society. There were anti-nomenklatura groups, anti-bureaucrats, free-marketeers, populists, democrats, intelligentsia, nationalists, and the old Communists, all forming parties, blocs, and alliances, but not forming a cohesive inter-communicating system. No discernable self-perpetuating system mind was possible, except possibly a tiny one centered on the nomanklatura. All of this only confused and bewildered the Russian people who became ripe for some form of authoritarianism. And even though many of Gorbachev's reforms were laudable, they were viewed by opponents and many of the Russian people as a sign of weakness. Again, living creatures including groups, move in for the kill when they detect weakness.

One of the least appreciated phenomenon of the post-war period was that there was one tenuous system mind in Russia that increased in importance as time went on, and Peter Reddaway and Dmitri Glinski do stress this factor. It was the Russian Mafia.[2] This mafia operated according to many free-market concepts, like property, contracts, and markets, etc. However, even though they had their own rules, they were not put into place by legitimate government; so they were not part of the system and were considered bad guys. The only difference between them and the later oligarchs was that the latter *did* attach themselves to and later effectively took over the direction of the recognized government.

Reddaway and Glinsky point out that the Russian mafia was really the outgrowth of a kind of populism with a sprinkle of anti-authoritarianism that had always been present in Russian society during its period of tsar serfdom. It continued under the Communist system, and was in place all during the period we're considering: "... the Mafiya was the most organized expression of the anarchic-libertarian spirit in Russian history".[3] I don't think these are the best choice of words. The kind of populism prevalent in Russian history was not really anarchic because it was never specifically anti-government. Also libertarianism is a pretty articulate political philosophy, and I don't think Mafiya members were very much concerned with political theory. A better characterization would be gangster Corporate Socialism. But the important point is that when Russia's version of Economic Socialism came into being, the mafia could fit right in to the new order.

By 1989, things were falling apart fast. The economy was collapsing, riots were breaking out all over Russia, and the Soviet empire was falling apart with many of their own republics itching to break away. The Berlin Wall in East Germany was torn down, and people from all over Eastern Europe were streaming westward. Gorbachev tried for the next few years to hold things together, but it was hopeless. In 1991, he was pushed aside by an upstart from the Communist party, Boris Yeltzin. With all other parties in somewhat disarray, Yeltzin stole the show from Gorbachev and won the election of June, '91. In Yeltzin, there was a bit of an appeal to all points of view: nationalism, democracy, liberalism, conservatism, authoritarianism, etc. He was a Russian Ronald Reagan whose words probably had little meaning even to himself.

There was a key moment in Russian history in 1991, when a group of hard-line Communists from the old guard tried to bring off a coup. Recognizing a real con artist like Ronald Reagan who was nothing but a big sack of one-line cliché's, the Bush administration favored Yeltzin. Finally, in a desperation move, the hard-line nationalists formed a line of tanks leading to the Parliament building in Moscow. In what looked like the ballsiest move of the 20th century, Yeltzin got atop one of the tanks and stared them down, declaring the coup illegal. After this showdown, Russia would be in the hands of Boris Yeltzin.

What happened next has mystified most historians and commentators of the Russian transition. Yeltzin got together with leaders of the nomenklatura and other followers and totally dismantled the Soviet Union. Now why would an authoritarian do such a thing — make his empire smaller. I have a not-so-informed theory about this. Even though the system mind around Yeltzin was very weak, probably the last thing it wanted was real democracy. Since political inputs from the periphery of the Union might not be controllable and might try to insert some democracy into the evolving state of affairs, Yeltzin and the system mind around him chopped off these potential democratic threats in the bud. The highest priority of a system mind is self-perpetuation. And since the system mind around any kind of market economy revolves around its most powerful nodes, the system's direction was towards National Socialism in which the leading nodes own and control as much wealth and power as possible just as in the US. This is the path Yeltzin and the evolving system mind took during the next 10 years in Russia and is continuing today. As we shall explain presently, this is exactly what US policy towards Russia encouraged.

Now, there was a group of young men, mostly economists, led by a young man named Yegor Gaidar, known as the "young reformers". They held symposiums and conferences, and wrote literature as to what Russia needed. They thought of themselves as idealists, which they were on paper and in public pronouncements. But behind the scenes, throughout the '90s, many of them were making a fast buck allied with various kinds of currency speculators and black marketeers.

The truth of the matter is that Yeltzin hadn't the vaguest idea of how to proceed. And as happens over and over in history, the people who rise to the top in revolutionary situations are people who understand only one thing: how to manipulate and intrigue their way to raw naked power. This was Yeltzin to a tee. He was just an old semi-educated Communist party hack with a low animal cunning. Just like Ronald Reagan, he was the perfect man for the incipient system mind that would evolve. He outlawed the Communist Party because it was organized and he dismantled the Union in order to chop away any democratic threats. Yeltzin maintained power exactly like Reagan: with a bunch of clichés and street slogans with absolutely no understanding or comprehension. And right on schedule, what this did in effect was pave the way towards National Socialism which is exactly what Russia wound up with.

In my opinion, the genius of Boris Yeltzin lay in his ability to straddle and capture both the populist anti-government sentiment that had always been present in Russian society but was now in disarray, *and* the familiarity and acceptance by these same Russian people of a capo — a tsar who could take control of things, clean up the messy political picture and bring back stability. But it was apparent that Yeltzin had very little idea what economics was all about and had no real plan to move the economy forward. And along with many of the young reformers, he was the perfect piece of the puzzle for an evolving system mind.

At the beginning of 1992, Gaidar was appointed to Yeltzin's cabinet. In the following years, Gaidar would alternate between a sincere individual patriotic desire to improve his country, and a cog in the growing system mind. The views of the young reformers were shaped by what they learned studying western economists who had gotten famous pimping for the system. These included people like Milton Friedman and von Hayek, who, along with Karl Marx, were part of a long tradition among some intelligentsia that the only things that exists are ideas and theories. This is why supply-side theorists like Friedman were never concerned about the destructive effects of their theories on practical affairs, nor even whether they were right or wrong in practice. As long as they got famous and their theories accepted by the powerful nodes in the economy, that was proof enough of the validity of their theories. In Latin America, Friedman's theories backed dictatorship, torture and killings and still most often eventuated in disastrous economic results. But when torture and murder is perpetuated by a dictatorial National Socialist regime, the system mind propaganda outlets tell us "they're on their way to democracy".

In my opinion, Friedman and Hayek were the leading advocates of Economic Socialism whose theories were the perfect formula for the road to National Socialism. They passed themselves off as economists, which is a joke. Friedman was rarely right about anything, not employment, not the money supply, not the banking system, and certainly not policies for developing countries. But due to the American Constitution and Roosevelt's Capitalism after WWII, progress along the path to National Socialism in the US was slow. However, with no momentum vector of this sort in Russia and no working Capitalist institutions, the growing system mind in Russian was free to take a much quicker path towards National Socialism.

With the parties, blocs, and fronts that had a democratic, populist, and progressive bent being in disarray, Yeltzin was able to take a more authoritarian course and institute pretty much what the young reformers wanted. Gaidar instituted what was called "shock therapy", which would be a quick jump to Capitalism that might involve some short-term pain, but would bring about a Capitalist utopia down the line. Anyone with an ounce of knowledge of complex organic systems realizes that these kinds of systems cannot *jump* to an entirely different structure in a discontinuous way without dying. What should have happened in the '90s was a slow transition with Capitalist institutions gradually *replacing* Communist institutions. This is what a living organism does. If we, as persons, change the direction of our lives, our bodies don't kill off all its cells and grow new cells on the spot with a new direction. Our bodies gradually, day by day, *replace* individual dying cells with new ones so that the function of all the body's organs can continue without break-down or loss of function.

This is where the American system mind came into play. A whole army of advisors, investment bankers, and economists sprang to life in the US who were going to save Russian Capitalism. Sincere Russian leaders were too dazzled by the economic success of the US to see that this army of helpers wasn't going to send Russia down a path of economic success that would compete with the US. What they would do was to *use* the Russian nation as a national guinea pig to spearhead a drive towards National Socialism which would be *pushed* from behind by the neoconservative system mind in the US, and *pulled* from ahead by events in Russia. Every single step taken by American advisors would be in this direction. (The same thing has been going on in our foreign policy towards China.)

The first signs of inspiration coming from Economic Socialists of the Friedman Chicago school was the deregulation of prices of many commodities and goods and services. This created a massive hyper-inflationary spiral. Prices rose over a *thousand* percent in the first year. This wiped out the savings of most Russians, so that there was less money for invest-ment in new small businesses and even less for Consumption. This caused a flight of capital, as profits from what businesses left were put in foreign banks as a hedge against inflation. When large firms of the Communist era were privatized, there would be a clear path for the nomenklatura and an oligarchy getting its hands on most of the Russian economy. They, in turn, would have the financial power to rig the rules in their favor — a perfect blueprint for National Socialism. You'd have to be either crooked or stupid (or both) not to see the effects of this; and Friedmanites are not stupid. Reddaway says: "…by the 1990s, conditions were ripe for the [professional class] to lead the entire country in turning away from the Byzantine and autocratic past and embracing the best the west had to offer. Shock therapy destroyed this moment…".[4*]

The most essential core ingredient for viable Capitalism is a consuming class prosperous enough to clear markets: *an attack on the consuming middle class is an attack on Capitalism itself.* Roosevelt had created a prosperous middle class in the US and saved Capitalism. But the elimination of such a middle class in Russia was exactly what the international community led by the US was prescribing for Russia. This was the formula initiated by Ronald Reagan and continued under George Bush. Whatever system mind was evolving in Russia at the time was being encouraged and guided by droppings from neoconservatives like Milton Friedman who were part of the *American* system mind. All diplomatic, economic and political pressure from the Bush administration, international institutions like the Group of 7 and the IMF (International Mutha-Fuckers), was directed towards destroying Russia's incipient middle class — a sure-fire path towards a crippling National Socialism. As a result, the Russian system mind took the same direction as it had in the US, only in a more exaggerated form.

An important voluminous report was commissioned by the G-7 calling on the work of all international development organizations — the IMF, the World Bank, The Organization of Economic Cooperation and Development, etc. — strongly opposing "…privatization measures that would give large numbers of citizen's a real stake in ownership…",[5] in addition to demanding the removal of any monetary and price restrictions. I want someone to explain to me how such a blatantly self-interested piece of crap with obvious destructive effects on real democratic Capitalism in Russia, contradicting the most basic principles of Econ. 101 — how you explain all this without the concept of a system mind. Even the mildest independent suggestions from various Russian groups that deviated in the slightest from the party line were met with threats from the western international community of "economists" to deny financial support to Russia.

The obvious results of all this free advice to the Russians, of course, was that real income of Russian workers was cut in half in '92. Again, with neoconservative theory stuffed into their brains coming from the US, they didn't seem to worry about the fact that you're not going to get a viable Capitalism if you starve the average Russian of income to clear markets. This important initial move put Russia on a collision course with disaster that could not be averted no matter what later policy was. These initiatives left Russian oligarchs a clear path towards ownership of the Russian economy on the road towards National Socialism. Historians of the period, Chrystia Freeland and Peter Reddaway, don't stress this point sufficiently.

---

* Reddaway calls the professional class the middle class, which most writers do. But even though there wasn't much of a real middle class in Russia at the time, I think we should reserve the name 'middle class' to the class between the working class and professional class, as we do in the US.

Opposition to Yeltzin all through this period consisted of a myriad of political parties, blocs, and alliances criss-crossing one another in a panoply of theories, political agendas, and special interests. Nodes of the system were collapsing and communication between nodes became sporadic. There was never a strong unifying theme that could coalesce everyone into a viable political opposition. And Yeltzin was good at playing one group off against another. Reddaway and Glinsky criticize the quality of opposition to Yeltzin all through the '90s as fragmented, disorganized, sometimes corrupt, showing its "moral and ideological decay". In my opinion, this is a bit unfair. Instead of unifying on the basic premises of pure Capitalism, liberals have for a hundred years had their brains paralyzed by the mind-numbing crap peddled by Karl Marx from whom they learned that Capitalism was the enemy. So they too have never had a unifying theory to get behind. The result is they never win power on their own steam. It is only when conservatives get greedy and collapse the system that liberals are elected to patch the system back up to the howls of conservatives who caused the collapse.

In Russia in the following months, it became apparent that the young reformers had relied too much on economic theory. They needed a *political* thrust to institute further measures. They started a political party called Russia's Choice led by a guy named Anatoly Chubais, who was the political organizer the Yeltzin regime needed. Chubais was an archetypical in-your-face neoliberal as we described in Ch. 28. His view was that if Russia was going to become a truly Capitalist country, you have to have as many Capitalists as possible. After all, you could call Communism a form of Capitalism too if you stretch the definition: the Communist party in Russia was simply one big corporation.

Chubais's goal was to privatize the Russian economy and get all of its productive entities into as many private hands as possible. This was a noble motive. But he too jumped on the shock therapy bandwagon, which shows that among these neoliberal types, the theory is more important than the reality. How did he think he could get Russia's businesses into as many private hands as possible when the team of reformers he was associating with was destroying money in these very private hands.

In 1992, a voucher program was instituted. The Russian people could buy vouchers and use them to buy stock in Russian firms. This had the added attraction of bringing in much-needed revenue to the government. The problem was that inflation was rapidly evaporating the savings of the average Russian. Only the rich, foreign investors, the mafia, and the nomenklatura who had been running these firms under the Soviet system had enough money to buy significant chunks of stock in various companies.

But here again, Russia was soaked in hundreds of years of corruption that had built up an enormous momentum vector. It was magnified by the Communist system whose economic directors in industry got by through lying, cheating, and covering-up how their firms were really being run. So when Russian businesses were privatized, it became apparent that the nomenklatura had been completely mismanaging their businesses and using them mostly for private gain. Businesses often refused to pay taxes and debts to other businesses. It was a snow-balling effect that sent most businesses reeling. Many businesses didn't even have the money to pay their workers, which inspired the Russian joke: "We pretend to work and they pretend to pay us". (There's a better joke about Communism as compared to Capitalism: Capitalism is a system in which man is exploited by man; whereas under Communism, it's the exact opposite.) Here again we find that a discontinuous jump to privatization just about killed these firms. The net result was that much of the money Russian people invested in businesses, shriveled away.

There *were* some businesses that were succeeding however. But the problem there was that the nomenklatura from the old Soviet system was in a position to grab these businesses. Even though workers in these companies could use their vouchers to buy stock, they couldn't hold on to them. Most businesses were failing and there was high unemployment. So directors even of successful businesses were able to keep wages very low because workers were lucky to have any job. So gradually, by offering workers special foods or cigarettes or vodka or whatever, they would be tempted to sell their stock to the director. Often, workers sold their stock just to survive. Of course, often the directors got the money for these perks by stealing from the company itself since there was very little regulation. Also, western investors were in a perfect position to buy up stocks of Russian companies because they better understood how to judge their future viability. All kinds of fast-buck operators moved in to steal anything valuable from naïve Russian workers. The average Russian either got stuck with worthless stock or found himself getting conned out of stock that turned out to be highly valuable later on. A privatization plan would only work if it was detailed, well thought out, and ideally motivated. You're not going to get anything of the sort from the one-liner droppings of the Milton Friedman Chicago school.

Gradually, most of the stock in successful businesses fell into the new class of owners. Reddaway says, "Most Russians got little or nothing for their vouchers, and the promised 'peoples capitalism' never materialized".[6] A study showed that about "two thirds of the medium-and large-sized Russian companies had ended up in the control of their old managers after privatization."[7] Since the nomenklatura had been part of the political system under Communism, they, along with the rising oligarchs, were in a perfect position to be in bed with the new political system. This is exactly the core of Corporate Socialism, which became the basis for a new system mind and the engine of Yeltzin's political bandwagon throughout the '90s.

What we should notice in this regard, is that when it comes to the interests of the ordinary Russian, he must succumb to the iron laws of the market and its crushing meritocracy. However, when it came to the elites from the Communist era who mismanaged many large companies, instead of a pruning process occurring as under real Capitalism to weed out corrupt managers, showing markets to these Bolsheviks is like showing a cross to Bela Lugosi. But there was another factor that *did* greatly expand the evolution of a real system mind, and it was not due to anyone's suspicious motives.

In the late '80s, a guy named Chernomyrdin (his last name is enough to identify) organized the oil and gas industry into a government company called Gazprom. Right off the bat, Chernomyrdin was appointed prime minister in 1992, and his buddy Vyakhirev was appointed head of Gazprom. Stocks in the company were divided between employees, investors and the government. This part was okay, but here again we have the standard model for Corporate Socialism: important government leaders in bed with heads of big companies.

After the dismantling of Communism in 1991, this one company was really the center of the Russian economy. It controlled 30% of the world's known gas reserves, it accounted for 8% of the entire GDP of the country and it supported about 6 million people.[8] As such, Gazprom became the model for all other resource extracting companies and the model for the coming National Socialism. But Gazprom was a natural resource company and taking advantage of the earth's farts is not like engaging in complex production techniques or even running distribution companies engaged in marketing strategies. So while the value of most Russian businesses was falling because of incompetence of non-market oriented executives from the Communist party, resource extraction was not hampered in this way.

Following Gazprom's lead, other companies got into the natural resource business called *geologies*. In its methods and status in the economy this was the core of a new system mind. Of course, American advisors and investors were drooling at these developments. This was the precise model in play in the American system. At first Gaidar and the young reformers were opposed to Gazprom's enormous power and its ties to the government. After all this is not really Capitalism. However, they too jumped on the Corporate Socialist bandwagon.

Other industries that don't require the absorption of technology into modern production methods nor complex systems of organization for production are banking, real estate, foreign trade, and communications. It is in these industries that fortunes were made by what become known as the oligarchs. We can name a few of them. Mikhail Friedman in foreign trade and oil; Vladimir Potanin in banking; Mikhail Khodorkovsky in business banking; Boris Berezovsky in communications, television and publishing; and Vladimir Gusinsky in publishing and television. All of these men became filthy rich because of their connections to high public officials in government especially Yeltzin. What is very interesting to me about this group is that a Russian word actually evolved to refer to the political influence, connections and communications between these new Economic Socialists (oligarchs) and the government: *blat*. This word could also be used to described the resulting National Socialist system mind.

At this time, Yeltzin and the young reformers were working at breakneck speed to privatize everything before the failure of their agenda became apparent to most Russians who might throw the bums out. The mood of the country was reflected in the mood of parliament, which was increasingly hostile to Yeltzin's agenda. So Yeltzin cut them off at the pass. He dissolved parliament in the fall of '93, which accrued even greater powers to the Yeltzin team in the Kremlin. With a weakened parliament, there was no check on the degree of collusion between the growing private sector lead by the oligarchs and the Kremlin. The government was increasingly incapable or carrying out its normal functions like controlling its expenses and collecting taxes. This was the perfect climate for a final leg in the journey which was outright National Socialism where leading economic elites pretty much control the agenda of the government. In few short years, Russia had taken the path that the US took following the Civil war culminating in almost complete control of our government by important economic nodes of the economy under the three Republican presidents in the 1920s. This resulted in the crash of 1929 and the subsequent Great Depression.

What Yeltsin's people were really creating was not Capitalism as an organic system with coherent rules, but a kind of *Frankenstein* monster. Peter Medvedev is one of the few commentators who really understands the organic nature of a producing economy.[9] Communism had built huge factories in Russia, and even though information flows were uneven and choppy because of the top-down organization of the economy, there was some semblance of a system mind. It was a very inefficient system, with no freedoms and so unacceptable for a modern advanced society like Russia, but it had some semblance of an organic system.

However, during the '80s under Gorbachev, many of the nodes of the economy were cut loose from the system, and shock therapy finished the job. Big factories were given more latitude in managing including prices and wages, which the nomenklatura used to enhance its own wealth and power. The banking system was also given more autonomy. Trade and imports was a growing sector not fully integrated in the Soviet system and controlled to a great extent by the mafia. Then there was the growth of the oligarchic sector of the economy involving resource extraction starting to make its own rules. You had small businesses totally unprotected and having to lay off workers. You had a shriveling consumer class losing jobs and savings. And you had government racking up huge debts unable to find a coherent set of rules for a privatized economy. Yeltsin and his young reformers, in effect was trying to sew all this back together into an organic whole. But all they got was *Frankenstein Capitalism* because parliament was unable to maintain the proper functions of government in its relation to the new status of economic entities. The oligarchic-nomenklatura system was increasingly able to dominate the economy, maintaining its power and growth by making its own rules. The rest, not being part of an organic whole, was slowly dying.

Many conservatives have claimed that you can't make progress in development without authoritarianism. They would point to Russian history in which reforms came about only under powerful tsars like Peter the Great, Alexander the Great and Catherine the great. In modern times there is Stalin, Hitler and Mao Zedong. Well, like any application of the laws of thermodynamics, you don't get something for nothing. These dictators may bring about more rapid modernization and industrialization, but it is at the expense of strengthening the momentum vector towards either Communism or National Socialism. Although economic development in all western countries took place under conditions of Economic Socialism, there was always enough democracy to patch the system back up after major collapses. And this is why the path towards National Socialism in the west has been relatively slow and has still not been completed.

However, other countries where modernization was brought off by dictators have yet to see even a momentary delay on the road to National Socialism. At present, China and Vietnam are right on schedule, notwithstanding the neoconservative apologetics for supporting these systems, especially China, as "on the road to democracy".* As we mentioned above, the cover headline of an issue of *The Economist* blared, "China's dash for freedom".[10] Tell that to the Tibetans. Don't you love the fantasy world of these neoconservative reptiles? In Russia, the very first moves of the young reformers, inspired by leaders of Economic Socialists in the US, were to put Russia on the fast track towards National Socialism and they too are right on schedule. Some of these same apologists thought that Putin would get rid of the oligarchs. Fat chance — only when they personally cross him.

With the Russian economy plummeting and Yeltsin's popularity right along with it, he decided to co-opt any possible coalescing of opposition in parliament. So he declared an illegal and unconstitutional emergency rule in April, '93. The American system mind reacted right on schedule by putting forth its leading propagandists in the American media to tell the American people that Yeltsin was the good guy and parliament was just a bunch of old commies. The truth, of course, is that Communists in parliament had *supported* most of Yeltsin's agenda from the start. The real opposition in parliament was led by people who were more interested in getting Russia on a democratic track than a Communist agenda. Peter Reddaway says, "...the deputies of the Congress...were broadly representative of Russian society at large with its... desire for justice..., while Boris Yeltsin's elitist entourage had very little in common with the majority of Russians." [11]

The American reaction led the way for all western governments to follow suit. The rationalizations were just sickening. Reddaway says, "Forced to choose between constitutional legality and shock therapy, the United States and its G-7 allies chose...shock therapy".[12] Promises of aid and loans started to flow in to Russia from western countries and all the international organizations, IMF, World Bank, etc. in support of the Yeltsin regime.

All during '92 and '93, the opposition continued in disarray and fragmentation as we have described above, unable to see that what Yeltsin and his IMF-American supporters were pushing had nothing to do with Capitalism. With unquestioning support of the international community led by the people working for Bill Clinton, Yeltsin moved gradually towards a real coup. When the American system mind saw that parliament had elements that questioned the fast-moving drive towards National Socialism, it moved to squelch parliament. The Clinton administration publicly encouraged Yeltsin to disband parliament and compared Yeltsin with Abe Lincoln, no less. The same people in the Clinton administration who worked to push an agenda that included support for Economic Socialists in the financial services industry, would later pop up under Barack Obama. And just as in Russia, this was accompanied in the US by support for apparatchiks in local government

---

* Notice that since we don't need Cuban business to buy our paper, you'll never hear these same conservatives bragging about Cuba being "on the road to democracy", even though it has the exact same system.

accompanied by neglect of the middle consuming classes who were losing jobs and income. This attack on Capitalism, of course, required the usual massive theft from the future to prop up demand, which the IMF was more than happy to arrange.

I personally think that Clinton was suspicious of Yeltzin. Clinton is a pretty smart guy. But the culture of Economic Socialism initiated by Ronald Reagan was so engrained and entrenched in society by the system mind propaganda outlets that Clinton was in no position to buck the trend. So, being the kind of Teddy bear he was, Clinton stayed on the same tracks Reagan laid down and supported Yeltzin. With the American system behind him, in Sept., '93, Yeltzin dissolved parliament, the Supreme Soviet impeached Yeltzin, and the battle was on.

By Oct. '93, there had been bitter disputes with parliament over legislation. It wasn't so much between Yeltzin vs. supporters of parliament. It was pro and anti-Yeltzin. The human animal is wired to follow a single leader and in situations like this, the top dog has a great advantage. All Yeltzin had to do was bribe the head of the army to his side. There were demonstrations, counter-demonstrations, marches, takeovers of buildings, shooting, and some killings. Finally, the army stormed the parliament building and put down any resistance. Propagandists in the west were overcome with jubilation. But this destroyed the entire constitutional order of the post-Communist period. *The Nation* said, "The US government and media, with few exceptions, again acted as Yeltzin's cheerleaders as he smashed the country's first-ever popularly elected, fully independent legislature. Yeltzin was destroying Russia's best chance in history to create a legislative branch capable of off-setting the nation's centuries-long tradition of unchecked executive power", under various tsars, which has continued to the present day under Putin.[13] The entire US policy towards Russia in this period is a poignant example of the system mind using Russia to point the way towards a future National Socialism.

In any event, elections were called for in Dec., '93 which were disappointing to Yeltzin's supporters. However, here again the Corporate Socialism thus far established enabled the economic system to override the political system giving Yeltzin dominance over parliament which became pretty much a rubber stamp. For the next few years, Yeltzin was pretty close to a dictator. As Reddaway and Glinski say, Yeltzin had also "blocked the development of an independent judicial branch, reduced the power and revenue base of local self-government, and by 1994, had imposed a regime of Byzantine authoritarianism on the country".

By the time we get to 1994, a Corporate Socialist system mind was completely entrenched in the new Russia. And Yeltzin, who had started out talking like a democrat and a real man of the people had been completely absorbed into this system mind in the same way as Barack Obama's mind was absorbed into the American system mind within days of being elected president. Important economic players, the oligarchs, were so strong and the government so weak that they were able to pull off what Freeland calls "The sale of the century". The program was called loans-for-shares and it was nothing but a big Grand Theft scam. The oligarchs would loan the government money in exchange for the remaining stock that the government held in the bigger industries controlled by the oligarchs themselves. These were the big companies in oil and gas, nickel, banking, communications, and a few others. The oligarchs were able to pass rules that allowed them to grab the only valuable stock the economy had for bargain basement prices. Instead of raising money for the government, it wound up losing money. And since the oligarchs really designed the whole scheme, you can guess the prices they paid. And to top it off, a lot of very valuable firms wound up in the hands of western firms, whose Corporate Socialist bedfellows in politics had conveniently been pushing for this very kind of privatization all along.

This is a prime example of Economic Socialism exactly as was practiced under George Bush where the government lost hundreds of billions propping up the stack of fraudulent paper our own Wall St. oligarchs had printed up and gambled on according to rules they passed being in bed with government actors. The oligarchs were really in the driver's seat now and simply steam-rolled over any resistance. The 1996 elections were looming and the Yeltzin government needed all the help they could get for reelection. By 1995, the plan was going full speed ahead.

Actually the Russian state was in such bad shape that the fake Communist candidate for president running against Yeltzin was thought to be a shoe-in. Government parties received a crushing defeat in the parliamentary elections of Dec. '95 and so even the west thought he would win. The vast majority of Russians were worse off than under the old Communist system. At least back then, they had a right to a job, some health care and education. Approximately half the population was below the poverty line. The economy had shrunk to half what it was in 1989, and some of them had witnessed the total rip-offs the oligarchs had schemed. So the oligarchs had to move fast. They came together in a meeting called the Davos Pact. They chose Chubais to manage Yeltzin's campaign, even though he had been on the outs with some of the oligarchs. But they all saw the threat to their respective rackets and formed a united front. Even the young reformers joined in.

Then an interesting and crucial series of events took place. Hard-liners in parliament had been angry at Yeltzin for dissolving the Soviet Union. They came up with the idea of dissolving parliament and calling off the elections. That would put them in a position to better influence Yeltzin and the course of events. Yeltzin's campaign wasn't going well but Yeltzin was not about to give up power. So he was tempted to go along. But the oligarchs seemed to have convinced him that winning an election would look much better for all of them and that they could achieve this with their team running the campaign. After all, if the Americans could get a no-nothing like Ronald Reagan elected president, why couldn't they do the same thing for Yeltzin, especially since they had even more control over the means of propaganda than Republicans had in the US. Besides, they had all the money in the world to finance a campaign. Here is a prime example of the system mind understanding the power of propaganda. Yeltzin probably had a slight aversion to a dictatorship, but Freeland's impression in interviewing many of the players later on was that if Yeltzin really thought he would lose the election, he would have called it off. And if George Bush could have done so, he would have done the same thing. With more democracy in the US, Bush had to start a war to get reelected.

The oligarchs mounted a completely western style political campaign. Since they owned the means of communication and understood the importance of propaganda, they presented Yeltsin as a man of the people, pressing flesh as he went along in the campaign. They suppressed coverage of the opposition and there were many violations of the law by the Yeltsin camp. They addressed every detail and spent billions bribing and cajoling key groups. As Freeland describes, "Russia's most popular psychics — clairvoyants, crystal ball readers, astrologists — were put on the Kremlin payroll to convince the highly superstitious Russian masses that a Yeltsin victory was in the stars".[14] What is most funny but sad is that the oligarchs had so much power over the government that they were able to use the election to make even more money using Yeltsin's campaign chest as a means to launder money from their illegal activities. The result was that with almost complete control over the means of propaganda, vast amounts of money, bribery, thievery, intimidation and fraud, Yeltsin stole the election of 1996.

Another interesting episode occurred before the run-off election. There was a power struggle between what was called the party of war lead by Korzhakov and the oligarchs supporting Yeltsin. The party of war consisted of hard-liners who wanted to recapture the Soviet Empire and included the secret service apparatus, a system of informers, wiretappers, and the revamped KGB. If the party of war had won out, there probably wouldn't be a run-off election. The sad fact was that Russia was facing a fork in the road as between a country run by a militarized dictator, or a bunch of fast-buck operators who would lead Russia into a hundred-year future of National Socialism. This was basically a battle between forces controlling the secret police and forces controlling the means of propaganda, and the latter won out, which shows the importance of propaganda.

From the time of the dissolution of the Soviet Union through the '90s, Russia scrunched all of American history between the Civil War and the Great Depression into 10 years. After Yeltsin's election win in '96, Russia looked good to the west because there was money being made. Investment money was flowing into Russia from all over the west to buy up stock in Russian companies and the stock market boomed. The problem was that it was all going to the top 20% (actually to the top 5%) exactly as happened in the in the US before the Great Depression.

With Yeltsin's rapidly deteriorating health and no effective opposition, the oligarchs were in almost complete control of the government. Freeland hits the nail right on the head: "Early on all of the oligarchs had learned that the way to make fortunes in the new Russia was by manipulating the state. In 1996, they took that one step further and began to run the political process itself"[15]: *the exact definition of National Socialism*, which she doesn't see. And just as in the US during the corresponding period, there was weak government that was putty in the hands of economic elites who got new rules passed into law that allowed them pile up more money and economic power at the expense of the rest of society.

For example, Luzhkov, the powerful mayor of Moscow, was also an oligarch with vast economic holdings. Guzinsky was given controlling interest in the biggest company in Russia, Gazprom, the huge oil and gas company. Gazprom proceeded to make favorable loans to expand Guzinsky's TV channel. Another oligarch, Potanin, was made Deputy Prime Minister. Berezovsky became head of the Kremlin's Security Council. These players go back and forth sometimes playing the economic game, sometimes passing new rules as government authorities, then back again to take advantage of the new rules to accrue even more wealth and power in the economic system. This is pretty much the situation in the US after the Civil War but attaining even more momentum under Reagan and Bush. Of course, the US with somewhat stronger political institutions saw a brief stall in the constant drive towards National Socialism under Teddy Roosevelt who was acting outside the system mind. But this interlude in American history was short lived. The system mind led by the old conservative gang was back in power with the election of Warren Harding in 1921. And the next 11 years saw the government pick up the Economic Socialist banner right where it left off in the 1800s, as a weak glob of putty in the hands of important economic nodes who climbed in bed with political actors in Washington to rig their own rules. The subsequent vicious attack on the working class caused a rotting of the foundation of the system and the lack of purchasing power among the lower 80% eventually led to the collapse of 1929.

The same thing happened in Russia. After Yeltzin's election in 1996, for the next few years, tons of money were made by the oligarchs on the stockmarket and rigging their own rules. But it was all on paper. The foundation of the economy was rotting. Many businesses were still managed by the old red guard communist nomenklatura who had no idea how to run a business in a market economy. In the financial sector, bankers and oligarchs were playing the same game of buying, selling, and betting on ever increasing piles of fraudulent paper, much like happened under George Bush. But the worst of it was that none of the new wealth was trickling down to the masses of Russians. The top 20% were doing fine and buying new western goods, fancy clothes, wines, cars etc. Many millionaires emerged. But the average Russian was going nowhere, and his purchasing power was gradually eroding, certainly not keeping up with the explosion of paper financial instruments, stocks, loans, derivatives, etc. The paper explosion was unsustainable, just like under George Bush.

To add to the problems, many of the young reformers like Gaidar who were always in bed with the IMF/international community, were brought into the cabinet with Chubais. This enabled a new round of shock therapy supported by IMF loans. Of course, these loans were conditioned on Russia following the system mind of the west, whose purpose was to not only inflate away more savings of the middle class, but to further indebt a sinking government. This was consistent with the ability of the oligarchs to treat the government as nothing but a means to achieving wealth by passing laws with rules to their advantage. The courts were a joke too.

Leading the charge was Chubais who started shutting down or taking over TV stations and newspapers that didn't spout the party line. It's the same old story with these megalomaniacs starting with Hitler, Stalin and Mao Zedong at the top of the list all the way down to lesser evils like Pinochet in Chile, the Shaw of Iran, and even Lyndon Johnson in Vietnam and George Bush in Iraq. Once they get a hold of some reason-box *theory* to cover up blatant self-interest, there's no amount of human misery and degradation, destruction and killing that will be imposed on a people in carrying out the theory. Here Chubais and his "reformer" friends along with a small number of oligarchs are making huge fortunes on the basis of quack supply-side *theory*, while the entire rest of Russian society is going down the drain, losing jobs and life's savings, and they never once question the theory.

In any event, in 1996, and '97, the government became less and less functional with no real direction. Reddaway calls it the "years of drift". They couldn't even collect taxes they were owed. As a result, to keep some government services going like pensions, it had to start borrowing and printing up more paper, again just like under George Bush. Because it was a disorganized, motley mess, sometimes the government had to pay 50% interest on their loans. Investment capital was flowing out of the country in torrents. The government was running out of money to support the ruble while interest on the national debt was growing. The Russian ship of state was springing holes faster than it could be patched up. But it was too late for patches. The government had been borrowing all along and with tax revenues not keeping up, the debt burden grew increasingly onerous. The slightest crack is like a tiny crack in the wall of a dam, which grows at an accelerating rate until the dam bursts.

Finally, in May of '98, the dam burst and the stockmarket crashed. The only way out of the mess was either to devalue the ruble or default on government paper, both very unattractive alternatives. So another patch was tried, an IMF loan of $22 billion. But by this time the government was a virtual sieve. Nothing could stop the economy plummeting. Investors were stampeding out of the country, which put further pressure on the ruble. And just as under George Bush, the pile of paper the oligarchs created was toppling over and there was no way to prop it up. The Central Bank was losing $300 million a day and lesser banks began to fail. Even the top 20% were losing wealth. As demand at all levels of society shrunk, businesses began laying off workers creating another downward spiral.

Finally, in Aug. of '98, there was no way out and the government announced both a devaluation of the ruble and a default on much of the government debt, which had become a Ponzi scheme anyway. This crushed investors in government paper including foreign investors. Immediately the ruble plummeted to less than a third its former value. People rushed to turn their rapidly disappearing savings into dollars which only made matters worse. Thousands of businesses involved in trade lost their cash flow and folded. With demand dropping, thousands of workers were laid off. By 2000, Russian GDP dropped 43% from the 1990 level; and there was a tenfold increase in poverty to where 40% of the population was living in poverty.[16]

Of course, the top 20% having more to lose, lost a lot. Yeltzin was still trying patches and appointed one prime minister after another. One of them, Primikov, seems to have had a sincere desire to clean up the corruption in the Russian system; but as you might expect, when Washington saw a glitch in the drive towards National Socialism, it prompted Yeltzin to dump Primikov. This game would go on until a strong man was hit upon who would take control of matters. Just as in the Russian revolution of 1917, what emerges in these situations is not a problem solver, not a man of ideas and knowledge, not a man of insight, but a man whose entire being is dedicated to the attainment of raw personal power. That man was Vladimir Putin, who immediately pulled off a Ford-Nixon disgrace by giving Yeltzin immunity from prosecutions in exchange for Yeltzin sneaking him into office. Within months, by suppressing the press, emasculating parliament, and intimidating the oligarchs into joining in, Putin had set himself up as the new tsar; and since this was modern industrial times, a National Socialist tsar. This was the American system mind plan for Russia all along. Remember the pudding.

After a whole book of excellent analysis and story-telling, this is where Freeland's book gets mushy. She descends into the usual mumbling about how things could have gone differently with just the right array of patches: balance the budget, liberalize prices more, less perks to company directors and on and on. It's like the guys writing whole books on how we could have won the war in Vietnam with bombing here, an official there, more money here and more army there.

But Reddaway and Glinski are even more astonishing. After over 600 pages of excruciating detail describing the play of hundreds and hundreds of Yurassoff Russian names, they say "...the West had no clear-cut or consensual understanding of its interests as a whole vis-à-vis Russia...".[17] Shows that too much detail totally obscures reality and clouds the mind. Their own book shows that a think-tank of experts couldn't have come up with a more *consistent* and *effective* policy attending to the most minute detail to send Russia towards a crippling National Socialism. One tiny example: in 1994, an Accounting Office was set up to monitor federal expenditures and to look for crime and corruption in government. They were doing some good work, but Reddawar and Glinsky admit that the reward for their efforts "...was a deafening silence about its reports...".[18] But it didn't escape notice of the Western allies of the young reformers, who "...conducted a campaign of innuendo...", concluding that nobody had to pay attention to the Office since they were nothing but a bunch of Commies anyway. In this whole period, the West didn't miss a single trick in pushing the anti-Capitalist, National Socialist agenda: destroy the consuming class, support an oligarchy that controls the government by rigging rules for further power and control, piling fake paper into a dysfunctional economy, support increasing authoritarianism to squelch dissent, and allowing the productive nodes of the economy to fall into the hands of a bureaucratic collectivized nomenklatura with fraudulent privatization. Did I leave anything out?

People educated in the west get the full force of a system mind so that they absorb massive doses of propaganda all their lives starting with the educational system, all directed towards inculcating the belief that the success of the West was due to Economic Socialism, euphemistically called Laissez-faire Capitalism. It is this same system mind propaganda infecting the minds of western thinkers that allows Reddaway and Glinski to say, "...Western policy...was not intentionally harmful...", even though it didn't "...show the wisdom and foresight they

displayed when assisting the destinies of Western Europe and Japan after World War II".[19]
These guys' perceptions are so distorted by being embedded in a swamp of Western propa-
ganda that they are incapable of seeing that the "wisdom and foresight" in our treatment of
Western Europe after WWII was the result of the *Roosevelt* administration's promulgation of
Democratic Capitalism not only in the US, but in Europe as well. The indisputable evidence
for this was the creation of a middle class and independent rules for the economic game.
Whereas, after the '80s decade of Ronald Reagan's Economic Socialism, the American system mind by this time was using *Russia* to lead the world towards National Socialism in the
exact same way that conservative Republicans in the 1930s prevented Roosevelt from moving
against Hitler so as to give Hitler a free hand to establish National Socialism in Germany as
the wave of the future. We need some real historians here.

It was also this same system of propaganda that had enough financial support and
enough expansiveness to reach the ears of potential reformers in other countries. It is so
invasive and so extensive that it prevents most people from seeing that throughout our history, far from Economic Socialism contributing to the success of an economy, it actually
drags the system down from time to time and actually sabotages economic progress. It
takes continuous massive doses of system propaganda to give credit for our economic success to the practices of Laissez-faire, which is code for Economic Socialism. And the young
reformers were in no position to see through this haze of propaganda.

By allowing economic players to make their own rules, the result is *always* an economic
collapse. In the 65 years between the Civil War and Roosevelt, the lot of the bottom 80%
of the population did not significantly improve at all. And this was during an Industrial
Revolution that produced remarkable technological progress and productivity. All the benefits went to the top 20%, with the result that system collapsed periodically and eventuated
in a really big one in 1929.

In distinction to the American crash of 1929, when the Russian system collapsed in
1998, a tsar-style National Socialism crystallized within few years. In the US, our democratic institutions enabled us to vote in the Roosevelt administration that brought back
some semblance of Democratic Capitalism and created an unprecedented post-war boom
and a prosperous middle class for first time in the history of the *world*.

But Freeland also misses the significance of the most interesting and most incisive
aspect of the whole episode. People point out that the oligarchs lost their fortunes as well
in the collapse. But they didn't lose everything and they didn't lose control over their companies. Even though they were weakened, the rest of society including the government as a
viable rule-keeping entity, was weakened *even more*. This point cannot be stressed more. As
soon as the oligarchs perceived that Putin was going to become a strong man, they immediately began climbing in bed with the new government and attaching themselves to Putin.
The result was that their influence on government could go on unabated. Even though the
pie shrunk considerably, their *share* of the pie actually grew, as we discussed in Sect. 30.7.

The Economist discusses a watchdog group, Transparency International, who gives
Russia one of the worst marks in the world for corruption: "80% of Russian businesses

pay bribes", which comes to a $300 billion dollar business. [20] "Corruption has become so endemic that it is perceived as normal…". Many businesses in Russia have hooked up with criminal gangs to drive out competitors.

Corruption in Russia is due to a blending between economic players and political operatives, with economic players taking ever-increasing roles in making the rules of the game. Often nobody knows who really owns a unit of production because there are no rules to make this determination. We discussed *The Economist* term, *hybrid* firms, which they inadvertently describe as blurring "…the line between the public and private sector.…"[21] But of course, they say nothing about the fact that these "hybrids" can influence their own rules of the economic game, which is the definition of Economic Socialism.

Hybrids are just one of many ways to blur the distinction between the economic means of production and the political system that is supposed to enforce the rules of the game. Nobody really knows which large assets are owned or controlled by top people in the political system in Russia. The whole system is a fluid amorphous syrup of state owned companies, private companies with political figures heavily involved, politicians controlling companies they have a financial or ownership interest in, and private producers teaming up with politicos to rig the rules in their favor. This is exactly why the US wanted influence in setting up the Russian system and why our foreign policy has favored China in many ways. An MIT professor has a book claiming that this is mostly what is going on in major industries in China, and that this really isn't Capitalism.[22] Well, in my opinion, this is exactly the definition of Economic Socialism. These countries are the spearhead of National Socialism that our own system mind is using to lead the way for us.

On the political side, with economic players in bed with politicos, democratic institutions are gradually eroding away, Masha Gessen details some of these moves: "Vladimir Putin has announced sweeping political reforms that will eliminate all direct elections except those for president, who … will effectively appoint members of parliament." [23] Also, the courts have been intimidated into submission. All of this is the exact definition of National Socialism, and once you take the fork and get a vector going towards National Socialism, there's no turning back. Only another revolution will put Russia on a track towards Democratic Capitalism. And I don't mean a Russian spring like occurred in 2011 led by the usual liberals, dissidents and hippies. I mean one involving the lower 80% of the population. This is not likely because the Russian people are inured to a culture of authoritarianism that's been in place for hundreds of years.

Peter Reddaway mentioned a number of models the Russians could have adopted instead of what they did. He mentions the French model of basic mixed democracy wherein the government went into business in certain industries like aerospace, railroads, nuclear power, etc. with huge government companies. He also mentions the Japanese model based on MITI wherein the government is a planning and investing partner of certain private sector businesses.[24] But he doesn't notice that all the instances he mentions occurred in countries with a strong feudal past giving them an important ethic and sense of responsibility.

Without this, economic and political power in the same hands invariably leads to authoritarianism and corruption. Russia is a perfect example.

There are two very necessary social ingredients for a viable Democratic Capitalist system (besides the obvious requirement of private property). The country must have a strong ethic usually from a feudal past. When there was a period of reformation throughout our history, the US has been able to patch the system up without corruption. Everywhere in the world where there isn't a strong feudal past — Russia, Africa, Muslim countries, India to some extent — instead of Democratic Capitalism, you find crippled economies under some kind of Fascism, National Socialism or Communism, all with massive amounts of corruption.

After it was all over, Gaidar blamed the Russian people and their "cultural inferiority". But without a feudal past, it would have taken a sequence of extremely delicate measures and subtle political initiatives to bring about a viable Capitalistic system in Russia. They certainly weren't going to get it via leaders like Gaidar listening to the world's leading "economists" who make their living pimping for Economic Socialism. And when all the smoke cleared away, Yeltsin and Gaidar and the rest would see that the version of Capitalism they had was a mafia-oligarchic-nomenklatura shadow economy.

Additionally, just as in our own collapse of 2008, I don't for one minute accept all this is as bad judgment, mistakes, misunderstandings and the rest of the reason-box crap spewed forth by western economic apologists. In my opinion, they know this is not Capitalism, and know exactly how it will all shake out even though this knowledge stays in the bottom of their brains. It doesn't take a rocket scientist to see that if you take a system where the political system controls the economic system and replace it with an economic system that has taken control of the political system, what kind of improvements are you going to get? Small gains in technology, entrepreneurship and business energy will be massively overwhelmed by the ability of economic elites to make their own rules. This allows them to strip of the country of its valuable assets and sneak their ill-gotten gains out of the country with massive leakages that have to be replaced with billions of borrowed money most of which they proceed to again steal, further reinforcing their economic and political positions. Some of this trickles down to the top 20%, while the bottom 80% gain nothing but inheritance of massive debts to international vampires.

You have to feel sorry for the poor Russians. I happen to like Russians. I like their sense of humor, they're ability to write well, (which I wish I could do) and to understand the human condition. They lead the world in quality literature. But after hundreds of years of tsarist authoritarianism along with a feudal serfdom that never allowed a social ethic to congeal, now at a crucial point in modern history where things might have taken a road towards real Democratic Capitalism, they're the victim of a western system mind that drove them on the road to a crippling National Socialist state that will go on for another hundred years at least.

The only thing that will prevent Russia from reverting to a third-world country is that their National Socialist system will be continually propped by a vast store of natural resources which will increase in value. Sunnysiders are already talking about how our new-found gas resources will lead us to the promised land. They are dreaming. Gains from these resources will only go to the larger nodes in the economy to buy and sell members of congress who will proceed to make their own rules. To prop up demand, there will be continuous theft from the future. At some point in this century, our system will collapse. Khrushchev might be right after all. Even though the US will probably always have more freedoms than Russia, we might wind up in just as bad a shape.

[1] "The Chaos at the Door", *The Economist*. Apr. 1, '00, p. 23

[2] Reddaway, Peter; Glinski, Dmitri, 2001. *The Tragedy of Russia's Reforms*, US Institute of Peace Pr. Washington, D.C.

[3] Ibid. p. 112

[4] Ibis. P. 307

[5] Ibid. p. 179

[6] Ibid. p. 248

[7] Ibid. P. 91.

[8] Freeland, Chrystia, 2000. Sale of the Century, Crown Pr., N.Y.

[9] Medvedev, Roy, 2000. *Post-Soviet Russia*, Columbia Univ.

[10] *The Economist*, Aug. 2, '08, Cover

[11] Reddaway and Glinski, p. 375

[12] Ibid. p. 396

[13] Vanden Heuvel, Katrina, "Yeltzin's (Real) Legacy". *The Nation*, May 21, '07.

[14] Freeland, Op. Cit. p. 213

[15] Ibid. p. 240

[16] Doder, Dusko; "Russia's Potemkin Leader. *The Nation*, Jan. 29, '01

[17] Reddaway and Glinski, Op. Cit. p. 589

[18] Ibid. p. 598

[19] Ibid. p. 590

[20] Ibid. p. 10

[21] "The rise of the hybrid company, *The Economist*, Dec. 15, '09, p. 78.

[22] Huang, Yasheng, *Capitalism with Chinese Characteristics*, Cambridge, Univ. Pr.

[23] Gessen, Masha, "Red to Brown". *The New Republic*, Sept. 27, '04

[24] Reddaway and Glinski, Op. Cit. p. 281

CHAPTER 32

JFK

―――

ONE OF THE MOST INTRIGUING event of the 20th century was the assassination of President John F. Kennedy. There was a very official government commission appointed to investigate the assassination and hundreds of books were written about the event. But the public was never satisfied that a complete accounting had been rendered by the government. A vast majority of opinion to this day thinks there was some kind of conspiracy. This is an interesting phenomenon in itself. The fact that the public has remained suspicious even now shows that the event never appeared random or accidental.

My reason for a chapter on this case is that in my opinion, the Kennedy assassination not only illustrates a system mind, but was another fork in the road of American history just as the fork that occurred during the Reagan administration. It sent us down one fork that we will never go back to and will continue on this fork into the indefinite future. We will explain this fork as we go along.

Another equally interesting observation about the people who got interested in the case and reported or wrote books on it, is that they fall into two distinct groups. This really shows what a binary device the brain is. It doesn't like being on the edge. It likes conclusions. We'll call the first group the simple solution group. They think there was nothing amiss in the assassination and that the conclusions are just what the Warren commission said: no conspiracy of any kind and Oswald was the lone assassination. Such definitive conclusions should make us a little suspicious right from the start because the case has too much complexity for any definitive conclusion like this. A leading proponent of the simple solution theory is Vincent Bugliosi who has written a humungus book giving this position.[1]

The second group thinks there had to be some kind of conspiracy because the facts don't add up, and there are too many very unlikely events leading to the assassination. There are many conspiracy theories, starting in the early days with Mark Lane. I have read quite a bit on the case and I have to say, it is an amazingly complex set of events. There is not one piece of evidence that isn't conflicted by opposing evidence. There are few pieces of the puzzle that everyone agrees on.

Regarding Bugliosi's defense of the simple Warren Commission conclusion, I can't say his conclusion is wrong. However, there's something fishy about spending fifteen hundred pages on the most minute detail to convince us. He reminds me of a Coca Cola collector who wanted to make sure he wound up with the best stuff, so he simply bought everything. For example, we learn that Bobbie's wife Ethel "…took their lunch of clam chowder and tuna-fish sandwiches at an outdoor patio" (60). We also learn that Oswald was wearing brown socks in his casket (318). The book is mostly such meaningless detail. What is the purpose of this?

Bugliosi is a defense lawyer, and I hear a very good one (I heard he got Thomas off who betrayed Jesus.) The purpose of so much detail is that by hammering the reader over the head for 1500 pages of minutia, he will throw in the towel, give up, and just accept the conclusion Bugliosi wants out of clear exhaustion. How could anyone write hundreds and hundreds of pages of mind-boggling irrelevant detail and never once think to ask, what is the *explanation* for this controversial assassination?

Right off the bat he tells us "… why would any members of the Warren Commission and their staff stake their good reputation on a report they prepared which they knew to be fraudulent?" (xix). This is a ripe example of the binary lawyer brain: it's either totally innocent or "fraudulent". Even though there is no evidence the Warren Commission lied about anything, this does not at all entail that it told the whole story. In any event, after steamrolling over us with the Warren Commission report, he now has a basis for a position he will defend. *Then*, anyone who disagrees in any way like a conspiracy has to prove his case with a preponderance of evidence. Since nobody has been able to provide overwhelming evidence, Bugliosi wins his case because his client, the Warren Commission is still innocent since it has not been proven guilty beyond a reasonable doubt.

But this is not a court case. The Warren Commission is not on trial. Even Oswald is not on trial because he was killed before a trial. The Kennedy assassination is a natural event in the world of events, just like any other natural event, although a very rare one. When science wants to explain natural events it does not start out with a theory that fits with current economic, political or religious forces, and coerces everyone to accept it unless they can prove it wrong. This is what the Church did in the Middle Ages about astronomy, but nobody thinks the Church was doing science. And this is exactly what the Warren Commission did. The entire government and the major media propaganda outlets put its weight and force into blasting us in the face with thousands of pages of the Warren Commission report and proceeded to insist that we must accept it unless proven otherwise by a preponderance of the evidence. If you're really doing science, you don't start out with a pre-conceived story at all. You simply *construct* a theory that best fits the facts. Sometimes theories are wrong and get replaced by others. We explained the scientific method in Sect. 9.2. Aristotle had a theory of motion that was proved to be wrong. Newton had a theory of motion that best explained events we see in the world. Turns out, Newton was right.

But the scientific method is not a strong point of lawyers, even if you line up 30 of them. These people simply do not have the conceptual tools necessary to properly analyze the Kennedy assassination. They know nothing about science, physics, math, or statistics. A number of tests conducted by the Commission were completely bogus that a real scientist would have caught. What we will try to do in this chapter is give a theory that best fits the known facts, using probabilities and logic. The theory presented here is not one that must be accepted until proven wrong either. It is just another alternative, which is why I don't need a 1500 page book.

The first thing a story has to do is describe the cast of characters. The main character was Oswald shooting from the top floor of an old school depository building *behind* Kennedy's car. Then there was the FBI and its officials; there was the CIA and its operatives. There was the Secret Service whose job it is to protect the president and the Dallas Police Department. There must have been a committee of some sort designing the parade route. There was the morning newspaper and its writers and editors. There was a Fair Play for Cuba committee. There were various right-wing groups and economic interests who hated Kennedy. There was Jack Ruby who killed Oswald, and the Dallas mafia who some claimed was in contact with Ruby. There was Oswald's Russian wife, Marina, and her friend Ruth Paine and Lyndon Johnson. These are most of the cast of characters in the story.

First of all, we should clarify what a conspiracy is, since the word gets thrown around so promiscuously. A conspiracy is where two or more of the parties in the cast of characters are in contact or cooperation in some way relevant to the event. Let's put the cast of characters into 15 categories, which would make 105 different pairs. (For those of you who know the math, the formula is 15!/2!x13!). It would be fair to say that a conspiracy is where a reasonable number of *pairs* of players are communicating in some way. Is there any evidence for this? I don't think so, although this doesn't mean there was not a conspiracy. Lack of evidence of a conspiracy is not evidence for a lack of conspiracy.

How about mini-conspiracies? This is where a single pair among the 105 was connected in some way. An example of a mini-conspiracy is perhaps someone in Government persuaded the editor of the daily newspaper to put details of the parade route on the front page. Another would be if FBI or CIA or Russian operatives arranged to have a drink with Oswald in a local bar and get him all juiced up about the unfairness of American policy towards Cuba and blamed Kennedy. Another would be where someone among the above players pulls strings to have a motorcade route that takes such as unusual detour. Another is the police tell Ruby that Oswald will be available all weekend right out in public. Another is one of the players asking LBJ if an investigation he would authorize would cover up any plan to kill Kennedy; this might be subtly what actually happened. There are 105 different possible mini-conspiracies. Is there evidence for any of them? Not direct evidence, but some think there was some circumstantial evidence.

The sequence of events is almost unbelievable. First of all, Oswald was a very unstable guy who had tried to defect to Russia for a while, claimed to be a communist, married a Russian girl, changed his mind about defecting, came back to the US, visited the Russian embassy in Mexico City, sent a threatening letter to the FBI, (that was conveniently lost) finally landed a job in the old School Depository Building which was a mostly empty old building to store books. He had bought a rifle that his Russian wife knew about.

Three days before the assassination, the motorcade route was pictured and described in detail on the front page of a Dallas newspaper. The motorcade route was to go down Main Street the usual way a parade goes. Only this one takes a right turn onto a smaller street and then a sharp left onto a very small street, Elm Street, where the Depository building was. This little detour onto Elm Street formed a little triangle called Dealey Plaza.

Kennedy was shot while riding in the back seat of a convertible either from behind from the Depository building or from ahead of Kennedy's car, or both places. This is one of the controversies. Kennedy was rushed to the Parkland hospital in Dallas and was examined and a *preliminary* autopsy performed by three doctors. This was Friday, Nov. 22, 1963. They made certain observations, took some photographs, and made some notes, some of which, again, were conveniently lost. However, Kennedy people and others insisted that a complete autopsy should be performed in Washington DC and the body was flown there. In this autopsy by a number of doctors, notes, photographs and x-rays were also taken, and there were opinions that disagreed in important respects with some of the doctors in Dallas. Everyone, even Bugliosi, admits that this autopsy was a complete mess, performed by people not highly trained, and whose procedures were a nightmare that minimized the amount of accurate information that could be gleaned. And this was the most important crime in American history.

In the meantime, on Friday, Saturday and Sunday, Oswald was paraded around the Dallas police station like a newly found species of animal. He was pushed through crowds with seemingly no accounting of who was there or if any arms were present. Not to worry though — Bugliosi assures us about Jack Ruby, "…the thought of shooting Oswald never enters his mind" (186). Of course, lawyers are in the business of knowing what's in other people's minds. (I want to say parenthetically, that the biggest source of injustice in our criminal justice system is shysters designing procedures based on what some people *think* about other people's *thoughts.* We discussed the ACLUs shenanigans in this regards in Sect. 29.15. What kind of justice are you going to get by judging people's *meditations?* All legal procedures should depend solely on observable behavior.)

Finally, on Sunday, Jack Ruby who had been carrying a gun all weekend, went right up to Oswald in front of a whole nation of TV viewers and shot and killed Oswald. Down the drain went any chance of finding a possible conspiracy. Immediately, it was decided to have a Commission to determine the facts of the assassination. They proceeded to write 26 *volumes* of excruciating detail related to the assassination, most of it completely irrelevant.

It is at this point that I think the concept of a system mind is relevant. We have to first ask ourselves, what would the system want the American people to believe? Well, the system mind being run mostly by the more important neoconservative and wealthy nodes in society, would want the American people to trust their government as it sends more and more wealth to the top 20%. They would want them to believe the government always works in the best interests of the American people; that it is very transparent in its operations; and that we should all believe in its integrity. What the system mind would like in the case of the Kennedy assassination is an explanation of the event that is simple, palatable, easy to digest, with no untoward ramifications whatsoever. The purpose of commissions like this is not to discover the facts, nor explain the event, nor get to the bottom of things. *The purpose of commissions like the Warren Commission is to work up an instruction manual, telling the system propaganda outlets exactly what to say to the public regardless of truth or completeness of the story.* This is exactly what the Warren Commission produced. In fact, a think-tank of highly paid analysts and consultants could not have come up with an account of the assassination that better met the needs of the system mind. The Commission's conclusion was that Oswald was the lone assassin. And a long expensive trial was avoided by a patriotic American who took Oswald out. End of story: no conspiracies, not even a mini-conspiracy; all conflicting facts explained away. This doesn't mean that the Commission is wrong. In fact, I tend to accept most of the Warren Commission myself. But it does nothing to explain the assassination.

What is remarkable is that Bugliosi is totally unaware that in typical lawyer speak, these important political players actually *ordered* the Warren Commission to come up with the simple solution. Of course, they worded this order in a way to make it look like they wanted an unbiased analysis, but their words are right there to see. Although the Warren Commission did not lie, nor introduce fake facts, they did not ask one single question that would be relevant to a complete *understanding* of the assassination. And Bugliosi's book, which is a complete apologia of the Warren report, is a mirror image of the report. What I've done here is only sketch what a proper analysis would look like, not that I have done it.

First of all, the most important overall question is this: if the sequence of events as described by the Warren report and Bugliosi's book are random, unrelated events totally devoid of a single mini-conspiracy, what is the probability that this sequence would have occurred? The way this is done in probability theory is to take each event in the sequence, look at each probability and obtain a final probability for the whole sequence. Now I'm not an expert in parades or guarding a president. So my probabilities are not going to be highly accurate.

First of all, if we look at the most important motorcades of celebrities in the past 50 years in the US, what percentage of them have a detour going off the main straight line direction of the motorcade making dangerous sharp turns around Dealey Plaza? This is an extremely important question. And of course, it goes right by an old nearly empty Depository Building that nobody bothers to guard.

After WWII, there were a number of motorcades for Dwight Eisenhower. There have been thousands of parades for popes, sports teams winning championships, foreign dignitaries, and American leaders including presidents. These motorcades almost invariably start in a highly guarded location, and proceed to take a straight-line trajectory right down a main street like State St. in Chicago, Broadway in NY, Pennsylvania Ave. in Washington. The motorcade ends again in a highly guarded location. The Kennedy motorcade should have *ended* in the Dealey plaza where Kennedy would have been transferred to an armored vehicle just like happens in all major parades. Why was Dealey Plaza conveniently *part* of the motorcade which left Kennedy totally unprotected going by a totally unguarded old building — not only old, but mostly empty as well? What is the probability that such a route would be chosen if you really wanted to put great importance on the president's safety? Maybe the probability of this is say, one in 10.

When plans were being made for a motorcade in Dallas, there were two choices for a luncheon after the motorcade, a Women's Building, which was the safest of the two locations, and a Trade Mart in the north of town, which was less safe in many ways. Texas was all Democratic at the time, but the *conservative* wing of the party wanted the *less* safe Trade Mart building and the liberal wing of the party wanted the safer Women's Building. Surprise, surprise. Bugliosi, of course, doesn't even raise an eyebrow.

At one point, Bugliosi says it wasn't the practice for the Secret Service to check out "hundreds of buildings" along a motorcade route. But we're not talking about buildings with people working in them on every floor. You can't shoot from a building full of working people. Oswald had the 6th floor of the depository building *all to himself.* I'll bet there wasn't more than *one* nearly empty old building along this route like the Depository building to check out. And it was located *right at the corner* of a dangerous sharp left turn — a turn that probably hasn't popped up in a thousand motorcades. You would think some Secret Service agent would at least be assigned to check out this dangerous building along *their* motorcade route. No Secret Service agent took a *glance* at the dam building. Another low probability.

Then, given that there was to be a motorcade route shown in the paper, what is the probability that a minor detail like a tiny detour would be shown in all its glory on the front page of the newspaper three days ahead of the motorcade? Why not simply show the motorcade going down Main St., especially if you really wanted to protect the president? Well, there is an answer to that, which after 50 years of crap from a million sources I finally learned by accident. The owner of the newspaper was an avid right-wing Kennedy hater. Bugliosi and the Warren commission conveniently suppress this highly important fact.

Oswald and Marina had been moving all over the place, with Oswald engaging in all kinds of crazy extremist political activities *that the FBI knew about.* He was in different places in Russia, different locations in Dallas, then a move to New Orleans, then back to Dallas. The FBI had kept track of every minute move of Oswald for a number of years. He had tried to defect to Russia, had joined a fair play for Cuba organization, *even wrote threatening letters to the FBI.* He had bought a rifle, which the FBI didn't look into. Oswald had tried to kill a General named Walker a few months before and his wife knew about it. The number one suspect, of course, was Oswald, but no authority, especially the FBI, investigated the prime suspect for such an attempt. A little effort by the FBI might have at least brought in Oswald for questioning and learned about a rifle. Another probability.

For a month before the assassination, the chief FBI man was buzzing around the Oswald residence getting information about Oswald, even finding out that Oswald had gotten a job in the Depository Building *right on the motorcade route.* But the minute he got the job in the Depository building, all tracking of Oswald stopped: no investigating, no questioning, not even an account of his whereabouts. What is the probability that not one single official, not in the FBI, CIA, the secret service, or the Dallas police was ever assigned to check on Dallas' number one extremist in the last days before the Kennedy visit? The FBI and Secret Service are not there to look at the clear blue sky, or to wonder about what a nice guy the president is, or how they're going to get laid. These guys are there *solely* and *specifically* to be thinking about who and how someone might harm the president. But the FBI doesn't tell anyone about its very suspicious file on Oswald. They don't say a word to the Secret Service nor the Dallas police nor a word about a letter Oswald sent to the FBI threatening to blow up an FBI building. (The FBI later destroyed this letter so that people wouldn't think they were negligent, a pregnant example of a system mind.) When the president's advance man in Dallas enquired with the Secret Service's Protective Research Section who might be a security risk, not one name came back. What is the probability that information about a crazy, unstable, extremist prime suspect for a major crime is not shared with other law enforcement agencies, especially with Kennedy coming to town? And then not even used by the agency that has the information? Another low probability.

On the morning of the assassination, Oswald took his rifle to work with him wrapped loosely in paper. He leaves his wedding ring home. It appears this was a planned assassination. Not having any deep understanding of this assassination, Bugliosi inadvertently says there was no question that "everyone in the ...Depository Building had to know that the presidential motorcade would pass by the building that Friday" (784). Amazing. So what's the probability that the FBI who knows where Oswald is working, does nothing about surveillance of Oswald by anyone, not the secret service, not the FBI and not the Dallas police? Oswald takes a gun to work and the FBI knows nothing about it.

The night before the shooting, Thursday, Oswald stayed at the Paine residence, and a friend drove Oswald to work on Thursday instead of the usual Friday. Oswald tells this guy and others who see him with the package that it contains curtain rods. Was he going to hang curtains in the depository building? This was obviously a gun package: what other long slim object needs to be sloppily wrapped in some improvised paper? Oswald exhibited other suspicious behavior the morning of the assassination. None of these people who know Oswald to be a peculiar guy, alerts the police. What's the probability of this?

On the morning of the parade, there was a virtual peanut gallery of people who testified that they saw Oswald fooling around in a window in the top floor of the Depository building. One guy even saw Oswald wielding a rifle there. Another guy saw Oswald actually shooting the rifle. After a thousand pages, Bugliosi admits that the special Secret Service agent in charge told the Warren Commission that "when you are driving down the street ...and you have buildings on either side you are going to scan your eyes up and down" the buildings (1443). So what is the probability that not one agent among hundreds ever entered or inspected a dangerous building like the Depository, even if Oswald hadn't been working there? It would take just one guy? Even without an assignment, what is the probability that no agent ever bothered to look up at the Depository building to see Oswald bigger than life as any number of bystanders saw? Again, another probability much less than one. (Of course, maybe we can excuse the eyesight of the Secret Service agents, since most of them were out the night before getting drunk.)

Not only that, but by another coincidence, a contingent of secret service people who *should* have been in Dallas protecting the president were conveniently assigned somewhere else. Another probability added to the list. Fifteen hundred pages of excruciating irrelevant detail and Bugliosi never comes close to asking a single one of these questions. And he complains about conspiracy theorists who at least *try* to explain the assassination.

According to marine records, Oswald was an excellent shot but not an exceptional sharp-shooter. The rifle he used was a decent quality rifle but far from the most accurate that could be obtained at the time. He paid only 12 bucks for it. According to Bugliosi, Oswald took 3 shots in a matter of a few seconds, two of them very accurate. Later on, various marksmen were invited to make similar shots in the allotted number of seconds. And these were real sharp-shooters. Two out of three of them could not reproduce Oswald's performance. So what is the probability that Oswald was the only shooter and got off the three noted shots? This probability would be a lot less than one.

Next, the evidence. Various photos and x-rays and doctor testimony at the time in Dallas suggested that one accurate shot to Kennedy entered his neck from the front and exited in the back as though the shot was coming from ahead like the grassy knoll. But there seems to be conflicting evidence and testimony that the bullets entering Kennedy were from the back and exited the front, suggesting that the bullets were coming from the Depository building. What is the probability that at least one of the bullets was coming from in *front* of Kennedy's car? From the objective evidence, this probability certainly seems greater than zero.

Next, look at the Ruby assassination. A real researcher into this event would look up the top 100 most important assassinations in the last 50 years. These would include that of Jack's brother Bobbie, Martin Luther King, Malcolm X, the Beetles guy, among many others. The first question is, in how many of these assassinations is the prime suspect paraded around in public among crowds of people hundreds of whom have direct access to the suspect? Even in courtrooms, precautions are taken to prevent people on the victim's side from getting at the suspect on trial. But not here, for the most important assassination of the century. Also, in what percentage of these assassinations is the assassin killed immediately afterwards so that nothing can be gleaned from his testimony? Even if there was another such assassination, it is another very low probability.

Now, you are free to put probabilities on all these events. There are a number of lesser events I've left out. I've made some rough estimates of these probabilities. A thorough analysis of this assassination would go into detail in order to make a more educated guesses as to these probabilities. This was never done, and there's nothing close to such an analysis in Bugliosi's book. To get the final probability that an assassination could be brought off like this one, you multiply all the probabilities of the various events together. My estimate is that there is less than one chance in 10 *billion* that this total event could have taken place in the way suggested by the Warren report and Bugliosi's book, which is that these events are all unrelated, innocent, random events. What this means is that the chances that the Warren Commission report and Bugliosi's book tells you all there is to know about the Kennedy assassination is about one in 10 *billion*. This is why it's a waste of time to read the 26 volume Warren Commission.

I would suggest that the whole framework of the Kennedy assassination and the Warren Commission lies in the needs of the system mind at the time. Kennedy was a liberal politician at a time when there were rumblings of a civil rights movement and right after all the hatred and recriminations of the McCarthy witch hunt for communists. Kennedy had sent troops to guard the entrance of a black student entering the University of Mississippi. There was hatred in the country over Kennedy's sympathy for black people. The cold war with Russia was in full sway and Cuba was their client state. Many Americans thought the US should simply invade Cuba and conquer the place. Kennedy also wanted to withdraw troops from Vietnam. Avoiding wars is always a source of extreme hatred among many people. There was a whole list of grievances that enemies of Kennedy had at the time, especially among the more important and influential nodes of the system mind and especially in the south. And the most important consideration is that all of the agencies like FBI, CIA, Dallas police, as is only natural, have a very conservative bent. That's just the nature of cops and spooks.

So what did the system mind do? Well it didn't plan an assassination and it probably didn't create a conspiracy to commit an assassination. What it *did* do was to arrange for a very high *probability* that the assassination of President Kennedy would take place. With half a brain, one look at the scene of the assassination will bang you right in the face that the Dealey plaza is probably the most pregnant, the most inviting, the most ripe, the most advantageous location for an assassination of a celebrity that ever occurred in the history of the US. I want someone to show me a better place to get away with an assassination in a motorcade than Dealey plaza. You'd have to be totally unconscious not to see the danger of such a location. The Plaza has a number of places a shooter could position himself, not only the Depository building and other buildings, but the grassy knoll, a picket fence, a parking lot and railroad yard behind, in addition to underpasses and bridges at the end of Elm Street. If the system really wanted to *protect* Kennedy, which is its overt job, Dealey Plaza and especially the empty depository building would have been crawling with secret service, Dallas police, FBI and CIA in every nook and cranny. Instead, the few authorities on the scene conveniently had their heads in their butts throughout the whole slow trip through Dealey Plaza, not once looking around for danger anywhere. Bugliosi doesn't question any of this.

Bugliosi employs various arguments to shoot down the many conspiracy theories that have people shooting from all these places. But Bugliosi never asks himself why would a motorcade be designed to go through a location where it is very plausible that so many people *could* be shooting from so many places? On top of it, the scene is advertised right in the newspaper days ahead of time. Bugliosi states flatly as though a matter of fact, that more than one shooter would indicate a conspiracy — a good example of lawyer thinking. It is important to point out that *five* shooters would not prove a conspiracy.

If I put a little map in a New York paper of a little place along the Hudson River where I found some gold, would the crowd of people showing up the next morning be *conspiring*? Would they have to talk to each other? A number of parties show up at the local beach on a hot summer day. Do any of them have to conspire? The beach is what in complexity theory is called an *attractor*. It *attracts* people under certain circumstances with no necessary connection between them at all. Dealey Plaza was a monumental *attractor*. The scene was so pregnant for an assassination attempt that I'm surprised there weren't more shooters all over the place, including another shooter in the Depository building. Maybe there were, and none of them would ever have to know each other.

Bugliosi has all kinds of untoward motives for people who have conspiracy theories. But when it comes to the Warren Commission and all the supporting testimony, their motives is as pure as the driven snow. But what about the millions of ordinary people who distrust the Commission? It never seems to occur to Bugliosi even once that the reason for so many conspiracy theories and people believing them is that the whole sequence of events is too unlikely to be explained by the simple solution. The fact is that Delealy *Plaza is just too ripe a place for an assassination to have occurred innocently at random by a lone assassin.*

It is perfectly obvious from the way the investigation was handled that the Warren Commission knew it's job the day they were appointed. Let's say an objective observer, like God, were to pick a commission to investigate the Kennedy assassination. Here is a case that involves flesh wounds, weaponry, biology, physiology, ballistics, physics, mechanics, probability theory, statistics, and logic. What's the probability that seven consecutive people would be chosen for such a commission *each of whom is a shyster*? Not one plumber, or carpenter or physicist or statistician, but 7 consecutive lawyers, whose only education is how to twist the facts to fit their case. The probability of this is another billion to one. But there's more. Guess about the three men chosen to coordinate the testimony, organize the information, and act as liaison? Three more shysters. If this weren't an incredibly tragic event, it would be a big joke. But there's even more. The next 20 or so people chosen to work on the commission are? Guess what? More lawyers, to a man. Now we're down to a probability of one in a *trillion*. You have to wonder how conscious Bugliosi is when he says, "...every conceivable pain was taken to select people who were totally independent, *which is hardly the way you set out to organize a truth-concealing commission*" (his italics)(342). This is what happens to the brain when you spend a lifetime practicing law, which is why we don't say that lawyers *do* law: they *practice* at it, but never really get very good. *None* of these lawyers had any relevant education. They were all trained to do the exact same thing: twist the facts to fit their case. In fact, if you wanted to *maximize* truth-concealment, 30 consecutive lawyers is *exactly* who you would pick for the job.

After the assassination, the world, especially Europe and Russia, and even the American people, was a swirl with rumors of a conspiracy or something fishy about the whole affair. This was not acceptable to the system mind. The job of the Warren Commission representing the system mind was to promote the simplest, easiest to understand, most uncomplicated story they could conceive of in order to convince the public that the government is something they can trust, is transparent in its operations, and looking out for the best interests of the American people. It is no accident that not one single question relevant to *understanding* the assassination was ever asked by the report. What it did was to *distract* the public away from the real issues and onto a barrage of irrelevant detail that would beat readers down and channel them into the irrelevant questions they were supposed to ask, and into answers they would accept including the simple solution.

But without knowing a thing about the facts, the media praised it to the moon. If you want proof of this, just read Bugliosi's book. This doesn't mean that the simple solution is wrong. What I'm saying is that an objective analysis of the Kennedy assassination was irrelevant to the work of the Commission. They knew what their job was from day one and they never strayed from that agenda, which was to promote the simple solution, not get to the bottom of the facts and thoroughly explain the assassination. It mattered not one iota whether the simple solution was true. Their job was to promote it, whether it was true or not. And as we mentioned, they were subtly instructed and guided to the simple solution by the system (and some think Johnson's instructions were not very subtle). Earl Warren, who had a degree of intellectual honesty, resisted mightily from being on the commission because, in my opinion, he subconsciously knew good and well his job was all laid out for him and what the conclusions would be. But Johnson leaned on him heavily and he finally relented.

So what theory best fits the facts? I can only give my opinion, but it's an opinion that is not distracted by the Warren Commission and Bugliosi's thousands of pages of irrelevant detail to clog up our minds. First of all, there was eyewitness testimony from FBI, Secret Service agents and many bystanders that they heard shots and saw smoke coming from the direction of the grassy knoll. There are doctor reports that the wound in the front of the body in the neck was an *entry* wound and that a wound in the back was an *exit* wound as would be the case if shots were coming from *ahead* of Kennedy's car. However, most of the evidence does point to the fatal shot to the head coming from behind. (Now when it was time to determine where shots were coming from, Bugliosi rejects many bystanders' opinion that they were also coming from the grassy knoll because a later test of the plaza revealed that there was a cacophony of echoes all over the place. However, when it was time to determine the *number* of shots fired, the echoes quiet right down to where we can ascertain with certainty that the 3-shot witnesses are to be believed over the 4-shot witnesses. I think Bugliosi did his analysis after 5 shots.)

The doctors in Washington after some fuzzy testimony finally agreed to write an autopsy report that the shots were coming from *behind* Kennedy, as would be the case if Oswald were the shooter. But everyone agrees that the Washington autopsy was incompetently performed, making the observations quite questionable, another example of the system mind at work.

In view of all the tangible evidence and eyewitness testimony, the explanation of what happened that *best fits all these facts and evidence* is that there were 3 shots from the depository, possibly a 4th from the direction of the grassy knoll. The first shot missed; the second, an entrance wound to Kennedy possible coming from ahead like from the grassy knoll, although possibly not; a third hitting Connolly; and the last, the fatal shot to the head. This best fits all the facts of all these wounds in my opinion, although this is a very close call because Bugliosi is very convincing that all shots came from Oswald. We will never know.

The second and third shots were so close together in time that they couldn't have come from the same gun. Also, the Zapruder film seems to show there were two separate shots, although close together. Of course Bugliosi doesn't like the Zapruder film because most crimes are solved without films. Anyway, the Warren Commission conveniently melded them into one shot, which is the source of the magic bullet theory. A photo of Kennedy's jacket shows an exit hole a full six inches below the collar line, whereas the front wound was about at the collar line.[2] But if the second and third bullet were the same coming from Oswald, this bullet would have had to enter Kennedy from a downward angle in the back, rise slightly to come out where it did in his neck; level off for about 2 feet so that it would hit Connolly at about the same level of the back as it hit Kennedy, go through Connolly, then take a sharp drop downward to hit his wrist and finally his thigh. It is possible that one bullet did all that is attributed to it, but just on the mechanics of what this bullet is supposed to have done, the trajectory for one bullet certainly has a less than 1 probability. Bugliosi explains this away by saying the president was bending forward. He would have had to be lying down on his stomach for a shot from Oswald from behind to take this trajectory. It was only recently that I learned that Kennedy was wearing a back brace that would have prevented him from bending forward — a fact *rigidly* suppressed by everyone commenting on the event right to the present day. *Additionally*, the Zapruder film shows no such bending forward, just as you would expect in a motorcade. (It is interesting that when evidence seems to support Bugliosi's claims, he gives us photographs and x-rays. When it conflicts with his claims, he gives us worthless sketches.)

Even a dummy like Gerald Ford saw that this trajectory was pretty unlikely. But the interesting thing about dumb people is that they have no conception of what it's like to be smarter. So Ford simply changed the report raising the entry wound in Kennedy's back up to his neck, thinking that nobody would notice — a pretty funny note of the whole story. But it shows even Ford saw the fishiness of the single bullet theory. Also, three of seven commissioners did not believe the single bullet theory, but were persuaded to go along so as to have a unified report.

About the last fatal shot to the head, there was massively conflicting testimony from forensic specialists, doctors, and autopsy people. Much of this evidence points to a shot from behind as from Oswald. However, from the Zapruder film, it appears that the first motion of Kennedy's head upon the bullet hitting him was a snap backwards in the same direction as the bullet, indicating a shot from ahead. In fact, assuming Kennedy's head to be in a fairly relaxed position, it snapped back by the right amount for the momentum of the bullet to be transferred to his head. In my opinion, Bugliosi's momentum test was bogus.

Well, we'll hesitantly accept the last shot as Oswald's, although it is amusing to note that Bugliosi doesn't think we need the Zapruder film because, after all, 99.9% of crimes are solved without a film. This example of lawyer logic is a palpable explanation of why 30 straight lawyers were chosen to analyze the Kennedy assassination. (Another example of lawyer logic is that the Warren Commission never examined any of the tangible evidence. The reason is that they would have to release this evidence to the public which would invade the Kennedy family's privacy. The Government's interest in our privacy takes some amazing twists and turns. Here again, if there was a conspiracy or anything untoward about the event, the system was going to make sure it would never come to light.)

And the needs of the system mind were carried out even after the assassination. Bugliosi very cleverly induces his readers into thinking that it was just bad luck that Ruby got to Oswald. Yes, Ruby by chance, got past a police guard to get into the basement of the police station where they were going to transfer Oswald to a car to go to the county jail. This was another unlikely event. However, what Bugliosi is careful not to stress is that the police station was crawling with newspeople and reporters almost non-stop from Friday, the day of the assassination, till Sunday when Oswald was killed. Few if any of these reporters had their credentials checked each day. In fact, Ruby could have killed Oswald on Friday just as well. An important fact is that right after the assassination, the police received *two* anomalous calls threatening to kill Oswald. One lonely cop suggested that, for safely, they should transfer Oswald in the middle of the night when nobody would be around. But the system mind would have none of that.

For an hour before bringing Oswald down from upstairs to the basement to be put into a car, there were throngs of people swarming all over the place. They had been told when Oswald was going to be moved. Crowds like this are like a basement flood. You try to put a sandbag here, but the water scoots around and flows over there. You put up a barrier here and the water finds a way to flow around over there. Crowds flow the same way. The police would push back the crowd here, only to see them expand somewhere else. It was an impossible situation. Anyone with half a brain could see that a shooter could very easily pose as a reporter, meld in with the crowd, and pick off Oswald when he appeared. Bugliosi puts the emphasis on Ruby. Ruby's actions were not part of the system mind's plan, nor anyone's plan. It was a freak occurrence. What he doesn't see is that the whole scenario was a perfect system mind set-up (another attractor) for someone to kill Oswald. Whether or not there was an actual player is beside the point. If Oswald didn't get killed on Sunday, the system would have kept pushing him through unchecked crowds until he got killed even if it took a week of parading.

Bugliosi is a lawyer. Every day people are put in jail on the basis of what *in reality* is basically circumstantial evidence. The reason is that without foul play of some kind to explain a crime, the crime is just too improbable to have occurred randomly and innocently. Bugliosi is passing himself off as a scholar not an entertainer. But his "scholarship" amounts to telling us that the whole thing was a string of coincidences. What he doesn't tell us is that the probability of such a string occurring coincidentally and at random is near zero, which is a lower probability than any of the conspiracies. And where is his scholarship when it comes to the Warren Report, an official government document, which is a lot more fraudulent than Garrison who was just one low-level man.

At the end of his book, Bugliosi gives a two-page list of the coincidences between the Kennedy the Abe Lincoln assassinations. They were elected exactly a hundred years apart and both were followed by a Johnson. The implication is that coincidences happen. But this is an irrelevant analogy. There are no causal ramifications tying together events a hundred years apart, which is why they are coincidences. The probability that any particular conspiracy theory is correct be be very low. However, any one of them is still more likely true than that the Warren Commission is the whole story.

This assassination story brings out an important qualification about the system mind. The system mind is a very coarse device. It does not deal in detail. To give a good metaphor, the system mind sets the *stage* for what it wants and needs. It creates the choreography, the set, the lighting, the backdrops, and the set pieces on the stage. It *invites* players to read the script but does not run the details of the actual players. The backdrop starts with the political climate engendered by some of the leading nodes of the economy at the time and by the system mind it created. The witch-hunting and devil-in-our-midst thinking had some effect on all Americans and all nodes of the system in this period, many to the point of intense hatred of Kennedy. It was this system mind that increased the probabilities of each event so that the string of events becomes reasonably likely without a conspiracy.

There were hundreds of opportunities to impede the assassination, but the system mind stood by and allowed Oswald to move closer to the final event. The Dealey Plaza stage was only an *attractor*, totally overlooked as such by every government agency. There might have been no players reading the script set up for them or there might have been three. It was a piece of bad luck that everything fell into place and Kennedy died. But the important point is that the system mind only sets the stage and the backdrop and *invites* and *attracts* the players. It does not *run* the players. Players may or may not mount the stage and read their scripts. Even when they do, the minute details of their actions are not relevant. The important point is that whatever the details, *the assassination came off because a setting was created by the system mind that would be highly conducive to an assassination of JFK. The system mind didn't kill Kennedy directly, but it did create the perfect backdrop for it to happen.*

But the action of the system mind didn't stop with the staging of the assassination. It very cleverly set the stage for the squashing of important evidence by facilitating the killing of Oswald. The system mind created a perfect set-up for both killings, and it was just bad luck that there were players who read their respective scripts. The very day of the assassination, the system went about setting up a new stage as to how the system would present the whole event publicly, that would acceptable to the American people and best for the country. Bugliosi is quick to question the motives of conspiracy theorists. But he is totally oblivious of the blatant fact that there was enormous pressure on everyone who was part of the system — the media, all the lawyers, all the doctors, and even some who testified before the Commission to agree with what a moron could see was the theory the commission was aiming for and what the system needed.

Fortunately for the system, as information about the assassination began to leak out from various agencies over the years, it became apparent that there was probably no conspiracy. It was only then that further investigations took place. If there had been any evidence of a conspiracy, all we would ever have gotten would be the Warren Commission report done by a bunch of motivated lawyers who never saw any tangible evidence. I hope Bugliosi lives long enough to see how much information is going to come out about events leading to the invasion of Iraq.

Bugliosi doesn't like conspiracies, but not only is the stage for an assassination the product of the system mind, but every single initiative taken by authorities *after* the assassination was also the product of the system mind. The real conspiracy is creating a commission to investigate such a natural event with 30 consecutive lawyers. This is fraudulent just for starters. If you had to cover up a conspiracy, this is exactly the way to start. Then they conveniently avoided any questions that would assist us in *understanding* the assassination. They never took a glance at the Zapruder film. They never looked at tangible evidence. It took them six months to interview Jack Ruby. What this shows is that the Warren Commission was not going to take the *slightest* chance that the Zapruder film or any other tangible evidence might show anything but the simple solution. To best describe the Warren Commission, we have to refer to our discussion of intentionality in Vol. I. *The Warren commission was a complete cover-up because that is what its intention was and that's what their actions were*, regardless of whether or not there was anything to cover up.

In reality, it makes little difference if there was a conspiracy or who was in on it. TV talking heads go through reams of detail about Oswald's guilt. *Who gives a crap?* The details we touched on in this chapter were sifted and screened and talked to death by thousands of hours of TV documentary distractions about the mechanics of the assassination. But they are not the important issues in *explaining* the assassination. If you want to see a real conspiracy, just look at the detail in the Warren Commission report. Look at thousands of TV documentaries right up to today's 50th anniversary where we find the usual puff-jobs smothering the important facts and distracting us from the important issues with millions of bits of irrelevant information, all coming from authoritative talking heads. But that's not a conspiracy either; it's just the way a system mind works.

The important issues are who designed these attractors and how did a highly motivated newspaper publisher to make them known to everyone. How did these attractors come about and how were they ignored? That's the real issue. If we know every minute fact surrounding the actual assassination, what would we do about it? But we can do something about preventing attractors for important events, and this is what the system mind is designed to squelch.

Oliver Stone made movie about the assassination that Bugliosi attacks with extreme vigor for being inaccurate, misleading and dishonest. Well, in my opinion, people making movies get a little slack in their interpretations. They are in the entertainment business not the scholarship business. Even if Stone is all wet, the movie does point out the enormous number of highly improbable events all strung together. And if for no other reason, this, to me, is a more telling contribution to an analysis of the event than Bugliosi's 1500 pages of irrelevancies.

Bugliosi suggests that Oliver Stone's movie was harmful to the country. I want to know what was the harm? Maybe it actually did a service to the country by suggesting to people that they shouldn't take government "investigations" at face value. The real harm to the country is people like Bugliosi whitewashing the fraudulent Warren Commission report and setting a precedent that the government could use the modern means of propaganda for future cover-ups of government misdeeds, especially the design of attractors for events the system needs and wants. Since JFK, there have been numerous events with the same official government commissions and "investigations" papering over law-breaking. It was after this event that Johnson, with the use of television, was able to crank up the war in Vietnam on the basis of a pure lie. For years, the system mind propaganda outlets would sugar-coat the Vietnam war and government "investigations" would white-wash what was really happening until people finally got weary of hearing how we were winning every day in a never-ending war. Then there was the Iran-contra scandal. In the next chapter we will discuss another major attractor that was used as the basis for a fraudulent trillion dollar invasion and war.

What the Warren Commission report did was take us down a new fork in the road of American history where modern means of communication, television, could be effectively used to assuage people's concerns and get them to accept whatever lies and distortions the system needs at any given time. Even in 2014 and the 50th anniversary of the assassination, the media is right back in place papering over all the important details of the JFK assassination. The practice of the system covering up important details of major events with sugar-coated explanations all started with the Kennedy assassination and the Warren Commission report.

[1]   Bugliosi, Vincent, '07. *Reclaiming History*, Norton Co., New York, NY.
[2]   Galinor, Stewart, '98. *Cover Up*, Kastrel Books, New York, NY.

CHAPTER 33

9/11

———

THERE IS A VERY EERIE resemblance between the events leading up to 9/11 and the JFK assassination. With JFK, a whole sequence of intrinsically unlikely events had to happen all in a row for the final event to take place. If any one of these events had been missing there would have been no assassination. Many forces in society were inimical to policies of the JFK administration and the resulting flows of information created a system mind that swept up all the players into raising the probability of each event in the sequence, making the assassination highly likely.

The 9/11 attack was similar. At the time, the system needed a terrorist attack and the thousands of flows of information among hundreds of Bush administration players created a mind made up of these players doing their parts towards enabling a terrorist attack. Before getting to the meat of this chapter, I want to warn the reader that I'm going to tell the 9/11 story in broad terms to illustrate something of how the system mind works. This will not be a detailed scholarly chapter. It's about concepts, not minutia. If you are interested in detailed facts, there are a number of extremely scholarly books written about 9/11 listed at the end of the chapter.[1] In these books you will find documents, quotes, references and enough footnotes to strangle the Nike shoe company. The authors are quite careful in distinguishing facts from opinions, and I will try to do the same.

A short summary of the analysis we will present in this chapter can be summed up in three phrases: the system *needed* a terrorist attack, the system *invited* a terrorist attack and the system *got* a terrorist attack.

33.1 INVOLVEMENT OF THE MAJOR NODES OF THE ECONOMY

This is a good time to discuss the various levels of involvement of the players or nodes relevant to an important event. They form a continuum like the red to yellow continuum we discussed in Sect. 6.3. At the top are *conspiracies* where relevant players are overtly participating in the planning and execution of an important event. The next level down is *complicity*. This is where important players are actually *cooperating* in making an event come off by performing key moves that *contribute* to the overall carrying out of a planned event. They don't perform the major activities that comprise the event, but they interject key details that are necessary for the event to occur. Then there are *facilitations*. This is where players simply cut a clear and convenient path for others to carry out the event in question. Even though they don't perform any overt contributory activities, they stand by and *allow* important contributions to the final event to occur. Then there is what we are calling a *system mind*. There are no conspiracies or overt cooperative behavior or even actual conscious activities that contribute to the final event. However, by being part of a system mind, the behavior of the relevant players, without conscious thought processes, creates a big picture scenario, a kind of mind, that will most likely bring about the final event.

One way to judge complicity and facilitations is the following. If a player would have done exactly what he did *if* he actually were a conspirator, then that player is complicit or a facilitator. There are plenty of actions around 9/11 that fall into this category. Before starting on research for this chapter, I would never in a million years have guessed the mounds of evidence that point to a conspiracy or at least complicity or facilitation. Of course, the system mind media outlets were extremely *complicit* in completely burying important details because wars make ratings go up and many corporate sponsors make fortunes on the king's wars.

The view presented here is a more conservative view that the 9/11 attack was a product of the system mind. However, there are so many suspicious events surrounding the attack that most competent writers I have seen claim that the level of involvement of government players rose to the level of *complicity*, or at least, facilitation. In my opinion, these views are quite plausible because there are mountains of evidence that supports them. But we will take a minimalist approach.

33.2 The System Mind and 9/11

Since this was such an important event in our history and subsequent developments in our society, we should briefly review how a system mind works in relation to the 9/11 attack. We have explained the system mind with analogies to the brain. When your mind thinks, "I'll get up to go get something to eat", millions of neurons in your brain are firing impulses back and forth with other neurons. Each neuron, which is a node in the brain, is just a little package of chemicals. They have no knowledge. They cannot talk. They cannot make plans. They do not think. The mind you have is the result of billions of tiny neurons firing impulses back and forth. Thinking about something to eat is something your *mind* does. Of course, how all that buzzin', bloomin' firing away that the neurons do — how this causes your *mind* to have thoughts is the mystery of the mind/body problem as we discussed in detail in the first volume.

The system mind works in exactly the same way. Both involve information flows traveling between nodes of the system. If the complaint is that we can't explain how a system mind emerges, remember, neuroscientists have been working for a hundred years on how our own minds emerge from activity in the brain, and have not yet come up with a satisfactory answer. So don't expect that there are any better answers as to how a system mind is created by billions of flows of information between the nodes of the economic system.

The nodes of the brain are individual neurons. The nodes of the system mind are individual people, institutions, and agencies. Bush and Cheney were nodes in the system. They were probably not thinking and talking about a terrorist attack any more than the neurons in the brain think about getting something to eat. It's the whole system of neurons firing impulses between one another that creates the human mind. It is the fact that all the nodes in the economy sending information back and forth between them that creates a system mind.

A good question you may have is how do we know there is a system mind? And even if we believe something like this, how do we know what it is thinking? We do this the same way we attribute minds to other people. Recall in Sect. 6.6, we discussed the problem of other minds. You should go back and read that section if you really want to understand the system mind. We attribute mindedness to other living creatures on the basis of intelligent behavior. Intelligent behavior includes displaying motives for what we do; indicating desires for what we want; showing we have beliefs that guide our behavior; and having the ability to maintain ourselves and to perpetuate our existence and fulfill our goals and desires. It is on this basis that we attribute minds to other living things.

We use the exact same criteria for attributing a mind to our economic system. We look at the behavior of the system to see if there is a tendency to fulfill certain goals and needs; and to see if it tries to reproduce and perpetuate itself. If you see that what the system does is always in line with its interests, you have pretty good evidence that something like a mind is in play.

33.3 Motivation of the System Mind

In the chapters on Russia and JFK, we looked at evidence for a system mind. In this chapter we will look at further evidence. So let us look at some of the wants and needs of the American economic system and the ways the system would benefit from a terrorist attack so that the system mind would have the *motivation* to invite and facilitate one. This would be evidence that there *is* a system mind.

One of the goals of the system mind, as we have stressed is control over the population. This is done by making the almighty job the core of people's identity, and to control the thinking and values of the population so that it is in line with the interests of the major nodes of the system. The best means to achieve this objective is by conducting permanent war as we will discuss in the next Chapter. The war on terrorism is a perfect war, and this can be greatly magnified by invading and conquering smaller countries of the world. Invasion and conquest not only enables permanent war, but it also enables another goal of the system mind, which is to control and micromanage these societies to the advantage of the system.

The Bush administration had been making plans for Iraq's oil. However, the American people don't always support outright imperialism. In a 1997 book, Zbigniew Brzezinski noted that "the pursuit of power is not a goal that commands popular passion.... What would make the American public willing to make the economic and human sacrifices needed for imperial mobilization, would be a truly massive and widely perceived direct external threat." [2] This pretty much tells the rat pack in the Bush administration that what they needed was a New Pearl Harbor.

As an aside, Pearl Harbor was a very incisive example of the system mind at work. There is not space here to go into detail, but briefly, Roosevelt's economy had sunk back into recession in 1937 because Republicans cut off money for job creation and restricted the money supply. Also, Japan had invaded China and was obviously looking to take over control of the Pacific Ocean. Our military had advised moving the fleet out into the Pacific to deter Japanese aggression in Asia. But there was no need for the fleet to be moved from San Diego where it was safe, to Pearl Harbor which was a confined body of water with limited access, which was an obvious trap. It would have difficult to safely get the fleet out of the harbor even with a warning. But there was no warning. The system mind had arranged a complete surprise attack.

The country needed a war and it also needed a war with Japan. But there was no groundwork propaganda campaign against Japan. The only way the American people could be put on a war footing was as a reaction to a major surprise attack. Our intelligence had cracked the Japanese code and knew an attack was imminent. But the mind of the system lost the information. Every morsel of information concerning an attack was misinterpreted, suppressed or ignored. The attack worked like a charm for both sides. Each side now had an "enemy". Young men ran to recruitment offices to join up and fight the "Japs". The US quickly mobilized for war at a frantic pace. This momentum eventually won the war but the question will always remain, did we have to sacrifice the lives of two and half thousand young men at Pearl Harbor to get us into a war with Japan? This question was never considered because the war wasn't started by individual decisions. It was started in an optimum way by the mind of the system at the time. One of the most eye-opening experiences I've had was to see how the producers and writers of the movie *Tora, tora, tora* gave many details of the workings of a system mind without themselves having conscious awareness of the concept of a system mind.

By the time we get to 2000, the system mind had become extremely sophisticated with many more flows of information and a more articulated version of its interests. It used that sophistication to arrange for George Bush to be elected in 2001, which, of course, occurred because the Supreme Court blatantly violated the Constitution that specifically gives the states powers to manage their own affairs, especially elections. They went right down into Florida and cancelled any democratic determinants of the election and picked Bush as the new president.

Right from the beginning, the economy was tanking. The stockmarket was dropping, unemployment was increasing and the economy was heading towards recession. The Bush administration was losing popularity and its agenda for goosing the war on terrorism was undermined with the result that reasons for conquering and controlling other countries were weakening. Things were not looking very good for the administration. The bad economy and bad ratings were *pulling* the administration towards a nice juicy war and the needs of the system for more imperialism around the world was *pushing* in the same direction. A terrorist attack could be the perfect basis to circle the wagons and the perfect excuse to carry out its international agenda abroad and bail out the domestic agenda at home. Wars have the added advantage of allowing spending of huge amounts of money. This is not only part of the conservative Republican agenda of crippling the economy with mountains of national debt, but it enables many large corporations to make huge profits producing war materiel.

This is exactly what transpired after the attack. The Bush administration used the shock and horror of the attack to direct people's emotions towards "fighting back". So immediately, with the complete connivance of the corporate system mind media, the administration established a connection between the attack of 9/11 and the countries it had been preparing to invade, namely, Iraq and Afghanistan. One of the leading propagandists for the system mind, Richard Perle, said, "State Sponsors of Terrorism Should Be Wiped out Too".[3] Of course, the facts of this situation were totally suppressed by the system mind media propaganda outlets. The terrorists came from Perle's friends, Saudi Arabia and were trained in *Pakistan*, no less. Iraq and Afghanistan had absolutely nothing to do with it. In my opinion, people like Perle have no intention of ridding the world of terrorism; their motive is to *create* terrorism as a vehicle to carry out their domestic and international agenda, which is Economic Socialism at home, and invading and killing people in smaller countries abroad. And they know the system propaganda outlets will back up any story they concoct regardless of the facts.

Another propagandist for the system mind said "...these attacks have been described as the 'opportunity of the ages' ", and provided a 'New Pearl Harbor'.[4] Condolizza Rice told the National Security Council to think about "how do you capitalize on these opportunities".[5] Now a statement like this might be pretty embarrassing to the administration. However, they don't have to worry about mistakes like this because they can be confident that the paid whores of the system mind will completely suppress such mistakes.

There were other motivations for wars against Iraq and Afghanistan even without the motivation of cranking up the war on terrorism and to have a distraction from the tanking economy and falling ratings. In Sect. 30.4 we mentioned the neoconservative think tank suggesting plans for invasion, conquest, and killing. Many of the people in this group wound up in the Bush administration. They even sent a letter to Clinton "urging him to adopt a strategy aimed at the removal of Saddam Hussein's regime from power".[6] "Paul O'Neill, Bush's former Treasury Secretary, has said that the Bush administration had from the outset planned to attack Iraq, partly for its oil." [7] All the administration needed was a nice juicy terrorist attack to justify the plans. In fact, various neoconservatives made allusions to the idea that what was needed for all this militarism to proceed was a new Pearl Harbor, which is exactly what we got and what Griffin titled his book.

In Afghanistan, there was a consortium of oil companies who wanted to build a pipeline through Afghanistan. "...the Talaban was originally created by the CIA, working in conjunction with Pakistan's ISI (Inter-Services Intelligence), with additional financial support from Saudi Arabia." [8] Millions of taxpayer dollars were spent to create and solidify a Talaban government, the purpose of which was to have a strong stable government that would enable the pipeline to be built. But the Talaban began to discourage the pipeline project and the pipeline consortium fell apart. Without it, Afghanistan was ripe for a weak, corrupt government, which the system mind needs for safe havens to recruit and train terrorists as we will explain in the next chapter. Not only that, but the Talaban had been replacing opium crops with wheat and other legitimate crops. The removal of the Talaban would allow Afghanistan to continue supplying drugs to our kids, enabling hundreds of billions of dollars to be made by the neoconservative money-laundering banks that support it

So removal of the Talaban was a top priority for the Bush administration. A BBC report had senior American officials saying, "military action against the Talaban would go ahead by the middle of October", a month after 9/11.[9] This is just one of a large number of telling facts surrounding 9/ll that were never reported by the mainstream media propaganda outlets.

In general, there was such massive motivation for the system mind to bring on a terrorist attack that you can't blame the critics for various conspiracy theories that suggest that important administration players had to be actively facilitating an attack. But this would require conscious participation. Our view is that there was no need for the players to be conscious of playing their parts. They were simply part of a system mind that needed a terrorist attack, invited a terrorist attack and got a terrorist attack. Before we get into the details, we can see evidence of a system mind in the usual Commission that was set up to examine the event.

33.4 The 9/11 Commission

Immediately after the attack, there was the usual preliminary investigation in 2002 called the Joint Inquiry Report. The Joint Inquiry report was carbon copy of the Warren Commission. It was not a real investigation to answer important questions about the event, but an instruction manual as to what a more comprehensive report to come later should say, and what media propaganda outlets should feed the American people. David Ray Griffin says, "A more sweeping investigation was not undertaken because the congressional leaders acceded to requests from the White House that the scope of their investigation be limited." [10] It is exactly the way the Bush administration put pressure on the CIA for "evidence" of Saddam's WMDs. In an article in the NYR, Mark Danner reported how "...Sir Richard Dearlove, the head of M16, Britain's equivalent of the CIA, had just returned from a high-level consultation in the United States". ..."Bush wanted to remove Saddam, through military action, justified by the conjunction of terrorism and WMD. But the intelligence and facts were being fixed around the policy" [11]

Many of the critics of the Commission report make a big deal over the fact that the guy in charge of the Commission was part and parcel of the Bush administration ideology, its goals and its implementation. But this is not the important factor. By its very nature, a Commission is made up of politicians, lawyers, and public figures who are involved in a myriad of information flows involving important nodes of the system. The result is that Commissions become part and parcel of the system mind and become the most exemplary evidence of a system mind that we can point out. This is why they invariably come to conclusions that wear down, smooth out, and paper over inconvenient sharp edges, which allows the smooth continuation of the operation of the system. By their very nature, if there is anything at all suspicious about events, you know good and well a commission is going to cover them up, avoid asking embarrassing questions and ignore key evidence, just like happened with the JFK Warren Commission.

But just as with the Warren Commission, a substantial majority of Americans never accepted the Commission report as telling the whole story. A 2002 Atlantic Journal-Constitution poll indicated that "...almost 50 percent of the respondents...suspected that the Bush administration was covering up advanced warnings it had received".[12] A CBS/*New York Times* poll indicated that "...an astonishing 72 percent of the American people believed the Bush administration to be guilty of" some kind of lying or cover-up.[13] What really surprised me is that in one poll of residents of New York State, 30% of *Republicans* thought that "some leaders in the US government knew in advance that attacks were planned on or around September 11, 2001, and...consciously failed to act".[14]

There are two categories of facts relevant to the 9/11 attack. There are technical matters and there is human action and behavior. We will be stressing the latter because these are more relevant to the creation of motives and goals of the system mind. We'll mention briefly a few technical aspects that make things look like some kind of conspiracy was afoot.

33.5 TECHNICAL ASPECTS OF THE 9/11 ATTACK.

The official Commission explanation of why the towers fell was that the heat from the jet fuel fires melted the bolts holding the steel structure together causing them to give way and for the floor of the attack to collapse on the one below. But the first floor that collapsed should have been slightly delayed when it hit the next floor down if only briefly, and the collapse should have picked up speed only after a number of floors had given way. But this was not the case. The whole building collapsed at about the same rate as free fall, which points to a demolition. Critics have speculated that the buildings were really demolished by a system of pre-placed explosives right after the planes hit. There is the testimony of many witnesses including firemen, who claimed that they heard explosions in the towers before they came down, indicating a demolition. *Fire Engineering* magazine said, "The destruction and removal of evidence must stop immediately".[15] But of course, all the evidence was taken away as quickly as possible and sold overseas before any thorough investigation could take place. What's the explanation for this?

Also, there are experts who claim that the heat necessary to melt the bolts to where they couldn't take the load was much more than could be produced by a jet fuel fire that was intense only as long as the jet fuel lasted, which was only a few seconds. Photographs of the north tower show that after the initial explosive fire, mostly smoke was coming out of the building, not a prolonged intense fire that would be needed to heat the bolts for them to give way. Some experts claimed that considering the reinforced steel structure, the strength of the beams, the number of bolts, etc. these planes could not have brought the buildings down as alleged.

Then there is the energy consideration. If the buildings simply collapsed, you would get a lot of big concrete blocks and slabs. But there was none of that. A hundred thousand tons of concrete pulverized into powder that filled the air and made breathing impossible and covered the area with a foot of dust. To pulverize this enormous volume of concrete takes a tremendous amount of energy, much greater than the potential energy of the weight of the falling buildings. There were scientific experts who claimed that only an explosive demolition could provide the energy to pulverize that much concrete into powder.

Even the steel structure was in small pieces as though there had been explosives. As a former architectural engineer, this fact is very puzzling to me. There should have been long spans of steel columns sticking up in the debris. As most of you witnessed, the many photos of the collapsed buildings showed no signs of these columns. There seemed to be only lots of small pieces of metal amongst the rubble. But farther down, the site contained pools of molten metal that stayed very hot for many days. Where did the energy come from to melt huge amounts of metal into molten pools except from high explosives?

Then there is the symmetry argument. These were very tall, thin buildings, constructed symmetrically. However, they were hit *a*symmetrically, on one side of the north tower and on the corner of the south tower. This should have caused the buildings to topple over. But they didn't. They fell completely symmetrically right in their footprints. This is a very powerful argument. I claim that if you showed a photo of these buildings a microsecond after being hit so that you couldn't see planes hitting them, out of a thousand architectural and structural engineers, every single one would believe the cause of the buildings coming down was a symmetric demolition. Photographs of the buildings pulverizing as they came down looked exactly like those demolitions of old large hotels you've seen dynamited down. Of course, rubble from this building was removed as quickly as possible to prevent any kind of thorough investigation, a perfect example of a system mind.

Then there was the smaller building 7 of the World Trade Center (WTC-7) that collapsed without being hit with anything not even parts of the two towers that disintegrated pretty much in place. This is the most mysterious event of all. The collapsing towers made a rumble, but not enough to bring down another steel reinforced building many hours later. Also, firemen were warned to stay away from this building as though someone knew they were going to be demolished.

Now listen to this, and ask yourself if you ever heard this important fact. For 8 years prior to 9/11, security for the WTC was provided by a company called Securacom, in which the president's younger brother was a principle. Then 5 days before 9/ll, security bomb-sniffing dogs were stopped. If the crews of this company were setting dynamite charges during this period, there would be no warning from bomb-sniffing dogs. Another fact: on the weekend of Sept. 8-10, the power was off on the top floors of the south tower. During this time, there were no security cameras or security locks on doors, plenty of opportunity to set dynamite charges.

All this clearly points to a conspiracy. On the other side of the ledger, if you accept a demolition theory, who set up the demolition? It would take tons of dynamite to be brought in and set in key places in the buildings and wired up. This would engage a very large crew working many hours. Even if the younger brother's security firm did the dirty work, how is it that in all this time, nobody anywhere sent a note to a newspaper suggesting something was afoot. It's almost impossible to keep a secret like this among a large group of people for a long period of time. This is strong evidence against a demolition theory. Also, I think many of the skeptical experts very much underestimate what total junk these buildings were. In my opinion, these buildings were unsafe without planes flying into them and should never have been built; they were crap in every way: architecturally, structurally, materially, and aesthetically. A good earthquake or hurricane that put some torque on these buildings could have brought them down the same way.

When we turn to the Pentagon attack, again there is evidence on completely opposite sides that seem equally strong, but equally convincing. The hole in the Pentagon was only about 18 feet in diameter, about the size of a fuselage, but too small to fit through the wings and tail of a huge Boeing 757 which is the plane officially designated as hitting the Pentagon. Not only that but there were no large pieces of such a plane outside the building, nor found inside either for that matter. Photographs of this part of the Pentagon right after the crash show no signs of wings, tail, engines, anywhere on the site. All that was found were small scraps of metal. So if there was a plane that hit the pentagon, where are the larger parts?

However, physical evidence suggesting a torpedo shaped missile and not a large plane invites the question: what happened to the Boeing Flight 77? If a missile hit the Pentagon, and Flight 77 landed safely, where do we get a bunch of people showing up with dead relatives who were flying that day? Conspirators would have had to land that plane somewhere, kill all the passengers, dispose of all the bodies, chop up the plane, and dispose of all the parts. Too much can go wrong with such an operation resulting in getting exposed, which would bring down the government. And most importantly, how could such a gigantic operation come off without anyone involved ever saying peep? In my opinion, on the basis of this technical evidence, you could come to any conclusion that suits you without looking totally off-base. Regardless of your opinions of the theories of the 9/11 commission critics, you have to admit there are a lot of questions that cry out for a thorough investigation and explanation. But we're never going to get it.

However, the analysis here does not rely on these technical aspects of the event because there is plenty of evidence of a system mind at work to keep us busy enough as it is. So we'll go on to the *human* aspects of the event and the parts played by the players. In this regard, there are three categories of information that the system had available to prevent the 9/11 terrorist attack. First there were general warnings from a variety of sources. Second, there were specific plans of an attack that the system learned about but completely ignored. And third, there were actual intercepts of communication between players that were or could have been involved in a terrorist attack. These too were suppressed and ignored.

33.6 INFORMATION AVAILABLE THAT COULD HAVE PREVENTED THE 9/11 ATTACK.

At the very beginning of the Bush administration, everything that could have done to *facilitate* 9/11 seems to have been done; first by doing nothing to prepare for one, and then ignoring all warnings of an attack. The very first thing the Bush administration did upon taking office to facilitate a terrorist attack was to drastically cut anti-terrorism funding. In the next few years, every piece of information that could have enabled authorities to *disrupt* the hijackers' plan or to even put them on the trail was conveniently ignored. For example, "On December 20, 2000, Richard Clarke, a counter-terrorism expert, submitted a plan to 'roll back' Al Qaeda in response to the bombing of the *USS Cole*." [16] The Clinton Administration passed the plan on to the incoming Bush administration who proceeded to reject "the plan and took no action". [17] Here we had a terrorist attack on the Cole and also on the WTC, and when a very responsible and experienced official warned that something should be done to prevent further attacks, his ideas are ignored. In fact, the more evidence that accrued pointing to terrorist attacks, the less was done to prepare for one. The system did everything it could to minimize the chances of disrupting a terrorist attack. The closer we got to the attack, the deeper asleep was the system.

Also, it turned out that the 9/11 hijackers had been "living, working, planning and developing all their activities in Laurel Maryland, which happens to be the home of the NSA, the National Security Agency. NSA, had been tracking their communication for months before the attack and had reason to believe they were planning an attack. French and Italian intelligence had warned Cheney and the CIA that the 9/11 people were real live terrorists who had planned other terrorist attacks. These weren't just your ordinary angry Muslims. These guys were known terrorists. Not only that but none of the agencies involved, FBI, CIA, NSA shared any information they had obtained. Any coordination at all of this information would have pointed to a terrorist attack. Again there wasn't one minute of surveillance or investigation and no one was brought in for questioning. These agencies take billions of dollars away from research into a variety of diseases like cancer that could save thousands of lives in order to spy on the American people. But known terrorists are allowed to run around the country with no investigations at all.

There were reports that some of the hijackers had taken flying lessons and asked only how to fly planes with no interest in how to land or take off. Again, no investigation. On top of that, a number of the 9/11 gang had broken laws. They had forged passports, and lied about their activities in the US. Again, no investigation, no indictments, not even comprehensive surveillance. And this was for actually breaking laws.

33.7 FACILITATE BY NOT DISRUPTING SPECIFIC PLANS

Lots of people in and out of government pointed out that the WTC was a perfect target for a terrorist attack. And there were numerous warnings from a variety of sources that specifically warned that a terrorist attack was immanent, and sometimes the exact time and location was indicated. Several presidential briefings warned of an imminent attack. The administration did nothing about it. Is this facilitation? "Russian President Putin later stated that in August, 'I ordered my intelligence to warn President Bush in the strongest terms that 25 terrorists were getting ready to attack the US, including important government buildings like the Pentagon... We had clearly warned them' on several occasions, but they 'did not pay the necessary attention'." [18] "...a memo provided by Great Britain" warned "that Al Qaeda had planned an attack in the United States involving multiple airplane hijackings." [19] In July, '01, "the Taliban's Foreign Minister informed US officials that Osama bin Laden was planning a 'Huge attack' inside America that was imminent and would kill thousands".[20] More specifically, there was a story of a government agent, Randy Glass, who, in July 1999 "recorded a conversation with an ISI agent named Rajaa Gulum Abbas and some illegal arms dealers" that took place near the WTC. "Abbas reportedly pointed to the WTC and said, 'those towers are coming down' ". [21]

Julie Sills, an agent for the Defense Intelligence Agency (DIA) was in Afghanistan and had gathered information about the Talaban and Al Qaeda. But she was investigated and her security clearance was pulled. "On August 22, '01, John O'Neill, a counter-terrorism expert who was said to be the US government's 'most committed tracker of Osama bin Laden and his Al Qaeda network of terrorists', resigned from the FBI, citing repeated obstruction of his investigation into Al Qaeda".[22] In fact, instead of Al Qaeda being investigated, O'Neill was investigated. All in all, *anybody or anything or any facts that got in the way of a smooth flow of events leading to 9/11 was pushed out of the picture.* What does this tell you? And you wonder why there are conspiracy theories.

On September 13, 2001, Attorney David Schippers — who was the Chief Investigative Council for the US House of Representatives' Judiciary Committee in 1998...publicly stated that he had attempted to warn Attorney General John Ashcroft about attacks planned for 'lower Manhattan' six weeks beforehand.... Schippers said that *the dates and targets* of the attacks as well as the names and funding sources of the hijackers were known by these agents months in advance".[23] "Schippers said further that the FBI agents told him that their investigations had been curtailed by FBI headquarters, which threatened the agents with prosecution if they went public...". [24] If this isn't complicity or facilitation, how do you explain such behavior except by some sort of system mind? Not only that, but the Commission didn't even mention Schippers in their report.

To cover its tracks, "US intelligence agencies...would later claim that the highly specific messages received two days before 9/11 were not translated until afterwards".[25] Specifically, "In the period from September 8 to September 10, 2001, NSA intercepted, but did not translate or disseminate until after September 11, some communications that indicated possible impending terrorist activity." [26] Of course, critics don't believe the NSA in this regard. However, this is exactly the sort of thing a system mind would do.

Anyone who appeared to be a crowbar in the gears of a smooth-moving machine leading to the attack was shunted aside. On July 10, 2001, Phoenix FBI agent Ken Williams sent a now well-known memorandum to the counterterrorism division at FBI headquarters, warning "that Osama bin Laden's followers might be taking flying lessons for terrorist purposes". [27] "He recommended a national program to track suspicious flight-school students. FBI headquarters, however, did not institute such a program." [28]

"In mid-August of 2001, the staff at a flight school in Minneapolis called the local FBI to report suspicion that Zacarias Moussaoui...was planning to use a real 747 'as a weapon'. After the Minneapolis FBI agents arrested Moussaoui,...they asked FBI headquarters for a warrant to search his laptop computer." And even though the French had warned the FBI that this guy was a terrorist, "senior FBI officials said that the information 'was too sketchy to justify a search warrant for his computer' ".[29] But it was perfectly okay to invade the privacy of millions of Americans including little old ladies, illegally spying on them *after* the attack. In addition, no follow up, no questioning, no investigation. The agents in Minneapolis persisted and requested permission for a search warrant through FISA. It appears all the FBI did was to "...remove the evidence that Moussaoui was connected to Al Qaeda. ... Minneapolis FBI legal officer Coleen Rowley asked: 'Why would an FBI agent deliberately sabotage a case?' ...Other agents in the Minneapolis office joked that those at headquarters who blocked the request, 'had to be spies or moles...working for Osama bin Laden'."[30] A very ironic observation, because as part of a system mind, *that is exactly what they were doing, at the very least.*

"On August 28, 2001, the FBI office in New York, believing Khalid Almihdar — who would later be named as one of the hijackers and had been involved in the bombing of the *USS Cole*, tried to convince FBI headquarters to open a criminal investigation. But the New York request was turned down...."[31] Here we have tons of reports, interceptions, messages, and warnings from various FBI agents as to the exact date and location of a terrorist attack, as well as warnings about specific terrorists running around the country engaging in suspicious activities, and absolutely nothing is done by heads of intelligence agencies to try to prevent the attack. Intelligence agencies don't bother to translate messages involving key players, *within a few days of the attack.*

Another FBI agent, Robert Wright, had been tracking a terrorist cell in Chicago. In January, 2001, in spite of his belief that his case was growing stronger, he was told by headquarters to close the case. Wright then announced that he was suing the FBI for squelching a book he was writing about the case, alleging obstruction by FBI headquarters. He concluded, "September the 11th is a direct result of the incompetence of the FBI's International Terrorism Unit". [32] This is just another example how a system mind operates. Every node of the relevant parts of the system mind is subconsciously doing its part to enable the attack to come off.

However, these warnings by individual FBI agents are examples of how sometimes people act outside a system mind. An FBI agent in a faraway city is not involved with as many flows of information as the central office. So there are times when their own individual psychologies will propel them to do things outside the interests of the system. But of course, the warnings of these individual agents were totally ignored or squelched and were never interviewed by people and agencies at the heart of the system mind. Not only that, but the 9/11 Commission never bothered to interview any of these agents.

33.8 FACILITATE BY IGNORING INTERCEPTS

Even when there were specific intercepted messages pointing to a terrorist attack, nothing was done to follow up the information gleaned. In 1995, "Philippine police found an Al Qaeda computer with a plan called Project Bojinka, one version of which involved hijacking planes and flying them into targets such as the World Trade Center, the White House, CIA headquarters…." [33] In 1999, the National Intelligence Council, which advises the President and US intelligence agencies on emerging threats, said the same thing. A Turkish-American translator, Sibel Edmonds, testified to the 9/11 Commission that "… the FBI had so much information about a terrorist attack involving airplanes within the next few months that there should have been an orange or red alert". [34] She had written reports "…suggesting deliberate FBI sabotage of FBI investigations and even collusion with organizations that the FBI was supposed to be investigating…". [35]

Again absolutely nothing seems to have been done about these warnings while the hijackers were running around Scott-free making plans for the attack right under the noses of all these government agencies assigned to protect us — well, almost nothing: she was fired after writing a letter to the Department of Justice. Not only that, but the people doing the squelching were promoted. After the attack, this woman's willingness to give testimony as to what she knew about government negligence was totally squashed. She and a colleague tried to get the Judiciary committee and the 9/11 Commission interested in names they could provide that could shed more light on the runup to 9/11. Nothing was done to follow up on her information. This is the way the whole investigation went ahead: squashing any leads and any avenues that might shed more light on the attack.

"Shortly before 9/11, the FBI reportedly intercepted messages like, 'There's a big thing coming' and 'They're going to pay the price'. On Sept. 9, a foreign intelligence service reportedly passed on to US intelligence an intercepted message from bin Laden to his mother, in which he told her: 'In two days you're going to hear big news, and you're not going to hear from me for a while'. The next day, Sept. 10, US intelligence reportedly obtained electronic intercepts of conversations in which Al Qaeda members said: 'Tomorrow will be a great day for us'." [36]

"Mohamed Atta, considered the ringleader of 9/11, was allowed back in the United States three times in 2001, in spite of the fact that he had let his visa expire in 2000, had violated his visa by taking flying lessons, was known to have terrorist connections, and was under FBI surveillance." [37] "One of those intercepts was reportedly made by the National Security Agency (NSA), which had monitored a call during the summer between Mohamed Atta and

Khalid Shaikh Mohammed, believed to be one of the architects of Project Bojinka…" [38], who later became the mastermind of the 9/11 attack. "A CIA report on June 12, 2001, said that KSM 'was recruiting people to travel to the United States to meet with colleagues already there so that they might conduct terrorist attacks on Bin Laden's behalf. On June 22, the CIA notified all its station chiefs about intelligence suggesting a possible al Qaeda suicide attack on a U.S. target over the next few days'." [39] Then "in an intercept of September 10, 2001, Atta reportedly received final approval for the 9/11 attacks from Mohammed." [40] If the NSA had said that they had translated it when it was received, that would be open evidence of a conspiracy. So the NSA had to say this intercept wasn't translated until *after* the 9/11 attack. Well, why in hell not. Here's in intercept between two known terrorists the day before the attack, and they don't bother to translate it. The Commission doesn't raise an eyebrow.

A number of money transfers were made to Mohammed Atta. But guess what? These intercepts were supposedly not translated until *after* 9/11. With all the warnings, all the knowledge of terrorists running around, all knowledge of an imminent terrorist attack, and messages between key players is conveniently not translated. But wonder if they were translated? You would then have evidence of facilitation, at least, maybe participation — which might explain why they weren't.

In sum, there was all kinds of information in possession of various government agencies of an imminent terrorist attack. They even had information as to the exact location and the exact date. But not one twitch was done to stop it from moving along. With all these warnings and intercepts, as we shall see, it is impossible for the whole system to be so unprepared on 9/11 without an explanation involving something like either outright complicity or a system mind.

33.9 THE GO AHEAD

But the most suspicious event surrounding the attack is that in very subtle ways, Al Qaeda was told that they could go right ahead with their plans because they would never get caught. And this accounts for why the whole operation was so sloppily prepared and executed and very little care was made to hide preparations. This is probably the most interesting piece of evidence supporting a system mind. But how was this opinion communicated to Al Qaeda? Well, there were a whole series of emails sent out that would be available to the hijackers. Recall our discussion of the *message* in a piece of communication back in Ch. 3. The message is the *meaning* that is being conveyed. Regardless of the exact words, the message in various emails available to Al Qaeda was that the country was unprepared for a terrorist attack. Now this seems like a pretty innocuous statement. But we have to stop to think about this. Is there ever a circumstance where you tell an enemy about your weaknesses? Did any army general in WWII let the enemy know that he was weak on his right flank? But here people sent out emails to the effect that we were totally unprepared for a terrorist attack. This was a subtle message to Al Qaeda that since we were unprepared, they could go ahead with their plans and get away with it.

33.10 DAY OF THE ATTACK: 9/11

On the day of the attack, Flight 11 left Boston around 8 in the morning, and at 8:21, flight attendants called in to the Federal Aviation Agency, FAA, to say the plane had been hijacked. The official procedure when anything like this happens is for the National Military Command Center (NMCC), and the North American Aerospace Defense Command (NORAD) to be immediately informed. They would have "scrambled" fighter jets from the nearest airport to intercept the hijacked plane, try to guide it back on its flight pattern, and to shoot it down if orders are not carried out. This procedure is carried out dozens of times a year. There are reports that "NORAD fighters were scrambled on 129 occasions in 2000".[41] Griffin also says, "If normal procedures had been followed, accordingly, Flight 11 would have been intercepted by ...no later than 8:30, 16 minutes before it ... crashed into the WTC" [42] at 8:46. Why not on 9/11? Critics claim on this basis that somebody in authority had to give orders to stand down or delay the procedure.

The first version of what happened came from the Chairman of the Joint Chiefs of staff who didn't think fighters were scrambled at all until after the Pentagon was hit, which was at 9:38. But on Sept. 18, NORAD claimed that they weren't notified about the hijacking until 8:40, which means the FAA was sitting around for 20 minutes before informing NORAD, which does look like there were stand down orders. This clearly violated standard procedure for the FAA which requires immediate notification to the military, NORAD.

The final version in the Commission's report says that after 8:21, instead of the FAA doing something constructive about the plane itself that had reported being hijacked, the FAA spent the next 13 minutes making a whole bunch of phone calls around it's chain of command looking for approval to intercept from some high-level government official. The excuse is they wanted to make sure the plane was really hijacked. This has nothing to do with normal procedure, which is that when *anything* suspicious occurs observing a plane, the military is notified *immediately*. Being reported that you've been hijacked is a lot more than suspicious behavior. As usual in cases like this, the 9/11 Commission blamed FAA behavior as due to incompetence and mistakes. Again, just as with the JFK assassination, we have a string of events that are highly improbable all happening on this one day. It is obvious that the whole system, including the FAA, was acting *precisely* the way it would be acting if it had orders to fake a reaction and delay. This doesn't *prove* complicity, but it does illustrate a system mind.

Also, NORAD compounded the delay because there was another 6 minute delay before the planes took off, during which time it was making calls to get authorization (that it absolutely did not need). The planes were supposedly ordered to take off about the same time as the crash into the tower at 8:46. Not only that, but the planes must have taken their time because they were supposedly still 71 miles away when the south tower was hit. The explanation was that for fighters to go after and shoot down a rogue plane would have required permission from the highest levels of government (Secretary of Defense, President, etc.), who, it appears, conveniently couldn't be reached in time.

But normal procedure does not require such high-level orders. Then to add to the delay, "NORAD inexplicably gave this order *not* to McGuire Air Base in New Jersey, which is only 70 miles from NYC, but to Otis Air National Guard base in Cape Cod, *which is over 180 miles away*", which is more than *twice as far*.[43] Of course, the planes got to New York too late.

The Commission says there were no planes at McGuire for this purpose, which means there are only 2 bases with 2 planes each in the entire Northeast quarter of the US ready to deal with a hijacked plane, Otis on Cape Cod, and Langley, Virginia. Most people with half a brain wouldn't believe a word of this crap, because it would mean that the most populated quarter of the country, including New York and the nation's capital, are protected by 4 planes. (Someone found out that at the time, Andrew's website said it was home to the 121st Fighter Squadron of the 113th Fighter Wing. After 9/11, the website was conveniently modified.) The Commission response is exactly what a system mind would say. We might add that after the Pentagon was attacked, fighters *were* scrambled from Andrews to respond to the Pentagon attack. It is pretty easy to see that if there was any evidence of a conspiracy or facilitation, the 9/11 Commission was going to cover it up. This is understandable. But what is absolutely disgusting is that the mainstream media supposedly operating "in the public interest", never reported any of these highly important facts, especially after spending 3 years investigating and reporting on every minute detail of Bill Clinton's private sex life. Griffin does not stress the role of the media sufficiently, in my opinion.

Flight 175 had also been hijacked. FAA officials said they notified NORAD sometime between 8:40 and 8:43, about the same time the first plane hit the north tower that *this* flight had veered off course. NORAD should have had fighters intercepting this plane, especially since they already had fighters in the air going after the first hijacked plane, which, by this time, had already crashed into the WTC. Not only that, but nobody bothered to warn the people in the south tower that a plane had been hijacked. As we mentioned, these fighters didn't take off from Otis until 8:52, 6 minutes *after* NORAD supposedly heard of the hijacking. And not only that, but they were told to go after the *first* Flight 11 that had already hit its target instead of the second Flight 175 which was still in route. And as we mentioned, the planes were not scrambled by close-by McGuire, but from Otis 180 miles away. But there was still time to intercept the second Flight 175 which didn't hit the south tower until 9:03, but it appears the fighters took their sweet time getting there because they were supposedly still 70 miles away when the south tower was hit, and didn't get to New York until 9:25.[44] "These same pilots, flying planes capable of going 1,500 to 1,850 miles per hour, on that day were evidently able to get their planes to fly only 300 to 700 miles per hour." [45]

Even the 9/11 Commission saw that this version of events sounded pretty fishy. So they simply revised it. The new version said that NORAD's delay was due to calling Florida to find out where the hijacked planes were. But of course, the FAA had already told them that the planes were heading towards New York, and not only that, but Flight

11 had already hit the north tower at 8:46. The Commission simply ignored the testimony of people who claimed that NORAD was aware of Flight 11 hitting the north tower and so *did* know where the planes were headed. On top of this, the new version had the FAA not knowing that Flight 177 had been hijacked at 8:43 when they supposedly notified NORAD. But there is evidence and testimony that the FAA did say enough about the behavior of Flight 175 for NORAD to get planes in the air at once. So the Commission simply settled on an account whereby the FAA really didn't know the plane had been hijacked until 8:55 and notified NORAD at 9:03. This delay was supposedly due to the FAA calling around other centers and people not picking up the phone. We can see from all this that the Commission had no real interest in the actual facts, but simply concocted a best-fit story. They knew they could do such a half-assed job because the media would never say a word about real facts

Finally, after two planes had already hit the WTC, an interconference call was set up at 9:20, according to the Commission, connecting the FAA, NORAD, and the military. But an important person in the FAA testified that this call was initiated at 8:50, when there was enough time to get interceptors in the air to go after Flight 175. But the Commission denies that any important information was exchanged during this call, in particular about Flight 77, even though the north tower had been hit at 8:46. This is all unbelievable. What were they talking about?

Flight 77 that supposedly hit the Pentagon, took off at 8:20 and disappeared from contact at 8:56. The FAA knew that the plane was either hijacked or in trouble in some way at this time. At first, NORAD claimed that "...the FAA did not notify it that Flight 77 had been hijacked and was heading toward Washington until 9:24." But this is a full "34 minutes *after* the FAA lost radio contact ...and 28 minutes after the plane disappeared from its radar." [46] Who do we believe, the FAA or NORAD, or neither? But even at 9:24, which is 13 minutes before the Pentagon was hit, there was enough time to get out of the exterior of the Pentagon building. This is why Griffin titled his book, *The New Pearl Harbor*. But again, if the FAA didn't tell NORAD until 9:24, a delay of 34 minutes, this was still *after* the first Flight 11 had hit the WTC, which should have put everyone everywhere on extreme alert. But nothing effective seems to have been done for half an hour before the Pentagon was hit at 9:38, which was over half an hour *after* the second tower of the WTC was hit, as well as the north tower. All the fighters that had been scrambled to intercept the first two flights 11 and 175, could have very easily continued on to Washington to protect the Pentagon. No such orders were ever given. The Commission's excuse is that the military was never specifically told by the FAA that there were actual hijackings; and this is *even after planes had hit the WTC in the most spectacular attack on the continental US in our history.*

But this account is discredited by one of the FAA executives, Laura Brown, who testified that during the interconference call sometime after 8:50, NORAD *was* notified that Flight 77 was in trouble, possibly hijacked. Richard Clarke also claimed that the interconference call was made before 9:15. As a result of this and other contradictions with NORAD's claim, the Commission finally decided to state that NORAD was *never* informed about this hijacking until after the Pentagon was hit. Not only does the Commission claim that this call was made after 9:29, but that this important interconference call never talked about hijackings, *which had already occurred*. When facts didn't fit the theory the Commission was promoting, they simply rewrote history with new facts that did.

Supposedly at 9:24 NORAD immediately scrambled planes, but again, it appears that they didn't take off until 9:30 — more inexplicable delays. Now the north tower was hit at 8:46 which was the most important attack on the continental US in our history. Why weren't planes immediately scrambled from *anywhere* to defend the nation's nerve center in Washington DC? There is no explanation. But that's not the worst of it. Guess where they were scrambled from? They were scrambled from Langley, ... "which is 130 miles from Washington, rather than from Andrews Air Force Base, which is only 10 miles away and has the assignment to protect Washington" with F-16 fighters that could provide capable and ready responses to a civil emergency.[47] Even then, however, Griffin says that since F-16s can fly at 1,500 mph, "they could have traversed the 130 miles to Washington in slightly over five minutes, leaving them almost three minutes to intercept...".[48] But instead, "these planes are said not to have arrived until about 15 minutes after the Pentagon was struck at 9:38,"[49] when they were still 105 miles away — all very convenient. The Commission said that the pilots didn't know which way to fly. But even more importantly, the Pentagon is protected by lots of missiles. And yet for some inexplicable reason no missiles were sent up towards Flight 77, a Boeing 757 which had veered off its path and was flying in a totally uncontrolled way. Remember, this was half an hour *after* two planes had already hit the WTC, and everyone in any position of responsibility should have been on extreme alert. But nothing was done. The Pentagon is probably the most well-defended building on the face of the planet. Griffin says that "...any non-military plane, not having a friendly transponder sending out a 'friendly' signal would have been automatically shot down by the Pentagon's battery of missiles." [50] Griffin adds, "How does the official account explain the fact that in this case it was not defended at all." [51]

And you wonder why there are conspiracy theories. There is no plausible explanation for *anything* the system did to respond to the events of that morning, especially when you consider that *every-day standard operating procedure* would have easily prevented these crashes into the WTC. This is why critics charge that orders had to be given from higher-ups to counteract standard operating procedure in order to *facilitate* the hijacked planes reaching their target.

But to finish the story, there was another Flight 93 leaving at 8:42, over Pennsylvania. Hijackers had gotten control of the cockpit and it was known for sure the plane was hijacked by 9:34, almost an hour after the WTC towers had been hit. Supposedly the FAA heard people on the plane saying they were going to die. Now this time NORAD claimed it was notified by the FAA of trouble on this flight right away. But the Commission in its attempt to put all the blame on the FAA denied this claim, even though there was testimony that the plane had been trailed by an F-16. The Commission claims that the FAA was calling around for the next half hour between its various centers to decide what to do, and as the debate dragged on, nobody ever told the military to get after this flight.

But remember, there were interconference calls going on in the 8:50 – 9:30 time frame, supposedly more than one. But supposedly, nobody bothered to talk about Flight 93 still in the air heading for Washington during all these calls. It appears from the Commission that the military refused to participate in the FAA interconference call, and then didn't bother to include the FAA in its own interconference call because a rookie was in charge. In fact, there is a ton of contradictory claims about what was said on these interconference calls. It was claimed that nobody in authority in the FAA was in on the calls; that nobody from the FAA bothered to mention Flight 93; that inexperienced people were at the helm; that the military wasn't paying attention some of the time; and the calls were filled with irrelevancies. And remember all this was *after* two planes had already hit their WTC targets. Somewhere in all this, there are monstrous lies. How could people not be talking about hijackings when two planes had already hit the WTC? But nobody had to worry about lies, including the Commission, because the system mind outlets could be counted on not to say a word about all the conflicting claims.

Finally, the FAA and the military finally got their big shots in contact, and supposedly Dick Cheney gave the okay to shoot down the plane. But this was at 10:10 or later, which is *after* Flight 93 had hit the Pentagon. But Richard Clark claimed that key people from the FAA and the military *were* in contact during these calls and discussed the hijacked Flight 93. Griffin adduces other evidence that the order to shoot down Flight 93 came adequately in time for an interception. A high-powered think tank could not have scripted a better scenario for all the players to result in a terrorist attack than what occurred on the morning of 9/11.

But there is plenty of evidence that flight 93 *was* shot down by fighters even though it was far away from any important target. The passengers on this plane, who included a professional pilot, had decided to try to take the plane from the hijackers. A call from one of the passengers judged that three male passengers were succeeding. But they weren't given a chance to take over the plane. If they were, there would be hijackers and possibly evidence as to the details of the whole terrorist attack. What this shows is that the system mind had decided by this time that there was enough spectacular terrorist attacks and enough loss of life to make a "New Pearl Harbor" and get the population all excited about terrorism. So now it was time for the system mind to show some efficiency in protecting us. This shows that when the system wants to shoot down a plane, there was a very quick, effective, and decisive response in doing so. But none of this effectiveness applied to the other three flights. Not only that, but "...when the cockpit recording of Flight 93 was released, the final three minutes were missing".[52] Very convenient.

This, of course, put the Commission in a bind. Either they admit the plane was shot down, in which case, why didn't they wait to see if the passengers had taken over the plane so that key evidence would be saved. *Or*, they admit the military and the FAA fiddled and diddled for half an hour and did nothing to go after the Flight. They chose the last scenario as the lesser evil, not that the real truth played any role whatsoever in the Commission's decisions. We will probably never know what really happened in detail on 9/11, but one thing is very certain: aside from a conspiracy theory, the 9/11 Commission was a total cover-up and a fraud.

33.11 Aftermath of 9/11

Osama bin Laden has been a cult hero of all insurgents, terrorists, and potential terrorists all through the 2000s. But he was never captured, even though there were many times when his whereabouts were pretty much known. As long as bin Laden was instrumental in recruiting and planning terrorist attacks, he was of great use to the system mind, even though the west had to pretend to be looking for him. So bin Laden had to hide quite securely. This prevented him from planning terrorist attacks. And when his usefulness to the system for drumming up terrorists ran out, it was just a matter of time before he was found and killed to the great fanfare of whoever was in power, who happened to be Obama.

But while he was alive and active, he was the focal point in Bush's efforts to drum up support and money for the "war on terrorism". There is something amusing about this. When Osama bin Laden wants to recruit a bunch of young Muslim men for Al Qaeda, he holds up a picture of George Bush. When George Bush needed to crank up the war on terrorism, he showed the country a picture of Osama bin Laden. The two were pretty much in bed with one another, using each other in the exact same way to drum up support for their respective killing sprees.

33.12 Explanation from the 9/11 Commission Report

The Joint Inquiry report concluded that the malfunctioning of all these players involved in all these events and transactions were simply the subject of "misunderstandings" and incompetence. After the attack, FBI director Mueller said "there were no signs that I'm aware of that would indicate this type of operation in the country".[53] This was a complete lie, of course, but we can understand a cover-up after the fact. But how do you explain the total facilitation of many players in the FBI and elsewhere *before* the attack? *Every single measure that could have intercepted the 9/11 attack was suppressed or asleep on this particular day.* A former British Minister, Michael, Meacher, said, " 'US authorities did little or nothing to pre-empt the events of 9/11' even though 'at least 11 countries provided advance warning to the US of the 9/11 attack' ".[54] In my opinion, all these players doing their own little part were just part of a system mind that needed a terrorist attack, invited a terrorist attack, and got a terrorist attack.

David Griffin has written a scholarly book on the 9/11 Commission report. What we are really left with is one long string of coincidences, involving mistakes, misunderstandings, incompetence and, "...distorting, or completely omitting dozens of facts".[55] For example, Griffin mentions a story reported by a Gerald Posner to the effect that a certain Al Qaeda operative, Abu Zubaydah, "was being interrogated by two Arab-American agents who were pretending to be, like himself, from Saudi Arabia. According to Zubaydah, "…at least three members of the Saudi royal family knew that Al Qaeda attacks on America were scheduled for 9/11".[56] Again, the 9/11 Commission brushed off all these relationship as coincidences and took no steps to investigate any of it.

Even after the attack, the system mind went right back to work to hide the facts surrounding the attack. There was a constant stream of obstructions, overlookings, and negligence that prevented further investigations by the 9/11 Commission into the hijacker's activities before and during the attack supposedly all by coincidence. The Commission never subpoenaed the security tapes of the Pentagon showing where the plane allegedly struck, and were never released to the public. On the other hand, "The Commission, for example, goes into great detail about Osama bin Laden, and rise of al-Qaeda, and the lives of the (alleged) hijackers".[57] What is really fishy is that many people who tried to further a more complete investigation or tried to uncover more facts were either fired, demoted or squelched. What does that tell us? On the other hand, every single individual who did *nothing* to prevent the attack was never punished and some were promoted.

There are millions and millions of flights each year in the US. And it is precisely because there are millions of flights that a very low probability event can happen. And even then, it happens only every 4 or 5 years. Winning the lottery is highly improbable as well. But they sell *millions* of tickets, which is why someone usually wins. If they sold only a few tickets, nobody would ever win the lottery. But there is not a terrorist attack every few seconds in the US. This is why it is almost impossible for this terrorist attack to have occurred simply on the basis of a string of unlikely mistakes or incompetence. If there were millions of terrorist attacks each year, then just like with airplane crashes, you would get one once in a big while due to a string of unlikely innocent mistakes or incompetence. But not with just a few terrorist attacks each year. There has to be more to it.

To show the total inadequacy of the 9/11 report, a number of relatives of the victims of the attack have tried in many ways to get to the bottom of what really happened on 9/11. Griffin says, "In the meetings in New York in May of 2004, in fact, family members expressed even greater disgust with the commission than before". [58] Every effort by these victims to get crucial answers to obvious questions have been stymied, and I might add, *with the complete and active cooperation of the system mind media outlets*. Nothing about the whole affair smells as bad as this, especially when they are always passing themselves off as true reporters of world events "in the public interest". When you compare the effort to uncover every minute detail of Bill Clinton's sex life with their efforts at getting the truth of what happened on 9/11, you have a lot more on your hands than another coincidence.

33.13 SYSTEM MIND

In my opinion, the explanation of 9/11 is that all the relevant government agencies and officials are involved with massive flows of information at all times. The whole intercommunicating system forms a mind in the same way as the communicating neurons of the brain create a mind. This mind arranges for all means to be taken that would enable a "New Pearl Harbor".

The 9/11 Commission, being involved in massive amounts of flows of information, is part of the system mind, which is why it is a total fraud. The purpose of this commission was the same as that of the Warren Commission: to provide a complete cover-up and white-wash *in case there was complicity or facilitation by players in the Bush administration*. If there was anything illegal or untoward in the activities of players in the administration or all relevant government agencies, I can assure you the 9/11 Commission was never going to let it come to light. Of course, this doesn't show that there *was* such complicity or facilitation, but only that *if* there was, the commission was going to squelch it.

Another piece of evidence for a system mind is that the Commissions appointed to investigate these kinds of historic events are always made up of people who are part and parcel of the system. This was true of the Warren Commission as well. Griffin points out that the head of the 9/11 Commission had "...close personal, professional, and ideological ties to the Bush White House", [59] as well as other members. It appears that "nearly half of the Commission staff members had ties to the very agencies they were charged with examining".[60] Griffin also details how the Bush White House "wanted no investigation into this attack, and then, once he was forced to accept this investigation, seemingly did everything in his power to delay and obstruct it". [61] Is this facilitation? However, these points are not really the most important facts surrounding the event. The most important point to be brought out is that every single individual chosen for these commissions is *invariably* heavily involved with the flows of the system, which explains why their conclusions are invariably exactly what the system needs to paper over the event.

That's why even a thorough investigation would have trouble getting a handle on the whole affair. If we went to Dick Cheney and asked him why he didn't have surveillance on people who he was warned were actual terrorists, what would he say? He would simply say that he didn't suspect anything. You would get the exact same response from relevant people in the CIA or FBI. And what can you do? What could you convict people of? All you could say is that they should have done this and shouldn't have done that. Very likely, none of them ever sat down with another high up and talked about a terrorist attack, let alone figure out how to bring one about. Just as the neurons of the brain have no knowledge or direct involvement with what the mind is thinking, probably none of the people who could have done something to prevent the attack ever did anything to discuss, plan, allow or in any way consciously abet the attack. All the nodes of the system mind do their own individual little part any one of which is overtly very innocuous. But when you add it all up in a complex system of information flows, you get a mindedness that is very apparent. It gets things done that perpetuates the system.

But, in my opinion, the most underrated factor in the whole affair is the system media mouthpieces. No matter what kind of fraud the 9/11 Commission engaged in, no matter what kind of complicity or facilitation there might have been by government, no matter what kind of conspiracy there might have been, all parties concerned could count on the system mind mouthpieces to completely cover it up, which is exactly what they did. I remember tuning in as much as I could to TV news of 9/11. But in reading these books about 9/11, I was amazed by the amount of suspiciously improbable events that made up the whole story that were totally ignored and suppressed by the mainstream system mouthpieces. If the system has a mind, the mainstream media is clearly part of it; and the reason is that they make money on killing and wars that boost ratings. They were not going to say one word that might interrupt Bush's path to war.

There have always been rogue governments coming to power throughout history for the simple reason that people trying to get to the top of political systems are raw, naked power-seekers. But people in the media are supposed to be motivated by dedication to adequately educate and inform "in the public interest". And even though media people are individually often admirable people, it shows that *a corrupt system with good people will always greatly underperform a great system with corrupt people, such as the Supreme Court.* It's the *system*, stupid.

To sum up, at the beginning the Bush administration, the system mind needed a terrorist attack to justify aggression, humiliation, invasion, and conquest of Muslim countries to provide a continuous supply of terrorists and continuous war. The main purpose of the war on terrorism is to have permanent state of war to cover up a system of Economic Socialism that provides gross inequality, maintained by continuous monitoring of the citizenry; and to create a new category of crime that the system could respond to in ways that dilute our constitutional protections. At the beginning of the Bush administration, *the system needed a terrorist attack; it invited a terrorist attack; and it got a terrorist attack. End of story.*

[1]   Ahmed, Nafeez Mosaddeq, 2002. *The War on Freedom*, Tree of Life Publ, Joshua Tree, Cal. Chossudovsky, Michael, 2002. *War and Globalization: The Truth Behind September 11.* Global Outlook, Canada Meyssan, Thierry, 2002. *9/11: The Big Lie, Carnot, London*

[2]   Griffin, David Ray, 2005. *The 9/11 Commission Report*, Olive Branch Pr., Northampton, Mass., p. 127

[3]   Griffin, David Ray, 2004. *The New Pearl Harbor*, Olive Branch Pr., Northampton, Mass., p. 129

[4]   Ibid. p. 130

[5]   Ibid. p 130

[6]   Ibid. p. 93

[7]   Ibid. p. 94

[8]   Ibid. p. 90

[9]   Ibid. p. 91

[10]   Ibid. p.148

[11]   Danner, Mark, *The New York Review of Books*, Aug. 11, '05, p. 60

[12]   Griffin, David Ray, 2005. *The 9/11 Commission Report*, Olive Branch Pr. Northampton, Ma., p. 2

[13]   Ibid. p. 3

[14]   Griffin, D.R., 2004

[15] Griffin, D.R., 2005, p. 30

[16] Griffin, D.R., 2004 p. 76

[17] Ibid. p. 76

[18] Griffin, D.R., 2004, p. 70

[19] Ibid. p. 71

[20] Ibid. p. 70.

[21] Griffin, D.R., 2005, p. 114

[22] Griffin, D.R., 2004, p. 77

[23] Ibid. P. 84

[24] Griffin, D.R., 2005, p. 51

[25] Griffin, D.R., 2004, p. 73

[26] Ibid. p. 73

[27] Griffin, D.R., 2005, P. 89

[28] Griffin, D.R. 2004, p. 80

[29] Ibid. P. 80

[30] Ibid. p. 81

[31] Ibid. p. 83

[32] Griffin, D.R., 2005, p. 91

[33] Griffin, D.R., 2004, p. 68

[34] Ibid. p. 189

[35] Griffin, D.R., 2005, p.288

[36] Griffin, D.R. 2004, p. 72

[37] Ibid. p. 85

[38] Ibid. p. 72

[39] Griffin, D.R., 2005, p. 265

[40] Griffin, D.R., 2004, p. 72

[41] Ibid. p. 248

[42] Ibid. p. 5

[43] Ibid. p. 9.

[44] Griffin, D.R., 2005, p. 177

[45] Ibid. p. 142

[46] Ibid. p. 42

[47] Ibid. P 43.

[48] Griffin, D.R., 2005, p. 147

[49] Griffin, D.R., 2004, p. 42.

[50] Ibid. p. 199

[51] Ibid. p. 42.

[52] Ibid. p. 143

[53] Ibid. p. 82

[54] Ibid. p. 156

[55] Griffin D.R., 2005, p. 277

[56]   Ibid. p. 279

[57]   Griffin, David Ray, 2005, p. 13

[58]   Griffin, David Ray, 2004, p. 192

[59]   Griffin, D.R. 2005, p. 281

[60]   Ibid. p. 286

[61]   Ibid. p. 285

CHAPTER 34

The System Mind and the Perfect War

——

IN SECT. 25.1, WE MENTIONED the fact that one of the goals of the system mind is to keep all new wealth and income going to the top 20%. Also, to get the most work for the least pay, the system wants the private lives of its citizens to be devoid of all human relationships — no friendships, no relationships, and no marriages. In this way, people's private lives will be cleaned out making room for the system's 12-hour workday jobs. In order to carry out the system's economic agenda, it must maintain the right propaganda going into their heads so that they vote in just the right ways. This means constant surveillance and control to make sure people have the right views, the right voting patterns and the right behavior conducive to the agenda of the system. A very pregnant way to maintain this whole agenda is to distract people's thinking away from their economic and political interests in the little time they have to think about anything outside their jobs. One way to insure this is through what we could call the perfect war, which is a permanent state of war. The war on terrorism fills the bill to a tee. It accomplishes all the major goals of the neoconservative agenda. Let's see how.

Wars are very primitive affairs and involve our most primitive inner brain emotions of conquest, aggression and territorial control. These are our oldest and most powerful emotions. They enable people, especially men, to identify with the projection of power, which creates a strong identity as we discussed in Sect. 20.5. All of this keeps brain energy at the bottom of the brain energizing the most primitive thoughts and emotions, and takes brain energy away from more existential considerations like the quality, meaning and purpose of life. This is why the American system has a strong motivation for a permanent state of war.

However, wars are tricky business. There is a certain logic to the concept of war that works against the idea of permanent war. Wars are supposed to end with a win; and you win it by defeating an offending army and removing its government. This is an important point. Conventional wars against nations with governments and armies are not good wars because you can't keep them going. If you try to keep them going by creating a stalemate like China did in Vietnam, the citizenry gets antsy and wants out. Then the system no longer has a nice perpetual war. The system mind must pick its wars very cleverly so as to maintain them over long periods of time, even though wars are supposed to be fought, won, and ended quickly. Since WWII, this has been very difficult to bring off until quite recently. One valiant attempt at permanent war was the cold war with Russia.

No sooner had WWII ended, but the cold war started. Now there were segments of Russian society and segments of American society who would have tried to negotiate differences in a more peaceful way. But the system mind in both countries very quickly pushed these elements aside. The US began to circle Russia with nuclear warheads and the Russians had to respond by building their own nuclear arsenal. Russian leaders began to clamp down all over Eastern Europe maintaining very repressive Communist dictatorships. Both sides revved up the rhetoric. In the US, there was the McCarthy period which kicked off a long and very truculent period of anti-communism. Russian leaders talked of burying the west. This started an arms race and a rhetoric race that lasted for over 40 years. It very much suited the needs of both systems.

The cold war had some excellent qualities from the point of view of the system, but it also had some weaknesses. Since it didn't involve armies and shooting, no one would be conquering or subduing populations. So it could go on forever. But its major drawback was that it wasn't a hot war where the king's men could invade, conquer and kill. It totally failed to meet the inner brain needs of neoconservative reptiles, which is for killing, destruction and conquest. It could stir up a bit of patriotism, but not enough to create a real distraction from people's quality of life or their place in the economy. So why did the cold war end?

As we explained in Ch. 31, while Reagan was building up the military in his first term, Gorbachev was keeping pace with his eye on the cold war. It was in the middle of his *second* term that Reagan changed course. Possibly, as his Alzheimer's progressed, energy in his brain increasingly accumulated in the bottom, specifically in the fear areas of the limbic system. This might have been pure luck. If it had accumulated in the aggression areas, the cold war might have turned hot with disastrous consequences for the mankind. But as Reagan's fears grew, he became extremely fearful of a nuclear exchange and he began to tone *down* the cold war and negotiate with Gorbachev. This allowed Gorbachev to turn some of his attention to reforming his economy which led to the end of the cold war.

Vietnam is a graphic illustration of Law VI in Sect. 2.1: if you have a big army, you need a war for it to fight. An army without a war is like a gun without a bullet. The system tried mightily to keep the Vietnam war going. Reports came out every day that with just a little more time, money and manpower, we would win. But as explained in Vol. I, this was a proxy war with China whose army was bigger than the entire population of the US. But it wasn't a perfect war because the American people got tired of it. A protest movement got going among young people that contradicted the goal of the system to mold each young person into a good corporate 12-hour day work slave — no hippies, no drugs, no protests. Try as it might, the system mind could not keep the Vietnam War going.

But starting right after WWII, the system had been preparing a better war to achieve its purposes. All along in Palestine and Middle East, the American system mind was laying the groundwork for the most *perfect* war that could possibly be devised from the point of the system— the war on terrorism. The reason why the war on terrorism is a perfect war is that the enemy is not a nation or an army. It is the lone individual. For thousands of years, the definition of 'war' was a military engagement involving some kind of organized group. Even in barbaric times before the Roman and Greek empires, wars were fought between tribes of people organized in some loose way; but always between an ethnic, religious, racial, tribal or geographical *group*. That's the essence of war. And the goal of wars involving groups is to remove opposition leaders and substitute leaders amenable to the leaders of the home team.

But terrorism is not a group, nor tribe nor ethnic population. It's an *idea*, a way of performing aggressive violent actions. There may be leaders, but there is no government, tribe, geographical area, or religious group to defeat and replace. Its essence is that it involves *individuals* as opposed to groups. When individuals are killed, they can easily be replaced one by one without disrupting the big picture.

'War' is an emotion-laden word that can motivate people even when the causes are just. We have had a war on poverty, a war on cancer, a war on Alzheimer's and a war on AIDS. So it is perfectly understandable that people who support the terrorism threat are going to make it into a *war*. But since the supposed enemy is *individuals* who can be replaced one by one as they are lost, you have the perfect conditions for perpetual war. All you have to do is make sure there is a continuous supply of terrorists. *This is the most important point we can make: The war on terrorism requires a continuous supply of terrorists.*

Recall in Vol. I, Ch. 16, we talked about concepts. The central key concepts in the war on terrorism are two-fold: *recruitment and weak corrupt governments*. Recruitment is necessary to have a continuous supply of terrorists, and weak, puppet government are necessary to have a fertile ground for the *training* of terrorists. In the media mouthpieces of the system mind, you will never hear them mention either concept with all their babbling about these kingly wars.

It is very important to realize that terrorists are usually young men who are often quite bright. And being a terrorist most often means committing suicide in the process. Why would a young man with his life ahead of him ever sign up to something like a terrorist organization that often means his death? The answer is you need to show him some grave injustice or humiliation to his people by bringing off some noteworthy international injustice.

Palestine has been the perfect place to kick off the war on terrorism by providing ammunition for terrorist organizations like Al Qaeda to recruit terrorists. This is what the set-up in Palestine was for. Whenever the system mind needs a new supply of terrorists, it simply lets loose some right-wing book-wavers in Israel to take some land, torture some Palestinians, or put up some walls to humiliate the Palestinians. Immediately, somewhere in the Muslim world, a new layer of terrorists is recruited for the anti-west cause.

This is the motivation of the system mind in the US. But why would Israel support this policy? That is a very complicated question. Given the geopolitical situation in the Middle East, is Israel foreign policy inevitable and unavoidable. Perhaps they're in a vector trap so that their train is on a track to disaster and nothing can be done to change its course.

As we mentioned, in my opinion, Israel's foreign policy is running them right into another holocaust. It is the Israelis who ought to take a good hard look at the situation they face.

There has been a dual policy towards Muslim countries that can be pulled into the war on terrorism. Preferably, it will attempt to set up National Socialist semi-puppet governments that will sell raw materials to the US cheap. Or, the system can initiate some eye-catching event like an invasion or attack on some Muslim country, as happened in Iraq and Afghanistan. Then by establishing puppet governments running these countries, you can count on them to crack down and inflict some grave injustice on some segment of the population once in a while with the full cooperation of the US. This will be a great source of terrorist recruitment.

If the system can't set up a puppet government for whatever reason, it will promote the exact opposite: a very antagonistic anti-American government that we can then call the "enemy", which will create fertile ground for any future invasion, conquest, attack or any other form of belligerency. This conforms to Law I international relations from Ch. 27. A perfect example of this is Iran in the 1950s.

Here's what Wikipedia says about Iran: "In 1953, Iran, or Persia as it was then called, had a functioning democratic system. A successful coup by the CIA and British Intelligence overthrew the democratically elected government and replaced them with the hereditary Shah of Persia. His abuses and misrule led directly to the Islamic Revolution and the problems we have encountered with their Islamic government ever since." This is pretty accurate. (Isn't it amazing how efficient the CIA is in removing legitimately elected governments. But when a blatant war criminal, Assad in Syria, was slaughtering his people even using poison gas warfare, the CIA was helplessly sitting by. This is what we steal 100 billion dollars a year away from vital cancer research for.)

In the '90s, there were amenable leaders in Iran that the US could have negotiated with to iron out differences. But because of the Iranian revolution, the system mind under the Bush administration did not see Iran as a country that could be eased into the puppet government mode. This pushed the policy to the exact opposite pole as an "enemy" government by cranking up anti-Islam rhetoric. Max Rodenbeck reviews a number of naïve books detailing some of this history: in 2002, "when the popular reformist administration of President Mohammad Khatami sorely needed some friendly signal from America to counter its increasingly aggressive conservative critics." "But instead of being rewarded for its condemnation of the Sept. 11 attack or its vital assistance in ousting the Talaban from Afghanistan...Iran found itself melodramatically branded by George Bush in a State of the Union speech as a member of an 'axis of evil' ". [1] This kind of event gets passed off by this book's writers as "missed opportunities". Yeah, right. It was a *great* opportunity to create a nice new juicy enemy, a country in which to recruit, support and train terrorists.

The system mind needed an anti-west leader in Iran to weave an aggressive foreign policy around and there was no stopping it. And sure enough, system mind threats brought about the election of a guy named Ahmadinejad who ran the exact campaign that got George Bush elected: we got be strong and stand up to the infidels in the west who want to destroy the Muslim people. Just as Bush got the conservative religious fundamentalists and the hard-line foreign policy capon vote in the US to get elected, Ahmadinejad got elected with support from the very same religious fundamentalists and conservative hard-liners, anti-dissidents, assorted government thugs, and the military. And of course, he got elected in a fraudulent election by a bunch of Supreme Ayatollahs in the exact same way that Bush got elected by our own fraudulent Supreme Ayatollahs.

The really funny part was to watch American conservatives in the media and on sewer radio loudly supporting Ahmadinejad's opponents in Iran — students, intellectuals, liberals, women, minorities, and anti-war protesters marching in the streets. These were the *very same people* marching in *US* streets back in the '60s for our own civil rights movement. Of course, back then, these conservatives wanted to club and kick these hippies out of the country. I never heard one peep out of the major system media propaganda outlets about this gross hypocrisy.

Everything went exactly according to script in both countries. Ahmadinejad got elected in Iran on the basis of standing up to the great Satan, and Bush got elected in the US, on the basis of fighting the "axis of evil". And neoconservatives of all stripes (actually only 2 stripes: two white ones down the back) have had a field day drumming up anger in the American people against Iran. This will be meat for terrorist recruiters. But this is the exact agenda of the system mind: it needs an important Muslim country like Iran as a source of terrorist recruitment. Remember, you can't have a war on terrorism without terrorists.

Then with his rhetoric going full steam ahead, Ahmadinejad was able to crank up his nuclear program. This is not in the interests of anybody especially the west. But it does provide a perfect excuse for any type of military adventure the system may need in Iran in the future. I don't want Iran to have nuclear weapons any more than you do. But how much of an argument does the west have against Iran's nuclear program? While George Bush threatened the world with nuclear weapons, and England, who invaded dozens of countries killing millions of human beings is allowed to have them without a murmur, Iran must not have nuclear weapons. After all, they're just a bunch of barbarians and you can never tell what they might do. The massive hypocrisy of the situation is another great source of terrorist recruiting propaganda for a long time to come.

If the west were making even a *vestigial* attempt to reduce its enormous stockpile of nuclear weapons, it would have moral justification to prevent Iran from getting them. But of course, the neoconservative system mind in the US and Britain are not going to allow "appeasement" and "disarmament". Obama is trying to negotiate an end to Iran's nuclear ambitions to the howls of neoconservative capons who want an excuse for more war, killing, and conquest to spruce up an ever-shrinking sexlife. But conservatives in Iran prop up their regime with the exact same rhetoric. They brand liberals in Iran as appeasers who want to disarm Iran and make it a victim of US aggression.

After the Iranian revolution in the late '70s, terrorism began to wane somewhat, although there was a small terrorist attack here and there. The '90s under Clinton was somewhat quiet again although he continued the usual fake attempts to solve the Palestinian problem, which only served to enrage the Muslim world. If he had come right out and admit we don't give a crap about the Palestinians, there would be less of a reaction among Muslims. It was plain that his foreign policy was never going to do anything significant to settle it, while allowing the Israeli's to stick it in the eye of the Palestinians from time to time. In my opinion, it was this total hypocrisy that provided the recruitment tools Osama bin Laden needed to organize Al Qaeda, who, somewhere along the way, began planning terrorist attacks.

With the election of George Bush, the system was just itching to crank up more more war, more conquest, more killing and most importantly, a new supply of terrorists. The opportunity came with the 9/11 attack, which was probably invited. On the basis of total distortions of facts by the system mouthpieces, Bush was able to associate 9/11 with Iraq, of all places. This mind-boggling lie was perpetuated by the media for the sole purpose of keeping the war on terrorism going. Hussein ran a bad government, but it was a *strong* government, which is why he had to be replaced by a puppet government that could act as a training ground for terrorists.

The usual semi-conscious political commentators couldn't figure out why Hussein was left in power by papa Bush. As Law IV shows, you always leave a situation in limbo so that it can be used as a focal point for future intrusions, invasions, or other forms of foreign adventure. An intact Saddam Hussein could be used as a means for a continuing war on terrorism, so they left him in power. Of course, the media had to cover up the fact that when Hussein was murdering and gassing Kurds and other minorities in the late '80s, Hussein's atrocities were totally ignored by the Reagan administration and totally suppressed by the system mind media propagandists. Donald Rumsfeld was quoted as saying: "we can work with this man". We'll probably never find out exactly where Hussein got the weapons systems he used to kill his own people. But you can make a good educated guess.

9/11 was the perfect world-shaking event the system needed to crank up the war on terrorism. In Ch. 20, we explained the motivation of the inner brain people in the Bush administration for invading Iraq (another illustration of Law VI). The Bush administration as part of the system mind was preparing for wars in Iraq and Afghanistan from before the election. All kinds of planning went into arranging the propaganda blitz to get the American people on board. Of course, they knew they would have complete cooperation from the system mind mainstream media. But also intelligence and background information had to be arranged. Recall in Sect. 33.4 we quoted the head of Britain's M16 as saying, "Bush wanted to remove Saddam... But the intelligence and facts were being fixed around the policy".[2]

Finally, with no congressional initiation, nor approval from the UN, Bush invaded Iraq. It really violated every human device for preventing this sort of thing. It violated international law, it violated the UN charter, even the US Constitution. The blame really lies in two places: the Supreme Court for allowing it and the system mind media propaganda outlets that allowed it to be sold to the American people without the faintest of inhibitions. By invading Iraq, the system mind had reinvigorated recruitment for the perfect war, the war on terrorism.

A NYR article reported that "In February 2005, CIA Director Porter Goss told Congress that 'Islamic extremists are exploiting the Iraqi conflict to recruit new anti-US jihadists,' and those who survive will leave Iraq experienced and focused on acts of urban terrorism".[3] This is how we wound up with ISIS. Another *NYR* article reported that "According to a recent National Intelligence Estimate, in April, 2006, a large body of all-source reporting indicates that activists identifying themselves as jihadists ...are increasing in both numbers and geographic location' ".[4] In the same issue, "Peter Bergen and Paul Cruickshank found in 2007 that the Iraq war had brought about a 600 percent increase in the average number of Jihadist terrorist attacks throughout the world." [5] "...an aide to General McCrystal, estimated roughly that every civilian killed creates an additional twenty insurgents".[6] Anatol Lieven details all this in his book saying, "It has above all been the US-led campaign in Afghanistan which has been responsible for increasing Islamic insurgency and terrorism in Pakistan since 2001".[7] What these very responsible commentators don't understand is that this is precisely the purpose of these invasions. When it's very much in the interests of the system to have a war on terrorism, and invading Iraq and Afghanistan causes a jump in terrorist recruiting, what is the explanation for these facts fitting so well together except for some kind of system mind?

Of course, the CIA found no evidence of Al Qaeda in Iraq under Saddam. And they found no evidence for WMDs as well. But after months of brazen arm-twisting, George Tenet, head of the CIA, finally relented. The whole story is detailed in an article by Thomas Powers.[8] You ought to read this. The idea that paid killers can operate against American interests and criminal minds are in a position to fix our intelligence after 200 years of constitutional protections, including a waste of hundreds of billions of taxpayer dollars, is a national disgrace.

Even collecting intelligence was a fraud. Defectors who insisted that Iraq had abandoned its nuclear program in the mid-90s were dismissed as untrustworthy. However, a complete pathological liar who hadn't been in Iraq in decades was treated as the last word in reliability. Eight years *later* in 2011, CBS 60 minutes had an exposé telling us that Chalibi really was a liar. Facts that involve the lives of millions take many years for our system mind propaganda outlets to get the news. But the details of Bill Clinton's sex life were reported within minutes. Here again is a classic case of a system mind. The system mind conveniently claimed Saddam had WMDs because it was in its interests to do so, and it arranged for all pieces to come together. The final coup de grace came when the Iraq war turned into a quagmire and Bush blamed Tenet for "faulty intelligence". Of course, Tenet was furious. It shows when you play with the devil, you get the devil's justice. Tenet and Powell are probably the most pathetic figures in all of American history.

Tenet wrote a book about it all a few years later and when interviewed on TV, the host asked him why he let the fake case against Saddam go ahead. There has never been a lamer answer, which, of course was totally swallowed down by the network host. Tenet said the CIA *believed* Saddam had WMDs. Of course, he didn't have to face the pregnant response that the CIA is in the *fact* business, *not* the belief business. Beliefs are for people in the

Santa Claus and fairy godmother business, not the *fact* business. Powers says that policy-makers in the Bush administration "…know what they want, and they are making sure the CIA knows what they want, and they aren't going to let it alone until they get what they want".[9] Yes, but in my opinion Tenet and the CIA are part of the system mind as well. Tenet had to *pretend* to resist only because he was sitting on fake evidence, just like the TV host has to *pretend* he's in the journalism business. So even though they had no evidence of Hussein's WMDs, the CIA fell right in line in allowing their non-existent reports of WMDs to be used by the Bush administration to support invasion and conquest. But after 9/11, a good percent of the American people couldn't care less who Bush was attacking. As mentioned in Ch. 20, he could have attacked Brazil or France with stories of terrorism and WMDs. As long as he was killing people to get even, he would have been supported in the same way.

When it came to means to enrage, humiliate and degrade the Muslim world, the Bush administration left no stone unturned. When US forces got to Baghdad, there was may-hem. Tearing up the remnants of the Hussein government was fine. But then our forces did nothing to prevent the total looting and pillaging of much of Iraq's cultural history and archeology. *A sure symbol that an invading force has a native population slated for extinc-tion, ethnic cleansing or elimination is to first destroy their culture and history.* One of the first things European settlers did to American Indian tribes was to chop down their totem poles. The *first* thing the Nazis did before killing the Jews of Europe was to fire their university professors who convey a people's culture and history. This tells us what the Bushies had in store for the Iraqis when they symbolically allowed their famous museum in Baghdad to be looted and destroyed. Donald Rumsfeld announced on TV that we can't worry about "a bunch of old pots". In my view, that is all the symbols of Iraqi culture and history meant to this political hack. Archeological sites all over Iraq were looted and destroyed beyond rec-ognition, discussed in an excellent article in the NYR by Hugh Eakin.[10] And we're talking about the Tigris and Euphrates River valleys that are the cradle of civilization going back eight *thousand* years. Conveniently, all ministries of the Iraq government were looted and destroyed, all except one, which, you might guess, was the oil ministry.

By looting their famous museum, Bushies symbolically showed that their intention was not only to try out new war toys, but to so enrage young men of the Muslim world so that there would be a fresh supply of terrorists for the system mind to go after making lots of money in the process. If you don't like explaining the huge number of details all pointing in the same direction some of which we are discussing, as the product of a system mind, how do you explain the difference between invading Germany and invading Iraq? The day after Hitler was dead, great pains were taken to preserve what was left of all European cultures and histories. The allied armies in Germany after WWII were probably the best-behaved armies in the history of warfare. And this was after Adolph Hitler, *supported by a large per-centage of the German people, caused the deaths of 60 million people.*

But the American people eventually started to turn against the war in Iraq. It had hunkered down to a pretty steady state occupation and puppetocracy. Besides the economy had tanked, and it was more difficult to get people distracted with patriotism and support for a far-away war when their economic situation was deteriorating. What's even more important, neoconservatives can't identify with the limited power of an occupation. They need massive projected power: big bombs, big destruction, big killing, big torture. As we have mentioned, this is the one glitch in the thinking of the system mind. It has trouble figuring out how to keep wars going continuously. But it is clever in giving it a good try. So the system mind decided that the best way to keep war going was to shift the scene to a new war, the war in Afghanistan, which killed two birds with one stone.

The main reason for Bush invading Afghanistan was that since the Taliban was a strong government, it could not be effectively used as a terrorist breeding ground. Terrorists had been training in tribal areas of *Pakistan*, not Afghanistan, which of course, has a very unstable and weak political climate. On Mar. 16, '12, some ambassador got on the "liberal" PBS and lied right through his teeth, saying the 9/11 terrorists were from Afghanistan, which justified the invasion. The 9/11 terrorists grew up in Saudi Arabia and were trained in *Pakistan*, and had absolutely nothing to do with Afghanistan. Ironically, the ambassador has a name something like "crock", which is exactly what the host on this fake PBS program swallowed.

The Talaban in Afghanistan was a brutal, dictatorial government that was cruel to women, but it was a *strong* government. And the Taliban did not welcome Al Qaeda as our system mind propaganda outlets led us to believe. Just as with Saddam Hussein, no strong government wants a rival political movement running around in their country competing for the support of the people. One of the reasons the Talaban was a strong government was that it was partially created by the ISI, Pakistan's intelligence service *with the help of the CIA* in order to expel the Russians. As we discussed in Sect. 33.3, once this was accomplished, the strength of the Talaban government began to become a hindrance to the US system mind. The main purpose of Bush's invasion of Afghanistan was the *removal* of a strong government and to install the usual puppet government. And 9/11 was the perfect excuse for doing so. Bush's invasion of Afghanistan accommodated the two ingredients we mentioned for the war on terrorism. It provided terrorist recruiters ammunition to create hatred for Americans among young Muslim men. And it enabled a weak, corrupt puppet government to be installed in Afghanistan that could provide a breeding ground for terrorist training. Remember, you can't have a war on terrorism without terrorists.

When Obama was elected and emerged from meetings with the system as a complete zombie, he quite naturally picked up in these wars right where Bush left off. His excuse was that Afghanistan is really different from Iraq, not pointing out, of course, is that the difference makes conquest in Afghanistan even more unlikely than in Iraq. And although Obama has some *personal* beliefs in the futility of these wars, he wasn't strong enough to resist the constant pressure from neoconservatives and the military for more troops, more destruction and more war.

As his ratings dropped and his stimulus package turned out to be a big giveaway to the very people who got us into the economic mess, Obama needed to distract the American people, especially neoconservatives, with an uptick in the war on terrorism. He needed a new batch of terrorists and the escalation in Afghanistan was the perfect way to do it. With the invasion of 30 thousand more troops in the "surge", this becomes a blatant occupation for the sole purpose of control. On the basis of this invasion, Al Qaeda and the Talaban were able to recruit thousands of additional terrorists and insurgents, which is exactly the purpose the system had in mind in the first place. As reported in *The Nation*, Howard Hart, a former CIA station chief in Pakistan told the *New York times*, "...the more troops we send in, the greater the opposition".[11] We can see why this guy is a "former". Here's what a very sober British ambassador said: sending more troops "would have perverse effects: it would identify us even more strongly as an occupational force and would multiply the targets [for the insurgents]".[12] You can't say it better than that. What he doesn't realize is that this is the whole purpose of invasions. What starts out as the policy of nice-guy advisors and nation-builders initiated by non-system thinking of a few people like perhaps a president, degenerates into a palpable conquest and occupation. The surge of troops was a great Christmas present to Al Qaeda and to neoconservative capons who derive their sex lives from wars, power, killing, torture, and conquest.

Why should things be any different in Afghanistan than Iraq? Afghanistan is not only 50% larger than Iraq, but it is very mountainous — a perfect place for the system mind to keep the war on terrorism going. Iraq is mostly open spaces, so it's easy to subdue the population and you don't have much of a war anymore. Afghanistan has very rugged terrain with mountains, valleys, caves and hideouts that are easy to attack from. And most importantly, a little fact you will never hear from the media system mind, Afghanistan is in a perfect location to be supplied by China and Russia. You could never conquer the place without huge numbers of soldiers. That's why it's a great place to keep the war on terrorism going.

But the genius of Barack Obama is his ability to keep up the war on terrorism with less costs. His way of doing this is to substitute drones for invasions. Drones are relatively cheap compared to the cost of invasions which costs hundreds of billions of dollars. In 2008, in three separate strikes, drones attacked and killed people in two wedding parties and an engagement party.[13] *The Nation* reported that the Bureau of Investigative Journalism "estimates that the United States has killed on the order of 3,000 people in 319 drones strikes, some 600 of them civilian bystanders and 174 of those, children".[14] To show the real motivation for drones, a number of independent reports discussed in a NYR article all come to about the same conclusion. "the elimination of 'high-value' targets — al Qaeda or 'militant' leaders — has been exceedingly rare — fewer than fifty people, or about 2% of all drone deaths."[15] They call civilian casualties, "collateral damage". It's the exact opposite. Collateral damage is the terrorists they get, which is why nobody has to provide the slightest evidence that people killed are terrorists. There is officially little collateral damage for the simple reason that the system counts anybody of military age who's killed as a 'militant', or "enemy combatant" in Cheney's phrase.

All reason box explanations cover up the real *cause* of drones, which is to create terrorists by *inflicting* terrorism. As Jennifer Gibson's report says, "Drones terrorize the civilian population…".[16] This article also suggests that Muslim leaders view drones coming from the sky as an attempt to "appropriate the powers of God", which is blasphemous. What makes drones so effective is that they kill a lot of innocent civilians whereas invasions mostly kill soldiers whose job it is to kill or be killed. Even when they get the one guy they're after, they also wind up killing a bunch of innocent women and children. Whenever civilians are killed in this way, it starts up what I think is the most important factor in wars of occupation — *gossip*. In fact, there's a theory claiming that language itself got started so that people could gossip.[17] This is a very underrated theory. Wars are such intense and stressful episodes that people revert to all kinds of primal behavior and gossip is just one form of reversion. This is the case with all wars, but especially where you've been invaded. During WWII, people in European countries invaded by Hitler thought about and gossiped about *nothing* but the war. The war occupies their entire lives and brings their thinking down to very primitive narratives.

The killing of innocent civilians is why gossip over drones is much more intense than over invasions with only armies fighting. This is why you can create many more terrorists for the buck with drones than with invasions and conquests, which cost hundreds of billions of dollars. There's the added attraction that drones can be kept secret from the American people. Some have called it a shadow war.[18] There is no trial for people targeted with drones, no evidence has to be produced, and no results confirmed. People pushing drone buttons can kill anyone they please on the basis of rumors with no accountability. Yet Obama can assure the American people that we're ending the wars in Iraq and Afghanistan. It's a clever move. He can get the anti-war vote by getting armies out of these countries, and yet get the killer vote by creating more terrorists to chase down.

Another ingenious way of creating terrorists for the war on terrorism is with the use of torture. Out of the clear blue sky, the Bush administration rounded up a bunch of young Muslim men, brought them to Guantanamo and started torturing them. Whether or not these men were terrorists or how many actual terrorists there were was entirely irrelevant. The system mind saw that the best recruiting tool for producing terrorists was to let the Muslim world see that the Bushies was torturing young Muslim men; and not only torturing, but to put salt in the wound, they allowed photos of *women* doing the torturing. Women are second-class citizens in most Muslim countries, and to see a woman torturing a Muslim man was probably the most rage-inciting spectacle you could possible display to young Muslim men. Why would the system mind depict *women* torturing Muslim men — in fact, why would the system mind even *choose* women to torture, unless it wanted to bring about the maximum anger among Muslim men, motivating some of them to terrorism? It was absolutely no accident that the photos of torture got out. If it were in the interests of the system mind to keep the torture secret, I guarantee it that would have not been a single photo of torture spreading around the world.

But they did get a bad publicity rap, especially from Europeans. So when Obama got elected, he promised to clean up the public image and stop the torture. He said, "we don't torture". But of course, creating terrorists by humiliating and torturing Moslem men is just too pregnant a way to create terrorists for Obama to give up. So his idea of stopping torture is to do a better job of hiding it — but only from the American people. Even by 2015, Obama still hasn't closed Guantanamo nor stopped the torture policy. He's just shifted it to other countries. They are now hidden from the American people, but certainly not from the Muslim world, which again probably enrages young Muslim men more than when the US itself was doing it. Reporter Anand Gopal details all the new ways torture is continuing in secret detention centers around the world, many in countries with dictators that Obama is friendly with.[19] The whole purpose of torture is as a recruitment tool to create more terrorists. Remember, you can't have a war on terrorism without terrorists.

Let's see what a special agent in charge of counterterrorism in the FBI says about torture: "I don't remember any information that was relevant coming out of Guantanamo,"... and that "torture and coercion gets you, in the vast majority of cases, wrong information that takes you off on a wild goose chase".[20] You will never in your life hear this extremely important statement from the system propaganda machines. This is backed up by an official commission that released its reports in April, '13, and in Nov. '14, saying the same: little valuable information.

In analyzing terrorism throughout history, historians tell us that terrorists operate in small cells. They may have a big picture leader like Osama bin Laden, but it is the individual cell that is the basic structure of a terrorist organization. The cell may get a go-ahead from leaders, but the cell plans the *details* of a terrorist attack by itself, operating in total secrecy even from other cells. Members of a terrorist cell talk and plan in person — not through emails and phones. Duh! On top of that, once a plan is hatched, if anyone in the cell is compromised in any way, the plan is scrubbed. If one of the 9/11 hijackers had even been questioned, the whole plan would very well have been called off. The reason is obvious. If a member of a cell is captured, he may divulge the current plot and endanger other members of the cell. So no matter what a captured cell member may divulge during questioning or torture, this information is going to be obsolete because by then, the old plan has been scrubbed and a new plan conceived that the captured member knows nothing about. This is why this FBI agent can say that *no valuable information is gleaned by torturing members of a terrorist organization*. This author says that Bush's policies "have greatly increased the pool of jihadist terrorists around the world".[21] What these guys may not see is the whole *purpose* of torture is not to get reliable information, but to create more terrorists.

But goosing the situation in Palestine, invading Muslim countries and torturing Muslim men are just some of the *means* for the system mind to enable the recruitment of terrorists. Then to fine-tune the number of terrorists necessary for the day, the system uses speeches and social indicators. This has happened a number of times. You arrange for some important foreign policy player to string together words that so enrages the Muslim world that you get a new batch of terrorist recruits. A perfect example of this was when George Bush sent his secretary of State, Condoleezza Rice, to make a speech in Iran in May, 2006.

In order to understand the importance of this speech, recall back in Ch. 3, we talked about the *message* in a piece of communication, which is the *meaning* that it is intended to convey. The exact words of Rice's speech are irrelevant. The important point is the *message*, which in my opinion, runs as follows: "Lookie here, I'm a little white girl from the United States. We get to have nuclear weapons — not only that, but enough nuclear weapons to kill off the entire population of the world many times over and we might very well use them. You people here are just a bunch of Pickaninnies. You don't get to have nuclear weapons." (It was also Rice who announced to the world that it was okay for her to use a pre-emptive strike but other nations "should [not] use pre-emption as a pretext for aggression".[22])

And this was during an administration that was fighting tooth and nail against test ban treaties, was sprucing up our nuclear arsenal and opposed any kind of nuclear reductions. If the goal was to really stop Iran from developing nuclear weapons, the last person you would send would be a woman who knew nothing about nuclear weaponry nor much more about foreign policy than what the Bush administration programmed into her. Women in the Muslim world are close to second-class citizens. Sending a woman on this mission was throwing salt into the wound. In my opinion, if the goal was really to stop Iran's nuclear program, you would send a very seasoned, senior *male* who was a known activist for nuclear *reduction* to make a speech to the Iranians, not a girl programmed by an administration dedicated to war, invasion, conquest and killing. But the purpose of the system mind sending a *woman* to Iran with this speech was not to stop Iran's nuclear program at all, but to generate another batch of terrorists. Of course, this little ploy worked like a charm. Within a few months of the speech, the CIA reported an uptick in terrorist recruiting. If you don't want to accept a system mind, you have to come up with an explanation for sending an administration puppet, and a young woman at that, to lecture the Iranians. This has sent Iran in the direction of continuing to develop nuclear weapons, which, of course, insures that there would be a nice juicy enemy in case the system needs to attack Iran.

In Sept., 2012, Hilary Clinton made a similar use of words. She was sent to Israel to give her blessings to Netanyahu for taking more Palestinian land and extending settlements. The *message* Hilary sent to the Israelis is that continuing the new settlements is a fine idea. Of course, Netanyahu got the message because the settlement plans continued right along. Within a few months, CIA reports indicated that Al Qaeda recruitment was "gaining momentum". There was a near terrorist attack on an American plane. A terrorist attack in Afghanistan killed a number of CIA people. Immediately, crooked politicians were talking about having to execute "new means" to deal with terrorism. We all know what the "new means" are. The translation in plain English is to compromise our rights and constitutional protections to go after the terrorists that US foreign policy creates.

I want to say parenthetically, the whole time I was growing up, the CIA were the bad guys. Vietnam protesters and liberals everywhere blamed the CIA for replacing elected political figures like Mosaddegh in Iran, Arbenz in Guatamala, and Allende in Chile with fascist dictators who killed thousands. To show you how far our foreign policy has drifted from American ideals, now we have to rely on the *CIA*, no less, when we want accurate information about US foreign policy. We've come a long way baby. People like to blame the CIA who they don't vote for, for bad things instead of the political crooks who give the orders, who they do vote for.

But recruitment of terrorists is only the beginning of the game. You then have to have places for potential terrorists to train. The system has an answer to that as well. You simply set up puppet government in countries you've invaded and destabilize other countries. This is why in parts of the world where terrorism is a possibility, Bush's foreign policy and even Obama's is to destabilize governments and support corrupt governments. The invasion of Afghanistan had the added bonus of destabilizing Pakistan that leads to a weak corrupt government which become breeding grounds for terrorist training. Within a few weeks of the invasion, there was an uptick in terrorist attacks within Pakistan. Right from the start, Pakistan was labeled by the system mind as a pregnant source of terrorist training. They got off to this start by hosting the training of the 9/11 terrorists. Christian Parenti says: "But the slow and steady destabilization of Pakistan by the US — on the one hand bombing it, while on the other feeding its corrupt political class…who it then feed the country's paramilitary religious fanatics — is a confused and failing policy…." [23] It's the same old story with these commentators. The US is always "misguided", "confused", "failing", "contradictory", etc. The reality is that this system policy is very consistent and very directed and remarkably successful in its mission, which is to create a perfect breeding grounds for terrorist recruitment and training in as many countries as possible. And where there are not weak corrupt governments, their policies have been to create them, which is exactly what occurred in Afghanistan and Iraq. A bevy of commentators couldn't understand why our initial occupation of Iraq was so inept. In an article called "The Mess", Peter Galbraith details the occupation of Iraq: "… Washington sent to Baghdad a steady stream of American conservatives, mainly young people with no relevant experience, … and no knowledge of the region".[24] But this is exactly the effect of a system mind. By botching the invasion and occupation, you maximize the outrage of their tougher young men, which was the whole purpose of the invasion in the first place.

Also, the more incompetent, uneducated and uninformed the CPA (Coalition Provisional Authority) was, the more corrupt and ineffective would be the puppet government it set up. It was screened and chosen by the CPA who best cooperated with the occupiers. There were instances of civilian contractors committing atrocities against Iraqi people with no repercussions at all.[25] These details are of no consequences to the popularity of the war or even world opinion. But it has a great effect on the tough young men of Iraq, where it becomes a total humiliation and sends them over to the resistance and the weak corrupt government they live under is a perfect place to train terrorists. And this is exactly what is in various CIA reports. Before the invasion the CIA found no Al Qaeda in Iraq; but after the invasion, Al Qaeda was all over Iraq recruiting new terrorists from all over the Muslim world, leading finally to a new and even more brutal terrorist organization called ISIS. That's what we get for our four thousand dead, thirty thousand maimed in addition to a trillion dollar cost while Americans live in orange crate houses that get blown away in a windstorm destroying their entire life history.

Of course, we never hear the real nature of these puppet governments. Since they get ratings with wars of any kind, it's in the interests of the systems' media mouthpieces to completely suppress the nature of the puppet governments that invasions set up. What helps in this regard are fake elections in the invaded country. These elections consist mostly of women and old men. And why not vote? Things are always bad in these underdeveloped countries. Elections are like a new toy. There's nothing to lose, and maybe things will improve. What determines the path these countries take is not a bunch of old people voting for which puppet will reign, but what their tough young men will be doing just like what happened in the American Revolution. What is supporting the whole Hollywood set of fake elections, puppet governments, armies, and police is the American taxpayer. If the dollar faucet were turned off, the whole set would come crashing down into rubble.

An article in *The Economist* outlined all the ways the puppet government in Iraq is returning right back to the bad old days under Saddam. The press is squelched: "Journalists are prominent victims of Iraq's judicial system",[26] and dissidents are being rounded up, jailed and tortured. This is what all the loss of life in Iraq was supposed to replace. Wikileaks detailed the atrocities committed by the Iraq army against people they don't like. This puppet government is what motivated ISIS to invade Iraq in July, 2014. Now, the same media whores who supported the puppet government for 12 yeas now say it has to go.

The same in Afghanistan. The corruption is so great that "the US military's contractors are forced to pay suspected insurgents to protect American supply routes." [27] Aram Rostow in his report says that it's a big "bizaar", "a virtual carnival of improbable characters and shady connections, with former CIA officials, ex-military officers joining hands with Taliban and mujahedeen to collect US government funds in the name of the war effort". *The Economist* had a glowing article about the progress of the ANA (Afghan National Army): "Max Fergeson, who commands an American company...... is full of praise for the fighting spirit of these Afghan 'warriors' ". [28] I'm reading along and thinking maybe I'm be wrong about this wonderful ANA. At the end of the article, we get the catch. Propping up this Halloween army "...will require $6 billion- $8 billion a year after the foreign troops pull out...". With that kind of money, I'll bet you could get a couple hundred thousand hippies to pretend to be an army too.

On top of this, many in the armies in Iraq and Afghanistan are part of the government by day, and insurgents at night. There are stories of millions of dollars of arms of various kinds disappearing from the Iraqi army. Not only that, but there are men going into this army to get their hands on arms to be used to torture and kill people of different religious affiliation in what is known as "sectarian violence". [29] The new tactic in 2012 is insurgents joining the Afghan army to have access to killing *American* soldiers. In my opinion, this is the tip of the iceberg.

Not only that, but very often, after the invader leaves and things settle down, people who supported the puppet government are labeled "collaborators" and traitors and are often executed. After WWII, leaders of the puppet Vichy government set up in France by the Nazis were hung. Many leaders of the puppet Government Johnson and Nixon set up in

Vietnam had to be brought here after the war to save their lives. Our puppets in Iraq and Afghanistan will probably wind up living high on the hog in the US on all the money they stole from the US taxpayer.

There's a funny note to the Halloween armies under these puppet governments. Somehow their size is always 200 thousand. I don't know why that number is chosen. A few months before the last US helicopter left the rooftops of Saigon at the end of the Vietnam war, the South Vietnamese army consisted of 200 thousand men. The army in Iraq now consists of 200 thousand men. And guess how big the Afghan army is? Right — 200 thousand. When the dollars stop coming, these Halloween armies disappear in the time it takes to change uniforms. What ever happened to the 200 thousand-man South Vietnamese army, by the way?

The brain energy that motivates terrorism and insurgency is from one of the oldest very primitive emotion of territorial protection. The young men who are fighting there are motivated by millions of years of evolutionary wiring in all males from the higher primates to the lowliest of bugs to defend their territory and expel invaders. And they were up against the most sophisticated, the most deadly, and the most powerful military force ever deployed in history. But no matter the odds against them, they will resist and fight on forever any way they can including terrorism. The motivation is always the same: *expel the invader.*

There is an analogy with a pot of water. A pot of water is visible as it sits in one place. This is analogous to an enemy army. Our military geniuses look at this army and think, we can blast this army to oblivion in a few days, as our invasions of Iraq and Afghanistan showed. However, upon invasion, the home army along with the tough young men in the country atomize just like boiling the water in the pot will evaporate the water into invisible molecules of water vapor all over the room. They become an atomized guerilla force which, by any means possible including terrorism, can keep the invaders at bay for years. As soon as the invaders leave, the guerilla army condenses into a regular army like we have now in ISIS, just like the water vapor in a room will condense into a pot of water when the temperature in the room drops. This back and forth has been going on in Afghanistan for hundreds of years, and the hard-wired paid killers who determine our foreign policy learn nothing from all this history. Now in 2015, neoconservative capons running for president want to go after ISIS. Of course, ISIS would be easy to destroy as an army. They would simply atomize into a guerilla force keeping the US at bay for another 12 years just the way Al Qaeda did for the last 12 years.

The Bush-Obama foreign policy of lawlessness has been successful beyond all expectations. What started out as a small group of maybe a few thousand fighters centered around Osama bin Laden over the Palestine issue has mushroomed after 12 years into terrorist organizations like ISIS in every Muslim country across the Afro-Eurasian world. All this was happening right under the noses of propaganda outlet reporters who, to keep the money flowing, were lying through their teeth for 12 years telling us that we were winning and it was just a matter of mopping up. Everyone gains in the war of terrorism: the military gets war, the military-industrial complex makes money and the propaganda outlets get ratings. The losers are the American people who pay for it all and whose kids get killed and maimed in the process.

But what about the social costs of the Bush-Obama foreign policy? As we discussed at length in Ch. 20, the mental lives of our soldiers were in total disarray upon serving in Iraq. They are pumped up with mounds of propaganda about preserving our freedoms, getting terrorists, and helping the Iraqi people. But when they get there, it slowly dawns on a small part of their brain, depending on the individual, that they are there to kill, conquer and control. This is what caused the tremendous amount of mental illness, social deviance, and suicides from the Iraq invasion. Now you add to that the reaction of some of the young men of the invaded country, and you have a self-perpetuating situation.

Of course, in the process of expelling the invader, there will be American soldiers killed by Iraqi and Afghani young men — some of it with suicide bombs. And since these tactics appear sneaky and dastardly to Americans, a few of our soldiers with mental abnormalities will go haywire. In one of the most important articles about the war, Michael Massing reviews a number of books that discuss the mini-war crimes and atrocities committed by some American soldiers.[30] These stories about as sad a story you are ever likely to find. As we discussed in Ch. 20, you puff up young American soldiers who aren't highly educated or self-aware with a lot of pro-war propaganda and then put them into the reality of Iraq and Afghanistan and you're going to get mental disorientation, instability and social deviance. And when they see their buddies getting killed in an unconventional way, it triggers off totally irrational and murderous impulses. Sometimes whole households are murdered who are innocent of anything to do with the war.

There is one question that really perplexes me, which is, what is the thinking of our military. One of our generals there, Stanley McChrystal seemed like a sincere, honorable military man. (One thing we should note, starting with that irrepressible moron, Westmorland in Vietnam, our generals kept getting better.) Do people like McChrystal really think he's going to rid the world of the Talaban and Al Qaeda? He was sensitive to the fact that you have to win over hearts and minds and carve away the *support* given to his enemy by the general population. He tried to do this by reducing the drone attacks and tightening up on casualties to civilians. But there is one factor that I don't think he does see, and neither do most others.

The kind of person who would collaborate with an invader is not the kind of high-minded, idealistic leader that has motivation to engage in legitimate nation-building and reform. They are going to be money-grubbing crooks who want raw power even if it's temporary and who stand to spend the rest of their lives in luxury at the American tax-payer's expense if they can't hold on to power. Now in 2014, the system TV war mongers are blaming the crooked Iraq government for ISIS. They don't have to worry about the fact that it was these same media whores whose propaganda inspired the installation of this same puppet government in the first place.

Reform and nation-building is what you get, if you get it at all, from people who *resist* the invasion, like Simon Bolivar in South America, Mahatma Ghandi of India, Charles De

Gaulle of France, and George Washington in the US. Their heroes are existential philosophers like Albert Camus and Jean Paul Sartre who were hiding in caves and sewers trying to sabotage the Nazi invaders in WWII to *expel* the invader. What McChrystal and Obama would like is for Afghanistan's George Washington to be on *their* side. They are dreaming. If Afghanistan has a George Washington, he is hiding in the hills and caves trying to kick out the invader exactly the way our *real* George Washington was trying to kick out the British occupier. And remember, the British in the colonies were not bad occupiers. In fact, all of our important institutions are copied from the British. They weren't sending in drones and killing innocent civilians either. That didn't stop George Washington from rounding up some tough young men and kicking them out. (And by the way, the British called George Washington and his men terrorists too, because they fired from behind trees instead of lining up honorably and firing from right out in the open like the red-coats. A British general here said, the "insurgents...with a wontonness of cruelty...carry depredations and distress wherever they turn their steps".[31] Sound familiar? Pretty much what the US is saying about the Iraqis.)

In Cuba, in spite of burdening his country with years of Communism, Cuban history books in the distant future long after Communism in Cuba becomes a bad memory, will present Castro as a national hero just like George Washington. And for only one reason — not because of the way he ran Cuba, but because he kicked out the foreign occupier.

What our policy makers and our think tank experts don't see is that *by its very nature, you are not going to get idealists, patriots and incorruptible people to form a government that collaborates with an invader,* no matter how nice the invader is. The puppets various American presidents have set up in Vietnam, Chili, Iraq, and Afghanistan, are no George Washingtons. They are precisely the kind of venal, corrupt, small-minded and power-hungry crook that you would expect of a collaborator who persecutes and marginalizes other tribes. Instead of an inclusive organic system, you get *organized* tribalism to replace *un*organized tribalism.

In my opinion, Obama and McChrystal might have been acting outside the system as idealists who want the best for the people of Afghanistan. On the other hand, these very honorable men are also part of the system mind, and the big-picture reason to be in Afghanistan is that the system mind needs continuous war. Also, we're not saying that US occupation of these countries has *no* beneficial results. There has been some progress in building modern institutions like courts and elections, etc. and considerable progress for women. However, as soon as the country is on their own without massive US dollars to prop up a Hollywood façade of puppet government, the country will revert to what it was for hundreds of years. In fact, it is probable that any gains that were made in the way of modernization could be swept away by the tough young gangs under leaders who control things by associating the gains with the invader and occupier as happened in Vietnam.

The New Republic magazine (Aug, 12, '10) devoted a whole issue trying to analyze the war in Afghanistan. These are the supposed experts. There is some good advice, and some insights, but in general, it is truly astounding how people build their views of reality not on perceptions, but on strings of words. The stark reality is that bottom of the brain energy motivating the administration's invasions was to kill, conquer and create pregnant grounds for recruiting terrorists. And regardless of all the reason box crap we hear from system propaganda outlets, *in reality, that's exactly what he did.* Of course as brain energy percolates upward in the brains of planners and soldiers, some of it sneaks into existential parts of the brain which accounts for soldiers giving candy to children and other good intentions and beneficial initiatives that dot the big picture. This is why the foreign policy of the US appears as a huge schizophrenic mish-a-ghass making it difficult to explain.

Seth Jones, an analyst in one of our think tanks has written a book about what we should have done in Afghanistan, reviewed by Dexter Filkins.[32] Now I used to work for think tanks when I was young and know something of how they work. They get paid big bucks by the government to either tell the government what it wants to hear, or tell us stuff so obvious that a drunk in the local bar could tell us the same thing. But because they get paid so much, they get to thinking they are saying something very original and important. Jones tells us we didn't spend enough money in Afghanistan to get a workable functioning state that would have earned the allegiance of the Afghan people. It's the same old crap. Just a nudge here, a push there, a few more soldiers here and a few more killings there, and we all live happily ever after. It's Vietnam all over with the same inner brain commentators and their sexual fantasies. Filkins says: "The central administration that existed in Kabul quickly evolved into a criminal enterprise, siphoning tens of millions of Western dollars..."(24). In Mar. '13, we get a report on reconstruction efforts in Iraq talking about billions of dollars of waste and fraud. Is this some kind of surprise, especially after the exact same thing happened in Vietnam?

Why didn't the US set up puppet governments in Germany and Japan after WWII? Even though the Japanese are Asians, there had been considerable western influence in Japan for two hundred years. But the most important consideration was that Roosevelt and even Truman were quite idealistic and wanted the best for the German and Japanese people. The result was that Truman allowed free and fair elections in both countries even if people running for office may not have liked us. Even communists were allowed to run. This sent a clear message to the people of the world that the US was for self-determination. This took them down a road leading to the camp of democratic civilized countries. If George Bush and his team of uneducated, unenlightened and uninformed neoconservative inner brain dinosaurs had been in charge after WWII, they would have installed right-wing puppet governments in Japan and Germany too. The result would be insurgency, civil war, dictators, and who knows what else.

Muslim countries have thousand year-old momentum vectors of fundamentalist religion dominating society along with the violence and corruption that goes along with it. It would take a monumental effort among the most competent of experts in many fields to change those vectors. No chance with the kind of killers that have dominated our foreign policy for the last 35 years.

And now we have a new force to promote policies that keep terrorist recruitment going. We have a bunch of guys preaching against religion detailing all the harm it has done in history. They claim that *science* will lead us to the promised land of world peace, prosperity and morality, no less. One of the leaders of this group is a neuroscientist named Sam Harris, who takes special aim at Islam which, he claims, is out for world domination and is "… undeniably a religion of conquest".[33] Well in actual fact, *religions* don't conquer anything— religious *leaders* conquer. This may seem a small point, but it shows that drumming up hatred for a few men is not going to make some these inner brainers happy. You have to indict *whole religions* and *whole peoples* so you can torture and kill *large* numbers of people instead of just a few law-breakers.

The fact is, leaders of *all* religions conquer people. But in its conquest period after the 7th century, Muslims conquered people by defeating armies, not by slaughtering innocents. Even though they put non-Muslims, Jews and Christians at an economic and political disadvantage in conquered lands, at least there was a degree of tolerance, and most importantly, let them live. When the western Roman Emperor Leo III started persecuting Jews and forcing them to be baptized, many Jews fled to *Muslim* lands to be able to continue to exist at least. Compare this to the Crusades a few years later when European Christians went into Middle East villages and murdered every living thing including dogs and cats.

Of course, he overlooks the fact that the whole Muslim world is a mess because of hundreds of years of invasions, conquests and killing by *Christian* European powers invading scores of countries killing people all over the world. It was Europeans who conducted slavery all over the world often using Christianity to justify the practice. Europeans came to the new world using *Christianity* as a justification for pushing aside the indigenous people and snuffing them out.

Oh, but Harris congratulates Bush for not killing hordes of Iraqis in the invasion, (only about a 100 thousand, including 20 thousand children). But the invasion of Iraq was not carried off by a handful of international criminals, but by government officials of a powerful nation state. Communism did the same while being anti-religious, and it's hard to compete with Marx's *scientific* Communism when it comes to conquest, anthropocide and crimes against humanity.

Nazi Germany engaged in its share of "scientifically" based eugenics, racism and human experimentation too in the name of "science", and "scientifically" based means of mass murder. But did we torture German prisoners of war or send drones into civilian neighborhoods because there might be a Nazi hiding? And we were fighting a *whole nation state*, not a small band of individual international criminals. The reason is obvious. Germans were white Christian Europeans deserving a modicum of international law.

Of course, there are radical Muslim groups everywhere in the world even in the new Arab spring countries who would like to snuff out any group of people not like them.[34] They are no different than leaders of every other religion throughout history. The bottom line is very simple — religion is a great amplifier: it takes basically good people and makes them a little better; and it takes basically bad people and makes them a lot worse. This is true of all religions. I sincerely hope that more moderate leaders will emerge in Muslim countries in the future. Of course, the US, goaded on by people like Sam Harris is making sure we aren't going to have much influence over events in these countries in a positive way.

As a scientist, Harris is especially offensive to people like me. If people like Harris want to spruce up their sex lives with more conquest, torture and killing of innocent human beings around the world, they should do it as the usual pissy-ass propagandists for paid killers — not as *scientists*. Led by the *Scientific American* magazine, science has recently been struggling to raise its status as a force for mankind's improvement. It doesn't need Harris's perverted idea of science-based morality. But Harris does have a way out for his views. He denies that humans have free will. So he can explain away his murderous views as the result of his mechanical brain uncontrollably clanking away as a deterministic machine.

The war on terrorism is the perfect war because you can adjust the intensity of the war any degree that you want depending domestic needs. Of course, the system will have to sharpen its efficiency in keeping the war on terrorism going. Iraq and Afghanistan are relatively large countries, and invading and conquering them costs hundreds of billions and thousands of lives. This is not an efficient way to produce terrorists and conflicts with the goal of a perfect war: *continuous* war.

In 2013, talk programs and newspeople were reporting about the "grave" situation in Iraq and Afghanistan. People like Charlie Rose have the usual bevy of word-mongering scribblers who are concerned with the "failures" in these wars, and "troubling" recent events like a resurgence of Al Qaeda. These people are inadvertently pushing the system mind explanation, which is very simple: we tried hard, but it's a difficult situation. As we said in Sect. 30.4, the way to judge motivation for a system action is to look at the palpable results. The reality is that *the invasions of Iraq and Afghanistan were one of the most successful system mind foreign policy initiatives in recent years*. The *purpose* was to create terrorists, to establish training ground for terrorists, to strengthen Economic Socialism, to enable the military-industrial complex to make more billions on war goods, to distract people from incompetent economic policies that send all new income and wealth to the top 20%, and to enable the media mouthpieces to get higher ratings as people tune in the hear about the ongoing war on terrorism. *Those are the results, and that is the motivation*. These invasions were a smashing success.

If you sincerely want a nation to develop, you leave them alone just like the Chinese. You send it advisors, scientists, entrepreneurs, economists, and health experts to partner and encourage like-mined people in the developing country. Even with these kinds of experts, it isn't easy to overcome ancient vectors when society is basically tribal and there is no feudal past. It takes finesse, planning and good-will. The easy stuff is sending paid killers into a country. Regardless of the reason-box diarrhea they spew forth, they are there to invade, conquer and kill.

But with massive federal deficits, political pressure mounted to end these wars. But one way or another, the system will find ways to keep the war on terrorism going. All you have to do is to come up with ingenious ways to attack and humiliate Muslim people around the world, which include assassinations, droning suspected targets guilty or not, torturing mostly innocent captives, and methods that we might not have even thought of yet. You can then find-tune the number of terrorists you need by allowing Israel to yank the tail of the Palestinians. All of this, of course, will enable terrorist organizations to stay in business. The last thing the system mind wants is to get rid of Al Qaeda and ISIS. Al Qaeda was the greatest gift to George Bush in his entire presidency, and Obama is still living off it.

Speaking of Palestine, we have heard for years about a "peace process". Typical of received opinion on this issue is a boring article in the *New York Review* reviewing a bunch of boring books about the pitfalls of the peace process. This review and the books reviewed are stuffed with phrases about American efforts as insincere, uninformed, "disengaged", "unprepared", "naïve", "overzealous", being "repeatedly outfoxed".[35] These people have their heads so immersed in words that they can't see the reality of the big picture. The American system mind has been extremely *consistent* in its agenda for 60 years now, and it's not naïve at all. Keep the situation fluid, hypocritically *talking* even-handedness while tacitly supporting everything Israel does so as to enrage young men all over the Muslim world.

Now this is a good time to remind you that there is no conspiracy here. Nobody meets behind closed doors to plan all this. Each player in the entire process is a node in the system mind doing its little part that is totally harmless in itself, but contributes to the making of a kind of mind — a system mind. Just as our own minds *emerge* from the activity of the brain's neurons sending electrical impulses zipping around, so a self-perpetuating system mind emerges with its own agenda on the basis of huge numbers of information flows, any of which is perfectly harmless. James Madison said, "no nation could preserve its freedoms in the midst of continual war". This is one of the most important quotes in this book. This is why the "continual" war of terrorism is so essential to the system mind's need to water down our basic rights and freedoms on its path to a National Socialist state.

1 Rodenbeck, Max, "The Iran Mystery Case". *The New York Review of Books*, Jan. 15, '09, p. 35

2 Danner, Mark, *The New York Review of Books*, Aug. 11, '05, p. 60

3 Cole, David, "Are We Safe". *The New York Review of Books*, Mar. 9, '06, p. 15.

4 Mayer, Jane, "The Battle for the Country's Soul". *New York Review*, Aug. 14, '08

5 Power, Semantha, "The Democrats and National Security, *New York Review*, Aug. 14, '08.

6 Lieven, Anatol. *Pakistan: A Hard Country*, Public Affairs.

7 *The Economist*, May 5, '07, p. 30

8 Powers, Thomas, "What Tenet Knew". *The New York Review of Books*, July 19, '07.

9 Armstrong, F.; Powers, Thomas, "The CIA and WMDs". *The New York Review of Books*, Aug. 19, '10

10 Eakin, Hugh, "The Devastation of Iraq's Past, *New York Review*, Aug. 14, '08

11 "The ethnic split:", *The Nation*, Sept. 9, '09, p. 14.

12 Ibid. p. 13

13 Gopal, Anand, "Who Are the Talaban". *The Nation*, Dec. 22, '08, p. 20

14 Cole, Juan; "The Age of American Shadow Power". *The Nation*, Apr. 30, '12, p. 26

15 Hamid, Mohsin, "Pakistan: Why Drones don't help". *The New York Review*, May 23, '13, p. 23

16 Ruthven, Malise, "Terror: The Hidden Sources". *The New York Review*, Oct. 24, '13, p. 20

17 Dunbar, Robin; 1997. *Grooming, Gossip, and the Evolution of Language*, Harvard Univ. Pr.

18 Cole, Juan, "The Age of American Shadow Power. *The Nation*, Apr. 30, '12, p. 25

19 Gopal, Anand, "America's Secret Afghan Prisons", *The Nation*, Feb. 15, '10

20 Bergin, Peter, "War of Error". *The New Republic*, Oct. 22, '07, p. 23

21 Ibid. p. 27

22 Cumins, Bruce; "Making the World Safe for Evil". *The Nation*, Oct. 28, '02, p. 27

23 Parenti, Christian, "With Friends Like These", *The Nation*, May 20, '13, p. 28

24 Galbraith, Peter, "The Mess". *New York Review of Books*, Mar. 9, '06, p. 29

25 Schahill, Jeremy, "Making a Killing". *The Nation*, Oct. 15, '07, p. 21

26 "Could a police state return", *The Economist*, Sept. 5, '09, p. 49

27 Roston, Aram; "How the US Funds the Taliban". *The Nation*, Nov. 30, '09, p. 11

28 "Plum Recruits". *The Economist*, Aug. 6, '11

29 Hayden, Tom, "The New Counterinsurgency". *The Nation*, Sept. 24, '07, p. 20

30 Massing, Michael, "Iraq: the Hidden Costs. *New York Review of Books*, Dec. 20, '07, p. 82

31 Breen, T.H.; "Our Insurgency". *The New York Review*, July 11, '13, p. 42

32 Filkins, Dexter reviewing Jones, Seth G. *In the Graveyard of Empires*. Norton Press in *The New Republic*, Mar. 11, '10.

33 Lears, Jackson, "Same Old New Atheism". *The Nation*, May 16, '11, p. 27

34 Marshall, P.; Shea, N. *Silenced: How Apostasy and Blasphemy Codes are Choking Freedom Worldwide;* Oxford Univ. Pr., UK.

35 Hussein Agha & Robert Malley, "How Not to Make Peace in the Middle east". *The New York Review of Books*, Jan. 15, '09, p. 42.

CHAPTER 35

Women's Liberation

————

IN THIS CHAPTER, WE WILL give some further evidence of a system mind. What we will be detailing is that the Women's Liberation movement piggie-backed on 150 years of feminism for the purpose of creating the perfect citizen from the point of view of the system. But first, let's look at a little history of feminism and how we got to the present state of affairs.

35.1 HISTORY OF FEMINISM

Modern feminism started in the late 1700s with a very small group of like-minded women in England. But the thrust of the movement really occurred in the US in the 1800s probably because if society was going to change in drastic ways, it could probably be accomplished more easily in a new country without thousands of years of precedence to struggle against.

It is interesting to ask the question as to why feminism started up in the first place. Well, these are the things historians fight about because most important changes in society come about from of a variety of reasons, all of which contribute to the final result. But we can consider what I think was a crucial motivating force in the early feminist movement. It's a pretty simple idea.

We have to realize that starting around 2 million years ago when earlier proto-humans entered the human evolution phase, there was probably a division of labor in the camp situations humans were evolving in. (The cave situation didn't come until much later and mostly in Europe. For most of this evolutionary period, hominids were evolving in little villages or campsites out in the open on the African pampas.) In any event, the division of labor had males protecting the group and hunting big game, and females raising babies and attending to camp duties like preparing food, clothing and shelter. This was a period of rapid growth of the human brain, which needs a great deal of protein to develop. This is partly why humans increasingly became meat-eaters and males provided much of the protein they needed by hunting large animals.

Since males were necessary for protection and protein, females were quite supportive in their relationships with males so that males could perform their roles. This meant support in every way, not only physically, but emotionally as well. This is why the motto among females all through the 2 or so million years of human evolution was patch 'em up, stand 'em up, and send 'em back out there. This motto gets hard-wired into the psyche of all pre-human females as we evolved into modern humans. And these mutual needs between males and females of protection and sustenance from males and nurturance from females is the basis for a primitive version of the family.

When we get to civilization around 8 thousand years ago in the Middle East, this division of labor and its accompanying roles for men and women became more articulated. Some version of marriage appears in most early tribes of people, even among pagans before the Greek and Roman civilization. The concept of the family emerged whereby this division of labor could be more institutionalized by the ties of marriage. A kind of social contract between males and females emerged that gave prerogatives to each side and responsibilities to match. Responsibilities sometimes included relinquishing various prerogatives. In western societies, the main responsibility of males was protection and support of families, especially physical protection. Of course, a woman might say that they were being protected against other males. That may be true, but it's protection nevertheless from aggressions posed by other tribes and from animal predators as well. This, of course, relies on the one major good instinct that males may have, as we have described: the emotion of *protection*. Males also had the obligation to support their kids, stay with their wives and keep their families together, at least in theory. What females got out of this implicit contract was protection and economic support from males, as well as fidelity and lifelong loyalty, at least in theory. What females gave up in the bargain was basically political and economic power, which is why they didn't have the right to vote or own property or have equal status in society until very recently.

Now people have argued ad nauseam as to the fairness of this contract. Many modern women would claim they were giving up a lot, and not getting enough in return. The fairness of this social contract is not relevant to our purposes here. However, we can note that for hundreds of years, women must have deemed the contract was *acceptable* because they passed it on to their sons and daughters. This did not have to be the case. We saw very graphically that when the Women's Liberation movement started in the late '70s, women stopped passing on the traditional culture to their children because they no longer thought it was in their interests. And the results were very obvious.

In any event, what occurred in the beginning of the Industrial Revolution in the late 1700s was that work in factories began its slow glide to become the predominant occupation by WWII. Not only that, but parliaments and other government bodies passed laws protecting women and created police forces to enforce laws. This was simply part of civilization. It was just a matter of time before women put two and two together and realized that it was *society* that was protecting them from the barbarians, not individual men. Also, they began working for wages so they didn't need men for the benefits of the old social contract. However, they were still giving up political and economic power. So the old social contract began to fray, as women began to petition and organize for equal political and economic rights. This is how feminism got started.

Throughout the 1800s, feminists tried mightily to organize women into a viable political force for equal rights, specifically, the right to vote. But they could never muster enough political clout to get the job done. It was a difficult job and you have to admire the courage and steadfastness of early feminists. Writers and historians claim that this proved the enormous degree of sexism all along in history. But a lot of it depended on the fact that all societies, even very primitive ones, have a degree of division of labor as a way to increase productivity. People had roles even *within* genders. Men workers specialized into various job categories. The roles assigned to women had been in place for thousands of years as part of the social contract. With the coming of advanced Capitalism, role-playing simply intensified. However, rights are a different matter. Even if women's roles could be justified as a division of labor, that doesn't entail that they should be denied *rights* to property, to vote and equality in education and job access.

But the goals of the feminist movement remained out of reach all through the 1800s. One of the ironies is that they had trouble getting even women to join the effort. Perhaps women during the Industrial Revolution were not at all anxious to get into the workforce and thought their best interests were to give up economic and political power in order to maintain their role as wives and mothers. Perhaps they saw that if they had equality before the law and with regard to job opportunities and equal power in other ways, they would lose the part of the old social contract whereby men were obliged to be loyal and supportive of their families, such as it was. Perhaps women in the 1800s formed a system mind. This doesn't seem likely because they were not part of complex flows of information. It was probably a Jungian universal consciousness or simply a cultural phenomenon.

In any event, even though the leaders of the feminist movement in the 1800s were intelligent, highly motivated, effective and determined, nothing much changed for the whole century and beyond. They met with stiff opposition from both males and females all along the way. We might mention a few of the leaders. The earliest was Mary Wollstonecraft in England. When things got going here is was Lucretia Mott, Lucy Stone, the Grimke sisters, and most importantly Elizabeth Cady Stanton and Susan B. Anthony. There are some good books on the history of 1800's feminism in the US (Marilley, '96; Freedman, '02).

The feminist movement reached a major milestone in 1920 in the US with the 19th amendment to the Constitution giving women the right to vote. The next steps were establishing equality before the law with regards to opportunity, employment, education, division of assets in divorce, etc. Now I don't see why women *didn't* have these rights all along as is clearly stated in the Constitution under the equal protection clause. But with presidents picking Supreme Court justices with their reptilian brains, the Court has been using the Constitution for toilet paper for hundreds of years. But in my opinion, this wasn't because they were men — it was because they were shysters. I don't think a group of scientists, for example, would have been so venal.

Finally, after all this time, we got a court that took the equal protection clause seriously and allowed the establishment of rights for women. But it took a great deal of law effort and petitioning to gain these rights which were achieved mostly in the 1960s. The Supreme Court who established these rights has since then been tainted with the title "liberal" court. When you actually *read* the Constitution as opposed to *"interpreting"* it into the toilet, you get stamped with a word that has the connotations of deviance and radicalism.

Of course, modern feminists would still say that in practice, discrimination and disadvantages against women continued. Well, anybody's rights and privileges can by thwarted by individual people in positions of power. But this is not the work of the *system;* it is the result of cultural biases in individual *people* that always lag behind progress made by the system. We have laws banning racism as well. The *system* has not been racist since the '60s, *until recently*. The current Supreme Court has ruled that that in effect, black people don't have an equal opportunity for higher education. They basically ruled is that it's okay to use race to the keep the black man out, but you can't use race to bring the black man back in. That's the kind of reptile we got on these Courts. We're back to pre-civil war injustices.

35.2 The System Mind and the Women's Lib Movement

With the introduction of TV, radio, telephone, mass culture, and massive new flows of information, a much more cohesive system mind evolved after WWII. It had more articulated ideas of its interests than ever before. With a "liberal" Supreme Court giving women the rights of equal opportunity in education, jobs, etc., the system took a look at this development and thought about what use could be made from current developments that would benefit the system.

The unit of production had been the family up till the Industrial Revolution in the 1800s, having been left over from feudal times of the middle ages. But the system received a huge boon in its desire to establish the lone individual as the unit of production with the establishment of women's civil rights in the 1960s. The system mind took one look at these historic developments and asked, how do we respond. What happened next was one of the most interesting glides in all of human history from the point of view of the system mind. *The Women's Liberation movement of the late '70s, piggy-backing on the 150 year-old feminist movement, was created by the system as a means to establish the lone individual as the unit of production and to design the perfect American citizen that would benefit the interests of the system.*

The system mind concluded that perhaps it was better if women not only had the *right* to equality in jobs, but would benefit if women could be actually *coerced* into the workforce. Market economies are always looking for workers, because more workers decrease the value of labor and, additionally, increases the number of shoppers to buy goods and services the system is making. With wives working, it allowed *family* income to increase in the bottom 80%, which covered up the fact that their *personal* income was actually dropping in real dollars starting with Reagan.

In addition to this, the system needed better ways to increase profits and to send new wealth and income to the top 20%. The way to do this is to get the most work for the least pay by getting more work hours per day out of employees. This effectively reduces wages. The system mind achieves its *economic* goals by having total control of the means of propaganda and by having a permanent state of war as we have discussed. The way to achieve its goals in our *personal* lives would be to initiate a movement that would create the perfect citizen who is a 12-hour a day work slave who has no personal life, no human ties, and no distractions from the almighty job. The road to this goal is to depreciate the value of families and existential relationships and to pare away any aspects of a normal meaningful life that could possibly be a distraction from the almighty job.

But such a movement needed leaders who would induce women into the new societal values. The same thing happened as after the black power movement discussed in Sect. 25.2. The system mind was taken by surprise by the success of the black power movement. But it reconstituted itself and gathered up the old radical black leaders, gave them big grants, made them fat, and stuffed them into suits with collars that almost choked them to death. The result exactly fit the needs of the system mind, which reduced economic rights of average blacks to where the difference between white and black wealth and income is worse than when the whole game started. Except, of course, the black leaders who were bought off to continue the game.

The same thing happened with the women's liberation movement. Intelligent word-mongering women were chosen by the system and given all kinds of economic opportunities to get them to preach the new gospel, which was designed specifically to make 95% of women into the perfectly isolated work-slaves meeting the needs of the system. In return for this dirty work, these libber leaders and their sisters at the top 1% of the talent ladder were offered high paying jobs all over the working world, especially in the propaganda business where lots of money could be made. New magazines were started and new books were written all spouting the party line.

If you hired a high-price think tank to devise a social movement that would achieve the goals of the system, what would its recommendations be? Its recommendations would be *exactly* and *precisely* the agenda that the Woman's Liberation movement actually put into practice. As we mentioned, it's first job was to break the natural ties between human beings, especially between men and women, leaving the almighty job as the sole focus in people's personal lives. Of course, there is a strong evolutionary tendency for men and women to be attracted to each other and to provide mutual support necessary for survival. So in general, the thousands of years of the old ethic whereby women's role in relation to men was to patch 'em up, stand 'em up, and get 'em back out there, had to be replaced by a new policy of knock 'em down and keep 'em down. So anything that created a means to knock 'em down was greatly encouraged. But the means for mutual support between men and women have been institutionalized in all cultures even the west for thousands of years. So this may not have been easy to bring off.

Well, the system mind is very resourceful, so the first avenue towards this goal was to engender strong emotions in women so as to create a *motive* for the whole agenda. The strongest emotion for this purpose is *anger*; and the best way to drum up anger was to emphasize victimhood of women in history. So we had 25 years of constant victimhood in every cultural media the system had at its disposal, from books and magazines to movies and TV news. Every tiny process, event, or condition in the past that was bad for mankind, especially women, was blamed on male *oppression*. Men were blamed for everything from cockroaches to dust and dirt to diarrhea.

For thousands of years, men had been coerced by society into an existential mode where their job was to protect their families. Of course, millions of years of aggressiveness would sometimes pop through and get expressed as violence to their families, both wives and children. But most of the time they stumbled through their jobs. The peak of this culture was the WWII generation who did a pretty good job of protecting their families and serving their wives. Of course, women libbers interpreted this thousand-year-old division of labor as just more "oppression". This provided the *motive* for the mistreatment of men and rest of the agenda.

The real feminists of the 1800s never talked about oppression in family life. In fact, Elizabeth Cady Stanton had a family with seven kids. They spoke to only one simple issue: they were citizens and as specified in the Constitution, were citizens equal to men; and as such deserved equal rights and privileges. A very simple agenda. In these respects, they mirrored the abolitionist movement and the men's movement of the times having simple narrow goals.

The men's movement was the union movement whose goals again were quite narrow: decent pay, the 8-hour day and safety on the job. The union movement didn't disparage families; it didn't depreciate women; it didn't call for promiscuity; it didn't encourage men to cheat on their wives; and it didn't blame problems of the world on women. In the same way, the early feminists never talked victimhood in every corner of their lives. There was almost no man-bashing. They didn't disparage motherhood or being a housewife. They didn't encourage children to start having sex when they were still children. They didn't hate men as a category and they didn't blame all the world's problems on men. Their anger was directed only at a *system* that perpetuated the specific denial of equal rights to women, not the whole category of men. In fact, they had many male sympathizers. It was a very simple agenda: equal rights.

Just as in the criminal justice system, what provided the *opportunity* for the new man-bashing was to tear down any cultural constraints and norms for human interaction that had been in place for thousands of years. This was done in the name of "freedom" and "liberation". Manners, chivalry, considerateness, reliability, loyalty that are usually prescribed by culture and religion were all devalued in favor of complete *freedom* to do what one pleased in any and all situations. Women were told, you don't have to be "nice" anymore, especially where opportunities arose that provided a means for payback. Once complete freedom from society's norms was established, it would be easy to create a nasty dismissive cultural milieu so that interaction between men and women would be as painful and stressful as possible. By the way, if you doubt the existence of a system mind, you have to ask, how is it that after thousands of years of the culture preaching the strict upbringing of children to encourage the recognition and abidance of cultural norms and religious dictates — how is that out of the clear blue sky you suddenly find the system encouraging parents to raise their kids *permissively* in the exact opposite way?

Coupled with the new freedom and "liberation" that allowed the opportunity for any kind of payback behavior was *incentive*. This was done by a constant reminder that women now had *power*. This much is fine, but it also insured that when the opportunity arose to mistreat men in any way, it would be done as powerfully and as aggressively as possible. Power is clearly an inner brain thing. *They* were going to run their lives and determine their decisions and design society to suit *them*. This will insure that when women started emphasizing freedom, freedom to be as nasty and aggressive as you please, freedom to be uninformed about the nature of men, and freedom to be as incompetent as they please, energy would remain in the bottom of the brain, thus reinforcing these very tendencies.

But the emphasis on power has another salutary effect for the system. Before liberation, when a woman got abandoned either in a relationship or marriage, she might be miserable and devastated. In this distraught state of mind, she would attract men's evolutionary tendency to come to the rescue. This phenomenon greatly improved the chances of such a woman to remarry or find someone else who might appreciate her. The system had to put a stop to this. By a constant stress on women's new-found power, it would maximize their rage when they got abandoned even though they often kept the anger at a subconscious level. But this anger would insure that future successful relationships with subsequent men would be difficult.

The new freedom provided the opportunity to break the natural ties between men and women. The *means* were to depreciate men in every possible way, and what's very important, to turn women from competent mothers, wives, and girlfriends into mindless ninnies who would be less attractive to men. Women were programmed with the preconceived idea that men are such lowly creatures whom you could never expect much from. It is amazing to watch TV stories, sitcoms, etc. in the '80s and '90s. Men are portrayed as stupid and clueless teddy bears that are good for hugging but little else. This sets up what in psychology is called *cognitive dissonance*. When a liberated woman runs into a man who may be well-informed, intelligent, talented, skilled, educated, or accomplished in any way, he will be briskly whipped out of the woman's life so as not to conflict with her preconceived ideas about how worthless men are. This will then reinforce cultural descriptions of men as pretty lowly creatures, not to be taken seriously.

Coupled with this agenda would be to program women to run their lives as stupidly and destructively as possible so as to lose respect from men. Women were told in every possible venue how brilliant and knowledgeable they are and that men are just a bunch of dumb dogs roaming the neighborhood. When you're told how brilliant you are, especially compared to men, there's much less incentive to try to improve the mind, ask questions, study, learn and to strain the brain. Remember, through millions of years of evolution, what got wired into men's brains was to look for females who would be the most likely to continue the male's genes. The main quality that this requires is *competence*. Men are wired to look for competence in women. So it was very important to the system mind to program women to behave as *incompetently* as possible in every possible way, *but only* in their private lives. The system wouldn't want incompetence in the almighty job. The best way to achieve this result would be for women to have the least possible understanding of men at all levels. Women were programmed to squelch the slightest interest in men's values, outlook, perceptions, motivations and general psychology. This would insure that women's interaction with men would be conducted as incompetently as possible. Recall, in Sect. 15.1, we explained the *theory of mind*. This is the phrase analytic philosophers have used to name the ability to understand the minds of others, their beliefs, perceptions, motives, etc. One of the goals of the system mind was to eradicate people's theory of mind. This insures that gender interaction will be carried on as incompetently and stupidly as possible.

If we look at the kind of programming the system would inflict on women to achieve all the above effects, there is one thing in common. They are all best achieved with the *brain's energy in the bottom of the brain*. We discussed this phenomenon in the Love chapter, Sect. 21.4. Victimhood produces first fear and then aggression — emotions at the bottom of the brain in the limbic system. *Freedom*, of course, allows primitive impulses at the bottom of the brain to hold sway over any kind of existential thinking. Power, of course, is always run by the emotion of aggression also in the limbic system. Since intelligence is in the existential parts of the brain, if most the brain's energy is in the bottom, there will be less intelligence in running one's life. Understanding, perceptions, and insight are again existential considerations seated in the most advanced part of the brain, and will be greatly attenuated when most of the brain's energy is in the bottom. Not only that, but when they start behaving as incompetently as possible, they would do it all with great gusto and aggression.

Our next step is to explain how the system mind was able to promote *essentialist* thinking and prevent existential thinking in women having the results we have enumerated. As we explained in Sect. 11.5, gender and sex is probably a half billion years old. It was about this time that nature began experimenting with sticking cells together to form multi-cellular creatures. It required a great deal more evolution to achieve the complexity in cells necessary to achieve a diverse array of creatures to fill many ecological niches. And this can be best achieved if genes can be reshuffled to create new and advantageous combinations that speed up the pace of evolution. Sexual reproduction accomplishes this task.

The point we are making is that sex, mating rituals, and reproduction are about as old as life itself. And these practices in early creatures were wired into the very earliest and most primitive parts of the central nervous system, what we've been calling the inner brain. And as we indicated above, the first goal of the system mind is to get women's thinking into the bottom of their brains. A way to do this is to conceptualize oneself in a gender way. Recall in Ch. 16, we discussed the location in the brain where we form concepts determines to a great extent how we interact with instances of that concept. In Ch. 21 on love, we discussed the location in the brain where concepts of members of the opposite sex lies. This applies to the concept we have of ourselves. If our self-concept is in the bottom of the brain, propositional attitudes, planning, imagining, and other mentality that involves the self, will tend to drag energy down to the bottom of the brain where the self-concept resides. This is exactly where the system wants it to be.

So how does the system get women to conceptualize themselves in the bottom of the brain? The key concept at the core of the woman's movement was the concept of WOMAN-HOOD. This caused women to identify themselves not as persons, but as *women*. By identifying herself as a *woman*, she will most likely be putting the concept she has of herself in the bottom of the brain where anything having to do with sex and gender lies. This explains why the system, acting through the liberation movement, constantly stressed *womanhood*. This creates a paradox. On the one hand, the movement stressed equality. At the height of the movement, people were running around claiming the men and women were exactly alike. What the leaders of the movement didn't realize is that it is only when you push energy into the *top* of the brain that men and women are alike. Men and women engage in art and music and science and literature in pretty much the same way. But these very human existential activities are late developments in evolutionary history and involve behavior that is not relevant to survival, mating and reproduction. It is in the *inner* brain where we find men and women differing the most. At the *essentialist* inner brain level, there are differences in the weightings of the different emotions causing different patterns of thinking and behavior that we see most incisively in animals. At the inner brain level, the important behavioral emotion in males is exploration. That's what hunters do. This is why men like interesting conversations and an adventure of the mind. At the inner brain level, females are wired motivationally only for sex and nesting; and behaviorally only for what's familiar for safety. This is why with all the energy at the bottom of the brain, men and women have never been as *in*compatible as now.

Consequently, the paradox of the woman's movement is that by stressing identification with the concept of WOMAN, the movement caused brain energy to remain in the bottom of the brain, thus amplifying the very gender differences that the movement pretended to dispel. And most importantly, among these differences is the criterion used to pick members of the opposite sex. By identifying herself as a *woman*, the "liberated" woman is not liberated at all. She is not free to choose her best course with regards to men because choices are only relevant at the existential level. She is really a slave to the hard-wiring of the inner brain.

Now this can be contrasted with the concepts used by early feminists. They stressed that they were *people*, just like men. And just like men, they deserved the same rights and freedoms. This was one of the most striking differences between real feminism and the system mind liberation movement. We should look at why it took a strong cultural movement to reverse a trend after WWII towards *existential* thinking as we discussed in Sect. 21.1 and towards the goal of mostly inner brain thinking.

35.3 POST-WWII ESSENTIALISM

A new and more sophisticated system mind developed after the war due to the great increases in flows of information through TV, mass markets, and mass culture. It immediately saw the need for more essentialist thinking to carry out the new needs of the system. The first order of business was to finish the job of turning the unit of production to the lone individual, and to attack on any form of human interaction and connection including marriage, leaving the almighty job in all its glory standing alone. This, in turn requires that the natural nexus between men and women be severed. These societal trends would be best actuated by encouraging the thinking of people, especially women, to drop to the bottom of the brain which gradually diminishes existential thinking. And an effective way to accomplish this is to promote *freedom*, as we mentioned. This in turn allows neglect of social and cultural norms; it lessens the ability to look outside oneself to perceive the needs of others; and it allows people to ignore the dictates of religious and cultural morays. It is no accident that a major social movement got started when it did and was called "liberation". This is exactly what the system needed at this point in history.

It takes effort to send energy to the top of the brain. This is why as people get older, many neurons die, especially those of the outer cortex where our existential thinking takes place. By the time people are in their 70s, there are so few neurons still alive that they think in very simple, practical terms. They have emotions, which involve the inner brain, but the rest of their thinking involves very few of the brain's neurons — only ones involved in talking about what the people they know are doing, etc. The system invented social media to turn young brains into old brains. Unless there are social forces pushing energy up in people's brains, their thinking will become very primitive, involving the simplest motions in their lives.

However, there is still the contradiction that if a free-enterprise system, whether Capitalism or Economic Socialism, requires technology, creativity and innovation in devising new products and production methods, why would the new freedom be good for all this? If freedom allows brain energy to remain in the bottom of the brain, how would we get the existential creativity that a modern economic requires? Well, here is a possible answer to this important question. It's a wild theory but might have some merit.

The most important change to occur in the history of technology and inventiveness occurred in the 1970s and 80's: the introduction of Information Technology. What is so different about the IT revolution from the all other technological bubbles coming before is that all technological spurts and bubbles involved infinite state devices. Machines and electronic devices involve infinite state physics, even though they it be infinite state *without a difference* as we explained in Sect. 9.9. What was really new and different about the IT revolution is that it involved devices that are *finite* state like smartphones, laptops, computer games, etc. The important point is that *it takes only a finite state computational brain to invent, produce, develop and program these finite state devices.* This is the major difference between the IT revolution and all technological bubbles from the past.

It's important to notice that the output of finite state devices is the simplicity of meaningless motion. As we discussed in Sect. 12.6, the primitive eye is basically a motion detector. It is only in the very last stages of evolution that we grew a visual cortex that can appreciate detail. This is why the part of the brain detecting motion is probably a lot older and are probably more strongly connected to the limbic system where emotions reside. This is why most human beings will usually choose motion over detail. Consequently, when the new

IT came on line, it fit right in to the needs of the system mind to keep energy in primitive motion detection parts of the brain and away from *detail*-oriented existential parts. Not only does the brain develop into a purely motion detector, but the parts of the brain that are sensitive to detail as well as parts associated with skills, knowledge, and most importantly meaning, stay underdeveloped. What energizes the existential brain is activities that create meaning like reading, hobbies, interacting with other human beings and perception of the detail of the world. But with IT, kids don't socially interact anymore where meaning can accrue. They spend on the average 7 hours a day on the computer or cellphone, with a constant stream of dancing and jumping meaningless objects.

This is how the concept of the computer geek got going which is a result of people using only the finite state computational brain. Studies show a great deal of obsessive-compulsive mental problems in the IT industry. Regardless of causation, this mental disorder probably comes from too much energy in the computational parts of the brain. When I studied and worked as an engineer *before* the IT revolution, there was no concept of the scientific geek. People working in science and engineering had broader intellectual interests. In grad school where most of the people I knew were scientists and engineers, you would find a history book, or a literature book, even a poetry book on people's bookshelves. But with most the brain's energy in the bottom, the geek has a very truncated theory of mind. This explains clumsiness in relations with women and why women came up with the concept of the "geek".

One of the most incisive illustrations of the computational brain that modern IT shoehorns us into is computer programming. Here we see how the mind of a programmer works. When using a computer program like the Word program I'm using now, you keep coming up against situations when the program goes off doing something that you have no use for. You've been using a certain font for months, but when you open a new document, you get a font you've never used in your life. The reason for this sort of thing is that the programmer has no theory of mind. He knows what *he* would want to do at your stage of a project, and he programs the computer to accommodate *his* choices. He has no idea that you have a different mind and may not want or need his "helpful" intrusions into your work.

This might explain why there was no contradiction between pushing for total freedom and the required thinking in the new area of technology. By allowing energy to stay in the bottom of the brain, it's no accident that a woman's "liberation" movement with all its freedoms got started at the very same time as the IT revolution. The system mind could not have asked for a more fortuitous set of circumstances. Even though women were entering the workforce in large numbers, it was no longer necessary to have existential thinking in the newly created jobs because most of them involved interacting with computers and other finite state devices. Not only that, but technology, have produced ever more specialized jobs involving less broad thinking. This is why you now run into the phenomenon of the totally uneducated Phd.

So instead a very existential woman's movement like the feminist movement before the '70s, the system mind guided a woman's movement into a totally *essentialist* enterprise, creating a *new woman* that was designed to the minutest detail for the needs of the system. The main force enabling these societal developments is to worship *freedom*, which puts energy in the bottom of the brain. In this way, there will less energy in the existential brain that does meaning and less successful interaction with other humans, especially men, thus freeing women to become 12-hour day, 6 days a week work slaves; and on the seventh, mindlessly buying junk the system produces — whose minds are too frazzled to keep track of their own personal and economic interests.

35.4 THE WOMEN'S LIBERATION MOVEMENT

Bottom of the brain thinking is a kind of *push* force, pushing women into bad choices and unsuccessful relationships with men. Marriage and family life requires work, as they say. This implies looking outside oneself to the perceptions, values and needs of other members of the family. And this, in turn requires meaningful existential thinking. Putting lots of brain energy in the bottom encourages inconsiderateness, ill-manners, negligence of the needs and perceptions of others, and resorting to primitive emotions like aggressiveness, control and stubbornness when problems arise. In addition, as we shall explain, inner brain thinking causes women to run their lives as incompetently and stupidly as possible making them less attractive and less deserving of respect from men.

But the woman's movement also had a *pull* force, which was to pull women away from successful relationships and marriages. This was done by totally disparaging and depreciating the value of family and replacing it with worshipping the almighty job. Marriage was to be disparaged, depreciated, demeaned and devalued in every conceivable way through all major media outlets, TV, movies, books, magazines, etc. For example, Diane Johnson, chief libber for the *NYR* disparages homelife as involving "making quilts and putting up jam".[1] Well, I've had every conceivable job at some point as a young man, and in my opinion, making quilts and putting up jam is more interesting and creative work than 95% of the jobs out there. But this is the point. The 95% of women in these jobs simply don't exist in the truncated brain of Diane Johnson. Art historian Pat Mainardi calls quilts "the great American art form", which is why some quilts fetch a hundred thousand bucks at auction because of the skill and creativity in making them. Here again we find a chief libber with a spectacular display of ignorance. The spirit of the woman who made one of the quilts I have lives on and provides pleasure for people long after she's gone and adds to our cultural heritage. What does one of Johnson's computer-pecking work slaves going to leave for posterity? A long string of 0s and 1s, that's all. But that's all Johnson's pet boss needs.

There was even more angry depictions of marriage characterized as "subordination", "subjugation", "surrendering her life", "subject of bondage", "men who diminish and despise", and even "slavery".[2] There were libber ninnies who got famous calling marriage "rape". *Ms. Magazine* had this forewarning blast: …prostitutes don't sell their bodies, they rent their bodies. Housewives sell their bodies…." [3] In the next issue we find this juicy description: "The man takes a body that is not his, claims it, sows his so-called seed, reaps a harvest [this libber was once somebody's very bad harvest] — he colonizes a female body, robs it of its natural resources, controls it, denies it freedom...so that he can continue to plunder it...." [4] There has to be something basically wrong with women when they can't see that a movement that depreciates a normal life choice of millions of young *women* (not men) coming up even to this day, is a total fraud.

Of course, every other issue complains about men not wanting to commit, but instead are held in disdain for "playing video games and watching television" and other infantile behavior. This major complaint about lack of commitment winds up being a complaint that men just aren't "forcing" women into roles as wife and mother as much as they should. After complaining about lack of commitment we get, "...but women of every group have almost no place where roles as wife, mother, sex object, hostess... or domestic aren't forced upon us". [5] Then there are articles blasting the media for daring to imply that women wanted marriage, commitment and families.[6] The typical libber's mind is a rubble heap of disconnected ideas, disjointed factoids, irrelevancies, contradictions, and massive illogic. This is exactly the way the system mind wants women to appear to men.

Then these mindless ninnies have the nerve to call themselves 'feminists', as though they are continuing the work of dedicated female human beings struggling for equal rights for 150 years before the '70s. And just who are the prostitutes here? In their semi-conscious state, these mindless robots have no comprehension that they are being highly paid to *prostitute* for a system whose major goal is to totally destroy perfectly legitimate choices of millions of young women coming up so as to force them into mind-numbing "careers" as 12 hour-a-day corporate work slaves, with their kids in the child abandonment center, or no families at all for most of them.

But don't be misled into thinking that prostitution is on the okay list for these libbers. In other contexts, the language used to describe prostitution is the lowest of the low: "screaming or a real or pretended pain to delight the sadist", "the conquering male viewer", "humiliated...by the obscene idea that sex and the domination of women must be combined".[7] Yes, it's wrong for men to have control over the views of women's bodies. But it was perfectly fine for a gang of dumpy libbers to have control over the views of *other* women's bodies. These libbers are all for choices, as long as *they* get to make *yours*.

But more importantly, don't think for one moment that they care one iota about the working class most of these girls are from. These very same libbers have reduced to almost nil the chances of a working class girl getting a nice, dependable working class guy like in the old days to have a stable family with. With a choice of "careers" available to working class girls as office work slave, hamburger flipper, cleaner, and fish head chopper, perhaps prostitution and pornography are not that bad by comparison. It certainly pays better. I'm not going to judge the choices of other adults. What really motivates these libbers' anti-prostitution anger is that prostitution is an outlet that enables men to get out of range of the target practice these libbers want to engage in. *That's* what has them all bent out of shape, not the real lives of working-class women.

Getting back to Johnson, what about the reality of home life? Some of these stories about men always dominating marriages in former times is just propaganda. There is considerable research showing that even in the Middle Ages, when a man fell madly in love with a woman who had qualities superior to his, so that he realized he was getting a good deal, the wife in these cases usually ruled the roost with the husband serving her. This was often the case in the famous WWII generation marriages. In my own family, my mother was superior to my father in every way, he was madly in love with her, and she was a total emperor, dictator, and overall high semomm. If there was a "slave" in my family, it was clearly my father. And I've observed this in many other families even among very male oriented ethnic populations.

Of course, there was wife abuse all through history because men often are not madly in love, in which case they dominated marriages and subordinated their wives. Probably the most important woman's movement in the 1800s was the woman's temperance movement because violence against women by drunken husbands was so prevalent. But abuse and violence attract attention whereas women ruling the roost doesn't get the same attention.

But by the WWII generation, the phrase 'American princess' was popular throughout the culture. This signified that by this time, there was enough equality that the distribution of power depended pretty much on who loved whom the most and who was getting the best deal. And women often came out on top and were assiduously served and catered to by their husbands. I have seen that over and over among that generation. And if we want a measure of life's success and happiness, just go out and meet women of that generation. Many of the senior women I met in the assisted living home my parents were in for a while had been married with kids and families. In spite of being quite old, many of them were bright, interesting, cheerful and above all *normal*. Their marriages could not have been that bad. Contrast that with the 50-year-old single libbers now who in spite of being a lot younger, are brain dead, mean, ill-mannered, with more hang-ups than an opera house cloak room. You know about the pudding.

Regarding choices, pre-liberated women knew that liberation means freedom from social constraints to develop each individual person. This implies not disparaging any choice a woman might make, including sexual practices. There were girls who chose to engage in quite a bit of sex if they choose. But virginity was a perfectly acceptable option and there was no way a young man could psychologically coerce a girl into sex if that was not her choice. Once the libbers got going, a young girl had to have a list of excuses for staying away from sex, and they were all easy for a young man to dismiss, given the state of the public dialog. Again, a girl had *fewer* options in her choice of sexual activity.

I remember very well before the '70s, if you went out with a young girl, she felt comfortable talking about her future in any conceivable way. Some would say they wanted a career; some would say they wanted to get married and have a family; some would say they would try to do both; and some would say they hadn't yet made up their minds. Any legitimate choice had to be accepted by the male world. The liberation movement made quick work of that. After the libbers got going, a girl would feel great shame telling her date that she wanted a family.

The disparagement of marriage and families was combined with the glorification of jobs. But they weren't jobs anymore. They were *careers*. This was pretty funny at times, but also pretty pathetic. So women as sales clerks, women pecking computer keys, women flipping hamburgers, cleaning hotel rooms, and working in noisy dirty factories — these women don't have *jobs* anymore; now they have *careers*. This is another illustration that the perception of reality by women can always be trumped by words. So by comparison with a *career*, the old saw of marriage and kids looked pretty boring. In my opinion, you have a career when you can't be replaced easily. Most professionals have careers because by building up a special skill and clientele, they can't be easily replaced. So the top 5% of jobs you might call careers. But a hamburger flipper, a career does not make.

Of course, the tremendous emphasis on "careers" even for hamburger flippers, produced a mass exodus of women into the job market. The percentage of housewives working about double since the 1960s, all enthusiastically cheered on by libber leaders. In her latest droppings, Diane Johnson characterizes marriage as "...frustrating their individual talents and ambitions".[8] The chief libber for *The Nation*, instructs her flock about the better life: "Women, like men, have a duty to their minds and talents and selves that cannot be fulfilled by living vicariously through husbands and children." [9] Yes, no more vicarious living, which means no love, no family, no husband to live vicariously through.

Cosmo stated that "60% of all women working are clerks, saleswomen, waitresses and hairdressers." [10] And who does the factory worker, sales clerk, hamburger flipper, paper-shuffler, cleaner, waitress, and fish head chopper live vicariously through? Their sexually harassing male boss or their slave-driving female boss? And what "individual talents and ambitions" are blossoming forth from the millions of women chained in little cubicles 10 hours a day surrounded by 0s and 1s machines? But reality is not important to the liberated woman. *Words* from her leaders are sufficient to create a full-fledged picture of reality.

What chief libbers really have their eye on is the top corporate female boss. They're basically ashamed of the rest and don't even like them, which is why they see nothing wrong with destroying their life's choices. And Diane Johnson understands that with the right words, her liberated audience is going to believe that a hobby like quilts that is rewarding, interesting, skill-involving and leaves something for posterity, is slavery while being chained up in an office 60 stories up pecking away at a computer 10 hours a day is a "liberated" "career". There is no amount of *un*reality you can't program into women's brain. What these libber leaders *really* want, of course, is a docile army of mindless female 10-hour a day work slaves doing the dogwork necessary to puff up the paychecks of their female heroes on the top of the pile. That's what Women's "Liberation" comes to.

But what is very interesting is that in spite of the rush to "careers", *Cosmo* noticed a strong sudden urge in women for babies. On the internet, we see in women's profiles just about every single woman around 40 wanting kids. Some of them give up on men and have a baby themselves or adopt one. There are many young women now who would very much like to have a family but cannot find a man among these infantile hunters who wants the same thing. It's like the canary in a cage. You open the door and the canary doesn't fly out. It just sits there as much as to say, I like it right here. Now that women are "liberated" we find that yes they want careers in the mechanical part of their lives, but as for the human part, the social part, they often want the same things they've wanted for thousands of years: a nice loving, faithful husband and some kids. Not all of them are like this, but a large percentage are. But we're in a period when they don't dare admit this to anyone for fear of appearing unliberated. Many of the young women in today's generation are having the worst time than ever before in history.

This baby craze was right in the middle of the women's movement stressing careers. Well, *Cosmo* has no explanation for this just as they have no real explanation for much of anything. But this shows how the thinking of women changed. Babies are the most primitive, earthy phenomenon in all of the human condition. It's been going on since life itself. The energy in the brain associated with anything to do with reproduction like sex, nurturance and pregnancy itself is going to be in the very bottom of the brain, actually in the top of the spinal cord. So even though there was a constant drum-beat for careers, society led by the women's movement was doing everything imaginable to keep energy in the bottom of the brain where there would be a great urge to have a baby. As one women said, "I was shocked by how suddenly frantic I became to have a baby.[11] By putting energy in the bottom of the brain, the libber movement put female emotions back two million years when they were basically nesters. That is also why they want a man even though they've been programmed to dislike them and never get one. This was all a very unintended consequence of the women's movement. You would think it would induce libbers to ponder this interesting phenomenon. But without an existential brain, the modern libber is incapable of pondering anything.

What is ironic is that when some of these semi-conscious libbers depreciate old fashion marriage, they are really suggesting that women are a pretty inferior lot after all. Diane Johnson says this about the bad old days of traditional families. "It could be that the reason American young people are so much a matter of concern — scribbling on walls, getting pregnant, gunning one another down in schoolyards — is that they had the rotten luck to be confined with some desperate, uninstructed, bored, addicted, immature, or lonely woman…. That such a beginning could be judged superior to one in which a supporting network of professionals… seems one of the more baffling mass delusions of our society". [12]

This is an amazing passage. Let's look at it in light of my own experience raised by a traditional mother/housewife. First of all, I think my mother very much appreciated the fact that while my father was out there in the ice and snow at five in the morning trying to keep his beat up old truck going and working like a slave all day, she was able to leisurely get up when she wanted and do pretty much what she chose for the day. Now there was housework, but with all the modern labor-saving devices, this had been minimized by her generation. My grandmother was a different story. She had an icebox. She had to scrub clothes on a washboard, sweep floors with a broom and wash dishes by hand.

But my mother had lots of free time and she put it to good use. She was in a book club and read enormously and took us to libraries often. A few times a month she would take us downtown to one of the great museums. I got to know the expansive (but boring) Field museum by heart. I preferred the Museum of Science of course and was fascinated by their model railroad. She took us to music lessons and learned to play a bit herself. (This later paid off for me.) She took us to art lessons and we spent lots of time in the Art Institute. She had hobbies refinishing furniture, cooking, and gardening. She even made a quilt once. She grew hot peppers that would burn the butt off an elephant. As little kids, we had a little patch of ground in the back yard we had to grow something in (not one of my talents). She did some community work. She had a little home business making women's hats in the '50s for friends and women in the neighborhood. She would charge 10 bucks for a hat. She was able to invest her 10 dollar a week savings back then, and by playing the stockmarket, worked it into over a million bucks in her later years, which none of us ever suspected she was doing.

She had a couple of girlfriends. Now this is interesting. I remember when I was just learning to talk, hearing my mother on the phone with one of her girlfriends. I heard words like 'Mesopotamians', 'Chaldeans' and 'Babylonians'. I couldn't imagine what those big words meant. Well, 20 years later, I'm in grad school reading some history, and there they are — those very words I heard as a 5 year-old kid and hadn't heard since. It was a real eye-opener. In general, I consider myself very fortunate to have been raised by such a mother. She created in us a degree of intellectual curiosity that finally enabled me to write this book.

Libber Judy Sullivan tells us that "…marriage, motherhood, and her genteel upper-middle class way of life were imprisoning her emerging self and threatening her sanity". [13] Well, I've had the miserable job of looking for a real human being many years among women who were "liberated" from this sort of "imprisonment" to enter the exciting "career" of corporate computer jockey. What I found with few exceptions were brain-dead zombies who perceive nothing, know nothing, question nothing, and learn nothing. They have the intellectual curiosity of a desert lizard. All they have is a computational brain adapted to their computer-pecking jobs.

I remember one of my first experiences after getting divorced. I'm sitting at the bar of a downtown restaurant. And right there at the corner of the bar are two youngish smartly dressed "professional" liberated women. I could hear every word of their conversation. For one straight hour they babbled on about the minutia of their mind-numbing office work. Who's filing whose papers, and who the boss likes and who did whose work. This is the conversation of the liberated women, and I'm thinking back to my mother talking to her girlfriend about the Mesopotamians and Chaldeans. I thought to myself, why bother talking. At least when men have this little to say, they don't say anything.

Because of the restoration work I did, I had to scour the business landscape looking for crazy materials. I've visited dozens of businesses making everything from plastics to rubber to copper rods to leather. Then there are the downtown office buildings reaching to the sky, filled with tens of thousands of paper-shufflers. Whereas my mother took us out into the world half of the days of the week in the summers, visiting museums and libraries, music and art lessons, site seeing, zoos, parks, shopping, etc., these millions of offices are filled with women *chained* in little cubicles pecking away at a computer 8 to 12 hours a day. And these air-conditioned office jobs are the good ones. These libbers tell us my mother was "imprisoned", whereas the "career" office worker chained in her little cubicle 10 hours a day is "liberated". Not only that, but traditional housewifery never reaches the level of "career"; that is until a divorce, in which case it becomes "unpaid labor" worth millions. The only reason these libbers can get away with such crap is that they know their brain-dead female audiences create reality not out of perceptions but with libber words.

Even among the majority of those considered professionals like nursing and teaching (the vast majority of women professionals), I want to know what these "career professionals" are doing that my mother wasn't doing. When we got sick, my mother had to do everything a nurse does to get us well again. Also my mother didn't have to teach the 3rd grade over and over like a teacher. She got to teach the 1st grade and the 2nd grade and the 3rd grade all the way up. She did such a good job of teaching me the 4th grade, I was able to skip that one. When a woman has certain tasks, responsibilities and duties at home where she can do them at her leisure and can get out whenever she wants to engage in a wide variety of enlightening endeavors, she's "in bondage", "subjugated", "enslaved", and "living vicariously". But when she does these *exact same things* on some job she is tied to 8 to 12 hours a day, under some slave-driving female boss, or sexually harassing male boss, she suddenly become "liberated" with a "career". Here again we find these libbers making dam fools of themselves in men's eyes.

I had always thought, especially because of my mother, that women might be superior to men. But these libbers have disabused us of that notion. In spite of a myriad of opportunities for self-improvement, creativity, and enlightenment, they are telling us that the traditional housewife back then was too empty-headed to take advantage of the opportunities to pursue any of these endeavors. She sat there "bored", "uninstructed", and "imprisoned", looking straight ahead helplessly racking up various forms of mental illness. If the modern liberated woman can get more fulfillment out of 95% of the actual jobs out in the world than they could with the opportunities my mother had, what does this say about the modern liberated woman? Is Johnson telling us that maybe Nietzsche was right that women are born slaves: if someone isn't standing over them on some dogwork minutia job telling them exactly what to do, they are lost and just sit there "bored and uninstructed" getting "addicted" and gathering various forms of mental illness.

But there's more to Johnson's passage. She's telling us that back then, women were "uninstructed", as opposed, we can suppose, to today's highly *instructed* libber. Well *instruction* is exactly what the modern libber has. She has no education: she has only *instruction* like a trained trick pony. Her "instruction" consists of some circuitry in the finite state computational brain that enables her to do her mind-numbing job. This is not education. We can illustrate what being educated amounts to with a bullseye drawing as shown in fig. 35.4. A truly educated person has many concentric circles of interest around the bullseye. Our illustration shows the interest of a mechanical engineer for example. The bullseye, of course, is mechanical engineering. But he also has some interest in other kinds of engineering like electrical, civil, or architectural engineering, which is the first circle of interest. In the next circle he has some interest in related sciences like physics and math. In the next circle he has some interest in other sciences like biology, geology, etc. Finally, in the outer circles he may have interest in literature, poetry, history or sociology, and then the arts. This is a picture of an educated person. Of course, as you go farther out from the bullseye, the interest decreases. But there is still some interest in the outer circles. This contrasts with the modern so-called educated person who has only the bullseye and nothing else.

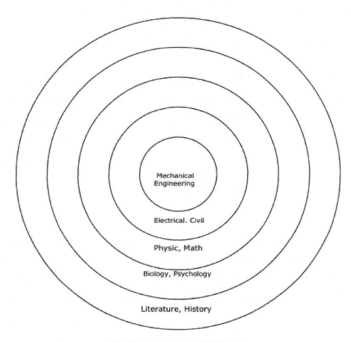

Mechanical Engineering

Electrical. Civil

Physic, Math

Biology, Psychology

Literature, History

Figure 35.4 Career Bullseye

I remember once a dating service was going to fix me up with a philosophy professor. Well, I'm thinking, here's the girl of my dreams. So we get on the phone and it turns out she taught Plato. She knew a great deal about Plato, which was fine. But along the way, I brought up Aristotle. Absolutely no interest in Aristotle. What about Wittgenstein and Bertrand Russell? She didn't even know who they were. Another time, I was getting fixed up with a neuroscientist. Again, visions of sugar-plums danced in my head: the girl of my dreams. Again we get on the phone, and it turns out she's doing research on the neurotransmitter acetylcholine. Well fine. So I brought up the problem of consciousness. Absolutely no interest. What does that have to do with acetylcholine? I brought the representation theory of mind, and memory. Again, no interest. Acetylcholine — that was it.

The modern liberated career women even with a phd is not an educated person at all. She's a *trained* person, an "instructed" person, to use Johnson's very words — a bullseye, and nothing more. We should inform "instructed" Diane Johnson that the reason why many traditional housewives were "uninstructed" was because they were *educated*, even though it may have been self-education like in my mother's case. I have no evidence of Johnson's education, but embarrassingly, she does have the right word to describe her modern-day coterie of "instructed" and trained liberated women. The training for her job uses a few brain circuits in the computational brain that are wired only for her very specialized job. The rest die a slow death. But I forgot; the modern libber doesn't have to worry about education, knowledge or intelligence at all. She has chief libbers telling her how brilliant and knowledgeable she is.

But there's more in Johnson's pregnant passage. First of all, the idea that a child is going to get a more enriched environment in the child abandonment center than being raised by somebody like my mother is the height of ridiculousness. Of course, the only child abandonment centers Diane Johnson knows about are the ones *she* can afford to put her kids in. And I'll admit, professionals in these high-end places sometimes provide an atmosphere superior to what many mothers could in the old days. But what about the child abandonment centers that the woman flipping hamburgers puts her kids in? And what about the rest of women workers?

And what about love? Maybe that's more important than the "professionalism" Johnson refers to. And, by the way, how much love can the liberated woman give to her child after her mind is numbed by her 12 hour a day job and commute? Oh, but I forgot. The libbers have a name for the one hour of the day the liberated career woman has to give her kids. It's called "quality time". Yes sir, after being exhausted, frazzled and burnt out by working and commuting 12 to 14 hours a day, the subsequent one hour she has with her kids is called "quality time". The system mind has a reason-box answer for everything.

But even regarding professional women, Johnson is still pushing child abandonment centers so the mother can have her "career", with her 10 hour a day computer-pecking job. This leads to another embarrassment for Johnson. In her semi-conscious state, she is really telling us that the modern liberated mother is such a mindless incompetent ninny that her kids are better off in the child abandonment center. Of course, the real reason the system mind wants kids in child abandonment centers is that there is very little fatherhood in the kid's life, and with the 60% of married women who get divorced, no father at all.

Scientific American Mind had an issue devoted to brain development among babies. This was an eye-opening issue considering all we hear about the superiority of mothers. The article concluded, "Faulty brain connections may explain why children who grow up without a dad often wrestle with behavior problems later". [14] Without a father to identify with, young boys will have very tenuous identities; a perfect setup for seeking an identity later on by joining the king's murderous war. This is showing up in school performance where young boys are falling farther and farther behind young girls. But girls have similar problems. Other studies show that *girls* who grow up without a father are more likely to start sex earlier and become promiscuous. [15] You can see why the system wants to get fathers out of the lives of their children.

Summing up, the combination of pushing women into inner brain thinking that would make relationships less successful, combined with the pull of the new career as opposed to the "oppression" of husbands, made marriage and family look like a pretty unattractive option — *the exact agenda of the system mind.* Let's look at the modern social milieu and the practices in place and how it all got started.

35.5 CHILD DEVELOPMENT AND ESSENTIALISM

The first step the system takes to bring energy to the bottom of the brain occurs right after puberty. Remember, a baby's brain is a totally essentialist brain. Even though it begins to develop right after birth, still, even when kids are teenagers, their outer existential brains are not fully developed. And in terms of our private lives, the system is going to make sure it stays that way.

The system was greatly aided by having the new technology coming on line actually tempting people away from time to read, to interact with other human beings, to engage in hobbies, arts, self-improvement and into finite state devices that feature meaningless motion. But there's worse to come.

An even more important way to keep energy in the bottom of the brain, is to render young people total sex objects. This is not difficult to do. Teenagers have strong sex drives to begin with, and in combination with a somewhat undeveloped existential brain makes it easy to keep energy in the bottom of the brain. And a very important means to reinforce this state of affairs is to stress sexuality. As we have explained, sex is as old as life itself. Sexual practices, sexual attraction, and sexual thinking are very inner brain phenomena. So emphasis on sex sets up a feedback loop. Sexual thinking brings energy to the bottom of the brain, and inner brain thinking encourages sexual thinking. This is where a system mind comes in.

For thousands of years, especially in the Christian west, the need for the family as the unit of production required intact families. So cultures evolved to keep families together and this requires very existential thinking to conform to the dictates of the church which was designed for families. This is why the church was so repressive towards sex. The medieval system mind knew that it takes existential thinking to enable men and women to understand one another, to be good companions and to maintain successful relationships. Mothers warned daughters that sex was powerful stuff and to be careful about sex. They encouraged young women to think existentially to distract them from primitive sexual thinking.

In order to reverse this state of affairs, the system had to evolve more *essentialist* inner brain thinking, which is encouraged with a great emphasis on sex. So it took the whole world by surprise to see a women's movement piggy-backing on the 150 year-old feminist movement making sex the focus of young people's lives. Women were told to throw off the chains of a male dominated world "suppressing women's sexuality". Since when did men ever "suppress" women's sex lives? Males have been trying get laid since homo habilis. I don't remember reading Susan B. Anthony advising 14-year old girls to "express their sexuality". Almost no older woman was going to accept early sex as in the interests of women. There must be something basically wrong with women who never got suspicious of a movement fraudulent enough to complain about women's sexuality "suppressed" by men. What's wrong is that women create reality out of words, not perceptions, and the libbers had the propaganda outlets on their side. Any woman piping up to question the new modus vivendi would look like a cactus in the cabbage patch.

We also have to look a little more closely at the definition of 'woman'. It turns out a woman was a female of any age. I remember, one of the first women a dating service fixed me up with after I got divorced, severely reprimanded me for referring to my 12 year-old niece as a "girl". She was a *woman*, and I better learn the new vocabulary or I would never make it in the new liberated world. Yes, I said, we tell 12 year olds that they're *women*, and they go out and do womanly things like getting laid, getting pregnant and then society has a mess on its hands.

Well, human males and females have natural programming right after puberty to get interested in sex, think about sex, and do lots of sex. This was left over from evolutionary times when young people started making babies right after puberty because life was less than 40 years. So the system mind media started splashing sex around in every conceivable way. Sex thoroughly soaked every program no matter what it was. It doesn't take much to bring the energy down in a modern kid's brain; the tremendous emphasis on sex encouraged by the libber movement is more than enough to do the job.

An example of the incredible promotion of sex for kids is Jessica Valenti's book *The Purity Myth*. In my opinion, it's hard to find a dumber libber than this one. First of all, where's the myth? She labels people who want young girls to take it a little slower for sex, "the virginity movement", which she calls "sexist", and regressing to "gender roles". More stupidity. What gender roles? Traditionalists are not saying that early sex is good for boys. They're saying early sex is not good for *everybody*, but more destructive for girls. Then comes more stupidity. The traditionalists are creating a "backlash", you see, "hell-bent on rolling back women's rights". Fourteen year olds are "women", and have a "right" to do womanly things. And what rights is she talking about? As a matter of law, it's illegal to have sex with 13 year-old girls. Does she want to give these girls the *right* to break laws? This kind of talk only devalues the whole idea of rights, which, of course, is the purpose of the system mind.

To encourage kids to start sex in high school creates an initial state of mind in males that is hard to redirect later on. Before puberty, members of the opposite sex are a different species; boys and girls often ignore one another hanging out mostly with their own gender. The boys have no idea about the thoughts and feelings of the girls their age. Girls are just moving objects because there is not a fully developed theory of mind. Puberty comes on like tsunami and they are very much unprepared to interact in a human way with the opposite sex. That's why they have very little to talk about. The system was determined to redirect brain energy right back down to the bottom. The best was to do it is by glorifying sex.

The result of this massive sex propaganda onslaught is that by the '80s, two thirds of high school girls were having sex. And probably the rest were thinking about it much of their waking hours. A *Cosmo* survey had 87% of girls having had sex before 19, and 30% before 15.[16] The purpose of this campaign is to encourage the conceptualization of members of the opposite sex as sexual objects, which keeps brain energy in the bottom, exactly where the system mind wants it to be. At any stage in life, energy in the bottom of the brain starves the existential brain of energy to have an elaborate theory of mind and to interact successfully with other persons, as well as making everyone less existentially developed. All this is reflected in a growing divorce rate. Even marriages that do exist have a much lower average quality, which is what you hear from hair-dressers, shrinks, dating service owners and businesswomen who get to hear women's stories.

Now in my generation before the sex revolution really got going, there was very little sex in our lives. So when we started getting interested in girls, we had limited resources to "get the girl". This forced us to develop other means to attract girls. Of course, being physically attractive helped. Another important way, of course, was to be a good athlete. But very few guys in high school are notable athletes. I was on the track team but nobody cared much about track. Other ways to make a hit with the girls was through character. Being a nice guy helped, being cool helped, being reliable counted, and being chivalrous counted. But the most important means to be attractive to the girls beside attractiveness was to be an interesting person in as many respects as possible. And this requires as much existential thinking as a teenage guy can muster. It gave us a little incentive to read, to think, and have something interesting to say to girls.

I remember my high school and college days especially in the summers. We used to hang out on street corners with a bunch of kids that included girls. When I think back to those days, we really had pretty decent conversations given the fact that we were really too young to know much. But we tried and put up a pretty good show. And there was a slight attraction to the guys who were the brightest in the group. Because we were interacting with human beings as opposed to computers, we accrued a great deal of meaning to project to people and states of affairs in the world. Even in school, we were able to project more meaning to what we were required to read, thus paving the way for more meaning to accrue.

Now modern kids can pass finite state tests with very little meaning associated with the concepts they are dealing with. Studies show that kids now spend 7 hours a day on the computer, looking at pornography, playing computer games, and exchanging "texts", which is what we can call *ants and bees talk*. We brought up this concept back in Sect. 3.4. The ability to have concepts and project meaning to them is an ability found only in humans because it requires the use of an existential brain which only humans evolved. But it isn't going to be used when there is very little meaning in playing with computers or engaging in ants and bees talk. They learn some finite facts to pass tests using their computational brains, but there is very little infinite state meaning that accrues in their school experiences. In spite of only having to use the computational brain to pass tests, SAT scores keep dropping. This is result of raising kids whose time is mostly taken up interacting with finite state devices. Their brains become finite state devices as well.

Libber leaders even thought of the detail that equality of attitude should pervade every aspect of life, not just regarding rights and prerogatives like the early feminists promoted. So young boys don't have to think of girls as special anymore. In fact, they're just like boys: wanting sex and being abnormal or hung up in some way if they don't. When you see young people together now, they hang out all equally. They live in the same dorms and interact in the same way. The boys ignore, push around, neglect, and mistreat young girls in the same equal way that they mistreat each other. They order them around like they're servants. Some even think they're doing a girl a favor to have sex with them. The whole milieu is designed specifically to render girls less *special*.

Of course, throughout history, males were taught that females were *special* in many ways. This is why when I was a teenager, even though we treated the girls pretty much as equals, you couldn't swear in front of them or touch them in any inappropriate ways. Well, the libbers were going to make quick work of that. We're all equal. Not only that, but "women" (meaning 13 year-old girls) want sex too. You no longer have to worry about a girl's feelings any more than you worry about the feelings of the crazy guys you hang out with.

Besides all this, males are programmed from evolutionary times to transfer genes to females and that's it. There were no "relationships" in evolutionary times. Even among today's primates, males and females don't pair off. What is important to realize from this evolutionary story is that the bonds between male and female humans is a relatively new thing in evolutionary history; and for that very reason, these bonds are not innately hardwired. If all a teenage guy is going to use is his spinal cord to run his behavior, girls are going to be conceptualized as moving depositories and not much else. It takes a strong existential culture to get kids, especially males, to conceptualize others in a human way. And cultures all over the world evolved to do just that. Females were always wired to care for the young. What was needed in the last stages of evolution was for *males* to be less promiscuous and more family oriented. And in my opinion, *the main purpose for humans evolving cultural systems in the first place was to get males to do the right thing regarding their offspring*. We can't emphasize this too much. Human culture was necessary for dealing with *males*. Let's explain this.

For millions of years, females of all mammal species took care of and reared the young. This tendency is certainly wired in because it appears in animals too primitive to have much of a rational brain. Now nobody knows how much of a mother instinct there is left in human females, but we can say for sure that they have some innate brain structure that enables them to learn pretty quickly how to care for the young. Males are an entirely different story. In many mammal species, even in an advanced family as the cat family, males do not participate in protecting and rearing the young. Male lions and tigers can very easily kill their own young. Even among the advanced primates like gorillas and chimpanzees, it is quite common for males to kill the young under certain circumstances. Males among advanced primates are wired to protect the entire group, but not specifically their own young. They don't even know who their own offspring are.

As human evolution proceeded, there was selection pressure for a large brain to provide the adaptability to learn what was necessary to survive in complex environments. Well, the more adaptability you need, the more flexibility is required in the wiring of human babies at birth, which means less hard wiring. This results in a greater degree of helplessness. Nurturance became an increasingly complex job for human mothers which required very diligent and attentive care. However, since males got into the nurturance game much later, there was simply not enough time for males to evolve the same degree of complexity in cognitive skills and emotions necessary to adequately care for increasingly helpless human babies. This is where culture comes in. The substitute for innate abilities in males is *learned* abilities. In my opinion, the initial purpose of human culture was to enable *males* to participate in the care and protection of their young.

Of course, there was no marriage a million years ago. But there was a gradual pairing off of males and females which did eventually result in marriages of some sort in early civilizations. Additionally, it was necessary that culture should accrue over the generations and be maintained. This is why no matter what human culture you look at, there are strong cultural practices like marriage to turn basically wild male hunters into adequate human fathers and husbands who would care for and protect especially their own young. Because of this fact, this became the real definition of *manhood*. But when we come to recent times we see the gradual disappearance of cultural morays and constraints. What we see is a noticeable difference between males and females in their attitude towards the young. Females by and large continued to try to care for and protect their young. It is males who have changed drastically in this regard. They may be better fathers while married, but we see increasing numbers of men abandoning families in favor of some new adventure that strikes their fancy. Without cultural constraints and prohibitions to keep men attending their families, this will get to the point where there is no difference between modern males and the lions and tigers of the jungle. This is not what real *human* manhood is all about.

Women's Lib leaders claim that men designed the culture to their advantage. But in evolutionary times, *nature* designed the culture, taking into account some the basic wiring in both males and females. And it designed culture to optimize the chances of survival, no matter how it turned out. Human survival was too tenuous for the past 2 million years for considerations of gender power to enter into the equation. The fact that most cultures give males more power might simply be because this distribution of power was optimal for survival in evolutionary times. Gender equality was a much lower priority for female mothers than passing on a culture that would coerce males into contributing to the care and protection of the young.

But there is an even more important issue regarding culture. In my opinion, you can't have culture with total equality between the sexes in every conceivable way. There's an interesting logic to this we must elucidate. By definition, culture includes rules: rules of comportment, rules for society's institutions and social arrangements, rules for manners, for obeying laws, and most importantly, rules involving male-female interaction. But rules apply only to *subgroups*. A constraint in a sport that applies to *all* players is not a rule; it is part of the *structure* of the game. You could call it a structural rule, as opposed to a *play* rule. A play rule only exists when it applies to a subgroup. Only receivers can catch the football.

Only the batter can run the bases. In basketball, only the guy who got fouled can throw free-throws.

The same applies to culture, the most important grouping of which is males and females. The behavioral aspect of culture requires *rules* that apply asymmetrically to men and women. A constraint that applies to both like both must work or wear clothes is not really a rule but part of the structure of human societies. In the past, there were many asymmetries. All the rites of passage were different. Responsibilities were different. Men were more responsible for support. Women were more responsible for child rearing. Men were required to treat women differentially as opposed how they treat each other. All the rules of etiquette imply asymmetry regarding men and women. Men used to have to bow and kiss the hand of a woman being introduced. Men could pursue and women could not. Women couldn't be sexually aggressive. As an aside here, as brought out in Sect. 28.5 on gay marriage, this is why *contracts* reflect culture and its values: they are *asymmetrical* cooperative agreements to carry out some endeavor.

Now many of the traditional rules were sexist in that they put women at a disadvantage, although not all. Some of them look pretty inappropriate in modern times. However, to have a *culture* to speak of, there must be *some* rules that apply asymmetrically to men and women. It's as simple as that. If you remove everything that is asymmetrical, you no longer have a complete culture. In my opinion, one of the purposes of equality of everything promoted by the system mind acting through the women's movement was to rid society of any signs of culture whatsoever.

Also, it must be stressed that culture is an existential thing. It is not hard-wired. The rules of a culture involve existential differences in treatment between the genders only on the basis of cultural roles. These are not *essential* differences. And so when you remove culture, males are going to revert to their habits from millions of years of evolution to spread their genes far and wide, not attending to families and not very attentive to females. And they are going to *conceptualize* women as essentially different, which can be a source of real sexism. And this is just what we see in modern times as culture has gradually been washed away with the great encouragement of the Woman's Liberation movement. If there was any liberation going on, it was *men* who got "liberated". The women's movement has replaced cultural *existential* differences relevant only to behavioral interaction, with conceptualized *essential* differences, which is why there is probably more sexism now than ever before. And it is a more virulent kind.

In addition to the cultural imposition that coerced males into attending to families, cultural forces evolved to keep males and females together to raise children. We could call these forces, *cultural glue.* They are simply rituals, patterns of behavior and psychological forces to keep males and females together while raising children. One of the chief sources of glue once Capitalism got started and began putting pressure to achieve the lone individual as the unit of production, was sex. Up until the woman's movement the church had considerable power over people's private lives and greatly coerced people into saving sex for marriage. This was possible because there is probably a bit of monogamy hard-wired into females in the first place. During evolutionary times, the most likely source of food and protection was from the male the female had sex with most recently, which is the most likely to be the father of the upcoming baby. So there might be some monogamy programmed into females, although it is hard to know how much. So a culture that restricts sex to marriage partners was probably never a great strain on women; that is, until the libbers came along and bragged about women wanting to cheat just as much as men. But in spite of 30 years of massive doses of libber propaganda everywhere we look, women are still looking for "monogamous long-term relationships".

One of the main purposes of the great emphasis on sex by the woman's movement was to remove sex as a source of glue between men and women. In reading woman's magazines going back to the '80s, it's amazing the degree to which sex is pushed. The result is that various studies showed that into their 20s, a substantial percent of women had upwards of 20 or 30 sex partners. Many women had a *hundred* sex partners in college and early 20s. Well it doesn't take a rocket scientist to see that if a girl is going to have sex with dozens of men, there is nothing very special about sex with a particular guy at a deep level of psychology, which means no longer a source of glue. There were probably many marriages that stayed together perhaps like my parents, simply because the two people had never slept with anyone else. However, whatever sexual monogamy provided in the way of glue between men and women, was going to be dissolved by the system mind acting through the woman's movement. The way to do that is to get kids started as soon as possible in the sex business, so it can never be a source of glue.

Another source of glue stemmed from religious and ethnic similarities: marriage partners were often from the same village or ethnic neighborhood even as late as WWII. This was a source of friendships, family relations and social interaction. Having these mutual factors in their lives gave them things to talk about and mutually relate to that were special and so meaningful. This was also a source of glue between men and women.

But the most important sources of glue relate to communication. As we discussed in Vol. I, Sect. 12.3, all through evolutionary times, a female's depiction of the reality of the larger world came from words of men coming back from hunting parties and negotiations with other tribes. The downside to this practice is that women became wired to use *words* to create their representations of reality. This has important ramifications but the most important benefit is that by the process of communicating about the wider world, bonds were created between males and females. This is why most cultures allow men to be older than potential female partners. Being older and being better able to interact with the detail of a wider world, enabled men to communicate about the wider world. This practice also encouraged women to conceptualize men in terms of their more existential qualities like character, knowledge, education, experience, talents, skills and accomplishments, which creates very meaningful glue. This extended all the way to modern times. In the famous WWII generation, men led conversations and women trying to keep up did extensive brain searches for additions to the conversation. And she had the option of asking questions. This created a race to the top in both genders. The libber movement was design specifically to trash this entire agenda. Conversation is usually carried along by questions, and since asking a question implies that the other person knows something you don't, the liberated woman is not going to admit anything like that. Energy in the bottom of the brain not only wires women to accept only ants and bees talk that appeals to familiarity, but it also enabled women to conceptualize men as a bunch of dumb dogs roaming the neighborhood. Any attempt at conversation that is original, provocative, complex or interesting is summarily dismissed because it conflicts with this preconceived notion. This has killed meaningful conversation, which was a major source of glue throughout history and encourages a society that leaves the lone individual available for her almighty 12-hour a day computer-pecking job.

35.6 FINDING A GUY FOR A FAMILY

After the early 20s, women seem to divide into two major groups. The first wants marriage and family, and second wants to develop careers and thought they would put off marriage and family until after their careers were established. Then in their late 30s, they would go out, pick out one of those dumb dogs roaming the neighborhood, take 'em home, clean 'em up, put 'em on the end of a leash and make a baby. On the internet, the majority of single women who are around 40 want a family. They think a man who wants a family is going to look for a 42-year old woman with her scrambled eggs with womb to make a baby. Statistics show among unmarried professional women over 40, only 1 in a 100 ever does, and it probably doesn't involve babies. Even *Ms. Magazine* admits, "After the 40-year mark, a single woman's likelihood of marrying dwindles to a stingy 1 percent." [17]*

But among the group who wants to start a family, they have most of their 20s and 30s to do it. It's a matter of finding a guy. But here again the system has guided the process of finding a guy for a family so as to result in the best possible outcomes for the system, but the worst for families. As we discussed in Sect. 21.3 on love, male choice best optimizes the viability of marriage because males are more existential by nature, and they are choosing mating partners on the basis of the same existential qualities that they have been using for millions of years: competence, health, fitness and beauty (which are correlated with good genes), just as they were the basis of male choices millions of years ago.

But, of course, the system mind has no intention of allowing good, stable long-term marriages because they are a distraction from the almighty 10 hour-a-day, computer-pecking job. Male choice was deemed "oppressive", as was anything else that wasn't in the interests of the system. So what the system did was to give women the power to pick because for tens of millions of years, females of all mammal species were gene sniffers, which is what the bottom of the brain is designed to do. And the circuitry to make these choices

---

* Some Libbers have violently disagreed with this statistic saying that twice as many unmarried professional women over 40 get married. So now instead of one in a hundred getting married, we have *two* in a hundred getting married. That's real progress.

became hard-wired because the inner brain where sexual attraction and lust reside is mostly hard-wired.

As we emphasized in Sect. 21.3, the best genes for protection, hunting, and all around fitness among early hominids, were those of males who were the best hunters, the fiercest, the most physically active, the most mysterious, and most important, the most promiscuous and least emotionally handicapped by monogamy. Women are so strongly attracted to taken men that they think nothing of sleeping with and stealing even their best friend's husbands and boyfriends. Nietzsche once remarked, "woman, as yet, is not capable of friendship". He must have seen the liberated woman coming. A huge percentage of stories in women's magazines involve women sleeping with a friend's husband or boyfriend. It's so common that libber magazines have gotten totally inured to the idea and don't even question it. But it all shows what a primitive creature the modern liberated woman really is.

This might seem to contradict what we said in Sect. 21.7 that the inner brain is wired for safety and is attracted to familiarity. But keep in mind that safety is related to dangers that could come from *strangers* invading the camp situation in evolutionary times. We even see this in the animal world. A male lion suitor is often from a different pride. He sniffs around and circles the female sometimes for days while the female is hissing and snarling at the poor guy, whacking him upside the head here and there. But by hanging around and becoming familiar, the female finally feels comfortable enough to do it.

But the violence and fierceness women are attracted to must be from males who are considered part of their group or where there is some degree of familiarity. This is why rape is most perpetuated by men the woman already knows and has some degree of familiarity. In fact, during the 2 million years humans were evolving, a lot of sex was either rape or close to it. There's a certain part of the brain that probably got wired to be attracted to the power rapists display. This also explains why in women's magazines going back 40 years that I've read, a good percentage of stories told by woman writers was how they couldn't break loose from a man who would often display violence sometimes resulting in physical abuse and injury. It is important to note here that these are men that are already very familiar to the woman. Not only that, but a surprising number of interviews show women having sexual fantasies of violence and even rape. O.J. Simpson got thousands of letters of romance and even sexual interest from women in all walks of life. But in my opinion, this was because OJ was already somewhat familiar to people by being a celebrity and a star football player. OJ projected power and fierceness, exactly what turns on the 2 million-year-old inner brain of the liberated woman. OJ would have had lots of trouble before the '80s, but after that, he could have a ball as long as he stayed out of jail.

One time Oprah Winfrey had a show featuring a bunch of college guys who had committed date rape. They were pretty nonchalant about it all. They were asked, aren't you worried about your reputation for future dating? Hell no, was the answer. They would go back to college and get dates just as before. All they had to do is engage in some ants and bees talk to establish some familiarity and the girl would be off on another date rape. There weren't many date rapes when I was in college because the kind of guy who would do a date rape, couldn't get a date.

But without a working existential brain, the modern liberated woman is not only free, but "empowered" to put the energy in the bottom of her brain which will be attracted to qualities of the 2 million-year-old man. This was fine in evolutionary times where the purpose of gender relations was getting the best genes into the next generation, but is entirely counterproductive in the modern world. What women need in modern times are men who fall in love, are loyal and faithful and dedicate themselves to their families. These are the qualities pre-libber women found desirable in a man, qualities that make for good long-term companions. This took existential thinking that is aided by strong cultural practices and learning, which is what culture used to do before the libbers came along and dispatched eight thousand years of human culture. But with most of the brain's energy at the bottom, the liberated woman is rendered helpless in directing her feelings and behavior and is hard-wired to try to conquer the man who turns her on.

Thus, when the modern liberated woman faces the job of picking men for whatever reason, they employ four main components: a spinal cord, two glands and a crotch. It is with these same organs that females chose males 2 million years ago also when females had very underdeveloped existential brains. As one women said in an interview in a *Cosmo* article, "I don't decide whether I will or want to be with a man. My vagina decides". [18] This is the most important quote in this entire book. The liberated woman lives in a vaginacentric world: the universe revolves around the vagina and everything else is peripheral. Recently in fact, there have been a whole slew of books and articles glorifying the vagina. And rightfully so, since it is the main organ used by the liberated woman to run her private life including picking men.

So when the liberated woman uses her vagina to choose men, she will conceptualize men in the bottom of her brain and love will amount to nothing more than conquest and control. And she becomes hard-wired not to let go. Some of the violence and abuse she endures is simply because she can't get the concept of the man out of the bottom of her brain. In the literature they call this *obsession*, which doesn't explain anything, but only names the problem. And men get away with anything they please because there will be no social consequences from a strong culture, which libbers have dismissed as being oppressive. Pre-liberated women used their *brains* to pick men and the vagina got dragged along. Now the vagina picks the man and what little is left of the brain gets dragged along. Naomi Wolf talks about the "profound brain-vagina connection". What she neglects to tell us is that it's a one-way connection — from vagina to brain.

Of course, men pick on the basis of appearance and sexiness too. But that doesn't hurt them nor marriage. They get into relationships on this basis and either they fall in love and marry, or they go on. They don't really lose either way. But when there was such a thing as courtship, men, who are much more perceptive than they're given credit for, are not biased by sexual attachments from getting a fairly objective view of the woman's existential qualities. But in today's world, where the liberated woman is using her vagina to decide womb to pick, sex totally distorts the perceptions of what a man really is. Now I am not saying that women should not do the picking, but only among real suitors. Recall our definition of a suitor is a man with sincere long-term interest. What I am saying is that there is a cost to picking because it contradicts the way humans are probably wired.

I remember a conversation I had with a woman running a dating service for women. Almost verbatim, she said, "as well as women are doing in their work lives — as doctors, lawyers, engineers, managers, administrators, financial services investors, etc. — their personal lives are a mess". Of course, she didn't understand this seeming incongruity. The reason is simple. In their jobs, they are using circuitries in the middle level computational brain. Even though finite state, it is complex enough to handle skills and most modern jobs. That's why even libbers can be successful at them. But in her private life picking men, the liberated woman makes a mess of her life. Accurately judging other people for intimacy requires a working existential brain. This particular organ is missing in the liberated woman.

What is even more interesting is that there are articles describing how the most intelligent women make the worse choices. Articles had titles like, "Smart Women, Dumb Choices". I think there was even a book called *Smart Women, Foolish Choices*. What is the explanation of that? Well, one of the characteristics of smart people is their brains generate a lot of energy. And if this energy is kept in the bottom of the brain it will amplify all the tendencies we have enumerated.

But no matter how bad the liberated woman's choices are, being a woman, she is still *optimistic* that she will be successful. In Sect. 21.11, we discussed the fact that in general men are more past oriented because a hunter has to remember where he's been. Females of all species prepare for the future appearance of a baby, which engenders very future-oriented thinking. Over time, this would select the emotion of *anticipation*, which is present in all mammals. Additionally, to put up with the pain and inconveniences of pregnancy and the work in preparation for a baby, the woman has to believe that raising the baby will be successful. This would cause nature to select for an *optimistic* disposition. This also helps keeps a person's spirits up and helps get through the vicissitudes of pregnancy and life itself. This is why sociological studies show single women are happier being single than men.

But optimism has its downside. Often women especially younger ones who are interested in having a family may be too optimistic about the boyfriend they have. They discount signs of danger with the belief that things will straighten out, difficulties will be overcome and blemishes in the relationship will fade away. And so with a feeling of optimism they marry the wrong man. Even after marriage, optimism can keep them many years in hopeless marriages feeling optimistically that things will improve as soon as the clouds clear. Most times they never do.

Even into a woman's 40's, unattached women are often optimistic about their future. Mr. Right is going to come along, even if it takes 30 years, because it's in the stars. (Optimism continues till the day she passes on. There are 80-year old women in the back room of the nursing home still optimistic that Mr. Right will come along.) This is why only about one in a hundred unmarried professional women over 40 ever gets married. Since the real Mr. Right is coming in the future as promised by God, or the Women's

Movement or the local fortune teller, the liberated woman will find something wrong with each prospect. Her optimism has enabled her to believe the promises she's received about the magical appearance of Mr. Right and that she shouldn't "settle" before he comes along. In fact, in today's world, men find themselves getting rejected by female clones they don't even want. This explains the one in a hundred. My motto regard is simply this: *Realism may create some short-term pain, but it avoids long-term disaster.* But why aren't men just as optimistic.

Well, first of all, there is no evolutionary advantage for men to be optimistic. In fact, males engaging in large animal hunting in evolutionary times would be more successful and stay alive longer, if they were not optimistic, but *realistic*. It wouldn't pay to optimistically think you can bring down some big animal if the odds are against you in reality. Nature would select men who were *real*istic about the chances of downing a large animal, vs. losing your life in the process. Thus, I think men have some basic wiring that leads more to *realism* than optimism.

This is probably why some young men get married. The idea of making a commitment for a long time not only to a woman, but to constraints on freedom that commitments entail, is a pretty scary thing to most men. But young men have identity problems, which can be alleviated by becoming a "family man". So they have forces in them that are also contradictory. But the fact that each of these forces neutralizes the other, allows young men to rely on their basic realism. When I was in my 20's the idea of marriage was pretty scary to me as well, although I wanted to do it sooner or later — preferably later. But when I met a particular girl, my realism told me that I would never find anyone better and I was probably right.

So why aren't older men more realistic? They don't do very well being single, so they should very much want to settle down. One explanation is that perhaps evolution has wired men to follow the example of women because women were their first and most important examples. We have to remember that we all start our lives very dependent on mothers who are women. Mothers can do all kinds of wonderful things. She can eat without spilling and drooling. She can tie her shoes. She can even use the toilet without falling in. In the millions of things babies have to learn, the mother is there to show the baby how to perform by setting an example. The every-day process of mothers setting the example for their children establishes a kind of *mutual world*. They are both doing the same things in the same way in the same world. This in turn creates strong bonds between mothers and their children upon which is the love Freud talked about. *If a mutual world can be established by the process of setting examples, there will be bonding and love.* And keep in mind, the essence of this process is setting examples. Boys start out having great respect for women and in the old days found it extremely easy to fall in love early in the game. This is exactly the source of bonding and love that the liberation movement was designed by the system mind to destroy. If we look at the good things men have done in human history, loyalty to their wives, providing shelter and safety for their families — these behavior patterns were established by women setting the example.

When we come to modern times, men have discarded their basic realism, and have become overly picky because that's the example women set. If we compare today's practices with practices before WWII, we see that pickiness was never a very pronounced tendency among adults. All through the early modern period, men most often found someone to marry quite early in the game and were realistic about who they could get. Young women simply picked from among their suitors as we discussed. Older people, especially widows and widowers, pretty quickly found someone to marry if they chose that course.

Remarriage statistics are very misleading in this regard. Before WWII, religion and ethnicity were very important in people's lives. Many people who became widows or widowers never remarried because their religious or ethnic values led them to believe that they should stay loyal to their spouse even after death. This shows up in the statistics. But those who did want to remarry did so with considerable ease. If this is the case, why weren't men overly picky? In my opinion, with no picky example to follow, men's basic realism usually enabled them to find a suitable mate within a reasonable time. But in today's world, men are simply following the example set by women. Also, in the great age of greed ushered in by the Ronald Reagan maybe the whole cultural milieu around us has made everyone greedier.

So with a dose of greed spiced up with a pinch of optimism, the liberated woman searches for a family man. Since she is constantly reminded how much power she has, what she does is make a picture puzzle of her life with very complex pieces with lots of squiggles and squaggles. There's one very complex piece that's missing where a man is to fit in. And by dangling the sex card in front of prospective men, she can demand that they reconfigure themselves so as to fit snugly into this space with no overlap and no spaces between pieces. You might guess what the missing piece is. With her new-found feeling of power, what she wants for the missing piece is a dumb dog on the end of a leash who barks when told to bark and sits when told to sit. In fact, I was surprised to learn recently that in a fit of self-awareness, finally a woman has written a book called, *My Next Husband Will Be a Dog.* I love it.

But this whole attitude among women amplified by controlling the public dialog, is getting the modern liberated woman nowhere as the stats show. So now libbers are writing books asking if we can do without men? They write articles like "the extinction of men", or "end of men", or "who needs men". The reason we can do without men is that with all the energy in the bottom of the brain, liberated women see very little of reality. The fact that we just got through an IT revolution in which men started the major hardware and software companies, men invented the chips, circuits and logic devices, men designed the protocols, men designed the operating systems and browsers — all this means nothing to the liberated woman.

Before liberation, men were awarded over 95% of new patents. But now that women are going to college more than men, and have the same opportunities to think outside the box, men are still awarded more than 95% of patents. As basically camp-dwellers, females are wired for multi-tasking, which is the opposite of what you need to invent which requires single-minded concentration for long periods of time in new and adventurous directions.

Oh! But I forgot. The patent office is a hotbed of sexism. Actually women have invented a perpetual motion machine and a way to turn aluminum into gold, but the patent office won't award patents because of sexism.

Women's role in evolutionary history was to attend to a variety of thoroughly familiar menial tasks, not to think in new and adventurous ways. The liberated woman amplifies these basic tendencies which is why she wants only familiar ants and bees talk and is perfectly happy with her 10 hour a day computer pecking job. On the other hand, men's brains are wired on a knife edge between doing what worked in the past vs. adventuring to new lands, new hunting grounds, new campsites and new ways of doing things. The downside to this is that their whole personalities are on a knife edge between constancy and adventure. But adventure borders on peculiarities. This is why men are hard to deal with. They easily fall into peculiar and destructive habits and impossible hang-ups.

The basis for some of this "who needs men" literature is that women are starting to take the best jobs and making more money than men. During evolutionary times, males were pretty lazy, hunting when they felt like it. Females on the other hand were continuously busy in the camp environment. This is why women are probably better workers. As a result, once men opened a whole field of information technology with new products and new methods, with all the energy in the bottom of their brains, women have very well-adapted computational brains to effectively do the finite state jobs a hi-tech economy creates. The cost is a dying existential brain resulting in a private life that is capable of only ants and bees talk.

Let's follow the career of the liberated woman as she attacks the job of finding a man. Well, there are a number of venues: dating services, personal ads, bars, clubs, vacation tours, and now, most importantly, the internet. Since the internet has been the most rapidly growing in recent years, let's take a typical liberated woman looking on the internet. Let's call her libber Lizzy.

Well, libber Lizzy gets on the internet and scrolls. There are thousands of mugs: men who have died in the last king's war, men who are married, men who are in jail, men in insane asylums, men who have become gay since the last census, and men who are headless. So she starts with Bill. The spinal cord asks the crotch, do you want to screw Bill? Crotch says, no. On to the next mug who is Tom. Again spinal cord asks the vagina, do you want to screw Tom? Vagina again says no. Next is Mark. Again spinal cord asks crotch, do you want to screw Mark? Absolutely not. Lizzy sometimes spends hours scrolling on the computer just looking for someone her vagina picks. In fact, Lizzy rarely gets past the photos of these men. Once the vagina says no, all human contact ceases. It has been programmed into the hard-wiring of the inner brain of the liberated woman, just like a computer, to maintain a default position of rejection. There is no curiosity to give anyone the benefit of the doubt to see if there are existential qualities that makes a long-term partner. Besides, since Lizzy has no theory of mind, she thinks men think are just like her. Since Lizzy wants a LTR (long-term relationship), men must want the same thing. So she can dismiss any individual man who enquires because she thinks she has hordes of eager suitors to pick from, not realizing that most men's plans for a liberated woman is a few months of new sex.

Finally, up pops Pete. Again, spinal cord asks the vagina, do you want to screw Pete? *Yes*, comes the brand new decisive answer. At last, libber Lizzy has her man — *piss pot Pete*. All looking can stop at last. Here's the man she was promised by that handful of liberated lezzies who infest the city of New York. Piss pot Pete. He's da man. And he is right there, bigger than life. Pete has that animal vagina magnetism that reaches Lizzy's threshold of transcending the basic tendency to reject strangers.

Well piss pot Pete, being an attractive, youthful, successful man checks out libber Lizzy who is an attractive young woman. Piss pot Pete says to himself, not bad. And as primates have been doing for 10 million years, primate Pete is not going to pass up a good thing. At this point, Pete has absolutely nothing on his mind that extends past one day. This illustrates the fact that men and women have different agendas. Women really have one agenda: a nice reliable, loyal man to get into a "long term relationship" with, which often is code for marriage. Men have two agendas, which is very lucky and convenient. The first is to get laid and the second is to find Ms. Right with whom he will trundle off into the sunset. So he starts out on the first agenda. If it evolves into the second, fine: he has his life partner. If not, he still has the first agenda.

Anyway, Pete exchanges emails with libber Lizzy. At this stage in the game, it is very important that Pete not ruffle the bottom of Lizzy's brain, which is wired for safety from strangers as we discussed. After all, Pete on the internet is really from a different tribe. In pre-liberated times, the need for familiarity was solved by the practice of *courtship*. Courtship also overcame the basic tendency to dismiss strangers. Not all suitors were successful of course, but courtship allowed the man with serious long-term interest to get started and created a period of time during which a real suitor could use his best existential skills to earn his way into the woman's heart. The purpose of denying sex during courtship was to get women's thinking to the top of the brain where existential qualities necessary for stable marriages would be noticed and any verdict from the vagina ignored. The last thing on the mind of the courted woman was sex because her vagina would summarily dismiss her less than totally cool suitors.

This is why the internet is such a disaster. Appreciating existential qualities requires real people interacting in a three-dimensional world as occurred through thousands of years of evolutionary history. But by offering only a two-dimensional photo of men, the internet insures that only the vagina will be active in picking men because a two-dimensional depiction is sufficient to show the five major qualities the vagina was attracted to a million years ago: violence, mystery, promiscuity, distraction and youth (sexiness). All human qualities that evolved the last hundred thousand years ago are ignored.

Anyway, as a result of needing familiarity to keep the bottom of Lizzy's brain from getting upset, Lizzy's idea of getting to know Pete is to exchange information about the minutia of their lives, which means only ants and bees talk. They want to tell and hear the same stories ad nauseum. This relaxes the spinal cord which is how Lizzy can feel comfortable. Since ants and bees talk say very little about Pete's real nature, it has the dual advantage of adding to Pete's mysteriousness. Any sentences that are complex, provocative, original, or interesting in any way would be summarily rejected by libber Lizzy and Pete would get cast out of the kingdom. Pete's emails must be as stupid and vapid as he can make them if he is to "get the girl". There's even some poetry to show sensitivity. Of course, Pete has been using these strings of words for years and they have been perfected to elicit the best possible response. They have absolutely no meaning to him. But they have some computational syntactical meaning to libber Lizzy, since the part of the brain that does evaluation and perceptiveness is long gone, leaving only a primitive language processor that goes crazy over the syntax of Pete's sentences that show his charm, sensitivity, empathy and sex appeal. This is clearly da man. So off they go to start a "relationship".

Deborah Tannen has written a bunch of books about talk between men and women. I think one of them was called "*You Just Don't understand*". Well, you can't expect a bunch of dumb dogs roaming the neighborhood to understand anything. What Tannen just doesn't understand is the most important thing about communication between men and women. To put it simply, women use conversation as a means to establish familiarity which is why they love ants and bees talk. Men use conversation to have an adventure of the mind often about the wider world. This is why modern men and women are pretty incompatible, especially at the inner brain level.

It's an impressive fact that over the years, whenever men came to where I was living as plumbers, carpenters, electricians, etc., I was always able to get into quite interesting conversations with them. Now these were not highly educated men; they did not have phds in magnetohydrodynamics. Although some of them were quite bright, most were just average guys mostly high school grads. But they welcomed the chance to have a stimulating conversation different from what they could get from their ants and bees chattering wives. The liberated woman wants no such thing. In meeting tons of liberated women for coffee, I often get severely reprimanded for not talking enough about them, or not talking enough about me. All they want is familiar personal stuff: how they feel and life stories, even though they've heard these stories hundreds of times before with only a change in names. This is reflected in the literature they read. I've read hundreds of articles in 40 years of a number of women's magazines. I can assure you that it's mostly ants and bees talk itself. He did this and I did that; then he ran here and I ran there. The remarkable thing about these libber magazine articles is they never describe the *content* of any conversations in their stories as opposed to *form*, which is the way a piece of communication is delivered.

In general, content is existential stuff concerning meaning, thought processes, abstract interwoven concepts, propositional attitudes like beliefs and desires. *Form* is basically essentialist stuff involving primitive emotions, their expression and body language. In the women's magazines, even the content of the article itself is often ants and bees descriptions of who did what to whom. The deepest they go is some pop worn out Freudian psychology.

What is remarkable however, is the complete lack of any mention of content of conversations *within* the stories they tell. One writer commented, "…it's amazing how soon you run out of things to talk about".[19] Well, you're going to run out of things to talk about a lot sooner if all you ever read are these women's magazines and all you engage in is ants and bees talk. They go into great flowery descriptions of *form* aspects of communication. For example, they'll describe how the girl "snuggled close to him, and as he spoke, his eyes glistened, and his body relaxed". Or, "as he spoke, I could feel my heart beating with increasing rhythm, and my mind fluttered from item to item like a bee in a flower garden". I've read tens of thousands of sentences like this in women's articles. Sometimes as I'm reading, my brain is saying loudly "WHAT THE HELL IS THIS GOD DAM JERK SAYING, with his 'alluring lips'." We never find out. Many of the stories are about affairs, romances, relationships, sex in thousands of positions, and you wonder, what did these people talk about. So it is with libber Lizzy. She expects piss pot Pete to give up his freedom for his entire life to listen to her mindless chatter. If Pete is going to have to listen to ants and bees talk from women in his life, at least he's going to change the spinal cord and crotch once in a while, which is exactly what he does.

But insisting on ants and bees talk is a new thing among women. It wasn't always this way. Back in the 1700s, aristocratic women in France got together and engaged in complex conversation. Led by people like Mme. deRambouillet and Madeleine de Scudery, they would discuss philosophy, literature and the issues of the day. There are number of books on the subject.[20] But the modern liberation movement is going to snuff this out. Their job was to kill meaningful thought and conversation. Besides, since the liberated woman already knows everything, there's no need to engage in intelligent conversation especially with men.

By trying to make Pete appear as familiar as possible, Lizzy thinks she's "getting to know" Pete. But to know someone, you have to have a complete picture because women want to deal with *whole* persons. But with only ants and bees talk, Lizzy has a very incomplete picture of Pete. As she fills out the picture of Pete into a whole person, she adds all the qualities she *wants* Pete to have, so that she winds up with a complete person. Down the line with much pain and suffering, she will feel betrayed and abused when she discovers that the real Pete has absolutely nothing to do with the concept she has created of him.

Men, on the other men can deal successfully with *partial* people. The advantage is that men are free to make abstractions about a larger world, without conversations being bogged down with personal trivia. Additionally, because of our evolutionary past, men are wired for exploration, hunting and adventure as we mentioned. That includes an adventure of the mind now and then. What men want is a little originality, some sparkle, some spice, a new way of looking at things, a new perception, some new knowledge (as long as it doesn't threaten their ego).

Men have the tendency to favor conversation about more abstract matters and the wider world which may be how language, as opposed to a system of symbols, got started. Really getting to know a person involves understanding how they perceive the world, how they value states of affairs, and how they react to counterfactuals in their lives. In prelibber times, when men were the "oppressors", they led conversation and women felt obliged to keep up, which means coming up with reasonable responses to men-led conversation and asking questions. Since women have always controlled the sex department, women responded that if we have to bring something to the table, we're going to expect men to do the same. This created a race to the top.

The most natural way for women to suddenly grab power was to reverse all trends of the pre-libber world. Since men used to lead conversation upward, the only way libbers could show their new-found power was to lead the conversation in the opposite direction, downward, which effectively creates a race to the bottom. So any attempt by the man trying to lead the conversation upward would be met with icy stares and would be immediate squelched. Besides, anything outside of ants and bees talk might involve seeing that the man has a brain and she has been programmed to conceptualize men as dumb dogs roaming the neighborhood.

Since the liberated woman really doesn't like men, she understands nothing about him. She doesn't understand that romance to a man means something special — a new way of looking at things, a new perception, a new string of words, a new piece of information. Newness, originality, sparkle, creativity; all this means nothing to the vagina which is programmed for power, promiscuity, distraction and familiarity. They want to hear the same tired crap they've heard hundreds of times. That's what they think is romantic.

I remember a few years ago, I was trying mightily to trick a liberated woman into an intelligent conversation. She was in some kind of fabric business. So being in New England, I wrote an email about old mills and the fact that New England was once the Mecca of weaving, spinning, and the textile industry, and some other relevant history. Well I was severely reprimanded for engaging in what this ninny called "trivia". To her, the real meat, the real core, and the real essence of conversation was personal junk minutia. What she wanted was ants and bees talk about how many brothers and sisters I have, what they're doing and where I've lived and where I've traveled, yada, yada. It's all about particulars. To her finite state computational brain, ants and bees talk is the essence of communication. I tried to talk about something abstract or something one of us can learn about. I'm trying to find out if this libber has a brain, which she never does.

What is amazing is that these liberated women have droned on about their personal lives hundreds of times before. And as is usually the case 99% of the time when there's no connection, they have to download all this meaningless data from their computational brains without a trace of learning left afterwards. If a relationship starts, there are hundreds of hours lying around in bed, driving around, etc. when you can bring up the trivia from each other's backgrounds. Why waste an hour on personal minutia when there isn't going to be a follow-up. But that's the incompatibility. The woman is using the hour's conversation to get familiar and she's very uncomfortable with any talk that's complex, unusual, stimulating, provocative or in any way interesting that may ruffle the bottom of her tiny brain.

And they get their way because the liberated woman has the sex card. For hundreds of years, women withheld sex not to beat men over the head with, but to create a period of time for courtship as we mentioned, to encourage meaningful conversation and to get commitments, which is a perfectly reasonable goal. But now sex will be used as a training device. We can see why the idea of "expressing your sexuality" was such an important staple in the liberated woman's arsenal of tricks after thousands of years of warning young women to be careful about sex. Her liberated sisters write books and articles and TV shows blasting sex, sexual parts, sexual practices, sexual anything right in men's faces. They come on like a bunch of crotch-grabbing nymphomaniacs just aching for sex. But first, a man must read his script which can be very strict. The woman in the fabric business was sending me a message: "I got the pussy and if you want to get laid, we're going to get to know each other on *my* terms". Of course, this sets up a totally artificial means of communicating. So in emails, if there is one word off the beaten path, the man will be summarily dismissed. If he shows any signs of excellence in any way, he will be banished from the sex line. Any attempt at interesting conversation will be rejected with the thought that "I don't want a know-it-all".

The modern day libber has taken real meaning completely out of men's behavior. Men read their scripts like zombies ascribing absolutely no meaning to anything they say or do. Of course, piss pot Pete doesn't mind any of this, which is why he can bring off his behavior so successfully. His agenda is to get laid, and he isn't overly concerned about how much he "knows" about his sex partners.

But for the time being libber Lizzy has her "relationship" and is in seventh heaven. Of course, she thinks she's in love because there's a strong feeling. But the strong feeling is the result of energy in the bottom of the brain where much of the brain's energy originates and it's the feeling of lust and sexual conquest, not existential love. But libber Lizzy has been trained to ignore existential love. That's not the real thing. The real thing is the *feeling*. In fact, in modern times, both men and women don't look anymore for a certain kind of person. They look for a certain kind of *feeling*, which, of course, is the feeling of conquest and control. What the person is is almost irrelevant. It's the *feeling*. This means that unbeknownst to semi-conscious libber Lizzy, this feeling at the bottom of her brain is not going to go away easily, which means a good chance of emotional slavery.

Ms. Magazine tells us that women "are expected to try to understand and explain what love is". [21] The reality is that these libbers have no idea what love is. And when they spot it, it's a signal for attack and demolition. Nobody complained about men not falling in love among pre-libber generations. It's only when women got liberated and became too angry and incompetent to fall in love with that people started complaining about men "not understanding love". Men understand enough about love to know that after 30 years of constant victimhood and man-bashing, a man with half a brain is not going to waste any real love on reptilian libber Lizzy.

Anyway, a month or so later, in the middle of the *feeling*, along comes Mr. Right. Now Mr. Right is the man who would fall in love with libber Lizzy, marry her, have a family, be a good loyal companion till death do them part. But all libber Lizzy's vagina sees is a possible kill. Libber Lizzy has been reading for years about centuries of male dominance and oppression. And now she has a live one to pay back mankind for oppressing women for two thousand years. She isn't even going to have a cup of coffee with Mr. Right. Besides Mr. Right is a little shy. He does not show the qualities chosen by females 2 million years ago. He doesn't have a square jaw. He doesn't project raw power and fierceness. He says something creative and intelligent once in a while which scares the crap out of the bottom of Lizzy's brain. If Mr. Right says one word that is unfamiliar, or one value that conflicts, or one piece of knowledge that Lizzy has been programmed to belief men have none of, he will be dropped right in the middle of a conversation. Remember, manners and thoughtfulness are components of the old "oppressive" culture that Lizzy has been "liberated" from. Besides, Lizzy wants no evidence in her life that men might have a brain to conflict with her preconceived idea that men are a bunch of dumb dogs roaming the neighborhood.

You could say that Lizzy is going to miss out on some really quality men with her modus operandi. But Lizzy isn't going to miss out on any quality men because Lizzy doesn't *see* quality men. At the inner brain level, all men are pretty much the same, just as in Lizzy: a spinal chord, two glands, and a crotch. The existential qualities that make for a quality man simply don't compute in libber Lizzy's computational brain. It's just a matter of which ones fit into the puzzle.

But the worst disadvantage Mr. Right has is he's in love. Of course, this state of mind creates fears — fears of loss, of being rejected, of not measuring up. And fears cause hesitancy, mental conflicts, emotional gridlock, all of which are turn-offs to Lizzy's spinal cord and vagina which are attracted to boldness, power, and confidence, just like 2 million year ago. The only conceivable way Mr. Right would have a chance is if there was courtship and if there was a culture that encouraged Lizzy to give such a man a second chance. The liberation movement made quick work of destroying those practices.

You might think that Lizzy would have a little curiosity about Mr. Right. How can she be so sure he isn't Mr. Right? After all she knows almost nothing about him except he's interested. But right off the bat, this is a disadvantage. In pre-libber days, an interested suitor was a resource, someone you could count on, someone who might be a life partner. But to the liberated woman, a suitor is a symbol of *oppression* — oppression by a system that's trying to run her life and foist some unwanted man upon her, and she will have none of it. Besides, curiosity is clearly an existential emotion on the exploration limb of the emotion tree, and without an existential brain, Lizzy has no such curiosity. All that aside, she's got piss pot Pete all wrapped up. He's da man.

There is no way any man is going to remain a good, loyal, long-lasting family man, unless he's very much in love at the start. We have used the idea of a *momentum vector* in Sect. 26.3. When a man starts a marriage, there is a momentum vector consisting of his ability to stay focused and loyal to his family and a good companion for his wife. Momentum equals mass times velocity. Mass is the degree of love the man has for the women; velocity is the length of time this love has existed. If he starts out very much in love, there can be enough momentum to carry him forward for a lifetime, which is why you see 85 year olds walking the beaches in Florida after 55 years of marriage. These marriages weren't all perfect. But the one thing they had in common is a large momentum vector in the man. I've seen interviews with these older couples. Invariably the woman says, "well, I didn't like him at first. But he was persistent, was chivalrous, reliable and very nice, and finally won me over". That was the purpose of courtship.

Everyone knows that it is very difficult for a man to stay loyal and faithful to one woman for a lifetime, especially now with a myriad of temptations. Women age sooner than men; they have kids which is not the greatest body sculpting activity; and they have menopause which often kills their sex lives and can make them crabbier. Still, we had life-long marriages in the old days. The reason is that a man in love with a strong momentum vector had a reasonable chance of courting the girl. This is the way successful marriages took place for thousands of years.

But libber Lizzy is not going to be "oppressed" by real suitors. Besides, she's got piss pot Pete who she has conceptualized in a totally essentialist way, right in the bottom of her brain, just as she would have 2 million years ago when she didn't have an existential brain. This is why in the women's magazines I've read, most of the articles are related to sex and nothing but sex. The really ironic thing is that the libbers who write these lurid articles in women's magazines and books complain about being "objectified" by men. But their own behavior implies that the only thing that counts is sexiness and power. The liberated woman presents herself as a one-night stand. In actuality, that's all she really is. Noticing existential subtleties is beyond the cognitive abilities of today's liberated woman. When she goes into a room full of people, she isn't thinking about the level of consciousness of people in the room, or how they see the world, or what their values are. There's only one thing on her mind: who's screwing who; who owns who? That's it.

Also with Pete stuck at the bottom of her brain, Mr. Right as no chance of getting started. The brain is like a funnel in this way. The farther down you go, the less room there is for concepts of men. When you get to the bottom, there's room for only one male concept just like the vagina has room for only one man. And she has her man right there: piss pot Pete. In the *pre-libber* generations, women had fully intact existential brains, which has infinite capacity for lots of concepts, lots of perceptions, lots of creative thinking, lots of meaning. Women of those generations dated lots of men. In this way they could process a number of men at the same time and with a working existential brain, they could perceive a great deal of meaningful detail about the men in their lives. Also, they would give just about any man some bit of a chance. They would gradually weed them out until they boiled it down to the best man. And since this man had to compete with other men, he had to sharpen up his existential qualities to maximize the chances of "getting the girl". This process would give a woman an optimal chance of getting a decent man.

Now I've had women friends who say, this was fine in the old days when sex was dis-couraged. But with sex in the picture, how can they process more than one man at a time. My answer is simple. List your men from 1 to 10 and possibly sleep with number one. You can see the others on a friendly platonic basis and they can use the time to try to charm their way into the woman's heart. Sometimes they succeed. If you lose them, that's a good sign of lack of long-term interest.

But even when a young woman wasn't interested in a guy, lots of times he would get another chance. I'll relate how men and young women interacted in my day. Let's say a guy met a girl at a dance and managed to get her phone number. He would usually call. But suppose the girl wasn't interested. Well, since she was smart enough to know that an interested man is a resource, even if a very tenuous one, she would talk for half an hour or so. When the guy would ask her out, she made excuses: she is busy with a project, or she had too many dates lined up, or any excuse that sounded okay. So the guy might ask if he could call again. She would say, sure, maybe in the next season. Now since this was a very light and airy existential way of rejecting the guy, he would not conceptualize the girl at the bottom of his brain so that he wasn't obsessed and couldn't get interested in anyone else. He would get the message and most of the time would look for someone else. But let's say he doesn't find anyone and he's still interested in our girl.

Well, after a number of months (not wanting to be a pest) he would call again. If the girl still wasn't interested, the same thing would happen, but she would be very nice and take time to talk a bit. Well, after 2 or 3 such calls, usually the guy would have found someone else. What was interesting about this process is that if the girl didn't have anything better to do, or if one of their conversations went pretty well, she might go out with the guy just for a lark. Once in a while, a second impression was positive and led to the couple starting to date. Often this resulted in life-long marriages simply because the man had a strong momentum vector.

Well the system mind had to put this sort of thing in the trash. Any means that could result in very close life-long marriages is anathema to the system mind. Now if a guy calls and the girl isn't interested, she barks (liberated women don't talk, they bark) "don't call here again", and slams down the phone. The liberated woman is not going to be "oppressed" with suitors. And besides, women are liberated from the oppressive duty of having to be "nice". So, libber Lizzy kicks Mr. Right right in the balls, knocks him upside the head, and dispatches him forthwith, often in the most humiliating manner. After all, she's got her man: piss pot Pete.

After a number of experiences like this, Mr. Right does not have the psychology to be Mr. Right anymore, and women who get interested in him in the future are going to get the same deal as libber Lizzy is going to get from piss pot Pete. I know men pretty well, and I can assure you that there are a substantial proportion of men who get this kind of treatment *once*, and they're out of the social scene sometimes for years. In either case, it's a victory for the system.

Of course, in libber Lizzy's semi-conscious state, she is totally unaware that the next liberated women, using the same body parts to pick her man, is also going to pick the same piss pot Pete. So will the next libber, and the next, and the next. Pete can get a nice new girlfriend every month or two. As we have discussed regarding reptiles, the spinal cord of all creatures, even humans, is pretty much the same. Our uniqueness comes from a developed existential brain. But libber Lizzy's existential brain is just about gone, and she isn't in the habit of using it anyway.

Libber Lizzy's semi-conscious state also prevents her from asking the simple question, why would piss pot Pete pull his world down around just himself and libber Lizzy for the rest of his life, giving up his freedom in the process? That's why the internet is a disaster for everyone. The internet supplies Pete with a new supply of attractive mugs every week. This appeals to Pete's hunter-gatherer wiring that got firmly cemented into his brain over two million years of evolution. Semi-conscious Pete is not going be able to resist the temptation of hunting and gathering instead of hunkering down on one women till death do them part.

We discussed the information-meaning approach to this in Sect. 16.13. The Universe of Discourse in the relationship with Pete is very narrow. Libby Lizzy hasn't had an interesting, unusual, provocative, original thought or perception in 20 years, often never in her life. There is no meaning in what transpired between herself and Pete because nothing special ever happened that might stir the natural adventurousness of men. In Sect. 16.13, we discussed the concepts people have of one another. What creates meaning of a person's concepts are representations with high information content because of a large universe of discourse. But because there was never anything special about their conversation, Lizzy's interaction with Pete will have low information content and so little meaning.

If course, libber Lizzy has an answer as to why Pete will stay. She thinks she's special, not realizing that her ants and bees talk is being repeated by millions of other libbers at the very same moment only with different names. After all, she's been told by chief NY libbers peddling books and magazines how unique and clever she is. But additionally, there's a built-in tendency in women to conceptualize people primarily as an *essence* — a soul. This soul is a very static eternal thing — a beautiful gold statue beneath the skin. The outsides of a person can move and engage in a variety of activities. But the soul stays constant as a glowing gold statue. This is why women like a static world laid out before them where little changes.

Essentialism is built into human cultures all of which invent some kind of a soul concept. Once humans were able to abstract time, the idea of an afterlife would proceed. The only way to explain afterlives is through an essential soul that lives on in eternity. I remember as a kid, I asked my very Catholic mother what heaven was like that we were all striving to attain. Well, she said you sitteth at the right hand of God. I asked, "but what do you do at the right hand of God". Her answer is that you *behold* God. This sounded pretty boring to me. I wanted to go where I could climb trees and play my guitar and carve wood. But we still strove to get into heaven because the alternative was made out to be worse.

Things like intellectual curiosity, character, education, accomplishments, skills, talents, knowledge, conversation — anything existential — are all peripheral to the soul, which is the core of their essence. They want to find a "soulmate" who will *behold* this soul for eternity and live on love. Nothing special has to happen except everybody *beholding*. And libber Lizzy, of course, thinks her soul is special because she's been told she's *unique*, even though there is not a shred of evidence for this.

I've had occasion to observe a number of women who you could tell very much wanted a man or a relationship or marriage. They go around half in a daze, never once in years of thinking ever ask themselves, why should a man pick me? They are waiting for their "soulmate" — someone who appreciates her soul just as it sits there, shining in all its glory, but doing absolutely nothing. Of course, if libber Lizzy had one ounce of perceptiveness, she would see that there is absolutely *nothing* special about herself at all. All of our specialness resides in our existential brain and libber Lizzy's existential brain is gradually disappearing from lack of use.

And of course, in their role of pimping for the system, leading libbers encourage this kind of essentialist thinking. Once *Cosmo* magazine had an article about how to hold on to a man.[22] Libber magazines are great at assigning women self-esteem, without ever giving a clue as to how to create a real self that anyone could esteem. Being energetic and constantly in motion are characteristics that are attractive to females about *men*. On the internet, women's profiles show them running, sliding, sailing, rolling, climbing and jumping, and not the slightest evidence of *thinking* or *wondering*. Motion is irrelevant to most men who are attracted to a stationary target who has the competence and attentiveness to get his genes into the next generation. The bottom line is that having no theory of mind, these libbers haven't the faintest, dimmest idea how to hold on to a man. They barely know how to hold on to a *woman*.

In any event, after the thrill of the initial sex wears off, Pete returns to his real self. As a *Cosmo* article details: "Then the nightmare begins". He "vanishes for days on end, then flares into anger at your slightest complaint". "He humiliates you in public and degrades you in private." [23] Then on a given day, Pete is gone. Lizzy emails. No answer. She calls. No answer. She leaves messages. He doesn't respond. All she wants is a little closure. But Pete, being a primitive animal himself, is done, and this is the good ending. If things continue, it might be worse because Pete simply doesn't care anymore. But libber Lizzy isn't going to give up. Her concept of Pete is hard-wired into the bottom of her brain and it isn't going to come out very easily. She's in conquest mode, although she thinks she's in love. Sometimes it takes years of frustration, misery, abuse, and neglect before she can finally pry loose piss pot Pete from the bottom of her brain.

Of course, since victimhood is much more effective in motivating women in the system's efforts to break bonds between the sexes, Lizzy has to come out the victim in these relationships. Even the prestigious *Scientific American Mind* had an article explaining and justifying attachment to Pete with the usual crap.[24] They've got all sorts of fancy names now, like "traumatic bonding", "power imbalance", "victim dynamics", to justify Lizzy's attachment to Pete. (In today's liberated world, you have to sterilize and euphemize women's dumbest qualities.) Without an existential working brain, Lizzy has picked Pete with her vagina that is attracted to Neanderthal man; and with the concept of Pete in the bottom of her hard-wired brain, Pete can get away with almost anything, sometimes extreme violence and abuse.

But let's say Lizzy does finally manage to break loose. She immediately reports to chief libbers in New York City. She might even get on Oprah Winfrey to tell the world that women are in charge now; and to prove it, she just "kicked her man to the curb". Women's magazines provide statistics about how women are dumping their boyfriends and initiating divorces more than men. In the meantime, men don't say a word — any way, anyhow, anywhere. In fact, it helps their case if the culture depicts women controlling the public dialog. Men don't care about the public dialog; they care only about reality. But the system mind knows that women create their reality by hearing words. So by giving women total control and power in the public *dialog*, and giving men total power in reality, everyone will be happy.

A male friend of mine said to me that all his male friends say that their relationships last only 5 months or less. Well, duh? With no existential brain with which to learn, the liberated woman is incapable of learning or questioning anything. She gets passed from man to man to man like an Indian peace (I mean, piece) pipe and never learns anything. Of course, not wanting to take responsibility for breakups, these men talk as though some unseen force had just disrupted their wonderful relationship and it was beyond their control.

But of course, over millions of years of evolution in crude times, vaginas got used to very rough treatment. The vagina is quite prepared for Pete's neglect and abuse. But more importantly, the vagina is built for resilience. A number of books have been written recently about the lives of young girls coming up. They are being treated like little slaves by the young boys and are passed around like the Indian piece pipe. But in spite of this, they seem to be doing better than expected. Girls and women are tough as nails from millions of years of mistreatment and getting bounced around. Maybe it's worth some mistreatment in order to have the freedom to whack a man whenever women feel like it. However you look at it, the social milieu we have was created by women, for better or worse, which brings up a very incisive illustration of a system mind.

Nowhere in the culture, not in books nor articles nor magazines nor TV nor even in sociology literature, will you find one tiny allusion to the new social milieu brought about by the woman's liberation movement — a nasty, rude, brutish milieu that is probably the biggest change in gender interaction in a thousand years. So when Lizzy gets dumped in an email after a 2-month "relationship", instead of complaining to her friends about the bad treatment, she now actually *defends* the nasty world she's in, saying, "it didn't work out", like it was all very nice. After getting treated like dirt by man after man, she now says she's "met some wonderful people". That's what she has to say about a world that *she* helped create. They are trapped because there's no longer anyone to complain to. It's all quiet on the western front.

Anyway, libber Lizzy bounces back and is in the game again. But did she learn anything? Absolutely not. Learning takes place in the existential brain and libber Lizzy is missing that particular organ. Lizzy does the same thing over and over. After 2, 3, or 4 of these "relationships" in her 30s, nothing is ever learned. Libber Lizzy simply cannot transcend her vagina's attraction to Neanderthal man. But let's say libber Lizzy tries a different venue. She's going to hit the disco scene. This is similar to meeting a man in person for a cup of coffee. The main difference here is that there are no emails, just conversation. Well, because she is dealing with strangers, the inner brain is on constant alert. Any attempt to make intelligent conversation is quickly rejected. To appease the inner brain which, as we have mentioned, is wired totally for safety in women, the man can't say anything that isn't totally familiar, which pretty much means ants and bees talk. From this kind of totally canned, meaningless, rehearsed conversation, libber Lizzy thinks she's going to find out what the new Pete is all about. She is straining to find out what her decision is going to be whether go or quick dismissal. She waits painfully for the decision, which, of course, is going to come from the vagina. Finally, at some point in the conversation, there is a slight twitch of the body. The vagina has made a decision. We'll call it the pussy-click, or to avoid crude names, crotch-click. The decision is either yes or no, up or down just like the old Roman emperor at lion feeding time. I have experienced this myself, but since I'm addicted to slightly intelligent conversation, I rarely elicited the crotch-click.

Now if the decision is yes, libber Lizzy immediately becomes interested in anything Pete has to say. If Pete wants to talk history, libber Lizzy loves history. If it's sociology, she's interested in that as well. How about consciousness, modern economics? She'd love to hear about it. Of course, none of this has ever made the slightest impression on libber Lizzy's shrinking brain before. She can't even ask an intelligent question. So the same scenario repeats itself. The concept of Pete gets embedded in the bottom of her brain which again puts her in conquest and control mode. But Pete, an attractive guy, isn't going to succumb to entrapment. So it's again a tug-of-war in which Lizzy slowly makes a slave of herself. But since there is absolutely no glue in her relationship with Pete, he grows tired of her mindless chatter, and again drifts off. Either that or Lizzy takes more years prying herself loose.

Without a theory of mind, all Lizzy knows is that *she* is bonded to Pete. Of course, she doesn't have the self-awareness to understand that the glue in this relationship is due to of sex. Self-awareness is again an existential ability and Lizzy's existential brain has been slowly dying away. So Lizzy has no way of knowing that sex means nothing to Pete in terms of creating glue for relationships. In fact, in males, sex actually *dissolves* glue. Let's elaborate on this point.

For males, when it comes to sex, sexual encounters are like the telomeres in our DNA. Every time a cell duplicates itself, a telomere falls away from the DNA, one by one. When all the telomeres have dropped off, the cell can no longer duplicate and is programmed to die. This is exactly the way sexual encounters are in men. With each prospective women, under normal circumstances, there are N number of times that a man will want to the have sex with this particular women. When N is reached, a man will not want one more sexual encounter.

The one difference between sex and the telomeres in our DNA is that N can change depending on the glue in the relationship. If glue is continually being made by the interaction between the couple, N can actually increase. Whereas sex for women may *create* glue, sex for males actually *dissolves* glue. And if the glue isn't replaced somehow, after a while there is no glue left, and finally the number N is reached.

We see this is many of the stories in the women's magazines. The young woman talks about "chemistry" and sparks when they first met. They got into a torrid relationship or marriage. They made love twice a day for many months. Then it begins to tail off, and now the woman is on Dr. Phil complaining that the husband doesn't care about sex anymore. What has happened is that the sex they were having was dissolving glue faster than new glue was made. Lizzy has no way to know that there's nothing in the world that grows stale more quickly with men than sex, no matter how sexy the woman is.

The second thing Lizzy is totally unaware of is that even though a man has to pass the crotch test in women, men have a very simple crotch test. Does he want to go to bed with the woman even once? This creates in interesting asymmetry, which we discussed in the Love Sect. 21.3 and above. We can imagine a large circle that contains all the men who would be willing to get into a relationship with Lizzy, even one-day relationships. There are some very attractive men in this group, including men who's number N for Lizzy is exactly 1. For Lizzy as an attractive young woman, the big group could contain thousands around a good size American city. They are very attractive, professional, seeming nice guys, men about town, men everyone wants. And they have the qualities Lizzy is after: distraction, busyness, power, promiscuity, mystery, etc.

Inside this large circle is a much smaller circle. These are the men with existential qualities who would marry Lizzy, have a family with Lizzy and provide a loyal, faithful lifelong companion for Lizzy till death do them part. Well, after sleeping with a number of tall, dark handsome men in the larger set, the men in the inner set seem total lowlifes to Lizzy, producing the emotion of *disgust*.

Years ago, women couldn't lure a man from the larger group because she couldn't initiate aggressive behaviors. She couldn't wiggle her butt and go to bed with men in the larger group simply because young women were told by the culture to wait until marriage for sex. They weren't even supposed to show interest in a strange man. Now even though this was a constraint on a woman's freedom, what it did was to force her to choose from among her real suitors. Women had to get used to lesser quality men, but *men they could get*. In this way, when she married one of her suitors, this was a guy who had a lot of momentum and many marriages in those days lasted a lifetime. Of course, having no existential brain to perceive subtleties, Lizzy *thinks* men in the larger group are suitors, not realizing that most of them have very small N and are light-years away from marrying her. But winding up alone with the almighty job is the main goal of the system mind.

Of course, mothers in the old days were very much aware of the ways of men and got across the message that these dashing, handsome, successful men were probably not going to stick around. In fact, there was often a kind of exploitation in the opposite direction. In my grandmother's generation, mothers often coerced their daughters into marrying very ordinary men because the mother thought he was stable, reliable and a "good man". But by the time we get to the peak of civilization in the '60s and '70s, women were free to get involved with whomever they fell in love with. But because of old traditions, they still couldn't go out and grab some hot-shot man simply by spreading their legs. This is why it was the peak of civilization. The culture encouraged women to pay attention only to their suitors. From the traditional days, they had an understanding that sex means nothing to men and that the man they could get for a few months is a lot more attractive than who they could get for a lifetime. This is why there was a high percentage of really good marriages, families and holding hands at the age of 85.

Well the system mind was not going to put up with women marrying their suitors because there was a chance it would result in a good lifelong marriage, which is anathema to the system mind. This is why libber leaders programmed women to denounce the old culture as being stifling and oppressive; women should be free to pick whomever they chose. This sounds nice, but what it does is get young women accustomed to a level of quality in men who are never going to stick around because either they can get a series of new girl-friends, which is always exciting, or they can do a lot better than brain-dead libber Lizzy.

Libbers talk about "exploitation" in marriage, even though you get a family and a home out of the deal. In my opinion, there's no more incisive example of *exploitation* than to program women to entertain only men they have absolutely no chance of getting so that they wind up with nothing but that almighty job. Libber Lizzy will never stoop to even getting started with her real suitors. They are resisted, obstructed, ignored, humiliated, neglected, dejected, rejected, deferred, denied, disparaged, depreciated, and finally dismissed. In fact, the new freedom allows libber Lizzy to push a suitor's face right into the ground. She can "get" her choice who is cuts above her suitors, so why bother with them. Now, how can any human being can get neglected, abused, and abandoned by the hot-shots in the larger group over and over and not take some notice of the trend. But remember, the ability to abstract is a very existential ability and libber Lizzy does not have a working existential brain. But I want to say a word of sympathy here.

As we mentioned above, women are wired to be nesters and gene-sniffers. This is as old as life itself. They can't help themselves. When they have a choice between Mr. Cool in the larger group and Mr. Right in the much smaller subset who can't hold a candle to Mr. Cool, it might be pretty difficult to resist the temptation. So over and over, Lizzy's vagina grabs the man with the best genes using million year-old criteria. Many of these men spend a grand total of one night with Lizzy. But without an existential brain, libber Lizzy has no organ to learn with.

Men never face this situation. If a woman accepts a man into her intimate life, as long as he behaves normally and stays pretty much what he was when they started out, there's a high probability that she will stay. By and large, consistent well-behaved men rarely get the gate from women who know them well. Women generally do not end good relationships. What this means is that men know pretty well the level of quality they can get.

What makes things worse is that females of any species do not have as much selection pressure in evolutionary times to develop a sense of *fairness* so as to better judge compatibility. When primate *males* and even other mammal species like wolves, bears, etc., fight over territory or females, they don't go all the way. They have evolved rules that prevent killings because the group needs as many individuals as possible. For example, when one member of a fight wants to give up, he just saunters away, or sometimes he displays his neck to the winner. This is a sign the fight is over. The winner assumes his position of authority, and there's no need for further violence. Rules of the game like this get wired into all males.

For females the situation is entirely different. When a female is attacked in any way, she has to be wired to protect her babies. This means a fight to the death. If she lets up for one moment, the aggressor may come back with further attacks and may win the day. This wiring prevents the evolution of a sense of fairness. We see this in many divorce proceedings. The man is usually not totally fair because he has an ego and is often self-centered, but there is some vestigial attempt at fairness. So he usually offers *something*. There was a famous case of a couple who got divorced and he had earned 90 million dollars. After viewing an interview with a modern-day ninny wife as she waddled down the street with chief ABC libber, Lynn Sherr, it was obvious to me that she played absolutely no part in his making 90 million dollars. She was a nanny at best. Well, he offered her around 23 million, which was summarily rejected.

With no energy in the existential brain to see reality, the modern liberated woman has no idea as to what is fair in a relationship. So she goes from one extreme to the other. She can number her boyfriends, one, two, three, etc. For the even numbered boyfriends, libber Lizzy is in conquest mode, and allows the man to gradually make a slave out of her, holding out any kind of emotional commitment. She washes, she cooks, she pays for things, she's on 24 hour-a-day call for anything including sex. When she gets abandoned at some point, she reacts the exact opposite way to the next odd numbered man coming along. He gets very little, she's cautious, she's stingy, she's tentative about sex. Lizzy has no way to know what is fair and how to divide things up in an equitable way.

There are many examples of the lack of fairness in women, even intelligent ones who should be able to transcend primitive wiring. Katha Pollitt, chief libber for *The Nation* demands that the wife in a divorce, "gets 50 percent of the husband's income for life plus legal costs. And, of course, she gets automatic full custody".[25] But Katha dear, you forgot the ball and chain. See, here is the housewife with the privilege of having the time and opportunity to lead a complete life similar to the life my mother led, with time for cultural interests, hobbies, intellectual pursuits, at-home small and comfortable businesses, while the husband is off 12 hours a day humping it on some miserable job. And *he* becomes the life slave, and loses his kids to boot. Oh! But I forgot. The poor "uninstructed and bored" housewife is sitting there looking straight ahead all day collecting mental illnesses, which of course, is the husband's fault for which he has to be a slave the rest of his life. But if she had been free of this life of "uninstructed and bored" housewife, she would have sprung to life with resourcefulness, intelligence, and ambition to climb to the top of the career ladder.

To these semi-conscious libbers, the housewife has to be compensated for "lost rungs on the career ladder". Yes, all those rungs on the "career ladder" leading all the way up to chief hamburger flipper, sales clerk, cleaner, factory worker, secretary, computer jockey, and fish head chopper. Then there are the thousands of offices filled with women in little cubicles in front of a computer 10 to 12 hours a day. The only ladder I ever saw in these places had one rung on it. But of course, the 95% of women in these jobs don't count to libber leaders. Their assignment is to be docile work slaves for some libber boss puffing up her profits.

I've had millions of jobs, some very good ones like economic analysis, statistician, management consulting, business report writing, etc. None of those jobs were as interesting, fun, rewarding and informative as taking care of my kid sister full time one summer when my mother was very sick. Now I would rather be a Supreme Court justice, CEO, or chief engineer than taking care of my kid sister, but those are at most 5% of all jobs. Now, my mother with exceptional abilities might have been a billionaire hedge fund manager if she lived in today's world, which could be considered superior to raising a family at home. And she did feel somewhat frustrated all her life because she didn't have the opportunity for formal education and career. But the grass always looks greener and I'm sure my mother had a rosier view of these jobs in the corporate world than was really the case.

Fairness depends on choices. In the old days, a wife may have been coerced by society or a husband into raising kids at home. If this was not her choice, then a case could be made that she should be compensated in case of a divorce for lost rungs on the ladder. But Pollitt is writing in modern times when women *choose* their course. And if they *choose* to be able to enjoy all the advantages of being home raising kids, this becomes a *privilege* that the husband is *supporting*. To force him to continue supporting *more* privileges after a divorce again shows the libber's innate inability to judge fairness. Judges handing out settlements to Pollitt's specifications have caused marriage for people over 40 to come to screeching halt, which is the system's agenda of ridding society of marriage altogether. I'm sure hard-wired Pollitt sees no connection in this regard.

Fairness involves determining values whether states of affairs, objects or behavior. As evolution progressed, the tendency to obey rules played some part in the thinking of all males, which evolved into the ability to determine value. Human males on hunting parties had been running into other tribes for millions of years where they had to negotiate trades and privileges. Males became wired to judge value in these kinds of negotiations, which is why they have a better idea of their own value as human beings. Females never experienced situations where value had to be judged. We see this in the field of job categories. We hear in every possible media outlet, day in and day out about men making more money. Men make more in some instances because they have extremely physically demanding jobs. Most women don't want to have their kidneys shaken loose bumping up and down driving an 18-wheeler 12 hours a day. But what I learned in a very obscure place is that in the jobs men have, they are more than *10 times* more likely to get killed or severely injured on the job. In the debate over equal pay in 2014, not one media talking head said one word about this very relevant fact — a great example of a system mind.

The system knows that men are smart enough not to blame women for injuries. It's the nature of the jobs. However, the system also knows that the liberated woman is dumb enough to explain unequal pay *not* by the nature of the dangerous jobs men have, but to *blame men*. Making women into *victims* increases the animosity women have towards men making good relationships less likely.

A similar thing occurs regarding housework. When these libbers hire nannies and other household help, they pay them slave labor wages and often treat them like slaves as well. But when a libber does the *exact same* housework while often enjoying a high standard of living provided by a professional husband, this is called "unpaid labor" and is suddenly worth millions. These are just more examples of libbers having no sense of fairness and no ability to judge value which washes away respect men used to have for them.

Whether it's making herself a sex object as a teenager, to the inability to converse in anything but ants and bees talk, to picking men with the spinal cord and crotch, to glorifying the career idea as applied to mind-numbing jobs, to creating a nasty singles world, to acting as though they know everything when they know almost nothing, to thinking that men are a bunch of dumb dogs roaming the neighborhood — everything she says, everything she does points to stupidity and incompetence. And they wonder why there's no more courtship and men have no respect for them. The whole purpose of the evolution of culture was to insure that females behave intelligently and competently *before* marriage, and males behave constructively *after* marriage. This is why the system mind acting through the women's movement had to quickly dispatch any vestiges of traditional culture.

35.7 REACHING 40

Finally, Lizzy reaches 40, and there's very little existential brain left. But she has a very functioning computational brain that enables her to do her corporate job. Now, in women, even numbered decades are the hardest to get through. (In men it is the odd numbered decades.) So 40 is a moment of truth and with the last morsel of existential thinking Lizzy can muster, she takes stock of her life. What does she find? Too many bad men — too much giving, too little getting. She puts her foot down. From now on, Lizzy is going to get tough. No more nice, sweet, accommodating emotional slave as has been the case for the last 25 years. (Of course, Lizzy has no way to remember how she treated men her vagina *didn't* pick.) Besides, she's armed with lots of libber words telling her as Cristina Nehring warns in her book, *A Vindication of Love*, not to "settle" for mediocre relationships. Lizzy is supposed to find true and lasting emotional love. When Lizzy was young, it was possible to fall in love with her because she was a little cute and girlish and engaging. But now that she's over 40 and angry about all her experience with men (who *her* vagina picked), this semi-conscious libber doesn't tell us how, after 30 years of victimhood and 24 hour-a-day man-bashing, men are going to fall in love with the rude, angry, no-nothing, mean-spirited ninny that Lizzy has become.

Now, in looking for Mr. Right, since libber Lizzy is not supposed to "settle", and with women now in control of picking men, Libber Lizzy has to determine the value of herself as a human being as well as prospective males. This is especially important because she has been promised what she "deserves" which is an *equal* relationship. What has happened in this regard is a great example of Jung's Universal Consciousness. Almost immediately at the start of women's lib, every woman who got liberated came to the same conclusion.

Since women are generally younger than comparable men, this becomes the only variable to measure the total value of a human being. The variable is AOC — age of crotch, which is really a measure of sexiness. Without a theory of mind, libber Lizzy thinks she can con piss pot Pete into valuing himself solely on age, totally disregarding all the existential qualities that men consider when valuing other people.

You can read a thousand articles in women's magazines, and every one that discusses attraction to men mention the same qualities. The width of his eyes, the squareness of his jaw, the slimness of his hips, his pheromones, the taste of his skin, the smell of his clothes and on and on. Of course, these qualities are going to be superior in the younger man. All existential qualities a man may have — his character, intellectual curiosity, values, personality, intelligence, knowledge, wisdom, education, perceptions, skills, talents, accomplishments, goals, etc. — all of this means absolutely nothing to brain-dead Lizzy. As long as her AOC is less by any amount, she is more valuable by her scorecard, even though most of these liberated women haven't had an interesting, provocative, original or perceptive thought in 20 years and whose abilities extend to sliding down mountains and rolling along sidewalks. Of course, with total disregard for the man's scorecard, libber Lizzy has no chance of getting what she has been programmed to "deserve", which winds her up exactly where the system wants.

This again is an example of stupidity among these libbers. Not only do men age more slowly than women, but more importantly, men can substitute power or money for lost youth, which accounts for many older successful men being with young attractive women. Highly successful women making millions have no better chance getting a quality man than the average woman. She simply can't substitute power and money for loss of youth. Two women I met over 50 said the exact same words, "after 50, women become invisible". There are certainly exceptions, but in our youth-oriented society, older women are clearly at a disadvantage, even if they are successful financially. This is why pre-libber women had an instinct to know that talk about age is not in women's interests. In my family, nobody ever knew how old my parents were at any time of their lives until the very end. We didn't even dare ask. Ages of *any* adults were never mentioned. Only kids had ages.

But the libber movement was run by women mostly in their 30s and 40s; and not having a time concept, thought they were going to be young and sexy forever. They can't look forward to the day when they themselves would be cast aside and irrelevant. Not that they cared one wit about older women in the first place. Of course, when they were in their 20s and 30s and sincerely wanted a family, libber Lizzy might give an older man a shot. But as Lizzy gets older, and subconsciously realizes nobody is going to want her for any length of time, now all of a sudden she wants a man "of comparable age". The liberated woman is still talking "rest of her life", even though the average length of a marriage is only about 6 years and the average length of a relationship a matter of months. On top of that, as we have mentioned, only about one in a hundred unmarried professional women over 40 ever gets married in the first place. So if a 40 year-old woman takes even a 65 year old man, she would most likely get a good, loyal, faithful 20 years out of the old bastard who is going to appreciate the younger woman. What will she get out of a man her age? A few years maybe, usually a few months, during which time there is abuse, negligence, and final abandonment if she finds anyone at all. No, the stated motivation for the younger man is just reason-box bologna. The real *cause* for wanting the younger man is that the younger man is the sexier man. It's still all about sex because that's the only consideration in Wolf's vagina-brain connection.

So in determining value, libber Lizzy harkens back to when she was 32 and met piss pot Pete who got in her pants and had a "relationship", at least for a few months, until he got bored with her mindless chatter and drifted off. Well, this establishes a life-long standard that all future men will be compared to. After all, it's all about self-esteem and she has been warned never to "settle". This leads to an interesting question. Why are single and divorced women the most attractive women of their age. If you go to a large gathering of married people, many of them happily married, you don't find the kind of attractiveness you find on the internet. In fact, it's amazing how plain and dumpy many happily married people are. Even *Ms. Magazine* noticed this: "...women who were exceptionally beautiful when young were found to be less happy in their middle age than women who had been average-looking...." [26] The explanation for this is that in their 20s and 30s, the most attractive women are able to pick and get their man. Of course, this is only a delusion. What they could get for the long haul doesn't come close to what they can get for a short fling. The plain woman can't do this because she would get creamed if she went out hunting. So she is forced to choose from among her suitors, however few there are. So she winds up with a decent guy and a decent marriage. Of course, her guy is pretty plain too; certainly not a piss pot Pete, but a good loyal companion for the long haul.

With no way to compute value, Lizzy can't see that perhaps the guy her vagina has picked could probably do better. Once I saw a very graphic illustration of this. Oprah Winfrey had a program with a line-up of middle-aged women probably between 45 and 60, all showing great signs of wear and tear. Each one had a heart-rending story about how a handsome, dashing, charming 28 year-old stud came along, swept them off their feet and wound up taking their money. They were "devastated". Of course, the libber crowd was outraged by these horrible stories. There wasn't one word to the effect that what would a dashing, handsome 28 year-old stud want with one of these women having absolutely nothing special about them. There wasn't one soul in the audience, including Oprah, who saw that these were not really *fair* relationships because these women had very little single's market value. Oprah is very bright, and I wondered how she could put on such an embarrassing show.

Now men get conned out of money as well, especially on the internet. When I was on the internet, every week I would get a dripping letter from some 28 year-old girl in Russia or China, saying she thought I was handsome and sexy. They would send sexy photos of themselves to up the anti. Some of these women are in business and probably some guy is sitting there writing love letters to me. After a number of emails, they would announce they just have to "be with me". They just happen to be short on money. Now, the question is this. Do men fall for this con? My guess is that maybe a few do. But here's the difference. Men have some sense of fairness and value. If they get conned, they know they got greedy and most of them learn.

With her new attitude, Lizzy joins dating services, gets on the internet and jumps right into the singles game with gusto. Now that Lizzy is over 40 and has been deprived of her rightful ownership of a dog on the end of a leash, she's even angrier and more dismissive. Of course, Lizzy's has no way of knowing that since she subconsciously suspects that nobody is going to want her, she's decided she really doesn't want a man. Additionally, because of her instinctive hatred of women, she is going to make singles venues so nasty and painful that other women, even sincere ones, are not going to have a chance to meet a decent man either.

Often Lizzy's profile says: no liars, cheaters, abusers, or players. I wrote to a few asking, do you expect a liar to tell the truth about being a liar. Never get an answer to that. Even a nasty answer would be appreciated if it showed some originality and sparkle. But the liberated woman is a flat-liner: you put an MRI on her head and all you get is a flat line, hmmmm. Of course, unbeknownst to libber Lizzy, what she is really doing is making an exact list of the men her vagina picked in the past. The few pre-libber quality women I've known never had any cheaters, abusers and players in their lives. But without an existential brain that perceives subtleties, libber Lizzy has no way of knowing what she's picking and getting. This is another casualty of the liberation movement that gave women the power to pick. First you destroy their minds, then you give them the power to pick: a perfect combination for disaster.

Mr. Right will have even less of a chance now. He can't even establish a little friendship so that there may be a small opportunity for courtship. On the basis of a few surface comments in a few emails, you may think you are connecting with a real human being — one with a complete mind with deep interests in the amazing detail of the world: art forms, great literature, history and historical objects, culture, architecture, anthropology, etc. Perhaps there's a reference in emails to early American quilts, or a reference to WWII, or a reference to the architecture of the early 20th century, or reference to fashions in the 1800s. It could be from among *billions* of such topics. You are all excited. You might even get one semi-intelligent email. But it's always a big letdown. You find that her interests in all these areas are as shallow as piss on a flat rock. It takes an existential brain to have deep interests in these topics. As soon as this woman decides that you do not fit precisely the exact space in her life puzzle, or if she gets a stronger pussy click from another mug, you are expelled from her life like the cork from her wine bottle.

I have had great friendships with older men. We are not going to *own* one another or get married or have sex. The relationship consists simply of exchanging thoughts, perceptions, ideas, knowledge, etc. about the interesting detail of the world. That's all there is. But it is enough to maintain friendships for life. This is not possible with the liberated woman. She understands *only* ownership of a dog on the end of a leash. All other considerations are peripheral including the basis for any real friendship. And they wonder why men have so little use for them.

A big problem in the philosophy of mind is free will as we discussed In Ch. 17. It is impossible to know if we really have free will or if we are just complex robots. One thing is for certain, however. If we have free will, it would reside in the existential brain. The bottom of the brain has only hard-wiring. A reptile has no free will. He simply responds to his environment in a programmed fixed way. But since libber Lizzy has no existential brain left after years of neglect, she has no free will either. She's exchanging emails with a pleasant, intelligent guy. All of a sudden piss pot Pete pops up. Can she transcend the temptation and continue with Mr. nice guy?

Drumroll please. No, she cannot. She reacts to the new piss pot Pete the same as the old, just like a boa constrictor would react to a bigger rabbit and forget the smaller one. So having no manners, no socialization, and no understanding of the social milieu she's creating, she ignores Mr. nice guy, leaving him hanging in midair. He thinks he's in an intelligent conversation, but he's talking to the wall. Lizzy is gone and she's gone in the rudest way possible. Why not? Men are bad guys anyway, and besides, she's got piss pot Pete lined up.

In evolutionary history, pain in females was often associated with having a baby. So females evolved to withstand some pain. However, as hunters out in the bush, pain in males meant injury; and since they would usually be either alone or among other males fleeing for their lives, injury often meant death. So males evolved to be very pain-averse, which pre-liberated women understood. In social situations, clubs, parties, dances, etc. they would always make sure that even unattractive men were comfortable. They would talk to or dance with men they weren't attracted to just to maintain a pleasant atmosphere to keep even the shyest men in the game. In Lizzy's profile, she wants a "kind, caring, sensitive," professional man (that she "deserves"). But without a theory of mind, Lizzy has no way of knowing that this "kind, caring, sensitive man" is not going be on the internet week after week waiting to be ignored, humiliated and rejected by hundreds of mindless liberated clones like Lizzy.

Of course, these semi-conscious libbers don't realize that the nasty singles world they have created is driving more and more professional men into the world of prostitution, which has really taken off with the internet. Why should a professional man take the neglect and abuse he gets from libbers on the internet, when he can rent a pretty, sexy 25 year-old who has enough brain cells still alive to carry on a conversation on top of some choice sex.

But for the few attractive men Lizzy is generous enough to pick, she has a carrot and stick approach to pound them into the perfect man, which is a dog on the end of a leash. For the carrot, Lizzy has sex and a bunch of affectations designed to induce men into the web. But, of course, without a theory of mind, Lizzy has no way to know that most of these affectations just make her look stupid. So, for example, Lizzy pretends always to be busy, especially with her job. Of course, men play the busy game too because, as we explained in Sect. 21.3, in evolutionary times, women were attracted to the busy male. So women think they will be attractive in the same way, another example of a lack of a theory of mind.

The really remarkable thing is that people are made to actually feel proud of being total work slaves. On the internet, you see everybody making a grand display of how busy they are. They can't afford one minute for a human piece of communication. This is the new manhood. I remember working as an engineer and mathematician in my 20s in high-powered consulting firms, as a top-secret analyst. This was the cold war and there was tremendous competition with Russia. But when 5 o'clock rolled around, everyone put down their pencils and went home to their families or girlfriends. We didn't care if the Russians were coming. Today's 12-hour a day job would have been a sign that you were too stupid to get a real job that allowed you to get home and interact in a human way with your family like everyone else. You would be ashamed to be in this kind of situation. But the system mind made quick work of that ethic. Now people are actually bragging about the fact that their lives consist of some 10-hour a day computer-pecking job and they just don't have time for human interaction. Real manhood now consists of being a work slave to some robotic boss who's a cell-phone away from the giving you the next task.

There were many other ways chief libbers had to convince women they were "special" when, in reality, Libber Lizzy is just another liberated clone. Women were told they are brilliant. I remember myself after I got divorced getting fixed up by dating services with liberated women. During conversations over coffee, a number of them expressed concern that they might be "intimidating" me. Now that might be possible if they were capable of saying *one* sentence that was complex, original, interesting, or provocative. But right before their very eyes was the *reality* that their conversation consisted of nothing but ants and bees talk. However, they had been convinced *with words* by leading libbers that men are dummies, "intimidated" by the brilliant new liberated woman. And they don't mind making total fools of themselves disagreeing with the most obvious facts about the world. And why not, since men are just a bunch of dumb dogs roaming the neighborhood anyway. In a million other ways, the liberated woman is programmed to look stupid. The system knows that men are not going to respect a stupid woman, especially when he usually started off life with a woman who could do all kinds of things he couldn't do.

Another fraudulent way to look special is to become a sexy 25 year-old, since men have the reputation of liking younger women. But the over-40 liberated woman thinks that by acting as though she is 25, that will make her *be* 25. After all, men aren't very perceptive and can easily be fooled. What is really pathetic about this is that they don't even know how the younger woman really acts. The younger woman often is *too* accommodating because possibly she sincerely wants a family or a life partner. I've had the experience of going out with young women starving in grad school insisting on paying for some of the entertainment. The 53 year-old *thinks* the younger woman is in the driver's seat barking out signals and running the show and being waited on hand and foot. So even though she's making 150 thousand dollars a year, when the bill comes she conveniently has to take a whiz. (But men should be chivalrous: whenever that happened to me, I didn't say a word, I paid the bill, went home and drew a line through her name.)

Another way to look special is to come on like they have a bevy of suitors clamoring at their door and they just don't have much time for the guy in view. They ask for phone numbers and never call. They give phone numbers, but are never there and too busy to answer messages. For thousands of years, females set the standards of comportment, manners, and etiquette. The liberated woman has no interest in such "oppressive" social constraints. She is the rudest, coarsest most ill-mannered specimen of the species since Neanderthal days.

But Lizzy isn't through. She also has the stick to remold the men of her choice out the amorphous clay she has been led to believe men are. Libber leaders conceptualized men pretty much the way their fathers were: nice sweet guys who loyally served their families in a fairly adequate way. However, these fathers, as good as they were, weren't perfect, and besides they often believed in a division of labor with their wives at home raising kids. This was just the cultural norm established over thousands of years. Well, leading libbers decided that with just a knock on the head here, a whack on the butt there, and a kick in the crotch there, they could pound into shape the basic clay making up their fathers and mold the perfect man. This again shows that the lack of understanding of the basic human male in these libbers is profound, it is deep, it is unremitting.

So one of the sticks Lizzy will use to reconfigure a man to fit into her life puzzle is to demand that she be able to instantaneously trample into the man's life who must immediately clean out his life of all other female contact to make room for Lizzy. I've had the experience a number of times making a date for coffee with a new woman for the following week. But let's say on Saturday night, she emails me or calls and I'm not there. That is the end of it. My life is supposed to be cleaned out for her and anything less is immediately rejected. If she suspects the slightest contact with other human beings, you get summarily rejected.

When I met my x-wife, I was dating two other women, and she was dating two other men besides me who were after her in college. We couldn't expect each other to immediately clean out our lives to make room for the new man or woman. We each took a number of months to gradually and patiently *earn* our way into each other's hearts and finally after a year, to exclusivity. The reason, of course, is that we each saw something *special* in the other, something worth putting some effort into, something worth fighting for and something worth accepting some inconvenience for. You had to *earn* privileges by a display of human existential qualities. This milieu is completely gone. Libbers are sending the constant, incessant and invariable message that no man is worth getting excited about who deserves a little slack until they get to know one another. They refuse to recognize any existential qualities. Only one variable is recognized: AOC – age of crotch.

So what is men's response to the new modus vivendi? Well, the good ones simply refuse to play. They meet people in traditional ways or spend their time in the massage parlor. Through business dealings, I was in contact with lots of middle-aged men who were professional, intelligent, normal, etc. — all around pretty good catches I thought. I would ask the single ones about the internet, and invariably they would laugh and say they tried it for a few weeks, but couldn't meet anyone, and didn't like the whole process and were gone. But of course, this means that there are only a few quality men on the internet until they figure out what the score is. But who *is* on the internet? This is an interesting question.

I was in contact with a number of women friends who were on the internet. I would get online from time to time to do some amateur sociology for this book. One night a woman friend was commenting about how often when she meets men from the internet, they don't listen to her conversation; their minds wander; their eyes wander. We figured out what was happening. There is a group of men on the internet who have a slight touch of autism. It isn't enough to be diagnosed because it's just a touch. But the symptoms are recognizable. The reason they stay on the internet is that they don't have a fully developed theory of mind. They don't know that they are being used and abused. They just accept the world as it is and struggle to make the best of it.

The second category of man on the internet is the elephant-skinned. He uses the buck-shot approach. The hunter sends up a bullet filled with little pebbles called shot towards a flock of birds. Most of the pellets miss but once in a while one of the pellets hits a bird. The elephant-skinned operates similarly. He has no respect for women and rejections just bounce right off his elephant skin. He has put his pride behind his goals. He grovels in the dirt and allows himself to be molded into the exact dumb dog Lizzy is looking for. Of course, the string of words he has perfected has no meaning to him. But once in while it twangs some libber's spinal cord and he scores. He has a relationship for a few months and moves on.

The last category of men on the internet are the players. They pretty much resemble the elephant-skinned, except they're better at it. They have perfected the art of *playing* the spinal cord of the liberated woman. So given these kinds of men on the internet, with no theory of mind, Lizzy has no idea what men's reaction to all this toughness and nastiness will be. In fact, I was surprised myself at the extreme reaction men had to the new society of liberated women. To understand men's reaction, we have to bring up a concept we talked about in Sect. 19.4 called *catastrophe* or *switching* theory. This is where it is important for mammals to switch emotions from aggression to fear or vice versa when the situation changes abruptly. What this implies is that mammal males, especially, are wired to live on a knife edge. Most of the time they are in idle mode. But the slightest change in their perceptual field can switch them from idle to aggression or fear in a heartbeat.

I remember, a woman a dating service fixed me up with saw that I was newly divorced. she looked at me with the sternest of looks, and warned that "things aren't the way they used to be". It looked like a threat. And it did scare me. I had heard of the women's movement and concluded that w*omen* had all the power now and I better clean up my act. No more sexism and men running the show. What I didn't realize until later is that men being on a knife edge of civility, fell immediately to aggression. Yes, women were a lot tougher now. No more accommodating, sweet and gentle cream puffs who treated men with the utmost care. But because women had always set the example, men cranked it up a notch and got even tougher as a reaction to the nastiness of the libbers. With the added testosterone, women are never going to outdo men when it comes to nastiness.

In the past, men controlled the public dialog because they were more dominant in general. So their public visage was somewhat rough. However, their private visage was often quite tender. There were many men who got married because the girl cried. But because women now control the public dialog, men have switched from being tough in public where they are now quite tender and intimidated, to being tough as nails privately. But since the public dialog is all that's important to brain dead libber Lizzy, she thinks she's gained something.

Of course, when libber magazines want to use violence against women as a talking point to get more rights or privileges from the system, they are quick to point out the increases in violence against women. From a women's crisis center, "Violence is not diminishing, it is increasing at an alarming rate." [27] *Ms. Magazine* said, "What is shocking is that reports of woman-battering in the U.S. are increasing".[28] In a survey, about half of the women "... have experienced some form of sexual victimization". [29] However, when it's time to assign blame for the nasty singles world *they* have created, they write books and articles about how much worse it was in the bad old days. Rape? Why, in the old days, everyone got raped in college. It was part of the curriculum. Abuse? All girls got beat up once or twice in college. Women coming up are too young to know how things really were.

In the 4 years I was in high school, being very active, and hanging out everywhere, I never observed one case of sexual harassment. I never saw a case of physically man-handling a girl. My observations are just a random sample. That doesn't mean it never happened, but I never observed it, and I hung out with the worst possible crowd of guys who got kicked out of everything at some point or other, some even going to jail. So what I observed was a typical sample.

A woman has a choice in this regard. *Either she creates a nice world for herself to live in, in which case, she has to endure the horrible prospect of men also living in a nice world. Or, if she wants a nasty world for men to live in, she's too stupid to realize she's got to live in the same nasty world.* But maybe after a couple million years of getting bounced around and mistreated, women are tough enough to take it in return for the freedom to whack men when they feel like it.

But what about the bottom half of society. These libbers are totally oblivious of the fact that the lives of working class women have degenerated into total chaos and terror. Without a highly intelligent existential brain to create a sense of self-awareness, working class men, who are in the majority, are complete inner brain random motion machines. Without a strong culture guiding their values and behavior and a crippled marriage institution too weak to provide identity for men, they create a life for working class women of total terror, abuse, discontinuity and abandonment. And it is driving huge numbers of working class young women into prostitution, drugs, and other forms of hopeless lives. And you never hear a word about these broken lives from the corporate media who pay chief libbers big bucks to pimp for the system.

An interesting piece of evidence as to where men's thinking has gone is that with thinking in the bottom of the brain, men, especially younger ones are in a constant hunter and conquest mode. In this mode, they view any other male as a threat, just like in evolutionary times. How did this come about? Unlike bugs, among mammals, one female cannot reproduce the entire next generation. *Each* female has to reproduce. This creates asymmetry between males and females. Because making a baby is a very complicated endeavor involving hugely complex chemical processes, each female among mammals has a limited number of eggs. What this means is that in order to reproduce the next generation, *each* female must reproduce. So the female genes getting into the next generation aren't restricted to the best genes among them.

However, since the male is contributing basically only a package of DNA, he can produce enormous numbers of sperm. So the male with the *best* genes can procreate the entire next generation with no help from less fit male genes. What this amounts to is that females are contributing the *quantity* of the next generation because each female is reproducing regardless of how good her genes are. Males on the other hand are contributing the *quality* of the next generation because only the best genes among males will continue on. But this creates another asymmetry. There is a small amount of competition among females but this isn't a very important competition because sooner or later the alpha male will get around to all of them. However, competition among males is going to be quite fierce. We see this among the higher primates like the gorilla who fight and compete for who is going to be the alpha male whose genes alone will be passed on. However, the last stages of evolution ameliorated this situation because all proto-humans had to cooperate. Males ran into other villages and had to negotiate. This puts energy into the top of the brain, which will enable males to overcome the tendency to compete and often get along pretty well. In the existential '50s, 60s, the culture was designed to get energy *out* of the bottom of men's brains. As a result, there were very close friendships between men that often lasted a lifetime. Men basically liked each other. If you went to a dance in pre-libber times, you would see young men in little clumps shootin' the crap. It took real self-awareness to get them to overcome their natural fears to ask one of those mysterious scary creatures with bumps on their chests to dance. It was much more comfortable to interact with their own kind. But this shows that in an existential frame of mind, males are wired to be friendly with other males.

But the last 35 or so years brought about big changes in men's psychology. As brain energy sank to the bottom, existential considerations began to recede and with it went traditional male friendship. Of course this is a transitional period, so there are exceptions. Males are competing for females just like in evolutionary time, and as a result, males often view each other with suspicion and aversion.

I remember once talking to a young man who, because he had been raised in a more traditional family, was somewhat friendly. He was considering moving to another part of the country for a job opportunity. He was having trouble making up his mind whether to relocate. Well, I commiserated a bit and reminded him that it's tough to start up in a new location losing contact with old friends and having to make new ones. His answer was that he had been thinking about that and realized that he really didn't have any real friends. He was just being honest.

With few exceptions, there is very little *real* friendship among men coming up. Whenever any form of femininity is around, younger men will never complement each other in any way. With thinking in the bottom of the brain, any form of friendship, cama-raderie, or support is a kind of giving. Another man is viewed as a competitor and the inner brain, programmed for survival, never gives anything, especially to competitors. So young men don't talk much to each other. They are total strangers unless there is imminent busi-ness that requires words. If they see another man having a conversation with a woman, they have to break it up to rescue the women from this obvious sexual harasser. Who would have guessed things would take this turn — certainly not the sociologists, to whom *everything* that happens is a total surprise. But this is just what the system orders. Friendship is a dis-traction from the almighty job and must be dispensed with.

All of this applies to young women as well, but not as incisively. They are not compet-ing to be an alpha female, but for the best genes. Consequently, young women have closer friendships than young men. However, when it comes to genes, all bets are off. Women friends will think nothing of trying to steal each other's boyfriends, using sex along the way. Men see this all the time.

For all these reasons, the respect men had for women in pre-libber times is completely gone. They see that every every practice, every attitude, every policy is just plain stu-pid and self-destructive. So when young men start seeing women choosing men with their vagina and spinal cord and coming on with all sorts of abusive, dismissive and incompetent behavior, this fractures the ties established by their mothers between womanhood and com-petence. This creates a feeling of dissonance and unfamiliarity in males, which elicits emo-tions of either fear or aggression both of which are embedded in a disposition of disrespect. If it's fear, the man will withdraw completely, which is the explanation why enormous num-bers of normal men, especially the shy types, will not last long on the internet. If aggression is elicited, many men simply fall back on their innate wiring to copy the behavior of females. In fact, if you throw an additional sprinkle of testosterone, you get everything amplified. So when Lizzy is dismissive and abusive, men do the very same things. So where women are unreliable, the men are even worse. It's a race to the bottom.

Of course, if you press them, men will swear on the grandmother's graves that they love women and have the utmost respect for them. But the very fact that they allow themselves to be pounded into a mold to become a dumb dog shows that it's all just a façade: part of a game they have to play to get the prize. When they see what is expected of them — the blandness of all interaction, the display of fake emotions, the lack of intelligence expected of them — at a very deep level, all respect men used to have for women dissolves. The worst of this is not only a high divorce rate, but poor quality marriages and relationships that do exist.

Of course, the inconsiderate, nasty and heartless treatment of women in the private sphere was totally covered up by an exact opposite display in the public domain. In the pub-lic domain, men didn't write books and articles complaining about one single detail of the modern liberation-designed social milieu. There is no righteous indignation, no complain-ing, no dissent. Even when they're interviewed in the mass media, they bow and scrape and ask for penance. The self-flagellation gets downright embarrassing. They have absorbed all the new requirements to appeal to the new woman. This misleads women. One libber says:

"Any dumb blond…can fool the cleverest of men". [30] Men agree, while they wind up with the ultimate goal: conquest and control. The mistreatment they absorb in the beginning simply gets *internalized* and comes out during later stages of relationships where they take complete control. We can make a good analogy with the game of chess.

35.8 THE END GAME

In chess, there is the opening, the middle game and the end game. The opening is very important and they have been categorized. Then there's the middle game in which pieces are lost one by one until both sides have only a few pieces left. The rest is the endgame, which determines the winner. The genius of grandmaster players is often their ability to strategize an endgame.

The same is the case for the connection between men and women in the new era. In order to be successful, men allow women slated for conquest to completely control the opening. In fact, they pretty much grovel in the dirt. Women can be as nasty, aggressive and mean as they please. They can demand total adherence to the script, which is a dumb dog on the end of a leash. And the man is using all his brain-power to concentrate on what will get the girl and nothing else. They obey orders, lose all sense of pride, and succumb to every detail demanded of them. But with all the energy in the bottom of their brains, women can't abstract into time, which is a very advanced human capability. They don't see that men completely control the endgame, which is the longest part of relationships. In fact, with no responsibility for what they do, men can concentrate on perfecting their openings to achieve the short-term goal of conquest. The middle game proceeds quickly and then the long endgame in which they are in complete control.

Men even talk about feelings. Of course, the feelings they talk about are the feelings they are *supposed* to have. The liberated woman is not going to be turned on by real feelings since many of them are associated with weaknesses of various kinds, which is a total turn-off to Neanderthal woman. It was in the interests of females in evolutionary times to have functioning, fighting, hunting and protecting males. A sign of involvement in these aggressive behaviors is physical injury. Men don't understand this. This is why when a man gets injured, he tries to cover it up. He thinks it's a sign of weakness that he doesn't want women to see. He doesn't realize that physical injury is a sign that he has been doing his job of hunting and protecting. This is a turn-on to females. This is why females are attracted to nursing and why they rarely abandon a physically injured man.

But *emotional* injury is very different. An emotionally incapacitated male is of no use in meeting any of the needs of keeping babies alive and genes propagating. The feelings script is just another training device to turn a man into a dog on the end of a leash. Men even learned to cry on demand. But any man with an ounce of knowledge about women knows that real tears will get you the gate accompanied by the emotion of disgust. Through millions of years of evolution, females got wired to be attracted to the *functioning* male. And he can't function if he's all curled up in the corner mourning his sad life. But if tears were the new requirement as one more training device, they could learn to produce them too and on demand.

Also, men must completely clean out their lives of any trace of other women because the women who have picked them have the concept of the man in the bottom of their brains, which means they're in ownership and control mode. To satisfy the bottom of their brains, every detail must be in order. To use our above metaphor, she wants a man that exactly fits the missing piece of her life's puzzle. If there is the slightest misshape of the puzzle piece, the man will be expelled.

Almost overnight, it appeared that men in every corner of the country turned on a dime. There would be a whole new vocabulary. Their ants and bees talk was squeaky clean with political correctness. No more sexist talk. No more talk about marriage and kids; only about careers. They learned whole libber scripts and memorized volumes of victim statistics. The new conversation was simple and harmless to the inner brain of the liberated woman. Of course, this was easy since men never at any time projected much meaning to the words they say. They don't use one word, one phrases, one sentence that could cast aspersions on women or ruffle their inner brains. Their ants and bees talk involve agreeing with everything the woman said. Of course, the liberated woman understands none of this. All the liberation in the world is not going to change millions of years of evolution. Women are still using words as the means of creating representations of reality. If it were different, the women's movement would never have gotten off the ground in the first place. One problem however, is that the liberated woman has no feedback to what she says.

In the old days, there was little sex. So a guy realizing he wasn't going to get laid no matter what he said, could be more natural and more objective about his views, opinions, and beliefs. You could treat women as persons and not as gender-carriers. You could disagree with a woman just like you could disagree with a man. Of course, without the sex card, women did the best they could and didn't reject new facts or evidence that might conflict with their opinions. This provided feedback to women so their views and opinions couldn't drift into no-man's land.

There is an analogy with the hearing-impaired. Over time, pronunciations gradually drift away until they cannot be understood. The label of deaf and dumb was not a nice phrase. It indicated that the hearing-impaired person could not speak. Today, there are schools where teachers provide *feedback*. Through instruction for the proper positioning of lips and tongue, they can keep the hearing-impaired on course with near correct pronunciations. They now have two languages, which some research has shown enables the brain to stay alive longer.

The liberated woman gets no feedback to what she is saying or wanting or believing. Men's agenda is to get laid, not to provide intelligent feedback. She can drift away saying into believing the most outrageous things, and there's no feedback to keep her on course. So they can clamp down with a very strict script that men must adhere to if they want to get laid, which is always held out as the carrot as the liberated woman has presented herself as a raving nymphomaniac. And of course, since men have long-since lost any respect they may have had in the past for women, they don't really care what the script says.

But it's worse than this. By never getting corrected or never presented with anything that might conflict with their ridiculous beliefs and opinions, the liberated woman gets the impression that she's well-informed and a genius. She's never wrong. She doesn't have to think, study, ask questions, or strain her brain in any way. The result is gradual loss of brain neurons so that by the time she's in her 40s there's very little existential brain left. But the liberated woman just itching for sex doesn't have to worry about feedback: men will read their scripts to a T.

There is one disadvantage to women controlling the opening: men don't get to pick. As a result, men don't get to marry the woman of their choice with a large momentum vector like in the post-WWII generations — one that enabled women to rule the roost with a husband dedicated to serving his family and holding on to his prized wife. Now they are constrained to women who pick them. This probably goes against evolution as well. In evolutionary times, when a male was being chased it was often by a dangerous animal and he had a good chance of dying. This might be why men are averse to being chased. But what good does picking do women? All it does is make life quite easy for men. No more work, no more courtship, no more chivalry. Just see which vaginas pick them and read the script. This is how the midgame goes.

But during the long endgame, without a strong momentum vector, the man will just relax into a half-negligent mode at best and an abuse mode at worst. As libbers gradually washed away the old culture, men were able to rid themselves of any degree of responsibility for what they do, unless they feel like it, which happens during the opening, but often fades during the endgame. Many studies show that 75% of men cheat on their wives. You add to this the fact that the libbers have completely destroyed marriage and family as a source of identity in men, and you have a pretty motley population of husbands. Why should they care about and put effort into something that adds nothing to their identity and sense of self?

There are billions of words in millions of sentences in thousands of books and magazine articles produced in prodigious quantities by various libbers that I've read. But only once in a great while a little stem pops up through the blanket of libber propaganda everywhere we look that describes reality. In a book review, Gayle Green quotes Lillian Rubin with a testimonial of what one women thought of liberation. "When I come home from work… and the house looks like a disaster area, I could kill him, not screw him" …"these guys are oh so liberated, but it's all words, nothing but words"… "I hate to say it, but woman's lib has really screwed things up". Wendy Shakit says in *Return to Modesty*, "…a lot of young women are trying to tell us that they are unhappy; unhappy with …their sexual encounters, with the way men treat them". This describes the real world of women's liberation.

What is interesting is that the pre-liberated woman understood all this — they may have had a kind of system mind. It sure looks that way. They attended to every detail that was in their interests. First of all, the pre-liberated woman before 1976 had a working existential brain which enabled her to have a time concept. I remember my x-wife being in a lot less of a hurry for sex that I was saying that there is just a brief period of time when she could be coy and unattainable. After that I would be in the driver's seat for the rest of our lives. Pre-liberated women had an instinct that men control the end game and to optimize their fate during the long endgame, women realized it was best to treat men with tender lovin' care, gentleness and consideration during the brief opening to set the example. The liberated woman has no such understanding because without a frontal cortex, she has no time concept and no awareness of an endgame.

Because of previous stereotypes, women still hadn't achieved equal status in the eyes of society. However, by the time we get to the civil rights movement of the '60s, women had secured all the rights men had. They had equal access to education, jobs and professions. This turned out to be an optimal combination. Young women were told in many quarters that they were inferior and yet had the opportunities to show they weren't. So they studied, they got degrees, they thought, they asked questions, and they learned whatever they could any way they could. They were curious about the detail of the world. These women were as an advanced human being as had ever existed. Men conceptualized young women as *special*. The comparison with today's world is startling, where we find no chivalry, no courtship, no pursuit, no energy. Young men wander around like dogs in the neighborhood they're supposed to be, totally oblivious of the needs of young women, unless they find one they temporarily want and go into conquest mode.

The opening among pre-libber generations was attractive enough for young men that they not only courted and pursued, but they were anxious to marry the young women of the day because they were special and easy to fall in love with. And many of those marriages lasted a lifetime. People ought to take photos of these 85 year-olds still married. They would be like photos of dinosaurs. In pre-libber days, men could have abandoned their wives for a young chick. Some did of course because it is a great temptation. But most stayed in their marriages even though wives lost more market value than their husbands. The reason is back to *respect*. Men respected women for doing the best they could. They learned as much as they could, they were competent home managers and mothers and they retained bright, cheerful personalities their entire lives. Compare this with the snarling, rasping, brusk, indifferent, and dismissive no-nothing libbers men had to deal with in the '80s and '90s. This is why their relationships last a matter of months. If men are going to have to put up with these libbers, at least they want to trade in the vagina once in a while for a new one.

And most importantly, women just plain liked men in the pre-libber generations. And it certainly made an impression on men during the opening. When I was in grad school, we used to have spaghetti and dissert parties. Young women were anxious to come see us. These were not sex parties, but just social get-togethers. The young women of the day thought we were cool; they liked spending time with us, and thought males were fascinating creatures. They just plain liked us. Compare with now where after 30 years of continual man-bashing from a handful of libber leaders, today's liberated woman doesn't really like men. I have communicated with hundreds of liberated women. You can call a woman that you met a while back just to have a friendly conversation maybe get some dinner or coffee. It may be someone you didn't follow up with or someone who wasn't interested in me. In the vast majority of cases, there's nothing much going on in their lives. But once it's determined by the vagina that you don't fit into the puzzle, that's the end of it forever. She is too busy to bother with friendship like men have; she does not want intelligent conversation; she does not want intimate communication; she only wants a dumb dog roaming the neighborhood that fits snugly into her life's puzzle, and nothing more. And she thinks men are too stupid to see that she really has no other use for them, and yet expects long-term relationships being served loyally and faithfully till death do them part. The liberated woman is delusional.

In pre-libber days, I ran into high school grads who were delightful to be with. They did some reading, they paid attention to the detail of the world and they asked questions. They did the best they could. Their brains weren't clogged up by all kinds of *form* thoughts like, do I want to screw this guy, who's doing the talking, who's asking the questions, who has more to learn, are men smarter than women, am I being oppressed. They engaged in normal conversation without regard to who had what between their legs. Contrast that with these libbers whose brains are so clogged up with peripheral *form* garbage that they are unable to engage in normal conversation concerning *content*.

I have to relate an experience in this regard. When I was in grad school, I was lucky to have a friend who happened to work in the administration office of a quality women's college. She snuck out a copy of the mugbook for me to peruse for each class of women coming into the college. Well, I would just pick the nicer looking ones, not having anything else to go on. I would call and say that I had gotten their names from someone close by after a Sunday dinner. Well pre-libber women had enough of an existential brain to realize that if you have a male at hand who seems interested, you check him out. So I always got into great conversations with these girls. I was pretty well-educated by the time I was in grad school, so no matter what they were majoring in, I could converse about it fairly intelligently. In their conversation, they could concentrate on *content*, and not have to worry about *form*. They weren't worried about who knew more or if they asked a question, they would feel oppressed. Conversations with them were like you might have with any intelligent person irrelevant of gender.

Anyway, I kept track of the girls I talked to in this way on little cards. Well, the result is that I called 147 consecutive young women over a 6 year period and talked at length with them. In those days, if a man made one sentence that was original, complex, provocative or interesting in any way, he got a date. I got a date for coffee with *every one* of them. Now, of course, when we met, some liked me, and others not. I had my preferences too. Their policy was that if a reasonable man is interested, check him out. This is not rocket science. But it is beyond the cognitive abilities of the liberated ninny. If she is in a bad mood, or just got dumped by a jerk her vagina picked, or was executing the man-bashing program chief libbers had programmed into her, she would bark that she wasn't interested; or she didn't talk to strangers. Often they would slam down the phone.

The latest craze is for libbers to write learned books about how gender is "socially constructed". You wouldn't believe the semi-conscious word-mongering in these books. The reality is that pre-libber people had only *role* assignments based on gender. So young men *behaved* differently towards women because of different roles, but did not conceptualize them as *essentially* different. There was very little *identity* gender. People's *identities* were defined by their existential qualities: skills, accomplishments, intelligence, perceptiveness, talents, education, social abilities, personalities, etc., all of which has nothing to do with gender. But under the veneer of superficial behavioral equality, the women's movement actually allowed and encouraged men to conceptualize women *essentially*, as a separate species inherently different. This only encourages a new kind of sexism not based on cultural rules of interaction and overt behavior, but on the basis of *essential* differences. It doesn't show up in superficial behavior, but it certainly shows up in the endgame. Unless a man conceptualizes women as creatures who are essentially *special* in some way, he will never make a very good or lasting companion. But that is the exact goal of the system mind.

The irony is that this "socially constructed" gender they piss and moan about *was exactly what was created by these very same libbers. They* are the ones who began defining people on the basis of gender, making a big deal out of *womanhood*. They coerced women into conceptualizing themselves at the bottom of the brain where sexual identity, mating stances, sex and reproduction all lie. The thinking of the liberated woman revolves entirely around the vagina. If you don't believe this, read women's magazines from the past. This "socially constructed" *identity* gender quickly replaced very innocuous *role* gender and has clogged up interaction between men and women to where it's a strain to even interact with each other.

35.9 THE STEPFORD SINGLE

The unmarried liberated woman is the perfect *Stepford* single. They have no real emotions. They are always happy. Happy, happy, happy — just like citizens of *Brave New World*. They are optimistic: Mr. Right is going to come along; it's just a matter of time. They love their job. They love their dog. They love their friends and family. When you bump into them in the elevator, they don't say, excuse me; they say, "I love my dog', "I love my job". And what do they like about their jobs? They involve incredible minutia and mindless procedures that fit perfectly with their finite state computational brains. It's such a great fit that they put in 12 hour days, 6 days a week; and the 7th is spent buying the junk the system is peddling.

Stephanie Coontz says that "consumerism was not spread by the liberation movements of women...." In fact, it "...has generally *opposed* consumerism".[31] Although it didn't *initiate* consumerism, it clearly welcomed it with open arms. The proof is that they can charge three times as much for women's shoes with three times less materials. If you price products, you'll see every woman's product is twice as expensive as an analogous product for men. The reason is the liberated woman can't see the *detail* of what she's buying. It's only words that count, and if the shoe has the name of some gay Italian on it, she'll pay three times as much.

In their private social lives, their talk is an exact copy of one another. In their profiles on the internet, they all say the exact same things: I have a sense of humor, I love to travel, I love wine. And speaking of traveling you might think that these women had valuable insights from all their traveling. We know about Alexis de Tocqueville, the most famous travel writer of all time. He was a French aristocrat who came to the US in the 1800s and traveled around the country. His books are famous for the insights he had about the new country, its people and its character. You won't get anything like this from the liberated woman. The reason is obvious. Without an existential brain, there is no meaning to project to the sense data they see in their travels. All they see are colors and shapes. Oh! And tastes. When they talk to brain-dead men about their travels, the conversation consists of name-dropping of the places they visited. The deepest the conversation ever gets is to talk about what they ate in a particular place. And yes, the wine they drank.

Among the thousands of liberated women I met in the past 15 years, and thousands of hours of conversation, *I never heard one sentence from one libber that showed any degree of perceptiveness, abstraction, insight or originality about the people they saw all over the world.* Now I can call up my x-wife and various girlfriends I had in the pre-libber days and get an education on some topic with plenty of interesting sentences including their own theories. But all you get from the liberated women is ants and bees talk or empty stares.

The liberated woman is the dumbest, rudest, most unconscious, least educated, least knowledgeable ninny to come on the human scene in approximately 65 thousand years. This is exactly the goal of the system mind: to make women as unattractive and undesirable as possible. And it shows up in national statistics. Whereas women from the pre-libber generations got married like water falling over Niagara, as we mentioned, among professional women in the liberated generations, only about one out of a *hundred* unmarried professional women over 40 ever gets married. Then they complain about commitment. Who in their right mind is going to spend the rest of his life with a lot of (bad) form and absolutely no content.

The liberated woman is a Stepford single work slave designed to the exact specifications of the system mind. When the woman's movement started, we were promised *greatness*. There were periods in history when there was great art, great science, great literature, etc. But if we look around in modern times, where is the greatness? Where are the great architects, great literary figures, great classical music composers, great artists, etc. Both genders are producing people with stratospheric IQs who can do excellent work as engineers, doctors, lawyers, information technology gurus, etc. But most of the work in these professions requires only a high-IQ computational brain.

Greatness requires the use of the existential brain and since kids' brains are fried by motion, we are getting less and less greatness out of people. Now we're not getting any greatness out of men either for the above-mentioned reasons. However, the women's movement promised to transcend social trends and give a dazzling display of greatness. Well, where is it? Even social consciousness is gone? In the '60s, when young women perceived the perfidy and mendacity surrounding the Vietnam war, the message in those days sent to young men was, "if you wanna get laid, you better come to the protest march". In this way, men who make a more robust impression, got into the anti-war movement, all of which ended the war in Vietnam.

Where were the libbers during the Iraq invasion and conquest? I'll tell you where. Instead of being on their *feet* protesting the unconstitutional invasion of Iraq, they were on their *backs* "expressing their sexuality". Aside from that, they were sending their boyfriends away to Iraq to get their arms and legs blown off to spruce up the sex lives of the people who sent them there. Now libbers are writing books to brag that women are just as good as men at going half-war around the world to kill people. That's what we got out of Women's Lib.

In the intellectual sphere, whenever I run across anything women did that approaches the level of real greatness, I find it's a pre-libber woman. It is interesting to compare generations. In pre-libber times, in the area of physics, we had Madam Curie who is the mother of modern physics because she was the first to speculate about the subatomic level. In the field of anthropology, we got Margaret Meade who is the mother of modern anthropology. She wasn't always right, but she was still a pioneer. In the field of primatology, there is Jane Goodall, again a pioneer in her field. Then we have Annette Karmiloff-Smith in cognitive philosophy, whose work is greatly underrated. In the most important fields affecting our very lives and our future as a viable form of life on earth are environmentalism, health and urbanization. Here again we find Rachel Carson who got the whole modern environmental movement going with her famous book, *Silent Spring*. Then there's Sara Josephine Baker, who pioneered the modern health agency.[32] She saved the lives of thousands of children from sure death in the unsanitary conditions of overcrowded urban life. We have Jane Jacobs another pioneer in the field of urban planning and urban life. She devoted her life to try to stop the outright theft of people's property by male judicial vampires to give to people who destroyed the organic growth of cities with their meaningless buildings. These eyesore beehives are already falling apart. *There isn't one woman from the liberated generations even close to the stature of these women.*

In the field of literature, where we once had Susan Sontag, and Hannah Arendt, now we have the ninnies that wrote the "*Rules*". Sontag was an amazing women not only in her literary life but her private life as well.[33] In fact, Elaine Showalter, in her book, *The Jury of Her Peers*, shows that in the mid-19th century, the literary marketplace was more dominated by women writers than any period since then. In entertainment, where we once had Billy Holliday, Ella Fitzgerald and Sarah Vaughan, we now have Britney Spears. Even in the less serious field of sex icon, there's no comparison. Where we once had Mae West and Marilyn Monroe, two very classy women, we now have Anna Nicole Smith, one of the most disgusting sows to ever waddle down the pike.

When we come to national leadership in politics, we once had Eleanor Roosevelt, Madeleine Albright and even Nancy Pelosi. Regardless of their politics, they are competent. In terms of mankind's progress and improvement, especially minorities, Eleanor Roosevelt was the greatest figure of the 20th century. But what do we get from the libber generations? We get Ann Coulter and Condoleezza Rice, who, in my opinion, joined up with paid killers to go halfway around to the world to kill people, including children who females are supposed to nurture and applaud neoconservative reptiles who climb in bed with Washington politicos in a big Corporate Socialist gang-bang enabling them to steal *trillions* from the middle class and from *children* who can't defend themselves with the vote. All to puff up profits of their heroes on Wall Street. Oh! I almost forgot Michelle Bachman, who wants to cut EPA funds so we get more pollution causing another massive increase in birth defects in children. Where's the greatness, or even a semblance of nurturance?

35.10 LIZZY AFTER 50.

Well, Lizzy is now 53, and the bell doesn't ring anymore. Our culture depreciates anything old, especially people. She will spend the rest of her life basically alone. And that's if she's lucky. With current trends in unemployment, Lizzy could very well wind up getting thrown in the street at the age of 52 to be replaced by a younger worker who is paid less. But even if she keeps her finite state job until retirement, what will represent a lifetime of work? A gold watch, which, exactly represents all the meaning Lizzy has accrued over her life of modern work slave.

But this reality has no impact on libber Lizzy because regardless of her actual situation, she has a constant chorus of leading libbers telling her that her life is wonderful. And words mean more to the liberated woman than perceptions of reality. Let's look at what Katha Pollitt says: "There has never been a better time in all world history to be a 53-year old single women looking for romance." [34] See, presto chango. But let's look at the *reality* of the typical 53-year old single woman, instead of a libber leader's empty words.

First of all, she probably isn't a chief libber for a national magazine. I'm sure Katha Pollitt can have a fling whenever she wants simply by going to a New York party filled with neoliberals blowing smoke up each other's butts about how great they are and discussing the next scheme to stick it in the face of the average American. Of course, there will be nobody at these parties to remind them of their total political impotence and how the political landscape created by 35 years of neoconservative dominance has made real liberalism almost dead and rendered their hero in the White House a zombie with a completely neoconservative agenda.

Our 53 year-old has a "career" life of a mind-numbing job shuffling papers working 10 hours a day. Not that this is bad. With only the computational brain left that still functions, she "loves her job" (and her dog), and will love the minutia of the finite state jobs that our future economy will create. I've had many occasions to talk to tons of these "single 53-year old" liberated women. Except for a rare exception, they are mostly Stepford singles. They have manufactured emotions and finite state brains capable of nothing more than ants and bees talk.

But what is the reality of the *private* life of Pollitt's 53 year-old? Well there's absolutely nothing going on. Now that she is subconsciously aware that nobody wants her, she is going to really kick ass. The few stragglers who might enquire about Lizzy on the internet are dismissed, humiliated and rejected with even greater gusto, unless it's another piss pot Pete, who is now looking for a younger woman. She thinks she's punishing mankind, being unaware of the fact that men on the internet are not going to be disturbed one iota being rejected by the kind of old crab mindless ninny Lizzy has made herself into. The last time Lizzy got laid was five years ago when a piss pot Pete entered her life. It lasted for about 4 months until he wearied of her mindless ants and bees talk and drifted away. Five years before that, she had a relationship that got abusive within a few months, and it took her a few years to extract herself from that. That's it for the last 10 years, although there may have been one more piss pot Pete thrown in. I've talked to women who hear women's stories of where there was nothing in the past 10 years. As one very down-to-earth woman I met for coffee said, "after 50, you become invisible". Of course, if this woman were plugged in to the *words* of libber Katha Pollitt, she would think her life was filled to the brim with suitors.

But it's even worse. For 35 years now, leading libbers have complained about "exploitation". Women were "chained" to these male-dominated marriages, "bored and uninstructed". Exploitation is an interesting concept. We have to distinguish *physical* exploitation from *mental* exploitation. If you control only the body, the person will try to escape, as did Southern slaves when the Civil War started and tried to join northern armies. This was *physical* exploitation. But they weren't *mentally* exploited, which is worse: you're not totally human, but a mindless robot puppet manipulated by others. You don't even know your own interests and will not even listen to parties trying to improve your lot.

Because of libber leader's propaganda, we now have Pollitt's 53-year old liberated woman, having no workable existential brain, stupid, mean-spirited, and looking in every nook and cranny for victimhood she can bitch about — we have this pathetic creature perfectly happy with her 10-hour a day, mindless computer-pecking job. Once a week, she gets together with cackling friends for dinner. With their finite state computational brains, the only things to talk about are their mind-numbing jobs (which they all love). They complain about the dearth of quality men. Why can't they find an equal, which means equal in age since that is the only variable vaginas care about. She is happy. Robots are happy too: you just program them that way. She delights in articles in magazines that glorify the single life. She is a complete clone of the system mind in every detail. She will continue this state of mind right into the back room of the nursing home with a constant need of a diaper change. Is there worse exploitation?

In the meantime, the 53-year old traditional wife and mother has been living a reasonably comfortable suburban life raising her kids and following some of her interests and hobbies. What Pollitt calls exploitation has produced some meaning in this woman's life. She has someone who loves her, even if only marginally in some cases. She got to watch the slow development into an adult human being from a little sack of chemicals which provides a great deal of meaning to her life. She had the opportunity for many interesting endeavors at home like my mother engaged in. And she had kids who in the last third of her life might be a source of comfort, help and companionship. She knew a number of other married people, friends and relatives that she and her family would visit.

I remember as a kid, Sunday afternoons with my overweight, but fantastic cook, aunt. There would be kids playing, people cooking very delicious home-made Italian meals with boiling pasta fogging-up the windows. There was interesting conversation that wasn't impeded by everyone being constantly alert as to who had what between their legs. There would be kids whose parents had the opportunity to see every step of their development into adults. There is meaning in all this, infinite state meaning as opposed to the finite state goings on in Lizzy's computer-pecking job, cell-phone and her version of doghood, which is some mutilated breed. When one of her kids has a baby, our traditional mother gets to see motherhood all over again with a grandchild. Now, there is twice the chance that she will have company and help as she enters old age and she will have real people with real lives to keep track of.

Of course, you will never anywhere in the popular mass magazines see an article glorifying this woman's life. However, since men are totally out of control because of any semblance of an example to follow, maybe our 53-year old is just as well off as the traditional mother. Besides, her finite state brain doesn't need all the complexity involved with having a family. All she needs for her finite state job is her computational brain. It's pretty easy to get through the first two thirds of life without a significant other. What about the last third between 60 and 90? It is the last third of our lives that the differences really show up, and we have yet to see that last third of Pollitt's 53 year-old's life.

I've had occasion to see over and over, when people get old and their brains began to shrink, what they need is someone who cares about them and provides a modicum of companionship. And even people whose marriages weren't good can have some semblance of a normal life in the last third of their lives if they have a companion they've been with for 40 or 50 years. There wouldn't be a couple in the world more incompatible than my parents, but in the last third of their lives, which is a long time, they had someone who cared about them and kept them company even if only meagerly. When Pollitt's 53 year-old liberated woman looks back on her life, what will she have to show for it? No marriage, ephemeral love, spotty companionship, no family— just the almighty job consisting of a very long string of 0s and 1s. What will occupy her emotions and thoughts, especially her hopes? Where will meaning come from? Of course, with only a computational brain left, there really is no place for meaning to be. We have yet to see the dementia and barrenness of the liberated generations when they get to the last third of their lives. Sociologists are going to have a field day. To me, this is *real* exploitation.

My family got to know the people running my parent's assisted living home because they had children and grandchildren and someone was coming to visit them every day. On holidays and many Sunday's, we would take them to a sibling's house for dinner. They were all shriveled up now and not saying much. Even my very bright mother who used to incite very interesting conversations was getting somewhat quiet. But as they looked over the 20-foot table they could see teachers, artists, musicians, doctors, economists, engineers, consultants, and Wall St. millionaires. There were many bachelor degrees, a number of Master's degrees and Phd's. There were life's accomplishments all around the table. And even though they had no formal education at all, they could look over this whole spread and say to themselves, "we are responsible for every single thing that ever happened with people around this table". That is infinite state meaning.

Compare this to where will Lizzy will wind up, which is in the back room of the local nursing home drooling from her mouth and peeing in her pants, whom nobody ever goes to see especially the way we are raising young people. People who ran my parents place saw that a substantial number of people in the home never had anyone come to visit. That was one of the most eye-catching trends in modern society. The reason is that by maintaining a constant supply of unemployed workers, the system can induce people to take jobs all over the country. Lizzy used to brag about nieces and nephews. But they are now living far and wide, in no position to visit Lizzy. The purpose of course is to fragment and scatter families and friends because they are distractions from those almighty jobs.

Oh, but wait. There is a savior coming on line that will save the day. Within 20 years there will be robots that can completely replace everything the older liberated women conceives as being essential to being a human being. Computer chips are getting beyond what anyone in my generation ever dreamed of. They will make a robot that could engage successfully in any kind of conversation libbers are capable of with only their computational brains left. After all, that's exactly what the robot has: a computational brain. It will have more than enough capacity to engage in the liberated woman's ants and bees talk and will be better companions than their demented woman friends. The robot can even fake emotions every bit as well as piss pot Pete with the appropriate words and facial expressions.

There will even be a choice of personalities. There will be talkative robots, quiet robots, funny robots, enthusiastic robots. There will even be robots to write women's liberation books at less expense to the publishers. Now it will take longer to build a robot whom she can cuddle up with in bed. But she has a dog or two for that anyway. For a little more money, there will be rent-a-man agencies where high-earning liberated women can rent a nice man who assumes the role of dog on the end of a leash. All she has to do is provide some food, a mat and a litter box.

Lizzy doesn't know it (because Lizzy doesn't much of anything), but *she has been programmed from her earliest days by the system mind to lead the exact life she has led and to wind up in the exact position she's in.* Libber leaders really don't like women as a species. They identify only with the top 1% of women who are CEOs, business owners and bosses who are the only ones who really count. They bitch about the "glass ceiling" the 1% are up against. They will never say one word about the concrete floor *90%* of women are up against. Their job in pimping for the system is to create a docile, mindless, slave workforce to puff up profits of the top 1% they identify with; someone who lacks any semblance of an existential brain; someone who knows nothing but thinks she knows everything;

someone who nobody will ever want so that the center of her private live is the almighty 10-hour day hotel cleaner, chained-up computer pecker and fish head chopper who "loves her job". It took men struggling against the system 150 years of union organizing, getting beat up, shot at, fired, and deported, to finally win the 8-hour day in the 1930s. Women's liberation comes along and within a few years we're back to the same 10-12 hour day that existed in the 1800s.

One more thing. Recall we discussed the *homeostasis* of the mind in Sect. 22.2. This is where the mind is designed to seek a steady-state equilibrium. When people have highs due to fortuitous events, their happiness is always dragged down after a while to an equilibrium state. The other side of the coin is that after horrible losses, the mind has a way to pick itself up and ascend back up to this steady state. Because of the great losses women suffered throughout evolutionary history, homeostasis of the mind is especially pronounced in women. This is why it almost doesn't matter how they run their lives. Women are so resilient that they are almost as well off in a great situation as in a bad one. No matter what they do, they always seem to bounce back to an equilibrium steady mental state of manufactured happiness. Being demented and not seeing reality, they're probably just as well off as married women with their brain dead old husbands. The purpose of this chapter is not to push some kind of life for women, or whether the lives they now lead are an improvement. My only aim was to show that Lizzy will lead the *exact* life that the system mind has programmed her for right to the very end. You make the call.

35.11 GENDER PROSPECTS

All market economies rely on selling goods and services and they always deteriorate into an economic imbalance that doesn't send sufficient income to the bottom 80% to clear markets. To sell what it can, the system must have competitive prices. And the way to reduce prices is to get as much work for as little pay as possible, which means a work force consisting of single-minded 12 hour-a-day work slaves whose lives consist of almost nothing but their jobs: no distractions from the almighty job — like friendships, relationships and above all, marriages. This in turn implies severing all meaningful ties with other human beings especially those of the opposite sex. And the way to achieve this result is to have men and women conceptualizing each other in the bottom of their brains, where most of the primitive emotions of aggressiveness, stubbornness and fear reside. This leads to behavior centered around conquest and control as opposed to existential love, because inner brain thinking is lumpy, coarse, finite state and devoid of meaning. The way to do this is to encourage anger and aggression motivated by victimhood of all kinds; and to encourage thinking related to sex, sexual roles and practices.

Depriving the existential brain of energy insures that women's behavior will be as incompetent, inconsistent and stupid as possible, making them quite unattractive to men, as well as turning men into tough, rude, inconsiderate, unreliable and negligent partners. This results in short, incompatible relationships devoid of meaning. It would also prevent women from their important social role of setting the example not only for men but for children and friends.

Now, the emphasis on career has improved the public lives of women at the top of the career ladder. Of course, this was the work of 150 years of true feminism culminating in the civil rights laws of the 1960s that gave women equal rights. This progress had nothing to do with the Women's Liberation movement that probably actually retarded progress in the career area by turning many women into slave-driving bosses and insufferable co-workers. But realize this. The system mind is not inherently sexist. It doesn't care what's between people's legs. In fact, it actually *coerced* women into "careers" because it needs to establish the "career" as the sole source of identity especially in men. The system mind has nothing against whatever benefits women as long as it benefits itself first.

In the future, the system mind will continue to pare away any historical means men had for forming a solid reliable identity. One of the main contributors to identity in the past was a strong sense of *self*. Recall in Sect. 16.7, we defined the *self* as all the experiences that left representations in the mind/brain. The self is a big part of our identities because it contains our past experiences, which is really our personal histories. Of course, the history that contributes the most infinite state meaning is the result of having people in our lives that we know well and have experiences with. This contributes to our concept of our self, and consequently to our identities. This can happen with only a limited number of other persons. There were true friends when we lived in villages where the contact was slow, steady, constant, deep, and extended over long periods of time. Only in this way did infinite state meaning accrue. With more meaning in their experiences, there was more meaning in the representations that make up the self. This enables the identity formed around this self to be more meaningful and stronger. It is a strong identity that enables men to have the constancy, reliability, and sense of direction that women need. Modern social media talks about "friends". This is a joke. There is almost no meaning at all with today's internet "friends".

Since the self is an accumulation over time of represented experiences, the system mind will continue to try to erase any indications of time passing which entails destroying people's past. One of the first habits our early ancestors got into after the evolution of the time concept, was to use this concept to talk about the past. All early tribes of people were discovered spending a lot of their conversation about the past and many of their rituals and beliefs involved the history of themselves as a people and their great leaders and heroes from the past.

One of the major means the system mind has to erase the past is to destroy meaningful vestiges of the past. This especially includes great old architecture, which we see constantly being torn down and replaced by meaningless beehives with no evidence of human involvement. Even in our public dialog, the system mind media outlets never say a word about history or the past. You get some on the history channel, but you rarely hear a word from the system's propaganda outlets about anything historical.

The system does all it can to depreciate anything old to be replaced by the newest junk in the present. To clear markets, the system must encourage a throw-away society and this attitude invades personal relationships as well. You throw away the old girlfriend and get a new one. You throw away the old wife and get a new one. And by coincidence, this is exactly the modus vivendi of prehistoric males. Once early males planted their seed, it's on to the next one. It was *females* with babies to feed and protect for a reasonable period of time who guided culture so as to interject permanency into human relationships. The bottom line is that the needs of the system just happen to fit with the goals of *males* and not with the basic goals and needs of females. This is not a conspiracy against women, but simply the luck of the draw.

Another very important element in men's identity in the past was through cultural means that valued various skills and relations with worldly artifacts. Objects are reality and the history of objects is evidence of human executed skills in the past. It is by executing skills in manipulating, creating, and fashioning real objects that there would be tangible evidence of a man's existence and a strong contributor to male identity. Before the Civil War when most life was either rural or village, men could point to the houses they built or the furniture they made or any other lasting objects that they exhibited skill in making. Compare that with today's myriad of office jobs. At the end of a year or even of a working life, what does the average worker have to show for his or her labor? Nothing but a long string of 0s and 1s. Again, we see a vacuum in men's identities that was once filled by human skills is now filled by the almighty computer-pecking job which is the final goal of the system mind. And as our job identity grows, our personal identity and our home identity shrinks, until there is very little identity left other than the almighty job.

In modern times men have very fragile identities which means weak circuitry in the frontal cortex that can absorb the lurches and plunges caused by catastrophe theory in the bottom of the brains. They are here, they are there with a moment's notice. They are madly in love, then on a dime, they don't care, or they're off with another woman. They are friendly but in a moment they can betray their so-called friends. Their brains are on a knife-edge that easily leads to peculiarities and bad habits. This is an impossible situation for women, whose most important need is for constancy and reliability. Without a strong sense of identity, men make poor companions and negligent husbands. This is the exact goal of the system mind.

And to make sure that our lives consist only in the present, the system mind even tries to remove the future. It does this by making the future unpredictable. For tens of thousands of years, human males had the role of "breadwinner". This was a major source of identity. But even breadwinning jobs have no permanency. The average length of a job now is less than 4 years. First the system makes our identity consist solely of the almighty job, then it turns around and makes that very job as tenuous and unpredictable as possible. Men are under constant threat of losing their identities by losing their jobs and businesses.

Women have less of a problem in this respect. No matter how much equality we get, there will never be as much pressure on women to be "breadwinners". The fact that women make less money where that's the case means only that women can buy less junk they don't need. I've never heard of a woman suffering intense psychological damage and identity problems because she makes a few bucks less. In fact, *highly* paid women who lack motherhood or femininity have more identity problems than many women at the bottom of the economic ladder where most poor women have it together enough to hold down jobs, raise their kids and keep a roof over their heads. Motherhood and femininity is their source of identity, not the paycheck.

However, men at the bottom lead lives that are a total mess. When a man is told by society that he isn't an adequate breadwinner, he loses a major source of identity. This leads to identity fragmentation and all kinds of personal dysfunction. They become depressed and turn to alcohol, drugs, and gambling, ruining their lives as well as the lives of their families. The vast majority of homeless men are there because they could not keep up with society's criterion for a "breadwinner".

All of these societal trends were encouraged and coerced by a women's movement that the system mind fashioned by piggy-backing on 150 years of feminism. I would say that the Women's Liberation movement was the most successful social movement in the history of mankind. There is no better evidence of a system mind than the emergence of a women's movement that achieved every single goal of our economic and political system. The great success of the women's movement of the '80s and '90s has been completed. There is no need for further stridency from leading libbers. We don't hear much of the old rhetoric anymore.

In 20 years or less the system mind can declare total victory. First of all, there won't be marriages, except among gays. Right now, half of adults are single and a third of adults have never been married. The libber movement wants people's personal lives to be totally devoid of anything meaningful, leaving all waking hours available for the almighty job. We have home computers and cell phones to keep people in constant touch with their jobs. Good marriages tend to motivate people to get home to their families. The system does everything it can to remove family as a source of identity. If we have man-woman relationships at all in the future, it will be a bunch of Neanderthals interacting with a bunch of automatons.

The system mind will have so depreciated and demeaned motherhood and by implication, parenthood, that parenting will not be a source of identity for men or women. Women at least have some instinct to take care of their babies. Males have no such instinct, and with the constant drumbeat by leading libbers depreciating parenthood and families for 35 years, there will be no contribution to identity in men by being a parent. Whatever new people we get will come as a result of women visiting the local sperm bank. They will live in building complexes and with the help of Johnson's "professionals", will raise each other's kids. Men will hang out in local bars, massage parlors, and internet pornography sites, with no responsibilities at all. There will be nothing important to distract from the almighty 10 hour-a-day job as the sole source of identity. Men might participate in children's lives, but only periodically when they feel like it. The lack of identity development in young boys will make them perfect targets for the current king's murderous war.

Some libbers come right out for this state of affairs. One of them doesn't even like the idea of families. Stephanie Coontz wants communities to raise kids. [35] Another one, Elinor Burkett is against families and people with children getting privileges.[36] (I might add that when this libber is old and shriveled up in bed all alone in the back room of some nursing home drooling from her mouth and peeing in her pants, it will be a young person who some *other* woman took the trouble to lug around for 9 months, who incurred huge costs to feed, clothe, and educate, and who is now coming in to wipe the drool from her mouth and change her diapers. But without a time concept, these inner-brain libbers can't see that far ahead.)

For younger people coming up, is there any chance that current trends in people's private lives would be reversed or improved in any way? Probably not. The liberated woman has no time concept. So only the present exists, and she can be as mean, nasty and brutish as suits her fancy in the present because she can't see a future. The only hope for improvement would lie in future generations of women who might resume women's progress that was being made by pre-libber generations. But the system mind is not going to let the cultural norms established by Women's Liberation go away easily. Just one point. The younger women coming up are mostly very sweet and very polite, and some quite bright and can still get excited over an interesting conversation. But they still have too much energy in the bottom of their brains, which gets antsy when hearing too much that's too new. In my opinion, younger generations of women coming along have more to overcome in order to become complete, productive, and creative human beings than the feminists had during the entire 1800s. Of course, they will do fine on their finite state very specialized jobs, but will we get any greatness? As sexist as the system was in the 1800s, it wasn't able to decapitate the brightest of women who were total and complete human beings and who persisted in their goals until they won. But the cultural norms, habits of mind, and disastrous use of brain energy established by the libber generations is going to be very difficult to overcome. It is highly unlikely that we are going to get two or three generations of Kamikaze young women who take it upon themselves to set the example for human conduct, especially between the sexes, until men can be brought back up to speed.

Regarding women in particular which is the subject of this chapter, women's libbers baldly stated that women should "take power". As is often the case with these libbers, they think you gain power by putting a stake in the ground ala Karl Marx. By making themselves into incompetent, mindless ninnies, the liberated woman has less power in relationships than ever before in history. As opposed to libber propaganda, power in families throughout history depended on who loved whom the most. Even during the Middle Ages, when the man was madly in love, the woman had power in the family. This state of affairs continued right into the postwar years. This was the result partially of women choosing from among their suitors, as we have stressed. People who want power have to earn it. The way you earn it in the case of gender is for women to be attractive, competent, likable and engaging human beings — the kind a man can fall tremendously in love with and want to spend the rest of his life with. That is the only *real* way for women to have power over men. But since the liberated woman creates reality out of words, all the system had to do to satisfy them is to show women with power on TV with women punching men out, martial arts, and other kinds of violence against men. That's all they need. And they can no longer even complain about the system because they know it was *women* who designed it. They are trapped.

Lastly, we have to ask, what has 35 years of pandering done for women? The system mind has used the liberation movement to create a nasty world in which women wind up as mindless 12-hour a day work slaves in either a bad marriage with out-of-control kids, or as a single who nobody wants. Beneath the veneer of the public dialog, there has never been a time in history when women had less real power in our private lives. Now if you're a woman, and if you think that the world created by the women's movement is in the best interests of women and this is the kind of world you want to live in, then you will probably ignore much of what's in this chapter, and that is perfectly fine. But if this is not the kind of world you want to live in, then maybe you ought to question what the system mind has brought us.

1   Johnson, Diane. *The New York Review of Books*, Oct. 23, '03, p. 35

2   Dworkin, Andrea. *Ms. Magazine*, June, '79

3   *Ms. Magazine*, Nov. '76, p. 71

4   *Ms. Magazine*, Dec. '76, p. 101

5   *Ms. Magazine*, July, '72, p. 18

6   *Ms. Magazine*, July, '86, p. 42

7   Steinhem, Gloria. *Ms. Magazine*, Nov. '78, p. 53

8   Johnson, Diane. *New York Review of Books*, June 21, 2012, p. 23

9   Pollitt, Katha. *The Nation, Feb. 27, '06*

10 *Cosmo*, Feb. '79, p. 112

11 "The Rush to Maternity". *Cosmo*, Sept. '86

12 Johnson, Diane. *The New York Review of Books*, July 16, '98, p. 20

13 Sullivan, Judy. *Mama Doesn't Live Here Anymore.* P. 35

14 Mossop, Brian; "How Dads Develop". *Sci. Amer. Mind*, July, 2011

15 *Scientific American*, May '14, p. 46

16 "Sex Facts". *Cosmo*, Jan. '89

17 *Ms. Magazine*, July, '86, p. 54

18 Bakos, Susan; "The Totally Sexual Woman". *Cosmo*, May, '88

19 Dr. Loy McGinnis; "What to do When your Man Won't Talk". *Cosmo*, Mar. '79

20 Craveri, Benedetta, "Talk". *The New York Review of Books*, Jan. 20, '00.

21 *Ms. Magazine*, Feb., '79, p. 28

22 "How to Attract men". *Cosmo*, Feb. '89.

23 Star, Cima; "The Cruel Lover". *Cosmo;* Aug. '79

24 Bressler, Allison, "Mind", Sept., '14, p. 38

25 Pollitt, Katha. *The Nation*, June 9, '97, p. 9

26 Porgrebin, Letty. "The Power of Beauty", *Ms. Magazine*, Dec. '75

27 *Ms. Magazine*, Apr. '82, p. 46

28 *Ms Magazine*, Sept, '93, p. 33

29 Sweet, Ellen; "Date Rape". *Ms. Magazine*, Oct. '85

30 Graham, Sheila. *Cosmo*, May, '72 p. 155

31 Coontz, Stephanie; 1992. *The Way We Never Were;* Basic Books, NY, NY.

32 Epstein, Helen, "The Doctor Who Made a Revolution. *New York Review of Books*, Sept. 26, '13

33 Schine, Catherine; review of *Sempre Susan* by Sigrid Nunez. *New York Review*, July 14, '11

34 Pollitt, Katha. *The Nation*, Nov. 28, '05

35 *The New Republic*, Aug. 16, '93

36 *The Nation, June 12, '00.*

CHAPTER 36

The Future

——

WELL, WHERE ARE WE HEADED? We will explain in this chapter where we're headed, but to put it briefly in two simple words: We're screwed! Let's see how. Regarding the system mind, it will continue to articulate and strengthen on the domestic scene because of increasingly sophisticated information flows. What is interesting though is that on the foreign affairs side, any vestiges of a system mind will continue to weaken. With increasing secrecy surrounding the president, and neoconservatives on the Supreme Court needing an all-powerful king to identify with, the president will accrue increasing powers, especially to make wars. After all, a king without a war is not much of a king — certainly not one who creates the greatest display of power for neoconservatives and helpless peasants to identify with. Barack Obama started out as a liberal community organizer, even though this covered up his megalomania. But upon becoming president, he continued on the tracks laid down by Ronald Reagan to accrue increasing powers.

36.1 FOREIGN POLICY IN THE 21ST CENTURY

Being a political animal, Obama began talking about timetables to bring troops out of Iraq and Afghanistan. The interesting question is, what will the system mind arrange for these and other developing countries this century? What it will attempt to do all over the developing world, especially Muslim countries, is to promote a dual policy. As discussed in Ch. 34, on the one hand, it will attempt to set up National Socialist puppet governments either by invasion or internal intrigue that will sell raw materials to the US and provide a source of cheap labor to reduce the value of labor in the US. This is the policy implemented in Iraq and Afghanistan.

In a very insightful article, Michael Klare discusses the new strategy.[1] There was a document called the Quadrennial Defense Review, the Pentagon's Congressionally mandated overall strategy for the future, released in Feb. 2010. You have to love the language in these kinds of reports, like, our objectives in the future is "insuring that US forces are flexible and adaptable so they can confront the full range of challenges that could emerge from a complex and dynamic security environment", wherein "...US forces will work with military forces of partner nations...". [2] When you translate all this militarese into plain

English, what they are saying is that in case bigger wars like in Iraq and Afghanistan aren't sustainable for creating terrorists because they get too much attention and cost too much money, we may have to change strategy and make smaller wars in smaller countries. These "partner nations" of course are puppet governments American presidents will install in these countries. Smaller wars will be less obvious to the American people, but very well known to potential terrorists. This policy has already started in the small country of Yemen. There's the usual drone attacks. The gossip starts filtering into all levels of society and more recruits are added to Al Qaeda.

On the other hand, if the system can't set up a puppet government for whatever reason, it will promote the exact opposite: a very antagonistic anti-American government that we can then call the "enemy", which will create fertile ground for future invasion, conquest, attack or any other form of belligerency. This conforms to Law I of international relations from Ch. 27. This is the situation in Iran. Currently, neoconservative hard-liners are pushing for military action against Iran our newest "enemy". Conservatives even invited Netanyahu to come to the US and drum up support to put the US on a path to war with Iran — a very fertile source of future terrorist recruitment.

The policy that best paves the way for the creation of "enemy" governments is to promote a lawless world as we discussed in Sect. 27.4. Recall, in the last chapter we talked about how babies follow the example of mothers who are the authority figures. Among nations, our large economy and strong military makes the US the leading authority figure in the world. We see this in a million ways, where kids all over the world are wearing American jeans and listening to American music and following American social practices.

Just like Ronald Reagan laid down the tracks for Economic Socialism in the foreseeable future in domestic affairs, George Bush laid down the tracks for the world's foreign policy for the rest of the century, *which is a lawless world*. The example the Bush administration set is that any strongman can round up a bunch of killers needing a war. We see this in Africa and the Middle East, but it will spread to other areas as well in this century. In a lawless world, the powers in the Afro-Eurasian continent where five of out six people live, can do anything they want while world opinion is in disarray. In my view, this is not in our national interests.

In any law-abiding community like a state or even small town, when a crime is committed, people count on a police force to uphold the law. They point to courts with independent judges and juries. There is no propaganda. Opposing lawyers don't start calling each other names. They simply present evidence. In a law-abiding international community, there would be international lawyers, evidence, a world court with judges and juries to come to a decision that all members of the international community would support. We find none of this in today's lawless world. When a putative crime is committed like invading Iraq or Putin invading the Ukraine, propagandists on both sides pop up like weeds whose rhetoric is light years from that of a lawful international process. The reason that talk of laws and courts is totally absent from both sides is that there are no international laws and treaties for human rights are dead. It all got repealed by the Bush administration with the active cooperation of the system mind propaganda outlets.

This led to a remarkable example of the mind of the system in deflecting attention away from the *lawless* world created by the Bush administration. Henry Kissenger and fellow propagandists came up with a new system line. As they see US power diminishing due to unsustainable costs, they are unhappy that the US will not be able to continue dominating the existing *world order*. The system now describes the lawlessness initiated by the Bush administration as "disorderly". Of course, the "orderly world" these inner brain reptiles are mourning is one whereby any Anglo-American "leader" can take armies anywhere in the world to invade, conquer and kill hundreds of thousands of "natives" bringing them to civilization. As lawlessness spreads to all corners of the world, the system describes this as a "disorderly world". When only the US and Great Britain were doing it, we had an "orderly" world, you see. This is a shining example of a system mind.

In the Ukraine situation, David Brooks of the NY Times was griping because Putin had upset an "orderly world". When he spoke with righteous indignation, you could tell that his compartmentalized brain was light years away from Iraq. *The Economist* chimed in that "…Mr. Putin had driven a tank over the existing world order". [3] The world order these Brits are upset over is one where Great Britain for 300 hundred years could invade over *150* countries right up to the present invasion of Iraq, killing millions of people. Semi-consciousness is really handy at times.

Truth is not the issue. The issue is language. Every sentence from these guys and from Russia is the organic language of a lawless world: people on our side are freedom-fighters, people on the other side have been infiltrated and turned into terrorists. Our elections are squeaky clean, theirs are a fraud and rigged. Our governments are democratic and legitimate; theirs are illegitimate. Our rhetoric is truth, theirs is propaganda. Their killings are terrorism, ours are "mistakes", to use David Brooks' very word. In their Ukraine article, *The Economist* mentioned Russian "propaganda" and "information wars" five times, while they themselves engage in the *exact same rhetoric*[4]. These lawless world advocates are comically solipsistic: they have no awareness that the other side is hearing the exact mirror image of what our side is hearing. They are totally unaware that in the lawless world they promote, *nobody*, including themselves, talks about international courts where truth is established by independent judges and juries, not propaganda.

Of course, you could say that we've had a lawless world for a long time led mainly by the British. But the US got into the act too when Teddy Roosevelt invaded the Philippines to rescue them from the Spanish empire, which was all but gone by then. Marines murdered thousands. The sinking of the battleship Maine in 1898 was blamed on Spain which was a total lie, but used as the excuse to invade Cuba. The reason Cuba has suffered under Communism for the past 65 years is as a reaction to a series of brutal right-wing dictators the US installed in Cuba for 50 years after the Maine. There was a respite during the Roosevelt period where the Democratic party led by Truman tried to establish a law-abiding world guided by the United Nations with a world court. But the game started up again with the Tonkin Gulf resolution that enabled Johnson to invade Vietnam and kill millions.

There was a window of opportunity in the last half of the 20th century in which Democracy and rule of law made some progress. But this window was slammed shut with the Bush administration's invasions of countries on the basis of outright lies. *The Economist* had a big fat article to explain the new direction away from rule of law and democracy.[5] Among pages of word-mongering there is one sentence of reason-box diarrhea to justify the Iraq invasion.

And now in the Ukraine we have some of the results of the lawless world the Bush administration initiated. On Mar. 2, 2014, we saw John Kerry blustering about Russia's invasion of Crimea totally unconscious of the lawless world his own government promotes. Every sentence Kerry used was an exact duplicate of what critics of the Iraq war had been saying for years. This is a great example of the system mind's lack of a time concept. The system could not see that the tsar it set up in Russia could become a loose cannon in the future in charge of a nuclear arsenal to boot. The missile that shot down a civilian plane in July, '14 had to come from Russia. In my opinion, this was Putin's Hiroshima. I don't care how many military experts you come up with, moral considerations should always precede military ones. Truman should have dropped the first atomic bomb on a military installation. Even if it didn't work, it would at least have shown that morality comes before killing. In my opinion, Truman did it as a subtle message to Russia at the time: *hey, look at mine.* In the same way, Putin is telling the west that if they get too pushy, missiles could fall into the hands of terrorists and bring international air travel to a screeching halt. This would be the mother of all sanctions. I'm sure this never occurs to our military geniuses. Unlike nuclear, missiles are easy to make.

But even now, what does Kerry propose we do about the Ukraine? He threatened economic sanctions and a mild military threat. As we approach a 20 trillion dollar national debt, part of which was to create a lawless world by invading countries of no threat to the US, where is he going to get another couple trillion dollars for more wars? Russia can prop up its National Socialism forever with their unlimited natural resources. They don't need a successful economy.

In the current lawless world, instead of the world rising up in *unison* to support the findings of a world court with independent judges and juries to determine facts and truths, the world went to sleep in *Unisom*, each country taking a position in its own interests instead of recognizing international law. South America and Africa slept through it all; China signed a big oil and gas contract with Russia, and India said nothing. Only Europe who had set a precedence for lawlessness over a 400 year period culminating in Nazi Germany, said a few tentative words, worried about their gas supply — which is a bit of an irony. One of the few things *The Economist* got right was that "Mr. Putin has got most of what he wanted". They better get used to this kind of admission, because in the lawless world they promote, the west will lose more and the Afro-Eurasian powers gain more in every confrontation because they're there and we're isolated in the west. *The Economist* entitled their Dec. '10 issue, "The

Dangers of a Rising China". See, the Brits who write *The Economist*, are scared shitless that Chinese National Socialism might start doing what British Economic Socialism has been doing for 300 years, namely, invading, conquering and killing people all over the world.

Kerry went right on lecturing the world, especially Russia, as though Iraq and Afghanistan never happened. Even if some of Putin's actions violate international law, where are the international judges and juries to determine this? Ranting by propagandists like *The Economist* aren't an answer to a lawless world. They are part of it. Kerry and Obama's rhetoric mentioned international law knowing full well that the Bush administration repealed all such international law. In 2003, when the UN said that it would be illegal to invade Iraq, Bush told the UN to go screw themselves. Hearing Kerry and Obama's rhetoric, the tone was that events in the future would be guided *not* by crisp international laws and principles judged by independent international courts, but by propaganda wars, sanctions, threats, force, killing, military confrontations, possibly nuclear, exactly as in a lawless world.

When Russia suggested a referendum in parts of the Ukraine, Kerry said it was illegal because it should be a nation-wide referendum. This completely contradicts one of the supposedly historic principles of US foreign policy for self-determination. If Kerry had the slightest interest in international law, he would be pushing for a UN monitored election to see what the Crimeans and eastern Ukrainians really want for themselves. But instead, he supports a US policy of bottling up Russia which is simply part of a lawless world where you push, threaten and intimidate. Does Kerry want a "nation-wide" referendum in China as to whether Tibet and Taiwan can maintain some degree of independence?

Part of a lawless world is mob rule. Mobs have overthrown elected governments in Egypt, Libya and Ukraine with coups. That's the end of real democracy there and most Muslim countries. In Egypt, dissidents are being rounded up, tortured and given fake trials. You would think that the US would coax these forces to at least *pretend* to have some rule of law with procedures like impeachment. Our foreign policy puts a seal of approval on these lawless coups including the one in Ukraine. It's only an opinion, but I believe mob overthrows of elected governments and coups are the direct result of a lawless world established by the Bush administration as part of a system mind that welcomes lawlessness as a foundation for the war on terrorism and the spread of National Socialism.

Of course, the system mind propaganda outlets love invasions, wars and killings because they make money with the higher ratings you get from wars. Not only that, but it keeps the "war on terrorism" going strong. It's showing up in refugee numbers. "The UN High Commissioner for Refugees (UNHRC), Antonio Guterres, shows that "armed conflict around the world really is getting worse… at the end of 2013 more than 50m people had been forced to flee from their homes…the largest count ever". [6] This will get worse this century.

Of course, in the compartmental brains of writers for *The Economist*, there is no tie at all between these numbers and Bush, allied with their own murderous hero, Tony Blair, whose lawless invasion of Iraq for the sole purpose of trying out new war toys that kill people, got the whole international lawless game going. As usual, they were cheerleading the bloody mess.

And after all the smoke cleared away in Iraq, in order to justify the four thousand American lives lost, tens of thousands of dead Iraqis including 20 thousand Iraqi children, the system mind had to spout the lie that US foreign policy was "winning", in spite of many CIA reports of increasing recruitment of jihadists. It showed Martha Raditz of ABC almost every week from Iraq or Afghanistan (maybe she was standing in front of *pictures* of Iraq and Afghanistan), telling us that the internationally illegal and unconstitutional war was working: we were getting the terrorists; they're just about all done. We can stick a fork in them. This lie had become so much a part of Washington thinking that they believed it themselves. So when a bunch of terrorists in a very complex plot invaded the US embassy in Benghazi and killed a number of Americans, the Obama administration's first response was, it couldn't be terrorists: they're all dead. So they made total fools of themselves blaming mob violence inspired by somebody's bad movie.

But then, all of a sudden there's a jihadist force large enough to invade and take over half the country of Iraq. *The Economist* asks, "How could all his happen when Iraq's government, which spent about $17 billion on its security forces last year...can call on a national army of nearly 200,000 men trained and largely equipped by America, backed up by police and paramilitary brigades of more than 500,000?" [7] This is the exact performance of the army of a puppet government.

This invasion didn't stop the Sunday morning war-whores. The new line was that this is a whole new game because the new jihadists have a new name. This provides a wedge to crank up the American people to support another 10 years of war. After all, they need better ratings. At first, intelligence and some authorities said that ISIS was posing no threat to the homeland. Well, this was unacceptable to the system. Now, without bombing, ISIS might take over some swaths of territory. But then what? They have no end game. They are an army of killers. As history has shown dozens of times, killers don't know how to run governments. Just look at Lenin, Mao, and the puppet governments the US set up in Vietnam. They would burn out just like Napoleon and all such armies. But such ripe fruit is a great temptation to the system. Dropping bombs on them maintains them as a viable fighting force attracting kids from all over the world to join the effort to fight the great satin. This has the potential of generating thousands of new terrorists for the "war on terrorism" and to attack the homeland. So the no-threat experts were pushed off the stage while the system mind came up with *new* experts who asserted that ISIS really was a threat to the homeland. But if ISIS so much more brutal, how will it be easier to defeat them than the jihadists in Iraq that the army fought for 10 years — *and* with boots on the ground? But I forgot. The Jihadists who blow arms and legs off are the really tough guys, impossible to conquer. However, ISIS, who only chop heads off, are such cream puffs we can defeat them by dropping a few bombs. The system is not bothered by contradictions.

This invasion caught the system mind by total surprise. But these ISIS fighters are not new recruits. They have been training in Iraq and Syria under various names for years while the propaganda outlets were lying through their teeth that Al Qaeda was on the way out. Obama hesitated over what to do, but he recovered with a speech that we were going to destroy ISIS. The response to this speech was a very incisive example of a system mind. Without a conspiracy, every single system media talking head had the same reaction to Obama's speech: he was "reluctant" to engage militarily. These media whores are demanding a lot more blood-thirsty leader than Obama. Even the stooges on the "liberal" PBS had the same line. Not a single one of them reminded the American people that with boots on the ground, the US has been fighting jihadists for 10 years with hundreds of thousands of casualties and a trillion dollar cost to produce nothing but a puppet government and more terrorists.

But the appearance of ISIS was a ripe opportunity for the system mind's propaganda outlets to crank up more lawlessness, more invasions and more killing. After the election of 2014, many Republican were drooling at the mouth to crank up another 10 years of war, killing and destruction. And who better to send around to get interviewed was a guy who some people in Europe want to try for war crimes and who initiated the lawless world in the first place. I saw him interviewed by Charlie Rose. And of course, since Rose is also in the media business, he too gets ratings with wars and killings. The new lie was that Bush and Cheney left Iraq "in good shape". Cheney then blamed Obama for the sudden appearance of a whole army of trained terrorists out of thin air because he was "too soft". And of course, Rose sat there horsing down every bit of it. He wasn't going to remind his viewers that in 2008, the last year of the Bush administration, over 300 American boys got killed in Iraq and another 150 wounded, more thousands with all sorts of mental illnesses including suicides, to say nothing of hundreds of Iraqis killed, just like any other year of the occupation. But since Al Qaeda was gone, it all had to be the work of one lonely remaining magical terrorist who moved around invisibly with the speed of light.

As we discussed in Sect. 27.3, there is no foreign policy system mind capable of *understanding* world events. The emotion that should take precedence is on the exploration limb as curiosity to *understand* geopolitical events. When you invade and conquer another nation, you motivate the young men of the country with the primitive bottom of the brain emotion of territorial protection. They will be a guerilla force that is composed of individuals or cells that is an organic part of the population. They will fight any way they can. This is what went on in Iraq for 10 years with boots on the ground. As we discussed in Ch. 34, as soon as the invading force leaves, these fighters will organize into a more cohesive army which fights it out with the puppet government exactly as ISIS is doing. John McCain says we need boots on the ground as an army to defeat ISIS. What he doesn't understand is that as soon as we invade with an army, ISIS will dissolve and atomize back into individual fighters in a guerilla war just like water boils out of the pot into atoms in the air, and we're back to 10 more years of occupation and killing.

There is a great metaphor for the situation in Iraq or any other country the king invades, conquers and sets up puppet governments. It's like a coil spring. US foreign policy attempts to stretch the spring till it reaches the appearance of viable government. This takes money. As an estimate, it would probably take about a 100 billion a year each to bribe enough Iraqis and Afghans to maintain puppet governments and Halloween armies and give an appearance of progress because the opposition would be individual fighters in a guerilla force. This money would be stolen from vital research into preventing diseases that kill tens of thousands of Americans every year. And remember, this number must be spent year after year after year, for 10 years, 20 or 100 years. The minute you stop spending, the spring snaps back and most of their tough young men will spontaneously organize into an army like ISIS to expel the invader and replace the puppet government.

For hundreds of years we've seen the same story. *Any leader that colludes with the invader is not a nation-builder like George Washington, but a totally corrupt gangster seeking money and power.* Men join their Halloween armies to make money and stay safe, not out of patriotism. And now without the least bit of shame, after the propaganda outlets have been lying for years about the puppet government in Iraq with an image of freedom and democracy, these very same propagandists are blaming this very same government for ISIS and Maliki must go.

In general, *any government however installed that cooperates in any way with the invader, is going to wind up a target for the tough young men of a country for expulsion, even if it takes hundreds of years.* In Nov. '14, *The Economist* was berating Obama for not leaving enough troops in Afghanistan. [8] Again, they are scared shitless that Obama might impede the creation of a continuous supply of terrorists for their favorite National Socialist police state to chase after. In my opinion, leaving troops in Afghanistan is simply ear-marking the new government as another puppet government for young Afghanis to expel.

There another important point that you will never hear from the Sunday morning war worshippers. *The more brutal the invasion and occupation, the more brutal the resistance.* As we discussed in Sect. 27.2, when people are threatened, they turn to their fiercest leaders who have the best chances of protecting them. A prime example was the French occupation of Algeria. Both sides were torturing and murdering people in one of the worst atrocities of the 20th century. The invasion and occupation of Iraq killed a hundred thousand Iraqis, mostly innocents. Their cultural history was destroyed. Soldiers going haywire had invaded homes and killed everybody. Of course, these events are never reported in the system propaganda outlets. But because of atrocities like this, gossip spreads and eventually results in a brutal resistance which we now see in the ISIS force.

On the other hand, the British occupation of the colonies was quite mild. They didn't send armies and drones to kill thousands of innocent Americans. They didn't invade homes and kill all occupants. The result was a resistance led by George Washington, one of the finest human beings who ever lived. He, along with like-minded founding fathers established a constitutional democracy that is a model for the world. If the British King George III was like our King George Bush, our resistance would have been led by a bunch of Attillas the Hun or Genghis Khans.

In the lawless world Bushies created, there is no right way to go. The enemy in one country is a friend in the next. Our friends in a third country are enemies in a fourth. Among the rebels in Syria who we support is the enemy in Iraq. Friends in Iraq are the enemy in Iran. Any military action Obama were to take would not be the result of an international system of independent judges and juries, but would only continue right on the tracks laid down by the Bush team for a lawless world.

And we haven't seen the worst of it. Opinion-makers in the US are totally oblivious of the fact that Russia, China and India don't have middle classes with something to lose like in the US. The lawless world Bush initiated is harder to get approval in the US, not only because we have more freedoms, but because some middle class people do not want to give up their prosperity only to identify with a king. Peasants in Afro-Eurasian powers achieve identity not by being prosperous, but by identifying with the king's or tsar's *power*. After the Crimean incident, Putin's popularity soared in spite of sanctions. When China threatens Japan, their peasants roar approval of the current emperor. And what happens if our anti-Russian foreign policy provokes Russia and China into building an anti-west block, which they have already started. What happens if Russia starts arming with advanced weaponry the developing countries the American king wants to invade?

We simply to not have a coherent foreign policy system mind, which is then at the whim of drunks, draft dodgers, international bullies, war criminals, and paid killers, which the American system mind allows to worm their way into positions of power, all blessed by the Supreme Ayatollas. They will set the tone for the century ahead which will see lots of little wars, aggression, pogroms, anthropocide, mob violence, killings, coups, and overall lawlessness. In my opinion, an erratic and lawless foreign policy is not in our national interests down the line.

We might add that lawlessness is infecting the domestic economy as well. Obama gets on TV and announces that if the Republicans don't pass his agenda, he has to do it himself regardless of laws he violates. This practice has been picking up steam since Ronald Reagan. We see judges more and more breaking laws and trampling the Constitution. With the kind of presidents and Supreme Court reptiles we get, we're not going to see a law-abiding world any time this century.

But the worst thought of all is that possibly the majority of Americans don't care about a law-abiding world. They couldn't care less about the innocents the Bush administration was killing in Iraq. They swallowed like pabulum all the reason-box word-mongering they got from the system propaganda outlets. To this day, nearly half Americans think Bush was "protecting" us from evil. Evolution has wired people to accept whatever their own kind is doing to go kill the bad guys. Curing the many horrible diseases people die from, having safe secure homes to live in, preventing birth defects in their own children all seem to have a lower priority than getting the bad guys who are always easy to manufacture. It may all be hopeless and there may be no chance of a law-abiding world any time soon.

36.2 FOREIGN POLICY — SMALL DEVELOPING COUNTRIES

Whether it's through invasions, puppet governments, or simply leadership, all developing countries will be led in the direction of National Socialism because that's the direction of the US economy. With technology, there is some improvement in the lives of the upper segments of the bottom 80%. But as the world runs out of resources, water and land, their standard of living will reverse and start dropping. The march to National Socialism will proceed a little slower in the West because of our feudal past. But without a feudal past, most of the Muslim world and most of Africa, Russia and India will wallow in corruption, which again, results in most new wealth and income going to the top 20%.

After labeling Africa as "the hopeless continent" ten years ago, *The Economist* had a glowing article about how well Africa is doing, especially since Africa's road to National Socialism is clearer than in other parts of the world.[9] After all, a third of them are actually earning more than 2 dollars a day. But as usual, just about all the new wealth is going to the top 20%. Also, much of Africa's economies are based on natural resources. When all you have to do is dig stuff out of the ground, a few players can monopolize a resource industry without having to be real entrepreneurs. The resulting monopolies make it even easier for top economic players to climb in bed with political actors to make rules that send more wealth to the top. They may have the advantage of seeing developed economies and can easily make use of technological and scientific advancements that have been made by others. But it is their institutions that lack momentum vectors.

But to be fair, it might be the case that National Socialism is inevitable in many developing countries no matter what they do. The reason is that they are basically tribal and do not have a strong entrepreneurial class. The only way development can occur is to lure incipient entrepreneurs into starting businesses by allowing them to make their own rules. This is the case in the Muslim world. Even if a strong Democratic Capitalist government were to emerge trying to enforce independently designed rules, their incipient entrepreneurial class would simply sag down to inaction and the country would revert to its traditional tribalism. But by taking the Economic Socialist course, you will never get a middle class in developing countries prosperous enough to call Democratic Capitalism. This is case especially in countries like India and Russia and probably China as well.

36.3 FOREIGN POLICY - LARGE DEVELOPING COUNTRIES.

Regarding the world of large developing countries, India, China, Russia, Pakistan, Indonesia, etc., these countries are too big to turn into puppets, but also too big to turn into hot war enemies. But they are fine for cold wars, which is the relationship the US had towards Russia for 40 years. But that didn't bring the needed results to the system. So the new approach is to guide them in the direction of National Socialism. As we saw in Ch. 31, this is exactly the policy the US pursued in the Russian transition and the policy towards China now. National Socialism in these countries acts as a magnet pulling us in the same direction. However, it is interesting to notice two groups: China and Russia are coming from Political Socialism where the *political* system dominated as in Communism. India and Brazil are going towards the same end, only coming from an Economic Socialist market system where the *economic* system ran the show. Led by our Republican party, they'll all wind up in the same National Socialist boat.

In China, leaders of the Communist party say they need quick development, which means allowing their entrepreneurial class to have increasing say in making their own rules. Once you take that direction, you never go back. As leading economic players accrue more wealth and power, they take a bigger and bigger role in making their own rules and you never get a prosperous middle class. Only a tiny dribble trickles down to the lower 80% and that trickle will be gradually reduced to a drip. Numbers show inequality actually increasing in China.

The NYR reviewed a number of books about recent economic events in China. Developers climb in bed with Communist Party officials at every level to completely destroy some of the most interesting early Chinese architecture and urban neighborhoods.[10] Private property is an essential ingredient of a Capitalists system. In China it is almost meaningless. Millions of people were pushed out of their homes and peasants driven off their land to make room for the usual urban beehives that blight so many American cities — over a million in Beijing alone. The Chinese are very bitter about the Japanese invasion in the 1930s. The harm to Chinese culture and history by the Japanese was minor vandalism compared to the bulldozer that steamrolled over huge areas of Chinese history and architecture in major Chinese cities in the last 50 years. The Chinese people had no say in it.

In an article about economic development, *The Economist* stated that when income per head reaches a certain level, growth stagnation sets in.[11] The implication, of course, is that some unseen demonic force attacks developing economies when too much wealth trickles down to their devilish incipient middle class. They avoid like a plague the real reason for stagnation. As wealth increases, large and powerful economic nodes appear who proceed to climb in bed with political animals to rig the rules in their favor. Inequality grows as their incipient middle class get starved of income and can't clear markets. The economy has to rely on exports; but with many countries trying to do the same thing and economic growth stagnant in the developed world, the game of relying on exports peters out, resulting in stagnant growth in the developing economy as well.

The president of The Council on Foreign Relations has written of "the existing opportunity to integrate China into a U.S.-led world order". [12] What he is really encouraging, in my opinion, is an opportunity to integrate the U.S. into a *China*-led world order. This is shown by allowing every conceivable kind of junk to be imported from China made with cheap labor. This so-called free trade actually increases the power and influence of corporate interests in China towards integration with the Communist government and further reduces economic power of their lower 80%. This is the exact formula for National Socialism and US foreign policy is actively engaged in promoting it. It has the added attraction to the neoconservative system mind of reducing the labor power of our own working class who hemorrhage good paying manufacturing jobs.

Up till now, there has been just enough trickle-down of wealth and income in China to the bottom 80% to keep the lid on unrest. But as National Socialism deepens, China may have trouble keeping their natives from getting restless. Some of the books reviewed in the NYR article claim that the Communist party will lose touch with the people who will rise up just like in the Middle East and demand democratic reforms. This is a possibility, but the Chinese are smarter than the infantile dictators in the Muslim world. What you will see is the Chinese Communist party buying an interest in Fox News and using their expertise to design a propaganda line that keeps the peasants in their place. There will be Tea Parties in China just like here. Crowds of peasants will gather together to hear one-liner speeches which will motivate them to stay in their place while all new money and power goes to the top 20%, mostly the top 5%, exactly as in the US.

Russia is going in the same direction except by slightly different means. The Russian system is being propped up by lots of natural resources, especially oil and gas which are natural monopolies. Today in Russia, nobody knows who owns these natural monopolies, whether oligarchic private players, or government officials, or some combination of both. But they are in bed with one another rigging the rules so that all their wealth and new income is going to the top 20%. This prevents a no prosperous middle class, which is a hallmark of Democratic Capitalism.

36.4 THE EUROPEAN UNION

If you have any doubt about a system mind, just take a look at economic developments in Europe in the last 35 years since the reintroduction of Economic Socialism by Ronald Reagan in the 1980s. There has never been a more insidious racket in the history of economics than the European Union. It is a total scam. That well-meaning political leaders and even great thinkers like Jurgen Habermas don't see it, to me shows it's the product of a system mind directed by the same large economic nodes that direct the system mind in the US.

The European Union was designed by economic elites of Europe to have a common currency. This enables them to slosh their money around mostly undetected to avoid paying taxes. It was a complete invention by the important nodes of the European system mind to keep wages low and to distribute income upward to the top 20%. Even though safety nets enable demand to be maintained somewhat, the general redistribution of income upwards more than cancelled out the effects of a safety net. But as voters try to maintain the safety net the only way it could be maintained is by massive theft from the future. This was all unsustainable and led to breakdowns in Greece and Cyprus. But European economic elites realize that if they can continue propping up this scam, they can steal trillions from future generations. It's a classic example of making hay while the sun shines. The longer they put off the end of the racket, the more they can steal.

By its very nature, the EU contradicts the motivation for having a union in the first place. The major motivation for a union should be as a stabilizer to provide positive feedback. If a country in the union falls behind in efficiency or productivity or trade balance, there should be positive feedback to bring them back up to the rest. The EU actually creates *negative* feedback. When a country gets off course, instead of mechanisms coming into play that would regain equilibrium, existing mechanisms actually *amplify* differences. If Germany becomes more efficient at making goods, they will export more to France than vice versa. This will put downward pressure on French labor suppressing demand. To keep up living standards, the French will borrow and incur deficits putting pressure on interest rates. The cost of borrowing for French industry increases which puts them at an even greater disadvantage to German industry. Higher interest rates increase the burden of the ever-increasing national debt. A viscous circle ensues that amplifies the difference between French and German productivity and output. The EU creates the very conditions that it was designed to remedy. Elites running the racket even thought of a common currency to prevent an exchange rate mechanism to provide feedback.

European economies have been hemorrhaging capital into various off-shore tax havens, money-laundering schemes and dummy corporations. What European financial wizards effectively did was put a stop to *trade* wars between economic elites and substituted *labor* wars in their place. Competition has been pushed down to the middle and working classes who are pitted against each other in a big *labor war* to bring down the value of labor. This labor war is exacerbated by the free movement of labor keeping its value low. *The Eurozone was designed specifically to integrate capital and isolate labor by substituting labor wars for trade wars.*

And what has the EU done? Well as you might expect, financial wizards behind the whole scam have given big tax cuts mostly to corporations and the wealthy including themselves. Since it is easier for companies to move from one country to another, member nations have to compete with lower taxes to get them to stay. And now with the Europe aristocracies having declining numbers, they can play off the peasants against one another and gain a bigger share of the pie.

But money taken out of a country has to be replaced as we explained Sect. 24.4 just like in your hot water heating system. And this money comes from constant stealing from the future generations who are becoming economic slaves. And once you start printing up paper, the road is cleared for the financial services industries in all these countries to print up fake money in the form of derivatives. The profits made in this totally unproductive industry must be extracted from the middle classes in Euro countries, which reduces demand and requires ever more stealing from the future to prop up demand. Then to throw salt in the wound, Euro countries have *increased* taxes on the lower 80% often in the form of what they call a VAT tax (Very Assinine Tax). The VAT has reached about 20%, which is ridiculous especially in this age of recessionary conditions.

One of the rules of the game imposed by the "experts" in Brussels has been free trade. But all European countries are advanced economies. The differences in their respective efficiencies are relatively small, especially since modern technology can spread easily. There is little to be gained by trading. We are not talking about an advanced economy like Germany trading computers to 18th century Zulus for gold or diamonds. Nothing made in Germany that can't be made in France, and vice versa. Even in blind taste tests, most people don't know which is the French wine. In 2013, Cyprus collapsed. It turns out they have a banking system bigger than their entire economy. To put it in frank terms, Cyprus was a European money laundering operation. Elites can gamble on fake paper that financial institutions all over the world have been printing up, and can make huge bonuses, commissions, and salaries in the process. When the whole scam collapsed, there was a gigantic pissing contest as to who was going to get stiffed between investors, depositors and holders of paper. Billions were lost. Lo and behold, *The Economist* had a blurb asking "Where Did All the Money Go?" [13] Guess their lame answer? "It went with the growth that never materialized". This is exactly where the money went that investors gave Bernie Madoff: it went with the growth that never materialized.

There is an additional effect that is never mentioned. By rules being made in a distant capital, there is the psychological effect that people don't see their country as a cohesive population with national goals that everyone should support and cooperate with, but as a swarm of individuals each looking out for himself. True Democracy tends to reduce corruption because people are more likely to be socially conscious and law-abiding if they can express their interests in some way. Diluting democracy as in the EU only invites corruption.

The result of all this has been enormous imbalances in member EU countries economies and growing inequalities. *The Economist* unconsciously had an article entitled "Too many cars, too few buyers". But in the small print, they went on to say that the luxury car market is doing fine. BMW, Mercedes and Audi are "working flat out to meet demand". [14] However, at the same time, middle class companies, Peugeot, Fiat, and GM's Opel are all losing money. Does this tell them something?

At no time will any major media propaganda outlets say one word about the real causes of these enormous national debts, which is that all western economies have seen inequalities grow to where the consuming classes simply cannot clear markets. This is exacerbated by the loss of social conscience as we mentioned. To prop up demand they all have to keep stealing from the future. You have to ask, how can *The Economist* see Euro countries with the most advanced technology and productivity in the world requiring massive deficits year after year to prop up their economies, and never question the whole thing. Shows how naked self-interest clouds the mind.

In fact, Europe is in a vector trap. They have to keep their economies slow or interest rates would rise and interest on their debts would keep them in permanent recession just like in Japan. This is why neoconservatives running this euroracket have a new scam going called "austerity" to prop up the old scam. Austerity is a two-pronged attack on very tapped out middle classes who are their main customers. *The Economist* recommends "...any new taxes should focus on consumption".[15] The whole world recession problem was everyone wants to export and here's the *Economist* recommending stealing more from the very consumers who are unable to keep up Consumption, production and jobs. This is what you get from a Phd in economics.

Austerity involves cutting government spending to reduce their self-produced deficits. But as we have stressed, Government spending is somebody's income. These deficit-cutting measures promoted by system talking heads will never do what they're promoted to do. When you attack the middle class with less government spending, and many unlucky forces pushing income up to the top 20% (talent, women's careers, hi-tech, and free trade), consumption lags, production falls, unemployment stays high and most importantly, tax revenues lag. There may be less government spending, but its revenues are also depressed and you are right back where you started with deficits. This is happening all over Europe right now.

The neoconservative party line has won the day all over the west because they control the means of propaganda and that includes the BBC (British Bullshit Company). There is almost no one in Brussels who is defending the interests of the lower 80% in all these countries. In Mar., '12, *The Economist* wanted corporate tax cuts so that British business can start investing and hiring with all the cash they've been "hoarding". Yes, business is going to come to Britain to make things they can't sell because of a starved out middle class initiated by Margaret Thatcher.

These economists ought to study the second law of thermodynamics which basically says you can't get something for nothing. With stagnant economies, interest rates approach zero along with the cost of servicing the debt. But the debt to GDP can increase. How financial con artists managing the European Union think they're going to back up all the paper they've printed up with shrinking economies and *curtailing* the creation of wealth is a total mystery. But what the system does understand is that patching up the system will allow more time for financial elites to make tons of money and avoid huge losses when the whole scheme collapses.

What the world needs is customers, and nothing going on anywhere in the world is doing that. The European Union exacerbates these problems because it can create various combinations of countries to print up paper to cover up the failures in any one country. Future middle classes are being made into economic slaves to pay interest on the fraudulent paper printed up. The IMF (International Muthah-Fuckers) loves this crap. And you won't read one word as to the basic source of Europe's economic problems which is that their middle classes are not getting a large enough share of national income to clear markets.

But people all over Europe are slowly catching on to this racket. Great Britain decided to leave. The elites running the racket are very self-righteously complaining because they fear the end of the racket and want to steal even more from the future before it all ends. By the time the rest of the European people figure it out, they will be so mired in debt that they will have stagnation and recession for decades to come just like Japan. But it won't matter to the people running the racket because they will have already gotten their billions out of the system into secret bank accounts.

36.5 THE AMERICAN ECONOMY - THE DERIVATIVES SCAM

The Euro Union might have provided inspiration for our own massive swindle pulled off by Wall Street. As we discussed in Sect. 25.7, Clinton and Bush's "deregulation" which is code for Economic Socialism, allowed Wall St. to print up hundreds of *trillions* of dollars of fraudulent derivatives. These derivatives are not only unconstitutional, but they are a complete scam. The financial services industry buys, sells, and bets on this fake paper and extracts huge profits and commissions in doing so. These profits come from stealing from our children by having to prop back up the stack of paper every once in a while when it topples over. Then, the profiteers claim, like Sergeant Klink: I know nuhthink. Wall Street is a huge whirlpool sucking billions into the derivatives scam from legitimate roles in financing effective economic activity. Not only that, but it steals gobs of talent from legitimate occupations like medicine or entrepreneurship.

A very insightful article by William Greider details the shenanigans. [16] After hundreds of billions were stolen from taxpayers and our children on the basis of total fraud, not one Wall Streeter has gone to jail. There are people in jail for 15 years for robbing a candy store of 37 dollars, but not a soul from Wall Street is even indicted. And what has system mind zombie Obama has done nothing? Even as you read this, the stack grows higher, and next time it topples over, even more trillions will have to be stolen from future generations to prop it back up.

And remember, this derivatives scam accomplishes nothing in spite of the propaganda from the system mind media that the system would collapse without it. After WWII when we had an optimal economy growing at a real effective rate of over 4% a year, there were no derivatives. Companies got capital the old-fashioned legitimate way: by borrowing from banks and selling stock. Adam Smith didn't need derivatives for real Capitalism.

In a really good book, Philip Coggan goes into the detail about countries of the world having incurred tens of trillions of mostly pension debt that can't possibly be paid off. [17] Coggan says that government units all the way from little towns to whole nations will have to default at some point, leaving "promises" hanging in the air. Of course, this is a gross injustice. However, it isn't fraud in the same way as derivatives. Derivatives are unconstitutionally printed money that enable wizards in the top 1% to make economic slaves out of future generations who will have to pay increasing taxes to prop up the stack of paper and for bonuses and commissions.

36.6 SYSTEM MIND PROPAGANDA

As we have stressed, the system mind's objectives are to keep pressure on labor to maximize short-term profits. This means an optimal *real* unemployment rate of about 8%, which is about what Obama got down to. So there will be a need for a constant stream of propaganda excuses and justifications for a crippled economy. Since the American people have a short memory, you can bring back excuses that failed in the past just like a revolving door. The first bromide under Bush was tax cuts for business. This was going to "unleash" the private sector and wipe out the deficit. But every recession and depression we had in the last hundred years was bailed out by a technology bubble; never with tax cuts. All we got from Reagan and Bush's tax cuts were massive deficits to prop up the same supply side economics that had failed many times before. The next push was for "deregulation". This effort resulted in a Wall Street Socialist gang-bang that allowed *trillions* of fake paper money in the form of derivatives leading to the '08 meltdown.

So now the system mind has to come up with a line of crap that will excuse the crippled economy. Nobody under the sun could have guessed the explanation that ensued, but the mind of the system is always up to the task. In the middle of 2010, *The Economist* says, "What is holding back firms from investing is now mainly *uncertainty* (my italics) about demand" [18], says Radley of EEF, a manufacturing group. This was picked up by the system mind mouthpieces and spread like a plague including PBS. This brings out an interesting law of propaganda: when you tell the truth, you only have to say it a few times. When you lie, you have to repeat it over and over again 24 hours a day, 7 days a week, which is exactly the case with the "uncertainty" myth.

The reality of course, is that *un*certainty is the essence of Capitalism. A business owner is *un*certain about government changes in rules and taxes. He is *un*certain about whether he will be able to continue getting materials and resources he needs. He is *un*certain as to whether a new business will start up with a better product and successfully compete. He is *un*certain as to whether people will continue to buy his product as opposed to other products in the marketplace. He is *un*certain about social changes that may make his product irrelevant. What *drives Capitalism is un*certainty, because *un*certainty keeps businesses on their toes devising new products to stay in touch with consumer preferences.

What these neoconservative Bolsheviks want is the *certainty* you get from Socialism, as was the case in Russia and China under Communism. Under Communism, there was *certainty* as to what products would be made; *certainty* as to how much each factory would produce; *certainty* as to how much each worker would be paid because unions were not allowed; *certainty* about prices; *certainty* about taxes, interest rates and money supply; and most important, *certainty* that economic players would be in bed with political animals making their own rules and there would be no democratic inputs to create *un*certainty. Socialists love certainty and these neoconservative Economic Socialists are no different.

The problem in our present economic mess is that there is too much *certainty* and it was brought on by the very same Economic Socialists that got us into the mess in the first place. The reality is the *certainty* that with no money in their pockets because of unemployment, people *ain't gonna be buyin' nothin'*, and nobody with a business is going to invest to produce more goods that they can't sell. The local tavern owner is not going to hire another bartender because he is very *certain* that the workers in his neighborhood aren't going to get their good manufacturing jobs back so they could afford to stop in for a beer. The local Chinese restaurant owner isn't going to hire another waitress because she is *certain* that many of her old customers aren't going to come in for dinner when they are out of work or have had their paychecks reduced. This really is Econ 99, but beyond the cognitive abilities of these inner brain neoconservative reptiles.

There is only one way the system can grow without continuing unsustainable deficits is to reform the tax code and labor relations so that the bottom 80% gets 60% of after-tax national income as was the case during the great postwar expansion. Well, two Laborites in Britain suggested that the top tax rate there be raised. As Table 24.3 shows, when the economy was humming along in the '50s and '60s at higher growth, less unemployment, and virtually no deficits, the top tax rate was around 80%. But now when two guys "… propose raising the top tax rate from 40% to 50%" *The Economist* calls this "bash-the-rich measures".[19]

You can go back a hundred years in this paper, and you will never *once* hear these system mind propagandists describe a tax on the lower 80% as "bash-the-middle class measures", or "bash-the-working class measures". When you tax the consuming classes, which is the opposite of what you need in a recession, it's serious stuff — real economics. But when you try to put the economy into balance to avoid massive deficits, you're "bashing" the rich. Studies show that prostitute street-walkers feel a little guilty about what they do; not these "economists".

Of course, with high unemployment, there was enormous pressure on labor. The result was not only low wages, but we're back to the 10-12 hour day. This, of course, results in big profits for businesses. In 2012, it was reported that American businesses were sitting on close to a trillion dollars in cash. During Bush, this was the cash that business supposedly needed to create jobs. But where were the jobs now? And where are those Phds scribbling for *The Economist*. When it's time to come up with some new scam to bilk taxpayers out of billions of dollars, these economists have stratospheric IQs. But now that it's time figure out why companies are sitting on billions of cash money, they suddenly go dumb on us.[20]

And if anyone even *hints* of ways to spur Consumption, which even Adam Smith said was the engine of an economy, they are severely reprimanded. In 2006, *The Economist* was decrying what they see as new populism, "…based on bashing business, boosting the unions and meddling with markets." [21] See, Adam Smith's basic premise of a *Capitalist* system with businesses *not* making its own rules, this is "meddling". Part of this "populism", is a "priority on raising the minimum wage" and "new laws to make union organizing easier. …is based on a dangerous combination of nostalgia and sloppy thinking".[22] See, getting back to the post-war period when we had optimal growth, a prosperous middle class due to labor voting power and unions, a tripling of median family income and *no deficits* — all this is based on "nostalgia and sloppy thinking". History means nothing to a reptile.

And how does *The Economist* characterize the economic policies under the Bush administration allowed the biggest swindle in our history? "At their best, Republicans have … sound economics".[23] To these scribblers, unsustainability is "sound". Right in front of their olfactory cortex sits the actual numbers that in 20 years of Republican administrations, massive, unsustainable deficits were racked up in *every single one of those years*, followed by a huge economic meltdown.

Because our means of propaganda is in the hands of the largest economic nodes, the neoconservative system mind ideology is in total control. They have a whole industry of econowhores who have become the witch doctors of modern society and who blast away their failed economic theories at the American people. Public television features the same econowhores as you get on Fox news. Not one word is mentioned about the total lack of balance in the economy.

We mentioned in Ch. 30 how neoconservative doctrine hasn't changed in a 150 years. The results are always the same and I mean always: a crippled economy and either massive debt or a big meltdown or both. We could ask where does their doctrine come from. A leading light in this regard is Friedrich von Hayek, the Karl Marx of conservatives. In my opinion, Hayek was one of the leading intellectual prostitutes of the 20th century and the inspiration of a whole cottage industry of econowhores like Milton Friedman who won great fame and fortune pimping for the system. They're right about as often as a monkey throwing darts. The question here is, how conscious was Hayek of his motives for his grandiose theory. Hayek preached Laissez-Faire, small government, and rules spontaneously sprouting from the "volk" in an organic way. Laws arrived at in this way were incremental, evolutionary and decentralized. This is total horseshit, of course.

The real purpose of Hayek and other neoconservative economists' attack on government is to reduce government's powers to enforce independent rules of the game. That's what they're really after. His idea of liberty is allowing large nodes in the economic system to be *free* to make their own rules, which not only allows but actually *promotes* collectivization, exactly what we have seen in *reality* since the Civil War. This econowhore could talk about rules spontaneously springing up out of the misty sea of the volk because he knew his favorite economic elites would be free to climb in bed with politicos in a big socialist gang-bang to devise their *own* rules kept under tight wraps by the system mind propaganda machine. Hayek could then *pretend* that big bad government had nothing to do with it. The head-in-the-butt neoliberal is no match for the low animal cunning of these neoconservative reptiles.

Now maybe laws like the ten commandments sprang from the volk. But the laws guiding an economic system are specific and highly technical like capital requirements, disclosure rules, derivatives, environmental protections, etc. To Hayek, these rules are beyond the understanding and comprehension of legislatures which he labeled "constructivist rationalism", a completely meaningless phrase to begin with. But somehow, they were adequately understood by the amorphous swarm called the "volk". This kind of intellectual prostitution is going to be accepted only by people who stand to gain from Economic Socialism. Laws and rules don't spring from the volk, but from the back-room deals made by politicians in bed with economic players. And I don't believe Hayek didn't see this.

Hayek howled against *political* socialism in Communist countries and even Democratic Socialism of the Scandinavian countries. To him this was too much collective power in government hands. This much is fine, but he wasn't against collectivism in the *economic* system, which again shows the total lack of principles among these inner brain neoconservative. Hayek was against ordinary working people collectivizing in unions because that interfered with his "free" market. But it was fine for capital to organize and collectivize hidden from view. This was Hayek's idea of a "free market". If a union is a collective of workers, what about a corporation as a collective of stockholders? Hayek is a mirror image of Karl Marx:

muddled, dishonest and semi-conscious. Like all neoconservatives, his need was to identify with bigness achieved by collectivizing business into huge units. He was awarded a gaggle of prizes and got famous as most neoconservatives do basically by pimping for the system and papering over reality with volumes of word-mongering crap.

Throughout US history, the more conservative the government, the more collectivization, as is amply proved during the Victorian period and under Reagan and Bush. Collectives were broken up or prevented only under the two Roosevelts. During the Reagan-Bush era of intense Economic Socialism, the anti-trust division of the justice department was totally under hypnosis. As Smith recognized, competition is one of the essences of Capitalism. The end result of Hayek's "free markets" is an economic system composed of one big company. The only difference between this and Communism is in the nature of the sex lives of the rulers.

The ultimate goal of the system mind is National Socialism, the tracks for which were laid down by Ronald Reagan. This is why the US system mind is so supportive of the Chinese economy. But of course, they have to shoehorn it into the minds of people as a form of *Capitalism* to make it more palatable. They use phrases *invariably* describing China's system as some form of "capitalism": "crony Capitalism, "authoritarian Capitalism", "vulture Capitalism", "state Capitalism", etc. *The Economist* devoted a whole issue with the cover blaring "The Rise of State Capitalism".[24] The reason for this blatant propaganda campaign is very simple: to pass off the system's favorite Economic *Socialism* as some form of *Capitalism*. Again, no conspiracy here — just another pregnant example of a system mind.

The title of their special report is "Adventures in Capitalism".[25] The only adventure in Capitalism is their use of the word 'Capitalism'. 'State Capitalism' is a contradiction in terms like dark sunshine or boiling ice. When the political system owns, controls, or is in bed with the means of production, that is the very *definition* of Socialism. It has absolutely nothing to do with Adam Smith's Capitalism, which is specifically defined as a system of *private* ownership of the means of production guided by *independent* rule-makers and a prosperous middle class. In China, there is no prosperous middle class; important parts of the economic system are owned and controlled by the Communist Party; and most importantly, economic players are in bed with political actors to make their own rules, which accounts for the enormous pollution in Chinese cities. That's strike three. US propaganda about China's road to democracy is pure unadulterated crap by the American system mind to prop up National Socialism in China. This is the wave of the future and the main motivation for our country buying Chinese goods is to move their economic/political system along so that it can lead us in the same direction.

In the past 35 years starting with Ronald Reagan, the system media mouthpieces have been extraordinarily successful at achieving every goal of the system. But at least these media propagandists are getting paid by the larger nodes of the economy to bring about the goals of the system. What excuses do historians have who are securely tucked away in big universities free to do history? Economic Socialism is such a powerful system that even the history profession has been taken over by the system mind. There is good history of the pre-Civil War years, but history of periods after the Civil War is a national disgrace. It is being written by the system mind exactly as in China and Russia.

The whole period of Economic Socialism between the Civil war and Roosevelt is called Laissez-faire Capitalism even though the economic system during this period had nothing to do with any kind of Capitalism. Even with big improvements in technology, there was never a middle class, nor independent rule-makers. It is monkey see, monkey do history and continues right to the present day.

We have yet to see a history of the period after the Civil war that the least bit resembles reality. One fake "historian" has so little knowledge of economics that he thinks Roosevelt's reforms were "radical", a copy of Russia's "central planning". Central planning involves replacing markets with government agencies that *prevent* unionism and determine prices of labor and commodities by *decree*. Resources are allocated and production of goods and services *assigned* not by markets but by government planners. Roosevelt did none of this before the war.

What Roosevelt did was get economic players *out* of the beds of politicians making their own rules since the Civil War enabling people's representatives to make rules, as Adam Smith prescribed. Unionism and a minimum wage created a prosperous middle class for the first time in the history of the world. Social Security and jobs programs were just as Adam Smith described as "public works". He did all this while maintaining our most important freedoms. Central planning is what the Bush administration did to invade Iraq, which this capon probably drooled over. Of course, during WWII, there was "central planning" and security measures Roosevelt took were egregious abuses of power. However, the life of the country was at stake. This is no excuse, but it was the *Democratic* Party who tried to return to traditional rights and freedoms after the war, while conservatives were actually trying to dilute rights and freedoms in the infamous McCarthy period.

Historians have completely mischaracterized our economic/political system since the Civil War. It had nothing to do with Adam Smith's Democratic Capitalism. They completely paper over Reagan's return to the exact same Economic Socialism as in the '20s without a twitch. And what kind of history are we going to get about the Bush era's clear agenda of creating a lawless world where *any* power can invade, conquer and kill people anywhere in the world? *If historians can't keep knowledge that human beings have about themselves and their past free of system mind propaganda, who will?*

36.7 THE SYSTEM MIND AND BIG BROTHER.

Here's another example of a system mind. Remember Eisenhower's warning about a military-industrial complex as a result of the cold war? In this century, we will have a *terrorism-intelligence* complex to keep the "war on terrorism" going. It will involve about half trillion dollars a year. A quarter trillion will be spent creating terrorists by attacking or invading countries, drone-type killings, secret torture sites and propping up puppet governments. Another quarter trillion will be spent spying on everyone to track down newly created terrorists. Of course, the war on terrorism will benefit the neoconservative agenda to cripple the economy so that the top 20% can maintain the biggest share of the pie. And it will benefit the system mind propaganda outlets, who make lots of money reporting on the ongoing war on terrorism and other ramifications of a lawless world. All of this will continue to be paid for by stealing from the future, which is blatantly unconstitutional, until our national debt is to where we won't be able to afford rifles for our soldiers.

The basic reason the war on terrorism can accomplish all this is simply in the nature of a terrorist attack which is an eye-catching spectacle. The propaganda outlets can run on them for months. They really are scary. However, in terms of actual losses, a nuclear exchange, which we came very close to during the cold war, would inflict infinitely more damage on a country than a terrorist attack. It could end all of civilization. However, even at the height of the cold war, people simply were not noticeably worried about nuclear war. But a single terrorist attack, even if it kills only a few people like the Boston Marathon bombing, creates more fear and a lot bigger response. This is why the war on terrorism is the perfect war: it is really the first kind of war that enables the system mind to create a *new* category of crime and *new* methods of dealing with it. Other categories of international crime are of much less use to the system. Drugs kill thousands of Americans every year, many more than 9/11. Why doesn't our military send drones into Mexico to wipe out known drug lords, along with a bunch of innocent civilians? Why don't they drone truck drivers bringing in illegal immigrants? The answer is that the drug trade provides billions to be laundered through western banks. And illegals are a prime source of cheap labor and votes.

Child prostitution is another area of international crime. One night I heard Jimmie Carter (a fellow engineer) discuss this problem with Charlie Rose. I never knew it was so bad. *Thousands* of young girls are sold each year many of whom actually die of a myriad of causes including diseases, some right here in the US. These girls are sold into slavery not for something harmless like picking cotton, but for doing sex and often getting killed in the process. What are the libbers doing about this? Traffickers who kill kids in this way don't use a bomb like a terrorist, so these deaths simply don't count. But again, we don't invade Thailand and kill thousands of innocents because they have international criminals involving sex trade with children. The reason is that prostitution is a perfectly effective way for the system mind to do away with intact families. With a constant supply of nice young girls, it's very easy for husbands to be tempted into the world of prostitution.

All international crime involves cells and gangs of people engaged in illegal activities in the exact same way as terrorists operate. But because other categories of international crimes are less spectacular and shocking, the system mind can't use international criminals to wage a war that would chip away at our basic rights and freedoms and initiate new categories of international crime fighting. The American people would probably not give up their freedoms to go after illegal trafficking, drug lords, money launderers or child prostitution gangs.

Not only does the war on terrorism allow the system to water down our basic rights and freedoms, but it has the dual purpose of dismantling any semblance of international law. Aside from the effectiveness of drone attacks, it is against international law to kill innocent people in the process of getting an international criminal. It *is* acceptable to kill civilians of a nation whose *government* is engaged in international aggression. This is *top-down* killing to remove a criminal *top*-down government and civilian deaths are acceptable in the process as in WWII. But you can't hold whole populations of people responsible for international criminals operating at the *bottom* of society unless the nation in question is overtly harboring and abetting them. Killing innocents while going after individual terrorists or any other kind of international criminal by governments is *top-down* killings to get *bottom-up* criminals. This is what defines war crimes and violates international law. The US can't declare war on Mexican drug lords and send drones to kill them in residential neighborhoods, even though drugs kill many more Americans than Al Qaeda. That is because druglords are bottom-feeders and you can't invade countries and kill innocents on the basis of their criminality. What is internationally legal is to prosecute bottom-up individual criminals with *individual* bottom-up government agents. But they can't kill innocents in the process. If the US weren't the largest economy and most powerful military in the world, Bush and Obama would be on trial for war crimes.

Network propaganda mills amplify bottom-up international criminals into "wars" on the US. This is pure crap. *Individuals* don't declare or make wars, only nations do. The tiny fraction of Muslim terrorists is bottom-up individuals engaged in various kinds of international crime just like drug traffickers and prostitution rings. But they allow Obama to declare "war" on these bottom-up criminals the same way you can go after whole nations. It gives sewer radio wet dreams.

International terrorists should be kept track of, chased, caught, indicted, and tried exactly like any other criminal, which requires good old-fashioned police work by bottom-up agents of the FBI. If there's the slightest suspicion behavior, you get a court order for surveillance. In fact, up to now, all terrorist plots that have been stopped were discovered by the FBI using usual police investigative tools that are consistent with the Constitution. Even though they are the only agency that has actually *caught* terrorists, they are not of much use to the system. This is why the system mind needed a *new* category of international crime and a *new* agency that can bypass constitutional precautions.

If this same propaganda machine were in place in Abe Lincoln's day, there would be a "war on abolition" because abolitionists were "at war" with official US government policy that included slavery. If they committed a crime like John Brown did, neoconservatives would scream that there should be an "exception" and that they shouldn't have a right to a lawyer and a fair trial. (As I remember, even John Brown had a trial in those unenlightened times). Union organizers in the 1800s were also at "war against the US" and they wouldn't get constitutional protections either. And what about feminists? There were instances of destruction of property by feminist advocates in the old days. They were against national US policy as well and consequently "at war" with the US. The US would have had a right to have a "war on feminism". Obama and Bush could have sent in drones to kill Frederick Douglass, Samuel Gompers and Susan B. Anthony, killing innocents in the process. The US should be *promoting* civilization, not destroying it.

On Feb. 14, '10 network interview, Dick Cheney came right out and bragged about how the goals of the war on terrorism had been achieved. He said, before 9/11, terrorists were considered international criminals and have the right to a lawyer and a fair trial. However, after of 9/11, he was able to put terrorists into a *new* category of "enemy combatants". Now the usual rules don't have to apply. Enemy combatants can be tortured, imprisoned without trial without even council.

One by one you take away rights from each layer of criminal until suspects of any crime have no rights at all. We will be back to the Middle Ages when we had what we could call Dick Cheney justice. When a crime was committed, the police would pick up a suspect, usually someone a little peculiar, manufacture evidence, torture him until he confessed, and string him up to the cheers of the local peasants. Of course, this enabled real criminals to continue committing crimes, which explains the enormous crime rates in European cities during the Middle Ages.

Led by the Chinese model, the system mind will lead this country towards a neoconservative big brother National Socialism. *The NYR* reviewed books about how China "spends tens of billions of dollars annually...on domestic *weiwen*, or 'stability maintenance' ".[26] It ranges from the soft power of interrogations and "guidance counseling" to hard power of jail and physical abuse. This is why the US system mind is so accommodating to the Chinese economy. Their political system is the exact model our system wants for the US. You ought to be happy you're living in the US now because many of our freedoms and protections won't be around by the end of the century. All the system has to do is insure a steady flow of terrorists. James Madison, who cowrote the Constitution, said, "no nation could preserve its freedom in the midst of continual war". This is near the top of the list of the most important quotes you will ever read. The neoconservative-led system mind understands this completely, which is why it will do everything in its power to continue the war on terrorism. *The purpose of turning Muslim international criminals into a "war on terrorism" is to justify a lawless world of conquest and killing and to wash away basic rights and freedoms leading to a National Socialist big brother state.*

Of course, all this will involve bigger and bigger government agencies to mine the data that keeps track of all of us and to keep wars going that inspire the very terrorists they claim they protect us from. Well, guess what? There is a book by James Bamford telling us about a massive construction project which is to house the collection and storage of near an infinite amount of information.[27] They will have the capacity to snoop on every phone call you make, every email you send, what your values and opinions are, every magazine you subscribe to, and eventually brain scans that will be used to predict all kinds of bad things you *might* do. They will know every detail of your private life, including your sex life. This is exactly the scenario predicted in the famous novel, 1984. Naive me, I would have thought that this Big Brother government would be happening 25 years from now.

Another really scary book has been written about the new terrorism-intelligence complex. [28] This is an unbelievable book. They say, "Washington area had thirty-three large complexes for top secret intelligence work under construction ...since 9/11" (69). "After two years of investigating, Arkin had come up with a jaw-dropping 1,074 federal government organizations and nearly 2 thousand private companies involved with programs related to counterterrorism" (86). There are over a million people employed in this industry and they churn out over 50 thousand weekly or monthly publications. There's no way to know exactly how much they spend, but it's probably around a quarter *trillion* dollars a year. There are no constraining laws, no trials, no reporting, no accountability and no awareness of the American people. Whatever is done in the way of torturing and killing people, smuggling arms, propping up crooked puppet governments, and spying on the American people is done *in total secrecy*. At some point, they have probably spied on every single one of us. Even our representatives in congress are prevented from knowing how, where, and for what hundreds of billions are spent.

Priest and Arkin quote a senior military officer as saying, "The Department of Defense is no longer a war fighting organization, it's a business enterprise" (188). Additionally, it's a cesspool of Economic Socialism. People go back and forth between government and private contractors. There is no way this terrorism-intelligence complex could ever be dismantled. There's just too much money in it.

The incredible web of agencies, publications and employees produces an overload of information much of which nobody reads. Its purpose is not to catch terrorists which the FBI is more than capable of, but to add another layer of big brother government that has the best chance of getting past our Constitutional guarantees. Additionally, by insuring so much secrecy, this overload among a bevy of intelligence agencies is a total morass that prevents interagency communication. It also enables a terrorist to get through once in a while like the Boston Marathon bombers in April, 2013, which could have been prevented by the FBI. But the system has no incentive to stop *all* terrorist attacks. An occasional attack keeps the American people sufficiently scared into spending more money and manpower to "fight the war on terrorism". (In fact, these guys *were* known to authorities, but were allowed to go ahead anyway — another pregnant example of a system mind.)

The Boston Marathon bombing illustrates another incisive aspect of a system mind. One of the kids was killed, and the other was captured who initially made a statement to investigators that he did it to get the US out of Iraq and Afghanistan. This statement lasted exactly one hour. Immediately, the system mind went to work to totally suppress what the kid actually said and transform his statement into "anti-Americanism". Here again, there was no conspiracy, no telephone calls between the propaganda outlets, no agreement as to what to say. The reason, of course, is that his *cause* was the exact same *cause* as millions of Americans, which is to get the US out of Afghanistan. Of course, terrorism is terrorism no matter what the cause and I would be first one to favor the death penalty. However, his *cause* was the same as most Americans which is why it had to be totally suppressed. It was suppressed by a system mind and nothing more.

What is ironic about this event is that at the very time of this terrorist attack, there was a gangland style criminal named Whitey Bulger who was on trial for 19 murders *in the very same city of Boston*. Now here was a common criminal whose only *cause* was to kill people just for money. But he gets a bevy of fancy lawyers and a big trial and all his constitutional rights. This is after killing 19 people in cold blood *for no cause at all*. And nobody says peep about the whole court procedure that cost the taxpayer over a million dollars. But the statement of a kid who had the same *cause* as half of Americans is transformed into "anti-Americanism". Also, where was our multi-billion dollar terrorism-intelligence complex when it was time to catch two real terrorists? It was good work of the local police who found these guys, not our hundreds of big government, big brother spy agencies.

If someone were to ask me what factor in the world shows the most total hopelessness of mankind's progress and prosperity, it would be the Supreme Court and the intelligence oversight committees in Congress. Oversight *means* guiding the intelligence community to its original *function* which is to gather information to enable the government to understand, predict and respond to important world changes. But instead, the people attracted to this committee are neoconservative politicians who put intelligence agencies on the road to a police state. I worry a little about getting killed an auto accident or getting shot by an intruder into my home or even a terrorist. These are *personal* enemies. A much bigger worry to me are *enemies of the United States and what it stands for*, which are these big government intelligence agencies and the crooks in congress who support them.

The original *function* of these intelligence agencies is long gone. When it comes to important world changes like the Iranian revolution, Russian and Chinese transitions, the Arab spring, the Ukraine crisis, the ISIS invasion and anything else of major importance, these agencies for all their hundreds of billions in spending have been clueless and predict nothing. (A week before the Shaw of Iran was overthrown, CIA reported that he would last another 10 years.) The free press is ten times more effective in predicting world events than a faceless secret big government agency spending hundreds of billions. The reason is clear. By its very nature, a secret agency has very truncated input and output information flows and no feedback from society. This makes for a deranged system mind that provides no viable mental functions at all. It's like the mind of a brain in which the thalamus has been removed. And the more secrecy they get, the less viable they become.

The people in these intelligence agencies and committees think they're patriotic by "protecting" the American people. But in recent years, there has been over 50 *thousand* deaths from Alzheimer's, a half *million* deaths due to heart disease, and half a *million* cancer deaths, much of it caused by environmental mutagens. Who's protecting us from these *tens of thousands* of deaths? Last year, 40 thosand women died of breast cancer. Since 9/11 there has been a grand total of one half death per year due to terrorism. And yet, we have cut funds for the NIH and starved vital research of funds to find cures for diseases like Alzheimer's and cancer. We have cut funds for the EPA that tries to prevent genetic mutations leading to the diseases we have. But the one half victim per year due to terrorism has spawned a terrorist-intelligence network of a thousand agencies, employing over a million "analysts", spending hundreds of *billions* a year, most of which is stolen from institutions and research teams that could prevent *thousands* of deaths.

Under the leadership of intelligence oversight committees in Congress, the only system mind that develops in these agencies is designed first and foremost for self-perpetuation and growth, even though their function is long gone, just like a gigantic tumor. The cells of a tumor use their energy to multiply uncontrollably instead of differentiating to provide a function for an organ of the body. This is the exact role of our so-called intelligence agencies overseen by the worst of crooked politicians. Americans ought to demand that people getting on intelligence committees must first pass an intelligence test, which would eliminate most of who's been on them in recent years. If you're a bright kid working for one of these so-called "intelligence" agencies, my advice is to quit. Put your brains to work finding a cure for diseases that could prevent tens of *thousands* of deaths a year.

The only thing that will slow down the growth of these tumors is to run out of money. When our national debt reaches amounts like in Greece where we can't print up more money, or the system collapses, then there might be some political capital to stop creating terrorists for the war on terrorism. You can't leave our national security in the hands of these inner brain neoconservatives.

Just as a measure of Economic Socialism is the degree of environmental protection to prevent birth defects, so too the degree of an advancing police state can be measured by an important principle of law-enforcement. The principle is that breaking lesser laws in the process of uncovering violations of important laws should be exonerated and the perpetrators of the important laws prosecuted. But we see the exact opposite. Edward Snowden broke minor laws that enable the government to keep millions of secrets that shouldn't be secret in the first place. But what do we see? The Obama administration is going after Snowden who should be rewarded for his courage in exposing wrong-doing by the NSA that attacks the core of our Constitutional guarantees.

The system will keep constant pressure to probe any weak moment in our political lives to get a foothold towards creating a National Socialist police state. The Snowden affair and the Boston Marathon attack were such moments. If there were video cameras in the apartment rooms where these guys lived, we could have stopped them. In fact, we could prevent lots of crime including murders if there were cameras and brain scans in every room in every American house. Do we want to live like that? Every year, we sacrifice some victims of crime in order to live in a free society with a measure of a right to privacy. I would rather take a chance on a one in a billion chance of getting killed in a terrorist attack than have my every move and every thought monitored by some big brother government. Most of you would too. But eventually there's a good chance that the system will win out.

36.8 THE POLITICAL FUTURE

There is no way any of the trends discussed in this chapter can be averted. The two political parties have sunk into their own vector traps that prevent any change because with ever-increasing information flows, these traps will only strengthen and perpetuate themselves and the system that supports them. Since Ronald Reagan, the Republican Party has realized that the way to control the system is to control the major means of propaganda. You don't have to *do* anything for the economic benefit of the great middle class like even providing jobs, but only control the words they hear. Their historic agenda of crippling the economy provides more relative power and money to finance the means of propaganda that keeps everything in place. Their hand-picked Supreme Court vampires have even ruled that money flows that finance massive propaganda by the system mouthpieces can totally overwhelm the minor chirpings you get from the internet or personal rumblings made by small people. Not only that but bribery with more money flows has become incased in law. The result is that economic players will be in smaller beds with political animals making their own rules, which is simply a milder version of Karl Marx's system of the two systems being the same people. This provides even more relative power and wealth to the top 5% to finance the information flows necessary to keep the system mind alive and well.

In the private sector, historically the Democratic Party was the party of labor, fighting for better working conditions, the 8-hour day, health benefits, safety and full employment. But since Ronald Reagan, Democrats began to see that it was a lot easier to sit idle and welcome with open arms casualties of Republican Party policies that cripple the economy putting millions on the edge of poverty. They supported free trade that shipped millions of good-paying union jobs overseas. After the 2012 election, there was an epiphany. The Democratic party jumped for joy drooling at the mouth. The mass of illegal immigrants let in by Ronald Reagan finally paid off. The huge population of babies made by illegals along with millions on the "pathway to citizenship", are voting citizens near the poverty level. Add to that the casualties of Republican party economic policies and you have a huge voting block that Democrats can buy with a safety net financed mostly by stealing from the future.

The Hispanic culture is not like the old European immigrants of the 1800s whose modus vivendi was to assimilate as soon as possible and join mainstream America. They are a more cohesive group. The same is true for Muslim immigrants to Europe. This is amplified by the new cultural goal of "diversity". Now, immigrants are *supposed* to be different. And by being at bottom economic levels, this sets up a feedback loop. By being poorer, their lifestyles are a little different. This creates a bit of prejudice which prevents economic advancement. This in turn causes more clumping in their own neighborhoods and clutching to their own cultural practices. And because of lower economic status, their survival is threatened. Whenever the survival of any species of living creatures is threatened, they survive by multiplying. This puts their culture in an even worse light. However, they can gradually coalesce into a powerful voting block exactly as senior citizens have and vote themselves taxpayer moneys for "benefits". This new lazy man's solution to winning elections is precisely how Obama got reelected. It's in the interests of the new Democratic Party for our citizens *not* to be self-sufficient.

A small part of the Republican Party understands this. However, too many leaders in the party have taken too many bribes from the business community to go along with social conservatives, even though they know a good percentage of the American people don't want massive illegal immigration. The one-two punch of the two political parties will keep the system going well into this century. The Republicans cripple the economy with Economic Socialism, and destroy the value of labor with a constant stream of illegal immigrants and the Democratic Party comes along like Santa Claus with a long list of "benefits" to buy their votes. You really can't beat this combination, even though it is unsustainable.

36.9 THE LAST FORK: A CENTURY OF CONTRACTION

The most important weakness of market economies is that they tend to over produce: they can produce more goods and services than consumers can buy. This creates pressures on the demand side to constantly induce people to buy, using advertising, credit cards, etc.; on the supply side, by constantly trying to reduce operating costs to win over market share. This requires getting the most work out of employees for the least wages, which means making employees into working zombies whose personal lives are devoid of attachments, friendships, relationships or marriages; and whose public lives consist of 12-hour work days, 6 days a week, with a day off to buy the junk they are programmed to want. The values, culture, habits of mind and social practices that bring about this agenda are promoted by the major means of propaganda which are the system mind mouthpieces. Around the age of 60, the system will throw people away having various forms of dementia due to a lifetime using only a computational brain necessary to do the almighty job.

But even though it produces higher profits in the short run, in the process of starving out the consuming classes, demand for goods and services lags. Eventually the system collapses into a recession or depression. This has happened *seven* times since the Civil War, the last being in 2008. But once in a while, new technology creates a technological bubble that gets the system going again for a number of years. An interesting question is, is there a chance of a new bubble that will get the economy back up to speed that could put off doomsday.

Everyone I've ever talked to says, oh yes there will always be another bubble, because there always has been. After all, history repeats itself (except when it doesn't). I don't think many would agree, but I have a sneaking hunch that there will not be another bubble. We have to keep in mind the definition of a bubble, defined in Sect. 24.8. There will always be new ideas coming on line. But a new idea is not enough for a bubble. It has to be such a revolutionary idea that much more money is thrown at it than it really deserves. The Dec. '11 edition of *Scientific American* was devoted to "10 World Changing Ideas".[29] Yes, and I can assure you, everything here was light years from an economic bubble.

Take the green industry. A new idea is the wind turbine that generates electricity by wind power. It's a great idea, but it isn't producing a bubble. There aren't hundreds of companies going into business making wind turbines. The industry may expand a bit and maybe a new firm will pop up now and then. But the amount of plant and equipment and the number of workers will never be *more* than what is necessary to produce the number of wind turbines that can be sold. Already the industry is at an equilibrium level. The same in the drug industry.

A major piece of evidence for lack of bubbles is to look at the possibilities that basic physics suggests. When you look at the areas of physics that can create breakthrough bubbles, they have all been used up. The four basic areas of physics are thermodynamics, mechanics, chemistry and electronics. Thermodynamics produced the basic engine. It created three bubbles — the steam engine bubble, the railroad bubble after the Civil War and the auto bubble of the early 20th century. It has been varied, improved, modified and adapted in a million ways and there will be more variations, but there will be no more bubbles coming out of the engine.

The great age of mechanics was in the Victorian period. There will be greater use of robots which is already a mature industry. Again, no bubble. We had the chemistry bubble after WWII with plastics and chemicals. There will be new chemicals, but nothing to make the bubble that plastics and artificial fabrics made. Finally, we had the electronics bubble, TV, Hi-fi, etc., culminating in the PC, internet artificial intelligence and smartphone. This one is on its last leg. The only bubble AI has produced really is *artificial* intelligence and an artificial bubble on Wall St. AI has increased our standard of living in many artificial ways like cellphones and computers. But there is no bubble here. The industry produces as many cellphones as it sells and no more. Not only isn't AI producing a bubble, but these finite state devices will do nothing to improve parts of our standard of living that involves meaning like perceptions of art, beauty, skills, nature, literature, other living creatures and most of all, human relations.

As far as jobs, AI will replace millions of jobs that involve only finite state perceptions. But it will replace these jobs with AI jobs that require an enlargement of the computation brain at the expense of an ever-shrinking existential brain. There won't be a lot of difference between the mechanical robots and the human robots that design and program them. There's been an upsurge in AI as companies are going into great detail about how words and sentences are related in people's conversation. They are accumulating massive databases. But it will be a colossal failure with real humans just like the last three AI colossal failures, because it will always be a finite state system and no real meaning will accrue. But I'll bet right now they have programs that, with a decent photo, a guy will get a crotch click out of 9 out of 10 liberated women on the internet. But AI will not replace real humans in any job where meaning is required which will probably be enough to keep an economy going as well as a small infinite state human class. When a service I have won't let me talk to a humanoid, I switch out of the service. You should too.

Also, with an ever-shrinking existential brain where meaning can be accommodated, there will be increasing problems at the inner brain level especially the limbic system. There will be more problems with phobias, aggressions, fears, stubbornness, repulsions. Homegrown violence and terrorism will increase. The mental health field will explode.

The American economy is like a train on a track. In the short run, you can pretend to steer the train all you want, but the track is going to take the train where the track is going no matter how much you try to steer. Tracks create a momentum vector. The founding fathers wrote a Constitution that laid down track for the next 60 years during which time we had some semblance of Democratic Capitalism. The system was too simple for the Supreme Vampires to foul up, although they did a great job of maintaining slavery. But the resolution of the slavery issue during the Civil War required new tracks. Lincoln attempted to do this but he never got to finish the job. Instead, the new Republican president, Andrew Johnson assumed the job of laying down new track for the next 65 years. He was guided in this regard by the explosion of technology and growth of large financial fortunes as economic nodes. Even a relatively good guy like Grover Cleveland did not have the political capital to lay down new tracks. There followed a long period of intense Economic Socialism during which almost all new wealth and income went to the top 20%. Some have called it the first great Depression. There wasn't a hint of a middle class, only a very large, very poor working class. Had Lincoln lived, he might have been able to lay down a track of continued Democratic Capitalism. But we never got the chance to see what Lincoln might have done.

The crash of 1929 was another train wreck. Because the crash was so intense, Roosevelt had the political capital to lay down new tracks in the direction of Democratic Capitalism. Rules were made for the economic game independent of the players for the first time since before the Civil War. A new middle class was created for the first time anywhere in the world that could clear markets just as Adam Smith described. The Roosevelt revolution lasted 20 years after WWII, and was the greatest expansion of the economy in history.

After WWII, we had an optimal economy, and most importantly, employment was created by the *private* sector precisely because the bottom 80% was getting 60% of national income. The government was relatively small with no deficits because there was no need for big government to create jobs. Real income to the middle class was high enough, by and large, to pay for their own benefits without a Democratic Party buying votes with benefits.

But then the nation had an injection of just plain bad luck. The WWII bubble of electronics and chemicals ended. There was an oil shortage due to trouble in the Middle East and there was Carter's problem with the hostage taking. So the '70s were recessionary. Continuing collectivism in industry created monopoly prices. And it might also have been the case that labor in some industries had gotten too strong. Wage demands in the major industries like auto, steel, and mining might have exceeded productivity gains which set off an inflationary spiral.

The crime of the internet bubble was that Clinton could have used this economic boom to lay new tracks. But Clinton's main interest was power and popularity. If there was ever someone who was an "easy rider" it was Clinton. He didn't get off the train for one moment. Instead, Clinton and Bush afterwards used the internet bubble to further water down the rules of the game so that instead of reinvigorating the middle class, they used it to create a financial services economy based on total fraud requiring massive theft from the future to prop back up.

Being a relatively idealistic guy, Obama, upon getting elected in 2008, proceeded to get off the train to see how he might lay down new tracks. The response to this meltdown could have put us on a road to recovering a Capitalist economy just as Roosevelt did in 1929. But Obama was too weak-minded for the job. The new team he hired a to help him lay new tracks was a Trojan horse. They said to Obama, "hey Barack, it's really wet and cold out here in the rain. Forget the tracks. Let's all get back on the train to the smoking car, have a good cigar and a martini and enjoy the warm ride. Just give us the money". This is exactly what Obama proceeded to do, and he's been riding the train ever since right on the tracks laid down by Ronald Reagan. The job may have been impossible. The tracks were so deeply embedded with the Reagan culture that it would have been a difficult job even for a Roosevelt — no chance with a weak-minded Barack Obama.

Like all complex systems, the economic system's priority is its own perpetuation. Organic systems from simple bacteria up to humans reproduce and perpetuate themselves. Our economic system is no different. For 35 years now, Reagan's tracks have taken the national train down an Economic Socialist path that perpetuates the system: import millions of illegal immigrants to suppress the value of labor, attack unions, collectivize industry especially agriculture, pass rules that steal more and more from future generations and wash away the Constitution. It keeps *real* unemployment above 8% to create a climate of terror in the minds of workers so that businesses can work people every waking hour. But it won't let real unemployment get above about 12%, or voters might bring back a Roosevelt and his dreaded Democratic Capitalism. But there is no fear of a Roosevelt now. The system is so powerful that a potential Roosevelt would be turned into a system zombie within weeks of being elected exactly like Obama.

Even with this level of unemployment, there will be deficits. In fact, we can give a formula as to how much deficits and unemployment there will probably be. I'll only briefly describe the formula. The primary variable is technology, which is the starting point of the analysis. Each year, there are new ideas and new investment opportunities. On this basis, deficits and unemployment will be determined by the distribution of income. If the bottom 80% is getting 60% of national income, you can run the economy with low unemployment, no deficits and some growth, just like after WII. However, if the bottom 80% is getting only, say x % of national income, this will determine a combination of unemployment, deficits and growth. If you want low unemployment, this will require a large deficit. If you want a small deficit, then you will get high unemployment. If you minimize both, there will be no growth.

Under Obama, we had a few new ideas coming on line to create a few percentage growth in the economy. (If we used the GEP instead of GDP, there was no growth). Given this level, you look at the share of income going to the bottom 80%, which is now about 47%. This will determine a combination of deficits and unemployment. It turned out that with a deficit of about a half trillion dollars, you get between 10% and 15% *real* unemployment (not reported). If Republicans cut deficits by cutting government spending, unemployment will go up.

This implies that the more inequality you have, the more government spending you need to keep up demand which increases the deficit. This is why neoconservative doctrine is not only morally but economically bankrupt. They complain about "big government". But given the enormous inequality they delight in, big government is an absolute *requirement* to prop up demand and keep up employment. Even Reagan knew this much, which explains his massive deficits.

The Republican Party will continue to be the party of *crippling the economy by attacking the middle class* so their heroes in the top 5% get a bigger share of the pie. This has been the core of the neoconservative political agenda *in reality* for 150 years. As inequality grew continually after Reagan, size of government and deficits grew in step, *every single year Republicans were in office.* At the bottom of the brain, neoconservatives don't really want small government. They want *huge* government — big enough to project massive power to kill people all over the world, big enough to keep stealing from future generations to prop up failed economic theories and big enough to monitor the details of our private lives.

These neoconservatives simply don't understand Capitalism, the most important component of which is a prosperous middle class to clear markets. Since the Civil War, except for the Roosevelt period, their Economic Socialism has kept up a constant class war on the middle class. There's an organization, the American Legislative Exchange Council (ALEC) "…which brings together state legislators and corporate lobbyists to trade ideas and draft model legislation. The country's largest corporations…buy a seat at the table and pick up the check".[30] In my opinion, this is just another Economic Socialist institution to put political actors in bed with economic players making their own rules, rules that the citizenry knows nothing about and has no part in making. To cover up this racket, neoconservative nodes will continue to hire paid econowhores in the tiniest of media outlets to talk up policies that are the exact *opposite* of what they are actually doing in Congress.

The only reason for the economy doing a little better than would normally be the case is that welfare benefits concocted by local liberals have sprouted like weeds. The good side of this is that it helps keep up income to the bottom 80% and so props up consumption. However, keep in mind that no work is done for these benefits which shows up as a shrinking GEP. The motivation is to buy votes. As genocide picks up steam in an increasingly polluted environment causing healthcare costs to mushroom, the GDP will become a totally irrelevant measure. There is nothing in the agenda of either party that will bring back sustainable Democratic Capitalism and a financially independent middle class. The debate will take place in the smoking car of the train that is on the tracks laid down by Ronald Reagan.

We have experienced a century of expansion due to the world inheriting four important factors that were handed to us free of charge: technology, resources, good genes and a safe environment. Technology allowed production capabilities to rise to where any kind of gadget can be produced for little money. This was greatly aided by the discovery of vast amounts of natural resources: oil, gas, cement, iron, copper, zinc, etc., and most importantly, fresh water. These resources came to us basically free and provided substances for the manufacture any kind of physical object. And the economy was not dragged down by environmental costs due to toxic waste, rising oceans and weather events.

In the past, with almost a complete lack of medical technology, humans died like flies from every conceivable malady, some environmental, some genetic. In the year 1900, one out of ten babies died before the age of one. If a baby had the slightest genetic malady, it would most likely die. This implies that adults born before WWII, basically had strong genes. These are our senior citizens now. Thus the four ingredients of a vibrant, expanding economy were in place during the 20th century: amazing new technology, unlimited free resources, a strong gene pool and a safe environment. This is why the 20th century was a century of enormous expansion.

But the 21st century will be a century of slow contraction. The explosion of technology, resources, health, and agricultural expansion is pretty much winding down. Every year, except for newly found gas, natural resources not only become rarer, but become increasingly expensive to mine. In many places in the world, even in the US, fresh water is running out and will run out faster with fracking. Bill McKibben reviewed some books on this problem a few years back. Much of today's agriculture is irrigated by underground aquifers that are gradually running out.

Even in the area of technology, we have exhausted methods of producing things. We are as efficient as we're going to get. What is ironic is that a lot of the new technology coming on line in the last 20 years that so dazzled everyone is all in terms of 0s and 1s. But in my opinion, the most important aspects of life are health, the quality of personal relationships, conveniently located good jobs, the roofs over our heads, food we eat, and the accessories in our homes, *not* 0s and 1s.

Agricultural productivity increased dramatically over the last 35 years, but will it continue to keep up with growing populations? Each year, collectivized agriculture produces food with less nutritional value. Where is a tomato that tastes like one. In some areas, climate change is actually causing a *drop* in crop yields and there will be increasing stress on agriculture due to plant viruses and pests. Combating this will probably require genetically modifying food to the sacrifice of nutritional value. When it comes to breeding, you don't get something for nothing.

General global warming, although not as bad as polar warming, is causing infections and viruses to spread northward.[31] Tics and worms are also moving northward attacking northern animals like musk ox, polar bears, walruses and seals. Nobody knows the real long-term effect on northern peoples, but they could be catastrophic. We are really playing Russian roulette with large populations of all forms of life including people.

Polar warming will cause a continuous rise in sea levels flooding many areas of arable land especially along the world's coasts.[32] In this century, hundreds of billions of dollars will be subtracted from our standard of living to pay for prevention, like drainage and barriers, and for coastal reconstruction after ocean storm surges like Hurricane Sandy. Of course, these expenses will be added to the GDP. But this is an illusion because our standard of living will actually be dropping. In fact, the hundreds of billions will have to come from money people have available to spend on goods and services that constitute their standard of living.

Turning to our personal lives, years ago, even working class people like my parents had nice accessories in their homes which were sturdy buildings called brownstones that could take a tornado. In a typical working class home, you would find hand-painted china, hand-woven textiles, and solidly built custom furniture made of hardwoods. I've been in upscale homes of highly paid professionals where you find nothing but junk. What have taken the place of fine objects are finite state devices like smartphones, computers and ugpads, which most often transmit only ants and bees talk having minimal meaning. And I don't care how smart the smartphone gets, an intelligent answer is worthless without an intelligent question.

The houses we build now are made of piss, paint, plywood and plasterboard. Photos of the tornadoes in March 2012 were astounding. Everything blew away in a heap of rubble spread over miles of countryside ruining the lives of inhabitants. This is a poignant example of Economic Socialism. Developers climb in bed with politicians to make rules for housing construction so that orange crate homes on cheap flood plain land can be pawned off on the public who have no idea of possible losses, which is everything they own, their entire life history. These homes should never have been built. Not a peep was ever suggested by the system mind media.

The tornados in Oklahoma City in May of 2013 killed over 25 people including a number of children. What is so egregious about this is that the very same area was destroyed by a tornado 14 years earlier. You would think these citizens would learn something and spend their money on building sturdy safe homes. They didn't even allocate funds for a safe school to put their own kids in. As a result, the tornado killed eight kids in one of their junk orange crate schools. But during the coverage of the tornado, not one word was said about how the enormous damage could have been avoided or at least minimized with sturdy construction. But these media whores make money on wars, death and destruction, not on watching safe homes and schools being built. If you take away the screens, our GEP standard of living as judged by an objective 19th century observer would be falling off a cliff.

Right now the average middle class family has lost about a quarter *million* dollars over their working lives in taxes, low income, and loss of benefits to their standard of living. It shows up in a lessening of major components of a good standard of living: well-built homes to safely raise a family in, home accessories, leisure time for hobbies and personal interaction, quality food and viable genes. The money that used to go for all that is now going either to the top 1% on Wall St. or the bottom 20% for benefits to buy votes; or it went to politicians like Bush who spent their quarter million dollars to go half-way around the world to kill people, to create terrorists and then to chase down the terrorists their policies created.

And finally, we have said that health care costs for maladies with a genetic basis before 1976 are a legitimate addition to our standard of living. However, diseases like childhood cancer, auto-immunity and autism have more than doubled since then. We get better at diagnosis due to advanced technology. But it's a losing battle because mutated genes are causing rising incidences of disorders faster than diagnoses can improve lifespans, which is why lifespans have leveled off and by the middle of this century, will be plummeting.

Our seniors now are a cohort that was born in a relatively clean environment. As generations of people born after WWII come on line, huge amounts of wealth will go to diagnose and patch up people whose genes were exposed to the thousands of highly mutagenic substances that have been invented since WWII that biological systems have no resistance to. Healthcare costs will mushroom and by the end of this century could take up three fourths of the GDP in my opinion. As the GDP mushrooms, the system's propaganda outlets will pounce upon this as showing a growing economy. But it will be a mirage. Nobody is better off even with the best medical technology after genes mutate than before. This is why the GDP will become more a propaganda tool than a measure of our standard of living.

Keep in mind, these expenses will only patch people up. We are not going to find ways to fix mutated genes that get passed on. There is some progress with gene therapy working with various forms of RNA that can intercept a bad gene from being transcribed into a harmful protein. There's a treatment for hepatitis C like this. But I've heard it will cost 50 thousand dollars *a week*. These mushrooming costs do not indicate better health, but only reflect the degree to which society is committing genocide on the gene pool. But since people depend more on words than perceptions to create their pictures of reality, they won't complain. The propaganda outlets do a great job of covering up this major cause in the drop in our standard of living as well. Every word you hear in the media about health is a "war" on this or that disease, and the "fight" against cancer and other maladies. You never hear peep about the causes of the genocide due to lax environmental standards in the corporate world who pay these media whores. Government agencies predicting world trends in wealth and growth have been adequate in the past because they were measuring the effects of newly discovered resources, better agricultural methods, and technology. They have *no* experience measuring the *impediments* to wealth and growth we have outlined.

There are two basic reasons people don't see the loss to their standard of living. The first is to distract people by the "war on terrorism" as we discussed. The reason why the American people allot huge amounts of money to a trumped-up "war on terrorism" is that humans are wired for the major emotions of fear and aggression. For thousands of years, kings had no trouble rounding up a bunch of young men to go conquer far-away lands even though it meant nothing but death and injury. People are not wired to for strong emotions to have well-constructed homes with nice things inside that are safe from tornadoes and floods. After all, *our hominid ancestors lived for thousands of years in simple caves*. At the rate we're going, we'll be back in caves in the not-to-distant future. It doesn't bother them that infrastructure is weakening, that education is suffering and the quality of life is deteriorating. They won't mind putting money for these necessities into an aggression-motivated war on terrorism and a fear-dependent terrorism-intelligence network. It would take strong education to get people to attend to their real interests and the system mind is not going to do anything like that. We see this already in the Tea Party rallies who are often ordinary middle class people. They think the multi-billionaires who sponsor these rallies are going to take money out of their pockets and give it to a bunch of dumb peasants at tea party rallies. For a thousand years, the kings of Europe had the support of the peasants too.

The second major reason the middle class won't see a drop in their standard of living is that the system will continue to empty people's lives of meaning. Urbanization does some of this. When we lived in villages, interaction between people was slow, steady, constant, deep, and extended over long periods of time so that infinite state meaning could accrue. Now, with constant job changes, thousands go through our lives in superficial ways with no opportunity to develop relationships that accrue significant meaning. As a result, people in urban areas suffer twice as much mental and physical problems as those in rural areas, all of which will add unnecessarily to health care costs. [33]

The lack of meaning starts in the earliest years of the educational system. More and more we see computers and computer-aided educational methods in the education process. Education will continue to consist of *training* in the use of finite state devices. These include screen instruction, machine lecturing and any other finite state device the system can concoct. Finite state machines might improve the ability to pass finite state tests in mathematics, geography, and some branches of science. But this is really *training*, as opposed to education. When it comes to *infinite* state abilities involving meaning, like interpersonal relations, aesthetics and liberal arts education in literature, history, psychology, etc., which is what real education is all about, these educational aids will probably be a colossal failure.

As these kids grow up, communication between them will involve less and less personal interaction and will take place over finite state devices that greatly diminish the meaning of a piece of communication. Kids sit in the same room texting instead of conversing in the normal way. As adults, they will be distracted from their falling standard of living by an assortment of finite state devices with lots of meaningless motion to keep the addicted eye occupied. They will still be able to do their finite state jobs to the system's satisfaction. They won't even mind 3 or 4 hours commuting because there will be no real home life to get home to and they can babble away on their cell phones while commuting. Commute, compute, dispute — that's their lives, which will contain less and less meaning in the way of understanding, human relations, and human perception. If you compare the understanding of the world around us among libber generations of Ronald Reagan to the pre-libber generations, the comparison is staggering.

With nobody appearing very special in this kind milieu there will be fewer relationships, the marriage rate will continue to drop and will gradually disappear from society as a hindrance to the efficient working of the system. Communication between spouses will deteriorate to ants and bees talk having little meaning. There will be less glue holding people together, which will result not only in a high divorce rate, but poor quality marriages that do continue.

Appreciating complex relationships with other human beings as well as well-built and beautifully made houses and high quality objects inside requires the ability to project meaning to things in the world. This century's citizen will develop no such meaning and so it will not be part of the citizenry's standard of living. The perception of a falling standard of living might only show up if people can't afford the latest fashions. This is why there hasn't been outrage or protest with the falling standard of living among the bottom 80%.

There are a few reasons the economy has done a little better than our formula would predict. One is that with the center of people lives the almighty job or business, only the computational brain is necessary. And it is working every waking hour to think about the job or to figure out how to make money. Millions of businesses are started each year and some succeed. Even though it gives a bigger share of income to the top 20%, the boost to the economy enables less deficits and unemployment over what you would expect with the great inequality we have. But it's at the cost of our personal lives, which will involve less and less meaning. When some of these hustling bustling beetles get old, they will wonder where life went.

There's another downside. Meaning takes place in the outer brain which is where our sense of morality and rationality lie as we became persons about a couple hundred thousand years ago. With energy going mostly to the computational brain, and having spent a few million years as homo habilis, (tool user) humans can easily become addicted to anything with hand-eye coordination like computer work. Add to that the lack of moral guidance, it's no wonder there is so much cyber-crime. And it pays well. What's worse, even people working to fight cyber-crime get addicted the same way. It's a race to the bottom of the brain.

Lack of meaning in the modern brain also explains why our billionaires produce nothing of redeeming social value. Wall St. billionaires are really money-making machines. There is little meaning in their brains and in their lives. The robber barons of the 1800s were aggressive money-makers too, but they at least had enough meaning in their lives to support great works of art and architecture and left a legacy to our cultural heritage. They put up beautiful mansions on Park Ave. and in Newport, R.I. showing skills only humans are capable of. Today's Wall Street billionaires had a chance to do something meaningful on the site of the World Trade Center. Instead, we got a meaningless sky-high hard-on that New Yorkers need to identify with. That event by itself symbolically shows what has happened to the modern human brain.

This also explains the extreme rancor in our political lives. Liberals and conservatives always disagreed but not to the extent of the extreme hatred we see now. Congress has come to a stand-still and is filled with really despicable ideologues. The reason is that with less meaning in people's lives and only the computational brain using energy for the job, there is no energy allotted to personal relations, perceptions, interesting hobbies, learning, discussing, etc. Brain energy drops to the bottom and energizes primitive emotions of aggression, anger, hatred and greed, which is exactly what we see in politics.

The lack of meaning in our lives has also shown up in the field of genius. A guy has written a book about why genius is disappearing from society.[34] But what is also required for genius especially in the arts and literature is a rich, meaningful environment to hone the fortuitous gene combination. That is what is missing in today's world. The above writer hasn't noticed that we still produce IQ geniuses but only in certain areas of finite state knowledge like math, many of the sciences, and especially IT that involve only the computational brain. What we lack completely is genius in areas that involve infinite state meaning like history (which is a national disgrace), literature, the arts, especially architecture, psychology, etc. It isn't too bad now because we still have a few people left who were born in a meaning-laden world, but it will only get worse this century. If you want your kids to achieve some sort of greatness, *get the finite state devices out of their lives.*

36.10 THE NEW INDUSTRIAL FEUDALISM

In the foreseeable future, nobody is going to lay down new tracks. In my opinion, the tracks laid down by Ronald Reagan lead right off the cliff into the land of National Socialism which means a crippled economy, a hierarchical economy and a continuously monitored citizenry and a century of contraction in the GEP. What makes all this inevitable is that the core of both political parties agree on where the system will go, although their reasons may be very different.

The first thing we must emphasize is that systems always produce hierarchies over time and history if full of examples, the prime one being feudalism itself. The reason history produces hierarchies is that hierarchies are less complex and follow the second law of thermodynamics which says that systems lose information and complexity and become simpler with time. Democratic Capitalism, which is what the founding fathers designed with the help of Adam Smith, is a very complex system because it requires detailed independent rules to keep it in balance and to maintain a prosperous middle class. This is why it is such a fragile system and can easily degenerate into Economic Socialism.

What created progress for mankind are people who *bucked* the system. The founding fathers bucked the feudal European system with a Constitution that was very *anti*-hierarchical. They specifically outlawed titles and an aristocracy. Their vision for the country was one of a prosperous independent yeomen middle class across all segments of society. Jefferson articulated this view on many occasions.

But they could not remove slavery in their time. But as time went on, slavery actually intensified. Lincoln had to buck the system to remove slavery. But after the Civil War, the system gradually evolved a hierarchy of Robber Barons as the nobility, a small professional class, a new aristocracy class in the propaganda business with large newspapers starting up. On the bottom was a very poor working class of factory workers. The abuses became so bad that it brought in a temporary reformer in Teddy Roosevelt. But he couldn't buck the system for very long. The 1920s again produced the usual hierarchy. Franklin Roosevelt bucked the system and brought back a semblance of democratic Capitalism. But with Ronald Reagan the system again picked up where it left off in the 20s with the gradual evolution of a feudal hierarchy complete with a slave class of illegal immigrants. Since these are modern times, we could call it *Industrial Feudalism.*

This time the system is so powerful with the massive flows of information that even historic liberals have been pushed right out of the Democratic party and replaced by a very energetic neoliberal movement that is motivated by one of the strongest human emotions that Karl Marx used to gain notoriety: the desire to annihilate, to squelch, to crush the system. A strong emotion always blots out detailed perceptions of reality. So they have no idea what will replace the system they want to crush. The first order of business to them is to crush the system. And they have found a way to do it without all of detailed work old liberals did in the past to protect labor and our freedoms and maintain a prosperous middle class and a decent society. Simply overrun the system with as many people as possible from failed states and failed cultures. This method requires no real work by neoliberals.

But the new neoconservative *does* know the kind of system they want for the future which is *Industrial Feudalism* and a hierarchy just like in the Middle Ages. This is the exact opposite of what the founding fathers envisioned for the country. There will be a nobility at the top 1% who have a controlling share of wealth and income and, most importantly, are above the law, just like the Middle Ages. The nobility includes Wall St, who orchestrated the biggest swindle in our history and were actually *rewarded* with bonuses and commissions for their work. There were no indictments, no penalties, no punishment because they are above the law.

The next 4% will be an aristocracy of larger neoconservative nodes of the economy. They will intensify economic socialism by controlling the political system so that they can make their own rules and keep their share of the pie increasing, all facilitated by a crooked Supreme Court that has no interest in the vision of the founding fathers. Of course, the rest of the top 20% who are the professionals will do okay economically because of their talents and education. They didn't do badly as craftsmen and yeoman farmers even in the Middle Ages. The top 20% will have most of the income and virtually all the wealth of the country.

Included in the professional class in the top 20% of are the talking heads you see on the system mouthpieces. Some would put them in the aristocracy. They take the place of the clergy in Feudal times and guide society's values and beliefs, which as we have explained is a life devoid of all meaning you get from human relationships. Traditional religion and marriage is gradually being pushed out of society. By controlling of the means of propaganda, they will keep the natives from getting restless by telling us that we have ever-growing Capitalism, while the GEP continually shrinks. The system mind understands why words have become a bigger part of people's experiences and perceptions less. The famous books, *1984* and *Brave New World*, described how words, as opposed to perceptions can be used to create reality.

What we have now as a middle class will gradually shrink into a helpless peasant class living in orange crates they rent from the bank with junk inside, a cellphone and deteriorating social interaction. And just like in the Middle Ages in many parts of Europe, on the bottom, the system will import a future slave class of mostly illegal immigrants. The aristocracy has always needed a slave class to clean up their shit and to drive down the value of labor.

The two parties will insure that the peasants will vote for continuous doses of Economic Socialism. And they will vote to increase birth defects in their own children with an environment that keeps accruing pollutants that are highly toxic to biological systems. This is in addition to the massive taxes and debt they are passing on to these very same kids. Not only will it be difficult for the lower 80% to have the same standard of living as their parents, but much of their tax dollars will go to pay not for healthcare, not for environmental safety, not for better schools or courts, but to pay interest to foreign multi-billionaires who hold the debt.

The important point is that both political parties are now part of the system. They disagree on some peripheral social issues like gay marriage or abortion, but these issues are not the top priority of the system mind. That's why lots of citizens say, it doesn't matter who they vote for. A feudal hierarchy is the priority and in that they are two peas in a pod. To show this, in the political campaign of 2016, the enemy of the Republican establishment wasn't Hilary Clinton, but Donald Trump because he alone threatened the system. Of course, Donald Trump doesn't come close to the figures who bucked the system in the past, but in view of the tremendous increase in information flows and a strong system mind, maybe he's the best we can do at this point in history to buck the system.

The 2016 election also showed that the Republican establishment has seen that their agenda is better off under a fake liberal than under a conservative. This is why they aren't alarmed that the influx of an immigrant class who will be a voting block for Democrats, will be the end of the Republican party at the national level. The top priority for both parties is the system and it doesn't matter which party the president is from as long has he or she is a system person. This is why Hilary basically got a free ride while Trump got a political lynching from the media like I've never seen before in my life. The sad and really alarming fact is that Trump with all his warts and inadequacies is the only icon in the whole country who wanted to buck the system.

A very important book yet to be written is how did historic liberalism meld into neoliberalism and then proceed to climb in bed with neoconservatism pushing for a new Industrial Feudalism. The reasons have to be a little different. My brief take is that by supporting the little guy for a hundred years, liberals gained a great sense of self-righteousness: they had God on their side and there was no question of their being right. But self-righteousness leads inevitably to authoritarianism. Combine that with with their economic success as part of the aristocracy and professional class with women wanting careers, it all points to the need for a slave class to clean up their shit. The end result is a feudal hierarchy with a king perched on top and a slave class on the bottom. Hilary is now running for queen.

The only fly in the ointment is that the system mind has no time concept as we have pointed out. It thinks the money it steals from the future is free money. But the system is unsustainable and down the line, the country will be saddled with debt larger than the whole economy. We will have permanent recession just like in Japan. Sometime this century the whole system will collapse; and I don't mean a little shock like in '08, but a real collapse. But Industrial Feudalism will be firmly in place and there will be no reform movement. It will be something like a new Dark Ages and can go on for the same amount of time.

Francis Fukuyama thinks the world is asymptotically approaching Democratic Capitalism as a default. But Democratic Capitalism is simply too unstable and fragile. The default is National Socialism as a form of modern Industrial Feudalism and one of these days he'll write a big book amending his latest mistakes. The American people are up against three of the most powerful forces in history: a neoliberal movement that wants to crush the system by overrunning it; a business class who needs cheap labor which immigration gives; and a new clergy of media propagandists who need a slave labor class to clean up their shit. I don't see how the American people can possibly cope with this potent combination.

I want to apologize for too many concepts in these volumes. But there is an index. So at times, you might want to look up a topic and reread some of this. Finally, I want to thank you very profusely for plowing through all of this. I tried very hard to shorten it, and actually did cut out about a third of what I had originally written. But there was simply too much to cover and I want to thank the reader for attempting to get through it all. One last thing. If this book is successful, the word 'meaning' will become meaningless.

1   Klare, M. "Two, Three, Many Afghanistans". *The Nation*, Apr. 26, '10, p. 21

2   Klare Ibid. p. 22

3   "The New World Order". *The Economist*, Mar. 22, '14.

4   "Putin's Gambit". *The Economist*, May 10, '14, p. 49

5   "What's Wrong with Democracy." *The Economist*, Mar. 1, '14, p. 47

6   "Flight of the Disposed". *The Economist*, June 21, '14

7   "Why the Iraqi Army Crumbled". *The Economist*, June 21, '14.

8   "Don't Let History Repeat Itself", *The Economist*, Oct. 4, '14, p. 18

9   "The sun shines bright", *The Economist*, Dec. 3, '11.

10 Bernstein, Richard, "The Death and Life of a Great Chinese City". *New York Review of Books*, Mar. 26, '09, p. 40

11 *The Economist*, Sept. 24, '11

12 Mann, James; "America's China Fantasy". *The American Prospect*, Mar. '07, p. 12

13 *The Economist*, Apr. 6, '13, p. 82

14 *The Economist*, Feb. 18, '12, p. 65

15 *The Economist*, June19th, '10, p. 14

16 Greider, Willian; "How Wall Street Crooks Get out of Jail Free". *The Nation*, Apr. 11, '11

17 Coggan, Philip; *Paper Promises*. Public Affairs Pr.

18 *The Economist*, May 8, '10, p. 58.

19 "Desperate Measures", *The Economist*, Apr. 25, '09, p. 15.

20 "Dead Money", *The Economist*, Nov. 3, '12, p. 71

21 *The Economist*. Sept. 23, '06, p. 13

22 Ibid. p 13

23 "The Right Republican". *The Economist*, Dec. 31, '11

24 "The Rise of State Capitalism", *The Economist*, Jan. 21, '12

25 *The Economist*, Oct. 22, '11. P. 17 inside

26 Link, Perry, "How to Deal with the Chinese Police", *New York Review*, Nov. 7, '13

27 Bamford, James, "Who's in Big Brother's Database", *New York Review*, Nov. 5, '09

28 Priest, D.; Arkin, W. *Top Secret America*, Little Brown, Boston, Mass.

29 *Scientific American*, Dec. 2011, whole issue

30 Kusnetz, Nicholas, "Where Bad Bills Come From". *The Nation*, June 28, '10, p. 22

31 Solomon, C., "Pathogens Move Northward". *Scientific American*, Aug, '14, p. 60

32 Fischetti, Mark, "Storm of the Century". *Scientific American*, June, '13, p. 59

33 "Big City Blues", *Scientific American Mind*, Mar. '13, p. 59

34 McMahon, Darrin, *Devine Fury: A History of Genius*. Basic Books, 2014

APPENDICITIS V

Cognitive Science

———

THE BASIC PROGRAM OF COGNITIVE science is to ground folk psychology on a more scientific basis. The concepts of folk psychology are the terms we use in the everyday life for mental experiences like perceptions and emotions, thoughts and feelings, and propositional attitudes like needs and wants, desires and hopes, etc. These concepts are relevant to the explanation of behavior because of what is called causal efficacy. This means that our ordinary parlance relies on the notion that mental events like those just enumerated can *cause* some of our mental and physical behavior. The models proposed in cognitive science attempt to explain causal efficacy, using a more lawlike concept of causation. As we discussed in Sect. AIV.8, mental event concepts have fuzzy edges and the folk psychology concept of *cause* that guides the interaction between these concepts is even worse. What makes these concepts so fuzzy is that as they are used in ordinary parlance, they have infinite state personal meanings.

On the other hand, the only other world the cognitive scientist has to work with in this program is the world of physical nervous systems, with brain cells and impulses traveling between them. This is a world of infinite complexity which could never be modeled to achieve a scientific patina. What's to be done? What cognitive science attempts is to create a new level and a corresponding scientific model between the level of brain processes, shown on the bottom level in fig. 8.2, and the top level of the mental phenomena of folk psychology. This model would explain how various mental phenomena causally interact and would enable the prediction of behavior.

However, the major obstacle in this program involves meaning. If a cognitive science model is to be fashioned, it should accommodate highly complex meanings of the mental phenomena of folk psychology. On the other hand, if it is to be a *scientific* model, it should be a computable model with computable sentences so that explanations and predictions would be forthcoming. At first blush, this seems to be a contradictory agenda. Well, what cognitive scientists do is to fudge a bit and look for a Goldie-Locks version of meaning that will be full and complete enough to simulate the mental concepts of folk psychology, and yet small enough to be handled computationally. This impossible task keeps a lot of cognitive scientists and analytic philosophers employed.

AV.1 REPRESENTATIONS

The first stop on the road towards a cognitive model of folk psychology is in the area of *representation*, which is the central concept in the field of Cognitive Science as elucidated by Jerry Fodor. Representations are the tin soldiers of mind/brain theories of Cognitive Science. But what are they? A representation is a mental trace that must be some sort of isomorphic copy of what is represented, as explained in Sect. 12.3. The criterion for a mental trace being a representation is that it can be activated, producing some kind of copy of the original experience, like a thought, perception, or memory, etc. There is a philosophical theory about perception and related issues called *Representationalism* or *Representionism*. In my opinion it is the worse stuff to come down the philosophical pike in a long time and we won't waste any time on it. It totally misrepresents the idea of a representation, which has as an essential characteristic its resemblance to what is represented and its ability to be recreated at another time.

In fact, in the last 10 or so years, the word 'representation' has been mutilated almost out of existence the way 'identity' and 'information' have been. According to Dan Lloyd's definition of a representation, a bottle-capping machine has a representation of a cap and the bottle; and a baseball bat has a representation of the ball. This defines 'representation' right out of existence.

The first philosophers who introduced and used the term were Descartes, Hume and William James (Beakley, '92), which makes many recent analyses of representations pretty inexcusable. These early philosophers agreed that a representation must be a kind of copy, so that when it is activated, there is some kind of isomorphism between the representation and the perception that created it. At the very least, a representation should carry a lot of information about what is represented. If current writers want a different concept, they should come up with a different word.

But what about registrations? They too interact causally with each other and with other mentality and result in overt behavior. The first problem of a representational theory or any other cognitive science theory is that most mental experiences leave only registrations. They are mental traces that enable a creature to only *recognize* the object of a perception, not to recreate it. Such is the case with all gustatory, olfactory, tactile perceptions, and emotions. But whatever mental structures are present that enable recognition must have some information about what is recognized.

In what follows, when we mention representations, it should be understood that we may also be talking about registrations or even detections.

Our account of representations in this book is given in Ch. 12. But Jerry Fodor's representations are more elusive. In one of his earliest books, *The Language of Thought*, he doesn't make it clear at all what they are. He deduces that there must be a system of representations having rules and procedures just like number theory is a system of symbols with rules to determine how we can operate on the symbols to derive certain results. Thus in doing causal work or any other kind of mentality, the system of representations must have rules and procedures to guide their operations. This is his language of thought, Mentalese.

Regarding the questions in the text concerning how representations and registrations can be individuated and how they do causal work in the mind/brain, it is clear that they could be individuated in a number of ways. One way is by their pictorial or *qualia* aspect, which is a picture in the case of vision, or a sound in the case of an olfactory representation. But this would be a very coarse sieve. Another way is by their semantic aspect. My representation of seeing my new car means something very different to me than my representation of seeing my friend's new car and very different from the representation my friend makes of his own new car. They also might be individuated functionally: by what mental and behavioral events caused them and what effects they may have.

Regarding representations as Fodor introduces them, he says some really curious things about the complexity of his representations. He says there are "...an infinity of distinct representations...", and that "...there is no upper bound to the complexity of the representation that may be required..." (Fodor, '75, 31). 'No upper bound', implies infinite complexity. The reason is that the *semantic* aspect of a representation involves a meaning cloud containing an infinite number of representations involving very high information content. So the first question that arises is, how would an infinite number of representations each with an infinite meaning cloud be handled computationally? It can't, so it doesn't.

But Fodor is going try to elucidate a theory of representations using the usual computer analogy. He says, "I shall put forward this stronger doctrine as the view that mental states and processes are *computational*" (Fodor, '81, 226). With this computational assumption, there must be entities that are computed over. These are his representations — not really the whole representation, but only a skeletal version: "...a mental process, qua computation, is a formal operation on *syntactically* [italics mine] structured mental representations" (Fodor, '01, 11). Well, as we have stressed many times, the brain's processes probably involve infinite state entities and processes causally related according to natural laws and probably not algorithmic at all. We will see how Fodor tries to ditch the meaning aspect of his representations so they can be computed over syntactically.

AV.2 The Semantics of Representations

As listed in the text, the major questions regarding the semantics of representations concern the nature of representations, where they come from, how they get into the head, and the role of meaning in representations doing causal work. The question is what does this content include? As we alluded to above, representations and registrations have a semantic aspect, which as we have described, is a meaning cloud consisting of memories, knowledge, counterfactuals, etc. Now even though representations are handled as *mental* entities, we must keep in mind that they must somehow supervene on physical brain processes. And if meaning is infinite state, which is the view here, then the brain processes they supervene on must also be infinite state.

First of all, we should address the problem of how representations would be individuated. In this respect, a controversy has arisen between defining and individuating representations *externally*, which is called *broad* content, and defining them *internally*, called narrow content. McGinn says the externalist case states that "The environment is thus held to be constitutive of the very nature of mental states, determining what they *are*" (McGinn, '89, 3). *Internalism* based on *narrow* content individuates them only on the basis of what's inside the subject. McGinee says, the *internalist's* "...mental states are determined by facts relating to the subject considered in isolation from the environment" (2). This is also called *individualism* because all mindstates are dependent only on what's in the individual's head and not on the existence of outside states of affairs.

What brought up the controversy is that two physically identical persons could have different thoughts if the world is different. The externalist says "...a change in the environment...necessarily changes the content of his experience" (83). And he points to twin-earth where, since water is XYZ, there are different thoughts even though the twins are exact replicas. But at the perceptual level, these worlds are *not* different: their *perceptual* environments are the same. The worlds are different only at the causal level. But this has nothing to do with perceptions, thoughts, representations or anything else mental. McGinn is finally down to natural kinds concepts as being external. But that's again because they supposedly refer to "theoretical" terms, like atomic number 79 for gold. But the gold concept is still a perceptual one even though the *criterion* for gold is at the causal atomic number level. I have some experience with this. Even when collectors mistake a shiny yellow metal for gold and buy a fake, they try to get better at perceiving gold, which means perfecting their *perceptual* concept. Even if they discover a test for gold like a reaction to some acid, this isn't going to help improve their *perceptual* concept which is what they're related to in perception, memory and flea markets.

McGinn says that externalism is incompatible with what he calls substantialism. This is an interesting statement. Supposedly, it comes from the fact that substances don't "know" anything separate from itself: substances are "...ontologically autonomous or self-sufficient: they do not depend on the existence or their intrinsic nature upon other substances..." (16). But if a mindstate is identical to an infinite brainstate, how would we individuate them except by what in the world they represent? The same would be true if mindstates only supervene on brainstates. On the one hand, they are "autonomous or self-sufficient", implying internalism. On the other, McGinn claims that since it is a copy of an outside world object, "...it is constituted by its relations to distant objects" (21), whose properties exist "independently of minds"(41), which conforms to his definition of externalism.

But representations aren't copies of anything in the causal world. They are copies of perceptual objects and states of affair which are mostly manufactured by the mind. Our perceptual world depends somewhat on the causal world but once a representation is formed, the causal world can change in some way like XYZ water without changes in the perceptual world.

McGinn sums up: "The item that has to exist for me to *think* 'something is square' is the very *same* item that has to exist in order for the material object in front of me to *be* square, viz. the property of being square" (41). The real problem is that on either interpretation, how does this external property of being square become a property, component, content or "constituent" of anything internally mental. He rebukes us by stating that since the internalist is saying that *his* toys (which McGinn depreciates as "image" and "bits of cerebral syntax") can become constituents of mental content, why shouldn't the externalist be allowed to do the same thing with *his* toys, namely, properties that exist "independently of minds"? My answer, of course, is that the internalist's toys are already in his head where the mentality is sitting, and McGinn has no way to sneak the externalist's toys into it. Even if he could, all he would get is a causal world having little to do with representations.

McGinn's discussion of qualities like color, shape, etc., in my opinion is hobbled by the assumption that experiences can be internally labeled, like a square experience, independent of what's out there. McGinn says, "...round things produce ... experiences as of square things on twin earth" (60). This is incoherent. A square experience or sense datum *whatever it might be* is one you get from viewing certain piles of molecules. Round things on twin earth are things from which people usually create round sense data. So there are no "experiences as of square things" when seeing what most people get round experiences from, except in rare circumstances where there is a misperception. So even though his conclusion is that these experiences are not strongly externally defined, he has the right conclusion for the wrong reasons — the wrong reason that inner experiences are intrinsically identifiable and labelable, which they are not.

Conflating levels also induces confusion about introspection. He entertains the idea that "Perception tells us how the environment is; introspection tells us how the environment seems to us" (82). This is cute, but not really true. They both tell us the same thing, but neither one necessarily tells us how the environment is. The mind creates representations that can be activated. They have mostly the same content in the introspective activation, which is how it seems, as there is in the original perception. But McGinn says, "Why is introspection so much more reliable than perception...?" (90). I think it's the exact opposite. Introspection is notably *un*reliable about attributive mentality, e.g, postures like generosity and honesty, and multemotions like avarice and jealousy. In these cases, the *perceptions* of others are more reliable. Also, per Dennett, we can distort a representation by the time it gets to introspection. McGinn brings up misperceptions that can be corrected by bringing up lots of knowledge and introspecting other perceptions that can correct them. Well, yes; but misperception is a lot rarer than distorting perceptions through emotional needs, etc. before they get to introspection. But the important point is that regardless of reliability, McGinn still can't get things into the head through introspection any better than through perception. Having eliminated causal theories of content, he can only do it by a one-sentence fiat out of a whole book: "What makes the disposition the disposition it is cannot come apart from what makes the represented property *it* is" (70). "Cannot"?

Our account of perception is not easily categorizable because instances of universals like redness or squareness are *components* of sense data. Also, since their creation is initiated by causal piles of molecules, one could say that they are "dependent" on causal objects and so McGinn calls this "weak externalism". But then these components of sense data become *qualities* of perceptual objects out in the world. This is clearly internalist. In our view, since the perceptual object is the meat of reality for humans and are mostly a creation of the mind, there doesn't seem to be enough out there for perceptual objects to depend on to call this externalism. McGinn says that, "... if we hold the appearance constant, we do not necessarily hold the reality constant" (31). But the appearance *is* the reality under normal circumstances. What confuses the issue is that what's going on at the causal level is a different kind of reality, a *scientific* reality, which has nothing to do with *perceptual* reality — the most important kind.

I think these guys overlook something very important. As John Perry points out, we can have "... two identical structures, one of which was a valve and one of which was a device for pitting prunes" (Perry, '01, 84). This says that a history and function define what an object is, which is externalism. But the use and function of an object are components of content created by human minds in the past. Even though we can put a horse to work pulling a cart or running a race, its infinite state meaning potential intrinsically *includes* these possible functions. That is part of what a horse is *internally*. We don't need to know what *use* we're putting a horse now to in order to know what a horse is.

But even if we depreciate the ability of meaning devices to record their histories, we still have the problem of getting all that external stuff into the head. Michael Tye asks, "Which features involved in...environmental states are elements of phenomenal contents?" (Tye, '95, 141), which implies that they are qualities of real world objects. His lame answer is that "...colors we see objects and surfaces to have are simply *intrinsic*, [italics mine] observer-independent properties of those objects and surfaces" (145). "The relevant features [of real world objects] will be the ones represented in the output representations of the sensory modules" he calls, "*observational* features" (Tye, '95, 141). And so "...*phenomenology ain't in the head*" (151). But he admits that "Somehow, the visual system manages to ascertain what colors objects really have, even though the only information immediately available to it concerns light wavelengths." (146). Notice the word "manages" here. Another stretch word. Jaegwon Kim, the property maven, also talks about "properties of physical objects represented". But reflecting light waves of a certain frequency is the only relevant property causal objects have, and this property is not represented in the mind at all. What is represented is *color*.

So the question is, if meaning, including all those wonderful color and texture qualities starts out in the world, or even exists there, as Fodor and Tye imply, how do they know how good a job we are doing in representing the redness? On top of that, how do we *reactivate* a representation? When we do, there clearly is, at least, *some* kind of watered down homolog of the meaning and qualia aspect of the original. And since the original perception is long gone, this representation must have something to do with our brains or minds and so must be somewhere in or about the head. By what magic does the color of the red barn "manage" to become an element or component or quality of their perceptual representations in the head, with only photons going between?

Jerry Fodor finally winds up relying on getting this content into the head by some kind of inference ability of the mind. Sensory cortices of the brain, which he calls input systems — "...input systems deliver representations that are most naturally interpreted as characterizing the arrangement of *things in the world*. Input analyzers are thus inference-performing systems..." (Fodor, '83, 42). Now, if what we have to do to get a handle on "things in the world" is to make *inferences*, no less, that tells me that Fodor doesn't think meaning starts out in the head, so to speak. Inferences are simply good guesses spruced up with a little logic.

But Fodor is not opposed to changing his mind. In a subsequent book he has a thesis that mental representations, "are the primitive bearers of intentional content" (Fodor, '98, 70). In this book, he summarizes his theory of representations expressed in a number of theses. And there is some good news. It appears he has finally given up on the project of paring down meanings to computational size. "The account of the *semantics* of mental representations that my version of RTM [Representational Theory of Mind] endorses, unlike the *thinking* it endorses, is indeed non-computational" (11). Well, I'm breathless. After struggling through 8 or 9 books, we finally get the phrase 'non-computational'. In his next book, he even has some new terms to describe how big and fat meanings really are. He speaks of meaning being "global", and "abductive", in addition to "holistic". The reason for this epiphany, of course, is that the semantics of mental representations are infinite state. But doesn't his statement imply that we *think* without semantics?

But he also assumes in this book that meaning originates out in the world. It does look that way. The meaning of a cow seems to be hanging out pretty close to the cow. Perhaps Fodor's assumption in this regard is what induces him to hold an *informational* role for semantics, IRS. Somehow the new buzzword 'information' can accomplish what other brands of meaning theory couldn't, such as the ability to sneak meaning into our heads while nobody is looking. He says, "Pure informational semantics allows me *not* [italics mine] to

hold that one's inferential dispositions determine content..."(14). He doesn't even need to make inferences and good guesses anymore as he did a number of books ago. It's all going to come in on the back of those zippy little photons.

Well, first of all, even if water is H_2O, he admits they are different concepts. But since they are the same stuff, they should lend the same information. But then how could the concepts be different? This seems to sink IRS. But even though inference would seem to be less reliable than causation, how will a causal explanation of meaning getting into the head give a better result? Well, it appears, simply by fiat. Fodor does seem to set the bar high on this issue. He says, "informational semantics is untenable unless there's an answer to questions like: '*how* does... the instantiation of *doghood* cause tokenings of DOG?' I propose to call whatever answers such a question a mechanism of '*semantic access*' "(75). Nothing like a lofty name for a problem. Well, how do we get "semantic access"? In my opinion, the following pages of Fodor's exposition is not only the lamest you'll ever see, but, in my opinion, is really a *reductio* of his whole Theory of Representations as well as his theories of perception and semantics.

He first says, "Informational semantics says that "...the fact that DOG means *dog*...is constituted by nomic connection between two properties of dogs; viz. *being dogs* and *being causes of actual and possible DOG tokenings in us*" (73). This nomic stuff is mighty powerful. It's really going to be *gnomic*. Not only is it nomic, but reliable: "...it's the *reliability* [italics mine] of the mediation between dogs and one's *dog* thoughts that *justifies* one's knowledge claims about dogs" (76). All this is just a "fact about the world". First of all, what does a stretch word like 'constituted' come to? Also, justification is not explanation. This is supposed to be philosophy, after all. But what does 'reliability' come to here? How can a representation like DOG, along with its meaning, be "caused" by the magic of a dog in the world with its meaning of doghood, simply by bouncing off a few photons?

Secondly, how do we get his admittedly non-computational amounts of information necessary for "non-computational" semantics through finite state transducers like the eye? And even if you could, how will all of that be handled by a computational brain? The fact that TV exists demonstrates that there is only a finite amount of information coming into the sensorium at a particular point in time. This is why sense data are finite entities. However, meaning and semantics seem to involve infinite amounts of information. The answer is that he has swallowed down some version of the causal theory of meaning and discarded Inferential Role Semantics, IRS. (Of course, in my opinion, neither one is tenable because they both assume meaning is out in the world.)

Well, just in case his "meaning-making" factory isn't working 24/7, Fodor has a back-up. You simply ask experts about dogs, or wire-tap their conversations, or listen to gossip about dogs. We're never told where these guys get *their* dog meanings. The explanation suggested here by Perceptual Realism is what we have said about perception in general. There is no meaning in causal dogs or even DOG. The causal dog, by injecting finite informational physical items into the mind/brain, causes it to project whatever infinite state meaning it has accrued to the concept DOG out to the causal dog, creating a perceptual dog. It is the *perceptual* dog with its associated meaning that is the instantiation of the concept DOG.

The question Fodor's and Tye's accounts must answer is if their features are *external*, how does this content out in the world get copied into the mind so as to enable reactivation at later times? Somehow, somewhere, some way, the red of a red barn got into the head, and it has some attachment to the mental representation of the barn — or else we couldn't visualize the red barn. And the real red barn may be nowhere in sight so we can't cheat. Later Fodor expresses this problem as "the mind-world-connection problem" (Fodor, '08, 93) and implies that either there's nothing out in the world (idealism) or there's nothing in the

mind (behaviorism). Well, as we have explained, both places do exist, and it's the same stuff in both places because we put it in both places.

Robert Cummins does a good job of presenting various theories to answer this question but they all really stink. The first is the Similarity Theory of Representations: "The idea [here, representation] represents the red ball, and it represents it as red...because the idea *is* red and spherical and the redness and sphericity come from the ball" (Cummins, '89, 4). This is all very nice, except how does the redness get from the ball in the world to the representation in the head? Since we can't check the similarity because objects out in the world are noumena (causal objects), how can we ever be sure there's any similarity at all?

Another theory is based on "covariance", which is the idea that if two objects do things pretty much in tandem, they *covary*. This theory is often expounded in conjunction with a computations theory of cognition (CTC) as appears in Cummins. Well, as usual, the idea of computation has nothing to do with any theory of representation. If we clear away the usual 'computational' debris, what covariance theory basically says is that if you have some internal contraption or device that trips off whenever there is a detection of a certain category of object or process, then you have a representation of that object or process inherent in that contraption. Not only that, but the word 'meaning' is stretched so that the tripping mechanism *means* what is being detected. 'Meaning' is slowly going the way of 'identity' and 'information'. Well, in my opinion, this kills covariance theories right off the starting blocks. There is nothing said here about how much of a *copy* is inherent in the contraption or even how much information about the object is contained in the device. A detection does not make a representation or even a registration unless there is some kind of copy or some information about the object that can be used to recognize the object or recreate the representation. And to say that the thermostat *recognizes* the drop in temperature just because it changes state is a real stretch of the word 'recognize'. It's like the car that hits a telephone pole "representing" the telephone pole. A sodium atom may *detect* a chlorine atom and it might even be said to have a smidgen of information about chlorine because it has complementary valence. But it is a real stretch to say it *recognizes* chlorine atoms. In my opinion, recognition requires, by definition, a one-to-one mapping from a detection mechanism to what is detected. Lots of things can map to temperature, and lots of atoms map to chlorine.

But even registrations that don't require qualia and a copy create problems for covariance theories. Because of expectations, your internal contraption that is supposed to trip when you taste rotten water may trip when you taste beer because you're expecting milk. This is the famous misrepresentation problem, which we'll get to in Sect. AV.15. But even aside from this, covariance can only relate sense data to outside *causal* states of affairs, not perceptual objects. Covariance says absolutely nothing about meaning going either way. The seasons covary with plant growth, but neither says a thing about the other.

After reading all of Fodor's books, I get the impression that what may have motivated a language of thought, which he calls Mentalese, was this very problem of getting meaning "into the head". His Mentalese is already in the head, and it comes ready equipped with meaning, and just the right amount of meaning. So he may not want or need whatever meaning is out in the world, especially if it's too big a load. This reminds me of the New Yorker who is complaining about parking in New York to a friend: "the parking in New York is impossible; sometimes I drive around for an hour looking for a place to park." The friend answers, "I solved that problem: I bought a car that was *already* parked."

He says, "...the Mentalese story is that the content of thought is *ontologically* prior to natural-language meaning. That is, you can tell the whole truth about what the content of a thought is *without saying anything whatever about natural-language meaning,*

including whether there are any" (Fodor, '00, 68). With Mentalese propped up with a very anorexic content, he has simply lost interest in natural language. Of course, we are never told where his Mentalese gets *its* "content of thought".

Fodor concludes, "But the worry about representations is above all that the semantic...will prove recalcitrant to integration in natural order... will fail to supervene on their physical properties" (Fodor, '90, 32). Well, if semantics entails infinite state entities as his reference to "infinity of representations" (Fodor, '75, 31) shows, and he is going to squeeze them through finite state transducers into what he thinks is a "syntax-driven machine" (Fodor, '90, 23), the brain, he has plenty to worry about.

AV.3 PRODUCTIVITY OF THOUGHT

So far we have discussed the mind/brain's ability to create perceptual representations of experiences we have. This gives the mind a kind of copy of the original experience, albeit, a more watered down version; and we can recreate or reactivate a representation at a later time. But the mind has the ability to synthesize new representations out of pre-existing representations primitive and complex. The mind also has the ability to create new thoughts in what is called the stream of consciousness. This is called the *productivity* of *thought*. Fodor's language of thought does seem to accommodate the productivity of thought because it can mix and match any number of sentences and combine and permute them. Mentalese symbols from various parts of the mind/brain are brought together according to the algorithmic rules of the language of thought and synthesized into a brand spanking new symbol. He talks about languages like his LOT "...whose formulas have transportable parts, as against associative networks, which by definition cannot" (Fodor, '87, 139). This point is probably the best selling point that might tempt us towards a computational theory of mind (CTM).

Peter Carruthers defines CTM best as: "Human cognitive processes are classical computational ones — roughly, algorithmically specifiable processes defined over syntactically structured mental representations" (Carruthers, '05, 109). This theory basically conceives of representations as an ontological category of little lumps in the head that can be moved around, transported, combined and permuted just like in the computer. This is the appeal of computational theories. But it must be realized that computer sentences have no meaning to the computer. If meaning packages are infinite state entities, the computer couldn't move a meaning package one micron to combine with anything. CTM basically dumps flesh and blood meaning and starts darting and flitting syntactical skeletons all over the mind with great dexterity. This is not how the mind works.

Now although Associationism does accommodate meaning in all its glory, it does seem a bit inadequate to accommodate the productivity of thought. In defending his theory, Fodor simultaneously criticizes associationism in this regard. But in my opinion, some of the defects he points out about associationism are really more of a problem for his own theory. He seems to be saying that even though associationism may account for representations of existing complex objects in the world, how would an associationism model put together new syntheses of other representations in our imagination? How does associationism accommodate the productivity of thought. I think this is a legitimate crticism.

Annette Karmilloff-Smith has written an excellent book that discusses the possibility of representations recreating themselves in whole or part in other parts of the brain to do certain causal work and to participate in other mentality (Karmiloff-Smith, '95). These peripheral representations might not be as complete or as articulated as the original perceptual representation in the sensory cortex for the modality in question. But they would also be stationary entities inherent in the circuitry of the brain, just as the

original representation. Perhaps when we are imagining a state of affairs, we construct a new representation composed of a number of primitive elementary representations that are assembled in a spare part of the brain. This is the motivation for Bernard Barr's "conscious workspace".

What is very interesting about this scenario, however, is the question of what happens to the meanings of the various components of the new representation? Do these meanings get dragged along with their respective representations as they get incorporated into the new synthesized representation? Also, can the new representation do causal work? This is a very interesting practical question. I would say that when any representation gets recreated, whether in memory or in imagination, its neural ties to *some* meaning items would continue simply because the recreated representation maintains those ties through its reconstruction ties to the original representation. But this is very speculative. We discussed briefly in Ch. 14 how our own experiences may indicate that concepts we synthesize in our imaginations may not have the full meaning that representations of past experiences have. But if even only *some* meaning stays attached to representations as they are assembled to form new ones, and if the language of thought is algorithmic, then it is doomed as a means for the brain/mind to manipulate, operate on, and assemble representations using Fodor's LOT.

AV.4 Representations and Causation

Fodor next turns to the role representations play in our thinking. The second major problem for Fodor is that it seems pretty obvious that the meanings of our representations come into play when the representation does causal work either by causing further mental events or causing behavior. So he starts from scratch asking, "...how anything could have the properties that mental representations are alleged to have; in particular, how anything with representational properties could be a cause" (Fodor, '95, 84). He adds, "…mental processes preserve semantic properties of mental states…"(Fodor, '87, 154).

You would think that the last place he would go to sort all this out would be a finite state machine to make analogies. But that's exactly where he goes. Fodor suggests that a critical property of the machine language of computers is that the computer operates in "…such a fashion that the operations the machine performs *respect* the semantic constraints on formulae in the machine code" (Fodor, '75, 67). (Italics mine). "Preserves" and "respects" here are great examples of stretch words. Does it mean that mental processes can proceed without *destroying* semantic properties? Or *ignoring* semantic properties? Or maybe just pickling them in little jars where they won't be in the way? We are never told.

Now even though Fodor will wind up ignoring the semantic aspect of mental representations, he has to work up some credibility with his computer analogies by manufacturing some meaning in the computer. He has some partners in crime for this endeavor. He quotes Phillip Johnson-Laird: "we might speak of the intension [meaning] of a program as the procedure that is executed when the program is run" (Johnson-Laird). It's truly amazing what mental contortions these cognitive scientists perform to stuff meaning into the computer.

But Cognitive Scientists have another straw to grasp. A computer has a compiler which translates sentences of a program it is presented with into an internal computer language. And you might have guessed that somebody was going to milk some semantics out of this. Fodor expresses this strategy: "…the compiled (e.g. Machine Language) representation of a sentence is eo ipso a representation of its meaning…." (Fodor, '81, 205). Armed with "eo ipso", the cognitive scientist gets a little opening into which he may be able to sneak a pinch of meaning. Fodor says the compiler algorithmically translates a programming language into a compiler language "…that the machine 'understands'

"(116). And how do we know the compiler language "understands" the input language? The answer from the mountain top is, when the machine translates meaningless strings of symbols comprising the input language into meaningless strings of symbols comprising the compiler language, this, is *"understanding"*. If Fodor had this kind of "understanding", he couldn't write a bad comic book.

Hilary Putnam says, *"The mind uses a formalized language…both as a medium of computation and a medium of representation"* (Putman in Rosenthal, '91, 528). This is a total contradiction. A representation has content which is infinite state stuff and is necessary to do causal work in the mind; whereas by definition, computations are limited to finite state sentences and algorithms. The work that meaning-laden representations do is to bring about other mental processes and behavior, which involves their *causal* capabilities. As Fodor says, *"what perception must do is to so represent the world as to make it accessible to thought"* (Fodor, '83, 40). For how can representations represent the world including its infinite meaningful states of affairs and do the causal work they do with a very truncated version of meaning involving only computationally amenable entities with no meaning? The analogy between minds and computers is one of the biggest disasters in the modern philosophy of mind.

To me all of this shows the absurdity of trying to stuff meaning into the computer. There is absolutely nothing "semantic" about a computer. In fact, compiling into computer language makes things worse. At least the programming language has meaning to the programmer. When the computer syntactically translates this into machine language, now the symbols don't mean nothin' to nobody. As John Searle would say, the computer doesn't "understand" anything. At one point, Fodor does say, "…machines typically don't know (or care) what the programs that they run are about…"(Fodor, '81, 207). The computer doesn't represent anything because there is no intentionality and no meaning, *in the eyes of the computer,* of its symbols.

He is aware that the content of these representations may have to be more "robust" or complex than a computational kind of meaning would entail: "…the account of the *semantics* mental representations …endorses…, unlike the account of *thinking* that it endorses, is indeed non-computational" (Fodor, '98, 11). But his temporary enthusiasm for the semantic aspect of representations fades quickly mainly because he has the huge problem of how his finite "computational" language of thought is going to drag around the heavy load of meaning that seems necessary to do causal work. Well, at this point, it appears that rather than taking the semantic road to explain how propositional attitudes do causal work, Fodor would rather unburden himself of the heavy load of meaning altogether.

Pulling a WWII battle of the bulge breakout, he bursts forward the suggestion that we don't have to worry about the full measure of meanings because representations do their work on the basis of their formal (syntactic) properties *only*. (This is really the skinniest kind of meaning possible because it is really no meaning at all.) He says, "Thoughts have their causal roles in virtue of, inter alia, their logical form", which, "supervenes on the syntactical form of the corresponding mental representation" (Fodor, '01, 18). "…Hence, they have no access to the *semantic* properties of such representation…" (Fodor, '81, 231). Here we go again with another stretch word, "access". Can we bounce representations around the mind/brain without taking along their semantic aspect? Perhaps we can park them until the thinking is over so they won't clog up our minds. We are never told.

In any event, he proceeds to shrivel down the semantic aspect of representations to a dried up version he can stuff into the computer. He first squeezes down meaning to extension; then he tries to free representations from their semantic burden, and finally, he defangs the meaning of a representation so that it doesn't clog up causal work the representation does in his computer. Then he can claim the mind operates on its representations on the basis of syntax just like the computer. What this implies, for example, is that a person's belief that it is raining, which has as its content a raining state of affairs, causes him to take an umbrella, not on the basis of what 'raining' means, but on the basis of a meaningless string of symbols comprising a syntactical representation in the brain's language of thought. I just don't see it. And neither does Fred Dretske.

The reason Fodor is driven to syntax on which to base causal efficacy is, 1) To provide a way for the language of thought to cart representations around "computationally", without dragging along their semantic aspect. This leaves only syntax to do this job. And 2), with everything computational, he can march onward because "…the computational story about mental *processes* fits so nicely with the story that psychological *explanation* is subsumption under intentional laws…" (Fodor, '98, 13). It certainly does, just like Aristotle's story of the soul being in the liver fits nicely with his story of the mind being in the heart. The only way psychological explanation could be subsumed "under intentional laws" is if we were all finite state robots.

Let's take seriously for a moment the idea that manipulation of representations in our thinking depended on alienated "logical form". Let's go back to the *Productivity of Thought*. Fodor says: "…*using a productive language as a medium of computation doesn't require access to its semantics*…"(Fodor, '90, 188). Let's look at what our mental lives would be like if the stream of our thoughts transpired on the basis of syntax, disregarding semantics as Fodor suggests. Here would be a typical stream.

Jim bought a new car and took it to the pier.
John bought a new car and took it to the pier.
John bought a new *boat* and took it to the pier.
Gene bought a new boat and took it to the *river*.
Jane bought a new picnic basket and took it to the river.
Jane bought a new picnic basket and took it to the park.

And on and on. Even an ordinary guy like me has a slightly more interesting stream of thoughts than this. And what about Jerry Fodor? I don't know how important meaning is in determining such a stream, but I'm quite sure it's based on a lot more than "inter alia logical form". But then Fodor wonders, "...*how* logical form could determine causal powers" (Fodor, '01 16). Now that mental entities have only shriveled down content, he can make analogies with computers because the computer's sentences don't have any content either. Fodor is telling us that if we want to understand the mind of the puppeteer, all we have to do is investigate the mind of the puppet.

Fodor implies that the computer is going from state to state causally and moving its sentences around on the basis of the *syntax* of its sentences. And so if the mind is a computer, it will go from state to state causally and move representations around on the basis of syntax too. But in my opinion, Fodor is completely misinterpreting what the computer is doing. As explained in detail in Sect. AIV.8, *neither of them is using syntax to go from one state to the next* and so his computer metaphor dissolves into the cosmos.   In another book, he has another metaphor. He says, when you intend to make a certain sentence, P, true, according to the language of thought, "...you put into the intention box a token of a mental symbol that *means* that P" (Fodor, '87, 136). (In his last book, he gets organized so that all this stuff gets through finite state transducers and the intention box gets transformed into a filing cabinet.) See, once shorn of their semantic aspect, this computational LOT can do all kind of "tricks". You first take a representation out of its semantic box marked "meaning", you undress the representation of its meaning and you can then bounce it around all over the mind/brain doing their causal work in their syntactical underwear. But when do they get interpreted so that they appear as they do in our consciousness as beliefs with meaningful content? Either mental representations have a semantic aspect which stays with them throughout their lives of bouncing around in the mind/brain to do various causal work, in which case, how would this meaning get into the head; and moreover, how would it be carted around by a finite language of thought? *Or* they spend much of their lives roaming around the mind/brain as bare syntactical formulae, in which case, when do they get interpreted so as to appear to us in meaningful ways? What Fodor needs now is a little man in the head and before any representation is activated into consciousness, he would reattach the representation to its meaning, so that it would have the meaning it appears to us to have. But how would the little man find the proper meaning clothing when there might be zillions of meaning clothing hanging on hooks in the meaning box? Fodor has written a whole stack of books having hundreds of pages of excruciating detail but nowhere is the interpretation problem addressed.

Finally, Fodor grudgingly allows some meaning to sneak into the discussion. He calls it "context", as though con*text* won't clog up the computer as much as con*tent*. He realizes that the context of a representation is a global thing which would seem difficult to squeeze down to supervenience on syntactic properties. But Fodor thinks syntax is a *local* matter; and so not amenable to handle context. What I would like to question is, even if we allow *context* to be substituted for *content*, it is still a global infinite state matter. How will finite state computations handle context, even if syntax were global, whatever that would come to? The only avenue left is to shrivel down content so that it is no more cumbersome and no more causally effective than syntax. Let's look at the idea of "syntactically driven".

Now, at the level of physical *brain* processes involving neurons, impulses, etc., if you want to refer to physical causation where atoms and molecules push each other around as "syntax-driven", then I suppose you could suggest the brain is a syntax-driven machine. (However, if syntax is finite state stuff, this isn't true either.) I don't agree with this usage because the word 'syntax' should be restricted to systems of symbols and not extended to physical matter. But aside from this, Fodor is doing the philosophy of cognitive science here, and he is talking about *mental* processes, not brain processes. At this level, the mind is clearly not a syntax-driven machine. It is a *meaning*-driven system. At one point Fodor says, "Mental processes are causal sequences of mental states…"(Fodor, '90, 19). But, as we have shown, the brainstates that meanings supervene on are related *causally* according to physical and chemical laws having nothing to do with syntax which is irrelevant to the sequence of brainstates. Of course, physical causation between brain states must be interwoven with causal properties of mental states. How this happens is the essence of the mind/body problem. But even causality due to mindstates proceeds *on the basis of meaning.*

Fodor alludes to this general kind of theory of representations as "*naturalistic*", and he frowns on this approach: "…a naturalistic psychology isn't a practical possibility and isn't likely to become one" (234). Well, certainly to discover how the brain can assume an infinite number of states, and how it can then handle meaning, as well as how the causal properties of the brain can create consciousness — this is a tall order, I will admit. Fodor states, "…it's overwhelmingly likely that computational psychology is the only one that we are going to get" (234). In my opinion, a "*naturalistic*" theory of representations is a lot more likely than a computational model.

He ends Ch. 9 of *Representations* with the gloomy thought that "…truth, reference and the rest of semantic notions aren't psychology categories" (253). Well, they certainly are psychological categories. Psychology is the study of the mentality of folk psychology, in which meanings are necessary ingredients. In my opinion, our language and our experience indicate that our representations do have a semantic aspect, and that they do have causal effects on mental experiences and our behavior, and they do take part in psychological processes. The job of philosophy is to explain how this happens, not to snuff out the meaning

in our mental lives by stuffing the mind into a computer. After all, meaning is what it is to be human and to be human is to enable our meaningful mental life to *causally* affect our mental and behavioral lives.

But at some level of his mind, Fodor suspects that maybe you can't get rid of the semantic aspect of representations that easily. So at one point, Fodor says, "I have no idea what an adequate semantics for a system of internal representations would look like…"(Fodor, '81, 200). He finally admits that "What we're all doing is really a kind of logical syntax, and we all very much hope that when we've got a reasonable internal language…someone very nice and very clever will turn up and show us how to interpret it; how to provide it with a semantics" (223). And all's quiet on the western front.

What I find interesting is that in all the word-mongering books with thousands pages written by syntax peddling guys like Fodor, Tye, Kim, etc., never once do any of them explain the motivation for resorting to syntax as the means for mental phenomena to have causal efficacy and giving up on content, which seems to me to be clearly responsible. It must be pretty desperate times because lots of mentality has no syntax at all, such as emotions, dispositions, body signals, etc.

Fred Dretske at first *appears* to appreciate the meaning problem by accepting a robust kind of meaning for representations. Unlike Fodor, he doesn't try to get rid of meanings entirely, and he recognizes that they have a role in doing causal work: "If meaning, or something's *having* meaning, is to do the kind of work — if it is to help explain *why* we do what we do — it must, it seems, influence the operation of"… brain processes and physical behavior. But he admits, "Just how is this supposed to work…is …a mystery" (Dretske, '88, 80). However, unlike Fodor, Dretske doesn't think the business of causal work can be done solely on the basis of syntax. "It is the *semantic*, not the syntactical properties of these internal elements [like representations] that explain their impact on behavior, and it is for basically the same reason that a syntactical theory of mind ...is unsatisfactory" (Dretske, '88, 105). It's good to see a heavy hitter like Fred Dretske on our side in this issue.

But when he comes down to his own analysis, Dretske's solution is really a bait-and-switch argument. Instead of explaining how "meaning itself" can be involved in a cause, "The project is to understand how something's *having* [italics mine] meaning could itself have a physical effect" such as behavior (83). After tempting us with the idea of meaning, while we're not looking, he switches meanings to an anorexic version that can be in the head alright, while full meanings are stranded out in the world, even though we still "have" them somehow: they're in the mirror. He says that while representations "are located in the heads of some animals", its content or meaning is "not itself in the head, of course..."(77). Well how does it get there? At one point he suggests that his "central states" only have to "borrow" (in Rosenthal, '91, 355) meanings. This is possible because due to the ephemeral nature of perception, central states only need to sneakily "borrow" meanings *for only brief periods of time* when we're looking at things.

But he doesn't need this improbable explanation either because he has a new trick word that is going to solve all our problems. You guessed it: *information.* But of course, this isn't going to do it either regardless of how promiscuously you throw around the word. He says galvanometers have intentional states because they carry information about voltages and currents. Why "even the humble thermometer occupies intentional states" (in Rosenthal, '91, 356). But these are not *cognitive* states because the galvanometer "does not know anything" (359). And guess why? Well the galvanometer has *too much* information so that it can't tell which information is measuring voltages from information measuring currents or whatever. This is really pretty funny. All these bizarre statements have one source: meaning is infinite state stuff accommodated only by organic brains. Sense data also have information about the outside world. But just like the

galvanometer, they can involve only finite amounts of information, not enough for intentionality and meaning. This information may be *necessary* for perception but this information transfer is so insignificant as to be light years from meaning. A hydrogen atom after hooking up with an oxygen atom may have information about the valence of oxygen, but this information will say almost nothing about what an oxygen atom is like. You simply cannot squeeze infinite state meaning out of a finite state device, which is why galvanometers do not have intentional states. This is not a difference in degree, as Dretske suggests, but a difference in kind.

He continues with more analogies with devices like thermostats and gas gages. He will apply this model as he climbs the complexity hierarchy until we get to human minds. And we thought we had it bad with Fodor and his computers. The model is that a mechanism is "recruited" within a device, which he calls C for cause, that *indicates* something about what's out in the world, which he denotes as F. He says, "We want the fact that it indicates F to be an explanatorily relevant fact about C, the fact about C that explains, or helps explain, *why* it causes M" (the behavior in question) (Dretske, '88, 84).

He continues, "it is the fact that C means what it does, the fact that it indicates the temperature, that explains...its *causing* what it does. And its causing what it does...is what gives the indicator the function of indicating what it does and confers on it, therefore, the status of a representation" (Dretske, '88, 87). There's lots of stretch words here like a new use of 'represent' and 'recruit'. The thermostat is *designed* with a metal pancake to act as the cause, C. The F here is temperature, which acts as a substitute for meaning in the model, and, of course, is out in the world. Supposedly, when the mechanism *indicates* a low temperature, it throws a switch that executes an M, the movement that is the turning on of the furnace. This is how C is supposed to *represent* the temperature, F.

Wittgenstein effectively illustrated this distinction with a crossed-out left turn sign. The sign may symbolically indicate driving instructions, but people have to *assign* this meaning to the symbol. But even if we allow that C may *indicate* temperature, it clearly doesn't *represent* F because there is absolutely no correlative mapping between C and F as a basis for even the most mutilated version of 'representation'. And where is a meaning here for the representation? Indication does not imply meaning. C may have information that an observer could use to measure temperature, but that is only because the observer knows how to add just the right meaning. Send a metal pancake or even a thermometer to an Amazon tribe and see if they get some idea of how hot it is.

It is one thing to *indicate* F (and even this is dubious), the temperature, with some kind of meaningless detection, and quite another to *mean* temperature, and qualify as a complete representation. A representation has content, but bent metal strips have no content and is not a copy of any kind of anything like temperature, any more that the lantern in the Old North Church *indicating* that the British are coming can *represent* the oncoming British. Indications have no necessary correlations and do not have the kind of infinite state meaning necessary for the brain energy for causal efficacy of the mind/brain. The information that C has about F is light years away from enabling anything like meaning or representation.

To me this is just another example of mutilating relational words by taking advantage of the tight bond of causation. Just as the identity theorists can claim that when A causes B, A can be "identified" with B, now we have it that if F causes C to cause M, then C "represents" F. We lose a perfectly good word 'representation', but I don't see anything we gain.

As we go up the complexity scale from thermostats to gnats, to bats, to rats, to cats, to people and finally to philosophers, one by one, the components and relationships fall off the table, until when we get to people, there isn't much left of the model. Next he looks at bugs. The story here is how a species of moth will evade an approaching bat who eats moths. The meaning of F here consists of the location of the danger of the bat and the C is a mechanism of how the moth supposedly represents the location of this danger. The movement, M, is the moth diving and spiraling to evade the bat.

First of all, nothing is "recruited" here. Through evolutionary processes, the moth *evolves* a mechanism that enables it to dive and spiral away from flying things like bats. That's the way it's wired. The moth only *detects* the bat, and the detection mechanism doesn't mean anything and certainly does not represent the danger the bat poses. The moth may *recognize* the physical conditions that underlie danger, but this is not recognizing danger because danger is what these conditions *mean*; and the moth doesn't have room in his head for any meaning to add to his detections or even registrations. Information from the bat is *detected* and goes directly to motor areas of the moth's finite state proto-brain, which initiates evasive action. *At best*, C only *indicates* danger to the bat — it doesn't *mean* danger, and it certainly doesn't *represent* danger.

Next come rats and cats, who can illustrate meaningful behavior because they do learn. The rat pushes a lever when he sees a green light, F, and gets food. Thus the meaning of F is that food may be in the offing. Now the rat wasn't designed to have a C that indicates or represents even the sense data of a green light. Perhaps "recruiting" is not an inappropriate word here because, after a learning process of trial and error, the green light *picks out* or maybe creates just the right mechanism, C, such that by C causing the lever to be pushed, M, food appears. The question is, how does Dretske get meaning attached to C? Only by fiat: "... learning not only confers a function on these indicators, and thereby a *meaning*, but also shapes their causal role, and hence the behavior of the system...in terms of *what they mean* — in terms of the information they now have the function of providing" (Dretske, '88, 99). But C is only a meaningless detection at best. Picking out a physical mechanism, which is a finite state process, says nothing about meaning. The only information C can get is what it gets coming in on the backs of green light photons, which at best is only enough to *indicate* or *mean₁* food. It has no more information about food than a sodium atom has about a chlorine atom. So C doesn't *represent* the green light with its food meaning. Yes, the lantern in Boston's Old North Church *means₁* the British are coming in the sense of *indicates* by some previously agreed convention that puts the meaning into the lantern. But *semantically*, lanterns by themselves don't *meanₛ* anything in particular, let alone oncoming British. The whole sequence of events consists only of physical processes whereby the green light photons go into the rat's visual system where a detection is made, which, after a learning process, causes M, pushing the lever. In my opinion, the only way any meaning gets attached to the C mechanism in the rat's head is if the rat could put it there, which he probably doesn't have room in his head to do.

But when we get to good old garden variety representation theory, as when we see a cow, Dretske says, "...these internal indicators are assigned a job to do in the production of bodily movement...in virtue of what they 'say' (indicate or mean)..."(98). Well, who does this assigning? Assign is a very intentional verb. Indicators are picked out almost randomly in the brain and consist of sense data traces, as we discussed in the text. The causal cow can't pick out the representation that results unless meaning can get into the head and "recruit" or create the right meaningful representation. But Dretske has already told us that meaning " itself is not in the head". And if so, how did this meaning get there to do the "recruiting"? He says, "C is recruited as a cause of M *because* of what it indicates about F..."(101). And what does it indicate about F? Absolutely nothing regarding meaning, unless somebody puts it there. C is recruited only as an indicator and it is totally ad hoc to call this meaningful. The information it gets about F is carried by light photons and is at most enough to create a sense data trace. If C eventually winds up with the meaning of F "in the head" to do causal work, the rat has to be able to put it there.

In my opinion, all analogies with machines of any kind are not going to explain anything about mentality such as meaning and causal efficacy. Conscious mental events have a character that is unlike anything else in the universe. Dretske's model is based on physical devices in which something in the device acts as an indicator. But what is indicated is not meaning, but only the finite information necessary to create sense data, *at best*, and bare sequences of physical causally-sequenced events at worst, with meaningless detections and registrations in between. And sense data and detections are not enough to *cause* complex human behavior. You need a robust degree of personal meaning attached to the sense data to do that. I don't think Dretske has a viable theory of representations because he still has not given us a way for full personal meanings get attached to representations, and how they cause behavior. In fact, at one unobtrusive moment, he just about gives the game away. He says regarding the meaning of representations and PA's: "...however useful it might be for predicting what we are going to do, will not be part of the explanation of what we do" (Dretske, '88, 81). In my opinion, prediction and explanation are two sides of the same coin, and you can't do either using dried-up versions of meaning in terms of detections and indicators instead of real meaners.

But Dretske's discussion has the very interesting and very important ramification that if "meaning itself is not in the head", as he says, *there would be no such thing as intentionality*. Dretske discusses intentionality in the classical way. He says, "Our mental states not only have a reference, an aboutness, an object...that forms their topic; they represent that object in one way or another" (Dretske, '95, 31). This "one way or another" obviously refers to the meaning these objects have, which should include the qualities they have. He says, directedness (aboutness, intentionality) "is supposed to be a quality of the experience that is supposed to be intrinsic to the experience." (32). He even brings in the heavy hitter Husserl, who, as usual with German philosophers, solves problems by naming them. He is going to give us a term for this quality: *noema*. Then experiences having this quality of *noema* or directedness would have "a subjectively accessible quality that is such that if they have an objective reference…this quality determines which object it is" (33). But then he drops a bombshell on us: "If this is what directedness is supposed to be, it seems clear that experiences don't have it. When I am experiencing an object, nothing in my experience of it determines *which* object I'm experiencing…"(33). Well, I'll be. Out the window goes intentionality. I am very glad to see that finally *someone* in the field of philosophy admits to this extremely important conclusion.

Dretske next tries to sneak some meaning into the head by analogies with bodily sensations, which is a lot better than thermostats. To drum up meaning for pains he says, "…pains…stand to physical states of the body the way…visual, and auditory experiences stand to physical states of the environment" (103). This is clearly not the case. Visual perceptions project meaning to causal objects, and the resulting representations are copies because we create them that way. Pains are raw feels, just sensations, and even though there can be pain perceptions, there are no representations because we can't reactivate them. Pains don't help representations represent.

What is at the bottom of Dretske's and Fodor's program for cognitive science is to build a bridge over the river separating the mind and the brain. Dretske does it with indicators. Ray Jackendorff does it with a "computational mind". Fodor's theory for cognitive science is a version of this model in which mental phenomena are modeled in computational terms. But his representations can't carry the load.

It seems to me that representations of any kind, if they are some kind of trace from perceptual experiences, would supervene on *stationary* abstract properties of certain circuitry, which have an infinite state capacity. And through projections to other parts of the brain, the effects of the meaning circuitries of a representation may be felt all over the brain. This is why some sort of meaning Holism must be true. And as stationary entities, their full syntactic and semantic power can be brought to bear in relations that comprise propositional attitudes, in doing causal work, and as appearing to us as we relive our experiences. This is what the mind is all about. *They would necessarily involve the semantics and meaning they were created with in the first place.*

Metaphorically, the analysis here implies a kind of gravity field idea. (If my memory serves me right, I think David Hume suggested a model of this sort.) Gravity fields have varying degree of strength and effectiveness, which corresponds to the fact that our beliefs and desires have a wide range of influence on our behavior and thought processes. The content of a representation is an infinite cloud of other representations in various parts of the brain, mostly cognitive areas that are associated through neural projections with the representation in question. But as stationary things, when other mental processes come its way, it affects them in some way, depending on the strength of the representation and the projections to its meaning cloud in the same way as a body of matter affects the path of a moving object coming within its gravity field. Freud talked about traumatic childhood experiences that leave representations of perceptual experiences that affect behavior for the rest of a person's life. Then if there is a thought process, the neurological activity underlying the current thinking or behavior will "run into" the representation of the experience and will be affected or influenced in some way. The resulting thinking or behavior will be deflected and redirected, so to speak, just as the meteor in a large gravity field it encounters.

This model of representational activity does not involve computations in any way, nor a language of thought for that matter in which to "compute" representations. The brain is not a computational device, and not a syntactical device and consciousness is not created by computations. The brain is a *meaning* device, which comes about because it is an infinite state *causally-sequenced* system that performs causal work in the mind/brain on the basis of the causal properties of the neurological constitution of the brain and the causal properties of mental states. Before we get to propositional attitudes, we should mention a small point concerning the semantics of representations.

AV.5 Sense Data and Syntax

We have intimated that there is no meaning in sense data traces. But sense data do have various components, lines, colors, etc. Sense data components are created by the mind as a result of information coming in from causal objects. In Sect. AII.1, we mentioned the notion that these components of a sense datum have a particular arrangement. It takes information to specify this arrangement just as it takes information coming from causal objects to create the components of sense data in the mind.

There is no meaning in these components nor in total sense data traces. But it could be said that the arrangement of primitive components in a sense datum is a kind of meaning, since it does involve information to specify. We could call this artificial kind of meaning, *syntactical* meaning. But the arrangement of sense data components is not part of the meaning the mind projects to causal objects because the arrangement of components of a sense datum trace is already inherent in the trace. A trace of a triangle wouldn't be a trace of a triangle if it showed the 3 lines scattered at random. The information specifying elements and their arrangement is part of the information specifying the total trace. That a triangle can't be distorted (which is why they build bridges out of them) is part of the meaning of 'triangle'. But this meaning is not necessary to make a triangle sense datum.

But this kind of artificial meaning doesn't bother Fodor because it fits in with his idea that meaning originates out in the world. For if the mind needs a little more gadgetry in the way of rules to perform the necessary Frankenstein operation of putting together primitive elements to form percepts, "...there would not seem to be enough ambient information available to account for the functional architecture that minds are found to have" (Fodor, '83, 35). It's hard to tell here if what he is referring to here includes the rules of assembly we are concerned with, but I would assume so. And so comes to the rescue his Language of Thought, which conveniently has all the rules built in. And we don't have to worry about developing this language because we are born with it.

But for now, I would like to suggest that the establishment of complex sense data traces doesn't involve the assembly of primitive components. There is some experimental evidence that traces of individual objects are established as whole Gestalts. As the Concept Appendicitis will show, we can learn to *have* a complex concept, which consists of an arrangement of simpler concepts without having any notion of the simpler components. We are misled in this regard because after we have learned the *meaning* of a concept, like of a triangle, we can disassemble the concept into more primitive components and their arrangement. I think we do this on the basis of the *meaning* of the concept in question. In my opinion, when a child establishes a concept of a triangle, but doesn't know what 'triangle' means, he would not be able to know the triangle is made up of 3 lines put together in a certain way, even if he was able to pick out triangles. What is interesting is that the same issue comes up regarding syntax.

To describe whole states of affairs, we have sentences. The syntax of a sentence is how the nouns, pronouns, verbs, adjective, etc., are arranged in the sentence and how they are related. The suggestion we made in AII.3 is that the way parts of speech are arranged in a sentence requires information to specify and this might be considered a kind of meaning. Well, in my opinion, if this is a kind of meaning, syntactical meaning, it is the same kind of meaning involved in the construction of a total sense datum of a state of affairs. In fact, I think the two kinds of meaning are really two sides of the same meaning coin. *The syntax of a sentence — the way the parts of speech, nouns, verbs, etc. are arranged in a sentence — reflects the features, objects and components are arranged in a sense datum initiated by causal states of affairs.* This is the *foundation* of the mind's ability to perceive real world objects.

The information necessary to construct a sense data trace of a scene out of primitive elements and components, such as a TV picture, is the same as the information contained in the syntax of a sentence expressing the propositional scene. It seems to me that the phenomenon of the TV camera, which creates sense data traces, illustrates the *finite* nature of the information content of both a sense data trace and the syntax of a sentence. When Fodor says, "... purely informational semantics can be reconciled with a purely computational theory of mental processes..." (Fodor, '95, 17), this can only be done if we are talking about sense data traces having finite information content, which comes through finite transducers. This is all his informational semantics is going to give us. But mental processes like thinking involve representations of percepts having full meanings (however you call them, broad, abductive, etc). The amount of information in Fodor's informational semantics is not nearly sufficient to do anything with full meanings, which is why Fodor's informational semantics in untenable.

This is also why computers can deal with sense data elements and components. Computers can create primitive traces consisting of sense data objects, like triangles, and sense data components like shapes and colors on the basis of finite amounts of information coming from causal objects. The computer then makes the discriminations necessary to distinguish concepts and categories of objects. This is reflected in the fact that the finite state computer only comprehends the syntax of its sentences, even though it has no idea what the sentences mean, as John Searle says, and that Fodor almost admits in moments of weakness. And just as meanings cannot be delivered by information coming from causal objects, also no kind of robust meaning

can be squeezed out of the syntax of a sentence. (I have been very impressed with how this word program can correct my awful syntax. And it is doing it with finite state algorithms. When God created me, I was lucky to get a music module, but He forgot to install one of Chomsky's grammar modules in my brain. But it's good to know it's only a finite state module.)

It's a shame David Marr didn't have more time — he might have investigated the informational aspects of his perception theory. An interesting question is, which of Marr's 2D (the primal sketch) or 2½ D sketches is the traditional sense data? On one reading, it appears that the difference between the primal and 2½ D sketches is that the latter includes information as to the special arrangements of components of a sense data whereas the primal sketch does not. The view proposed here is that there really isn't a separate primal sketch, but that information coming into the eyes *includes* information about arrangement and that only one sense datum is produced by the visual system. Syntax reflects the information in the 2½ D sketch, but nothing linguistically corresponds to the primal sketch. There is no primal sketch syntax. Of course, this idea needs to be cleaned up, which there's no room for here, (even if I could do it).

If there is something to this view it may show why Chomsky posited that deep grammar is innate. He has looked at the languages of the world and observed that they have similar deep grammar. Since languages of the world evolved in a wide variety of circumstances, it might suggest that the only way this could happen is if the rules of deep grammar were built in at birth. However, if we look at syntax as the product of a need to represent the arrangement of meaningless sense data arrangements of causal objects out in the world, then since all the languages of the world evolved in the *same* world of causal objects, the syntax of deep grammar would have to be the same as well. This opens the possibility that rules of grammar are learned, which seems to me to be the case. Of course the only way to prove this is to look at languages in worlds where the laws of physics are very different. But we can't do this, and Chomsky's theories are safe for a while.

One of the most interesting results in cognitive science research is the fact that primates can handle meaning, but have trouble with syntax and so cannot do language in the fullest human sense. This is exact opposite of the abilities of computers. To me, this shows that organic living things, especially mammals, with their infinite state capacity, are able to confer meaning to their sense data experiences, whereas the computer cannot. On the other hand, the fact that primates have trouble with syntax, whereas computers do not, might show that the primate is perceiving things in the world as Gestalts which do not involve taking apart or assembling of sense data elements, and for which syntax is relevant. The computer, on the other hand, is not capable of perceiving Gestalts. Therefore, if it is to handle complex objects and states of affairs, it must be designed so as to look for sense data elements and to accommodate syntax corresponding to the assembly of these elements. However, there is no more meaning in the assembly than there was in the elements. But the primate does not have a language facility to represent the assembly as an assembly, but perceives whole Gestalts having whatever meaning accrues on the basis of Gestalt perceptions.

Alzheimer's patients are the exact opposite of primates and resemble computers. Various tests (Lieberman, '91, 120) show that they can handle syntax adequately but have forgotten meanings of words and sentences. This shows that their perceptual apparatus is still intact so they can relate the syntax of a sentence to arrangements of sense data elements. However, connections to meaning areas of the outer cortex are clogged and full meanings are inaccessible.

All of this may also explain why Quine's radical translation is impossible. Translation involves meaning. But the only meanings that instrumentally exist are personal meanings, which are infinite state entities. Even when public meanings are constructed, a translator would have to assemble a public meaning on the basis of personal meanings. And since personal meanings involve infinite state entities, this job could never be done computationally. But syntax is another matter. Computers seem to be able to translate sentences *syntactically*, even if they don't get the meaning right. Even the fairly primitive program being used to write this book often corrects my grammar, even though it has no idea what I'm saying, whereas sometimes I do. Since personal meaning involves various infinite state entities, accurate translation is not only impossible, but a goal that contradicts the very nature of the entities involved.

This might give some credence to Putnam's idea that you can't refer to real world objects. The mind does participate in building sense data traces consisting of sensory elements of states of affairs. These are Gestalt traces only, in that information about arrangement is not used by the mind for meaning analysis. In Appendicitis II, we explained that the syntax of a sentence enables us to *refer* to the arrangement of *causal* objects out in the world. Young babies and people who received sight as adults, at first see only sense data. Arrangements of sensory elements are inherent in the sense data trace, but not as arrangements *per se*. It may not even be appropriate to talk about arrangements at this stage. Awareness of the arrangement of sensory elements requires meaning, which is not present at the stage of sense data development. So even if sensory traces enable us to refer to causal states of affair, described by syntax, they certainly do not refer to *perceptual* objects and their arrangement. Semantics enables us to personally refer to perceptual objects, including the arrangement of elements, components and features, because a viewer takes part in creating these percepts by projecting his or her meaning out to causal states of affairs.

We *publicly* refer to real world objects because of an innate ability to direct the attention of other humans to causal objects our syntax refers to. The other person we are communicating with creates his *own* percepts by adding his individual meanings to these causal objects. After the smoke clears away, however, the world that one person perceives may be very different from what another perceives. This is why I've said that most understanding is *mis*understanding. However, humans have created great civilizations and technology because manipulating most real world objects does not involve complex personal meanings. Scientists and engineers around the world can adequately cooperate in creating scientific progress because they rely mainly on the *syntax* of their languages which refers to commonly perceived *causal* objects, and not on personal meanings they project to *perceptual* objects.

AV.6 INADEQUACIES OF BEHAVIORISM

When John Watson published his famous paper in 1913 introducing behaviorism with a bang, he was at the same time digging its own grave. By defining all mentality in terms of behavior, he was in effect shutting off the possibility that behaviorism could ever be an adequate theory of the mind. By his very program of eliminating references to mental phenomena like thoughts, perceptions, propositional attitudes, etc., he was in effect defining behavior not as actions having meaning, but really only movements, which, by definition, have no content. (We will get into an analysis of actions in Ch. 18.) This is only causal stuff. Movements are finite state causal processes and it is quite possible that computers could recognize and categorize movements. Movements could be reflected in the syntax of sentences describing them, again finite state stuff. And this explains why behaviorism could never get beyond rat psychology. As long as you're talking about the inputs and outputs of functionalism, or the stimulus-response of behaviorism, you're talking about causal level *movements*. In very simple devices like thermostats and computers, there is no meaning to what they do and all of their motions and operations are *movements*. This is why finite state devices without content can be predicted by other finite state

devices. Behaviorism works only if there is no meaning involved in the events in question.

This is why behaviorism was somewhat successful in analyzing mentality of simple creatures like rats and pigeons. They don't have the brain capacity to accommodate meaningful representations, let alone propositional attitudes. A rat can't project himself into a state of affairs at another place and time. Even if they make representations, which is doubtful since representations probably appeared 10 million years ago after the advent of rats, the content of them is so sparse, that it is highly unlikely that they would have causal efficacy. And the experiments the early behaviorists were conducting did not make use of the small amounts of meaning rats do have. The stimulus and responses in these experiments involved mostly movements having almost no meaning at all. If his brain processes that occurred between the stimulus and response do not introduce infinite state meanings but can proceed along solely on the basis of algorithmic laws of chemistry, then his responses will be movements, which can be analyzed computationally. That's why it was easy for early Behaviorists to postulate mentality with no content or significance at all and dispense with them so easily. Even when they experimented with people, their experiments were laughable. They were designed to turn a person into a rat, and lo and behold they got the same results as they got from the rat.

This is why you can get animals to do some extremely funny things, and they don't crack a smile. You put a funny costume on a dog or cat, and all it is to them is an annoyance. They have no meaning to project to the costume. And some of the experiments run by behaviorists were funny for the same reason. The animal is doing things that have very little meaning to the animal, but lots of fun to watch. The fact that these behaviorists didn't see the humor in their experiments says a lot about the theory of behaviorism. There's the joke about two rats talking, and one says to the other, "I've got my psychologist very well trained: every time I push this lever, he feeds me".

If everything could be explained by physical causation, like behaviorists did with their stimulus/response story, why would we evolve mentality like desires and beliefs in the first place? Of course, there is probably a lot less mental causation than we think, but there must be some of it, or why would we evolve mentality?

If representations and complex propositional attitudes with meaning enter into the game, as our causal cutter shows, and if the stimulus necessarily has meaning and so has causal efficacy to complex creatures like humans, then there is no way a behavioral analysis can predict or understand the response. This is infinite state stuff with causal efficacy, and no simple-minded behaviorist or even a functional analysis is going to predict anything. This is why armed with their whole arsenal of behaviorism's theory and tricks, Watson and Skinner couldn't do as good a job at predicting human behavior as well as an intelligent folk psychologist.

This is why Chomsky was able to demolish behaviorism with his own 1957 paper criticizing B.F. Skinner's work on linguistics. Chomsky showed that behaviorism's theories of language were inadequate. His analysis is quite detailed; but a simple overview would point in the same direction. The very purpose of language is to convey meaning. And if behaviorism is going to omit meaning, its linguistic stimulus will be considered only meaningless symbols. As such, there is no way it would be able to predict a response, even if we were to let the behaviorist get away with considering his response only syntactically as mere movements.

AV.7 The Semantics of Propositional Attitudes

Propositional attitudes are very important in human interaction, a mainstay of the mental phenomena that go into explaining and predicting human behavior. Thus they make up a good part of folk Psychology. Recall, we discussed folk psychology in Appendicitis IV.8. We do explain people's behavior on the basis of

hopes and intentions, beliefs and desires, etc. We discussed Propositional attitudes in Ch. 15. Also, as we stressed in Sect. 16.9, the ability to entertain propositional attitudes can be viewed as the essence of being a human person, as well as being the essence of language. If a system of symbols can express propositional attitudes, it qualifies as a language. So if you can come up with an analysis of content for propositional attitudes, you will probably have a theory of semantics.

We first have to define what a propositional attitude is. In *The Language of Thought*, Fodor brings up a number of points that add to problems incurred by making sentences as the objects of propositional attitudes. Also, descriptions of propositional attitudes can't be in any spoken language because how could a non-English speaker believe that John bought a Ford, when he can't say those words. Also, there is the case of the feral child who grows up in the woods with no human contact and no language. It seems likely that feral children (and adults) have beliefs but they don't have sentences in their heads at all. Of course, Fodor has a way out of this sinking ship. He passes the buck to his LOT, puts on his Mentalese life jacket and is saved.

So he chooses to define a propositional attitude as a relation between a person and a sentence or "formula" in an internal language. But he doesn't make clear what this formula is. In some of Fodor's accounts, there is only a *sentence* in Mentalese that is the object of a belief. But a sentence must either *express* or it must *represent* a propositional state of affairs. If a sentence is used to *express* a proposition, then the emphasis is on a possible state of affairs that may or may not exist. On the other hand, if it is used to *represent* a proposition, then the sentence is a kind of name for a representation which is then the object of the propositional attitude. Fodor seems to change his mind about this a number of times. He describes this as "...the solution is thus to take the objects of PA's [propositional attitudes] to be sentences of a *non*-natural language; in effect in an Internal Representational system," (Fodor, '81, '94) which "constitutes a (computational) language" (200) — *Mentalese*. But where does his sentence come from?

Colin McGinn says, "beliefs are relations to possible states of affairs..." which are propositions. Also, "Non-existent possibilities simply cannot be believed to obtain" (McGinn, '89, 39). But at what level does the "possible" reside? Not at the perceptual level because unicorns don't exist, and yet I can truly believe that unicorns have one horn. And not at the causal level either because if Sam has the belief relation to Cicero being bald, he would have the belief relation to Tully being bald because it's the same propositional state of affairs at the causal level where propositions reside. But he doesn't believe Tully was bald.

The belief expert, Mark Crimmins, seems to go back and forth in this regard as well. He comes up with the idea of a *"notion"*: Bill's Tully *notion* is responsible for the role that 'Cicero' plays in the proposition above. And Crimmins' notion seems to be individuated and identified at least in part by its content. But then, it seems to me, he's really shifting the game over to a relation to some kind of *representation* that represents the proposition in question. We will discuss the idea of notions presently. (It turns out that Crimmins' and Dennett's idea of *notion* is really a very bad substitute for a perceptual object.) In my opinion, 'believing propositions' is either just bad grammar, or a category mistake like believing in miracles. We don't believe in miracles, which are certain phenomena that exist; we believe in various *explanations* of miracles.

So the first question that comes to mind in Fodor's account is, how will Fodor represent the proposition in a propositional attitude? There has to be a lump somewhere in the mind/brain that will have causal efficacy in what we do on the basis of the belief. Fodor seems to think this lump can be a *representation* of a *proposition* like John buying a new Ford or a sentence in Mentalese expressing this proposition. But there are an infinite number of representations that could represent the causal state of affairs. We will call these *interpretations*. And he never tells us how we are to determine which representation he has in mind that will correspond to something abstract like the propositional object of the belief, which is at the causal level. A belief without a definite representational object of the belief that interprets a proposition, is like a picture frame with no picture. What a belief does is simply set up, like a big picture frame, the proposition the belief is about. The *object* of the belief, the representation chosen to interpret the proposition the belief is about is the picture. But neither Fodor nor Carruthers tells us how to determine which representation along with its content will be chosen to interpret the proposition the belief is about.

The question is how *do* I represent a propositional state of affairs like John buying a new Ford that I may believe happened? Do I represent this with a picture of John kicking the tires on a new Ford, or talking to the dealer, or sitting down wrapping up the deal with the dealer, or getting into his new car, or driving away in the new Ford? This is all personal stuff. Even though this was a particular causal event, the description must be some sentence describing the representation at the perceptual level that interprets the proposition. What representation would be used to be the object of my belief that you bought a new Ford.

As we explained there in Sect. 15.1, propositional attitudes are relationships between a person with a self and an *interpretation* of a propositional causal state of affairs. The proposition in a PA is a *casual* state of affairs and the interpretation is the object of the belief. Now when we entertain the propositional causal state of affairs, we surround this causal state with a meaning cloud. What we are suggesting is that the representation chosen to interpret a proposition in a PA is some representation taken from the meaning cloud surrounding the causal state of affairs. In turn, the chosen interpretation will have it own meaning cloud. These will be *personal* meaning clouds. Of course, the representation chosen to be the interpretation of the proposition will vary depending on the time the belief is entertained or activated. And there may be more than one of them.

This is why it is very difficult to determine PAs. For example, if you walk away from the façades of buildings, is it likely to be the result of a belief that junk can fall from a building at any time, even though this belief is non-occurrent and has never been activated. Somewhere in your head should be a representation consisting of junk falling from a building attached to a bit of fear. However, there is no way to know if any piece of behavior is being affected by such non-occurrent propositional attitudes and so no way to know we have them through any kind of functional analysis. Maybe I don't want to run into people coming out of the building. This is why PAs are so messy. The content, M, of a PA is the meaning of the representative chosen to interpret the propositional state of affairs, which is the *object* of the PA. Thus a propositional attitude is a three-term predicate {self, interpretation, value}, and this predicate could be used to individuate PAs.

We should also note that there is no need for language in this process. PAs most likely evolved *before* language, which is why pre-language children can have desires and beliefs. In our view, PAs directly involve representations that have the meaning we created them with, so there's no language barrier to overcome. However, if we wanted to describe with language the interpretation chosen, we could use the Tarski convention in Appendicitis II to do so.

Stephen Schiffer (Schiffer, '87) tries to discredit representations as the objects of propositional attitudes. But the only way he can tempt us in this direction is using a straw man. He uses Fodor's formulae in his Language of Thought as what a representation has to be, which is pretty gratuitous. And then he proceeds to show in inscrutable detail that this is not viable basically because there's no way for these formulae to gain the content of an actual belief. Well, as we shall illustrate in many ways, this is a problem with Fodor's LOT, not with real representations per se. The representations we use for the objects of beliefs have the content they have because we *create*

them with this content. So we don't need these huge inscrutable books to futilely try to attach content to our representations.

Regarding individuation, it is impossible to individuate propositional attitudes on the basis of brainstates or any other kind of physicality. Two people could have the same belief without anything in common at all in terms of what their brains are doing. Besides, as an infinite state system, brainstates could never be checked to see how they compare. This is why we probably can't individuate PAs semantically: meanings are infinite state entities. So how do we individuate PA's? One way is functionally through inputs and outputs. The first problem in this regard is that this analysis is circular. Also, we couldn't use the syntax of a sentence that describes the representation because that would not be a fine enough sieve.

It would be impossible to determine inputs and outputs of PAs on the basis of meanings of the representational objects of the PA. Part of what a belief in a John-bought-a-Ford state of affairs could mean to John is that he won't be looking for another car in the near future and won't be available to accompany a car hunt. We can't determine functional outputs unless we know what such personal meanings are. Even if we know some of John's behavior, which PA's do we define in terms of this behavior? The bottom line is that there is no non-circular way to individuate and tally up propositional attitudes to the satisfaction of philosophy. All we have are criteria for ascribing them. However, it is suggested in the text that representational objects of PAs and the involvement of the self can be so fleeting, floating and flimsy that there wouldn't be much to work with in defining a PA. It seems to me that we ascribe PAs on the basis of behavior, and only when there is no relevant behavior do we accept the reports of people about their mentality.

But even using behavior as a criterion, it is often difficult to determine what our PA's are? What things do we intend to do? There is no way to determine what our beliefs and intentions are. When I go for a walk, do I believe the sidewalk will support me? Well, yes if I'm asked. But what about before? Is there any detection, trace, representation or the slightest suggestion of a picture anywhere in my brain depicting myself falling through the cracks in the sidewalk? This is the situation with the vast majority of beliefs and other propositional attitudes. If you take a particular piece of behavior, which PA's does it define? If I buy a house, does this indicate I believe it will be a good investment, or want to be near a friend, or my job, or I'll like the scenery? These in turn depend on my desires and other PA's. Each PA like a belief involves further beliefs, desires, and intentions. Pretty soon your whole system of beliefs, desires, and other PA's will be involved, as Braddon-Smith and Jackson describe ('96).

Daniel Dennett says our beliefs consist of a bunch of core beliefs plus anything that can be *inferred* or deduced from these. Well, this is really tally by fiat. In my opinion, in order to have a non-occurrent belief or any other propositional attitude, there has to be a representation that is the object of the belief in your head somewhere. And there has to be the potential for inserting the self into this representation if prompted by the environment. If you don't have a representation of a state of affairs, and don't have an attitude attached to it, like it's a highly *valued* state of affairs represented as in hope, or a *feared* state of affairs represented, etc., then you don't have a propositional attitude.

The important topic, of course, is causation. Now Fodor acknowledges that the semantic aspect *does* seem to be involved in *causing mental and physical behavior*: "...propositional attitudes have semantic properties.... A philosophical theory of propositional attitudes must explain their semantic properties and their intentionality." (Fodor, '81, 18). Fodor points out that Folk Psychology is "...deeply committed to mental causation..."(Fodor, '87, 12). "...it is in virtue of its *opaque* content that John's belief that P plays its systematic role in John's mental life — e.g., in the determination of his actions and in the causation of his other mental

states." (Fodor, '87, 185). Where is this "opaque" content coming from?

But keep in mind that the meaning of the chosen interpretation is *embedded* in the belief relation, and so this meaning is not exposed as with ordinary representations. It's not the meaning, M, by itself, that will do causal work, even if we were to convince Fodor that a representation needs its semantic aspect to do this work. It is the total *belief* complex complete with a representational interpretation of the propositional object of the belief including its meaning and the attitude towards this object that will do causal work. You're not going to behave the same way when you hope it will rain, and when you fear it will rain.

But in spite of the enormous complexity of this project, most analytic philosophers make the problem even worse by trying to put propositional attitudes on a more so-called scientific basis just as we discussed for representations in general. The agenda is to fashion a scientific model which will enable us to explain and predict behavior just as folk psychology does, only more scientifically and effectively. Fodor does it with analogies with computers, Daniel Dennett does it by substituting crisper, cleaner concepts for the ones of folk psychology, and Stephen Stich does it by throwing propositional attitudes into the trash altogether.

AV.8 Meaning Holism

You might think that with the complexity of propositional attitudes, Fodor might give up his Computational Theory of Mind, CMT. But a computer is to a modern day philosopher like heroine is to the addict. He's joined by Hartry Field in this matter: The "...task of psychology is to state..." the scientific functional ramifications of propositional attitudes: what laws relate inputs to establishing PA's and laws as to how these PA's will affect behavior. Then he says, "...then semantic characterization of beliefs and desires are irrelevant to psychology: one can state the laws without saying anything about what the...sentences mean..." (Field in Block, '81, 102). Here we go again.

So now if Jim wonders whether Amy will say yes when he asked her to dance, Field is telling us that the *meaning* of his representation of dancing with Amy is not relevant to his beliefs about what she will say, nor to whether or not he will ask. I have no idea as to how these cognitive scientists come up with their conclusions in the face of blatant real world counter-examples. He tries to steer clear of real world situations and gives a sterling example that seems to rely solely on logic. He says if you believe that doing X will bring about Y, and you desire Y, you will also desire X. Now Joe believes that robbing a bank will get him a bunch of money, and he wants a bunch of money. We can conclude from Field that Joe will want to rob a bank. Isn't philosophy amazing? In my opinion, the establishment of propositional attitudes and their functional ramifications are based *solely* on content. And if there is anything remotely resembling a law relating all these mental items, it had better talk a lot about meaning.

Fodor may suspect this, so at some point Fodor goes on the offensive regarding meaning. As mentioned above, the views I have been defending are a brand of what has been called *associationism*, which is like the Naturalism discussed above. It's a simple idea that all the mental items constituting the meaning of a representation are "associated" with that representation, not only figuratively, but neurologically as well. It does seem to me that meaning is a neurologically global matter. The meaning associated with any representation consists of other representations that can be anywhere in the brain. They are attached to the main representation by neural projections, so that they can come to mind any time the representation is being activated. There are probably an infinite number. As far as mental work is concerned, any particle in the meaning cloud of a representation that is the object of a propositional attitude can affect other mental activity as well as behavior.

Fodor seems to suggest that when representations do causal work either by themselves or as the object of a propositional attitude, they have to be following rules; and as such, they have to be entities that participate in computational activities. Associationist theories don't seem to imply rule following. At one point Fodor compares association "...as viewed as a mechanical relation *among* mental contents"...as opposed to "...computational relations defined over them". (Fodor, '83, 31). To which the associationist says, that's me.

In my opinion, a representation can stay attached to its semantic aspect, and do its causal work just by sitting there and affecting in complex ways anything coming its way. It doesn't have to be *following* any algorithmic rules at all, in the sense of actively following a lead. We all obey the law, but that doesn't pin down anything we do. The earth doesn't follow or obey rules or laws as it goes around the sun like a duckling follows the mother duck, even though we talk that way. It *exhibits* a physical law. Any rule-following that *appears* to be present is part of a description that we, as human outsiders, interpret the process. A lion lying about in the jungle has a lot of meaning for animals that may come its way, and will greatly affect their behavior. The lion doesn't have to be following rules.

Fodor has further criticisms of the associationist view in his book *Psychosemantics*. But here again his motivation seems to be to depreciate the importance of a very robust meaning aspect of representations I have outlined so that they will comfortably fit in the computer model. Fodor has a notion, called the *epistemic liaison* of a term or sentence. P is in an epistemic liaison of a term if P is relevant to the semantic evaluation of the term. This might be pretty close to our meaning cloud. Fodor next defines *Meaning Holism* as the idea that the content of a propositional attitude, like a belief, "...is determined by the *totality* of its epistemic liaisons" (Fodor, '87, 56). So far, so good, except the meaning of a propositional attitude is its content and if this content is determined by its epistemic liaisons, then so will the content or meaning of any representation that is its object. And you would have holism of some sort. But you might guess that Fodor is not going to like meaning holism because it's just too big a load to stuff into his computer. He likes meaning *atomism*, whereby meanings are local gadgets, not extant enough to clog up his neat clean computer.

He seems quite alarmed that on the basis of these ideas, "… no two people (for that matter, no two time slices of the *same* person) ever are in the same intentional state" (57), such as the content of a belief, for example. This is because the meaning of a sentence such as "it is raining" includes any mentality associated with the sentence, such as "things outside will get wet", and "it's cloudy". And it will include all the personal associations, such as "this is the weather when my back hurts". Of course, this is what makes human beings a little more interesting than Fodor's computers. This is why differences between the personal meanings of the object of a belief of two different people will cause different behavior. But the beliefs are different not because the belief relation is different, nor the syntax different, but because the *content* of the beliefs are different.

Fodor's tack will be to attempt to depreciate the relevance of Meaning Holism. And you might guess what his criticisms will be. First of all, Fodor seems to think that somehow we have to have some objective way of individuating meanings or that we should have some way of determining an *objective* meaning, whether it's for a term or a content of a propositional attitude. This may be the motivation for neglecting personal meaning in favor of a public meaning, which may be more computationally manageable. Yes, that would be nice, and that would enable us to stick them into computers, and then the cognitive science community would jump for joy. But the problem we are concerned with is the role that the semantic aspect of propositional attitudes plays in causing mental and physical behavior of *individual people*. Mental causation does not occur in public; it occurs in mind/brains in the heads of individual persons. And so it occurs

on the basis of *personal* meaning, which are infinite in number. If this is the case, it would be difficult to individuate and identify them. But that doesn't mean there's no such thing as meaning. It just implies that meaning is not going to be easy to handle, especially computationally.

What may discourage Fodor from the implications of Meaning Holism is that we would have trouble figuring out which liaisons are going to be included in the term. "Since epistemic liaisons are what *individuate* beliefs, each belief has its epistemic liaison *necessarily*. But Meaning Holism …gives us no idea how we are to do so" (Fodor, '87, 58). Fodor suggests that by tracing one belief, which presupposes another, which implies another, which is related to another, and on and on, the epistemic liaison of a particular belief object will involve a person's entire system of propositional attitudes and meaning items, which is holism.

Epistemic liaisons for beliefs are just like the meaning clouds for individual terms we discussed in Ch. 3. In the case of a belief, on a given occasion, a representation will be chosen from the interpretation cloud around the proposition the belief is about, as explained in Sect. 15.1. The chosen representation would probably be the most important or relevant of all the representations in the cloud on a particular occasion, and will have the most responsibility for whatever behavior the belief causes on this occasion. Of course, on another occasion, a different representation may be chosen and altogether different behavior ensue. Whichever is chosen, this representation will have its own meaning cloud containing an infinite number of mental items having high information content themselves. *But there is going to be a weight on each item in the cloud that determines its potential effect on a particular piece of behavior.* Some mental items in this cloud are going to be more important in affecting certain kinds of behavior than others. Other mental objects are going to be weighted negligently because they would have very little influence on a particular mental or physical piece of behavior.

Of course, to determine the weight of a particular mental item like a mental memory image in a meaning cloud for a representation as the object of a belief, for example, you would have to take into account the meaning of *this* representation. This might involve another infinite number of further representations that would have to be evaluated as to its contribution to the causative power of the original representation chosen to represent the proposition in the PA in question. This process never ends because each representation involved has a meaning that involves an infinite number of further representations. We could imagine this creating a triangular tree forever expanding upward as meaning clouds multiply. Fodor would still call this a kind of meaning holism because sooner or later you are going to involve every representation and every propositional attitude the mind/brain has. But this is an unfair exaggeration because he seems to imply that each of the representations in a meaning cloud have equal weight in affecting the causal power of this meaning. This is certainly not the case. As we get farther away from an initial representation, the weights get increasingly smaller (or is it decreasingly bigger?) Far up the line of meaning clouds, the weights will become negligible. I don't think it is important to quibble about weights. The important thing to note is only that some items in this meaning cloud have more influence on a particular piece of behavior than others and some mental items would have absolutely none. My belief that 2 plus 2 equals 4 is not going to affect, in any way, my belief that China is in Asia. Of course, we could never accurately determine the weights of representations in meaning clouds, nor get to an infinite number of items in meaning clouds. This might be why Fodor says the problem is "...to explain how thinking manages reliably to preserve *truth*; and Associationism ...hasn't the resources to do so" (Fodor, '98, 10). This is a remarkable statement. What it says is that Associationism, which does admit infinite state meaning, doesn't have the "resources" to enable thinking and causing

behavior, but computations, which involve only finite state algorithms, somehow can!

But we know what the weighting evaluation process would be like and we can sample the first few layers of meaning clouds to get some idea of the causative power of a belief content. Just because there will be an infinite number of them doesn't mean we cannot talk about a particular item. The causal potential of a particular item in a particular content would be a weight associated with that item. We could determine whether a particular particle is included and how much weight it has simply by asking questions and observing a person's behavior, including verbal behavior. Of course, this process would never end. But this does not mean we are totally in the dark. What we do in practice is apply a cut-off point for the weights of items in a liaison, not counting those below the threshold. This gives us a reasonable basis for making educated guesses as to what people will do. It would also give us a way to individuate representations because it would be a finite process. It's the best we can do given the infinite complexity of liaisons and enables us to evaluate a meaning cloud in a rough and ready way. We could call this Partial Meaning Holism and it probably describes Folk Psychology.

Of course, if a different representation were chosen as the object of a propositional attitude, it would have a slightly different meaning cloud. But since all the representations in the meaning cloud for an interpretation of a proposition have a lot in common, all these meaning clouds will have a great deal of overlap. Even though the weightings of the meaning cloud of a particular representation will differ from representation to representation, these weightings will lie within a certain range. This is why when a person has a certain belief and chooses a particular representation to interpret the propositional object of a belief, his subsequent behavior will probably lie within certain limits.

This weighting theory might also solve what is called the frame problem. Peter Carruthers calls it the intractability problem (Carruthers, '05, 109+).

In solving a problem, a device might have to look through its entire database to find relevant sentences or representations. This would create a computational explosion that is "intractable". This is the motivation for Carruthers' massive modularity theory of mind. Representations and their content are probably global and modules would limit the number of items to be considered in solving a problem to only what is local. To me, this is not a solution at all because how will the right modules be chosen that would best address the problem at hand, to say nothing of the fact that central processing should be the last place in the world we'd find modules.

Weighting theory seems to solve this problem. For any problem at hand, representations would be chosen to be the interpretation of the propositions involved in the problem. The items in the meaning cloud for this representation would have an array of weightings that would best address the needs of the problem at hand, so that the vast majority of items would have nearly no weight at all and the mind/brain would not have to consider them. Thus a solution to the problem at hand would be tractable because the only items in relevant meaning clouds to consider would be ones with appreciable weights.

This weighting theory might also explain the disjointedness and incoherence of dreams which we mentioned in the text. An energy deprived cortex during a dream may not be able to put weightings on various meaning items in a meaning cloud that would be appropriate for the situation in real life. This might account for the story in a dream to wander incoherently. The wrong weightings might send the story off in crazy directions not in accordance with the weighting functions that were established during waking experiences. It might difficult to test this though.

In one paragraph, Fodor intimates a reductio as a result of an assumption of meaning holism. In the same spirit as the above quotes, he says, "…if *any* of the function of a mental state bears on its content, then all of its function bears on its content. But if all

function bears on content, then no two mental state tokens ever have the same content and there can be no such thing as psychological explanation by subsumption under intentional law" (Fodor, '90, x). But since Fodor's whole program is to wind up with "intentional laws", he intimates that rejection of them is out of the question, which puts meaning holism into suspicion. And so in throwing out the baby with the bath water, he concludes, "…we have, in fact, no very good reason to believe that epistemic liaisons *are* determinants of content" (Fodor, '87, 62). For, what criterion should we use to determine which ones should be included so that we could individuate them? And if we can't determine which ones to include, maybe we should give up the whole idea. But weighting theory solves this problem because in practice, it would limit the number of meaning items that would be considered in carrying out any kind of thinking or problem-solving. On the other hand, if mentality really does involve *infinite* clouds with significant weightings, there will never be any kind of *law* describing them because laws require finite algorithms. As we explained in Sect. AIV.10, mental causation is not lawlike in the same way as behavior of inanimate objects. Fodor doesn't seem to realize it, but we could start with this last result and run his deduction backwards and prove meaning holism. People are totally unpredictable in the detail of their behavior, which should tell us that there are infinite numbers of mental items in a meaning cloud each of which has great complexity. This is the very essence of being human. And just because meanings are not computationally manageable, doesn't mean we have to give up and depreciate what is really involved in evaluating meaning with the claim that either it involves everything or it involves nothing, which is where Fodor's theory winds up.

Fodor spends a whole book attempting to talk us out of meaning holism. He tells us that "If Holism is true, then I can't understand any of your language unless I can understand practically all of it" (Fodor, '92, 9). Also, he indicates that two people can't have one thought in common unless they have lots of thoughts in common. In my opinion, these are gross exaggerations. They stem from the idea that since the meaning of a sentence may involve a person's entire belief system, two people can't have the same understanding of a sentence unless they shared their entire belief system. But we don't need the *exact* same understandings. We can get by with approximate understandings most of the time because mentality is individuated in much grosser terms than Fodor is willing to allow. As we mentioned, propositional attitudes are individuated on the basis of the content of the interpretative representation which will be similar from person to person because based on a common causal world. Of course, we have different content for the representations we choose for the object of beliefs because they are always *personal* beliefs. This causes us to often misunderstand each other, but we do muddle on through most of the time on the basis of behavioral understandings which enables us to cooperate and often predict each other's behavior. The fact that our understandings are often inadequate and off the mark demonstrates that meaning does involve infinite state entities. They can never be computationally analyzed so as to compare thoughts and beliefs to determine their identity or even similarity. Fodor's extremely picky ideas about meaning identity and similarity are really unfair to the whole idea of meaning holism. It is very ironic that in this book, when Fodor wants to discredit meaning holism, all of a sudden, he is relying on a definition of meaning that does take account of its enormous complexity — what I am claiming are infinite state entities. Of course, when he wants to stuff meaning into the computer, it shrivels down to computational size. This rush to extremes pops up in much of his writing.

In his very difficult book on *Holism*, Fodor builds an entire edifice containing many extremely difficult concepts and deductions in order to discredit meaning holism. I may not fully comprehend much of his analysis, but I have a sneaking suspicion that his whole discussion is applicable to our *causal* world. The meaning of causal objects and states of affairs is the meaning provided by a whole *theory* in which causal objects are embedded. And this involves a means of confirmation that could very well imply computational procedures or at least a more manageable holism. But this analysis is simply not applicable to the *perceptual* world that very importantly involves meaning.

One of the more fascinating aspects of Fodor's analysis is that he seems to accept *belief* holism, but then he balks at *meaning* holism which he says isn't necessarily implied by belief holism. I just don't see this. If there is a holism of beliefs, isn't it because the *contents* of beliefs are holistic? There are only a finite number of propositional attitudes. If the system of beliefs and other propositional attitudes is holistic, what would explain this unless content is also holistic.

AV.9 PSYCHOFUNCTIONALISM

Next Fodor tries functionalism, which he calls *psychofunctionalism* (Norman Bates style). "The way to rid psychology of intensional idiom is to carry through the program of machine functionalism…"(Fodor, '81, 21). This is a new way for Fodor to pare down meaning so as to be computationally acceptable. You simply define the meaning of the object of a propositional attitude (or any representation) functionally on the basis of environmental inputs to a mind, mental activity, and subsequent behavior. This is a kind of "narrow" meaning, because it talks only about what's within the surface of the person. Actually, this is pretty close to the operational meaning people use for other people's propositional attitudes in predicting and explaining their behavior that we find in folk psychology. Fodor says that a functional analysis will give you a causal definition of only propositional attitudes *per se*, but not their content. So for example, you can define a belief in terms of its causal relations to other mental entities, inputs and behavior. But if we take the belief to be a certain relation between the subject and a mental representation, which is the object of the belief, how can we talk about which causal relations define the belief without taking into consideration the object of the belief including its semantic aspect? Is Fodor going to be a painting collector who collects only empty frames? If I believe it is raining, is this belief identified by being caused by seeing a clear sky? And will this belief cause me to add two and two, or to take an umbrella? Fodor says that the causal relations involved in a functionalist analysis will enable you to distinguish "...believing from wanting, but not believing that such and such from believing that so and so" (Fodor, '87, 70). I have a question for Fodor. Why would a person taking an umbrella better show that she *believes* it to be raining rather than *wanting* it to be raining, than it would show that she *believes* it is raining rather than that she *believes* it is sunny?

Fodor continues his criticisms of relating meaning to functionalism. He asks, if content is determined by functional relationships, "...just *how* is content constituted by function?" He incisively points out that "...the vocabulary that is required for the individuation of contents is, by assumption, *not* available for the individuation of functional roles" (76). This is very true. Contents are about meaning and intentionality, whereas, functional states are discussed in terms of inputs from the outside world, subsequent behavior, and other causation. He asks: "How do identities and differences among patterns of causal connection give rise to identities and differences of meaning? (77). A very good question. See, now that Fodor is refuting a particular theory of content, here functionalism, meaning blows up to monster proportions of complexity which couldn't possibly be handled by the theory. But when presenting his *own* theory of content, meanings again shrivel down to computational size. But aside from the complexity of representational content, we have to remind ourselves of the circularity in a functionalist account of meaning. How can we identify a belief with a meaningful object by looking at the potential behavior it might cause when the only way we can know what kinds of behavior it might cause depends on what the representation means?

If we really entertain the details of a functional analysis of meaning, it probably is the case that causal relations do not exhaust the meaning of a representation. But this does not give us the prerogative to conclude as Fodor does that "There is a short route from functionalism about meaning to meaning holism", (Fodor, '00, 70) which says that a representation would involve everything in a person's head. But Fodor here is neglecting the weights on items in meaning clouds that would provide some idea of a belief causing a certain piece of behavior.

In any event, without further ado, and without a single example, Fodor triumphantly announces that "...functionalism about *believing* (as opposed to believing-that-P) isn't a *semantic* doctrine at all" (Fodor, '87, 71). Well, it certainly is a semantic doctrine. It may be an anorexic doctrine, but it is a theory of how to define and identify a content of representations. But what is interesting here is that Fodor seems to be implying that functionalism isn't really up to the task of determining content because it's too coarse a sieve. Is this a tacit admission that meanings really are big highly complex things after all?

What all this shows is that the whole project of building a footing in the middle of the river between the brain and the mind, or alternatively, finding a level of description between the two levels, using the computer is never going to work. Mind events in the upper layer have meaning, and it is in virtue of meaning that mind events have causal powers. Computers don't do meaning, and attempting a theory of the mind without the key ingredient of meaning is like analyzing baseball without talking about the ball, or analyzing hockey without knowing what the puck you're talking about.

Carruthers distinguishes *cognitive* content from *semantic* content. To me this only furthers the confusion. I can't figure out what these contents would be unless cognitive content is personal meaning, and semantic content public meaning. These are really bad names. Carruthers thinks he can use a functional theory of meaning for propositional attitudes to substitute for meaning holism. He drops epistemic liaisons for a belief in favor of "...the set of conditionals about what the subject *would* think or do..."(Carruthers, '96, 116). He adds that "...these hypotheticals can remain true for a variety of individuals, with various different beliefs and desires, and there is no threat, here, to a content-based science of psychology" (116). Talk about a jet-speed flyover.

The question that cries out is, if we can't determine what a subject will do in the given real situation, how are we going to do better in hypothetical situations? The purpose of functionalism is to provide a theory of what a psychological state *is*; and it does a rotten job of that. But it can do this only if we already know what inputs and outputs are. Ostensibly, these would have to be determined by the *content* of the state. How can functionalism possibly determine outputs, especially hypothetical outputs unless meaning is put to work? I just don't see it. And if meaning is used to determine outputs, who needs functionalism?

AV.10 Semantics and Causal Efficacy

Well, slowly but surely, various setbacks in other approaches to the causality problem for propositional attitudes like beliefs, seems to finally have trapped Fodor into examining the real source of representational causality, which is their semantic aspect. But since he still has no way to get the meaning of states of affairs into our representations in our heads, he's going to sneak in content on the backs of neurological brain processes. It's like in the spy stories where you sneak in the spy under a load of hay on an old broken down wagon pulled by a couple of old broken down horses. What he is going to do next to entertain the idea of an "isomorphism" between causal roles and semantic roles.

Suppose you have the belief that John bought a new Ford. Around the representation that interprets the causal proposition of John buying a new Ford is a meaning cloud. The question is, how are cognitive scientists going to put this meaning cloud into a correspondence with its causal role? On what basis will they proceed? One piece of evidence that you can do this trick is that "...*you can deduce the causal role of a mental state from the semantic relations of its propositional object*" (Fodor, '87, 79). And what are these, pray tell? There is a whole cloud of meaning representations surrounding the proposition described by John buying a new Ford. Even if we could identify all these representations, how do we map this cloud to its physical causal role in producing a particular piece of behavior? And if we choose one representation for this cloud to represent the John-bought-a-Ford state of affairs, this representation will also have a meaning cloud of an infinite number of mental items. And they all have different weights in their power to influence the final effect.

Well, Fodor is going to do this by dovetailing PAs with the *causal* nature of neurological processes in the brain. He adds, if this can be done, "we can imagine a reduction of psychology to neurology..."(Fodor, '81, 166). This has the added attraction that if psychological processes are computational, we are more likely to buy the agenda that their causality may be lawlike. But he winds up with the same problem Chalmers had. Recall in Appendicitis IV4.8, Chalmers was forced into a corner, mumbling about voltages and circuits in the computer to try to manufacture some causality between the computational states of the computer. It didn't work for Chalmers and it isn't going to work for Fodor either.

But although Fodor certainly wishes all this could be done, he isn't convinced himself that it can be. He says, "...we can summarize the whole business by saying that neurology will not reduce psychology unless neurological descriptions determine the content of internal formulae" (171). (Internal formulae include representations). What he is saying is that we would have to ground the meaning aspect of a representation in the neurology of the brain as well. Well, this is clearly impossible if the brain is not a finite state computer. And if the system of representations is infinite state, you can't map that to a computer brain either. He adds, "…it is the intentionality of psychological predicates that primarily confounds …" this enterprise (172). That's putting it mildly.

However, if representations, whether alone or part of a propositional attitude, are infinite state and the brain is an infinite state system, as seems likely, the procedure to evaluate all the items in the meaning cloud and put them into correspondence would never end and so there would be no "deduction", induction or reduction. There's no way to map the indeterminacy of mental causation with the lawful causation between brainstates. But it appears that Fodor isn't sold on this mapping either. In fact, he says something that, in my opinion, dooms any such mapping. We "have no workable theory of meaning in hand" (Fodor, '87, 72).

It seems to me that *whether representations are "computable" finite state entities, and the brain is a physical computer, or alternatively, representations are meaning-loaded infinite state entities, and the brain is an infinite state causal device, you still have the problem of mapping computational states held together by the rules of logic to neurological states held together by causal laws.* There is no way such a mapping can be accomplished. What has to go, of course, is the computational theory of mind.

Fred Dretske tries a different shoehorn (Dretske in Grimm & Mererill). He is going to skip the problem of correlating meaning to neurology simply by directly assigning meaning to those same neurological processes. This is a category mistake if there ever was one. Meaning *supervenes* on brainstates. Brainstates have no meaning whatsoever. The problem with the causal efficacy of non-conscious meaning items in a representation meaning cloud concerns only the problem of formalizing infinite state brain processes. The physical brain processes that subvene meaning items are doing the causing in the usual physical way. But when meaning items become *conscious*, we have the additional question as to whether the consciousness of

this item can change things in any way different from what the brainstates it supervenes on are trying to do?

Dretske papers cover this problem by calling the physiological parts of the cause, "structural" causes, whereas the intentional mentality involved is a "triggering" cause. Fine. New names are good. But this does nothing to dovetail mental events with physical processes. Lynne R. Baker says mental causal efficacy is necessary for *explanations* which we do all the time (both in Heil & Meil, '93). Again, fine. The question is, are these explanations *justified?* Again, only if you can dovetail the mental with the physical.

Another escape hatch is to say that meaningful mentality like a belief is the reason or cause of a *person* doing such and such action. But in my opinion, this still requires that we dovetail the mental events that occur with what purely physical events are happening in the action that they supervene on. This still doesn't get rid of infinite state processes.

AV.11 Daniel Dennett and Abstracta

I think we have adequately shown that causal efficacy of representations and propositional attitudes relies essentially on full meaning and content. But now we have the problem that if this is the case, how does meaning get attached to our representations in the first place. Let us now look at Daniel Dennett's exposition about the role meaning plays in propositional attitudes causing mental and physical behavior. It very starkly brings out the problem of getting meaning into our heads. Dennett ('87) is much clearer in posing the problem, which appears in his book *The Intentional Stance.*

The brain, as an intentional theory and evolutionary biology show us, is a *semantic engine*; its task is to discover what its multifarious inputs *mean*, to discriminate them by their significance and 'act accordingly.' That's what brains *are for.* But the brain, as physiology and plain common sense shows us, is just a *syntactic engine;* all it can do is discriminate its inputs by their structural, temporal, and physical features and let its entirely mechanical activities be governed by these "syntactic" features of its inputs. That's all brains can do. Now how does the brain manage to get semantics from syntax? It couldn't (61).

But, of course, it *does* — as he himself tells us at the beginning of this multi-contradictory passage. And it does it the only way it can — by accumulating an infinite number of syntactical items. Dennett's answer to this conundrum is that the brain "cannot be designed to do an impossible task, but it could be designed to *approximate* the impossible task, to *mimic* the behavior of the impossible object (the semantic engine) by capitalizing on close (close enough) fortuitous correspondence between structural regularities — of the environment and of its own internal state and operations — and semantic types" (61).

Well, at least Fodor hooked up meanings in the head with the outside world on the basis of "inference". Dennett is going to do it on the basis of monkey-business luck, which we get by "mimicking". And where did we get such luck? We *evolved* it, of course. This is degenerating into another evolutionary psychology story. But unless babies are born with all that detailed and specific meanings in their heads, *pretending* to have meanings in our mental representations by "mimicking" a *real* semantic engine (where do we find that?) seems to me to be a pretty lame explanation of how the mind/brain has meaningful causal efficacy.

Dennett talks about the possibility of ourselves or nature designing such a "mimic", "...in the end all one can hope to produce (all natural selection has produced) are systems that *seem* to discriminate meanings by actually discriminating things that *co-vary* [italics mine] reliably with meanings" (63). Told you so about evolution. A co-varying device may *indicate* something about what's being detected. But *co-variance does not reproduce meaning.* We're back to the same problem Fodor and Dretske had. And if we take seriously the copy concept of a representation, we don't have

that either. The question remains, how do we know how well Dennett's putative representations really represent?

Stephen Stich wrote an excellent synopsis of Dennett's intentional stance theory in which he gives us a comprehensible description of Dennett's program (Stich, '81, 167). Although Stich's discussion refers mainly to Dennett's ideas about propositional attitudes, it brings out the general problem of getting meaning into the head. It appears that when all the smoke clears away, basically Dennett is going to solve everything at once: the status of the concepts of folk psychology, the meaning of the concepts of folk psychology such as the propositional attitudes, and how a syntactic device like the brain can accommodate these mental phenomena.

It took me a long time to figure out what Dennett is up to in this regard, so I may not be interpreting his strategy accurately. But it seems to me he is first going to anthropomorphize machines, then show that they can be broken down to finer levels of components until you get to a level with no meaning at all. Analogously, the mind can be broken down to such a level where all descriptions are algorithmic and deterministic handled computationally and scientifically, which is where he wants to wind up.

So in his *Brainstorms* book, Dennett introduces the intentional stance by anthropomorphizing computers, thermostats and other machines with talk about how it thinks, believes, expects, etc. In his own words, "...the thermostat will turn itself off the boiler as soon as it comes to believe the room has reached the desired temperature" (Dennett, '87, 22). Plants blossom when they *believe* it's spring. We could even invent our own stance, the love stance. The thermostat turns on because the room's temperature has gotten too low, and the thermostat *loves* for the room's people to be comfortable.

Now that he has us talking about believing and desiring machines, he next breaks down the operations of the machine into finer levels of description and components until you get to a level where everything is totally mechanistic. He likens this to a series of nesting boxes where "Eventually this nesting of boxes within boxes lands you with homunculi so stupid…" (Dennett, '78, 124). And now we're in the land of deterministic laws and hard scientific explanations, and he can proceed to make analogies to the mind/brain.

But this whole strategy is misconceived, in my opinion. This business of believing and desiring machines is just kindershpeil. These aren't real beliefs and desires at all. The whole purpose of analyzing PAs is to explain their causal efficacy. As we explained above, representations that are the object of PAs have *meaning*, and it is the *content* of the propositional attitude that is doing the work of causing our behavior. It is the *painting* in the frame that causes our reaction to the picture, not the frame, which is only a mechanism that constrains our gaze.

There is no meaning in anything the thermostat or the computer does at *any* level. He doesn't even have to open the first box because the first box, the whole dam computer, is stupid. These AI people have beat us over the head with anthropomorphic talk for so long that they even have Dennett talking about "data structures" that "understand themselves", no less (123). The reality is there's no more intelligence in artificial intelligence than there's a rose in an artificial rose. This is because all machines are made from inorganic substances, and so the lowest level of component are at the very least, atoms and molecules, but usually aggregates of atoms and molecules. There is only finite information content in components made from inorganic crystalline substances, and finite information content in machines made of a finite number of such components. At this level, all phenomena are "mechanistic" and deterministic, and can be modeled only algorithmically, no matter how tenderly you treat the dumb thing. This is totally inadequate to the job of accommodating infinite meaning clouds.

But it is likely that when it comes to the makeup of living things made of organic substances, the lowest level of components might involve macromolecules whose identification and other relevant properties might require infinite information content and non-computable processes. This is what enables organic creatures to accommodate intentionality. And consciousness may rely on *sub*atomic non-computable properties of quantum mechanics. If meaning and intentionality require such infinite information content, only living things made of organic molecules put together and related in infinitely complex ways would be capable of intentionality and might not ever be amenable to finite algorithmic models. This would account for the fact that after 50 years of incredible wizardry in computer technology outdoing anything any of us could dream of in the '70s, the computer still cannot do one drop of intentionality or consciousness; whereas the simplest of people can.

Dennett wants to think that when you get to the lowest level of macromolecules, you have processes that are mechanical and deterministic enough to describe with algorithms and computer models. He briefly entertains the ideas that "organic compounds" may have powers "…unrealizable in non-organic materials…"(198), and that biochemistry may be "essential" for things like pains. But he quickly douses these ideas: "These are both highly implausible vitalistic claims…"(198), as though it's pretty silly to think you have to be alive to feel a pain. This is a very *im*plausible definition of "plausible". He doesn't have one scintilla of evidence for this bold statement. The fact that pains are *only* observed in biological devices and *never* in non-organic devices doesn't seem to count as evidence for scientific, nuts and bolts Dennett. But it is palpably obvious that he has to be wrong somewhere along the way. If biological processes were algorithmic and finite state, how could you get any more meaning out of the brain than you do out of the computer, at *any* level of description? Dennett simply isn't digging deep enough into the nature of organic structures. He's only going down to the level of atoms and molecules which he conveniently assumes can be describable with finite algorithms. But if meaning involves infinite state structures, and consciousness requires noncomputable processes, he isn't going to be able to explain meaning *nor* its important effect, that of causal efficacy.

All the systems Dennett mentions, like thermostats, *can* be described using the intentional stance. But only because they do things that *appear* superficially like things people do. Anything that moves can be anthropomorphized, even a rock rolling down a hill wants to get to the bottom. But things like thermostats are finite state machines from top to bottom, and *the ability to understand, explain, and predict their behavior is already accounted for by the laws of physics and chemistry.* Dennett can dress up thermostats with his intentional stance because he already knows what they will do. Dennett's intentional stance has accurately predicted 14 thousand consecutive sunrises now.

The intentional stance just isn't doing any work. It reminds me of a little girl I once saw in a little toy car vigorously whipping the steering wheel right and left in the supermarket. But the steering wheel wasn't attached to anything and the car was going to go exactly where the mother pushed it. We can say the tree drops its leaves because it *believes* winter is coming. Does this increase our understanding of trees? How does something simple that really isn't capable of beliefs ever going to help us explain the meaningful actions of something infinitely more complex that does have beliefs? Dennett is really saying that to explain the mentality of complex living creatures, we have to go levels *below* the perceptual level. (But he isn't willing to wait for answers from very deep causal levels that are probably responsible for consciousness.) This much is fine. But how will this agenda be promoted by anthropomorphizing machines and then explaining the resulting *artificial* mentality? Dennett is trying to get us to accept chemical causal phenomena of the brains of living creatures as the only way we could explain their intentionality by showing us that this level works to explain the intentionality of

machines that don't really have any intentionality at all. My question is, how in the world will taking the intentional stance by anthropomorphizing machines going to get us anywhere in this project?

Dennett uses stretch words like "simulation" and "synthesis". What do these words come to except a lame attempt to sneak mentality into the computer? We don't have to synthesize pains in people, and simulated pains in people really are pretty much like simulated pains in the computer, which is like no pain at all. What Dennett finally comes up with is spaghetti and meatball pains as discussed in Sect. 14.7. I don't know if Dennett is successful in getting a pain into the computer, but his conclusions sure do create a headache in his readers.

So Dennett's next tack is pretty much the course taken by all these physicalist types. You just get rid of the excess meaning in our folk psychology mental concepts, like propositional attitudes, so they might be more amenable to scientific analysis. Mental entities of folk psychology are called *illata*. (Sounds like a mafia term.) Illata are "theoretical entities" like mental representations and propositional attitudes, which inhere in the mind/brain. They are pretty much what the mental phenomena of folk psychology are. (I may have these concepts mixed up, but I don't care.) Since illata come in bundles with infinite elements, they are too fuzzy and cumbersome for Dennett's liking. His solution to the meaning problem is going to be a variation of a method we described in Appendicitis II that's been used in philosophy for a long time to solve difficult problems: the blob.

He calls his blobs, *abstracta*, which are not part of the "furniture of the physical world", but are seen with a certain kind of squint, the *intentional stance*, although it "...sheds virtually no light on the underlying mechanisms" (Dennett, '87, 77). (As most philosophers in recent times, Dennett isn't going to commit himself to anything specific we can check, which is strange for a physicalist.) His program is to show how mental phenomena of folk psychology that we attribute to others (beliefs, desires, intentions, etc.) can be "mimicked" in terms of the notions of intentional stance theory, which he calls "abstracta". So we have beliefs$_{IS}$, desires$_{IS}$, and hopes$_{IS}$ that can be accommodated by a computational framework instead of folk psychology concepts. But in order to pare down the fuzzy edges of folk psychology concepts to make them crisper, more determinant and law-abiding than illata, he uses a rationality paring knife. As explained in the text, if anything, evolution actually selected for *ir*rationality, especially in our private lives But at one very surprising and unobtrusive point, Dennett says "...not only does evolution not guarantee that we will always do what is rational..."but "there has probably been some positive evolutionary pressure in favor of 'irrational' methods" (51). In my opinion, if Dennett thinks his stricter version of rationality will more than make up for the loss of meaning in his abstracta, he is paring the wrong apple.

But now Dennett has to explain how his abstracta blobs are going to do a better job of predicting and explaining behavior than the beliefs, desires, and hopes of folk psychology, especially since his abstracta are going to have *less* cumbersome meanings. Additionally, propositional attitudes like beliefs and desires are real cans of worms. This is why philosophers like Dennett and Stich bring in rationality. If there is one best piece of evidence that most mentality is infinite state, it's the study of beliefs and desires. Beliefs are in a many-dimensional space with extremely fuzzy edges. And unless an analysis of beliefs takes account of its infinite state nature, it is going to come up totally inadequate. I don't think Dennett is going to do any better at predicting and explaining what people do than the rest of us using ordinary folk psychology. I have a simple question for Dennett: *If evolution is so efficient and marvelous as Dennett implies, why didn't mother nature evolve the language of the intentional stance rather than folk psychology?*

But Dennett must not be overly convinced that the intentional stance is going to give us a kind of

meaning in his abstracta that can do any better a job of explaining causal efficacy than the concepts of folk psychology because he keeps on writing. His agenda is still to find a way for meaning to inhere in our representations and propositional attitudes. He begins by trying to soften us up by convincing us that our beliefs aren't all they're cracked up to be as meaningful mental phenomena. So he tells us our beliefs are pretty much the same as a frog's beliefs. Reminds me of Bonnie's description of Clyde's "rathah *pecuulia* ahdees about love-making — which is lahk no love-making at all."

Dennett spends huge quantities of time talking about what the belief relation relates, whether states of affairs, propositions, sentences, representations, etc. His problem is that all of these guys have mental or brain involvement, and if brains are only "*syntactic engines*" (Dennett, '87, 141), he's got the job of squeezing some semantic blood out of a syntactic turnip. How is this done? "Somehow, the syntactical *virtuosity* [italics mine] of our brains permits us to be interpreted at another level as *semantic engines*..."(142).

He seems to accept that there is no semantics at the input interface as well as the output interface, so how is anything semantic going to get cranked up in between. Here's the answer: "Moving towards the center, downstream from the transducers and upstream from the effectors, we can *endow* [italics mine] more central events with ...a partial semantic interpretation" (141). *Endow* eh? Is this a religious epiphany? or a pinup? Dennett constructs a whole network of nested boxes with syntactical elements in each one (written in mentalese of course). You add some bootstrapping, salt and pepper; and violá, you get meaning. If he weren't so wedded to the idea that the brain is a finite state machine, he might have thought of the idea that an infinite number of syntax boxes might do the trick. But whether you talk about boxes, brackets, networks, syntactical strings, notions, representations or any other trick, the only way you'll get any semantics is if you have an infinite number. The only possible way to get a drop of blood out of turnips is to squeeze an infinite number of them, and maybe that won't do it either.

Well, after much ado, he decides that *sentences* are going to be what beliefs are related to. And why? Because languages are "The only examples of (arguably) *universal* systems of representation..." (149). But along the way, he surprisingly states that there are an infinite number of sentences. This is an interesting claim because it could have suggested to him the solution to the meaning problem. But as with all these modern cognitive scientists and philosophers, the computer has such a hold on their thinking that they are driven to amazing feats of verbal gymnastics to try to get meaning into representations via the computer. But with his approach, he isn't going to get any farther with sentences as with any other kind of representation. For example, he has a little diagram, "Syntactical features + linguistic conventions Õ Character, and Character + Context Õ Content" (135), to show how we get from syntax to content of a propositional attitude. How do syntactic features and linguistic conventions, which have no meaning and content, give us character, which does, even if only a little bit?

In my opinion, no matter whether you're talking about sentences, states of affairs, propositions, representations or anything else, there's no complete semantics without a mind/brain putting it there. Not a fancy diagram, but a mind/brain. And how can a "syntactic brain" do anything of the sort? He's got the same problem Fodor has. As we've been saying all along, and Dennett seemingly alone states, "what we are looking to characterize is an intermediate position — halfway between syntax and semantics you might say" (152). This is an example of the underlying problem of finding a half-way level between mentality and physicality that explains mental phenomena. In my opinion, if such a level is ever discovered, it won't have anything to do with computers.

But now he tries a new kind of blob called a "notion" which is going to do what the abstracta may not have been able to do, in case we're really not as *rational* as he needs us to be for his intentional stance. But just as with abstracta, Dennett goes through great lengths to tell us what the blobs in this notional world are *like*, what properties they have, but never what they really *are*. It's a "...sort of *fictional* world...", and for some people, "...will contain notional objects having no counterparts in the real world" (153). In case you think it's a Hussurlean "bracketed" world or any kind of phenomenological world, it's better than that. It's really a "*hetero*-phenomenological" world that enables us to get some "partial semantics" under way. How? By creating a world that "mimics" real semantics. Back to monkey business. It's "...the apparent world of the creature..." (157). We also learn that stuff in the notional world isn't good enough to become part of propositional attitudes. So when a child believes that Santa Claus is coming, "...the child's psychological state...at that time is a notional attitude that determines no propositional attitude" (186). There goes our childhood Christmas fun.

At times, it might seem that Dennett's notional objects resemble what we have called perceptual objects. But he depreciates notional objects as not always matching "the real world". This is brought out by the characterization of the real world objects as "relational", whereas the relation with the notional world is only "notional". And so we have beliefs, and beliefs$_{IS}$. Now I think one of the motivations in Dennett's analysis is to patch up the Quinean distinction between de re and de dicto beliefs. This stemmed from the famous *substitution problem* first outlined by Frege, discussed in Ch. 14. Basically, a *de re* belief is *transparent* because you can see through to the causal level to refer, so that you can substitute different descriptions for a referent in a belief statement in the perceptual level, and you won't change the truth of the belief. This is because a de re belief is supposed to be referring to a kind of thing-in-itself (really at the causal level), so that the thing has to exist for a de re statement to be true regardless of how you describe it.

Dennett uses an example of Hoover a policeman who unknowingly wrestles with the real criminal at the scene of a crime, but has no idea who he was wrestling with. If the belief that he was wrestling with the real criminal is a de re belief, Dennett says, "it would be most disingenuous for Hoover to claim to have a suspect" (Dennett, '97, 198). Well, this is certainly the case. But in my opinion, the reason is that Hoover was wrestling with a *perceptually* innocent man, which is what causes his beliefs. The *truth* of his beliefs depends on the causal level where we find that the man he is wrestling with is a causal criminal.

But Dennett is going to patch up the de re story with a distinction of his own which is his relational-notional distinction. I don't see where this trick works any better than the one it's supposed to replace; but let's see how it works. Suppose Ralph believes there are spies. Dennett says this has two readings:

1) $(\exists x)$(Ralph believes that x is a spy) $\exists$ means "there exists".

2) Ralph believes that $(\exists x)$(x is a spy)

Dennett says there is a vast difference between these two: 1) is relational and false, but 2) is notional and true. Now it seems to me, if these really are two different readings both saying Ralph believes there are spies, I can't see any difference in truth-value between the two. If you're trying to see if they are equivalent truth-wise, you have to be consistent in what levels you're at in going from one statement to the other. If we start with 1), Ralph has a vague non-identified perceptual man he is imagining, who he believes is a spy. But Ralph also believes there is a *causal* man underlying whatever perceptual man he sees, who causes Ralph to believe a perceptual spy, which is 2), giving the same truth-value. However, if we start with 2), this says Ralph believes there is a causal guy somewhere who Ralph imagines perceptually is a spy. So there is a

perceptual guy (who may or may have a causal underpinning) Ralph imagines, who Ralph does believe supervenes on a causal spy, which is 1). Again we have the same truth-value. However, perhaps this analysis doesn't always work.

Ray Jackendoff plays this game with a more complex sentence, and he uses the opacity-transparent dichotomy. Suppose Ralph believes your dead uncle is alive. Then Jackendoff claims there are two readings of this belief, 5) is the transparent reading, and 6) is the opaque reading.

5) $\exists x$((x=your dead uncle) & (Ralph believes that x is alive))

6) Ralph believes that $(\exists x$((x is your dead uncle) & (x is alive))).
(Jackendoff, '83, 215).

He claims that 5) is false because a dead uncle doesn't exist, whereas 6) is true because Ralph does believe he has a dead uncle who's really alive. So there are two readings with two different truth-values. Again, I don't agree. These are slightly different readings, but we have to be consistent to see if one statement implies the other. If we're going to see if A implies B, it seems to me we have to read B the same way we have read A. Starting with 5), we have a perceptual uncle who is actually *causally* dead, but Ralph believes is perceptually alive. Again, since Ralph believes there are causal people underlying his perceptual people, he believes that there is an uncle who happens to be causally dead, but to Ralph is perceptually alive, giving the same truth-value. Now if we start with 6), we have Ralph believing there is a causal uncle, who happens to be causally dead, but Ralph believes is perceptually alive. This implies that the perceptual uncle he is imagining has an underlying causal uncle who happens to be causally dead, but Ralph believes is perceptually alive; again giving the same truth-value.

Dennett's notional idea presents even bigger problems for fictional characters. Dennett says the notional counterpart of the relational statement,

7) ($\exists$x) (x is believed by Tommy to have filled his stockings with toys), is

8) Tommy believes that ($\exists$x) (x has filled his stockings with toys)

Dennett thinks the notional 8) would not be "... committing ourselves to the existence of Santa Claus, which the relational claim [here 7)] would do" (Dennett, '87, 182). Well, in my opinion, if we interpret these existents as *perceptual* entities and not causal entities, these two sentences are again equivalent; 7) doesn't "commit" us to the existence of a Santa Claus. It commits us only to a *perceptual* Santa Claus who does exist, not a *causal* Santa Claus who does not. But Tommy knows there are usually causal people underlying his percepts. So he believes there is a *causal* guy causing the perception of Santa filling his stockings, which is 8). Even if we start with 8) and Tommy believes there is a causal Santa underlying the Santa he sees, then we have the perceptual Santa he sees and he's the guy filling his stockings; again the same truth value. But with Dennett's reading, he is now committed to the idea "...that no one has beliefs about Santa Claus, and no one could..."(186). (Now Dennett is probably smart enough to have figured out that there is no Santa Claus immediately after birth, but there was a Santa Claus in *my* life when I was very young, and probably yours too. In fact, Santa recently brought me one of Dennett's books!)

It seems to me, these de re/de dicto, opaque-transparent, and fine and coarse-grained distinctions are distinctions without a difference that were cooked up to avoid the famous substitution problem, which arises only because of confusion between perception and causal levels. Either a sentence has only one interpretation, which is indicated by the semantics

of the context or it is ambiguous. When the context really is different, then you get different statements and different truth-values. But so what. If a context gives ambiguous readings, all we have to do is to be consistent as to which level we're referring to in the two readings; and when we are, they have the same truth-values. Dennett's two readings are artificial and gratuitous assignments of perceptual and causal people designed to make their truth-values different. This MPC between perceptual and causal objects is brought out by an example Dennett gives of a guy who carries a penny around in his pocket at all times we'll call Amy. But one night an evil person switches Amy with another penny called Beth. Dennett considers the belief,

9) Tom believes of Beth that she is in his pocket. (195)

But then he says, this belief is "...strongly about Beth" (195) and true. And he has Dretske to back him up. Now I am very sorry, but this belief is not about Beth at all. Tom's beliefs are only about Amy because clearly, 'belief' is an intentional verb. Tom doesn't see causal Beth because nobody sees a causal anything. But causal Beth is inducing Tom to see *perceptual* Amy. If we interpret Beth in the sentence as *perceptual*, which, I think the context may warrant, then the sentence is false. If we *forcio grande* interpret Beth as *causal* Beth, because we're keeping track of her from a meta viewpoint, then this reference to the causal level enables us to say the sentence is true. But from Tom's point of view, the sentence is false because Tom knows nothing about causal Beth and his beliefs involve only perceptual Amy.

As we explained in Sect. AII.1 what confuses the whole issue is that historically people in all early societies were fishing for a causal man who would be responsible for our perceptual lives. This is the concept of the soul. So to this day, when people use proper names, they are probably referring to the essence of a person which is the modern day substitute for the soul, and which we are saying is the causal person. At the causal level, this essence is our DNA. In my opinion, this is the source of the idea of Kripke's rigid designator. It is an attempt to refer to what people historically have tried to refer to, namely the causal level soul or essence. This is why when people are involved, it is sometimes necessary to go to the causal level to determine truth. In my opinion, and as explained in AII, our beliefs, thoughts and references are always to *perceptual* objects, which are de dicto readings, and which are the subject of causal efficacy. Water has no soul. Propositional attitudes are relations to interpretations of *causal* states of affairs, not states of affairs themselves. It is only when we want to determine certain *truths*, like that the extension of water as determined by H_2O, or the reference of proper names, then we go to the causal level where H_2O sits. The problem, it seems to me, is that Dennett's notional objects are whole cloth creations, a blob theory, which is mostly to patch up the famous substitution problem. We still have the problem of how do we get meaning into anything mental, especially propositional attitudes, and how does this meaning figure in thought processes? So far, all we've got are abstracta whose anorexic meanings are obtained by straining to be rational and some monkey business involving "mimicking". It's time for you know what.

But Dennett has very different uses for the computer than Fodor. Fodor tried to show that the mind doesn't use meaning to do causal work, but, analogous to the computer, uses only the syntax of its representations. Dennett says the computer doesn't deal in meaning, can't represent anything, and knows nothing about intentionality. So he's pessimistic about a halfway notional level involving the computer. Whereas Fodor uses the computer as a chopping block to pare down the meaning of mental representations, Dennett says the style of his halfway level of abstracta "...will not be 'computational'; the items will not look or

behave like sentences manipulated in a language of thought". I agree completely.

He starts out by pointing out that if the computer *appears* to do anything meaningful, its intentionality is "derived". It is derived from the fact that human beings are always available to provide meaningful *interpretations* of what the computer is doing. In my opinion, this is a pretty second hand and artificial idea of intentionality. His analogy is that just as the computer's intentionality is derived, in the same way, *our* intentionality is also derived. (It appears as he nears the end of his book, he isn't really convinced that rationality and mimicking are going to be enough to get real meaning into our representations after all.) Since we can't get any meaning out of a syntactic devise, any more than you can get blood out of a turnip in a finite amount of time, the only option left to get meaning for our representations is to beg, borrow, or steal it from somewhere. And Dennett shows how we can do all three. You'll never guess what Dennett claims to be the fountain of meaning: Muthah Nature! To me this is the mother of all lame explanations.

First of all, he brings up *intrinsic* intentionality, which is intentionality that is inherent in a device and not derived from anything else. He takes on the whole list of heavy hitters in the field of mind/body philosophy and disagrees with them claiming that humans don't have intrinsic intentionality. For example, he quotes Tyler Burge as saying, "The meaning or content of an individual's internal states could not be different from what it is, given the individual's *internal* history and constitution" (Dennett, '87, 309). This seems perfectly reasonable to me, but Dennett says, "The falsehood of this thesis should not surprise us" (309). Dennett's rejection of this reasonable claim shouldn't surprise us either because he wants our intentionality to wind up being on no different a par than that of the computer. Dennett implies that the computer gets its derived intentionality because it was *designed* that way. In the same way, humans are going to get their intentionality because we are designed that way. "But then who or what does the designing?" Dennett asks (299). "Mother Nature, of course,...by natural selection" (299).

Of course, this is a pretty adventurous use of 'design', and Dennett implicitly admits this by putting Mother Nature's "designing" and "what Mother Nature had in mind" in scare quotes, which says, in effect, "I don't really believe this". Dennett's words like 'design', 'intentions', and 'purposes' are very intentional verbs. If the source of our derived intentionality is Mother Nature's "intentions", "purposes", and "designs", then there isn't going to be any derived intentionality at all because Mother Nature had no intentions and didn't *design* anything. The same designer designed the human animal as designed the man in the moon, which is no one.

But computer design and evolutionary design is a misleading characterization of both stories. Even though the computer is designed so that intentionality can be *derived*, the design is only necessary, but not sufficient for derived intentionality. When I got my computer home in a box, it didn't have one drop of meaning in it. The only meaning that design confers is what's in the mind of the designer, which I have no idea about because the designers have given up on user manuals. The derived meaning of the computer comes as a result of *my using* it. And I can assure you, the meaning I derive from my computer is a lot different from the meaning derived by someone who knows how to use it. Humans interpret and give meaning to what a humanly written program causes and describes, namely, what the computer is *doing*. That's why it is *derived* intentionality. However, if Mother Nature designed us, no intentionality automatically follows from our point of view because Mother Nature didn't have anything in mind except tautologically. Just as in the case of the computer, we would have to be *used* by something to get derived intentionality. There is no designer running programs through us. Also, nothing resembling a viable computer program could be shown to be what the brain is following in making transitions.

Just as with Fodor, Dretske, Chalmers and the rest of the gang, Dennett doesn't make even a vestigial attempt to show a possibility of such a program. But even if it were possible, who would interpret what we do to obtain derived intentionality? Mother Nature? The analogy breaks down.

There's another problem. What Mother Nature came up with as a result of selecting from a sequence of random mutations over millions of years is a fertilized egg, which, just like the computer, has no intentionality at all. It's a meaningless package of chemicals. Once the egg is fertilized, Mother Nature steps out of the picture, and in my opinion, there is no intentionality Mother Nature has conferred at this point. Meaning is highly specific. The items in a meaning cloud are particular representations left from particular perceptions and other experiences. It is highly unlikely that anything like this could be wired in at birth. Of course, if intentionality involves infinite state representations, Mother Nature had to "design" the egg to have this potential. But potential is not existence. And unlike the computer, as the egg develops, it experiences and learns, and thereby accrues the infinite number of representations constituting intentionality, *which is inherent in its structure*. Mother Nature doesn't interpret what we're doing, we are not running on a program, and nobody has to *use* the human being at any stage of development or at any time, or in any place nor interpret what we're doing in order for our mentality to have meaning. This is why we have intrinsic intentionality.

But let us take up Bertrand Russell's idea that the world could have popped into existence five minutes ago, "complete with memories and records". And let's suppose it was created or designed by God, (or God's attempted constitutional rework, an Intelligent Designer). Even Dennett has to allow for this possibility: "It may be a wildly implausible fantasy, but a possibility after all" (285). Also, "...the design process itself is the source of our own intentionality" (317). Who would we derive our intentionality from then?

God? Well, Creationists would jump for joy over this conclusion, and leave ole infidel Dennett fumbling for some rosary beads.

And so we still have the problem of how meaning gets into the representational objects of our propositional attitudes. It isn't going to get there with Fodor's computers, nor Dretske's thermostats nor Dennett's derived intentionality from muthah nature. Meaning accrues to representations the only way it can: by accruing an infinite meaning cloud of representations, which comes about through experience and learning.

AV.12 INDIVIDUATING PROPOSITIONAL ATTITUDES

Individuating propositional attitudes involves the same issues as individuating representations because a PA is a relation between a representation and a person with a self. So they can be individuated *externally* on the basis of broad content, or *internally* on the basis of narrow content. There is a lot of controversy in this area in the literature. One solution to the problem led by Stephen Stich avoids the issue by claiming there are no PAs in the first place. Discussing Stich's analysis will bring out the talking points of the alternative ways to individuate PAs. By "eliminating" PAs , we may be able to dispense with the rest of folk psychology. Considering the importance propositional attitudes in folk psychology, this is a cosmic undertaking. Is Stich up to it? Now if you were going to dispatch PAs to oblivion, the way to do it is to start with this eliminative conclusion, and work backwards to see what premises and definitions you need to deduce this conclusion. This is what Bertrand Russell accused Aquinas of.

We can use Stich's analysis to get back to the earlier problem as to what a propositional attitude is related to. Stich defines a propositional attitude as a relation between a person and a *sentence*. We can assume that these sentences could be in a language of thought. But what is Stich's view as to what this sentence does? As we explained back in Sect. AV.7, a sentence can't

represent a proposition unless it describes some *interpretation* of the causal propositional state of affairs.

But picking an interpretation can be dicey because it depends on whether we're after causal efficacy or truth. McGinn says, "The causal powers of a state... must be intrinsically grounded; they cannot depend essentially upon relations to what exists elsewhere" (McGinn, '89, 133). This is internalism. Jaegwon Kim disagrees: "To explain this causal-relational structure, we must resort to facts concerning the organism's relationship to its environment..." (Kim, '93, 297). He adds, "Thus, a psychological explanation... necessarily involves a *relational explanans*, which the *internal* biological theory of the organism is unable to supply" (Kim, '93, 296). This is externalism.

Fred Dretske also seems to be caught in this dilenema, even though he feels, "...the pull of the Internalist Intuition", and he seems to get halfway there with a cute metaphor (Dretske, '95, 151). He imagines a tornado hits the local junkyard, and when the winds die down, parts and pieces from all over the junkyard have come together to make an exact duplicate of his Tercel car (my car doesn't need a windstorm to be in the junkyard). But in spite of an atom by atom duplicate, he says the twin Tercel doesn't have a gas gage because of its history, but his Tercel does. But the meaning function of the gas gage gets into his Tercel only because humans designed it that way. But if so, he still has the problem of showing how it will get attached to representations of those of us who didn't design Tercels.

If you took anyone but a philosopher into the junkyard, he would say the twin Tercel certainly does have a gas gage who's meaning is that it measures the gas in the tank. Now it seems to me that if Dretske accepts the idea that we put meaning into objects by *design*, why doesn't he go the rest of the way and accept the account given here that all we have to do is look at the dam thing to make it a gas gage, which is clearly how we would ordinarily respond. In fact, the designers put the meaning into the gas gage *in order to* design it. The key concept here is *perception*, not design. The designers didn't put meaning and function into the gas gage because they designed it, but because that's the way they perceived it *while* they were designing it. Regardless of how something was designed, subsequent perceivers make it a gas gage in the process of *perception*, whose meaning doesn't have to get squeezed through finite state transducers to get to our representations. And we don't have to invent and design a new thermostat every time we need a dose of Dretskean meaning.

But McGinn has a trick up his sleeve that bolsters the externalist position which is to incorporate teleology. He says: "*the relational proper function of representable mental states coincides with their extrinsically individuated content.... Function fixes content*" (147). The function and purpose of an ability or organ or any physiological entity was selected for as a *general* system thing to do certain things. But information about this function or its evolutionary process does not get swept into representations the mind creates *using* the system. McGinn is saying if you want to understand one of my sentences, go find out about the printing press that printed it. What a mind/brain does today has no information about how the system it is using got here. As Bertrand Russell pointed out, the world could have been created 5 minutes ago complete with memories and records. Any meaning related to evolutionary processes of the mind/brain as a *system* has nothing to do with the content of particular representations we create as we live our lives. I think teleology is worse than history to individuate PAs. Let's look at a history story.

Steven Stich brings up the Watergate hearings. Suppose a person believes he saw the Watergate hearings. Then we build an exact replica of this original person. Now does the replica have the same belief as the original? Stich says, "The original may, for example, remember seeing the Watergate hearings on TV, but the replica remembers no such thing" (Stich, '78, 346), because, of course, the replica never got near

the Watergate hearings. This is an *externalist* account which assumes *broad* content. But since the replica *thinks* he remembers the hearings, his belief is a false one because he causally wasn't at the hearings. Then Stich adds a premise he needs, which is that if two beliefs have different truth-values, they are different beliefs, in which case, you can't reduce beliefs to internal physical states.

I would prefer to evaluate beliefs at the perceptual level and save truth as a causal level consideration. This would agree with Folk psychology which would say both are going to behave towards everything the same way including talk of Watergate because both their beliefs supervene on brain processes that are the same regardless of how they got there. This would give them the same beliefs.

Functionalism would seem to disagree because the two beliefs were arrived at in different ways and so different beliefs. Functionalism is a sort of half way position. But I would prefer not to consider truth-values when evaluating beliefs because I think truth is a causal level consideration. So, unlike Stich, I think it perfectly possible to have identical beliefs with different truth-values.

One of the most impressive papers I've ever come across is by H.W. Noonan (in Heil & Mele). I really wish I could write such a paper. He seems to prove that whenever you have a PA that depends on external states of affairs, it is always possible to have a description of this PA that is individualistically defined. Of course, he doesn't know how to do it, which is why it's impressive that he could figure a way to prove it's possible. But we can now see how this is possible. What appear to be external objects of PAs are really personal *interpretations* that may or may not have causal underpinnings. He's on the right track for hallucinations because the hallucinator has to have *something* he relates to since there is no causal object. But he doesn't keep it up and finally gives in to Burge about Pierre.

When Pierre is in Bristol, he thinks it's London; and so Noonan agrees with the rest that when he believes London is pretty, his belief is not about London but about Bristol. There's only one reason why there's ambiguity in all these examples: are we reporting on or describing a person's state of mind at the perceptual level, *or* on the truth of reality in a total historical flow for which we would look at the causal level? Both Frege and Russell and others tried to patch together some ad hoc way to make such a distinction. If we're reporting Pierre's impressions at the perceptual level and his subsequent behavior, then he does believe London is pretty. But if we're reporting about *truth*, then since causal Pierre is in causal Bristol, he doesn't yet have opinions about London. If his perceptual London were deemed ugly, his belief is simply false but not empty. We might add that when Pierre says "Londres est grande", he also believes that London is pretty only if his perceptual London is the same as his perceptual Londres. But for truth, if he doesn't know the translation of Londres is London, then he doesn't yet believe causal London is pretty. If someone tells us that Pierre doesn't yet believe London is pretty because Pierre doesn't know what causal 'London' really is like, we would unhesitatingly accept that as true.

Another ambiguous example brought up by R. Stalnaker (Rosenthal, '91, 576) is of a footprint in the sand, which has a ton of interpretations. Sam could believe that the indenture in the sand *fits* a human foot, which would be narrow content. But Sam could also believe the footprints was *caused* by a foot, which would be broad content. When viewing a footprint on Twin Earth, there is the same ambiguity. Only context clears up the content.

Externalities are relevant, but only when you want to determine *truth*, like what kind of footprint there is. But when we are interested in causal efficacy which is a perceptual level matter, internalism based only on meaningful *interpretations* of possible states of affairs is needed for predictions of behavior. Philosophers are always talking about laws and science and have as a goal to put psychology on a more scientific footing.

Well, the essence of science is prediction, here the prediction of behavior. What is relevant in explaining how beliefs actually *produce* subsequent behavior is narrow personal content no matter how it got there, which is independent of causal level truth conditions, public meanings, and externalism.

AV.13 Opaque/Transparent De Re/De Dicto Wide/Narrow

But this brings up an interesting point about *de re* beliefs. As we mentioned above, this *de re/de dicto* distinction and its partners the opaque/transparent and wide/narrow distinctions are more of those top hat inventions designed to paper over the famous substitution problem. Without the distinction between perceptual and causal worlds, these distinctions seem pretty ad hoc to me (and transparent too). Take the sentences:

12) Athena believes that Cicero was bald
13) Athena believes that Tully was bald
14) Athena believes of Cicero that he was bald.

Now supposedly 12) and 13) are de dicto sentences to be read "opaquely" involving propositions of some sort because you can't substitute names because the truth of Athena's beliefs depend on which name is used. 14) is de re because the 'that' in the sentence supposedly forces us to talk about the causal person Cicero. This is a conspiracy among philosophers and another example of MPC. In my opinion, none of these sentences is de re because they are not about the *causal* Cicero at all.

Now Frege's solution to the substitution problem was by veritable salvation, which says you can't substitute if the expressions were different *senses*. This is very lame because how can we ever know what the sense is in a particular case? Determining senses is clearly an undecidable criterion. Quine was even worse. He depreciated *de dicto* beliefs as not really involving reference at all because they are *opaque:* you can't substitute without changing the truth-value because it is about descriptions of things as opposed to things in themselves. Quine's approach says that the places for Cicero and Tully in 12) and 13) are syntactical and not really referential. This is just naming the problem, not solving it. So what Quine does is to rewrite sentences so that you can substitute a denotational identical like Tully and the belief will still be true. Well, some of his rewrites don't even make sense. And where a rewrite doesn't work, he simply states by philosophical fiat, that this is "...evidence of non-referential position..." (Quine, '60, 151). For example, Quine would write 12) as, Athena believes Cicero *to* have been bald, and now it is de re, and we can substitute. This is silly. Athena probably didn't believe Tully *to* have been bald either. Quine has a hundred tricks up his sleeve (Quine, '66, 185+) to rewrite sentences to avoid the substitution problem and they all really stink.

Mark Richard says the distinction falls into two types: it depends either on the "context" of the "historical situation", or on "abstractions from such situations" (Richard, '90, 162). But these are just labels for very ad hoc ill-defined categories in my opinion, because even with scores of pages of inscrutable prose, he has no basis to determine which it is. The bottom line is that most propositional attitudes are de dicto because they are reporting on people's impressions and perceptions which are interpretive *representations* and are always perceptual even if abstractly perceptual. And you can't confidently substitute for *any* perceptual object because they depend on the individual's mentality at a given time.

If Athena says that Cicero is bald, she is not saying that Tully is bald; the Cicero she is referring to is a *perceptual* person, not a causal person. As opposed to Davidson's overrated theory of sayings, Athena is saying something that expresses an *interpretation* of the proposition about Cicero's baldness. This is going to be a representation, which involves *perceptual* objects that Athena's mind creates, making the statement internalist and de dicto.

This is also why you can't maintain truth conditions under embedded propositional attitudes. Suppose Bill thinks that Athena believes that Cicero is bald, and Bill knows that Cicero is Tully. Is it then true that Bill also thinks that Athena believes that Tully is bald? Not in most instances. What Athena believes in the second "that" clause describes a representational interpretation of the proposition about Cicero's baldness that *Athena* chose. What Bill says must convey the interpretation *Athena* chooses because *Bill* is not referring to or interpreting the baldness proposition as he sees it. All Bill is doing is *reporting* something about how Athena sees, talks, believes and interprets the world. That's the default position. Of course, if you specifically direct our attention to the causal level for *truth* of Athena's beliefs, then Athena does believe that causal Tully is bald because causal Tully is causal Cicero.

Now wonder if Bill saw Athena kiss Cicero. Did he see her kissing Tully? This is a tough question. Again, this depends on the purpose of the report. I would say no in this instance because the context seems to point to Athena's *actions*. Bill has a theory of mind and is viewing an intentional *action*, not a movement. So he didn't see her kissing Tully because Tully is not in Athena's perceptual world. Our folk psychology description of this would be, she didn't think she was kissing Tully (Athena's perceptual world), but she really was (truth in the causal world).

Boer and Lycan ('86) and Richard ('90) go through incredible feats of logic to try to convince us to go downstairs to causal objects. They got concept roles and semantic roles and every other trick of the trade. They are really pleading with us, saying, ah come on now — when Athena believes Cicero is bald, underneath it all, and in reality, she really does believe that Tully is bald even though she may not know it, because Tully really is Cicero. But it's all in vain. Athena's belief involves her *perceptual* world. And there is nothing in any of Athena's representations of Cicero that *necessarily* has anything to do with Tully.

It has been suggested that a belief can be de re (the best kind) if you're acquainted with the object of the belief, so that your representation will come from an actual perception. Well, the belief expert, Mark Crimmins, intuitively thinks this is not only ad hoc, but too restrictive. And he valiantly tries to come up with some way or criterion to delineate one from the other. But after an incredible fireworks display of crisp cutting-edge logic and symbolism to analyze beliefs, he gets mushy when it comes to sentences like 12) and 13) above. He says the difference between sentences like these "…is no semantic difference in meaning or overt reference, but a contextual pragmatic difference…" (Crimmins, '92, 144). Well, when you're trying to do the impossible, it always requires a clever Fodor-style slight-of-hand; and Crimmins is up to it. If anyone dares to think that Athena can have the belief in 12), but not in 13), which would make them de dicto statements, we have an asymmetry we can exploit. Since the report asserts a positive belief of Athena's about Cicero, and a hand-waving disdainful dismissal of any belief about Tully, in "normal circumstances" this shows that Athena really knows, loves, and cares more about Cicero than Tully. Why, she doesn't even know that Tully is really Cicero — and she doesn't care. In fact, her denial of 13) indicates to Crimmins that she's a bit "confused" about Tully. On the other hand, what she knows about Cicero rises to the level of "information". *Well*, if it's *"information"*, no less, that Athena has about Cicero, we all better be prepared to back down right now. 'Information' is the royal flush of philosophical analysis these days. In any event, this allows Crimmins to dull down de dicto statements to where they can't cut any distinction at all. He triumphantly announces, "The names 'Cicero' and 'Tully', in *de dicto* reports, serve the *semantic* role of standing for Cicero. We suspected all along that after all the smoke blew away, Cicero would come out on top in the competition for Athena's affections and beliefs.

This is all pretty lame. Yes, probably most people know more about Cicero. Perhaps Athena's positive assertion about Cicero, and denial of Tully's baldness may indicate that she knows more about Cicero than Tully. But these assumptions are pretty gratuitous. The reporter of these beliefs has no idea what Athena knew about these guys. All we have are probabilities for Crimmins' "contexts" and "pragmatic role". Athena, in particular, may know a lot about Tully, and is quite sure he isn't bald, whereas she may have a mere *suspicion* that Cicero is bald.

Well, having failed to give an account to distinguish de dicto beliefs, how can Crimmins possibly come up with a criterion for de re beliefs? But he plods on. He says, de re beliefs must "… make no requirements at all about how an agent thinks of a thing" (171). The agent's report of a belief is "notionally uninformative" regarding what the believer believes. He's off to a bad start. Nobody makes belief statements with *no* meaning attached to the object of the belief. Athena's beliefs about Cicero and Tully involve *concepts* of those guys and concepts have meaning. So Crimmins tries to find a belief with no particular "notions": "The man standing behind us is a spy". But this doesn't make it either. You couldn't substitute George Bush for the man behind us because Bush isn't smart enough to be a spy. This is a hopeless endeavor and Crimmins begins to agree: "…it is likely that there are very few ordinary de re reports" (178). I would add, this is so almost by definition: beliefs have content no matter how small, because they involve *representations*. The only thing that could save Crimmins now is one of Fodor's watertight modules to seal off our beliefs from any contaminating meaning.

I would add there are no de re beliefs at the perceptual level except possibly for proper names under certain specifications. De re beliefs can occur only at the causal level where beliefs exist on the basis of the *theory* at the causal level. But I'm not sure of possible de re statements even at this level. Even if you know a lot about subatomic particles, if you believe that electrons revolve around the nucleus, do you necessarily believe that negatively charged fermion leptons revolve around the nucleus? I'm not sure of this. After all, this is a *quasi*-perceptual level.

Crimmins goes through an elaborate analysis which is basically that we can judge what the believer is referring to on the basis of context. If he weren't a philosopher, he would add body language, facial expressions, and tone of voice to the tools we use to determine reference. But it's been over 2 thousand years since Athena made any facial expressions or body language. What do we do with her beliefs? Crimmins is running out of gas, and he still has the fact that regardless of Athena's *notions* of Cicero and Tully, that they are bald is the same proposition because they are the same man. And if Athena believes *propositions* as Crimmins wants, she has to believe the same for both, which she doesn't.

But Crimmins is still twitching. He says if Athena really wants to refer to Cicero, she has to prep the listener with "pre-assertive" statements (182) that gets her all excited about the real Cicero. There has to be "providing conditions", which tells her listener that she really means Cicero, the stud, in flesh and blood, and no cheap substitutes. If she fails to impress the listener to the necessary degree of agitation over the real Cicero, her belief statement is summarily rejected as not involving a true proposition. Poor Athena then has to "withdraw" her tendered proposition and sit down.

I think there are times when there is ambiguity in making and responding to belief statements. There are certainly times when we have to clarify what we're really saying and what we're really referring to. However, for Crimmins and Dennett to be telling us that there is no proposition when it doesn't meet their standards is pretty unrealistic. We talk about fictional characters just as easily as we talk about real ones having a causal level basis. Our interpretations of propositions embedded in beliefs about characters real or fictional are every bit as valid as those meeting Crimmins' requirements.

The reason is that *all* propositional attitude statements, unless clearly specified, are de dicto and involve *perceptual* objects in the interpretative *representation* of the proposition in the PA. Only that will determine its functional ramifications: how the content has causal efficacy. They are going to have narrow content because the believer created the content of the perception in the first place out of what's physically in his head only. Perceptual objects caused by the same causal object can vary all over the park, which is why we can have great disagreements and misunderstandings about them. The only time the causal level is involved is under certain circumstances where you want to refer to a causal person or get to truth from a meta point of view. Braddon-Smith & Jackson comment on this matter: "Some have despaired of finding a single feature that can do both jobs — that, on the one hand, determines a belief's truth conditions...and that of, on the other, causally explaining the effects a belief and a desire have on behavior (Richard, '90, 178). This is a great summary of the problem, but not a solution. Briefly, the truth of PA's points down to the *causal* level; whereas causal efficacy is a *perceptual* matter.

Jerry Fodor is going to pull off a coup de grace with this distinction. He is going to show that not only "...under *opaque* construal that attributions of propositional attitudes to organisms enter into explanations of their behavior..." (Fodor in Rosenthal, '91, 489), but this construal fits hand in glove with the computational theory of mind whereby "mental processes are formal... and "have access to only formal properties of such representations..." (488). This is a difficult paper, so I may not be understanding it correctly. So, for example, since the belief that Phosphorus rises in the east is a different belief from one that Hesperus rises in the east, we should construe these beliefs opaquely. However, Fodor says, "Computational processes are, by definition, syntactical" (Fodor, '83, 40). So, if computational theory looks only at syntax, this will, in my opinion, refer us to the causal level where both planets have the same causal underpinning, namely Venus, and so be the same *transparently*. But he admits that it's the *opaque* reading that will determine behavior. This suggests taxonomy on the basis of content. However, he further tells us that the formality condition "... prohibits taxonomizing psychological states by reference to semantic properties of mental representations" (Rosenthal, '91, 491). So how can syntax, which the computational theory depends on, make the distinction that an opaque reading gives us for taxonomy, which requires content and determines behavior? Then he says, "transparency is a semantic notion" (491). Transparency refers to the causal level where there is no semantics at all but only means to determine truth. He says beliefs of different content can have different behavioral effects because "...different content implies formally distinct internal representations" (492), which can be different functionally. But the different content of the two perceptual stars does not imply *formally* distinct internal representations because *formality*, referring to syntax, sends us to the causal level where the *causal* stars are the same, namely Venus. If "formal" doesn't imply syntax which is at the causal level, then what does it mean? So, as opposed to what he says, coreferring expressions, like the context in which both Hesperus and Phosphorus both refer to the causal planet Venus, *are* formally identical. If so, how will his computational theory make the perceptual and taxonomical distinction between Hesperus and Phosphorus that he admits behavior depends on? He's really backed himself into a corner. Either "... mental processes can't have access to the truth value of representations..." (or to whether they denote), which is his computation theory of mind; *or* mental processes really do depend on content. He's not comfortable with either choice and I don't blame him.

Let us pick up the strand we left off with Fodor's attempt to explain mental causation in terms of the semantics of representations. We saw that Fodor finally gives in and allows meaning into the picture as a causal component of propositional attitudes. His next strategy now is to pare down meanings and the best way to do that is with the usual computer

analogies, which, of course, points to *denotation* as the basis for meaning. This approach is discussed in his book, *Psychosemantics*.

AV.14 DENOTATIONAL MEANING AND CAUSATION

After twisting in the wind for a whole stack of books, Fodor is finally going to allow some meaning into the picture. Not enough for causal efficacy, of course, but enough to try to placate the meaning boys. The best way to do this is to pare down meaning in representations and PAs to denotation. This will make it easier for Fodor's language of thought to flit around the mind doing causal work. Fodor says: "Learning a language ...involves learning what the predicates of the language mean, which in turn, involves learning a determination of the extension of these predicates" (Fodor, '81, 63). In my opinion, this is not true at all. I blame Carnap for this business of extensions defining meaning. In my opinion, meaning has nothing to do with extensions. Meaning is at the perceptual level and is responsible for causal efficacy; whereas extension is a *causal* level consideration, and there's nothing necessary between levels.

But Fodor needs this kind of idea for the meaning of representations because if meanings mostly involve extensions, then he can treat the *meaning* of a concept the same way as *having a concept*, which is probably a computational process that is amenable to his finite Language of thought. But, in my opinion, meaning in terms of extensions is not accommodating the full meaning of meaning. Above, we quoted his reference to an "infinity of distinct representations". On p. 79, he refers to natural language having an *infinite* number of predicates. He discusses a *truth definition* of natural language "... which associates truth conditions with each of the infinitely many predicates..." of the language (79). How can his computational model accommodate infinite state truth conditions? This has very little to do with extension.

He looks at Putnam's twin Earth story where water is made of XYZ. It seems that Earthers and twin Earthers, both have the same belief, and so the same propositional content, that water is wet, for example. Now if the content of beliefs is in terms of denotation and extension, and if the extension is different on the two planets, he is stuck with the idea about a twin Earther that "…'water is wet' means something different in his mouth from what it does in mine" (Fodor, '87, 27).

Fodor contrasts two views about the twin earth story. In the commonsense view, the beliefs of Earthers and Twin Earthers are "relational" and so their beliefs are related to two different substances, H_2O and XYZ, and so are different. This is an *externalist* definition. So having shown that common sense is not very common, he proceeds to show us that it doesn't make any sense as well. But since the two inhabitants are exact replicas, their brainstates are the same. The only way this can be is for the mentality of belief to violate supervenience, which is not acceptable even to Fodor most of the time. So much for the common sense view.

In what he calls the psychological view, the two beliefs are individuated *non*-relationally, so not related to the composition of water. As a result, the content of the beliefs is "narrow" because they don't include facts about things outside the mind like *causal* H_2O. With the composition of water out of the way, Earthers and Twin Earthers will have the same water beliefs which preserves supervenience. Seems the Twin Earth problem is solved. But Fodor doesn't want to accept any kind of meaning that doesn't include composition because Kripke has convinced everyone that water *is* H_2O. So he can't accept the psychological view either.

So, we have lots of combinations viewed either causally or intentionally. We can view beliefs individuated functionally by behavior; or by the content of the belief as relating to the extension of water which leads to the causal level and the composition of water, in which case we get different beliefs. And we can individuate brainstates on the basis of the brain's

microstructure, or on the basis of causally relating to a different environment, one containing H_2O, the other containing XYZ. Of course, only about half of these will preserve supervenience.

Now since Earthers and Twin Earthers are physical duplicates, the brainstates must be the same. If we add supervenience to the mix, which Fodor also accepts, what we have is that if the identity of brainstates "ensures the identity of mental states and the identity of mental states ensures the identity of contents, *the identity of the contents of mental states does not ensure the identity of extensions…*"(Fodor, '87, 45). But of course, in my view, the content of a belief, its meaning, has nothing to do with extension. Fodor is stuck: he's got different beliefs supervening on identical brainstates. Not only that, but now he can't explain the behavior of the twins because the same behavior is caused by different beliefs.

Fodor plods on: "what I'm thinking about when I think: *water*, is different from what he's thinking about when he thinks: *'water'*; he's think about XYZ, but I'm thinking about H_2O" (46). He calls this "anchored content" because it's anchored to composition. (At one point, Fodor realizes that ice and steam are also H_2O; and so he's stuck with the idea that ice is water, and steam is water. Guess what? He actually swallows this crazy result.) But people who know nothing about chemistry never think about H_2O or XYZ. Fodor's statement is simply not true in general. Fodor wants to insist that "…no difference in extension without some difference in content" (46). But the Twin Earth story blocks this idea, because when beliefs are individuated by intention, water and 'water' apply to the same *perceptual* stuff and the content of the two beliefs and resulting behavior would be the same even though the extension at the causal level is different.

He concludes, "The Twin Earth Problem *is* a problem, *because it breaks the connection between extensional identity and content identity*" (47). His only way out is to rely on "narrow" content which doesn't apply to extension. But he claims we don't know what the narrow content would be so as to allow water beliefs to be the same. He needs a "canonical way of reference to…" what amounts to extension. But he admits we don't have such a way. So he winds up with a " 'no content' account of narrow content". What we really wind up with is a no count account of content. The apotheosis of Fodor's analysis is: "…the home team gets to name the intension…" (52). Reminds me of Putnam's invasion of Twin Earth with his sample of real water, which, by force of arms, is H_2O.

The core of the problem is that extension is at the causal level, and content is at the perceptual level and you can't mix levels because each has its own concepts and there is no necessary connection between them. Fodor then admits of "a plethora — of unsolved problems about saving denotational semantics" (Fodor, '87, 87), and that *"A purely denotational semantics breaks the connection between content and behavior"* (89). And *"Purely denotational semantics doesn't solve the problem about individuating contents"* (91). The entire motivation for this denotational dead end is to squeeze meaning down into something less than what it is: an infinite slew of high information content mental entities.

After a big stack of books where he was only half-wrong and inconsistent, he's decided now in his last book to be all wrong and consistent (Fodor, '08). He no longer cares about the "connection between content and behavior". He says the beliefs of the earthers and twin earthers are the same, but they have different causal powers because that depends on syntax. Now he has the beliefs the same for the wrong reason that they depend on denotation or extension, and the wrong reason for causal powers as depending on syntax, which they don't.

A really funny addendum on this topic occurs in one of Fodor's later books, *The Elm and the Expert*. Having been totally unable to accommodate the twin earth story into his computational mind theory, he tells us to just throw out the story: "…XYZ is nomologically impossible" (Fodor, '95, 28). For 30 years or more, this entire gang of analytic philosophers has been coaxing

us to imagine universes with worlds where water is XYZ. Now Fodor tells us this is impossible. This tells me what I've suspected all along: that this idea of "logically possible" or "metaphysically possible" worlds is pretty wambling, whimsical, and worthless.

But Fodor's attachment to a computational idea of meaning in the form of denotation remains undeterred. By the time he writes *A Theory of Content*, he starts out Ch. 6 with the supplication that "The older I get, the more I am inclined to think that there is nothing at all to meaning except denotation" (Fodor, '90, 161). No wonder he wants to stay young. He then asks, "What's wrong with the idea that denotation is all that there is to meaning?" (163). Well, there's the small point that it is simply not true, as Oedipus shows. Frege suggested that a substitution like Jocasta for Oedipus's Mother in the beliefs about eligibility for marriage, were "unallowable". By fiat, Frege tells us that J and OM do not refer to real people but to propositions or attributes. Well, Jocasta is not an attribute of anything, but a perceptual person in the mind of Oedipus. These brilliant philosophers ought to question their theories of perception and meaning when they're stuck with ridiculous conclusion that Jocasta and OM have to mean the same to poor tongue-tied Oedipus.

Donald Davidson brings up a case of a guy shooting a murderer, who, unbeknownst to him is the bank president. He says, "…my shooting the escaping murderer and my shooting of the bank president were one and the same action…since the bank president and the escaping murderer were one and the same person" (Davidson, '80, 110). This is simply not true, and it's only being a philosopher that prevents him from seeing this. This was not the same shooting *action*. Shooting is an intentional action verb. He was shooting the *perceptual* escaping murderer, which is an entirely different perceptual person from the perceptual bank president. They happen to be the same *causal* person, but the shooter doesn't shoot at, believe in, dislike or in any way relate to causal persons.

Getting back to Fodor, we have Fodor making another stab at fitting the square peg of denotational identity into the round hole of belief content. What Fodor does is to fish around for some way "...for Oedipus to have two beliefs with the same content..."(Fodor, '90, 168). He invents a new concept for belief, which is a four-place relation, having in addition to the usual relation between a person and a proposition, also includes a "vehicle". (In *The Elm and the Expert*, he pares this down to three; the vehicle becomes a "mode of presentation", MOP.) In either case, the vehicle is just a particular token or symbol that stands for the particular proposition in question. Fodor's strategy basically involves prying apart the idea of a belief from the content of the belief, which, to me, is like prying apart a painting from the paint. Then with meaning a kind of an unimportant dangler, "...the proposition that J is eligible might turn out to be identical to the proposition that O's M is eligible *even though* believing the one proposition is a different state from believing the other" (Fodor, '90, 166). Then he can still claim that "...denotation is all that there is to meaning" (166) because the meanings of the propositions would be same while the beliefs can still be different. But this tricky move revolves around Fodor's usual proclivity to strip things of their meaning; and once lightened up, he can do ingenious tricks with what's left. But what is left? Fodor's vehicles being only syntactical objects, "formulae in Mentalese", are not full meaningful representations. When he sticks his vehicles back into beliefs, they have to have meaning of some sort. And while we're distracted by the vehicle talk, he very parsimoniously eye drops in a very anorexic drop of meaning based on extension. But this is nothing but what we've called syntax meaning, which contains only enough information to create sense data of *causal* arrangements.

If Fodor were looking at a freight train with some coal cars going from West Virginia to Indiana, he might say the *cause* of the coal cars moving to Indiana was that they were hooked to an engine on a track taking the coal to Indiana. Well, this might be true in a physical sense, but most people would say the *cause* is that the steel people in Indiana need coal to make steel, which is what their meaning of coal implies, and they bought coal from West Virginia. It matters nothing to either party what the vehicle is like, what kind of a coal car it is, or what RR company owns it, etc.

When I was a kid, I worked in an all-night job in the largest railroad yard in the US. Cars were always getting lost, sometimes with live cargo. I remember trying to console a car full of abandoned cows. It became obvious to me that the railroad people thought of themselves as moving *cars* around the country instead of moving *loads* around the country. And this is one of the reasons why many railroad companies went bankrupt in spite of the Federal government giving them buckets of valuable assets in the early days and giving them almost guaranteed profits.

The vehicle coal car has nothing to do with the meaning of the coal shipment. Without a load, there is no cargo and no meaning to what the car is doing. Fodor's vehicles are exactly the same. They don't cause anything to happen. Oedipus' two beliefs can't be different because we give them different names, which, to me, is all a vehicle can do on the basis of syntax. Beliefs are different or the same on the basis of their personal *content* and the causal work they will do depends not on the name of the object, but its content. Fodor says, "...difference of belief-state does *not* imply difference of belief content" (Fodor, '90, 172). Fodor thinks he can tell the difference between a car empty of coal from a car empty of hay. How else would we distinguish belief states except through content? We can't separate a belief from its content because a belief without content is no longer a belief, just as a frame without a painting is not a picture. Just as a coal car has to follows rules of design, wheels 5 feet apart, and certain weight capacity, etc., so too, the syntax of a proposition must conform to rules of grammar. But syntax has nothing to do with the effects of the content of a belief. The kind of vehicle used to transport coal is irrelevant to the causes and effects of the shipment, which are the meaningful intentions of the coal and steel people.

Donald Davidson would try to salvage this account by noting that just because Oedipus married Jocasta doesn't mean that this event wasn't identical to marrying his mother. This is very clever, but basically a bait-and-switch argument. It's a last minute swapping of Oedipus' perceptual Jocasta for the causal woman in the story. Oedipus, just like anyone else, relates to causal objects in the world at any given time only *through* the creation of perceptual objects which have the content he ascribes. Oedipus' beliefs are relations to *his* perceptual representations, in *his* world, not to vehicles which only name or symbolize a proposition that can have wide interpretations. The way we individuate Oedipus's beliefs and determine how his beliefs affect his behavior depends on Oedipus' *personal* meanings, and nothing else. Fodor can't substitute *causal* women into Oedipus' beliefs, because that's not what his beliefs are about. The perceptual woman he creates by attributing meaning to this causal woman depends on the situation. When it's sex and marriage time, his perceptual woman is Jocasta; when it's laundry time, it's his mother. If in Oedipus' perceptual world, he believes J is eligible and OM is not eligible, it can only be because J and OM have different meanings, in which case meanings are not determined by denotation. QED.

Joseph Owens elaborates Nathan Salmon's theory that beliefs are relations to propositions; and Jocasta and his mother are different "guises" of the one person in the same proposition (Owens in Anderson, '90). John Searle says these are different *aspects*, which begs the question, aspects of what? First of all, without being able to refer to the causal person, Salmon has no way to identify the proposition he's talking about. Even if he did, Oedipus has no relation at all to causal women who are neither Jocasta *nor* his mother. Salmon says there's a "...binary function *f* that assigns to any believer *A* and sentence *S* of *A*'s language, the *way A* takes the proposition contained in *S*..." (232).

Yes, and that "way" is already given by the sentence *S* that contains terms with *Oedipus's* meanings. Salmon can't fiddle with *A*'s meanings in *A*'s beliefs. But he isn't done: he's going to nudge clueless Oedipus along by showing him that Jocasta supervenes on his causal mother and now he no longer wants to marry her. But Oedipus was lining up his marriage 2,000 years ago, long before Salmon could help. (Salmon also goes back *three* thousand years and helps the Babylonians see Hesperus and Phosphorus as Venus to straighten out *their* substitution problem.)

The simple facts are that Oedipus doesn't see Jocasta as disguised in any guise at all. Even if there were something behind the guises, like causal objects, it wouldn't matter. Nothing behind Salmon's guises suggests any kind of guise other than what the sentence flat out says, which tells us what Oedipus, and not Salmon, *sees*. Seeing is intentional; and what you see is *all* you see. Also, these are not *aspects* of causal objects because causal objects have no aspects. Oedipus' beliefs involve *interpretations* of propositions containing only *Oedipus'* perceptual objects.

As recently as '07, this type of approach is still being milked and is reaching epidemic proportions. Ned Block now has Metaphysical MOP's, and Cognitive MOP's, interspersed with properties of properties of properties, reaching the moon. He implies that "Jocasta is eligible" and "Mother is eligible", as coarse-grained propositions are the same. But as fine-grained propositions, are different. It's the same old story. Whether you call these different propositions, or modes of presentation, or vehicles, or different descriptions, or non-referential (per Quine), or fine-grained, or guises, or aspects, it all amounts to explaining an important difference by giving out different names. Modes of presentations, guises and aspects are fantasies cooked by philosophers to solve their reference problems. Stephen Schiffer is on the right track when he claims there's no such thing as a mode of presentation (Schiffer, '87). But he builds a contraption to the moon to get some content into beliefs, which I suspect doesn't succeed (but am not sure).

Causal objects in the world don't "present" anything like a sales clerk *presents* his merchandise. And they aren't disguised. Causal objects send raw information to us and bow out of the picture. *These so-called MOP's are bad substitutes for perceptual objects, which individual minds create on a particular occasion, not what is "presented" to us, because the world doesn't present anything to us.* But let us leave the identification of meaning problems aside, and go along, temporarily, with Fodor's implication that meanings are out in the world. The question then becomes, how would they get into our heads?

AV.15 Causal Theory of Meaning Acquisition

We have talked about problems of how representations and propositional attitudes can *cause* mental and physical behavior. But there is a worse problem, it seems to me, which is how meaning gets attached to representations in the first place. And if Fodor's analysis of thinking is going to be in terms of a language of thought, so that sentences in the language of thought are being manipulated as the basis for thinking, how will meaning get to these sentences? In this section, we will look at the role causation has in the *production* of meaning and content that these mental phenomena wind up with, i.e., how their content gets "into the head" so to speak. Well, whenever things have to happen, it's a good bet to look at causation, because it is mostly through causation that things get moving. But will causation help Fodor in this regard? Not, in my opinion, for the simple reason that meaning isn't out in the world in the first place, but originates "in the head". Fodor has intensionality going the wrong way.

Now Fodor acknowledges the meaningful content of representations, and this may be the motivation for the idea of "semantic evaluation". To puff up the semantic aspect of a representational interpretation of a propositional attitude, for example, Fodor invites us to look at truth conditions. Truth conditions are clearly part of the meaning of a representation; maybe we can get truth conditions in a way other than through information coming from the outside world. Fodor says you can get truth conditions from the *context* of the belief. But context involves infinite state meanings out in the world. If "context" is all already "in the head", how did it get there? If not, how do you get all that conveyed through the finite amount of information coming into the sensorium?

Even if Fodor could somehow manage to get truth conditions part way into the head, how will they fare there? On his assumption that the brain is a computational, syntactical devise, how is Fodor going to get infinite state meaning out in the world squeezed down into a computational brain, or into something even smaller like the algorithmic content of his beliefs? He admits: "I don't know how to carry out this program" (Fodor, '87, 98). Well, don't look at us either.

In Ch. 4 of *Psychosemantics*, he attempts to see if the causation aspect of perception can provide some means to put semantics into the content of propositional attitudes. He calls this the *causal theory* of representational content. In his analysis, it is the *intentionality* of our perceptions that puts meaning into these experiences. This is something I can very much agree with, although intentionality, as we have described, is a mind-to-world process. There is *nothing in the world* that causes meaning to attach to sense data simply because what is in the world has no meaning to lend.

But Fodor has meaning going the wrong way, and so he must show that DOG means dog because dogs cause DOG to happen. (DOG here denotes a representation of a dog.) Of course the DOG representation must have content. So Fodor asks, "*how* does... the instantiations of *doghood* cause tokenings of DOG?' I propose to call whatever answers such a question a mechanism of 'semantic access'" (Fodor, '98, 75). So how does he explain semantic access? Simply: "...there is a nomic connection between *doghood* and *cause-of-DOG-tokenhood...*" (75). This is pretty bold because he's saying simply the sight of a dog carries information about dogs and actually *causes* a token of DOG to pop up in the ming/brain complete with DOG content according to *laws*, no less. This is the basis for his final version of a semantic theory, which is called *Informational Semantics.*

But of course, the problem with this theory of semantics is that states of affairs have personal meanings that are infinite in number. And it is *personal* meanings that are involved in our thought processes. How will all that get squeezed down through the finite state sensory transducers like the eye? Causation isn't in the business of making meanings. At one unobtrusive moment, Fodor makes a slip: "There is no reason for believing that percepts *are* reducible to transducer outputs" (Fodor, '81, 218).

The problem is that perceptual events don't cause *enough* information to be transmitted. In actuality, dogs provide only enough information to create a meaningless sense datum of a dog, DOG, and not enough to make a perceptual DOG with the meaning of dog. This is shown by the fact that young babies see only DOGS, not DOGS. There will never be enough information coming to us in this way to account for the full semantic aspect of a representation like DOG.

At times, Fodor is aware of the problem calling it the "Poverty of Stimulus" argument: "...there is typically *more information* in a perceptual response than there is in the proximal stimulus that prompts the response..."(Fodor, '90, 196). (This is the core of the matter and I admire Fodor's objectivity in criticizing his own stuff.) This is why Fodor is forced to resort to *inferences* in order to get a grip on what is really out in the world. He says, "... perception is smart like cognition in that it is typically inferential..." (198). Well it's obviously not smart enough because, as we discussed in Sect. AV.2, inferences are only good guesses. The bottom line is that neither Fodor nor Dennett has any way to check how good our hypotheses are, how

accurate our inferences are and how well they perform in representing the world.

But there's a twin problem that refers to the essence of any causal theory, which is what is the nature of the causation involved? Is his causation strict and lawlike, or is it fuzzy and indeterminate like that involving mental phenomena? Well, Fodor opts for a causation whereby "...causes have to be covered by *strict* laws". This backs him into the position that "...it must be *physical* laws, and not intentional ones, that cover mental causes", which entails that "intentional properties are causally inert" (Fodor, '90, 148). This is not an enviable position.

Now, he could hold onto his strict causal laws because the only thing horses are doing is causing the creation of meaningless sense data, HORSES. However, when the causing entity is infinite state, causation becomes the squishy kind. So he will have to "...give up on the idea that the causal responsibility of the mental is the nomological necessitation of the behavioral by the intentional" (149). And so, meaning becomes "causally inert" in doing mind/brain causal work. He's really backed himself into a epiphenomenalist corner. But our ordinary parlance has plenty of 'cause' talk. Do these locutions have no meaning at all?

There is an interesting story that vividly illustrates the impossibility of cause dragging along meaning when information from causal objects *causes* sense data to be established in the mind: how can there be *mis*representation? If seeing a cow *causally* creates a sense data trace, COW, to become a COW in the mind, how come sometimes we see a horse when there is really a cow in view, for example, when viewing the cow on a dark night. Here we have a HORSE representation caused by either a real horse, *or* sometimes a cow, in bad circumstances. But now we no longer have a misperception. (In philosophical literature, this is called the *disjunction problem.)* But misperceptions do occur in real life, so there must something terribly wrong with the causal theory of meaning. What we really need is a kind of causation, or a way of establishing representations so that our horse representation, HORSE, occurs only when viewing horses, and never anything else, like a cow on a dark night. But we don't have it.

By the way, Dretske goes a step further and claims that the essence of a thinking system is the ability to have misperceptions, which is equivalent to saying that a thinking system is, "...of necessity, something whose meaning is independent of its causes" (Dretske, in Chalmers, '02, 494). But inexplicably, Dretske doesn't then have an answer to where this thinking system *does* get its meaning. If it isn't caused as in the account given here, where does it come from?

Fodor next tries to see if his idea of informational semantics can be of any use in the disjunction problem, especially since 'information' is the new buzzword. He points out that some horse representations, HORSES, carry information about horses, and some don't, like when your HORSE is caused by a cow on a dark night. Information in the form of photons of light or sound waves, etc., Fodor calls psychophysics. And Fodor admits that "Psychophysics...can't... guarantee the *intentional content* of the mental state that you're in...because it can't guarantee that when you see the horse you'll see it *as* a horse" (Fodor, '87, 116). If this statement really sunk in, he might question his theories of perception. Since the only tie between the horse and our minds is psychophysical stuff like light waves, how does meaningful content of horsehood, get into our mind/brains when we see a cow on a dark night? If causation brought along meaning, the causation involved should bring along a cow meaning in this situation. But it doesn't because we wind up with a HORSE representation. This is why informational semantics is DOA. At one point, Fodor lamely tries to pump life into the causal chain: " 'Horse' means *horse* because that chain is reliable" (122). But the problem is that it can't "reliably" do anything *about meaning*.

Peter Carruthers tries to patch up this problem with "consumer semantics" which says that the "...

intentional content of a representation depends, not just on the information carried by that representation, but also on the consumer systems...are apt to do with it..." (Carruthers, '00, 142). First of all, if the representation "carries" information about cows, why does the consumer see a horse. And if it "carries" information about horses, where did it come from? But the worse of it is that if this content is going to depend on what the consumer is "apt to do with it", it would seem that the consumer is going to try to ride this cow instead of milking it. We aren't going to solve the misperception problem with semantics that pumps gratuitous meaning into meaningless sense data.

Ironically, Fodor tries a teleological solution. Horses cause HORSE representations because we *evolved* so that this would happen. He has an amusing story about frogs catching flies. Frogs evolved so that they snap at flies because flies are the filet mignon of the frog's menu. But then we find that frogs also snap at little black dots like beebees. Fodor says it doesn't matter how we describe what the frog evolved. We could say that frogs see beebees as flies. So the frog sees B V F as F, which is an example of the disjunction problem. Well, first of all, it *does* matter how we describe what the frog evolved, if you're really interested in evolution. (The frog story created a whole new career for Fodor.)

Now, if little black dots in the frog's environment were beebees, wouldn't he see beebees as beebees just as he used to see flies as flies? Fodor suggests that the frog is misperceiving beebees as flies. This is not true. He's not even perceiving beebees as beebees. If he's serious about evolution, the frog evolved the proclivity to snap at little black dots because they are, in fact, the *minimally* complex sense datum that *include* flies. In his world where all little causal black dots *we* see as flies, why should the frog expend the evolutionary energy to be able to discriminate flies from beebees (or any other kind of black dot) when there weren't beebees in the frog's environment? All he sees are little black dots no matter what *we* see. He doesn't even see flies as flies; this leaves individualism intact. All of Tyler Burge's detailed analysis about how authoritative we are in evaluating what's out there is beside the point because there's nothing perceptual out there. What's out there are only causal objects; they don't have any perceptual qualities at all, and this is a bad analogy.

But people can tell the difference between horses and cows because we evolved enough perceptual abilities to accurately see things as they are (perceive perceptual horses when there are actually *causal* horses present) most of the time. On seldom occasions when we make a misperception, there wasn't enough of a price to pay to force the evolution of better vision. (Bees, on the other hand evolved ultraviolet perception because it did pay for them to avoid certain perceptual mistakes.)

Fodor's next strategy is to try to find a difference between a horse causing a HORSE representation, and a cow under unusual conditions causing the same. But he starts this attempt with some very misleading statements that are the result of another promiscuous use of 'information'. He says, "...some "cow" tokens carry information about cows and some "cow" tokens don't" (Fodor, '90, 90). But what about COWS, (small caps)? Sense data of COWS have no information about cows, which is why they can lead to misperceptions. He says, "...information follows etiology and meaning doesn't, and that's why you get a disjunction problem if you identify the meaning of a symbol with the information that its token carry" (90). As Charlie Chan would say, "correction please." That is not why we get a disjunction problem. Meaning follows etiology just as much as information, because meaning is conveyed by and *contains* information. You get the disjunction problem because only COW tokens carry information about cows, and COW tokens don't. Perceivers add the *wrong* meaning to COW sense data and wind up with, say, a HORSE perception.

Fodor finally comes up with a clever way to differentiate between veridical and wrong perceptions. But it doesn't seem to me to do the job. He says that

the peculiar situation of seeing a horse for a cow is "*asymmetrically dependent*" upon the causal connection between horses" (Fodor, '87, 108) and HORSE representations. In other words, you would never see a cow as a horse and create a HORSE representation, if there weren't lots of times when horses accurately caused HORSE representations. Well, this is true. But so what? Of course, you wouldn't see a cow as a horse, if you didn't know what a horse is. This doesn't mean you can't see a cow on a dark night as a horse, even if rarely.

Fodor puts it in another way: in a world like ours where horses cause HORSE, then if HORSE didn't mean horse, nothing would. That may be true, but again, so what? Horses causing HORSE is still consistent with a cow on a dark night causing HORSE. Asymmetrical dependence is a fantastic idea and I'm sure it can be used to great effect somewhere. But not here. What we need are *sufficient* conditions for horses causing HORSE representations in order to explain that HORSE means horse. Fodor loves this new idea, but in the game he's in, he's carrying a turkey across the goal line thinking he's scoring a touchdown. We might add here that even if Fodor manages to get past the line, he's up again even more formidable linebackers. What about times when even a horse doesn't cause a HORSE representation?

When Fodor says, "Psychophysics naturalizes the semantics of a certain...set of mental representations" (Fodor, '87, 117), this would apply to sense data traces only vacuously. There are no necessary semantics in sense data to be "naturalized". If there were, you would have the same problem as with other kinds of representations that do have a semantic aspect. You would have situations where you think you're seeing red when you are seeing green. But if you think you're seeing red and you know what red means, you *are* seeing red, which is why you can't treat HORSEHOOD in the same way. The sense data concept RED stays RED no matter what you add to it. But a HORSE sense datum is entirely syntactical and involves only psychophysical laws that do not give us a complete HORSE concept with plenty of meaning. We *still have the problem of explaining how a horse can put meaning into a HORSE representation just by causing a sense datum, HORSE.* Fodor finally admits, "*we have no idea at all* what a naturalized semantics would be like" (118).

As you might guess, Fodor takes a shot at getting the computer to come to the rescue. The model is that a computer is somewhere *between* the sense data of a horse and a HORSE representation, between HORSE and HORSE. Can the computer do it? Only by fiat. "The computer's running through certain calculations" (123) leads to an accurate horse representation, a HORSE, decked out with all the meaning HORSE has. To me this is going from the sublime to the ridiculous. Here we have a problem that the brain, with its infinite capacity isn't clever enough to dress up the causal process of creating a representation with meaning, but the computer is going to do it with "certain calculations". I want to see this. But Fodor disappears behind the curtains.

In his book *Representation*, Fodor very cleverly tries to sneak meaning of representations or content of propositional attitudes into the head while we're not looking by means of learning situations where he introduces the idea of "fusion". But Fodor really needs to bring in the difference between causal and perceptual objects. I have probably not been completely fair to Fodor's discussion. His correct conclusions come about because if the content of a learning experience is out in the world, causation in not going to get it into the head and attached to the content of beliefs. And fusion is not going to help. Fodor tries to spruce them up with "robustness", and counterfactual histories. His conditions for robustness are pretty puny. History enters into the picture because for HORSE to mean horse, HORSES must have been caused by horses in the past. But if informational psychophysics doesn't bring in meaning on one occasion, how will it do so by piling up many occasions. If the newsboy doesn't bring

ice cream, he isn't going to bring ice cream simply by coming more often.

The misrepresentation story is just another example of the problem we have been discussing throughout these Appendicitis'. In my opinion, causation simply cannot account for the meaning that representations have, and that the objects of propositional attitudes, have. This seems intuitively obvious. Causation simply is not in the business of transporting meaning, and the information coming to us from causal objects is insufficient to account for the robust meaning our representations wind up with. In my opinion, as long as we conceive of real world objects in the traditional mind independent way, no amount of brilliance among philosophers whether acquiring beliefs, learning, fusion, confusion, infusion, refusion, deduction or induction is going to insure that our representations really represent.

This should have been intuitively obvious when Brentano first came up with the idea of intentionality. The mind supposedly reaches out and "grasps" the meaning of objects in the world. Well, how does it do that? If the brain is a syntactical device, which all these philosophers enamored with the computer want us to believe, why don't computers reach out the same way? Why don't computers do intentionality? The only answer remotely plausible is that as a physical syntactical device, the brain can't do anything of the sort — and for two reasons: if objects out in the world make meaning available anywhere, why would they make meaning available only to brains instead of threshing machines and computers? And even if objects had meaning somehow, how could it send infinite amounts of information through finite state transducers? It couldn't so it doesn't.

Our account enables us to explain how we misperceive things. There is no disjunction problem. We cannot see a horse-or-cow-on-a-dark-night, just as Hilary Putnam cannot see a cat*-or-mouse*. These are not perceptual objects. The brain doesn't *grasp* meaning, it *confers* meaning as an infinite state device, which how it can wind up with infinite state meanings attached to its representations that correspond to the meaning we attribute to states of affairs in the world. The causal theory of meaning fails because it can't account for more than HORSE upon seeing a causal horse. 'Horse' means horse because it is a symbol for a representation, HORSE, which includes the content that the perceiver creates. If the perceiver confers the wrong meaning to a causal object because of unusual circumstances, there will be a misperception and a misrepresentation. But Fodor isn't done yet. He's invented the idea of a *module* to get meaning into representations.

AV.16 MODULES

Fodor's discussion of information leads to the concept of a module. Fodor starts with the fact that objects in the world send *information* to our sense organs which not only cause representations to be created, but also serves to fix beliefs about what is out in the world. Now Fodor is too modern-posted to talk about sense data, but these initial representations created by transduced information coming from the sense organs are pretty close to sense data. At one innocuous point he says, "...the visual analysis system can report only on the shapes and colors of things..."(Fodor, '83, 87). These are exactly what sense data components are. They are created in sensory cortices which Fodor calls "input systems", since they create the inputs that will go to the brain's "central processor". But where does meaning get into the act? Now since Fodor's main purpose in this analysis is to get meaning into representations along the way, he chooses these input systems as a fine place to sneak meaning into the chain of events. I don't know why. It would seem Fodor would be better off having his "input systems" pass on their meaningless traces to a sense impression module. But he would still have the problem of getting meaning through the gates of *that* module. But he sticks with the input system module and so he has the problem of getting

meaning to sense data all cuddled up in this module. Well, it turns out, these input systems have other talents: they can make inferences, no less.

Now, in reality, we're still in the sensory cortices, and haven't yet gotten to central processors, alternatively called cognitive areas, and yet we're told about "inferences" about complex physical objects out in the world. And what does an inference mean in this context? The visual sensory cortex, somehow "infers" that there are certain shapes and colors out in the world. He also uses the term 'hypothesis' that these "input systems" form. Fodor says, "...it is possible to infer properties of the distal layout [sense data qualities] from corresponding properties of the transducer [eyes] output. Input analyzers [sensory cortices] are devices which perform inferences of this sort" (45). Of course, all this is going to require the usual "computations", but "...performing such computations is precisely the function of input systems" (45). It's the same old stuff.

Now even though all parts of brain are infinite state systems, perhaps creating a sense datum does not make use of this capacity and creates sense data by computational finite state processes. But the information content of a percept is infinite. As we mentioned above, Fodor refers to this as the "poverty of stimulus argument", which says that "...there is typically *more information* in a perceptual response than there is in proximal stimulus that prompts the response" (Fodor, '90, 196). (We can think of Fodor's proximal stimulus as something akin to sense data). In my opinion, this statement dooms most of his perception theories. So where does all this additional information come from?

We have to keep in mind that so far, we have no meaning and no sense impressions. We have only sense data, as far as I can tell. He says, "...*the operation of the input systems [sensory cortices] should not be identified with the fixation of belief.* ...Fixation of belief is *just* the sort of thing I have in mind as a typical central process...*in light of background information*" (Fodor, '83, 46). This sounds to me that we still have no meaning in the picture, and that the "fixation of belief", which *will* involve meaning and content, will come as a result of cognitive "central processes". But before proceeding with this program, Fodor stops to mention that the input systems he refers to, and which we can assume are sensory cortices, are *modules*. As we shall see, as modules, these input systems are at an even greater disadvantage in creating meaning.

Modules are *domain specific*, which is the simple idea that the visual cortex creates *visual* sense data, and the auditory cortex creates *auditory* sense data. Also, Fodor's input system traces are *informationally encapsulated*. This basically means that an input system can go about its work without interference from stuff wandering around the mind/brain like expectations or beliefs or memories, etc. He uses another concept, *"limited access"* to describe the idea that other mentality has limited access to what's going on in the various modules. So an animal is not going to see the sense data of a lion as the sense data of a lamb simply because he would rather see a lamb.

Now this idea of encapsulation can be abused. The account we gave of Perceptual Realism says that upon the creation of sense data, the brain *immediately* begins to add meaning to create a sense impression. Thus, the creation of a perception is very much affected by expectations and beliefs. But Fodor isn't careful in making this distinction. He mentions Z. Pylyshyn's idea of "cognitive impenetrability" of *perception*, "...meaning that the output of the perceptual system is largely insensitive to what the perceiver presumes or desires" (68). To me, this is blatantly false, if they are really referring to *perception* as the quote says, as opposed to sensation.

Fodor gives examples, such as the Muller-Lyer illusion in which our knowledge that the lines are the same length does not change the illusion that the top line is shorter. This is supposed to show that a sense datum trace that the lines are not the same length is totally unaffected by knowledge that they are the same length. This is because the system that is creating sense data is encapsulated. I would suggest that people

have completely misinterpreted the Muller-Lyer illusion because it proves the exact opposite. This illusion falls into a kind of schema that George Lakoff made famous. It is an example of the compression-tension schema. Our minds add the *meaning* to the sense datum that the corners in the top drawing are *compressing* the line, and so we see it as shorter, whereas our minds interpret the corners as *pulling apart* the bottom line and so making it appear longer. In my opinion, there may be sensation modules, but this example doesn't show it.

Now, it does seem to be the case that the language system *first* looks at bare auditory sense data, which may include syntax or form. He says, "...the language input system specifies...its linguistic and maybe its logical form" (Fodor, '83, 90). So maybe the whole issue is simply where the language input system ends and where central processing begins. This leads to the question as to whether there is some point at all in the language recognizing system where there is only syntactic information processing, which would define a module? Fodor obviously thinks there is. He says "...linguistic form recognition can't be context-driven [involving meaning] because context doesn't determine form; if linguistic form is recognized at all, it must be by largely encapsulated processes" (90). So we have a module.

It is at this point in the game that Fodor's analysis takes a much more controversial turn. He admits that an "interface...must take place *somewhere*", between the creation of sense data and the central processors, "if we are to use the information that input systems deliver in order to determine how we ought to act" (Fodor, '83, 102). Now according to the account here, the next thing would be for "central processors to gather up meaning and attach it to the sense data made in sensory cortices (Fodor's input systems). But since Fodor thinks meaning originates out in the world, and he likes the idea of modules, he has a different account of what happens next, which is that we make *hypotheses* and *inferences* about the outside world. He calls it the

"the fixation of belief". But where does this happen? Does he have an inference module? Also, inferences need information to form its premises. Where does this come from?

Well, at one point, Fodor tentatively suggests that possibly "...*anything that the organism knows, any information that is accessible to any of its cognitive processes*, is ipso facto available as a premise in perceptual inference" (Fodor, '90, 200). Now this information is exactly what constitutes items that can be attached to a sense datum to create a meaningful percept. But Fodor is going to use this information to make "inferences"; and so at this point, the process seems to become unencapsulated. There are mechanisms "...that look simultaneously at representations delivered by the various input systems and at the information currently in memory, and they arrive at a best...hypothesis about how the world must be..." (Fodor, '83, 102). These mechanisms are part of central processing. But the question that hollers out is, if we need all this information to make inferences and hypotheses, why couldn't we use this very same information to add to our meaning-bereft sense data in the first place? Fodor wants to hammer in a nail, so he uses a hammer to make a saw, then uses the saw to hammer in the nail.

Additionally, after all this "inferring" and hypothesis making, do we still have a "poverty of information"? Do we have enough meaning about what is out in the world to create a real perceptual representation? If I am looking at a cow, why can't I add my stored cow information to my cow sense data to create a meaningful COW sense impression and skip the inferences? What are the inferences going to give me that I don't already have? But Fodor can do a Freudian runabout on this issue: "...the principles of inference according to which they operate are 'inexplicit'", (Fodor, '90, 211) whatever that means. This stretch word cuts us off at the pass.

Now, if things in the world are such that we can fix beliefs about them only by making guesses and inferences, that commits Fodor to the view that these objects are *mind-independent* and inaccessible to immediate perception. And then, how can we ever check our hypotheses and inferences? So in his next book, *A Theory of Content*, he attempts to patch up his story. But his problem now is that if his input system is really a module, where is it going to get the information necessary to make inferences?

Well, it turns out that these input systems have their own little "proprietary data base", which is only a subset of all the stuff that's in the rest of our heads; and the input system has "...access *only* to the information in its data base" (201). Fodor is going to allow his modules to cheat — but only a little bit. This allows the whole perceptual process at this point to be in an encapsulated module because now it doesn't seem to need any outside help. Not only that, but the module doesn't even *want* any outside help: it isn't going to allow in any unfamiliar information from far away foreign parts of the mind like the stuff mentioned in the text: culture, ethical values, etc. He wants what's available to create meaning from inferences to be a few items in the proprietary database.

The question now is, who is going to do the highly skilled job of picking out which mental items are going to go into his very exclusionary databases? Also, now that our input systems have only a limited amount of information available in their databases, can they muster up enough meaning to explain how it is that people do see very meaningful objects in the world? His proprietary databases must have some remarkable meaning-manufacturing skills. And then, how can we be sure that the meaning our inferences work up corresponds to what Fodor thinks is really out in the world?

I don't think the module and encapsulating question is all that important. It does seem that there is a point in the sensory cortices where information is used to create sense data with virtually no meaning. Whatever neurology is involved up to this point could be called a module whose operations are encapsulated. This point may be only as far down the information channel as the end of the optic nerve.

Some recent work in this area has indicated that as far down as the primary visual cortex, meaning starts to sneak into the processing of information: "The primary visual cortex, in short, appeared to be able to exercise associated cognitive processes previously credited solely to higher cortical areas…"(Martinez-Conde, '07, 55). This is very important work in my opinion. And she was working with rats with not much meaning to work with. What this shows is that when sensory information reaches the first areas of the brain, almost immediately, meaning starts to flow in to sense data. If worse comes to worse, the eyeball is a module, and so is the ear, so we're not going to be able to take back the horse show blue ribbon Fodor got for the module idea. But if meaning starts gathering to our sense data almost immediately, as we experience every moment of our lives, the module idea is no longer a mind phenomenon, but only a transducer idea.

The brain is just too interconnected for modules to exist as Fodor would like. However, it appears that contingently, there is a lot of modularity not only in people's perceptions but in their reasoning processes as well. If this book has any merit, there's not much encapsulation in my brain. There's a lot of experimental evidence that young children do a lot of modular thinking (they call it massively modular). For example, they use almost exclusively, geometric information to reorient themselves after disorientation, ignoring non-geometric information (Carruthers, '05, 94+). But as the children grow older and neurons in the brain grow more dendrites and make more connections, this apparent orientation module becomes increasingly unencapsulated; modularity starts crawling up sensory input channels until as adults, the only clear-cut and universal modules left are sensory transducers and initial stages of sensory cortices that make sense data. However, in many people, interconnections aren't made, simply because their thinking is the same old stuff day in and day out. And this is why experiments can show modularity even in cognitive thinking processes and even in adults.

We should mention in this regard that most modularists also assume a Computational Theory of Mind, which we discussed in Sect. AV.3. But CTM creates a big problem called the Intractability Thesis, which says that to think and solve problems, the mind would have to plow through enormous amounts of information to pick out stuff that's relevant to the problem at hand. And so to cut down the amount of work needed, CTM theorists bring in the module idea which will shut off all irrelevant stuff. But of course, the first problem is, why should a tractable package of the module's "proprietary data base" be relevant to the problem at hand? In my opinion, this CTM-modularity idea is a dead end, and the basic reason is that it ignores meaning. When the mind is mixing and matching representations as we think and solve problems, what guides the process is the *meaning* of representations brought to mind. Representations will be chosen from meaning clouds that are relevant to the direction of thinking we are engaged in. This is what solves the Intractability Problem. To the extent that modules restrict their resources to syntactical objects, they have no way to guide the thinking process, and to the extent that other resources are brought in to solve the Intractability Problem, you no longer have a module.

And just as the words 'information', 'identity', 'representation', etc. have been beaten, battered and mutilated out of existence, the same has happened to the module idea. Much of this isn't Fodor's fault, who tried not to be promiscuous with his modules. Of course, some modules are legitimate like the concept recognition cylinders described in the text. But every function the brain has can be made into a module, just as you can manufacture beliefs out of whole cloth for trees and thermostats. Peter Carruthers ('06, 146) even has a "belief-generating module" for rats, no less. Beliefs are very meaning-intensive. Where does the belief-generating module get the *meaning* for the objects of its beliefs?

Many brain functions share one characteristic of modules: they are sensitive to only certain kinds of information. However, they invariably involve infinite meanings, which modules cannot accommodate because they're supposed to be computational and algorithmic. Carruthers says that animal's minds are massively modular. But this is because they don't have much meaning in their heads in the first place. Then he says, as humans evolved, "what one would expect is that each of those pre-existing modules would be considerably deepened and enhanced" (159). To me this is a stunning example of how the computer has been a hindrance against understanding the mind. It is very clear to me that propositional attitudes are mixed and matched by the mind on the basis of their *content*; and not some anorexic content supplied by some ad hoc "proprietary database". This content would *expand* as the human evolutionary line progressed and would be quite global, which precludes modules. It is the enormous increase in the capacity for *meaning* as brain size mushroomed with evolution that gradually blurred away Carruthers' massive modules.

Near the end of *Theory of content*, Fodor seems to drop the idea of a propriety data base, and gets down to just how we do get meaning into our sense data traces. He quotes Gregory's idea that "We are forced...to suppose that perception involves betting on the most probable interpretation of sensory data, in terms of the world of objects" (Gregory, 29). After more than 10 books, Fodor is now *"betting"* that the meaning we have on the basis of our inferences corresponds to the meaning that he thinks is out in the world.

The final version of his perceptual theory is, "sensation is responsive solely to the character of proximal stimulation and is noninferential." I agree with this much. But then, "Perception is both inferential and responsive to the perceiver's background theories" (Fodor, '90, 244). There we are stranded in midair wondering what we have.

He says about any theory we may come up with that the content of the theory "does not determine the meanings of the terms whose connections to the world the theory mediates" (Fodor, '87, 125). This seems to imply that what fixes meanings of terms and concepts like HORSE, is not any theory about what the brain is doing, but "*by what things in the world the theory connects them to*" (125). He puts the point succinctly: "For 'John' to mean *John*, something has to happen in the world" (Fodor, '90, 99). I believe the exact opposite: for 'John' to mean John, something has to happen in the *head*. It is precisely what the *mind/brain* is doing that determines meaning, and "what things in the world" there are have nothing to do with it, except to wake up brain's meaning factory into production. In my opinion, the solution to the meaning problem lies in the distinction between causal and perceptual objects, and unless Fodor recognizes something like this, he isn't going to solve problems of meaning. As we have stressed many times, meanings are "in the head", and as John Searle has said, there is nowhere else for them to be. And Fodor has no explanation as to how they get there.

Without living creatures, the world consists of a meaningless swirl of strings or quarks or somethings. Causal objects, by themselves have no meaning and no intentionality. Through a process of millions of years of evolution, the sense data components created by the brain's sensory apparatus interacting with causal objects are instrumentally correlated with a causal world around us that we are successful in interacting with. Sense data components do not *correspond to* qualities out in the world because causal objects *intrinsically* have no such qualities to correspond to. They become *part* of the content of the resulting perceptual object because the mind creates them that way. There is nothing to infer. This is why semantics is infinite state syntax. If you accrue an infinite number of sense data, you get a meaning cloud. It is their infinite number that creates meaning, which is why computers will never be able to do meaning.

The solution to the representation meaning problem is simply that since the representation is a copy of a sense impression we initially created, it is going to have the same semantic aspect as the percept we participated in creating in the first place. To answer Putnam, we automatically refer to objects we participated in creating by creating them in the first place. As we mentioned, a shoemaker automatically refers to the shoes he makes by making them.

AV.17 COMPUTATION VRS. MEANING AS MENTAL CAUSATION

Well, after 20 or 30 years wrestling with the problems we have been discussing in this Appendicitis, in his newer book, *The Elm and the Expert*, Fodor finally crystallizes everything down to the simple dichotomy of computations vrs. meaning. After spending half a lifetime depreciating and chipping away at meaning in a big stack of books, the first few pages of this new book are a tacit admission that meaning is pretty big stuff after all, and not easily cut down to computational size. Now he isn't going to talk about infinite numbers of meaning entities associated with our representations because that would admit too much. But if there is a "non-computational" aspect to meaning, which he finally acknowledges, what else could be the reason?

But all he has at his disposal is his finite computational language of thought that supposedly gives us our psychological life. So on the one hand, he has big fat meanings and on the other he has only computers to handle them. As Lenin said after the Russian revolution, (a weakly supported legend), "what's to be done?" Meaning is still lurking in the background like a huge out-of-work dinosaur. Will he ever admit that meaning is something that a computational model may not be able to take in and launder? Not yet. Besides he can acknowledge the robustness of meanings because they aren't going to get in the way anyway. In this last book, he has pretty much settled on syntax as the key to the meaning problem. But the computer isn't gone quite yet. The mind may not be a computer, but we still have the brain to talk about. Maybe the brain is a computer.

Well, he suggests that if intentionality (and meaning) is "external" in the sense that it is about the relation between what's in the mind and what's out in the world, then "... if intentional laws can't be computational, it also shows that it can't be neurological..."(Fodor, '01, 15). The reason, of course, is that the mind supervenes on the brain; and if intentionality is too big a load for the mind to handle, it will be too big a load for the brain to handle as well. But of course, how is this big load of meaning out in the world ever going to get into our minds or our brains if they're both just computers handling finite state algorithms? He asks, how could a computation, which "merely *transforms one symbol into another* guarantee the causal relations between symbols and the world upon which... the meanings of symbols depends" (12). A very good question.

He succinctly describes the pickle we're in: "It looks as though the best story about meaning we've got...can't be squared with the only story about mind we've got — viz., the computational theory. ...So it looks as though we must either give up on the informational metaphysics of content or we must give up on the computational theory of mind" (21). He says, "I particularly wanted to have both" (13). Now what in heavens name would motivate this unattractive desire? How much luckier is mankind if "psychological processes" were "computational"? Well, I don't think we even have a choice because, we have to *give up* both. In my opinion, once these guys wean themselves away from the computer, it will be clear that the mind is not a computer, the brain is not a computer, and nothing we all value as human is computational either.

But what follows in Fodor's book is really an irony. He seems to think that his assumption that the mind engages in computational processes is impeded by stories that, in my opinion, do nothing of the sort. But he thinks he has to find a way to get rid of them. He dispenses with the twin Earth story with the simple expedient that water can't be XYZ — by law, no less. Well, here we have Putnam's twin Earth spiraling through the heavens for over 30 years now; but finally, through recent astronomical observations, Fodor has determined that twin Earth has run out of XYZ, has dried up and dissolved into the dust of the cosmos. And God is never going to allow this experiment again.

The Oedipus story is even funnier. Fodor tells us in the story, "Something went badly wrong" (Fodor, '95, 43). *"Most people do not marry their mothers ..."*(45). Counterexamples don't count unless there's lots of them. The moral of the story is, "Oedipus was rash and he was unlucky" (46). Is this philosophy? Is Fodor implying that men are not supposed to want to marry women old enough to be their mothers? What would the Woman's Lib say about that? (Fodor should have talked about the Greek Koros, who wanted to marry his *daughter.*) As a result, since stories like Oedipus's are mere "aberrations", we can disregard them.

The last Chapter 4 in *The Elm and the Expert*, he says thoughts seem to have to be in two places at once: "They have to be, as it were, 'out there', so that things in the world can interact with them, but they also have to be, as it were, 'in here' so that they can proximately cause behavior" (83). This is the best sentence he ever made; but he tops it: "For it's the essence of mental representations that they face two ways at once: they connect with the world by representing it; and they connect with behavior by being its typical proximate cause" (83). The problem is "...how mental representations could be both semantic, like propositions, and causal like rocks, trees, and neural firings, is arguably the interaction problem all over again,..." (84). Yes, and he isn't going to solve this dilemena with computers

First of all, the semantic aspect of representations and the interaction problem certainly *overlap* but do not coincide. This is a very subtle point. The interaction problem, illustrated by the causal cutter, is how immediate conscious mental events like thoughts and feelings can cause subsequent behavior when the neurological substrate of these events should be causing the same behavior. However, lots of meaning is not conscious, by and large. If I see thick clouds in the morning, this means rain; and this may cause me to take an umbrella. But I may see the clouds and take the umbrella, *perceptio simplicio*, with no conscious mentality at all. Athletes play whole games in which there are all kinds of meaning caused behavior but no thoughts. It is through its *physical* substrate that meaning does its causal work in situations like this, and there is no interaction problem.

Of course, a particular particle in the meaning cloud of the raining representation could come to consciousness. I could activate a belief that thick clouds could produce rain, in which case, it is the *content* of the belief that does the causing. But it is unknown as to how much this image influences my behavior. The causes of much of our behavior are not conscious events but subconscious mentality having meaning which does causal work on the basis of neurological processes, which should delight Chalmers, Dennett and the rest of the "closed universe" gang.

So Fodor has some deep problems. On the one hand, he seems to think that the content of a representation is too wispy and airy to push around our big heavy physical bodies. On the other hand, he seems to think that meaning out in the world is just too heavy a load to get into our heads without first paring them down to computational size. Well, which is it? Of course, on the wispy view, once he gets them into the head, he may have to pump them back up with steroids so that they are again powerful enough to do causal work. Nothing illustrates these problems more than this: "...representations can mediate the worlds effects upon behavior because *the same properties of mental representations that determine their computational roles also carry information about the world*" (86). You won't find a relatively short sentence packed with more wrong stuff in it than this.

First of all, the informational theory of semantics is totally inadequate. The amount of information coming to us through transducers is finite — only enough to create meaningless sense data, as is suggested by the syntax of sentences. But this is a very long way from "information about the world" which involves an infinite number of high information content entities, and what's worse, counterfactuals. Second, the amount of meaning necessary to cause behavior is clearly more than what could possibly be handled computationally. Counterfactuals themselves are infinite in number. All of this certainly could not be explained by the syntax of representations. And finally, if you need a robust idea of meaning to do the causal work that the mind seems capable of, how does it get there if it starts out in the world? In his book, *The Mind Doesn't Work That Way*, Fodor bites the bullet and admits that cognitive science is in bad shape. But he can't escape the computer trap: "Mental processes are sensitive solely to the syntax of mental representations (because mental processes are computations)" (Fodor, '01, 24). Once again, in the battle over meaning, the computer, which has no meaning at all, wins.

Let's look at a real example. Take the thought that the earth is round. This representation is surrounded by a meaning cloud. One of the items in this cloud might be that you can travel round the world. What Fodor seems to be saying is that even if mental work could be done by items in this cloud on the basis of their syntax, here, the syntax of "you can travel round the world", the syntax of the original sentence, "the earth is round", cannot reach these meaning items because the syntax of "the earth is round" is local. But I think there's a worse problem.

Even if the syntax of the "earth is round" thought *were* global, it would still not be sensitive to the *meaning* of "you can travel round the world"; and to me, this is not enough to account for the causal work that the "earth is round" thought might do. What is there in the syntax of "the earth is round" that is going to pick up the syntax of "you can travel round the world"? This is an example of the famous "frame problem", mentioned above. He says, " 'The frame problem' is a name for … how to reconcile a local notion of mental computation with the apparent holism of rational

inference…"(42). The result is that since "…abductive inferences are nonlocal, hence noncomputational…"(44), syntax, which can only accommodate computations, is not going to be up to the job. He concludes, "…there appear to be mental processes…that respond to (irreducibly) nonlocal properties of belief systems; and we don't understand how such processes work" (45).

So he has two choices, make syntax more global, or pare down the meanings of "the earth is round". Having given up on the first, he turns to the second, and his approach is to miniaturize thinking by modularizing it. He says, "Start with Turing's idea that cognitive processes are syntactic. There's a plausible inference from that to the conclusion that cognitive processes are by and large local…; and there's a plausible inference from that to the massive modularity thesis" (91).

Ah, but wait: there's a fly in the ointment. He has a whole swarm of flies in the ointment, but he picks out one: beliefs. Beliefs seem to be all over the brain, and involve big chunks of meaning. And of course, beliefs, the most important mental entities for survival, have a wide range of content, and are certainly domain-general, global entities, whereas "Classical computations are sensitive, at most, to the local context; and so too are computations that modular mechanisms perform" (64). So how is he going to use modules to rescue him from this sinking ship? Modules are supposed to be innate, so how can we be born with big fat things like beliefs in these tiny little modules? He's on the run now.

Fodor says, "Innate modules thus require a detailed epistemic fit between what's in the mind and what's out in the world" (94). Yes, and they ain't gonna to get it *if* he's really talking about meaning. We are not born with encapsulated modules with the full measure of meaning "out in the world". Well, after 10 or more books, Fodor is done. He's run out of syntactic gas. Even evolution, which has been used to back up the wildest of stories seems of no avail. He finally concludes, "…Classical computations are intrinsically local and thus badly equipped to account for the abductive aspects of cognition" (79), or inference to the best explanation which is "…much of what the mind does best". Such global processes "can't be informationally encapsulated… and domain specific" (97). Well, like at the end of the old cartoons, "that's all folks".

In my opinion, the whole group of tied-together cliff climbers consisting of Turing machines, computability, modularity, locality, syntax and finite algorithms — this whole bunch is falling off the cliff, dragging each other down. None of this can accommodate an infinite number of meaning items containing high information content in a typical meaning cloud. And as far as I can see, it doesn't matter whether computations are local or not, nor how large the databases of modules are.

At the end of this book, he sums up what we can say with some assurance.

1). "A lot of cognitive inferences appear abductive. [read, big fat "holistic" meanings] If so, then a lot of cognitive architecture can't be modular" (98). I can't, for the life of me understand how modules ever got into the meaning act in the first place. As Fodor himself sometimes implies, modules are *pre*-meaning.

2). "Because abductive inferences are sensitive to global properties of belief systems, they almost certainly can't be driven just by the syntax of mental representations…." For, "… the syntactic properties of representations are ipso facto local, and it is a truism that global inferences aren't." (98). But it isn't representation's globality that overwhelms the "syntax of mental representations", but the infinite complexity of their meanings. Even if computations are not local, they still cannot accommodate the infinite nature of semantics and meaning.

3). "The cost of treating abductive inferences… that depend on logical form — that is, as determined by the *internal* ("local") syntax of mental representations — would be radical holism…"(99). Holism is "radical", no less. Not only that, but it is an indication

"that something has gone wrong with one's theory" (99). If Fodor took the trouble to sort the details of holism such as how meaning entities form a tree with weights, etc., he wouldn't be so terrorized by meaning holism.

The last sentence in this book is, "So far, what our cognitive science has found out about the mind is mostly that we don't know how it works." Amen. The account given here does try to address these problems. Meaning doesn't start out in the world, it's "in the head" to begin with in the form of infinite state neurological structures. It is the mind that projects meaning out into the world of causal objects which have no other meaning than what we project. *Without advanced living creatures, especially humans, there is no meaning inherent in the world.*

But regarding mental causality, there's a lot less of it than we think. Most mental causation is really physically caused. Any mental event that is brought to consciousness from the meaning cloud of a representation is usually a *reason* only and plays no causal role. Of course, such a mental event, on a particular occasion, *may* have a causal role, in which case, we do have the overdetermination interaction problem, which is the second most difficult of the mind-body problems. However, meaning is not what makes the interaction problem intractable; it is conscious mentality that creates the difficulty (the first most difficult problem).

AV.18 The Language of Thought

Now that we have discussed all the aspects of representations in doing causal work in our thinking, we have to get down to the question of what are the lumps that our thinking manipulates or computes over. Fodor calls it a Language of Thought, LOT. But what does it consist of; and what is the role of meaning?

As you might expect, a minute difference of opinion has been blown up into monumental proportions and resulted in two basic kinds of theories.

There's "*...the cognitive conception of language*, which sees language as crucially implicated in human thinking" (Carruthers & Boucher, '98, 1). Then there's the *communicative conception*, whereby we think in terms of a kind of non-linguistic lump, and use languages of various kinds to *communicate* thoughts to ourselves and others. In other words, these two theories say that either the lumps are language sentences themselves or something else.

Colin McGinn has a very fascinating dichotomy that might correspond to the same things. There is digital coding whose "features are independent of the properties of things represented"; and analog coding in which "properties of the represented states of affairs are somehow *reflected* in the features of the code" (McGinn, '89, 178). An example of digital coding might be auditory sentences, and analog coding might be visual representations. The problem isn't the fact that we're consciously constantly running words through our heads. The problem is what is the mind/brain doing when we're thinking but there are no words? It must be doing something because our behavior can be very complex. And what are the lumps and how do they do causal work in this sort of thinking?

Lots of writers seem to be enamored by the role of natural language in conscious thinking. Peter Carruthers says, "So there is no real reason to believe that young children are capable of complex thought prior to the development of natural language..." (Carruthers, '96, 44). He offers as evidence the fact that before a pair of twins had been exposed to language, their play was "rudimentary" and lacked cognitive abilities. But when put in environments where they could learn language, there was a marked improvement in the cognitive abilities. The same thing happened with congenitally deaf children with no language exposure who are suddenly put into a signing community. Carruthers explains this as due to conscious language providing more tools to sharpen cognitive abilities. This is also evidence that even their

non-conscious thinking after language acquisition may be partially in language which enables their cognitive abilities to improve.

Then there is counter evidence. The two sentences, "the dog bit the man" and " the man was bitten by the dog" express the same thought even though they are different sentences. So the thought should be something different from the sentences. Also, what about times when we seem to have a thought, but can't find words to express it? It does seem the thought is in some kind of lump that needs translation into language expression. Carruthers says simply that the language of thought is good old-fashioned English. But then what are animals and children using before they learn language? They engage in *some* kind of primitive thinking.

In my opinion, since any mental phenomenon, whether representation or perception or memory or belief, supervenes on brain processes, it is going to have some kind of causal effect. Carruthers' view of propositional attitudes is that "...we must be dependent upon the acquisition of a public language in order to be capable of conscious propositional thinking" (259). Also, language may better enable the use of concepts in thinking. Animals have concepts in the sense of being able to recognize instances. Language can be used to symbolize concepts — yes, but this still doesn't preclude the importance of other kinds of representations.

At times he makes an even stronger claim that only propositional thinking by itself, requires language. I don't agree with this order of things. I think it's the exact opposite: that primitive propositional attitudes are a *necessary* precursor, although maybe a concomitant, of language and possibly why language evolved in the first place. Pre-language children seem to have beliefs.

Carruthers seems to be implying that a propositional attitude can't really exist without being expressed. But if we look closely at what PAs are, all that is required for a PA is the ability to abstract a self concept into a different place and time *plus* some value on the imagined state of affairs. I don't see where language is necessary to do this. The higher primates have the *beginnings* of the circuitry to do PA's without language. They can handle the weaker PA's. Certainly, representations appeared long before PAs (we are saying around 10 mya). It seems plausible that there was a period of time — we're saying between a million and half mya — when our ancestors could create propositional attitudes but had only a proto-language to express them.

The *image* of a chasing lion is going to have a lot of meaning to all other mammals, especially humans. You don't have to mumble something like "I'd better get the hell out of here", to activate that meaning. And it certainly seems the case that a non-conscious representation of a chasing lion brought to near activation doesn't have to be translated into some crazy language to get us to seek safety, no matter how much babbling in language you are able to do.

I think that discussions of natural language representations involve certain confusion. When we hear a spoken sentence, we create an auditory representation. Since it is a stream or sounds, it might be an analog code. Fred Dretske in his important book, *Knowledge and the Flow of Information* says that our cognitive system translates a basically analog signal into a digital signal: "…we define a structure's semantic content as that piece of information it carries in (what I shall call) *completely digitalized form…*" (Dretske, '81, 184). This is only half right, in my opinion. The analog signal of an auditory representation is first recoded into a digital code, perhaps natural language sentences; but then shouldn't the *content* of this code again be analog because meaning is infinite state stuff. When he says, "Our own perceptual experience testifies to the fact that there is more information *getting in* [our cognitive systems] than we can manage to *get out*" (149), he is forgetting about the *content* that we add to the perceptual experience. Dretske's statement here applies only to concept *recognition* and sense data, which are not cognitive abilities at all because they don't involve

meaning. Sensory information is funneled down to the ability to recognize concepts, which may involve only finite state brain processes underlying sense data. This is not cognition.

Also, Dretske doesn't account for the fact that especially with experiences like our car story, we can often recreate a picture of the experience in great detail in our minds (activating a representation). Perhaps some information gets lost in the process which explains why the recreation is less vivid. But there seems to be comparable amounts of meaning in the perception as in the reactivation. Certainly there is a lot more information in the recreation than is involved in recognizing concepts and establishing sense data and their finite word descriptions. Again, a problem is that these philosophers are too word oriented.

The bottom line is that even though language symbols may be important in a language of thought, which is digital, that does not erase the role of content of these symbols, which may remain analog. And of course, in the case of many other auditory representations, there may be very little language digital encoding. Listening to music and recreating it in our minds is not listening to and recreating meaningless noises. There might be some digitalization into language like, the tempo is quick or the melody is pretty, but most is left in analog form.

But what about the thinking of non-linguistic creatures like artists, athletes, and babies? Athletes especially do a lot of thinking in their performances, but there are no signs of language use. They are likely thinking in visual representations or perhaps executing procedural programs not involving any symbolism. Rosemary Varley has studied global aphasiacs who are almost totally devoid of language abilities (Carruthers & Boucher, 128). And yet her studies showed that they are capable of considerable propositional thinking, like the ability to pass false beliefs and theory of mind tests and causality tests, although there was some impairment in these abilities. Higher primates would probably flunk most of Varley's tests, but only because they couldn't understand the instructions. But I'd bet they could do certain causality tests and they seem to have a primitive theory of mind with regards to the weaker propositional attitudes like wants and needs. They know when their babies want food. This would show that they do engage in some kind of primitive thinking without language.

In promoting natural language as the vehicle of thinking, Carruthers adds more gratuitous assumptions that don't seem to be necessary for his main theory. He says, "...it may be that in many of those cases where a thought is carried by an image of an object, an embedding in a linguistic context may be necessary to confer on that image a determinate content" (Carruthers, '96, 253). Also, "it appears quite impossible for images, as such, to carry content of any but the very simplest thoughts about the immediate environment" (253). This is pretty certainly not true. *All* representations whether linguistic or not, and whether conscious or not, have meaning clouds associated with them, a lot of which is not linguistic at all. It is the *meaning* of representations that gives them their causal efficacy, *not* whether they are visual or linguistic.

Pylyshyn tries to show that there is a lot about visual representations that isn't pictorial at all. Then he stealthily sneaks in factors that clearly are pictorial into the same bag, and throws the whole bag out the window. He says, "...there is no fundamental difference between the relations 'is to the left of' ...or 'causes' inasmuch as none of them is any more 'directly in the scene' than any other (Pylyshyn in Block, '81, 172). I disagree totally. All representations have associated meaning clouds, which may contain linguistically expressed facts involving cause or to the left of. There's a lot of stuff in these clouds that isn't pictorial, but this has absolutely nothing to do with whether or not the representation *itself* is pictorial.

All of Pylyshyn's examples show that in the case of *visual* representations, which are pretty wispy, washed out, and somewhat indeterminate, linguistic descriptions do help in getting information from the representation. This is a counterpart to Carruthers' point that language greatly enhances a child's cognitive problem solving ability. The ability of the visual system to record very *detailed* representations is a relatively new thing within the last million years or so. Many people don't have much of this ability at all. Additionally, this ability was evolving at about the same time as language was evolving. And since a great deal of the content of a *static* visual representation is in terms of their geometric relationships, it stands to reason that verbal descriptions of certain aspects of a visual representation might play a considerable role in adding to the ability to make reports about a visual image. This would be digital coding from an analog signal.

Of course, Daniel Dennett doesn't think we have images in the first place. We discussed in the text the untenability of this view. But clearly we have pictorial traces of a sort, at the very least, on the retina. So Dennett and Pylyshyn must believe that the retinal traces must get coded into some kind of linguistic digital code, and it is from sentences in this code that we can make reports of our past perceptions and experiences. But now we have a new problem. If the internal code is not English sentences, we have to have two more translation systems for translating English conscious speaking and hearing into the code, and translating the code back into English sentences to express our thoughts. There's even more. When we remember something, we get English sentences. Who does the translation between English and Mentalese? Owen Flanagan says, "It looks as if we need a bilingual homunculus... " (Flanagan, '84, 176). Stephen Kosslyn, who has done the major research on imagery, mentions Pylyshyn's requirement for having two codes: "...our ability to translate or exchange information between verbal and visual codes...requires the existence of a third 'interlingual' code" (Kosslin in Block, '81, 152), which is propositional in nature. This might lead to an infinite regress.

Print and poster collectors talk a lot about what's in their visual representations. They talk about objects in the scene, how they are related, where the vignettes are, the colors of the objects, etc. Some of this might be recorded in linguistic form. However, damage to a print is very difficult to encode symbolically. This is one factor that separates the appreciator from the investor. The appreciator compliments a good restoration because he can visualize the print before restoration and now compare it to what appears afterwards. The investor thinks he's being cheated. He consults his Pylyshyn playbook and can't figure out what the conservator has done because his imagery is weak and he has to rely on whatever can be done with symbolic information, which doesn't say much about the crazy kinds of damage that are not amenable to language descriptions at all.

Another fact against Pylyshyn's position is that there is no correlation between visual imagery talent and IQ. High IQ is mostly a matter of manipulating symbols and to think in symbolic terms. If Pylyshyn were right that reports of visual imagery is propositional and symbolic in form, the smartest people would have the best visual memories. This is not the case. In my experience, there is no significant correlation between intelligence and visual memory, in the same way that there is very little correlation between intelligence and musical ability. The most important jazz musician who ever lived was Louis Armstrong, who was not noted for his genius IQ.

Finally, there's evolution which Dennett loves to bring up. Humans evolved the ability to picture scenes in the first place so that they could scan a scene and have a quick way to see where food might be or a good place to hide or a tree to climb. These guys are telling us that our proto-human ancestors went through millions of propositions that they had stored about a scene to get one appropriate for the needs at hand. How many per second could they access?

In short, it appears there are two basic kinds of representations that are the lumps that we think in terms of: digital auditory language sentence representations and continuous stream auditory and snapshot visual pictorial representations. What makes people suspicious, I think is that it seems strange to have two very different kinds of representations as one language of thought. But I don't think the difference is important. A sentence representation is nothing but an auditory representation from hearing an English sentence and its work could be done with a digital code. An image is simply a *visual* representation from a visual perception. And they both have meaning clouds that can contain most anything. Since these are the only two modalities that create representations in the first place, I don't think it's anomalous that they should both be part of the make-up of the Language of Thought. Neurons of the brain really don't care what they're representing.

But whatever the internal code is, we still have to explain how sentences in this code do causal work in our thinking. People like Hartry Field put most of their marbles in the language basket, as do all wordmakers. So he talks about the syntax of the internal language whether a natural language or Fodor's language of thought as the factor responsible for the causal work the internal sentence does. The idea, I think, is that thinking requires mixing and matching and causality between whatever representations are being used in thought processes. This requires that you pick them up and move them around and make inferences with them, etc. This requires that your representations of thought, whether Natural Language or Mentalese, have a *syntactical structure* that identifies them and acts as a handle to pick them up. But I don't think this hurts anyone's theory in this regards because even languageless visual and auditory representations have a structure that corresponds to the syntax of sentences used to describe them. Recall in Appendicitis, we said the syntax of the Tarski sentence in quotes, guides us to a *causal* level state of affairs in the world whose structure is given by the arrangement of sense data elements. The meaning we project to this causal state of affairs is ascribed back to the Tarski sentence. So if we need to drum up syntax for our representations, all we have to do is look at the syntax of sentences used to describe them. This is why the syntax of a sentence describing a state of affairs corresponds to the sense data trace that a sense impression and its representation are built upon. These factors are used to identify the representation so as to do bring it to the conscious (or non-conscious) workspace to be used in thinking. What enables the causal work a representation does, whether pictorial, auditory, or linguistic, is *content*; and in this respect, linguistic representations are on the same footing as pictorial or auditory representations. In my opinion, what all the evidence points to is that our thinking is in terms of good old-fashioned representations, linguistic and non-linguistic, along with their content. This is something babies, animals and even philosophers can do. If enough meaning is attached to representation, they are conscious.

Let's look to see if Fodor can do any better with his Language of Thought. To motivate his arguments, he accepts Paul Grice's theory of language meaning in terms of beliefs and intentions, and other propositional attitudes. This is a communicative conception of language. Grice said that when you use a sentence to communicate meaning, like the meaning of grass is green, you "...intend your audience to acquire the belief that grass is green as a result of recognizing your intention in speaking" (Carruthers, '96, 74). Immediately, we have a problem that when you're trying to set up a belief in a listener, you have to account for the meaning of the object of the belief as expressed in a natural language sentence. But if belief as a propositional attitude is between a person and a natural language sentence, you would have a different belief for speakers of different languages, whereas we would want to say that the belief in an Englishman's mind that snow is white is the same belief that a German has when he believes that schnee ist weiss. The only way you can make these beliefs the same is if they are in terms of the same meaning the two sentences have.

In order to avoid this problem, Fodor simply throws out natural language as the vehicle of thought and substitutes a language of thought that is the same in all of us, even Germans. And the only way this could be is if we're born with the Language of Thought. If we wonder where his Mentalese sentences are going to get their meaning, Fodor simply spoons a small amount of meaning into them that we're born with. But not too much meaning so as to gum up his computer. It would also, supposedly, explain why humans can learn a variety of languages. They all get started with Mentalese already downloaded into the brain, and from there it is easy to learn other languages. As we discussed above, when do the "formulae", pick up their semantic aspect so that it can participate in the causal activity in our thinking? Also, when do these syntactic representations get interpreted so that they appear to the mind as they do?

There is no motivation for Fodor to have to avoid the problem with natural language sentences being different for different language speakers having the same beliefs. This problem could have been avoided in the first place if Fodor had taken beliefs and other propositional attitudes to be relations to *representations* and not sentences. Besides, representations, whether visual or auditory, have the same meaning as the sentences used to describe them. There will be overlap in meanings of respective representations in communicator's heads because they have a common causal state of affairs they all get information from. The purpose of communication is to set up corresponding meanings in communicator's heads, much of which are visual and auditory representations. you do it with ostension, facial expressions, body language, and words. Language is just one means, probably the most important one, to bring about a concurrence of *meanings*.

Fodor's last foundational pillar is the innateness idea. He goes into great detail to explain how one cannot learn a language without knowing one already. This is certainly true for learning new spoken languages. He then attempts to show that this is also true of the first language we learn: we must have an innate language of thought to learn English. But if the Language of Thought is innate, it had to have evolved before about 8 thousand years ago, when civilization probably brought evolution pretty much to a close. Fodor denies that you can "... learn a language whose expressive power is greater than that of a language that one already knows" (Fodor, '75, 86). This would imply that we cannot learn all the very complex predicates and meanings in today's language unless this richness was already present in the language of thought, which had to evolve long before this complexity. How, in evolutionary history, would LOT evolve the ability to handle today's complex concepts, such as in relativity theory, magnetohydrodynamics, quantum mechanics, and above all, Fodor's brand of often inscrutable philosophy?

As discussed in Appendicitis II, in my opinion, the basis of language learning is not a language of thought, but the ability to *refer*, which may have some innate aspects, but nothing like a whole new language. I think there is a language of thought, and it is simply representations we have of sense impressions and language tokens. We can explain users of different languages having the same belief that snow is white by seeing that they both have the belief relation to similar representations that are based on the same causal objects. This is the language of animals and babies who create representations right after birth. Also, as we have shown, representations are the objects of propositional attitudes, and it seems quite in line with this fact that representations are the language of thought.

From an evolutionary viewpoint, why would evolution go to the trouble of evolving a whole new language of thought stuffed into the poor newborn baby's head, when we have representations we accrue that can do the job just as well. Evolution never does anything more than it absolutely has to. Representations have the added attraction that they can be identified and individuated on the basis of the real world *object* of the sense impression; and by syntax in the case of linguistic representations. What does the actual causal *work* in thinking processes is the meaning of the representations employed, no matter what the modality.

Finally, we might notice that thinking in terms of representations enables translations between languages a lot more tractable than Quine and his followers tried to show. People think translation raises insurmountable problems. What philosophers overlook is that when two people are communicating in a single language, the same problems arise. The speaker's thoughts have to be described in natural language sentences with a certain meaning. Words of a speaker's sentence then have to be translated into a stream of representations that includes pictorial, auditory, and linguistic representations and concepts in the listener's mind. These representations and concepts and their meanings may be just as different as the meanings between translating languages. Then they have to be described in the language of the listener when he speaks, which adds another layer of indeterminacy. In my opinion, there's no more problem in translating *between* languages as there is in communication using the same language. No two meanings of representations and concepts are the same for two different people within one language; and the meanings of representations used to create a public meaning for translation between two different languages are just as dissimilar.

Martin Davies wrote a very difficult paper comparing Fodor's LOT and Carruther's NLT, Natural Language Theory (Davies in Carruthers, '98). First of all, I was happy to hear the way Davies addressed the interpretation problem we mentioned in AV.8. If the Language of Thought, LOT, is all syntax, when does it get interpreted so that they have the meanings they appear to have? Here's Davies: "When I hear a sentence in a language that I understand, I do not hear the sentence as a phonological object in need of interpretation; rather I hear the sentence as having a meaning. …I hear the meaning clothed in phonology" (230). This leaves us wondering how meaning got into vision when all we have to see with are finite transducers. Actually it's the other way round: we dress up the phonology (noise sense data) we hear with meaning. Davies' discussion tells me that Fodor really does have an interpretation problem.

What Davies brings out as that the crux of the matter is how do we know that there will be a correspondence between deductions and inferences, etc. going on at the perceptual level (Davies calls the personal level) and brain processes going on at the causal level (which he calls the sub-personal, information processing,). We keep running into this problem in many guises. Now Davies only talks about syntax not brain processes. But moving sentences around on the basis of syntax is going to use logic as does the computer. But brain processes proceed on the basis of natural physical laws. So in opposition to Carruthers, he implies that we can't be sure brain processes at the causal level obeying natural laws will allow a perceptual level thought process to go smoothly no matter whether perceptual level processes are proceeding along according to personal meaning or on the basis of logic and syntax. Similarly, how can Fodor's Mentalese proceed at the causal level according to either physical laws or the syntax of Mentalese sentences, correspond to supervening personal level thought processes involving meaning and emotions?

Well, what Davies overlooks is consciousness. He even seems to question why consciousness has anything to do with all this. And as we mentioned above, maybe Carruthers misses this point as well. Perhaps Carruthers likes natural language representations as his language of thought because they have syntax, we can introspect them and they have causal efficacy. But this isn't enough to solve the correspondence problem. What makes natural language representations the best candidates for a language of thought is their *consciousness*.

The whole point of consciousness is that it enables thought processes at the perceptual level to go in and affect the sequence of brainstates these thought processes supervene on so as to make the thought processes and underlying brain processes correspond. This is very wild theory as we have admitted. But logically, if consciousness can't do this, then there really isn't any detectable difference between conscious and non-conscious thinking, and we don't have to worry about perceptual level causation at all. We can go with Fodor, Dennett and the rest with a causal level LOT doing its job on the basis of syntax, alongside either epiphenomenalism or no phenomenalism at all, and we've solved the mind/body problem, the consciousness problem, and the LOT problem all in one fell swoop.

In sum, I think there are enormous problems with Fodor's Language of Thought with its myriad of ad hoc and unexplained connections between correspondents, English sentences, propositions, and Mentalese symbols. If natural language can't squeeze worldly meaning through finite state transducers, how will Mentalese do any better? Years into the future, after all the smoke has cleared away, it will turn out that Mentalese is really our old friends, representations, including representations of English sentences. And although language will always struggle with describing an infinite number of representations, it is better equipped to do so than some algorithmic Mentalese, which we have no conscious control over whatsoever. Representations have the necessary syntax to enable being picked up into the conscious workspace, and they have meaning that implements their causal efficacy; *and* their consciousness creates a correspondence between perceptual level thinking and underlying causal level brain processes. We don't need an innate language with a mountain of paraphernalia to stuff into the poor baby's head. After Fodor's modules, there's really no room for it anyway.

Concepts

———

AVI.1 Concepts and Induction

Fodor says, "Much of life of the mind consists of applying concepts to things." (Fodor, '98, 24). We should try to make our discussion of concepts consistent with our analysis of perception. As we defined in Ch. 16, we will denote sense data concepts with no meaning with small caps like STRAIGHT LINE, REDNESS, OR SWEETNESS. Full meaningful concepts will be denoted with large caps: STRAIGHT LINE.

Before we get into the details of concepts, we should first point out the important difference between *having* a concept and knowing the meaning of a concept, which is called "knowing a concept" or "grasping a concept". *Having* a concept, is simply the ability to pick out examples of the concept and probably involves only finite amounts of information from the causal level and shows up in the *syntax* of sentences involving the concept.

Knowing a concept is a lot more complicated because it involves meaning. But Fodor doesn't clearly make this distinction. At one point, Fodor defines concepts as "word meanings", which are constituents of thoughts. I don't think this is tenable. Concepts *have* meanings; they are not the same things *as* meanings. You can *have* a concept without thinking anything as with neural nets.

There is a little problem with our definition however. We have said that having a concept depends only on sense data, which may be subconscious. So we really couldn't pick out instances until enough meaning was added to the sense data to get a conscious perception, after which we can distinguish instantiations. Well, this is cheating a bit. However, a very minimal amount of meaning could be added to bring the sense data to consciousness where we could make discriminations and know what concept it is. However, the sense data concept can still exist subconsciously. The reason is that the amount of information necessary to instantiate a sense datum concept, whether primitive or complex, might be only finite and could be handled computationally. Causal objects send only finite amounts of information to sensory organs. So it is easy to *have* concepts which requires only finite information coming from causal objects. This is part of the *theory* that causal objects are embedded in. This is why it takes only finite amounts of information to determine extension which is a causal level concept. And this is why the Churchlands' neural nets can *have* concepts and why a TV set is able to create a sense datum picture.

Of course, the question arises, are computers learning to have concepts on the basis of primitive sensory qualities or entire Gestalts? Well, it seems that when shown an object, a computer gropes around and looks for primitive sensory elements like lines and colors and feels along to find out how these primitive elements are assembled into the total concept instantiation. Experimentation in this area has lead many cognitive scientists to posit that the brain/mind is doing the same thing. But I don't believe so.

But before we elaborate further on the difference between *having* and *knowing* a concept, we should ask, what is a concept anyway? Well, nobody seems to have a theory as to what they are that convinces most people. A simple definition is that a personal concept is an abstract category of *perceptual* objects in the world that have some essence in common. It must be stressed that concepts appear only at the perceptual level as categories. So they must be explained only at the perceptual level. The only concepts at the causal level are those necessary to define causal level theoretical entities.

Regarding the ontological status of concepts, in our opinion, a concept is a something: it exists in some way, just like thoughts and feelings exist in their own way. But whatever the status of concepts ontologically, we can talk cogently about *having* a concept and the *meaning* of a concept.

AVI.2 Sense Data Primitive Concepts

Let's look at the most primitive level of concepts which are sense data concepts. In Appendicitis V, we discussed sense data traces and perceptual representations. Briefly, sense data are mental traces that are created by the mind as it interacts with information coming from causal objects out in the world. Concepts come about because with a pinch of meaning, we can bring a sense datum to consciousness where we can see the components of the sense datum. Our visual system puts various components of sense data into categories that have some essence in common. It is irrelevant as to whether these categories have some abstract properties in common or even a justification of them. The brain does this on its own accord on the basis of the way it is wired to form concept cylinders. Of course this wiring came about through evolution, so there must be some instrumental basis for categories, but we don't have to worry about what this is. In any event, these abstract categories are our personal concepts. I hope this isn't circular. Thus the mind creates

instances of a primitive concept of STRAIGHT LINE on the basis of seeing certain causal level arrangements of molecules, and seeing this on many occasions. The personal concept formed in this way is made on the basis of these *instantiations*. In this way, we get primitive sense data concepts denoted with small capital letters, STRAIGHT LINE, CIRCLE, OR REDNESS.

It should be noted that the components that instantiate sensory concepts at this point in the perceptual process are only sense data components and, as such, have no meaning. If we add meaning, we then have instantiations of *perceptual* concepts. If we add meaning to the curved line sense datum, we get an *instantiation* of the total concept CURVED LINE. Fodor confuses this important point. He says, "… semantic decomposition of the lexicon parallels sensory decomposition of percept" (Fodor, '81, 217). Well, this might be simple carelessness. Semantic decomposition parallels *perceptual* decomposition, not *sensory* decomposition, because meaning is part of the perceptual process, whereas there probably is no sensory decomposition at all.

AVI.3 Having Primitive Sense Data Concepts

It should be emphasized is that *having* concepts can be attained by discriminating only *sense data* components. Of course, to do this may require a pinch of meaning to get the sense datum into consciousness. But the meaning present in percepts is not necessarily involved in discriminating them. You can pick out examples of a concept CURVED LINE only on the basis of having the concept, CURVED LINE often with very little consciousness involved. As explained in the text, having a primitive concept involves only a concept cylinder that picks out instances. Also, when we *have* a concept like RED, this is really a recognitional ability. But our perception analysis claimed that we *create* a quality such as redness when we see certain causal objects and project it out to the causal object. Is this inconsistent? For consistency, we have to specify that when we say we recognize RED, this is an abbreviation for saying we are again projecting our sensation of redness or our red sense datum to a causal object because we learned to project this sense datum upon exposure to red frequency light. *Having* a concept is simply the ability to project the same sense datum to similar piles of molecules.

Now Jerry Fodor applies his ideas about representations to learning and having concepts. For example, we form a concept of SWAN somehow and that all swans are white. Fodor explains, "…if we assume (a) that the organism *represents* the relevant experiences as experiences of…" certain animals which we see are swans and that all swans are white; and (b) "…the concept learning task as essentially involving inductive extrapolation [which] commits one to postulating a representational system in which the relevant inductions are carried through" (41); and (c) "that one of the hypotheses that the organism entertains about its environment is the hypothesis that perhaps…"all these kinds of animals are swans and that all these swans are white (Fodor, '75, 37). Fodor says that if every time you see a certain-looking bird, it is a swan, and you see it is white, you make an induction and a hypothesis that all the birds with this look are swans and they are always white. But how does a little kid make a fancy thing like a "hypothesis"?

This problem is brought out by the question of how the brain jumps to its final conclusion that certain birds are swans and that they are always white, without having the concept of white swans in the first place, regardless of how fancy a language it is using, and how many times it sees swans? Fodor papers over the whole problem with another fiat statement in his *Concept* book: we can think of "concepts as mental representations…" (Fodor, '98, 25). But how do we form a representation of a *concept* out of a whole string of experiences? Or a representation out of a bunch of other representations? Representations are copies of particular mental events. How will something particular

help us understand something abstract like a concept? Induction has always been a problem in analytic philosophy and it isn't going to be of much use in analyzing concepts either.

Fodor asks "…what, beside hypothesis testing, could explain why you generally get WATER from experiences with water and not, as it might be, from experiences with giraffes?" (Fodor, '98, 150). The reason is that it is interaction with *causal* water, H_2O, that causes water sense data traces to be created by the mind, not causal giraffes. This eventuates in *having* the sense data concept WATER. This is a *push* process and not a pull process as is induction. There is no one mental representation for a concept. Sense data traces caused by all the experienced instantiations of a concept *pushes* the growth of neurological cylinders in the circuitry of the brain so that we can pick out instances. The process never knows where it is going. Even though the cylinder formed from this one experience is pretty skeletal, it is a concept nevertheless. Also, the cylinders would be able to determine the extension of water because they *have* the concept WATER, even though it is only a sense data concept, and not a perceptual WATER concept. Fodor's account can't account for *having* a concept with one experience.

When science comes along and tells us that H_2O is responsible for establishing our WATER concept, then when we start to attach meaning to instantiations of WATER, we know we're attaching meaning to the right stuff and to the right ability. As we accrue meaning items during these experiences and we get an infinite number of them, we get a meaning cloud surrounding the series of cylinders in the brain which enables us to not only have the ability to pick out instances of the sense data concept, WATER, but know what water means. In this bootstrapping way, we develop the complete WATER concept.

Fodor's analysis suffers from confusion between causal and perceptual objects. He does come close to this distinction when he discusses natural kinds, but he draws lines in the wrong places. He talks about natural kind concepts and natural kind concepts *as such*. Is this a distinction without a difference? Well, ironically, he brings up poetry, no less, and the ancient poet Homer and his WATER concept. Fodor doesn't think Homer's water concept is the same as ours because our WATER concept includes knowledge that water is composed of H_2O, whereas Homer's WATER concept doesn't include this knowledge. Well, as we explained in Sect. AII.2, this knowledge is a very small part of the meaning of a WATER concept. Fodor says, "...WATER wasn't, for Homer, a concept of a natural kind *as such*; and for us it is" (157). I don't think this distinction is important enough for a separate ontology. He follows this with, "We're locked to *being water* via a chemical-cum-metaphysical theory, that specifies its essence, and that is quite a different mechanism of semantic access from the ones that Homer relied on" (157). This sentence is a real mess. Our WATER concept doesn't come from "locking" onto water, whatever that means. We add meaning to our sense data WATER concept to get our WATER concept the same way Homer did. We simply add a little more knowledge than Homer had, but that has very little to do with perceptual water. The chemical-cum-mumbo-jumbo theory, that "specifies its essence", is a theory about causal water, H_2O, and gives a criterion for determining the extension of water. A chemical machine could determine this but it has nothing to do with meaning even if we really had any Fodor-induced semantic access, *which we don't*. The meaning of 'water' and the concept WATER has to do with *perceptual* water, and very little to do with H_2O in most minds.

Fodor uses the knowledge we have of causal water to make a very unimportant distinction between Homer's no H_2O-WATER concept, and our H_2O-WATER concept to demarcate a natural kind: we have a natural kind concept and Homer doesn't. Well, in my opinion the idea of natural kind is a bit too important to waste on this small distinction. I think our concept analysis would profit a great deal by saving the natural

kind idea for the distinction between causal and perceptual worlds. H_2O would be a natural kind, and water not.

Sometimes in the literature, people talk about *comparing* a new representation instantiating a concept, to a representation of the concept. But there is no representation in the brain for a concept, and so there is nothing to compare with. The new representation either falls within the cylinder specifying the concept, or it does not, and either the representation elicits a response of recognition or is does not. There are no representations of concepts.

A question at this point is, should we identify the concept with the series of cylinders, or with an *ability* to pick out instances. We should keep in mind that *having* a concept is an elliptical phrase since there is nothing to *have* except an ability or an ever-growing series of neurological cylinders. Even though the series of cylinders may approach an asymptote, it never gets to the end of the process. This is a kind of "push" theory of concept attainment. You push along the development of a concept; but this doesn't imply that you get to an end product. Maybe the concept is whatever the cylinder is at any point in time.

We must keep in mind, however, that we are dealing only at the sensory level of sense data traces of instances of concepts. So far there is no meaning in this picture. This suggests that we really can't be using words and sentences to describe what we're doing because these things have meaning. We have to look at COW as a meaningless sense data neurological cylinder in the brain. Linguistically, what corresponds to the sense datum COW concept is the *syntax* of sentences using the word 'cow', and how 'cow' appears grammatically in sentences.

At some points, Fodor admits that *there is no particular representation that can be identified with the idea of a concept*. You can't be drawn to something during a process, unless what you're drawn to something that already exists. This is true, but our learning experiences with concepts get around this problem. After a child has experienced a lot of instantiations which he recognizes with his concept cylinder, the child can *learn* that 'concept' is a word for an abstraction such that all the instantiations the child could possibly ever experience, even an infinite number, create a category. This is part of the *meaning* of the word 'concept' and where we get the idea of a universal or an abstraction.

This analysis is supported by the idea that machines can *have* concepts. They simply feel along lines and corners for primitive concepts and features of complex concepts. For the arrangement of components of sense data, we discussed in Sect. AV.5 the idea that the finite information content may correspond to the finite syntax of sentences used to describe sense data and determine only *extensions*, and not full meanings. This is why cognitive scientists like Fodor think that *having* concepts is computational, and that the mind must have a language of thought to bounce components around in the mind and assemble them to create concepts. Fodor's computational theory of mind assumes the mind is doing the same thing. But this is not obvious and probably not even true. However, *understanding* a concept involves infinite entities and processes and becomes involved only during *perceptual* experiences, as opposed to sensory experiences.

AVI.4 HAVING COMPLEX SENSORY CONCEPTS

Now most causal objects in the world will create sense data traces in the brain that are made up of a number of primitive sense data components. At the first level, we have primitive sense data concepts like CURVED LINE, REDNESS, SALTY, BANG, etc. They don't have meaning even though we may have to add a little meaning to bring them to consciousness. For vision, there are levels of complexity of concepts. The second level above primitive are combinations of sense date components put together in a particular arrangement, such TRIANGLE made up of three STRAIGHT LINES connected at ANGLES. These are primitive

complex concepts because they are made of primitive sense data concepts. After meaning is added to a sense datum, the result is a perception in the mind which can also be an instance of a concept, a *perceptual* concept: TRIANGLE. Car wheels are made up of a bunch of circles and straight lines which are the spokes. So we get CAR WHEELS and when meaning is added, CAR WHEELS.

At the third level of complex concepts are *features* of objects, like the wheels of a car or the tail of a cow. At the next level are concepts like buildings, bridges, cars, beds, tables and chairs that have a number of features made up of sense data elements. Finally, we get to cities, companies, businesses, and nations which are the most complex concepts of all. What is common to all these complex concepts is that they are made up of a number of features which, in turn, are made up of sense data elements that are concepts themselves. Of course, if you go far enough, you get all the way down to the primitive sense data concepts we mentioned, CURVED and STRAIGHT LINES, SPOTS, RED, etc.

The important thing this model stresses is the holistic nature of concepts especially sense data concepts. The mind/brain, in initial stages of learning to have concepts, does not create representations of primitive elements, or even features, and then put them together to form the whole instantiation. At this stage of learning, to *have* a concept COW is not the same as having the concept of EYES-NOSE-EARS-LEGS-SPOTS-TAIL-ETC. ARRANGED IN COWLIKE WAY. The COW concept is an integral concept all its own. At times, Fodor seems to suggest that we *infer* the components of a complex concept. I don't think this is true at all. This brings up an interesting question. At the childhood learning level, if a child learns to have a COW concept, does this child automatically have the sense data concept EAR, for example, or TAIL or the BROWN color? I think he would if you named,,the feature, but if not, it's a close call probably depending on how observant the child is.

When neural nets learn to have concepts, nobody has been able to find out where the features are in the neural net's weighting functions. Even if we could identify connections of the net that are most responsive to a certain feature, this is a pretty creative idea of a representation, which is supposed to be some kind of copy. The net doesn't have a mind to make a picture. And even though our representations are neural systems of cell assemblies, brains have supervening minds which give us sense data copies having components. But it may be impossible to find how these components supervene on particular brain circuitry.

AVI.5 MEANING IN ARRANGEMENT OF COMPONENTS OF SENSE DATA CONCEPTS.

An important problem comes up at this point which is what is the status of the information contained in the way primitive components of sense data trace are arranged? As explained in Sect. AV.5, the position taken here is that this information is contained in the TRIANGLE concept. However, as experience with instantiations continue, this information can be utilized by the mind to add to the *meaning* of the total concept that it is made up of primitive components. Also, part of the meaning of the total concept can include the fact that the total concept is composed of meaningful components that can in turn be concepts themselves, functionally related in certain ways to form an integral whole. But in the initial stages of concept development, there may be very little of this meaning of the components dragged into the total concept. You don't have to know very much meaning of what a line is and what an angle is to learn the meaning of TRIANGLE. TRIANGLE is learned as a total gestalt and its meaning is attached to the growing series of neurological cylinders associated with the total concept. Meanings of components are not necessary, although they probably do enter concept meaning in some ways.

We are basically dividing the synthesis aspect of a concept into a finite information sense data portion that refers only to the physical arrangement of sense data components, and an infinite information portion that *eventually* includes the meaning of the components and how they are functionally arranged to form the integral meaningful concept. It may be difficult to make this division. However, if we keep with the view that meaning involves infinite information states, then the arrangement of components in a sense datum being finitely specified, would suggest that this is simply information necessary to create the total non-conscious sense datum and has not yet emerged as part of the meaning of the conscious perceptual concept. As we discussed this in Sect. AV.5, the functional relationship between components would be part of the meaning of a *sense impression* concept. Some of what follows lends credence to this view.

AVI.6 COMPLEX CONCEPTS AND MEANING

Let's turn our attention to the meaning of concepts. This is an area that is very puzzling, because writers on the topic talk about meanings of concepts as though a concept itself has a definite meaning. But it is *personal* meanings that are relevant to our mental and physical behavior. And of course, it is behavior that determines what we are and who we are as human beings. So, what is the personal meaning people have for their concepts? I don't know how philosophers would answer this because they never ask the question. We might shed some light on this question by looking at how a child builds up meaning for her concepts.

A child, in the course of learning about cows and seeing many of them in a wide variety of circumstances, builds up an infinite repertoire of sense data traces. As we have described, these traces create a growing neurological cylinder which enables the child to pick out instantiations of the concept. But other kinds of mentality form a meaning cloud around the cylinder, such as knowledge, beliefs, counterfactuals, truth conditions, memories, and any other mental items associated with the concept in the mind of a particular person. Of course, as a child learns, the individual representations created during perceptual experiences included in the cylinder will have meanings that get increasingly comprehensive as life goes on. An older child's representation established upon seeing a cow, will have associated with it greater amounts of meaning specific to this representation than those of a younger child. The suggestion here is that the total of all the meanings associated with the individual representations created by each perceptual experience instantiating the concept — this total meaning cloud is what constitutes the *personal* meaning of a concept like CURVED LINE or color.

Now that we have some idea of the meaning of a *personal* concept, we can handle *public* concepts pretty much the same as for public meanings we discussed in Appendicitis I on Meaning. However, I want to stress that I haven't heard of anyone who knows what a public concept is. But if we consider this task carefully, we find that there's no such thing as the public *having* a concept because the public does not recognize anything. What the public has are *meanings* of concepts and phrases used to express them. As discussed previously, a public concept meaning will be arrived at by lexicographers who crystallize a meaning that overlaps the personal meanings most people have.

AVI.7 ABSTRACTIONS

In the text we defined sense data concepts as *abstractions*. We have used the word 'universal' for the total public concept. The question for this section is, are there universals in this sense, and if so what is their nature? The very first sentence in D.M. Armstrong's very detailed exposition of universals is "It is argued in this work, first, that there are universals...which exist independently of the classifying mind (Armstrong, '78, xiii). Well, this tells me that he isn't even going to recognize personal concepts.

And yet his book is sprinkled with references to what could not be anything but personal concepts. The question to be answered is, how do we categorize things in the world into universals and what are the conditions for using universal words, called *predicates?* Armstrong discusses a number of theories to answer this question. For example, he says, "According to Predicate Nominalism, an object's possession of (say) the property, *being white,* is completely determined by the fact that the predicate 'white' applies to this object" (17). However, Armstrong seems to take the classical view that sensory qualities like color and shape are properties of objects out in the world. Of course, if this is the case, there is the problem that if the application of the predicate 'white' is in the driver's seat determining what things are white, how do we justify applying 'white' to particular objects?

This is why he rejects Predicate Nominalism. He says, "Each white thing has the same sort of relation to the predicate 'white' "(19). Then he says, "they have this type of relation to any token of the predicate-type 'white' " (19). Well, how do we characterize this "type" without an infinite regress. I don't see where white things have a *type* of relation to anything. White things have a *particular* relation to particular 'white' tokens, *unus restrictio.* We can even name it the *white* relation.

In Armstrong's account of perception, Predicate Nominalism has enough problems without manufacturing more. It still has the problem of explaining the *basis* of applying the word 'white' tokens to white things. Armstrong shows that there are similar difficulties with other kinds of nominalism. After a lot of meanderings, he opts for a view called *Immanent Realism* which is basically the rather simple view that there are particular things in the world which have properties that often instantiate universals. But he then has the problem that Fodor and Dretske had as to how we can be sure that our representations of instantiations of universals correspond to the right ones so that we can apply the right predicates to them? Well neither Armstrong nor anyone else is going to get anywhere with this if they think that concepts are out in the world, so to speak.

Of course, in the perception account given here, the explanation for our legitimately applying the predicate 'white' to white things is that the white sensory quality created by the mind/brain due to certain causal objects reflecting certain frequencies of light into the visual sensory organ — this sensory quality of whiteness is projected out to this kind of causal object. We learn to *have* a sense datum concept of WHITE, which is a personal concept that nobody else will ever know "what it is like" as we develop a neurological cylinder. We add meaning to our personal sense data instantiations to get a sense impression. Then we abstract a concept which has the meaning that the category created could include an infinite number of instantiations a person could have. 'Whitehood', or the symbol WHITE is the *name* or label we give to this concept. They do not "exist independently of the classifying mind" as Armstrong says, but are abstracted from personal sense impression concepts, which are clearly creations of the classifying mind.

AVI.8 Having Vrs. Meaning of Concepts

Fodor makes no attempt to make the distinction between having a concept and the meaning of a concept, and as a result his discussion is a real a mish-a-ghass when it comes to theories of concepts. He says he can't tell elm trees from beech trees. We'll assume he doesn't have an ELM concept *and* he doesn't have a BEECH concept. Then he says: "...there is *nothing that you have to believe, there are no inferences you have to accept,* to have the concept ELM" (Fodor, '95, 37). We can very much agree with this, but we have to keep in mind that this is true only if he is talking about *having* concepts, which is computational. He immediately jumps to the conclusion that "...psychological processes may be

computational even though externalism is true..." (38). I really wish these guys would keep categories straight. Psychological anything involves content, mental and at the descriptive level. Computational is finite state, syntactical and at the causal level.

The botanist could teach Fodor about sensory qualities like the texture of the bark, shape of leaves, shape and size of tree etc. Fodor could become very proficient at telling elms from beeches and *have* a concept of both without knowing important things about these trees. If all Fodor has done is to *have* these concepts, we certainly hope Fodor doesn't go into the tree farm business, or into the furniture business, which involves lots of "thinking", where you would have to know what these trees are. On the other hand, when the botanist tells him something about *content*, he may talk about cell DNA, means of nutrients rising through the tree, types of grain, means of photosynthesis, what the wood from these trees is used for, etc. This knowledge would be helpful to enable Fodor to *use* the wood from these trees but he may still not be very good at telling elms from beeches.

In another example, Fodor gives as a partial meaning of 'chair' as 'portable seat for one'. But he adds, "But someone might know this about 'chair' and still not be able to *tell* about some given object... whether or not *it* is a chair" (Fodor, '75, 62). This is an extremely interesting comment. What this says, and it is an important point, is that you can know the meaning of a concept, and yet not know how to determine its *extension*, i.e., without *having* the concept. But then Fodor changes his mind, and says, "Learning what the predicates of a language mean involves learning a determination of the *extension* [italics mine] of these predicates" (Fodor, '75, 63). I think he got it right the first time. In any event, this example and many others show that Putnam's and Fodor's view using extensions to determine meanings is not viable.

Also, we shouldn't confuse knowing and having just because sometimes you can pick out instantiations on the basis of knowing meaning. Blind people can often pick out instantiations on the basis of meaning without *having* a visual concept at all. They may have very elaborate meanings of concepts, more elaborate than sighted people, because not having sight induces you to become much more sensitive to meanings, as many novels about blind people illustrate. However, being blind would prevent a person from *having* a visual concept. But what Fodor *doesn't* point out it that the opposite is also true. You may be able to have a concept and determine the extension of a concept on the basis of recognizing sense data components and not know anything about content.

When a child *has* a HORSE concept on the basis of just a few exposures, but he doesn't yet know what the word 'horse' means, this ability will have no influence on most kinds of the child's behavior. He won't want to ride a horse, or feed a horse or call over a horse, because these types of behaviors rely on the knowing what a horse is, what 'horse' means. I learned to *have* the HORSE concept as a little kid on a farm one summer. I could tell horses from non-horses. But one day, my uncle said he was going to put me *on* the horse. I said to myself, are you crazy?

Fodor asks about the constituents of complex concepts, "...*which inferences constitute which concepts?* (Fodor, '98, 37). In my opinion, there are no inferences at all. A child learning to have the concept of a cow may not have a concept of an eye, a tail, brown color, or any other individual feature or quality. And he doesn't infer that the COW concept has features with their own meanings. Children form a series of neurological cylinders that enables them to recognize cows. Along the way in learning the meaning of the COW concept, we learn lots of things about cows. We might also learn to have concepts of components and learn the meaning of those components as being part of the total COW concept. Part of this meaning is to understand how features are assembled to form a whole concept. These are meaning-laden processes that are not necessary for having a concept.

Computers may be able to *have* concepts, but they clearly can't handle the *meaning* of concepts. Being only finite state machines, they cannot comprehend the idea that a concept can cover an infinite number of instantiations. So computers know nothing about universals. This is reflected in the fact that computers don't have real languages that involve abstracting from an infinite pool. There are no quantifiers in computer languages.

Returning to the having versus meaning distinction, there are some tricky examples that force us to keep the difference straight. What happens when we *entertain* a concept, like when we imagine a triangle? Do we imagine a general triangle or cow? Do we assemble primitive concepts? Since this is a conscious undertaking, it has to involve representations. If so what are those. When I imagine a triangle, of course, I get some kind of representation of a triangle, and it looks to be one I haven't seen before: a very clean, crisp triangle like the ones Plato talked about. And it doesn't seem to have much meaning, but possibly some. How is the mind arriving at this representation? Fodor would explain the synthesis by enlisting his language of thought that grabs representations of components off the shelf and glues them together. But what's on the shelf and how did it get there? I can't find anyone even talking about this problem. A wild but plausible idea is that we simply send some brain energy into the triangle concept cylinder and it takes a random path that subvenes a triangle that was never seen. Enough meaning is added to make it conscious.

Now as a child develops, her concepts will become more elaborate, and accumulate meaning. Part of this meaning is that instantiations of the TRIANGLE concept will have components put together in a certain way, i.e., lines joined at angles. This meaning will be part of the meaning cloud associated with the concept TRIANGLE. So on particular occasions when attempting to imagine an abstract triangle, perhaps this meaning may come into play and enable her to *synthesize* an imaginary triangle never seen before from component representations. However, when a young child who only has a TRIANGLE concept imagines a triangle, her concept is a sense data one only, which would not include the component aspect of meaning; and so she would not synthesize a brand new representation synthesized out of components of triangles. She would probably bring to mind a *particular* representation of a particular experience of seeing a triangle.

AVI.9 INDIVIDUATING CONCEPTS

Let's get to the problem of individuating and identifying concepts. He introduces a quality or characteristic of concepts which he calls Method of Presentation, MOP, that will enable us to individuate concepts. MOPs will have the added attraction that they will lend concepts causal powers in thought processes. He doesn't tell us what MOPs are, but slowly deduces what they must be by the process of elimination. But as we shall see, Fodor is like Bertrand Russell's characterization of Aquinas. He knows where he wants to go; he just works backwards until he arrives at the assumptions he needs, regardless of viability.

Fodor is still all wet when it comes to water and H_2O. He still thinks both have to have the same content because according to Kripke, water *is* H_2O. But somehow they are different concepts. What a mess. So he needs a way to differentiate these two different concepts which he thinks have the same meaning. And so he turns once again to Method of Presentation, MOP, which are going to be the key to individuating concepts. As we explained ad nauseum, we do not need to MOP up the water controversy because the water concepts are the same with the same meanings. Not only that, but there are no such things as modes of presentation because the world of causal objects doesn't present anything except puffs of air and light photons.

WATER and H_2O are different concepts because they not only have different meanings, but are at different causal levels. But is Fodor softening up on the water-H_2O issue? He says, "...*referents* can't individuate concepts because lots of different concepts can have the same referent" (Fodor, '98, 19). Thus, you can't individuate concepts with MOPS if MOPS are referents. Well, this is very clever. He's back to his old trick of demoting meaning to referents, which are veiled extensions. Of course, you can have lots of different concepts with the same *causal* referent, just like Jocasta and Oedipus's mother. What Fodor is quietly gliding past is the fact that these "lots of different concepts" do not have the same *meaning* because meaning has very little to do with reference or extension. Fodor is just knocking down a straw man. As we shall see, what you can't have is lots of different concepts with the same *meaning*, even though you may have a number of meanings for the same concept. The reason is that learning to *have* concepts comes first, which makes them lumpier. By the time we learn *meanings* of concepts, it's too late to make up new concepts for *every* different subtle meaning even though individual meanings sometimes give rise to new concepts. The bottom line is that meanings are not referents, they are not extensions, they are not out in the world, and they are not finite computational entities — just for starters.

Fodor has an additional factor to throw into the mix: causality. He says, "mental objects are *ipso facto* available as proximal causes of mental processes..."(19). Since concepts have something to do with mentality, this is supposed to suggest that MOPS are going to have to be something mental. (Now it's a mystery as to why Fodor doesn't apply this reasoning from the need for representations to have causal powers in the mind to the necessity for representations' content to be "in the head".) In any event, Fodor now has us backed into a corner. MOPS for individuating concepts can't be meanings because meanings are referents and referents are too skinny for the job for individuating concepts; they can't be public because they couldn't get at mentality to push and shove mental items around, let alone bodies. So what's left? You might have guessed it:

syntax. Here is something mental, enabling causation because "in the head", and something computers can handle. Isn't there a story of an ugly Greek god who, to win over his love, slays his competitors one by one, leaving the poor damsel stuck with him. The object of Fodor's philosophical love is syntax.

When Fodor sees meaning individuating concepts or causing mental or physical behavior, he looks for some difference in syntax and claims the work is being done by the syntax. This is incisively illustrated in the following sentence. "Morning Star beliefs have the same conditions of semantic evaluation as Evening Star beliefs, but they implicate...different syntactic objects and are therefore different beliefs with different causal powers" (39). I don't see this. If they have the same conditions of semantic evaluation, it means Fodor can see the Morning Star in the evening. (I want to see this.) Now Fodor knows a lot more about syntax than I do. But I don't see where these two star words differ syntactically at all, at least not enough to cause different behavior, like looking for these stars at different times of the day. (As an aside here, I'm only an amateur at philosophy, but I don't see how it is possible to decide matters of syntax other than at the causal level.)

As we explained in detail in Sect. AII.2, the Morning Star and Evening Star are entirely different perceptual objects with entirely different *meanings* that are responsible for their differently caused beliefs and behavior. The only way Fodor can shift the engine over to syntax is to demote meaning by equating it with extension so that the two stars have the same *alleged* meaning which renders meaning impotent to individuate concepts. Well, extensions have very little to do with meaning, and although extension is involved in *having* concepts, it has very little to do with the *meaning* of concepts, of *knowing* concepts. *Having* the concepts of these two stars does not enable you to tell them apart which is exactly the problem the ancients had. You have to know when and where to look for them. Only the *meaning* of these concepts will enable you to do that.

There are examples of the same syntax but different meanings and different behavior. In May, the bartender says to Jake that Tony Blair is driving by, and Jake keeps drinking. In June after Jake learns that Tony Blair is the Prime Minister, the same bartender says to Jake that Tony Blair is driving by, and now, Jake gets up to see what Tony Blair looks like. The syntax is the same, but meaning has changed and so has the behavior. It is *meaning* that is doing the work here. Perhaps there are examples where syntax does causal work. But neither Fodor nor anyone else has shown us an example to my knowledge. If syntax can't be shown to do causal work, and meaning can, I don't see what advantages there are to individuating concepts with informationally starved syntax when meaning will do just fine.

It seems to me, Fodor's is able to enlist syntax to do all the work simply because syntax does make some fine distinctions. Even though I'm among the billions of humans who don't fully understand syntax, it seems to me that semantics makes at least as many fine distinctions as syntax. Intuitively, it seems reasonable that you can make finer distinctions with infinite state entities than with finite state entities. Syntax involves finite information content, which is reflected in its correspondence with sense data concepts like shapes and colors which also have no meaning coming from the causal level. This enables us to discriminate *having* concepts, What creates confusion is that it is difficult to determine what is more basic and what derivative. It's like confusing fans and windmills. As a kid I learned what a fan does, and when seeing a windmill out in the country, I wondered why we needed to make a wind outdoors.

Having disposed of meaning as not being very meaningful, he can now leave the semantic load behind and induce syntax into doing the causal work concepts do. We looked at the untenability of this line of reasoning in Sect. AV.8, where we showed that WATER and H_2O are different concepts because the WATER concept is instantiated by *perceptual* water, and H_2O is instantiated by *causal* water. And they do their mental work on this basis. Meaning does a fine job of individuating concepts; why does he think syntax, can do any better?

One of the puzzling things about Fodor's discussion is that since MOPs are mental, then in order to do causal mental work, shouldn't that necessitate that concepts themselves be mental as well? But at another time, he says, "Concepts are *public*; they're the sorts of things people can, and do, *share*" (Fodor, '98, 28). It's the same confusion that arises regarding meaning. It's like the "public" bathroom, *the* bathroom, in the center of town that we all "share". Well, there are no public bathrooms in the center of town (except in France) and if there are public concepts, they never do any causal work. *Individuals* have concepts and act and think on the basis of the *personal* meanings of these concepts. This is why humans respond very differently to different instantiations of the same concept, whereas simple animals, who have mostly only sense data concepts having almost no meaning, do not.

The view in the literature seems to be that concepts are public and that we have to measure and define our personal concepts in terms of them. Two problems arise with this view. 1) How do we determine what that public concept is? 2) How do we know if our personal concepts are the same as the real thing out in public? The first idea that comes to mind is that they have to be *similar*. But Fodor shows that you can't determine whether two concepts are similar unless you already have the means to identify and differentiate the concept itself. Of course, he isn't going to provide these ideas a lucid description because he is really setting us up. What he wants to do is what he's been up to all through his books, which is to depreciate meaning. First, he tries to show that meaning can't individuate concepts, and now he's got us thinking that we can't even compare our concepts to see if they are the same or similar. Amidst all the confusion will arise the great Phoenix, MOPPING up the mess with syntax, which will perform every task we need.

You could think of a public concept (universal) as involving a counterfactual. A public concept might be the personal concept the average man *would* have, if there were such a thing as the average man. It is an abstraction made up out of the personal meanings people have developed. Of course, this public meaning, in turn, is used to teach the next generation of children to know the concept. They develop their own personal meanings in the process. This is why concepts can drift over hundreds of years. 'Awful' used mean full of awe.

To determine whether or not we have similar concepts, we can simply show pictures the way Quine did to determine meaning. The more two people agree on what falls under a concept, the more similar their perceptual concepts are. This is the same way that stereotypes or prototypes are established as explained in the text. There's no problem in comparing our concepts to something public because the public concept is an abstraction *constructed out of our personal concepts*. (We can stop looking for the enemy, because the enemy is us, said Peanuts, I think). If we want to compare with public concepts in our town, we just nominate someone to act as the average man.

The situation is somewhat different regarding causal objects. Our concepts of causal objects really are public because they are determined scientifically by finite state processes and are part of a finite *theory*. So our personal causal concepts are going to be exact copies of the public concept. There are no perceptual objects at the causal level. I've never seen any H_2O and I've never seen any H. Scientists tell me what they are, and I believe them.

Fodor's next gambit to corner us into accepting syntax as the way to individuate concepts is to get meaning out of the concept business by trading on the notion that words and sentences are not definable. To me, this would imply that no two corresponding concepts would be the same either. Fodor is again into his agenda of depreciating meaning. Of course, this would only apply to complex concepts that have alternative descriptions involving other concepts. But this may be the thin edge of the wedge to get syntax into the picture. Now this problem doesn't refer to compositionality which we'll get into in the next section. But here, the issue is meaning: whether a concept has the same *meaning* as its elements. Of course he doesn't even bother to define 'definition'. We'll just have to assume it's another string of words with the same meaning.

Regarding his assumption that you can't define words, phrases, or sentences, I agree with this wholeheartedly, even though he implicitly has to be talking about personal meanings. And he is really talking about *exact* definitions, as opposed to rough-and-ready definitions. Of course, in terms of personal meanings, no two words or sentences ever mean exactly the same, simply because they are infinite clouds and are never used in exactly the same way. Public meanings which are derivative upon personal meanings should reflect this fact, so that you can't have public meaning synonymy either.

Fodor tries to throw a fast ball by us before we even get settled into the batter's box. He says, "… practically all words (/concepts) are undefinable. And, of course, if a word (/concept) doesn't have a definition, then its definition can't be its meaning" (Fodor, '98, 45). He also says, "If there are no definable words, then, of course, there are no complex representations [here concepts] that correspond to them" (42). For, if there were, then the words in the definiens would express a complex concept which would have to be made up from the conceptual constituents corresponding to the words in the definiendum. And often they do not. For example, if the definition of 'bachelor' were unmarried man, then the concept BACHELOR would be a composite of two concepts, UNMARRIED and MAN. But as Pope John illustrates, he is an example of UNMARRIED, and an example of MAN, but not an instance of BACHELOR. But Fodor wants to wind up with the same meaning for 'bachelor' and 'unmarried male' in order to get meaning out of the concept business

altogether. I think Fodor has it backwards. It seems to me that once Fodor accepts that BACHELOR and UNMARRIED MAN are different complex concepts, his goose is cooked. The meanings of words that express concepts have to be *at least* as articulated as the syntax of sentences using them. So in cases where the syntax is the same, meaning is the only way to differentiates them.

Concept sieves can't be less fine than the words that express them. What this amounts to is that even though meaning may be an unnecessarily fine sieve to individuate concepts, syntax is too coarse. If there is a difference in syntax, this will create a difference in meaning even if only slightly or a different sense. Since syntax is finite state, and reflects only sense data components, and may enable us to differentiate *having* concepts, meanings could be very different and syntax would not be a fine enough sieve to individuate *knowing* concepts.

But is it really the case that words don't have definitions? It seems to me that words *do* have definitions and they are *public* meanings. What they don't have are *exact* definitions because they depend on greatly varying *personal* meanings. What Fodor is trying to get us to agree with is that since words and sentences don't have *exact* definitions, then the structure of their definitions do not exhaust their full meanings. And consequently, the corresponding complex concept that the definiens words or sentences express won't have a structure and an identity that conforms to the structure of the original concept. This might enable Fodor to break the connection between concepts and their meanings.

There is an analogy in physics. No two bodies can occupy the same position at the same time. Well, no two words or sentences can possibly have the exact same usage. So their definitions could never be *exactly* the same. But if all we could use were exact definitions, we could never distill public concepts (universals) and no child could ever learn a language. As we learn language, we get rough-and-ready definitions which gets us going in using the phrase. As we get corrected or approved as kids we build up a personal definition that is usable most of the time. That is part of the human condition.

But how will the syntax of concepts do any better in this regard, especially since words and phrases definitions are the finer sieve, and concepts the lumpier? How could you possibly find a difference between two concepts or between a complex concept and the sum of its constituents, how would you do it except through meanings. And if you use syntax to distinguish concepts, different syntax creates different meanings, even if only slightly, and you can still rely on meaning to individuate concepts. It seems to me, meanings can perfectly well slice the world thin enough to differentiate concepts because as he acknowledges, every word and every sentence has a distinctive definition.

AVI.10 COMPLEX CONCEPTS, COMPOSITION, AND DISCRIMINATION

Fodor's next attack on the role of meaning in individuating concepts and the promotion of syntax for this job involves composition. Composability refers to whether or not a concept is *composed* of some of its constituents or elements. There are two questions that must be addressed in this regard, and Fodor doesn't separate these questions. There is the question as to whether a putative composition is necessary for *having* a concept, and the second question as to whether composition is necessary for *knowing* a concept. For example, if you have the concept BROWN COW, would you have the sense data concepts BROWN and COW? If you know the meaning of the concept BROWN COW would know what BROWN means and what COW means?

A popular approach to concept identification and individuation has been what's called a *prototype* or *stereotype*, which we mentioned above. A concept is identified with a prototype. But prototypes are probably too lumpy to serve as a means to individuate concepts. The

pet fish example illustrates this as well. "...a goldfish is a poorish example of fish, and a poorish example of a pet, but it's a prototypical example of pet fish" (Fodor, '98, 102). Also prototypes of a pet and of a fish doesn't provide anything like a prototype of a pet fish. And so prototypes don't compose and couldn't be used to individuate concepts.

Concerning composability of complex concepts, it seems to me we have already rejected the idea that concept meanings compose because this really reduces to whether words for a concept are definable. This agrees with a *definitional* theory which says that a concept depends on its constituents *necessarily*. But for practical purposes, Fodor relaxes this requirement and allows that a concept depends on its constituents only *reliably* (whatever that comes to).

Fodor says, "...all concepts are individuated by their syntax and by their contents, and the syntax and contents of each complex concept is finitely reducible to the syntax and contents of its constituents" (Fodor, '98, 95). Fodor also says, "*the very inferences that are supposed to define a concept are also the ones you have to accept in order to possess the concept*" (111). Does This seems to say that concepts compose in both respects. Let's look more closely at this.

Regarding *having* concepts, our analysis suggested that complex concepts are not assemblies. We learn to *have* complex concepts as Gestalt wholes, not as assemblies. This is why in terms of *having* a concept, a complex concept is rarely the sum of some array of components. If you *have* the concept LINE and the concept ANGLE, I don't think you necessarily have the concept TRIANGLE. Equally, having the concept TRIANGLE, you don't *have* the two component concepts. This is supported by the work of Susan Carey on the role of definitions in cognitive development, which suggests that concepts are not built up or learned component by component. What misleads this line of enquiry is that after we have learned meanings, we *can* break down concepts to simpler components.

Even a definitional concept may not compose syntactically. If you can have a FISH concept and a PET concept, you'll probably be able to pick out pet fish and *have* the PET FISH concept. However, if you have a PET FISH concept, would you be able to pick out a cat as a pet? Probably not.

Knowing a concept probably has a better chance of composing. One theory enabling a determination of what constituents make up a concept necessarily or even reliably, is called *"inferential role semantics"*. Inferential role theory enables us to determine a bundle of features or qualities that would be necessary to identify and constitute a concept. This is composability by content. And at one point, Fodor says, "… Conceptual contents, however, *must* be compositional" (105). Thus, the *meaning* of PET FISH, would enable you to go pretty far in *knowing* the concepts PETS and FISH. So far, so good. He also says, "What PET contributes to PET FISH is the property of *being a pet*" (107). This seems to imply that if you know what PET means and what FISH means, you would know what PET FISH means.

But at another point Fodor says that "Inferential role semantics is bankrupt" (Fodor, '98, 108). For example, when we look at the composition of a complex concept, we get features and qualities that are concepts themselves. And the problem arises as to which of these are essential to knowing the concept in question, either necessarily or reliably. For example, the rough and ready composition of BOAT might be a LARGE, POINTY, OBLONG SHAPED, CONTAINER, MOVES THROUGH WATER. But this might leave out tugboats but include canoes. So there is a problem of whether this composition fills out the entire meaning of BOAT.

Since he has relaxed his criterion for composability to "reliably", meaning does a decent job of this and so provides a fine enough sieve to individuate concepts. This mirrors the way we learn concepts. We learn to *have* concepts on the basis of whole Gestalts. However, very importantly, the constituents of a concept and how they are composed is part of the *meaning* of a concept and meaning is built up gradually in children by seeing lots of instantiations and by learning counterfactuals and knowledge. Having a concept is overrated because it is only a sense data recognitional thing that doesn't get to the essence of a concept. Since only full concepts compose and not prototypes nor sense data, it seems to me that content would do an adequate job of individuating concepts.

Summarizing, having a concept depends on discriminating between sense data concepts, which correspond to syntax, which is a finite state game. This is why having concepts doesn't seem to compose and so is not a good way to individuate concepts. However, knowing a concept involves infinite state content, and this may explain composability. And it is its composability that enables *content* to individuate concepts. And this is why, in the end, Fodor's "informational semantics", being restricted to the finite state processes of sensory transducers, is not going to have the capacity to do much that is interesting. It won't give you the full meanings of propositional attitudes and representations, nor the content of perceptions, nor, in this case, the ability to individuate and identify concepts. Fodor also shows that compositionality is required to explain the productivity and systematicity of concepts.

AVI.11 INNATENESS

Let us take up the problem of the language of thought, and specifically, the problem of innateness in general. I want to say right off the bat, that I have never ever read anyone discussing innateness who knew exactly what he was talking about. It's another of those terms that has some vague meaning, but nobody wants to get specific and really nail a meaning down. The problem is brought out incisively in the case of concepts, which Fodor handles in his Chapter 10 on innateness in *Representations*.

His discussion like most others on this topic has a phantasgorama of ideas, but there is never a mention of a criterion for innateness. Let's restrict ourselves to simply having a concept. Fodor divides the answer to the innateness debate into two basic theories: Empirical and Nativistic.

He says concerning the Empiricist account that "primitive concepts are assumed to be sensory, and their acquisition is occasioned by the activation of the sensorium" (272). (The sensorium is simply all the sensory cortices in the brain). Now what does "activation" mean? Does this imply that there is something in the sensory parts of the brain and when you see a primitive concept, like the color red, you twitch this something, and you have the concept? But isn't this what Nativists are supposed to be saying? He says, "the Nativist says that the *triggering* [italics mine] of the sensorium is, normally necessary and sufficient for the availability of all concepts" (273). Where are the criteria for these stretch words? He introduces a new term: "on all standard theories the sensorium is an innately specified function from stimuli onto primitive concepts" (276). But what is the criterion for something being "innately specified" as opposed to simply innate?

Let's take a case most amenable to an innately specified analysis. These would be sensory concepts that seem to be attained with just one experience. Suppose baby sees the color red for the first time. Since sensory concepts like red are primitive, seeing red on another occasion would only reinforce the concept cylinder that seeing red created for the first time. This cylinder won't grow very much with subsequent perceptions of red. So the initial representation is pretty close to a concept cylinder, and this is whatever the sensorium gives you on the basis only of how it is constructed. But what about *innateness*?

Some Nativists seem to suggest that the concept cylinder was already in the brain before the experience. This is why they use the term 'trigger'. The metaphor is that all the experience does is to *wake up* this cylinder that was already there. All this is highly unlikely.

There are tons of evidence that show that new-born babies don't even have the concept of a physical object. On the other hand, there are examples of genuine innate concepts. We mentioned the Mongoose in the text. (The fact that simple animals with little meaning structures can have concepts shows that having a concept is a finite state process based on finite state sense data that even computers can do.) Very young babies don't display much of a reaction upon the first time they see a color. So it certainly seems plausible to say that all the properties of the brain's components, its synapses, neurons, etc., that accompany a concept cylinder are not there at birth.

So if we leave aside the highly unlikely eventuality that the newborn baby's brain is wired just as it would be if the baby had seen red, can there be any sense at all that the concept was innate? The only thing I can figure out from what Nativists say is that even though experience "triggers" the concept (whatever that means), the sensory cortices determine the *nature* of sensations of red, and this would be what "innately specified" would mean. So, for example, the visual cortex creates sensory concept cylinders of colors and shapes, whereas the auditory cortex creates sounds concepts. Seeing red for the first time will create a visual concept cylinder around a representation *innately specified* as having a color nature and Nativists and Empiricists can agree on that much. This still requires the experience of seeing red. Fodor says, "Both sides assume that the space of concepts potentially available to any given organism is completely determined by the innate endowment of that organism" (Fodor, '81, 277). Well, of course it is no great epiphany to proclaim that the visual system produces color concepts whereas the auditory system produces sound concepts. To me, this is not what the innateness question should be concerned with. It should concern the ontology of primitive concepts, which we could call, innateness *per se*? Do primitive concepts *per se* exist at birth? And what criterion should we have to make this determination?

Most of what we learn to do requires practice and development. If knowledge that or knowledge how were really innate, the neurological structure underlying this knowledge or skill should be there right from the start like that possessed by certain snakes. In stark contrast to "innately specified", this would be innate *simpliciter*, which is more of an ontological idea having to do with the actual existence, as opposed to the nature of the concept. An innate ability's underlying neurology is the final product that enables the ability to be manifested. If Nativists aren't saying we are born with the final underlying neurological structure, what criteria are they using to judge innateness in this ontological sense? The problem with Nativism is that they manage to avoid concrete talk regarding a criterion of innateness that is between the *innate structure* idea and the *innately specified* idea that would provide a sound foundation for the innateness concept.

AVI.12 INNATENESS AND EVOLUTION: EVOLUTIONARY PSYCHOLOGY

In view of the pronounced inability of new-borns to do anything complex involving knowledge, abilities, or even skills, the Nativist seems to be on weak ground. Since structure of some kind seems to necessary to get within miles of innateness and a new-born needs experiences to put it there, Nativists turned to *evolution* to explain how they could be born with any kind of structure underlying knowledge or abilities. This was part of the new academic discipline called Evolutionary Psychology that we discussed in Sect. 9.3. Archeologists find primate bones that resemble ourselves all over the world, but nobody really knows which, in any, of these bones are from our ancestors. But even if it could be proved that an elbow and an asshole that some archeologist finds in some cave was from a creature that was an ancestor to present-day humans, how can anyone tell what its environment was like?

I'm pretty conservative about these stories. I will accept an adaptation story that stems from some basic things we know for sure about our evolutionary past. Our primate ancestors certainly had innate *tendencies*, which we'll discuss next, like sensitivity to faces, imitation and the tendency to see objects as integral wholes, and to form concept cylinders. I don't think these are in dispute. As far as more complex behavior patterns, the only ones I would rely on are those that stem from the simple fact that males sought sex with females and females had babies. As we get away from these primitive behaviors, the stories from evolutionary psychology get more and more tenuous, until we arrive at stories that are pretty ridiculous. Cognitive scientists, who are not in the business of making cocktail party talk, are a bit more restrained in their reliance on evolutionary stories. They restrict themselves pretty much to cognitive abilities like concepts, knowledge and language.

Physiologically, humans seemed to have evolved from some primate line around 6 million years ago. As some line evolved off this primate line, the proto-humans that existed along the way were substituting intelligence for physical prowess including big teeth and claws and the ability to swing from trees. Our ancestor's skulls grew accordingly. But as they became more vulnerable, it became increasingly important to stick together and this in turn requires rules and procedures for everything they do. This is what culture amounts to. And as our vulnerability increased so too did the complexity of human cultures to meet the survival requirements of complex environments. We discussed this in Sect. 6.2.

As proto-humans spread around the world, they faced different environments and so what would have the greatest survival value would be *adaptability* to enable cultures to evolve that matched a wide variety of environments. What would be necessary for survival of a particular population would be the ability to *learn* the cultural rules necessary to survive in a particular environment. This implies a *minimum* of hard-wiring and innateness. Innate beliefs, even if true in some circumstances would, in general, actually be a *hindrance* to the ability of early people to adapt to new and changing environments. If anything, evolutionary stories tend to *dis*confirm the idea of innate knowledge. It is *culture* that becomes engrained, not the brains of people who had to have a *lack* of specificity in their brains to adapt to a variety of cultures.

But let's ask, are there any other ways we could address the question of innateness? Well, in my opinion, you can answer this question any way your little heart desires. If you are a Nativist, you point to the fact that there had to be neurons in the brain to change and axons in the right place so that certain synapses would be strengthened and certain dendrites would form new synapses, which create new circuits. In other words, the basic architecture of the brain must be such that our neurological cylinders can form the way they do. A lot of this brain architecture was there at birth, so, in this sense, you can say that some aspects of concepts are innate. So when the Empiricist accepts "innately specified" what is he accepting? It seems to me, it's either the *nature* of the concept, or the *potential* for a neurological cylinder. In either case, experience is still necessary to create the full concept.

AVI.13 INNATENESS DEVELOPMENT

In humans, the support for anything innate is adequately contradicted by the fact that in order to evolve adaptability, most of the hard-wiring that might have existed in our distance ancestors, probably got washed out of our genes. In view of the basic incapacities of new-borns, Nativists were again on the run. And they were dimly aware that sooner or later they were going to lose the debate. So they decided to change the rules of the game; and they did it in a clever way that prevents them from ever losing. What they said was that what we are born with are *potentials* to develop independently of any environmental inputs in certain ways towards certain knowledge and abilities. Richard

Samuels puts it: "...the acquisition of an innate trait cannot be explained by reference to any psychological process" (Samuels in Carruthers, '07, 26). Of course, children develop in a *sea* of "psychological processes". But Nativists assure us that none of these are affecting the inexorable development of the trait in question. And the reason this assures them of never having to admit defeat is that it will be almost impossible to ever prove that psychological processes *did* affect the development.

Realizing the weakness of this story, Nativists try to have it both ways. They know that there ought to be *something* at birth to enable development in the right direction. On the other hand, since new-borns show no signs of the knowledge, concepts, or skills, this headstart can't be the structure of the final product. So what is it? Nativists use all kinds of high-sounding terms to refer to what we start with, (if not the final complete structure) that sends the development process in the right direction. For example, Fodor, Bever, and Garrett in their paper in (Block, '81, 329) characterize Nativism as follows: "For the Nativist, environmental information serves largely to elicit behavior whose principles of organization are genetically coded." This is the mother of all loose talk. What are the principles of organization? Of course, the brain at birth has *some* architecture, which is "genetically coded". But what criteria are being used to decide whether the structure we are born with has enough correlation to the final structure after development of the concept or ability to call it innate?

Other such expressions are, "genetically determined information" and "distinct mechanisms". Steven Pinker says, "The mind is likely to contain blueprints for grammatical rules..."(Pinker, '94). What, do these kinds of expressions mean? Of course, genes include blueprints for laying out the neuronal layout of the brain. The question what is the difference between the new-born brain and the brain wired up with the rules of grammar? This is the key to Nativism. But we never see philosophers get anywhere near the idea of a physical criterion like this.

In my opinion, even if we had a clear definition of innateness in terms of structure or function, I don't see how we could demonstrate innateness or prove it one way or the other. If you put the emphasis on the fact that some kind of architecture is *necessary* to act as the substrate for the final concept or ability, everything will turn out to be innate for the simple reason that at the very minimum you have a brain in your head to get started. And brains are innate. If you believe that since experience is necessary for the concept to fine tune or twitch the circuitry (called "triggering"), or if you believe that relevant experience is still necessary for development to occur and you wouldn't be able to attain a concept without experience, you would be an Empiricist of some kind. To me, this would be a simple matter of convention. I tend towards empiricism simply because there is no concept without some experience. And if the Nativist is saying that development would occur leading to a final neurological structure *independent* of experience, the evidence is not on his side. Congenitally blind people who receive sight have not *developed* any visual concepts except for what is "innately specified". Feral children have not *developed* rules of grammar.

In the text, we made an analogy with building materials corresponding to the innateness of concepts and abilities, and the actual construction of a building which requires construction workers, analogous to environmental inputs children receive that lead to the development of concepts and abilities. The Nativist would seem to be saying that a building will assemble itself from building materials dumped on the construction site while the construction workers just sit and watch. All knowledge or ability involves an increase in complexity. What Nativists are saying is that a structure is going to increase in complexity all by itself with no relevant help, which is a violation of the second law of thermodynamics. If experience is necessary to provide the energy or information to cause the increase in complexity, what is left for the Nativist to hang his hat on?

Sprinkled throughout the literature are examples to convince us of innateness of certain concepts. In my opinion, they all really stink. There isn't one that's convincing. One of the most popular is that a baby is born with the ability to see in three dimensions. I don't agree with this at all. What shows the implausibility of this is that adults who have obtained sight through an operation of some kind, are often so scared because their initial experiences that they want to go back to being blind. The reason is that during their life up to the operation, they have developed representations of a kind of three-dimensional world through the senses of touch and motion. When they see what is probably a *two*-dimensional world with their new sight, it causes complete cognitive dissonance, which explains the fright. During their blindness, they didn't *develop* any visual concepts.

The best evidence for innate concepts is that some animals have them. We mentioned the mongoose. But it is usually animals pretty low on the phylogenic scale who learn very little as opposed to humans who have to learn whole cultures.

AVI.14 Epistomology and Ontology

There might be some parallels between the world of Platonic concepts and Kant's world of noumena and Transcendental Idealism. Kant basically said that we know we have to be constructed in a way that makes experience possible, (to make a very long story short). So there is a priori knowledge. But we can't really know what the basis of our experiences is, his noumena, because we have no way to be in contact with them. So do we have knowledge of the world around us? Carruthers says, "It is very likely that our experience is innately determined as representing a world of physical objects in space around us" (162). He's on the right tract here, it seems to me, but then he falls in line with conventional thinking that we can't know physical objects because we can't get a grip on them. Again pops up the confusion between causal and perceptual levels. As we have brought out many times, Kant's noumena are really causal level objects, and we learn about them through science which is very empirical. If our account of perceptual realism is correct, we know we have knowledge of physical objects because they are perceptual objects created by the mind. But is this *a priori* knowledge? In my opinion, the *a priori/a posteriori* choice is only a convention. Since we have to look at the world to experience real world objects, it could be said that knowledge of perceptual objects is *a posteriori*. However, it could also be said that before we open our eyes, we know that what we will see are perceptual objects. So in this sense, this knowledge could be said to be *a priori*. I just don't think it's important how we decide this.

But is this *innate* knowledge? No, because our *knowledge* of physical objects comes as a result of projecting *meaning* to causal objects. And if meaning is infinite state, there is certainly no innate meaning. And there could be no innate knowledge involving meaning that would be necessary to comprehend the nature of perceptual physical objects. What gets the ball rolling in the concept game are concept cylinders. They enable a learning child to clump objects into categories and *have* concepts. After seeing a number of instantiations of a concept and a bunch of learning, we arrive at the *meaning* that the category could contain an infinite number. This process is called abstracting, and I don't know how to analyze the idea of abstracting. Once we have this meaning, the category derived from the concept cylinder becomes what we call a *universal*. Then, whether we call universals *a priori* or not is just the convention of whether we consider concept cylinders innate. However, the Nativist can always manufacture an answer that our brain circuitry at birth is such that when a child sees an instance of RED, a cylinder forms from the representation of a red sense datum that enables the child to learn to *have* the RED concept. To me, this is a pretty flimsy idea of innateness.

AVI.15 Innate Tendencies

We should point out that up to now we have been dealing with innate knowledge or skills or concepts. There doesn't seem to be any innateness in this stuff that's worthy of the name. But there probably are innate *tendencies*. This idea is simply the proclivity of new-borns to react and behave in certain ways. Of course, right after birth, these tendencies are pretty inchoate. But they are noticeable as compared to something like rules of grammar for which there isn't the slightest twitch of behavior in the direction of these rules. For example, new-borns kick their legs in an alternating motion as a precursor to walking. The wiring for this motion is obviously innate by any definition. However, they move their arms in unison, thus presaging the later need for the arms to cooperate in carrying out motions like pushing, pulling, lifting, etc. New-born babies seem to have a fear of falling, a tendency to suck, and to imitate people around them.

There are also *tendencies* in new-borns to be sensitive to the faces of adults, follow the gaze of adults, and to imitate adults around them. Following the gaze may just be a special case of imitation. Sensitivity to faces is due to enlargement of a special part of the brain for being attracted to and perceiving faces. It has also been discovered that there are imitation neurons in the brain that perform a similar dance when seeing an activity as when actually *doing* the activity. So these tendencies could reasonably be called innate because they start up right at birth.

There is a tendency for new-borns to see objects as integral wholes that stay together over time. This is part of the tendency them to build concept cylinders right from birth. But perhaps this only indicates that the basic brain wiring is there at birth so that experience will make use of that wiring to see objects as Gestalts and to further build concept cylinders. However, there are still no concept cylinders without experience. In general, the evolution to humans required great increases in adaptability. As you go up the phylogenic scale, innate hard-wiring gets replaced by adaptability until you get to humans where there is probably very little hard-wiring at birth, and so very little that is innate. All that is left are some very basic tendencies to create concept cylinders, a few fears, a few motions, a few sensitivities, and some imitation. I think the washing-out process went much too far for anything as complex and intricate as rules of grammar built in at birth other than this stretch concept of "innately specified".

AVI.16 INNATE COMPLEX CONCEPTS.

The next question is, how does the Nativist and the Empiricist differ concerning more complex concepts, like the concept of a triangle, or a box, or a horse? The Empiricist says that complex concepts are just bunches of primitive concepts put together by what happens to be in the outside world. So, for example, the concept of a TRIANGLE would come about on the basis of a certain arrangement of the primitive concepts of lines, and angles. But the arrangement is new to the learner. So, how does the Nativist explain the acquisition of a complex concept, like a triangle? Of course, the Empiricist would say, for example, that a child can't tell cows from non-cows if the child has never seen a cow, and so doesn't have the concept. Certainly, if there are no innate brain traces corresponding to primitive concepts, there wouldn't be any for more complex concepts. So since the experience was necessary to set up the representational concept of a cow in the child's brain, we could conclude that the concept is not innate. However, even with complex concepts, a child seems to be able to *have* a concept, albeit a very rudimentary one, with just one experience. There seems to be something innate about this.

But Fodor verbiage suggests that he wants to talk about *knowing* concepts as well. The means to know concepts is a variant of the usual causal theory

of meaning: we can be "... *non*-cognitive about concept possession; it says that having a concept [read knowing] is ...being in a certain nomic mind-world relation..."(Fodor, '98, 124). This is legal, no less. But since the non-cognitive view has no meaning toys to play with (induction, inferences, hypotheses, etc.), he has to have a way to get meaning attached to instantiations of his concepts. (We explained the futility of trying to get full meanings through finite state transducers in Sect. AVI.9.)

But because of the confusion between having and knowing, to avoid the inductive knowledge based learning processes, he says, "you need a non-cognitivist view of concept possession" (125). True, but he doesn't think we have one "...because it is perfectly possible to be a cognitivist *about the possession of skills... that concept possession requires* (125), which would require meaning, inferences, induction, and the rest of the cognitive arsenal. This is simply not true if he's really talking about *having* concepts.

He ends this awful paragraph with the idea that "...*concept acquisition is mediated by hypothesis formation and testing*" (125). As Charlie Chan would say, correction please. Induction and hypothesis testing are semantic notions, and, as shown by computers and babies, has nothing to do with learning to *have* a concept, or "concept acquisition" in Fodor's terms. When a baby learns to tell swans from non-swans, there is nothing inductive going on at all. The baby doesn't form a final concept of a swan as being white or entertain the idea that all swans are white. The whiteness of swans is certainly reflected in the series of neurological cylinders the child forms on the basis of seeing white swans. This enables him to *have* the concept of white swans. The computer and neural net don't give the tiniest crap whether *all* swans are white. The baby and the computer have no way to represent the infinite number of possible instantiations of a concept having something in common to from a category. The fact that all swans have whiteness in common, is part of the *meaning* of 'swan' and SWAN. The computer, being a finite state device, has no way to represent this meaning.

But we don't have to get induction and hypothesis testing involved with learning concepts because it is "...primarily cognitivism about the metaphysics of concept possession [read meaning] that motivates inductivism..."(126). This is a mess. As we have stressed, we don't need cognitivism for concept possession. And if he's talking about learning concepts, we still don't need cognitivism, because we can get "nomologically locked" into the concept instantiations we see and get all the meaning we want. This gets pretty funny. This is really a dressed up version of the causal theory of meaning, which is the basis for his "informational semantics".

When it comes to induction, which gives only *portions* of meaning, somehow we lose the combination to the nomological lock, and we can't get this smaller portion of meaning into our heads. But when it comes to robust meanings, we can get infinite information content meanings of instantiations of COW to come through finite capacity sensory transducers simply by not squinting, keeping our eyes wide open and getting "nomologically locked" onto the poor cow.

But Fodor thinks there is an argument to show we need some kind of induction after all. (And we're going to show it with DOORKNOBS instead of COWS.) For how do we use the experience of seeing doorknobs to add to the learning of what doorknobs are, unless we have a concept of DOORKNOB in the first place? And this is where Fodor's confusion between having concepts and their meaning really gets his analysis stuck in the mud. He says, we have "...to live with the fact that it's typically acquaintance with doorknobs that leads to getting locked to *doorknobhood*."...So we still have "...to explain why it's those experiences, and not others, that eventuate in locking onto that property..."(127). (doorknobhood). This is a very important point, and he doesn't think

Darwin is going to help. Not that Fodor is dismayed. He doesn't mind at all that we have trouble hooking up meaning with their concepts because if he can show that it can't happen without induction, and induction can't happen without the concept, then we will be driven to a Nativist theory of concepts, which is where he wants to wind up anyway. But this retreat is predicated on the confusion between having concepts and their meaning.

He has noticed that for some primitive concepts, like RED, there is no worry about attaining such a concept because the "...*arbitrariness* of the relation between the content of sensory concepts and the character of their causes" (130). For once, it isn't important that he confuses having with knowing a concept. The reason is that whatever representation the brain establishes upon seeing red, even for the first time, *that* representation will be the personal RED concept. And it doesn't matter what it is. This is why the inverted spectrum argument we discussed in AIV.1 is so silly. Person A is not in the same brain-state when he sees azure as person B is when he sees brown because there is no such thing as sameness of brainstates.

So he's going to sneak in the concept of DOORKNOB hidden under the wagon load of sensory concepts like RED: After all, "it is encounters with doorknobs that typically occasion the acquisition of ...a complex concept like DOORKNOB"... just like "...it is typically encounters with red things ...that typically occasion the acquisition of...a *primitive* concept like RED" (131). And "...all that needs to be innate for RED to be acquired is whatever the mechanisms are that determine that red things strike us as they do..."(142). Well, let's make it a bit easier on Fodor and assume he's talking only about *having* these concepts. But what is it in innate circuitry that enables us to "acquire" the RED concept? Simply a brain? It is highly unlikely that we are born with brainstates with the complexity of a seeing-red brainstate.

But even if we made the leap of faith that we have the RED concept innately somehow, how will DOORKNOB come in on the same load? Even if he could "trigger" the RED concept, how could this kind of triggering going to get the full DOORKNOB instantiation recognized as an instance of DOORKNOB. There weren't any doorknobs around when the brain was growing this miraculous innate hard-wiring. So what he needs is "…some mechanism that reliably leads from having F [say, doorknob] experiences to acquiring the concept of *being F* [DOORKNOB]," (133) that doesn't involve dreaded induction. And we can't squirm out of this dilemma by looking at definitions because since there are no definitions, there is no breakdown of DOORKNOB into simpler component that may be easier to handle. He's going to have to "nomologically lock" onto the whole DOORKNOB in one grab.

But he isn't going to settle for nomologically locking onto the simple sense data DOORKNOB concept, he's going to explain winding up with the complete DOORKNOB concept along with "content", no less. "But the issue isn't whether acquiring [read knowing] DOORKNOB requires a lot of innate stuff… The issue is whether it requires a lot of innate *intentional* stuff…"(143). Unless he's talking about DOORKNOB as opposed DOORKNOB, it certainly does. Maybe Fodor is implicitly admitting that sense data concepts don't involve abstracting to knowing a concept with the content that all instantiations fall into a category. What follows is the pinnacle of his *Concept* book: what makes doorknob experiences into the DOORNOB concept is "…how it strikes us". Now, why didn't I think of that? Not only that, but if "…being a *doorknob* is a property that's *constituted* by how things strike us, then the intrinsic connection between the content of DOORKNOB and the content of our doorknob-experiences is metaphysically necessary…"(136), (which in philosophy is the U.S. seal of approval on meat). This is really pretty lame. But he's not done. He's going to bring up one of his earlier cannons from the rear. If we put this "…

account of the metaphysics of *doorknobhood* together with the metaphysical account of concept possession that information semantics proposes — having a concept is something like 'resonating to' the property that the concept expresses — then you get: *being a doorknob* is having that property that minds like ours come to resonate to" (137). We don't have to induct: we just "resonate". A new dance move? Maybe it's sexual. But it's nothing like that: we're born with minds that "resonate" with doorknobs. Maybe caves had doorknobs 50 thousand years ago. Fodor is really off his game here. He usually squirms out of impossible situations with more finesse than this.

But if Fodor couldn't get the meaning of a simple object like a token doorknob into our heads, how is he going to do any better with a DOORKNOB *concept* where there is an abstract entity of some kind that encompasses an infinite number of instantiations? Stretch words like "locking on", "resonating", "striking us the right way", are in desperate need of explication. Why wasn't he "resonating" when he was squeezing meanings of simple representations through our finite state transducers? The history of philosophy is full of stuff like this. Searle's consciousness as a "feature" of the brain is a typical example. Using words in these new and novel ways is great poetry and sounds creative. But they give us no idea what these adventuresome phrases come to and no real philosophical explanations.

But then the whole house of cards starts tumbling down: "…the innateness of the sensorium isn't the innateness of anything that has intentional content" (142). This little sentence pretty much puts innateness in its place. In fact, it's hard to see how it ever got into the picture in the first place. Our sensorium may be wired to create sense data traces of a particular nature, but there's no way we can be born with all the meaning a representation of a complex world already in our heads, especially the infinite nature of concepts. All he has left is "innately specified" and even this applies only to *having* concepts where no meaning is involved.

To polish off this house of cards, he then admits that "...the sensorium model of the acquisition of RED doesn't require that it, or any concept, be innate" (142). Now, even the simple sense data RED concept is breaking down under the load. First of all, it implicitly admits that acquisition, which is the *having* a concept does not involve meaning. And secondly, it admits that even *having* a concept does not involve anything innate, but only possibly something about its nature. But where does this leave Fodor? He says that "...properties like *being a doorknob* are mind-dependent" (147). Well, yes. Most of what's important to humans is mind-dependent — except the causal world of meaningless piles of molecules. What else is new? The rest of the *Concepts* book limps along with sentences like "...*being a doorknob* is just *having the property that minds like ours lock to in consequence of experience with doorknobs*" (148). And so we're back to "locking on".

The meaning of concepts presents a very difficult challenge for meaning no matter how and where we consider meaning to originate in the scheme of things. The meaning of concepts is the meaning of something abstract. How do we ever accrue such meaning? In my opinion, the arguments against induction are very decisive. The only way to see how induction can be avoided and still get a handle on the meaning of concepts is to start from scratch during early childhood when we learn to *have* concepts. Even though this is only an ability, it is a very important ability because it enables us to at least pick out instantiations of a concept. That is step one. If Fodor wants to say we have an innate wiring so that something like a series of cylinders form that enables us to have a concept, so be it. We probably do have evolutionary wiring that can be adapted for the job of building cylinders. But we don't know we're doing this, and when a child sees an instantiation of a concept, he doesn't know his representation is going to be an instance of a concept and part of the *meaning* of the final concept. But at the sense data concept stage, there is no

meaning, and so no sense that the child will wind up *knowing* the DOORKNOB concept as well as *having* it. It may even be wrong to call this a concept at all, simply because, at this stage, there is no concept *per se*, that the child knows about.

Now if we can pick out instantiations of a concept as children, we can attach or associate any meaning we obtain during perceptual experiences with instantiations. But the meanings we attach are not out in the world. They accrue in our minds as knowledge, representations of perceptions of experiences of the concept, counterfactuals, etc. An infinite number of mental items like these accrue associated with the neurological cylinders that enable us to know the concept. In a bootstrapping fashion, we gradually build up a meaning cloud for the concept.

There are some fundamental problems with the whole idea of Nativism. Basically, Nativist theories, of any kind, all say that there is something innate that gives us some kind of head start in attaining many mental abilities like concepts, perceptions, talents, capabilities, and intelligence itself. But what you will never find in any discussion about innateness no matter where you look is what does a head start mean, what does it refer to, and, most importantly, what are the criterion for having a head start? People argue a great deal in the literature about innate concepts, innate intelligence, innate rules of grammar, etc. But what are they talking about? We are never told, and the reason is simple: they really don't have any idea of what they are talking about. In all of Fodor's verbiage, there is no mention of what a criterion of innateness would be like.

The language used to describe Nativist theory is what applies for many complex concepts; "they are triggered but unlearned" (Fodor, '81, 279). Should this imply that before a child has seen a cow, he should be able to imagine one by "activating" something related to the concept of a cow that was there at birth somehow? But surely, nobody, even a Nativist, would say that. Does it mean that the first time a child sees a cow, he will recognize it as a cow because the concept of COW is somehow already in his head? Nobody, including the Nativist, would say that either. Well then, what is it that is innate here, and what is really in the child's head that gets "triggered"? Nobody who talks about this stuff will ever say. Fodor's chapter on innateness goes on for 60 pages of bewildering philosophical verbiage, and even though he is partial to a Nativist theory, he isn't going to touch these tough questions with a ten-foot pole.

Fodor says that Empiricists cannot show that terms for many complex concepts, like " 'table' or 'grandmother', or...'triangle', is analyzable (i.e., definable) in a reduction base where the non-logical base is — even prima facie — sensory" (284). To him, this implies that the Empiricist program "is now effectively a dead issue in philosophy" (284). I would say, not so fast, Jerry. For one thing, I think it's important to distinguish perceptual concepts from abstract concepts. Abstract concepts, like grandmother, are created through their *semantic* aspects. But perceptual concepts, like a triangle or table, are what we are mostly concerned with; and they are created through *perceptual* processes.

Fodor's versions of Empiricism imply a mental synthesis, as his description of the Empiricist Maxim: "...there's nothing in the mind except what's *either* presented to the senses *or* logically complex and constructed from sensations" (303). I don't see where there necessarily has to be anything "constructed" at all, or "analyzable" in terms of primitive concepts, at least in perception. Just because we can see that a concept is made of simpler parts, that doesn't prove that we learn it that way. Of course, Fodor hasn't answered the question of how even a primitive concept comes about. Fodor implies that the fact that since most "simple expressions of English are undefinable" (285) in terms of primitive concepts, that we can't learn them Empirically. Well, he hasn't convinced me.

Fodor says, "The flow of information in perception ought, fundamentally, to go in one direction: from the application of sensory concepts, via, processes of logical construction, to the application of complex concepts" (290). Now, it certainly seems the case that the visual cortex is processing information from each component of the concept in a different place. In fact, there is research that shows when a creature sees a square shape, there is a kind of rudimentary square that can be made out in the actual firing of neurons that are involved in the creation of the representation. So each line of the square would cause a response in a different place in the cortex. But there is no "process of construction" here. The brain isn't putting anything together at all. It's already put together in the trace that is formed, even if it is spread out over many areas of the brain.

I think the flow of information is the other way round. We learn concepts by creating whole gestalt representations of instantiations of a concept. It is only *after* we *know* a concept and know something of its meaning that we *intellectually* take apart a concept and argue about what primitive components may compose the total concept.

It is ironic that the one place where the computer might help us to understand some aspect of mentality, Fodor isn't talking about computers. When a neural net learns to *have* a complex concept, like TRIANGLE, there is no evidence that it is putting together line and angle components. It adjusts the strength of of its connections to pick out instantiations, but I don't think you can correlate these various strengths with particular elements and components of the concept.

Fodor admits that all programs for defining concepts analytically, by seeing what they may be composed of, "have failed". But what must be distinguished is having a concept from learning meaning. When we learn to *have* a concept, it is the Gestalt sense data concept we learn. But when we learn meaning, it is then that analysis may be relevant, and the question of the structure and definability of the concept comes into question. But by not distinguishing between having concepts and meaning, Fodor's analysis comes to an Empiricist dead end, and he is forced to entertain Nativist theories with their goofy ideas of innateness.

Now Fodor's analysis would allow for something like the growing cylinder theory of concepts. Of course, being a philosopher, it is not very important to him what the exact nature of this kind of theory. He dismissively refers to any such theory as being about "mental chemistry". Of course, there's no such thing as "mental chemistry", only *brain* chemistry, but in keeping with most cognitive science, Fodor isn't going to get his hands dirty talking about real brains. But there is motivation to this confusion at the heart of the innateness controversy.

Even though the instantiation of a concept, like a triangle, "triggers" the concept, it is certainly a partial *cause* of attaining the concept. A causal triangle out in the world does two things. First, it causes sense data traces to be created that are probably proximal in the brain. This enables a category to be formed by lumping together instantiations into a cylinder. This is *having* the concept. But regarding knowing concepts, he relies on J.S. Mill's discussion of concept formation and says about acquiring concepts like TRIANGLE that "... it arises from the prior concepts of mental chemistry, not by construction" (Fodor, '81, 305). This seems to accord with what we have been saying about learning concepts as whole Gestalts. But on the very same page, and relying on the very same guy, he says, "...the principles of mental chemistry are such that the availability of LINE triggers the availability of TRIANGLE" (305). But either way, "What, on the mental chemistry view, explains the contingency of a concept upon its causes is, of course, the principles of mental chemistry, which is to say, the *innate* structure of the mind" (305). This is

how Fodor arrives at a Nativist theory. But the question is what is it about this "mental chemistry", (read, brain chemistry) that makes this process innate by "triggering" and leads to the brain arriving at its concepts. This tells me that the only thing you can distill out this innateness talk is that creatures who can make registrations or representations have a brain — and the brain is innate! If we still have a Nativist-Empiricist controversy, what aspect of "mental chemistry" is going to decide the issue? All we have so far is "triggering" and "resonating".

One of the last things Fodor says about innateness is, "everybody accepts that simple concepts are unlearned" (315). (By everybody, he means cognitive philosophers like himself.) But what can Fodor point to as being in the brain at birth, except a bunch of neurons? Without seeing red, it is highly unlikely that there is anything resembling a red concept cylinder at birth; and since the first experience with red is somewhat after birth, shouldn't this imply that the concept was learned, in some way? But here again, nobody has remotely established what the criterion would be for a concept being learned.

It isn't that Fodor is a great enthusiast of Nativism. He seems to be driven to this theory because he can't accept the process of induction for building up of a concept, which Empiricist theories may imply. But I don't see that induction is necessary for even complex concepts. The brain doesn't have to know where the concept is going to wind up. It doesn't really care, so there is no need for a hypothesis. In very early stages of childhood, children typically have rudimentary concepts that are somewhat inaccurate. But as the concept cylinders grow, they will asymptotically reach a concept which is not only fairly accurate, but quite uniform among all children of a given culture.

When we come to more complex concepts, or even things like abilities or the rules of grammar, or intelligence in general, is there any sense that can be given about innateness? The example of the mongoose is instructiv. Can a case be made that possibly humans have some built-in wiring at birth that corresponds to having a concept, besides this goofy idea of innately specified? If so, what criterion would we have in mind for how much wiring would be necessary to say we have an innate concept? Let us look at an analogy.

In figure AVI.16, we have a simple picture that might appear on the back of a cereal box. It is created by joining dots in the order that they are numbered. Now in the first box, all we have is a bunch of dots — no picture of anything. In the second box, we have joined about 20% of the dots. Well, we still don't have a picture of anything recognizable. In the third box about a third of the dots are joined. You might barely be able to make out a picture of an elephant. In the fourth box, even though only half the dots are joined, we clearly see an elephant. The question is, what percentage of dots have to be joined before we see an elephant? Of course, this would vary from person to person. But it would simply be a matter of convention as to where we decided we had a picture of an elephant. There is no objective way to determine a criterion in any other way.

I think this is an excellent analogy with innate concepts, even if I say so myself. Let's say a child sees a triangle. She will have a representation of a triangle, which will involve a number of neurons hooked up in certain ways, new growth of dendrites, and new

synapses forming what we have called a concept cylinder. Now if we look at this area of the brain before seeing a triangle, there will also be a structure of neurons and dendrites and synapses. Neurons are spaced, and axons are laid out in certain directions determined by what are called pathmark proteins. Now let us imagine making up a brain simply by dumping about 100 billion neurons into a skull and letting the axons and dendrites fall randomly about. Now we have three different brains; the first is a totally random array of neurons and synapses; the second is a brain of a child at birth with whatever structure there is to the array of neurons; and the third is the brain of the child after a concept cylinder has been formed. The question is, do we have any quantitative measure to measure the "distances" between the innate structure from the random structure and from the concept-laden structure? And even if we did, how would we decide how relatively close to the innate structure the concept-laden structure has to be in order to anoint this distance as small enough to call the concept-laden structure *innate*? What kind of space would be required to put these brains in before even thinking about a measure of distance? You won't find thinkers and researchers who even talk this way, let alone analytic philosophers. Without such criterion and thresholds, what does this

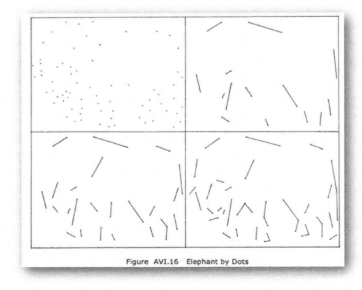

Figure AVI.16 Elephant by Dots

innate talk come to? It's just a lot of arm-waving babble with no definite meanings or criteria to any of the relevant terms.

We could apply this entire analysis to Chomsky's "innate rules of grammar". Chomsky did his pioneering work 40 years ago. Fodor thinks Chomsky's analysis "...makes perfectly good sense so long as what is innate is viewed as *having* propositional content" (Fodor, '83, 5). I can see that something computational, like the rules of grammar, could have some structure corresponding to them at birth. But it's a real stretch to say that something as complex as meaning has any kind of representation at birth. Chomsky says that grammar is *represented* in the baby's brain somehow. This more modest claim doesn't involve meaning in any way.

To back Nativist claims, for example, they say that all children wind up with the deep rules of grammar, in spite of a wide variety of environments they develop in. The Empiricist retorts, what wide variety? He would claim that the Nativist is cheating by restricting the range of environments to language-speaking communities *on this earth*. All children on earth develop in a world where nouns stay intact as they verb around in certain adjective ways. This common world is reflected in the grammar they learn which is quite similar at a deep level, says Chomsky. By the same reasoning, wearing clothes is innate too, because we're all born naked, and everywhere in the world, people wind up wearing clothes. And even though the clothing around the world is different, it's all clothing (at the deep level). But the Empiricist would ask, what about a world where nobody was talkin' to nobody? This is the world of feral children. Would the Nativist claim that rules of grammar develop in this very possible world?

Let's suppose that Fodor meant to say only that the syntactic rules of grammar are innate. But has anyone, including Chomsky ever discussed what *criterion* are being used to judge innateness. A new-born baby can't talk. So what basis is there for saying anything as sophisticated as grammar rules are innate? Of course,

there is some innate structure in the verbal areas of the brain, which has the *potential* for encapsulating, somehow, the rules of grammar. It's not a random pile of neurons and axons. But what measure is there on this structure, and how much of it do we agree must obtain to say this structure has rules of grammar built in? It's exactly like the question of how many dots have to been joined in the elephant picture to have a picture of an elephant. I don't even see discussions of these questions. I can just picture years from now, a Chomskian lecturer in a big hall in front of a flock of students. He drills a hole in someone's head, points into the hole, and says, "*there's* your rules of grammar".

But let's look at the initial stages of a child's language learning experiences. My own view is that the sentences told directly to a child are sentence-words as we described in Sect. 3.4. And they learn the meaning of the whole sentence-word. When a child's sentence is rejected or corrected by a parent, there are many reasons, only one of which is grammar. The meaning of the sentence may be confused, the sentence may be inappropriate for the situation, pronunciation may wrong, references may be incorrect, and on and on. The parent doesn't say to the child, you have a grammatical error. The parent supplies another sentence-word appropriate for the situation, and that's the end of it. At this stage, grammar may not be involved at all.

An interesting question is, how many different sentence-words is a child told between 2 and 4 disregarding substitutions of nouns? For example, "Jimmie played with his fire engine", and "Jimmie played with his car", and "Jimmie played with his baseball", would all be based on one sentence category. I would be surprised if a typical child is told more than 10 thousand different sentence-words between 2 and 4. (Chinese children learn to make 10 thousand little picture symbols.) These sentence-words are learned on the basis of *semantics*. The grammar would be irrelevant. The important point is that grammar isn't even an issue at this stage. If you look at tenses and conjugations, the rules involving the simpler verbs and nouns vary all over the place. There's no rhyme of reason to them. As one English language learner remarked to me, the rules of grammar only apply to the words you never use. A rule that applies only to seldom used words is not much of a rule.

Imagine 3 year old Joey with a baby sister learning English. So he hears his mother say that sis *played* in the afternoon. So now Joey wants to say that he was sleeping yesterday afternoon, and so he says "I sleeped yesterday afternoon". Mother quickly corrects him: you throw away one of the e's and add a t. You *slept* yesterday afternoon. Fine. So now the next day, Joey wants to say that he blew his whistle. But there's no e to throw away; but he makes the best of it and says "I blowt my whistle". Again he gets corrected: you *blew* your whistle. Joey accepts this since mother is a good cook. Then mother tells Joey to sit at the table and Joey says, "I sit at the table". But sis is different. Sis *sits* at the table. Now Joey is ready to apply his newly learned rule. He says, "I sat at the table yesterday; and sis sats at the table too. Now if little Joey is as smart as baby Chomsky, pretty soon he's going to say to himself, "screw this grammar crap. There's almost as many rules as words I gotta learn. I'm gonna learn the whole sentence in one gulp, which is easier anyway because at least sentences have meaning that helps me learn them. These rules o' grammar don't mean nothin' to me."

I was very happy to learn that some interesting research on language learning is consistent with the account given here. Rumelhart and McClelland created a model on a neural net to simulate learning tenses in English as a child would (in Goldman, '93b, 535+). They divide up the language-learning period into 3 phases. In phase one, they seem to learn the right tenses separately just as we are suggesting, even for very irregular verbs like give, come, take, go, etc. There doesn't seem to be any abstracting rules of grammar because most of the common verbs learned are irregular. To me this gives evidence that there's no rules of

grammar being learned in phase 1 at all because you have almost as many rules as there are verbs to learn and learning could be simply word-sentences.

At first Hilary Putnam could be interpreted as possibly agreeing that the child initially learns something like sentence-words. He clearly states that children's sentences are not corrected specifically for grammar but for being "...deviant-for-some-reason-or-other..." (Beakley and Ludlow, 399). But then he proceeds to fall into Chomsky's "carefully laid trap", quibbling about transformational rules like going from sentences like "Jim is tall", to the equivalent question: "Is Jim tall?" In this kind of quibble, Putnam is going to lose because once he acknowledges grammatical rules at this early stage of language learning, he's going to find Chomsky waiting for him at the finish line with just the right transformational rule.

To me, the whole idea of a two-year old child having complex transformational rules wired in at birth is pretty far-fetched. In my opinion, the above two different sentence-words are learned in very different circumstances. It's just a coincidence that their words happen to be reshuffled. What's the question for "the job is trying". "Is the job trying?" You could probably cook up rules to transform a horse into a cow as well.

Now after the age of 5 or 6 or 7, kids start making real sentences which are more complex. I've seen children's books from the 1800's that are very beautifully illustrated. These books, contain mostly sentence-words. But some of the sentences are more complex. And it is at this age that grammar mistakes start showing up with a vengeance. This is phase 2 of Rumalhart and McClelland's work. In this phase, around 90% of the verbs learned are regular. It is in this phase that the child begins to abstract rules like the regular verb rule that you simply add an 'ed' to the present tense verb. But the interesting thing is that the child starts to make mistakes on the irregular verbs she learned in phase 1. So for example, in phase 1 the child might learn that the past tense of took is take. In phase 2, she might send the past tense of take to tooked or taked. *The child never gets back to the performance levels for irregular verbs that was achieved in phase 1!*

What is even more interesting about this stage, is that when the child begins to use bigger words in more complex sentences, more uniform rules of grammar begin to appear and can be considered real rules because there aren't hundreds of exceptions. But then why do mistakes appear at this late stage? The reason is that when rules do begin to be abstracted, they create interference with the individually learned rules of irregular verbs in phase 1. This seems to show that irregular verbs were learned separately in phase 1 and there are *no rules learned or innate*. Of course, since Rumelhart and McClelland are leading competent academic researchers, they can't make the wild, cosmic speculations I can here. But I think their work could be extended to cover all the rules of grammar a child learns.

It is because the purported rules for sentence-words with little words are so complex while the rules for complex sentences with big words are so simple that we should question the whole idea of innate grammar. Why should complex rules be more easily learned in simple sentence-words when the young child should be least able to learn them, while the rules for more complex words and sentences are quite simple, and yet involve more mistakes at a time when the child is older and more advanced in every way? Something is wrong with this picture.

I personally believe that the rules of grammar are just another variety of abstraction. We build them up as we learn language in the same way we build up concepts of perceptual objects and other abstract concepts like MONEY or GRANDMOTHER. Rules are abstracted as we go along, and often never reach the competence of the baby with sentence-words. I can assure you that the guys I grew up with still ain't got no rules o' grammar built in, even now. And they're adults — at last. What did they have at birth? And when we look at typical mistakes in grammar, we see that semantics trumps syntax. We say, "I only made 5

bucks" instead of, "I made only 5 bucks". Some people say, I don't have no money because they're emphasizing the negative. How could meaning which comes much later trump syntax, which is supposedly hardwired in at birth?

Fodor, Bever, and Garrett's paper mentioned above adduces evidence in support of a Nativist position. They point out that grammar instructions don't help a child to learn grammar: "There exists some experimental evidence which suggests that explicit instruction in the child's first language fails to be facilitating…" in learning his language and grammar (Fodor, Bever, Garrett in Block '81, 332). Other studies show actual *less* progress in learning grammar in the instructed children as compared to the control group. In my not-so-humble opinion, this evidence points in the exact opposite direction from what these authors suggest, which goes to show about evidence. If children are basically learning sentence-words as is suggested here, then if you try to teach grammar to a young child, all you will do is confuse and obfuscate his learning the *meaning* of sentence-words and he would make less progress, as the studies show. But grammar instruction *does* help *older* children, who already know quite a bit of language. This should suggest that once children get past the sentence-word phase of language learning, and start making more complex sentences, they make lots of grammatical mistakes, and instruction would help in this regard.

I have one more piece of evidence for the sentence-word idea. Look at the following 3 sentences. You can say,

3) John gave a book to Amy. And you can say,

4) John gave Amy a book. Now you can also say,

5) John donated a book to the library. But you *can't* say,

6) John donated the library a book. Now why is this?

Stephen Pinker calls verbs like 'gave', "davitizable" verbs. For example, you can say John *showed* Amy his drawings, but you can't say John *exhibited* Amy his etchings. Nobody seems to have a good reason for this syntactical puzzle. The only peculiarity people have noticed is that davitizable verbs are short words which might suggest how we learn the rules of grammar.

We know that children love stories. One on the most impressive pieces of research on child development I've seen was done by Jerome Bruner — one of the truly great and very underrated thinkers of our time. He suggested that our affinity for stories might actually have an innate component. Humans are natural story-tellers and story listeners. One of the qualities shared by most stories, plays, and movies is that you first introduce the characters and then you tell a story involving those characters. This is what davitizable verbs illustrate. Of course, the sentence should read, 'John showed his drawings to Amy'. But in this form, the story of John and Amy, which is about showing drawings, comes before 'Amy'. So in saying this sentence to a child, the parent moves Amy up in the sentence so that the characters of the story, John and Amy are introduced *first*, and the story about what they did follows, just as is the case for any story a child hears. And so we get, "John showed Amy his drawings".

This shows us two things. First, children might very well learn sentence-words in which meaning is more important than syntax. If there really are less than 10 thousand syntactically different sentences, this is not beyond a child's learning abilities. It is only after a child has a quite advanced language facility that she begins to abstract the rules of grammar partially from early sentence-words, but mostly from more complex sentences that she hears and begins to make. By the time she knows what 'exhibit' means, she has sufficient knowledge of syntax to deem that "John exhibited Amy his drawings" is not grammatically correct. The sentence-word, "John showed Amy his drawings" does not follow the later rule that would

prescribe "John showed his drawings to Amy". The fact that the child learns the former suggests that at the early stage of learning where davitizable verbs are always short words, cognitive learning using semantics totally trumps grammar.

And how difficult is the abstracting anyway? We evolved the ability to create sense data of states of affairs in the world. Grammar is simply a reflection of sense data elements. If we can learn to abstract what material objects are doing and how they are related, which I would imagine even Chomsky wouldn't quibble with, why can't we abstract a grammar that reflects the very same things? At more advanced levels of perception and sentence creation, we make the same mistakes in identifying what objects are, what they are doing and how they are related as we do in the grammar that symbolizes these perceptions. If Chomsky could show that we're born with abstract concepts of how sense data elements are created, he might be more convincing. But this project has never gotten off the ground because there's too much evidence against it. The only reason he can make a case for language is that since language *symbolizes* states of affairs, it would be a much harder to master than mere direct perception.

Hilary Putnam attributes our eventual facility with grammar as due to "general intelligence". Chomsky pokes fun at this idea: "To invoke an unspecified 'general intelligence'...is no more illuminating than his reference, at one point, to divine intervention" (Chomsky in Block, '81, 356). Talk about the pot and the kettle. How specific is his "represented in the brain", or "genetically encoded", and the rest of the innate lingo? At least in the account here, right or wrong, we have given a general outline for a model of how we abstract rules of grammar. Where is Chomsky's model of how the rules of grammar are "represented in the brain"?

By the way, as an aside, we might make an even stronger claim, although we would be on somewhat shakier grounds. Perhaps even adults speak in sentence-words whose meaning is associated with the entire sentence. In the 90's after I got divorced, I was a single guy, and joined dating services and met lots of women. I had many hours of conversation with adult above-average intelligent people. How often did I hear a sentence that was highly unusual? I wouldn't at all be surprised if the vast majority of people use between 50 and 100 thousand different sentences, discounting substitutions of nouns and verbs, during their entire lives. Once in a while, in my experience, I would drop a relatively complex sentence in an average conversation. Almost invariably, it wouldn't compute. The listener would pick out one word they recognized, and spin a whole story around that word, totally disregarding the original sentence. Not only that, when people, including myself, try to make sentences over and above their usual repertoire, they make many grammatical mistakes. This book has lots of complex sentences that are out of the ordinary, and I'll bet there are tons of grammatical mistakes. I've already corrected hundreds of them. As I write this, I think the word 'what' is singular, so that the sentence "what I see in the zoo is/are lots of animals", should have 'is' and not 'are'. But to tell the truth, I haven't the faintest idea if this is true.

These brilliant linguists hang around with other brilliant linguists. I'm sure they have abstracted many rules of grammar over the years so they don't make mistakes. But when average people try to make a new complex sentence not included their 50 thousand sentence-word vocabulary, they make tons of grammatical mistakes. Knowing Chomsky's politics, I have a nice experiment for him, Katz, and their gang. Take all the political speeches made by George W. Bush running for president, as president, news conferences, and any time he spoke in public. Not counting substitutions, I want to know how many different sentences Bush ever made. I'm just a typical buyer in the market of ideas, although an informed interested party. Before I buy any of this innate stuff, I want to be shown two things. I want to see *some* criteria in terms of actual brain processes and structure that enables us to scientifically judge the innateness of anything. And I want to see a list of actual different sentences a typical young child hears.

Of course, we can make analogies which does give us some direction in our thinking about innateness. I think there is something to be said for a kind of innateness that corresponds to the quality of the building materials in the construction metaphor. We could call it "innately *qualified*". The ability to learn quickly and to rise to high levels of musical, artistic, linguistic, intellectual or athletic competence *does* depend on what one is born with. Even the architecture of the brain circuitry that *enables* neurological cylinders to form is innate. But all of this is only potential, depending on the quality of the materials at birth. But the best construction materials in the world, a beautiful piece of architecture does not make. A baby still needs environmental inputs to put these materials together and to create circuits that form the substrate of the abilities the child later develops.

In summary, at our present state of knowledge of the workings of the brain, and on the basis of the evolution of total adaptability of the human mind, the idea of innateness is pretty tenuous. The model given here is speculative although plausible. We simply do not know how we learn to have abstract concepts. And we have even less of an idea of how we come to know the grammar of our language. Without a theory, there is absolutely no physiological criteria at this time for the the idea of innateness, beyond the rather unenlightened idea of innately specified. The one ability that seems to have gotten the most attention in this regard is intellectual talent or intelligence. One of the really peculiar ironies about the study of intelligence is that, historically, the study of intelligence has been greatly impeded by the fact that researchers and writers in the field of intelligence usually have a below average amount of it. What is invariably studied is how much of intelligence is due to the environment and how much is innate. Through the use of very misleading statistical procedures, researchers come up with actual numbers in this regard. Often the numbers arrived at are that intelligence is about 80% hereditary, and 20% environmental. Well, this is pure junk science. By taking the samples in certain ways, you can come up with any numbers you want.

Let's say you're a hereditary enthusiast, you take twins, and make sure that they are constantly glued to together so that their environments will be exactly the same. It will turn out that all the variation in their later intelligence abilities will come out to be due to their heredity, say 95%. On the other hand, suppose you're an environmentalist. Then you take pairs of kids, (and they don't even have to be identical twins), and you raise one in normal society with normal environment inputs, and you raise the other in solitary confinement in total darkness with no environmental inputs at all. (By the way, this is a brutal picture, and there is on record children being raised this way by a demented parent). Well, guess what? It will turn out that more than 95% of the variation in intelligence will come out to be environmental. By playing with your sampling methods, you can get any numbers you want. There is a political motivation in some of this. People who run things, who had the opportunity of richer environments and good education and possibly better materials at birth, don't want to spend money on educating "slower" kids. So by showing that intelligence is most hereditary, it seems reasonable not to waste money trying to educate them. So they want a number for the hereditary contribution to be a high as possible, but not so high as to lose credibility. The number around 80% is usually chosen for the amount due to heredity. But the number 80% is really a measure of how correlated different environments are in modern American society. If they wanted the environmental contribution to come out higher, just raise one kid in a plosh American suburb and the other among the New Guinea headhunters. Even a kid growing up in extreme poverty in the U.S. in today's world has a rich environment compared to someone brought up among the New Guinea headhunters.

The stark scientific fact is that Intelligence is the result of a very complex interplay between genes and environment and both are absolutely necessary. There is no way to divide their individual contributions into percentages. By playing with the statistics, you can get any numbers you want. If Einstein's kids were raised with total sensory deprivation, they would have no intelligence. There is no way to quantitatively compare the variation in genes with the variation in environments, because they are two entirely different phenomena. It's exactly like arguing about what is more important to a piece of architecture, the building materials or the construction workers. You can get any number you want as to their relative importance. The only quantitative conclusions we can draw about intelligence or any other talent, is that our genes set the midpoint of a range and the environment sets where in the range we wind up.

Suppose Sam smarty is born with a potential of 10 IQ points higher than dumb Dan. So Sam's midpoint is 10 IQ points higher. But suppose Dan is given the best of schooling special teaching starting in infancy and a motivating environment: no stress, abuse, or pressures that may cause emotional impediment. In school, Dan will reach the top of his range. Suppose Sam is put in a very deprived environment: no schooling, no intellectual inputs, no perceptual enrichment and an emotionally stressful environment. Sam will probably test at the bottom of his range. This means that as adults it is quite likely that Dan will test higher than Sam.

There is another even more important point. We have assumed a range of about around 30 points depending on the difference between a rich environment and a poor one, *in today's society*. But this is a relative thing. If we went to extremes and considered totally deprived environments like solitary confinement, we would get an even greater range. This is why it is just plain silly to talk about the amount of intelligence due to genes or the environment. They are both necessary, and there's no scientific way to break down the respective contributions.

The only concession that must be made to the hereditary people is that there is an upper barrier to these ranges. But in my opinion, the top point of many of these ranges is pretty high on the scale, certainly where we would say there is an adequate degree of competence. But there are limits. I would have wanted to play the piano like Teddy Wilson. Well, I could have been given lessons from Teddy Wilson himself and practiced 8 hours a day for 20 years and I'm never going to be a Teddy Wilson. I tried pushing the envelope in one other field, pure math. I really studied and took some very advanced courses like Algebraic Topology (which makes you pee in your pants and your eyes water). But I could never get beyond a certain degree of comprehension in abstract mathematical reasoning. I think I got to the top of my range, but there was a limit I could never get beyond.

But the exact quantitative measure of these ranges should not be important from an educational point of view. The mission in education is quite simple: to bring each student to the top of their range, *regardless of where their genes determine the center of the range is*. The midpoint and even the range is irrelevant to education. The important factor is how far up the scale the student will move through education.

My policy when I taught in junior college was to grade mostly on progress, not on an absolute level of performance. If a student was intellectually challenged, but if he came to class and studied and showed progress, he would get a decent grade, even if, on an absolute scale, his performance was pretty sad. But I'm sure the educational system would strongly disapprove. The major purpose of education in the US is not to bring kids to the top of their range but to make sure they and the world around them understand that they're not too swift and shouldn't expect too much in the way of economic returns. This is why over the last 40 years when incredible amounts of wealth were created, not a penny of it went to people who were below average in school. When they tried to raise revenue in Massachusetts from a tax on rich people's yachts, they and their friends in the media (who also have yachts), howled and squealed on every news program on every channel for weeks until it was removed. When you're told you're good while growing up, you think you deserve the world. When the world tells you that you're below average, you will accept very little. *The main purpose of our educational system is to indoctrinate most students into not expecting much out of their working lives.*

Our presently organized education system has become nothing but an extension of the corporate personnel department who want to find out where people are on the scale. That's the motivation for all the standardized testing which has nothing to do with education but only serves to pigeon-hole people. As a result, students' ranges and the top of their range have become completely irrelevant. You don't get people to the top of their range by discouraging them. In my opinion, the relationship between teacher and student, especially regarding grades should be a private thing. Let the corporate world do its own testing, experimenting and tryouts to determine where to put people.

Free Will

AVII.1 THE WORLD AND METAWORLDS

THERE IS ONE FACTOR THAT gums up most discussions of determinism and free will. It is confusion between the world we live in together with the ordinary language we use, and a metaworld we can imagine. 'Meta' is a Greek prefix meaning over and above. An example of a metaworld would be the heaven that most Christians believe in. Our metaworld is a kind of abstract world that looks down on the ordinary world we live in and from which we can make various objective comments about our normal world. It is like a God's eye point of view.

In addition to this metaworld, we also have various levels of causal worlds we have discussed. But much of the writing about the free will problem in the philosophical literature confuses these levels. I was very eager to read a collection of important papers on the subject of free will edited by James Watson, aptly called *Free Will*. But it was pretty disappointing. Most of the entries drone on about the intricacies of the logic of free will *talk*. Very rarely is the issue addressed directly. Even when it is, there is the usual confusion between levels of phenomena.

Before continuing, we have to mention that there are three questions for the free will story. The first is, can we pop a thought into our heads at will out of the clear blue sky. If supervenience is true, this would seem to imply jumping into a brainstate not caused by a previous brainstate. This appears highly unlikely.

The second question is, can we interject a thought or thoughts into a sequence of brainstates and affect its course? This is the old problem of causal efficacy. The third is, can we somehow choose a brainstate from among a number that may all be physically possible without breaking hard causation and natural laws?

AVII.2 COMPATIBILISM

The *Free Will* collection contains an extremely difficult paper by Hilary Bok that illustrates what a tangle you get into by not distinguishing the various causal levels. Bok favors what is called *compatibilism* which goes by the motto, "...we act freely when we can choose among actions which it is possible for us to perform..." (Hilary Bok in Watson, '03, 132). About determinism, Bok says the above criterion is compatible with determinism as long as we are looking at things from a "practical" point of view, where only certain kinds of information about the situation are relevant, namely, information about what is possible and what we can choose. But when we put our *"theoretical"* hat on, it seems that determinism enters the room because it takes account of all considerations including the causal world.

If we can disentangle ourselves from Bok's inscrutable prose, I think the compatibilist is basically saying that we can let people play their silly little language games talking about freely choosing this or that; but from a meta point of view, where we take things seriously and where we are looking at atoms and molecules, everything grinds along relentlessly and deterministically, propelled by hard causality. But if we take language use more seriously, 'choice' is more than a sound. It seems to me that what the compatibilist is really doing is putting our choices and actions in the perceptual world and determinism in the causal world, and *keeping the two apart*. But from a meta point of view, this disregards the fact that *somehow* the perceptual world of actions and choices are interpretations of a causal world upon which the perceptual world must somehow *supervene*.

About a women making choices, Bok says, "...it does not follow from this [determinism] that she cannot perform any other action at T in the compatibilists' general sense unless we can infer the claim that she will not perform any other action from that [determinist] conjunction without referring to any claims about what she will choose to do..." (Watson, '03, 135). I am suspicious of overly difficult sentences like this (although I wish I could do it). After studying this sentence for a half hour, it seems to me it may be covering up a falsehood, and its falsity is the result of confusing causal with perceptual levels. It seems to me that the woman in the story *cannot* perform any other action if determinism is true because we really *can* infer that she will not perform any other action regardless of her "choices" because what she does depends on a causal world where billiard-ball causation reigns. She can paper over the difference between these worlds with talk of practical and theoretical worlds, but supervenience is still there under the paper.

As we discussed in Sect. AIV.3, even if we look at this person's actions as an *interpretation* of what is physically happening, still the physicality of those actions must supervene somehow on the determinist's world of causal objects. And if the causal world is deterministic, you don't have to refer at all to a person's deliberations and choosings to determine subsequent actions, because those actions are interpretations of this causal world. They will be dragged along by the

relentless sequence of deterministic microstates, which makes the compatibilists' theory pretty untenable. Bok says: "...any number of actions might have been possible for her in the compatibilists' general sense, but this fact has, from a theoretical point of view, no particular significance"(141). By her own definition of the "theoretical" world, it would include the causal world of atoms and molecules, and the only way she can possibly say this is to ignore supervenience. Regardless of what words we say, if determinism is true as Bok and the compatibilists claim, the *causal* woman in the story is going to do what the underlying causal world dictates and nothing else; and then we are left with a Putnamian conclusion that either freedom of choice talk is invalid, or it doesn't refer to anything real.

When characterizing the free will position, Bok is pretty vague. After page upon page showing off her inscrutable prose, only a few totally vague sentences are allotted to what free will comes to. She says libertarians "...argue that our freedom requires that we are able to choose among alternatives which are possible given all relevant information about our state, our circumstances, and antecedent events..." (132). (Bok calls Free Willsters, libertarians, for some strange reason. Libertarians don't conceive freedom as a universal prerogative, but a commodity in the marketplace: you get as much of it as you can pay for.)

Now what is "relevant information"? Is our state and circumstances described at the perceptual level or in terms of microstates at the causal level? If we assume she is talking at the perceptual level, then free will according to free willsters is the same as compatibilists', and we're still stuck with the problem of how you can have real choices when those choices supervene on a supposedly deterministic closed causal world? Apparent real choices must still supervene on a causal world, and the question is, how can mental phenomena interject themselves into an apparently deterministic stream of brainstates? Bok says that what we say in our practical world is of "no particular significance" to our theoretical world. But somehow, we have to tie the two worlds together because the practical world does supervene on the theoretical world. In any event, with all this vague talk, it's no wonder that Bok concludes that it's a toss-up as between compatibilists and free willsters: "...no appeal to our ordinary concept of freedom... will settle the issue between libertarians and compatibilists, since that concept supports both views..."(136).

Bok asks us to imagine a pocket Oracle, which can plug in all the initial conditions of a choice situation and in conjunction with the laws of physics will print out the next brainstate and consequently which choice we will make. (We will overlook the problem that such a computation is impossible since free will certainly requires an infinite state system.) Suppose at time T, faced with a choice, the pocket Oracle computes that you will raise you glass to drink. But if you can read the printout which says you will raise the glass, you "...may respond to any prediction the Pocket Oracle made by deciding to do something entirely different" (146). Of course, she points out that the Oracle would be accurate if you couldn't see the printout. Thus "...I cannot possibly know which of my alternatives you would call my only real possibility until I have already chosen one of them" (151). The happy conclusion is that we can dither and dather in our "practical" deliberations whether or not determinism is true. But the attitude we take towards free will and determinism in our practical language is irrelevant to the real question of free will from a meta point of view because the free will debate takes place in the *causal* world, which Bok's practical world totally ignores.

In all discussions I've seen about free will, there is some tendency to drive a wedge between our normal perceptual-linguistic world of deliberations, motives, and choices, and the metaworld of physical states deterministically driving each other. I. A. Melden may have started this habit. He implies that there is no place in our normal talk of deliberations and motives to bring up bodies, causes, and other physicalist concepts. The same is true the other way round. It brings

about "incoherence", "unintelligible", and other philosophers' insults. He says, " 'Could have done', and 'could not have done', 'helpless', etc. these are expressions employed not with respect to events occurring in the mechanism of the body, nor...Humean effects of neural events — but to *persons*", and to "questions of the freedom of human action" (312). This is all very sweet. But what about supervenience? Persons do include a physical body and all its little parts.

There is none of this touchy-feely talk of persons and actions in the metaworld of atoms, molecules and efficient causes. Someone in the metaworld may not know any language; but even if he does, he can chop things up and label them any way he likes. All he has to know about are atoms and molecules, movements and motions, and Melden's "Humean" causation. Further descriptions involving persons and actions are *contained in* and *constrained by* the relentless sequences of physical states that may be deterministically following physical laws. All he has to know is the laws of physics and chemistry as we presently know them, and would conclude that it's a deterministic world, just as most of these philosophers do from their metaworld stance. But that is the key. We just don't know the last word on the laws of physics and chemistry, philosophers' and scientists' brash confidence notwithstanding.

In my opinion, any free willster worth his salt would say there is ontologically some *thing* or *process* that can be called a will that our language refers to. Either we pop thoughts into mind/brainstates, interrupting the natural sequences of brainstates, or there is causal efficacy or we tip some kind of balance. There is no way at this stage of knowledge of physics to know whether or how any of this can happen. To hide behind "practical" worlds of ordinary language, or to drive a wedge between these worlds, or to simply ignore the supervenience of the mental on the physical, or to dismiss a view from the metaworld, or to just put our heads in the sand — all this says little about the free will controversy.

Bok says, "...a determinist cannot believe that all of her supposed alternatives are in fact possible *tout court*," and so "...a determinist who deliberates thereby shows that she has inconsistent beliefs."(152). (*Tout court* means taking everything into consideration including what may be happening at the causal level.) It would be more accurate to say they have inconsistent *behavior*. As pointed out in the text, people's expressed beliefs contradict their behavior because science has many educated people cowed into expressing *belief* in determinism. But willing has a *quale* aspect, which Bok totally disregards, and it's the *qualia* of willing that determine how we act and speak. In view of our actions and speech supplemented by this qualia aspect, free will is innocent until proved guilty.

Bok ends her paper with a definition of free will: "...a person is free if she is capable of determining her actions through practical reasoning; such a person is free to choose among all those acts which she would perform if she chose to perform them..." (164). The suspiciousness of this definition comes out when we are told this kind of free will is generous enough that "...we need not believe that determinism is false ...or that we are free in the libertarian sense" (164). To me this is like saying we have free will even though we may not. In my opinion, practical reasoning is nothing but an attempt to disregard the most important elements of the free will debate. Free will or determinism is a matter that must be decided at the *causal* level of micro-states. All scientific questions involve explaining a perceptual phenomenon in terms of what is going on at the causal level which it supervenes on. The feeling that we have choices and that what we choose is willed, is a perceptual phenomenon. A true free willster agrees that the free will question depends on what is going on at a causal level that the feeling and the choosing super-venes on. And unlike free will philosophers almost to a person, he doesn't disregard the *qualia* we experience when we make choices. This must be explained at the causal level. To disregard the causal level is not solving the free will question but just avoiding it.

Kadri Vihvelin (in Tomberlin, '00) has a very clever way to promote compatibilism. But it's a Fodor-style hand is quicker than the eye solution. He basically says that in evaluating the determinist claim that if Sam had done something else, the past would have had to be different, the counterfactuals involved are too messy. He says we have to use only counterfactuals where the past in constant. However, we still have natural laws to play with. Thus free willsters claim would be that, given a certain past and natural laws, Sam could have done otherwise; and the determinist claim would be that he couldn't. So his way of reconciling these is through the back door of laws, so that we can have determinism and still choose to do otherwise. What happens is that right before your choice, a little cosmic mind-reader steps up, reads your mind and arranges for new laws of nature that your choice will conform to. The question is, when does the cosmic mind-reader change the laws? If he changes the laws *immediately* before Sam's choice so that his choice is really *following* the new laws, which is what determinism says, then he's contradicting his premise that the past is fixed. It must that the new laws are created at the same time as the choice. But if the choice is really free and unpredictable, how would the cosmic mind-reader have time to change the laws so that the choice conforms to them? This is highly implausible. It would have to be that the choice *causes* just the right new laws so as to conform to them, in which case the new laws would have to *follow* the choice that is supposed to conform to them. This is pretty preposterous. But at least Vihvelin is aware that compatibilism, as it is usually propounded, is untenable.

Thomas Nagel substitutes a somewhat less vague dichotomy for Bok's linguistic realms of the practical and theoretical and doesn't see how we can escape the deterministic trap. He contrasts the "internal perspective" where we talk of autonomy and responsibility to the "objective perspective" that takes account of the world of historical causes and effects, from which we cannot escape from some kind of determinism. Of course, to me this is just a fuzzy way to refer to our perceptual world of human affairs as contrasted with the scientific causal world. And in spite of wanting to salvage some kind of freedom and responsibility, he is forced to conclude that in spite of talk of autonomy and agency and all, when it comes to the dictates of the objective perspective, "...nothing believable has (to my knowledge) been proposed by anyone" (231). He adds, "...compatibilist accounts of freedom tend to be even less plausible than libertarian ones"(231). I agree with this too.

And speaking of the causal world, the idea of a closed universe is so universal among most scientists and philosophers that even the few who supposedly believe in free will, often accept a subtle form of determinism. For example, in this same *Free Will* book, Galen Strawson states, "Nothing can be ultimately *causa sui* in any respect at all" (224). Well, probably, but this doesn't totally snuff out free will. (*Causa sui* is Latin, meaning, more or less, that nothing can be its own cause. He adds, "...determinism is unfalsifiable."(225). So is *in*determinism. Where do these people get these bluntly stated cosmic assertions?

In our mentality diagram, we have brainstates going merrily along until it comes to an empty-stomach brainstate. Now which is next, the want-food brainstate or the stay-thin brainstate? Our feelings seem to indicate that this is a toss-up which may indicate that the two brainstates are in a delicate balance. Perhaps the body/brain physical configuration creates a field or a non-physical entity that could tip the balance in favor of the want-thin brainstate which, in turn, could cause a stay-put brainstate and stay-put behavior. This entity or field is the will. Now this is a very simple-minded model, (I would be very shocked if anything like this were the case), but it does indicate a possible mechanism). Some would object that this field is still a physical thing created by physical processes in the body and brain. Perhaps, but it is still an encapsulation of everything a person is at the causal level and it is causing a choice of behavior. Couldn't it rightly be

said that this person is *initiating* his causes and enacting his choices? The *person* is doing the causing, and nothing is causing the person to do anything because any description involving brainstates will find them in a sort of suspended animation, not causing anything. The field aspect of the person tips a balance in a certain way. And there's also the possibility that this field is not physical. Also, these closed-minded closed universe types accept current astrophysics which postulates a big bang. This is precisely an uncaused cause. We are a long way from determining whether our explanation here is viable, and Strawson doesn't have a shred of evidence to exclude such an explanation. I still say, free will is innocent until proven guilty.

AVII.3 FREE WILLSTERISM

Timothy O'Connor is an abashed free willster, and he supports the idea with a long list of concepts meant to convey the meaning and thrust of the free will concept. He talks of "agency", "powerful particular", "volition-enabling", "initiator", and finally, just plain "will". The essence of these ideas is that an agent has a *property* that's an ability to initiate action out the clear blue sky. His phrases includes "...a power — one that in suitable circumstances is exercised at will by the agent..." (262); "...a sort of emergent property whose novelty consists of its capacity to enable its possessor directly to effect changes at will" (264). This seems okay. But when it comes to how this ability and this "will" comes about, O'Connor gets more controversial: he or she is "self-actualized" to borrow a phrase from A. Maslow. But if O'Connor were to be asked what is causing the agent's act of causing or initiating or acting, he says "... the very idea of there being sufficient causal conditions for an agent-causal event is unintelligible"(270); a strange statement for a philosopher. But in case it really is intelligible, he adds, "...it is strictly impossible for there to be sufficient causal conditions for an agent-causing event..."(272). He goes on to explain that things like our propositional attitudes like desires and beliefs, and other mentality like reasons and justifications, may enter into deliberations, but are not sufficient causal conditions. I certainly agree with that. (In fact, in Chapter 18, I will try to make the case that the *reasons* we give for our behavior have absolutely nothing to do with the actual *causes* of our behavior.) He explains that all these kinds of mental events may have "…an influence on the *production* of …"(277) our decisions and choices "…without themselves forming part of a causally sufficient condition for the action"(279). But it seems to me that O'Connor, along others in this important *Free Will* book ignore the real crux of the determinism controversy.

Our behavior involves physical stuff, our bodies, which are caused to move by brain processes. And physical stuff doesn't self-actualize. All the mental phenomena O'Connor mentions *including the will*, must somehow supervene on this causal level of physical matter, a detail most of these philosophers conveniently ignore. Owen Flanagan ('02) has written a whole book, much of which is about free will, and doesn't mention supervenience once.

Causes seem to be involved wherever things happen in the physical world. Of course, O'Connor has to invent a new kind of causation for his self-actualizing causation. This is okay at the perceptual level of mental phenomena including the idea of free will. But it doesn't remove the supervenience problem. And the philosophers in this book offer absolutely no model for how we can have free will at the perceptual level with self-actualizing decisions and choices and still conform to the dictates of the causal world that these decisions and choices supervene on.

In the same *Free Will* book, Rudolph Clarke attempts a model, although, being a philosopher, he is not going to get his hands dirty with an actual body/brain model. He starts out asserting that the agent-causal theory refutes determinism. This is because "Whatever happens now, past events caused it; but since they do not causally necessitate it, something else might have happened instead…"(288). Clarke

wants to avoid O'Connor's uncaused agent-causation, which looks fishy in our scientific causal world, while not admitting strict lawlike causation of the physical world. So, it appears to me that he has a Goldie-Locks causation whereby "…the occurrence of certain prior events will be a necessary condition of an agent's causing a certain event", but do not cause agent-causation in a strict lawlike way, but in the squishy way of ordinary folk psychology. How can he do this?

Well, he introduces probability theory and suggests the choices available to an agent have a probability distribution. Robert Kane suggests that choices of brainstates falling according to a probability distribution would be a matter of luck or chance, and hence "…not free and responsible actions" (304). There is no way to determine the probabilities of the various choices of brainstates in an infinite state system like the brain that is never in the same total state twice. Even if you could, what does this add to the free will debate? Suppose the probability of the staying-put brainstate is 99% and the probability of the getting-up brainstate is only 1%. So what? If the agent does get up, is he defying the probabilities?

In my opinion, probabilities add nothing to the free will debate. Either the probability distribution constrains the choice the will makes or it does not. If it does, then the will isn't totally free. If it does not, then it adds nothing to the determination of what choice will be made. If the physical situation allows either brainstate to occur without violating physical laws, so that something like a will can make a choice, then the probability distribution isn't telling us anything. A combination of mental events that would do the choosing in a deterministic way through supervenience. On the other hand, if the will really is free to choose the brainstate, then he's back with the uncaused causer idea of O'Connor that he started out criticizing. And the problem will not be solved with poetry that many of the papers in this collection resort to such as Kane's, "What is experienced phenomenologically as uncertainty corresponds physically to the opening of a window of opportunity that temporarily screens off complete determination by the past" (306). Now what is the mechanism underlying this kind of talk? So we have free will because deterministic mechanisms have been "screened off". After much ado, Kane finally gets the will into that act: "The indeterminism, therefore, does not have an external source. It is internal to her will" (318). And what is the mechanism that surrounds this will?

Peter van Inwagen uses a similar logic to show that the concept of free will cannot pass the gauntlet (in Tomberlin, '00). Wonder if God goes back after Alice chooses to lie or tell the truth, and reruns the decision. And suppose He does this a thousand times? Van Inwagen seems to think we would have a probability distribution for her decisions. From our point of view, what she does would look like chance even though each choice could be made by the will. Well, I don't agree with his basic premise at all. If God reran the choice, it would be the same Alice person field that would make the decision — and the *same* decision. Alice would be making the decision, not chance, and it could be a free choice. Just because you rerun the choice over and get the same result doesn't show subsequent choices to be determined or occur by chance any more than rerunning a movie over and over takes away the free choices, if they exist, of the people in the movie.

Even though the determinist position is contradicted by many mental phenomena at the perceptual level, the free will position is also tenuous. Many of the papers in the literature bring up the idea that a lot of decisions we might call willed, have causes, even if squishy causes. We say that Sue's desire to get a good job caused her to go to college. But if a desire has this causal efficacy, then how free is her choice? The problem here is that free will falls along a complete continuum. There are times when while lying along the river, we seem to be able to will any thought at all with no restrictions. And on a given day, we seem to be able to choose a wide variety of activities to do for the day, again without restrictions. Philosophers call this agent

causation. But at the other end of the spectrum, there are things we seem to will but seem quite deterministically caused. The violent death of Kim's sister in a given house may prevent her from driving by that house. We all have addictions. The smoker may have such an overwhelming urge to smoke that he says it's impossible for him not to light up. Is this man free to choose? The answer isn't clear to me. The compatibilist and the determinist can say that even though we don't feel as much pressure when we make choices, still all of our past mental experiences may pick our course of action in a deterministic way. They would say this even about picking the thought lying along the river too. And how could we ever disprove this without knowing a lot more physics?

Daniel Dennett's writing on this topic illustrates the confusion. He wrote a book, *Elbow Room* (Dennett, '84), which I eagerly read because I thought if anyone can solve the free will problem, Dennett could. But I was very disappointed. The problem is that Dennett, as many scientists and analytic philosophers, has a bent towards determinism as described from a metaworld. From a God's eye point of view, the universe is *closed* which we discussed in Sect. AIV.3.

But Dennett does recognize that our ordinary language is surfeit with free will talk. We talk about *choosing* a Ford over a Toyota; we talk about spontaneously getting up to go for a walk; we say we *decided* to go to the movies. So how will Dennett put the square peg of free will into the round hole of determinism? Well, Dennett is the poet of contemporary analytic philosophy and by using metaphors, "intuition pumps", poetry and confusion between our perceptual world, its causal world, and a metaworld, he tries to convince us that we can have a kind of free will in spite of a deterministic universe. But he does this by bouncing back of forth between the Earthly perceptual world we're in, and a metaworld from where we see that in terms of atoms and molecules, every state of the world happens deterministically. Dennett has finally run out of "stances".

Dennett does bring up the idea of randomness in physical processes. At the quantum level, there may be randomness in the choice of the next state following a given state of the universe. If this is true, the concept of determinism might have to be revised somewhat. In my opinion, I don't think it's important as to whether a totally physical universe has some random processes. Whether events are chosen mechanically or statistically, it's still physical causation we're talking about, and both conflict with the concept of free will. However, another possibility is that if there *appears* to be randomness in physical processes, there might be a fine balance between states that can be tipped one way with the slightest nudge and perhaps a choice is made physically like with the field idea. It is also possible that a mind event can go in and do the tipping.

Dennett starts with putting reasons, rationality, and consciousness into the fray. These are the fanciest mental things the brain can do. If you are given a reason for getting life insurance, you will have certain conscious thoughts about those reasons and certain feelings. These are all mental phenomena. So, will those reasons and other conscious thoughts directly affect the choice of subsequent brainstates in a causal way. Or will Dennett take us up into the meta-world from where we see that natural laws determine that each state of atoms on the Earth follows deterministically from the previous state according to physical laws. And this kind of determinism doesn't care if there are nice cuddly thoughts supervening on the sequence of brainstates. In Dennett's words, "if any act of mine is caused by physical conditions in the world, it is *ipso facto* not caused by a reason" (Dennett, '84, 27). Although he doesn't say it here, he does have a bias for thinking his acts *are* "caused by physical conditions in the world". In this view, *sounds* we make in giving the reasons for our behavior simply supervene on the deterministic sequence of brainstates. They simply tag along in an epiphenomenal way.

In our ordinary language, rational considerations play an important role in determining our courses of action. This would imply that these mental events having to do with reasons and rationality do play an important role in choosing brainstates. But Dennett doesn't really think any kind of mentality can interject itself into the relentless series of brainstates that will occur on the basis of strict physical laws. But how can he be sure of this? As we have explained with the causal cutter, it is possible that mental reasoning a person entertains can interject itself somehow into the causal chain of brainstates to affect the choice of subsequent brainstates and subsequent behavior.

Dennett is not going to be intimidated by rationality, meaning, or consciousness. "Others (myself included) are ...sure that whatever 'genuine consciousness' or 'real intentionality' comes to, it must lie at the reachable top of that pyramid of natural physical processes" (37). He tosses us a bone and ennobles consciousness and intentionality with being "at the reachable top". Of course, for Dennett, "at the top" really means up in the epiphenomenal sky harmlessly floating about not really doing anything.

In the context of his discussion, the physical processes he is referring to seem to be the usual causal deterministic sequences of brainstates. And he is going to explain our ability to convey reasons to others in the usual physically causal way so that we don't have to resort to "any mysterious, 'contra-causal', vitalistic way..." (45). This sounds like it's coming right out of the Churchlands' polemic tool chest. The purpose of this gratuitous put-down, of course, is to nudge us into the determinist camp. Not only is mental causation down the drain, but along with it goes the will to initiate thoughts. We can now disregard our whole panoply of linguistic terms related to mental causation, voluntary action, and, best of all, (or worst), free will.

He now brings us back down to earth where we have the concepts of control and deliberation and other ordinary language for the mental. We can salvage these concepts because they don't interfere with determinism. He says, *"determinism does not in itself 'erode control'"* (72). Also, "there is no incompatibility at all between determination and deliberation" (102). We can babble away with words like 'control' and 'deliberation' because they do no harm. They simply describe a bunch of thinking and behavior that tag along as they supervene on brainstates, which are the real stuff. This Earthly ants and bees talk is alright as long as we realize that Dennett can threaten at any moment to take us back up to meta-heaven where we'll see the whole Earthly machine, including computer-brains, rationality, and deliberations grinding along relentlessly. Besides, "Even if one knew one's decision was determined, but did not know what decision one was determined to make, ...there would be a sound rationale in favor of the policy of deliberating" (113). Why not? People don't have anything better to do than to harmlessly "deliberate", even if the results of the deliberations were determined.

Dennett proceeds to devalue a number of other mental terms like "seeing opportunities", "avoidable", "inevitable", "anticipate", "prevent", etc., by taking us back up to meta-heaven where all the goings on here on Earth are seen to be determined. He hunkers down to strong cases for free will as described by the phrases, such as "changing the course of history", or "I could have done otherwise". He asks, "What would it be to change the course of history?" (124). He then says, "It is often said that no one can change the past. This is true enough, but it is seldom added that no one can change the future either" (124). Now how come is that, prey tell? If you can't change the future, this would seem to push free will right off the stage. His explanation is, "The future consists timelessly of the sequence of events that will happen, whether determined to happen or not, and it makes no more sense to speak of avoiding those events than it does to speak of avoiding the events that have already happened" (124). I don't see this. If they're not determined, then aren't they avoidable or replaceable? It basically says, what will happen, will happen, and nothing else will happen.

This tautology, of course, is true only if you don't mention anything in *particular*, in which case, you're really assuming determinism.

Before events happen, we can cause things to fall into very wide ranges. Even though we can't avoid *something* happening, if we have free will, we can avoid something *in particular* happening. Dennett can make such a clumsy statement only because from a God's-eye deterministic point of view, the past, present and future might be all laid out in meta-heaven right before His eyes, and Dennett can look at future events the same way he looks at the past. But without this assumption, we can take a variety of different paths *beforehand*. The only time we are committed to particular future events is after they happen, in which case they aren't in the future anymore.

This reminds me of people who say, "it was meant". The guy either buys a Ford or buys a Buick, and no matter what he does, you simply get out your price tag and label what does happen as "it was meant" because *something* will happen whatever it is. And the phrase "it was meant" loses all meaning because it now applies to everything that does actually happen. Remember the law in language: a term that has universal *ex*tension (applies to everything) has zero *in*tension (meaning). This "meant to be" trick doesn't explain anything, and neither does Dennett. The phrase, "what will happen, will happen", has the same status.

He says, "those who claim to know that they have performed acts such that they could have done otherwise...must admit that they proclaim this ...fact without benefit of the slightest shred of evidence..." (136). Of course, the acceptance of my belief by everyone that when I chose to go for a walk, I could have just as well have chosen to stay indoors, is no evidence for Dennett. Friends don't look at me like I'm crazy when I say I could have stayed home. Ordinary speech ought to count for *something*, regardless of how little and even though it's only in the perceptual world. But Dennett will have none of it. The reason, of course, is that the universe is causally closed by fiat, determinism is true by fiat, and you better have some very good "evidence" to say otherwise.

The truth of the matter, of course, is that since we do not know the ultimate constituents of physical matter and its laws at the quark and string level, there is not one "shred of evidence" for a closed, deterministic universe. The little we know about quantum mechanics indicates a lot of crazy events, some of which depend not on a deterministic choice of outcomes, but on "observations" which implies consciousness, no less.

Dennett, assuages us not to feel bad about free will because it wasn't that useful an idea anyway. He says, "What good would it do to know, about a particular agent, that on some occasion...he could have done otherwise ...?" (137). Well, for one thing, we would know if we have free will or not, which is the object of his whole shifty book. Dennett looks at the case where Jones kills his wife and suggests, "given Jones's microstate at t and the complete microstate of Jones' environment...at t, no other Jones-trajectory [behavior] was possible than the trajectory he took" (137). This is nothing but a not-so-subtle plug for determinism, which makes totally gratuitous assumptions about how the world works. He then asks, "Now if you learned this [killing the wife], would you have learned ...anything about his character...or his likely behavior on merely similar occasions?" (137). Dennett's unqualified answer is a resounding NO. The reason is that since the brainstate Jones is in will never again be repeated, we don't learn anything about Jones because on another occasion with a different brainstate, we wouldn't know what Jones will do because of a different brainstate. What do they call this, the fallacy of decomposition? Or the fallacy of microscopy?

First of all, he introduces Jones in terms of his overt behavior and mental states corresponding to it. This mentality and behavior can be supervening on a great number of different brainstates. In the future, Jones is liable to be in the same *mind*state, which is a murderous mood, supervening on a different but similar brainstate, and liable to do the same thing. When we find out that somebody committed murder, we learn a great deal about his character, because character is defined in terms of *mental* qualities, especially proclivities; and it's the very mental qualities Dennett introduces us to Jones as having. Even if we restrict ourselves to brainstates, the brain being a habitual device, makes it more likely that Jones will be in a murderous mindstate and brainstate similar to the one he was in when he murdered his wife, than in a distant brainstate in the n-dimensional brainstate space. We have some idea about this because people who do bad things usually do more bad things. There's the man at trail for murdering his wife. The judged asked why he murdered his wife to which the man answers, "I always murder my wives". Most of the rest of his book is filled with the usual saw that even if determinism is true, we would still deliberate about our plans, agonize over our decisions, and we would still vacillate over our choices. But it would all be determined by previous physical states of the universe.

Dennett likes determinism, but wants to allow some kind of free will. Reminds us of Fodor who "particularly wanted to have both". I don't see how you can have both. If anything mental cannot affect physical processes, then free will from a meta-position, is in bad shape. However, if mentality can affect physical processes somehow, then you have a case for free will. At this time, we just don't know, and "we" includes Dennett. Again, free will is innocent until proven guilty.

A whole book could be written to question Dennett's conclusions, but for now, we will just touch on a few obvious problems. First, if thoughts are nothing but brainstates or epiphenomenal mind events caused by brainstates, why are some conscious and others not? What would be the difference between a conscious "physical" thought process and a *sub*conscious "physical" thought process? (to use Dennett's confusing terminology). If conscious events are all causally impotent, what physiologically differentiates the two categories? There is no neurological evidence that indicates a *physical* difference between brainstates that underlie conscious and non-conscious thoughts. But we know there must be *some* difference, which shows that unlike Frank Jackson's Mary, we don't know everything there is to know about brain processes. In the account in the text, it was suggested that since subconscious thoughts are only virtual, the physical basis of which are brain processes, they are *part* of the deterministic sequence of brainstates having no causal efficacy. Perhaps it is the *power to cause* subsequent brainstates and behavior that differentiates conscious thoughts from non-conscious. Perhaps consciousness and free will originate from the same physical properties, such as Penrose's quantum reduction process.

As we saw on a number of occasions, Fodor tries to convince us that causally related mind events can dovetail with causally related physical brainstates because our thinking is logical. But for him to think that brain processes will underlay a series of mindstates that follow a "valid argument" is a pipedream. People's thinking is mostly *not* logical, especially in their private lives. And what about dreams? While dreaming, we are not conscious, and so there are no conscious mental events on the top row of our diagram to come down and interject themselves causally in the series of brainstates transacting on the bottom row. And what do we find? I don't know about Fodor's dreams, but most people I've talked to (including myself), say their dreams are an incoherent mess, as described in Sect. 18.2. What this shows is that even though our thought processes supervene on causally determined brainstates, when they are not doing any causal work in driving along brainstates, the physically determined sequence of brainstates underlies a meandering story that is incoherent and certainly not a "valid argument".

At times when we do think logically in solving problems, inventing, or writing a Fodor book, mental processes are probably doing a lot of mental causation. MRI exams show that significantly greater amounts of mind/brain energy are expended to bring off this causally efficacious mentality, which may suggest that something very intriguing is going on physically when mental events are causally affecting our thinking. Until we discover what is really happening probably at the subatomic level, we are not going to solve the free will or the mind/body problem.

Now admittedly, free will and mental causation probably precludes a causally closed world. But so what? The proclivity of the scientists and analytic philosophers for a causally closed world is a bias "without the slightest shred of evidence", to use Dennett's remonstrative. Even now at the level of quantum mechanics, there is indeterminacy of physical processes. (The latest word on quantum mechanics is that we know probably less about it than we did 20 years ago.).

But the worst of Dennett's problems concern responsibility and morality. Dennett suspects that you can't hold people responsible for things they do if what they do is determined by physical processes underlying the relevant mentality. So he keeps asking in just about every page, why responsibility is such a big deal. The short answer, of course, is that it makes a big difference as to whether a law-breaker spends the rest of his life in the can. Linda Zagzebski thinks you can hang moral responsibility on behavior (in Tomberlin, '00, 240). She ought to watch defense lawyers. Often, they get greatly reduced sentences, like for the guy who assaults his daughter's rapist. Here the jury is asked to judge the psychological coercion of the intention, not the behavior. Not only that, but lots of punishments for crimes do depend on choices or intentions, and not on the actual behavior. There are many kinds of cases where I violently disagree with this practice myself. I think it's dangerous grounds to be basing crimes and punishments on the basis of *mentality* unless the mentality lessens the crime. It leads to a police state where people can be punished for having the wrong thoughts. There should be no such thing as pre-meditated murder — only pre-*planned* murder where the plans are in terms of behavior. The major reason for this practice is that high-priced shysters can get their white-collar criminal clients off on the basis of good clean *thoughts*. But then when it comes to the poor guy holding up a candy store, the system switches to behavior; and the guy with the gun is judged on the basis of the gun, not on the basis that his only intention for having gun was to intimidate, not kill anyone, which he did not do. If the system is going to punish on the basis of the gun, it ought to also punish on the basis of the white-collar *theft*.

Dennett is looking for "elbow room" between the dictates of a relentless physical universe grinding away deterministically and our normal everyday world of being held responsible for choices. Well, *there is no elbow room*. Either mentality can intervene in physical processes, even a little bit, or it can't. This distinction makes a very big difference because it involves our whole moral outlook and our systems of rewards and punishment and our whole criminal justice system.

Dennett spends the last 10% of this book in a high wire act trying to enlighten us about the justice, needs, and procedures of the criminal justice system. Why does he bother? Maybe he was determined to write this, so he's just going through his predetermined motions. He says about harms people can do to society, "if we prohibit the causing of these harms, and give force to the prohibition by threatening sanctions, we will thereby diminish the frequency of those harms" (Dennett, '84, 159). The question is, how can threatening sanctions change the behavior of potential criminals without going through their thoughts and feelings? Supposedly, determinism would dictate that the potential criminal reads about jail sentences, and this information goes into his brain and changes brain-states in such a way that the probability of committing a crime diminishes. But suppose he *does* commit a crime. If this was determined despite the warnings, why the punishment? If the poor fellow could not have "done otherwise", how do we morally punish him? We could say it would be to maintain credibility of the warnings for other potential criminals. Fine, but still, how could we morally punish *this* criminal for *this* crime, when he wasn't really responsible because it was determined to happen? Threatening loved ones of a potential criminal with punishment if he commits a crime might reduce the probability of his committing a crime as well. But we can't have a justice system that does that either.

Finally, Dennett refers to "the myth of free will" (166), although a convenient myth. At this point in our knowledge of the physical world, a closed universe is also a myth. As long as we do not know the ultimate workings of physical matter, I don't see why the evidence of our ordinary mental concepts and language use shouldn't bias us a little bit towards free will, even at the metalevel of analysis. As far as we Earth dwellers, although Dennett deems free will an "illusion" (168), he agrees that we are better off with the illusion than without. Well, this might be true, but we're inn philosophy where we're supposed to be interested in truths. Dennett titles his book *The Varieties of Free Will Worth Having*. Well, by the time he spends a whole book paring down and emasculating the idea, the varieties of free will he has left *certainly aren't very much worth having*.

Action

———

MELDEN RESTS HIS THEORY OF actions as behavior that is following or observing rules. Rules have meaning and I think this can be generalized by saying that actions are simple movements with meaning. The meaning can come from a number of different sources — rules are only one source it seems to me. The action can be motivated or caused by a propositional attitude where the interpretation of the proposition has meaning; or willed with certain meaningful intentions or goals in mind; or caused by an emotion with certain meaningful purposes.

Dretske has a breakdown that seems to confuse levels. When picking up a glass to drink, he explains, "Syntax alone may give you an explanation of R, my arm movement, but to explain why S_i [a mental state] *produces* R, why I move my arm, one must appeal to the semantics of S_i" (Dretske in Grimm & Merrill, '97, 57). Thus, if S_i is only a sense datum, this can be describable in terms of syntax but can explain only movements. On the other hand, if you want to explain an action, then S_i must be a meaningful belief or perception. This must supervene on an infinite state brain process that is causing the action, in which case it isn't describable by mere syntax.

Meldon looks at a typical action where a cyclist signals in traffic by raising his arm. Norman Malcolm says, "when one signals a turn, one raises one's arm" (Melden, 20). This is simply not true. The origin of this idea comes from Donald Davidson, who claimed that different descriptions of an act are the same act.

This is called the identity thesis for acts. Here, signaling and raising one's arm would be the same act. However, if we can individuate acts functionally they should be different acts. For one thing, the propositional attitude of *intending* to signal causes the guy not to raise his arm, but to signal. The guy did not *intend* to raise his arm, he intended to signal. He may signal *by* raising his arm, but the action is not raising his arm, but signaling. Seeing a motorist in his rear-view mirror caused him not to raise his arm, but to *signal*.

It is important to see the role of prepositions like "*by*" in accounts like this. "*By*" signifies that something is happening — the raising of the arm — but not that somebody is *causing* the happening. When the man signals *by* raising his arm, he is not raising his arm: the arm is a vehicle for the *action* of signaling, which is caused by the intention of signaling. If his intention was to raise his arm, then *this* intention would be the cause of the raising of the arm, and his action would be simply to raise his arm. He can do this when he's not in traffic.

Melden thinks 'cause' should only apply when there are lawlike relations between events, like billiard balls. So a finite state physical thing would *cause* in a lawlike way other physical events like movements. But what about *actions*? Throughout his book (*Free Action*), he bobs, weaves, and ducks to characterize the causal nature of propositional attitudes without using the word 'cause'. This is laudable. We used 'produce'. The English language has 27 words for 'prostitute', but none for 'cause' that has the necessary connotation of pushy-shovey force.

When explaining an action by giving its cause like a "motive" or "intention", he says these mental events explain because they "...provide us with a better understanding of the action by placing it with its appropriate context..."(Melden, 102). Well understanding should imply the involvement of meaning, it seems to me. Propositional attitudes were not discovered in Meldon's time, because he says of a man who desires food that the desire "... may excite the movement of legs, but will it explain his doing, namely, his *action* of walking across the street to get ..." some food (128)? The physical nature with which he characterizes his desire representation would not be enough to bring about, push, shove or, in any way cause, *actions*. It would cause things in a lawlike way alright, but it would only cause movements, not actions. And Melden does seem to admit that even if desires do cause actions, it is not in a lawlike way. This discussion to me holds the key to understanding the difference between syntax and semantics that we have tried to address. If the brain is a computer with an algorithmic language of thought as Jerry Fodor insists, then a representation would be a finite state brain complex. Then the question would be, where does an action which is movement with meaning get it's meaning if its cause is a finite state entity in the language of thought? It seems to me that both the infinite state meaning in the motive is what confers the infinite state meaning of the action.

Meldon describes this as a *gap*: "...in cases of human action there are gaps in the chain of physiological causes which are filled in by the doings of agents..." (meaning, actions) (57). This is the same problem of how mental causation can interject itself a sequence of brainstates. Melden is saying the only way the will or other mental causes can interject itself into a relentless sequence of lawfully determined brainstates is if there are "gaps" in the sequence. To me, this is an unwarranted assumption. In the account suggested in Sect.

14.1, the mental event *joins* a brainstate and together determines the next. This is wild speculation, of course, but it seems to me enough to show that "gaps" are not necessary.

Melden introduces movements of muscles. But this is a non-starter, in my opinion. The brain causes muscles to contract and the arm goes through a movement of rising. Of course, this is not the *action* of raising one's arm. Melden says, "...I move the muscles by raising the arm"(63). This is not true. We never "move muscles" when we're performing an act. Only the brain moves muscles. When we *flex* muscles, we aren't usually doing any act. Melden totally ignores the *qualia* aspect of willing, which is an important consideration. I can very easily tell the difference between flexing my muscles and raising my arm. In fact, that's easier than telling the difference between raising my arm and signaling.

This is the familiar story of confusing causal with perceptual levels. A *person* raises his arm *by* willing it. How this happens is partially explained at the causal level by a brain, impulses, and muscles causal sequence. But in this picture, the muscles contracting do not cause the action of raising the arm because the latter is a meaningful action involving mental stuff. Either the will or some meaningful propositional attitude, like intending causes the action. Melden admits: "...the rising of the arm — is one thing, the doing or the action of raising the arm is something else again..."(66). Of course, raising the arm does *involve* muscles contracting, but the brain contracts muscles, whereas the person raises the arm.

Melden tries to get an action going by introducing a *motive* and adding it to an arm movement. But then he says, "...if this motive is the motive for raising the arm, the motive, far from defining or constituting that action, presupposed it" (77). In other words, how do you define a motive without mentioning the action it's supposed to explain? He concludes that motives may bring about or cause bodily movements, but "...no action is being explained at all" (85).

I disagree. Muscles cause movements, but motives *do* cause actions and partially explain them. But he adds, nothing about a bodily movement "...could possibly disclose that additional feature that makes it a case of an action" (85). This is true, but then he says that if the motive is going to *cause* the action, it has to be law-like, and no kind of motive has this logical necessity. But that's the glitch in the explanation. Motives with meaning are infinite state events and *can* cause meaningful actions, which are also infinite state events, but only squishy causation can be involved.

He next looks at a prime suspect: an intention. He says an intention has to talk about the action it will cause and explain. In fact, in asking a guy his intention, he will use words that refer to or describe the action. But since an intention is a motive, he's going to reject intentions for the same reason: that we can't use 'cause' to describe the push an intention provides for an action. Melden still hasn't found an "internal event", which when added to the movement of the arm rising logically leads to the action of raising the arm. But the intention has infinite state content which can cause (although squishy) or produce the meaningful action.

Now the idea of propositional attitude probably wasn't invented when Melden wrote. So he disparagingly characterizes what we know as propositional attitudes like a desire, as "...some sort of causal factor, an itch, twitch, internal impression, tension or physiological occurrence..."(Meldon, 116). (I love philosophers' putdowns.) But since Melden tries to limit himself to using 'cause' when only physical events are in question, his representations would be physical, and, to these philosophers, a finite state (syntactical) thing. But the object of desire is obviously, even to Meldon, a meaningful real world thing, like a pretty girl. And so, to Melden, the object of the desire must be a separate entity from the itch or twitch. And if the desire is just a separate itch, that doesn't tell us anything about the object of the desire, just like a stomachache doesn't tell us anything about what we've been eating. And so his first problem is how we can logically hook the desire up with the *object* of the desire, such that any ensuing movements can be seen as willed actions because they are caused, and thereby explained, by the desire. He asks, what prevents us from hooking up the desire to the wrong object. So if Jim desires Kim, what's to stop him from going after Mary instead? Since the desire is an itch or twitch, "...what it explains, at best, is the bodily movement that occurs when the person raises his arm, not the action he performs..." (117).

Now this problem does not arise in the case of intentions because the object of the intention is actual behavior. So there is a logical connection between the intention and the object of the intention because the description of the intention like signaling is the same as the object which is also signaling, and the same as the signaling action which the intention should normally cause a person to perform. But we are not so lucky with a propositional attitude like desire. Meldon can't find an easy way to logically connect the desire with the object of the desire. And the behavior that would be motivated by the desire may not be logically connected to the object as well.

So without a link between the desire and the object of desire, if the desire were to *cause* some action, the desiring "...to do would be, indeed must be, describable independently of any reference to the doing" (128). *But it is so describable:* the desire PA *includes* the object of desire. The desire consists of a total picture, which includes the desiring person *being with* or *having* in some way, the meaningful object of the desire. But Melden isn't aware of what a PA is. So he is forced to fish around for the mystical link between the desire and its object, such that any action that is caused by the desire has something to do with the object of desire. Melden's answer to the magic link is, "...desiring anything logically implies ... desiring to get it" (121). This is a humean distinction without a difference. But Melden's very motivated mental gymnastics to hook the desire with the object of desire does show that the logical connection comes from the essence of the desire relation. The answer, of course, is that the representation of the object of the desire is not a meaningless itch, but a meaningful picture, image or even subconscious thought, which has an infinite state meaning cloud in mental space. This is what a propositional attitude is. This is what enables a desire to bring about or cause an action, which becomes the *motive* for the action. (Even if a squishy kind of causation.) What he is leaving out is the *meaning* of the object of desire. This is part of the desire and so enables the desire to encapsulate a meaningful description of the actions which the desire can be said to squishally *cause* and so to explain. But since squishy causation is also anathema to Meldon, he might not even accept PAs as a motive for actions.

Alvin Goldman wrote an excellent book about actions (Goldman, '70). But it was back in 1970 before propositional attitudes were firmly in place. So he too has trouble hooking a desire with the right actions. He is forced to add *beliefs* to the mix, so that an action will be caused by a desire if you believe it to be effective. He says basically that unless paralyzed, a basic act is something you do if you want to do it and believe it will be effective. But this is too restrictive. As we have pointed out, beliefs are tricky animals. You can desire a new Ford and go to the Ford store to look at them without believing anything. But beliefs just pass the buck; for how do we connect the belief with the object of the belief, just as with desire. We don't need beliefs if we

know the full composition of the desire propositional attitude. The *object* of the desire, owning a new Ford, together with the desire relation, will tell you which acts can be deemed caused by the desire.

But all of a sudden, the idea of *willing* sneaks into Goldman's discussion, without any analysis at all. He says about our act-types, "...our ability to exemplify them at will causally depends on certain processes, ... (69). As usual with the mind, there aren't many necessary connections between mental events. But aside from the fact that intentional or willed acts don't have to be caused by anything, even propositional attitudes — where does the willing come from? Surely not necessarily from desire-belief causation. We often say, when asked why we went for a walk, "no reason at all — I just felt like it".

As far as Dretske's analysis, our Tarski discussion in Appendicitis II indicated that the syntax of the Tarski sentence points to the sense data arrangement of states of affairs in the world. And this would include movement as opposed to actions. When we project meaning to the right side of the Tarski sentence, we can determine the truth of the left side. And by including meaning in our propositional attitudes as the causes of actions, we are simply embellishing movements described on the right side by the meaning in the propositional attitude that is causing the movement which is then an action which we can ascribe to the left side.

VOL. II INDEX

Made in the USA
Monee, IL
25 November 2019